AF361271

A HISTORY OF LAW IN CANADA

Volume Two

Law for the New Dominion, 1867–1914

A HISTORY OF LAW IN CANADA

Volume Two

Law for the New Dominion, 1867–1914

JIM PHILLIPS, PHILIP GIRARD,
AND R. BLAKE BROWN

Published for The Osgoode Society for Canadian Legal History by
University of Toronto Press
Toronto Buffalo London

ISBN 978-1-4875-4567-3 (cloth)
ISBN 978-1-4875-4568-0 (EPUB)
ISBN 978-1-4875-4569-7 (PDF)

Library and Archives Canada Cataloguing in Publication

Title: A history of law in Canada / Philip Girard,
Jim Phillips, and R. Blake Brown.
Names: Girard, Philip, author. | Phillips, Jim, 1954– author. |
Brown, R. Blake, author. | Osgoode Society for
Canadian Legal History, issuing body.
Series: Osgoode Society for Canadian Legal History series.
Description: Series statement: Osgoode Society for Canadian
Legal History | Volume 2 statement of responsibility: Jim Phillips,
Philip Girard, and R. Blake Brown. | Includes bibliographical
references and indexes. | Complete contents: v. 2. Law for the new
dominion, 1867–1914
Identifiers: Canadiana (print) 20189050683 | Canadiana (ebook)
20220402779 | ISBN 9781487545673 (v.2 ; hardcover) |
ISBN 9781487545680 (v.2 ; EPUB) | ISBN 9781487545697 (v.2 ; PDF)
Subjects: LCSH: Law – Canada – History.
Classification: LCC KE394.G57 2018 | LCC KF345.G57 kfmod |
DDC 349.7109 – dc23

We wish to acknowledge the land on which the University of Toronto
Press operates. This land is the traditional territory of the Wendat, the
Anishnaabeg, the Haudenosaunee, the Métis, and the Mississaugas of
the Credit First Nation.

University of Toronto Press acknowledges the financial support of
the Government of Canada, the Canada Council for the Arts, and the
Ontario Arts Council, an agency of the Government of Ontario, for its
publishing activities.

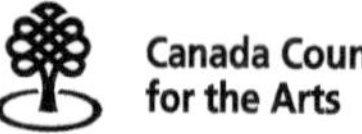

Contents

Foreword xi
Acknowledgments xiii

1 Introduction 3

PART ONE: THE LAW AND LEGAL INSTITUTIONS

2 The Constitution: Confederation, The *British North America Act*,
   and Post-1867 Developments 23
     The Making of Confederation: A Very Brief Survey 24
     The *BNA Act*: The Senate, the Division of Powers, the Judiciary,
       and Disallowance 27
     A Constitution Similar in Principle: Canadianizing the
       Crown 40
     The Meaning of Dominion: Imperial and International
       Questions 44
     Extending Confederation: British Columbia, Prince Edward
       Island, Alberta, Saskatchewan, and the North 46
     The Courts and the Remaking of the Division of Powers 54
     The Demise of Disallowance in the Era of Provincial
       Rights 71

3 Creating the Dominion Court System 74
    Establishing and Integrating Court Systems in the
      West 76
    The Founding and Early Decades of the Supreme Court of
      Canada 79
    Provincial Courts of Appeal 87
    The Fusion of Common Law and Equity 90
    Professional County and District Courts, and Lower
      Courts and Specialized Courts 94
    Judicial Numbers and Remuneration 101
    Judicial Appointments 104
    Public Perceptions of the Judiciary and Judicial Scandals 112

4 Sources of Law: Statutes, Codes, and Case Law 117
    Federal and Provincial Statutory Consolidations 120
    Federal and Provincial Statutes: Cross-Border Borrowings 133
    Case Law 135
    The *Civil Code of Lower Canada* 140
    The *Civil Code of Lower Canada*: Structure and Scope,
      Reform and Amendment 146

5 Quebec Civil Law: A Mixed Legal System in Confederation 151
    Family Law 154
    Obligations 165
    Property 177

6 The Legal Professions, Legal Education, and Legal Literature 184
    The Emergence of the 'Large' Law Firm 187
    University Legal Education 192
    Legal Literature 197
    Professional Governance: The 'Canadian Model'
      Established 205
    Towards Diversity? 209

PART TWO: INDIGENOUS PEOPLES AND THE NEW DOMINION

7 Canadian Law and Indigenous Peoples I: The Métis, the
    Numbered Treaties, British Columbia, and the Rebellion 217
    The Métis, the Red River Resistance, and the Founding of
      Manitoba 218

The Numbered Treaties, 1871–1907   229
British Columbia: Federal-Provincial Disputes over
    Indigenous Title   247
The 1885 Rebellion and the Criminal Law   255
The Trial and Execution of Louis Riel   257

8 Canadian Law and Indigenous Peoples II: The *Indian Act*, the
  Reserve System, and Assimilation   270
    Enfranchisement   273
    The Law and Practice of Reserve Protection and Reduction   283
    Governance of Indigenous Bands and Reserves   289
    The Criminalization of Cultural and Religious Practices   298

9 Canadian Law and Indigenous Peoples III: Education and
  Assimilation: The Origins and Expansion of Residential
  Schools   304
    The School System for Indigenous People, 1867–1883   306
    The Origins and Growth of the Residential School System to
      1900   308
    The Operation of Residential Schools   312
    The Revelations of Dr. Peter Bryce   323
    Why Were Residential Schools Not Abolished or Drastically
      Reformed?   326

10 Indigenous Law and European Law: Adaptation, Resistance,
   Avoidance   328
    The Gitxsan   330
    Kahnawà:ke   336
    The Six Nations   341
    The Métis   343

**PART THREE: BUILDING THE NEW DOMINION:
CAPITAL, LABOUR, AND A CRIMINAL CODE**

11 Law and Economy: Corporate and Commercial Law and
   Regulation   351
    Corporation Law: General Incorporation   353
    Corporation Law: Special Act Incorporations   365
    Debtor Creditor Law: Imprisonment for Debt, Bankruptcy, and
      Insolvency   371
    The Regulatory State: Banking, Mining, Railways   379

12 Labour and Employment Law 394
    Employment Law: Master and Servant 395
    Labour Law: Trade Unions and Workplace Dispute
        Resolution 398
    State Intervention in Labour Law: Arbitration and
        Conciliation 407
    Workplace Health and Safety 411
    Compensation for Workplace Injuries 415

13 Criminal Justice: Criminal Law, Criminal Procedure, and
    Punishment 421
    Making a National Criminal Law 423
    Criminal Procedure: Introduction and the Northwest
        Territories 429
    Criminal Procedure: The Decline of Juries 434
    Criminal Procedure: Trial and Appeal Rights 439
    Imprisonment: The Federal Penitentiary System and
        Intermediate Prisons 444
    Capital Punishment: General 450
    Capital Punishment: Women and Indigenous People 456

14 Property Law 461
    Métis Land Rights in Manitoba 462
    Homestead Settlement: The Canada Land Survey,
        the *Dominion Lands Act,* and Provincial Homestead
        Laws 475
    Title Registration: The Torrens System 485
    Resolving the Prince Edward Island Land Question 489
    Expropriation 492
    Land Use Regulation: Public and Private Law 495
    Nuisance: The Shifting Boundary between Public and Private
        Law 503
    Succession Law 508

**PART FOUR: LESS FAVOURED BY LAW: WOMEN AND
MINORITIES**

15 Women, the Family, and the Law 519
    Married Women's Property in Common Law Provinces 521
    Marriage 535

Contents IX

Divorce Law, Divorce Courts, and the Sanctity
    of Marriage   537
Parliamentary Divorce   544
Child Custody in Common Law Provinces   552
The Female Body and the Law   560

16 Minorities and Civil Rights   569
The Chinese and Japanese in British Columbia: Discriminatory
    Legislation, International Relations, and the Courts and the
    Rule of Law   570
Provincial and Federal Asian Exclusion Acts   580
Anti-Chinese Legislation: White Women's Labour Laws   586
South Asians: Indirect Exclusion   589
Black Canadians   594
Rekindling an Old Fire: Religious and Linguistic
    Minorities   599

Postscript: Law and Legal Institutions on the Eve of the Great
War   613

Abbreviations   617

Notes   623

Statute and Proclamation Index   747

Case Index   751

Name Index   755

Topical Index   765

Foreword

THE OSGOODE SOCIETY
FOR CANADIAN LEGAL HISTORY

This book is the second of a three-volume *History of Law in Canada*, by our editor-in-chief Jim Phillips, our associate editor Philip Girard, and R. Blake Brown, a three-time Osgoode Society author. The main theme of *A History of Law in Canada Volume Two* is encapsulated in its subtitle: *Law for the New Dominion*. As a new state on the global stage, Canada, expanding to the Prairie west and British Columbia in 1870 and 1871, sought to use law to weld into one nation several disparate settler colonies established on Indigenous lands. But unity was elusive: Canada had to recognize Quebec civil law, tried to override or replace Indigenous law, and faced challenges to its own authority, from the Northwest Rebellion to the claims of restive provincial premiers. This volume deals with all aspects of Canadian law and legal institutions in Canada's formative years as a dominion, with chapters on the constitution, courts and judges, sources of law (common law, civil law, Indigenous law, and statutes), the legal profession, Canadian law and Indigenous peoples, criminal law, law and the economy, labour law, property law, the law affecting women's status, and civil rights and minorities. Like *Volume 1* this book is a history of law and legal institutions, integrated with the other histories – social, political, economic, and cultural – that transformed Canada after Confederation. Like *Volume 1* it examines the interactions of Canada's three legal traditions – common law, civil law, and Indigenous law – but we see that Indigenous law played a decreasing role after 1867, as it was largely, though never completely, pushed aside in favour of Victorian certainties about the superiority of European law and culture.

The purpose of the Osgoode Society for Canadian Legal History is to encourage research and writing in the history of Canadian law. The Society, which was incorporated in 1979 and is registered as a charity, was founded at the initiative of the Honourable R. Roy McMurtry and officials of the Law Society of Upper Canada. The Society seeks to stimulate the study of legal history in Canada by supporting researchers, collecting oral histories, and publishing volumes that contribute to legal-historical scholarship in Canada. This year's books bring the total published since 1981 to 117, in all fields of legal history – the courts, the judiciary, and the legal profession, as well as the history of crime and punishment, women and law, law and economy, the legal treatment of Indigenous peoples and ethnic minorities, and famous cases and significant trials in all areas of the law.

Current directors of the Osgoode Society for Canadian Legal History are Constance Backhouse, Heidi Bohaker, Bevin Brookbank, Shantona Chaudhury, David Chernos, Paul Davis, Theresa Donnelly, Linda Silver Dranoff, Timothy Hill, Ian Hull, Trisha Jackson, Mahmud Jamal, Waleed Malik, Rachel McMillan, Roy McMurtry, Dana Peebles, Paul Schabas, Robert Sharpe, Jon Silver, Alex Smith, Lorne Sossin, Mary Stokes, Michael Tulloch, and John Wilkinson.

Robert J. Sharpe
President

Acknowledgments

A number of people read all or parts of this manuscript, and provided very valuable comments. We are especially indebted to the two anonymous reviewers for the Press and the Society, whose detailed reports were just what authors want – half a page of generous and enthusiastic praise and many further pages of corrections and perceptive suggestions. Bob Sharpe and Lori Chambers also read the whole manuscript and we are most grateful for their suggestions. Others who read chapters and provided very useful feedback, and/or furnished us with research materials, were Hamar Foster, Don Fyson, Mélanie Méthot, Chris Moore, Michel Morin, Sarah Pike, Dan Rohde, Arnold Weinrib, and Stepan Wood. Dr Nick Haisell compiled the index.

The Osgoode Society for Canadian Legal History has supported our work, and that of many other Canadian legal historians, for decades, and we are deeply grateful to that organization, and to Amanda Campbell, the Society's Directors, and its President, Robert Sharpe. Len Husband and Christine Robertson of the University of Toronto Press were unfailingly helpful in a host of ways. We also thank the SSHRC for the initial grant that provided generous support for Volume I and the impetus to continue with the project through subsequent volumes.

Jim Phillips was fortunate to have the assistance of a number of research assistants over the four years it took to write this book. He is especially indebted to Iain Wilson, JD University of Toronto 2021, who worked on a wide variety of subjects for two summers. Iain brought to the task legal training, an MA in Canadian history, a remarkable work ethic, unflagging good humour, and the friendship of a cycling companion. This book would not have been finished when it was but for Iain. Yuchen Liu and Tom Collins also provided very valuable help as summer research assistants. Other law students helped for shorter periods of time on specific tasks – Thomas Alexander, Justin Irwin, Katrina Kotarba, Alexander Packman, and Michael Wang. At various times Geoff Chambers, Daniel Girard, and Ben Savage all provided additional research assistance. Special thanks are also due to two remarkable librarians at the Bora Laskin Law Library, Sufei Xu and, especially, Sooin Kim.

Jim Phillips owes two debts that cannot be properly acknowledged in words. One is to Philip Girard, teacher, mentor, collaborator, co-author and, most of all, the best of friends, for almost forty years. The other is to Christine Davidson, whose love and support, and unflagging good humour, have sustained me through the writing of this book and difficult physical challenges. I dedicate my contribution to this book to her.

Philip Girard wishes to thank several research assistants who worked on this project over the years, especially Sebastian Becker, Luc Chabanole, Matthew Green, Anisha Nag, and Robert Mackenzie. He is also grateful for an Osgoode Hall Research Fellowship in fall 2020 that allowed him to make good progress on his portions of the manuscript. The insights of participants in the Legal History Workshop who critiqued several chapters presented there were always appreciated. Jim is very much the first author on this volume and working together on it has been a great pleasure, if at times also a slog. Philip dedicates his part in this book to Sheila Zurbrigg, whose support along the way has been invaluable.

A HISTORY OF LAW IN CANADA

Volume Two

Law for the New Dominion, 1867–1914

1

Introduction

In the half-century between Confederation and the First World War, what we now call Canada was both created as a nation state largely independent of Britain and transformed from a collection of three colonies/four provinces in 1867 to a federal state with nine provinces and two northern territories. By 1914 Canada occupied the whole of North America north of the forty-ninth parallel, except for the US territory of Alaska, Danish Greenland, and the British colony of Newfoundland, which did not join Canada until 1949. It also greatly expanded demographically. The provinces of Nova Scotia, New Brunswick, Ontario, and Quebec were in 1871 occupied by some 3.36 million settlers of European origin and perhaps 45,000 Indigenous people.[1] By 1911 Canada contained more than double the number of white settlers (about 7.2 million) and probably more than 100,000 Indigenous people. There is consensus that the number was higher when the Prairie provinces and British Columbia joined Confederation, but the Indigenous population declined in the later nineteenth century. In 1871 Ontario was the most populous province, with 1.62 million people, followed by Quebec (1.15 million) and Nova Scotia (388,000). Ontario and Quebec retained their positions as the most populous provinces in 1911, a total of about 4.5 million people, but a harbinger of the new importance of the West was that Saskatchewan now had the country's third-largest provincial population, almost half a million people. Indeed, massive immigration continued and the number of settlers living there went up another 30 per cent between 1911 and 1916.

Numerous other transformations accompanied these political, geographic, and demographic changes. By 1911 some 45 per cent of the white settler population lived in urban, not rural, areas, up from 31 per cent in 1891. A decade later, the relative numbers were almost equal. This rural-urban shift was both product and cause of a shift in the economy from a substantial reliance on farming, fishing, and the exploitation of natural products to a mixture of those sectors with manufacturing, mining, financial, and service industries. At Confederation most of the people of European descent could trace their family origins to Britain, France, or other parts of northern Europe. Those groups still made up the majority of non-Indigenous inhabitants in 1914, but they had been joined by not insubstantial numbers of eastern and southern Europeans, and by much smaller numbers of Asians and Blacks.

Arguably the most profound transformation of this period was that experienced by northern North America's Indigenous people. In 1867 only those living within the boundaries of the central and eastern colonies, on Vancouver Island and the lower mainland of British Columbia, and in Red River, were under British sovereignty, the last indirectly and mostly nominally. And while that meant the loss of large areas of their land base, it did not mean a significant diminution in their effective control over their daily lives. By 1914 every Indigenous person lived under Canadian sovereignty, as defined by Canadian law, including tens of thousands in the interior of British Columbia, the Prairie provinces, and the North. More pointedly, the Indigenous land base had been massively curtailed and the apparatus of the Canadian state intruded itself into every aspect of Indigenous peoples' lives.

In outlining these many and varied transformations, we are not saying anything that historians have not already said.[2] The purpose of this book is not to repeat their histories, but to add to them by writing a history of the law, of legal actors, institutions, doctrines, cultures, and ideologies, that accompanied and facilitated these and other transformations. The law was everywhere, as both derivative of political and social change and economic transformation, and as a contributor to them. In *Volume 1* of this history we saw that Britain and France took the law with them, in a variety of different forms, to many parts of northern North America. We also saw that, having arrived, they encountered other laws and legal orders, those of the Indigenous peoples occupying the land, and for centuries three legal traditions co-existed. In the period covered by this volume there was both continuity and change in the relationships among law, society, Indigenous peoples, and white settlers.

These shifts can be followed through the two main themes that animated *Volume 1*: legal pluralism and the role of law in balancing liberty and order.[3] The somewhat eclectic and tolerant approach to legal multiplicity characteristic of the eighteenth century, one accepting of custom as a source of law and comfortable with a layered concept of sovereignty, was already being transformed prior to Confederation. The more hard-edged and positivist view of law that emerged from the writings of John Austin, influenced heavily by Jeremy Bentham, proved extremely popular in the Anglo-American world following the posthumous republication of his 1834 work, *The Province of Legislation Determined*, in 1861. Austin argued that law should be divorced from morality and articulated a theory of 'law as command,' resulting in a conception of law as exclusively generated by the state in the form of either case law or legislation. A.V. Dicey would build on these ideas in formulating his theory of the rule of law, which also proved popular in the later Victorian period. These views, built around a more monistic conception of sovereignty, came to prevail over the older practices of legal pantheism seen in *Volume 1*. The main casualty of this new approach was Indigenous law, which, largely based on oral transmission and traditional practices, was increasingly seen by settler society as folkloric and not real law. Once delegitimized in this way, the Covenant Chain and earlier understandings between Crown representatives and Indigenous leaders could be ignored by settler governments. As seen in *Volume 1*, the giving of presents by colonial authorities as a mark of respect and a sign of renewing past agreements had ceased in 1858. The practice was minimally revived in the post-Confederation period, as a small aspect of the treaty-making that deprived Indigenous people of much of their land. It would not be long before the *Indian Act* sought to replace Indigenous laws and traditional leadership with norms derived from settler law, the goal being the eventual assimilation of Indigenous peoples. The efforts of various Indigenous communities to resist, adapt, or avoid these governmental measures are explored in chapter 10.[4]

Conversely, the legal pluralism that saw Quebec civil law co-exist with the common law elsewhere in Canada not only continued but was even strengthened in some ways while being challenged in others. The enactment of the *Civil Code of Lower Canada* in 1865 (in force as of 1 August 1866) provided a prominent anchor for the civil law in Quebec, a visible symbol of its renewal for observers inside and outside the province, and the focus for a growing doctrinal literature that enriched and clarified the law. Nonetheless, the subjection of Quebec law to interpretation by the Judicial Committee of the Privy Council and the Supreme Court of Canada after 1875 – courts staffed by a minority of civil law-trained judges – presented potential challenges to its integrity. Perhaps because it dealt with so many legal traditions around the empire, it was the JCPC that often seemed more solicitous of maintaining the distinctiveness of Quebec's civil law than the SCC. Even though the latter had two members from Quebec, calls for uniformity of Canadian law on a particular topic were sometimes met there with the simple interpolation of common law rules into the civil law. While accepting that Quebec possessed a mixed legal tradition that should not reject out of hand the adaptation of doctrines from the common law, civilian lawyers and Quebec judges were always alert to what they found to be unsuitable or incompatible importations. These struggles are explored in chapters 4 and 5.

Finally on the legal pluralism theme, Canadian common law itself existed in an imperial context where both English law and the laws of other colonial units circulated directly, through the movement of people, and indirectly through the transmission of ideas in texts, case law, and legislation.[5] It also existed on a continent where the federal jurisdiction of the United States and dozens of state jurisdictions churned out legislation and, especially, case law, in quantities that even Americans despaired of ever mastering. The views of Canadian lawyers, legislators, and judges towards English law were somewhat ambivalent in the later nineteenth century. The international reputation of the English judiciary was probably at its peak around the time of Victoria's jubilee in 1897, and their decisions were revered for the most part as being of high quality in both style and content. A number of English statutory innovations were adopted almost verbatim by Canadian legislatures, such as the *Bills of Exchange Act* federally and the *Sale of Goods Acts* by the provinces. Yet Canadians did not want to be bossed around. It was one thing to voluntarily adopt an English statute or doctrinal innovation, another to have it forced on them. When the JCPC announced in *Trimble v Hill* (1879) that Canadian courts were bound by English Court of Appeal interpretations of statutes that had been re-enacted in Canada, there was considerable resistance. As for American influence, it waned somewhat in Canadian case law in the later nineteenth century, apart from some particular areas where English law provided no guidance.

The issue of English versus American influence is discussed generally in chapter 4, but appears in many chapters in particular contexts.

While one of the three pillars of Canadian law – Indigenous law – went into partial eclipse during this period, and some Quebec writers protested the undue influence of the common law, nonetheless Canada maintained its legally plural heritage during our period. This was inevitable, given that the original four provinces, belonging to two European empires, had not been separated from them by a revolutionary event. Even though the conquest of Quebec involved a violent rupture with the French empire, subsequent measures culminating in the *Quebec Act* ensured that legal continuity would prevail. Thus, neither English law (in common law Canada) nor French law (in Quebec), even today, is seen as radically 'other' or foreign.[6] The Austinian concept of sovereignty, while influential in some respects, did not prevent Canadians from looking beyond their national boundaries to other jurisdictions for inspiration and advice. Legal pluralism may not exactly have thrived during this period, but it survived. The equation of one nation with one national law, much as it appealed to many Anglo-Canadians, would never work in the new dominion.

Our second theme, the role of law in securing a balance between liberty and order, is most evident in the settling of the West after the acquisition of the territory from the Hudson's Bay Company. The sheer difficulty of travelling to the western plains from either eastern Canada or British Columbia before the completion of the railway gave the dominion government an advantage in asserting its authority in the area. It could exercise a level of control over the settlement process that had not been present in the United States, where the plains were more directly accessible by would-be settlers, either by land or via the Mississippi and Missouri Rivers. It was imperative from the federal government's point of view that order precede liberty, that a legal infrastructure modelled on that in the east but suitable for western circumstances be established before large numbers of settlers arrived. The experience of events in the Red River settlement in 1869–70, with the creation of Riel's provisional government, the execution of Thomas Scott, and the military expedition that ensued, seemed only to confirm to those in Ottawa the wisdom of asserting its authority before a wave of settlers arrived. The rapid negotiation of the numbered treaties, the surveying of the prairies in their wake, the maintenance of Crown lands in the hands of the federal government rather than the Prairie provinces, the passage of the 1872 *Dominion Lands Act* to control land distribution, the adoption of the Torrens registration system to guarantee and publicize titles to the newly surveyed plots, and the creation of the North-West Mounted Police in 1873 formed a whole suite of measures designed to regularize and direct the settlement process over the vast area between Lake Superior and the Rocky Mountains. But the ostensibly orderly process that was to produce settler liberty did so by restricting the liberty of Indigenous inhabitants, resulting in violent confrontation. The dissatisfaction of the Métis, culminating in the Northwest Rebellion, led to the reimposition of settler law via military means – the ultimate weapon in restoring order.

A second area where order prevailed over liberty was the criminal law. Of course the criminal law exists to promote order and to restrain the antisocial pursuit of liberty, but these poles exist on a spectrum. The criminal law can be harsh and authoritarian, or it can be milder and more protective of the liberty of the subject where less serious or victimless crimes are involved. The enactment of the *Criminal Code* in 1892 was a significant aspect of nation-building in its attempt to provide an accessible and authoritative account of the criminal law for the whole country. From the various models in circulation at the time, however, the federal authorities chose the most authoritarian, that of Sir James Stephen. Although for the first time it permitted a right of appeal for a convicted accused, it also introduced the possibility of a Crown appeal from an acquittal – a Canadian innovation unique in the Commonwealth whose origins remain obscure. Via the *Speedy Trials Act*, initially enacted for Ontario and Quebec in 1869 but later extended to other provinces, the federal government also dramatically reduced recourse to juries. Juries were indeed subject to criticism from the public and professionals alike at this time, but the move to judge-alone trials for all but the most serious offences signalled the transformation of the criminal law's administration into an almost bureaucratic routine. A state-imposed order aimed at economy and efficiency largely replaced a centuries-old tradition of community involvement in the criminal justice process. The cessation of conducting executions in public from 1869 was also of a piece with this trend.

Within settler society, political and economic liberty expanded slowly, mostly for white males but also for some other groups. As noted in chapter 12, criminal sanctions for breach of labour contracts were largely abolished, and unions were no longer proscribed although there was also no obligation on employers to bargain with them. The removal of these restrictions would make possible the creation of labour-oriented political parties, though they did not emerge until during and after the First World War. The connection between property ownership and the franchise remained throughout our period, however. Until 1920 the federal franchise relied on the provincial franchise, and the latter retained some property qualification until the 1920s or later. 'Universal' suffrage for all adult males and females except 'Indian[s] ordinarily resident on a reservation' thus arrived together at the federal level in the *Dominion Elections Act, 1920*.[7]

The tension between liberty and order was especially acute within the family. The legal authority of the husband and father as head of the family was still almost as strong at the end of the period as at the outset, both in common and civil law. Yet this was also the era when women married in common law provinces saw a dramatic enhancement in their ability to maintain and manage their own property and wages independently of their husbands. Such reforms in turn helped fuel the women's suffrage movement, whose efforts came to fruition just after the end of our period. Within the sphere of family law proper, however – whether and how marriages could be dissolved, who got custody of children if it was disputed – liberty was seen as destabilizing. As will be seen in chapter 15, divorce was very difficult to obtain and male authority over children of the marriage largely upheld.

The sixteen chapters of this volume have been grouped into four parts, although there are numerous overlaps among the chapters and between the parts. Part 1, chapters 2 through 6, examines the core elements of the new dominion legal system. We begin in chapter 2 with the constitution, dealing firstly with the *BNA Act*, especially its provisions relating to the division of powers, the judiciary, and disallowance. The last is now defunct but it played an important role before the First World War, and one cannot make sense of some later chapters, especially chapter 16 on minorities, without an appreciation of how it operated. Chapter 2 also deals with aspects of constitutional law outside the *BNA Act*, especially the role of the Crown and constitutional conventions and the inclusion of new provinces beyond the original four. It does not, however, include Manitoba, as one cannot understand the creation of the original 'postage stamp province' without delving into the legal issues involved in the Métis peoples' resistance to incorporation into Canada without consent, a topic covered in chapter 7. Much of chapter 2 is taken up not with the *BNA Act*'s division of powers as written in sections 91 and 92, but with what those powers came to mean as the courts set about interpreting the rarely 'plain' language of the text.

By 1914 a document intended by the majority of its authors to create a strong central government and correspondingly weaker local, provincial ones, had become, through the work of the JCPC, the constitution of a federation in which legislative power was much more evenly divided.

The four original provinces had each long operated with well-established court systems, and localism in court structures was retained at Confederation through section 92 (14) of the *BNA Act*. But the *BNA Act* also introduced a degree of central control over aspects of the provincial courts, most notably in two areas – the appointment of most judges became a federal responsibility, and section 101 of the *BNA Act* permitted Ottawa to create a national Court of Appeal and additional courts 'for the better administration of the laws of Canada.' Parliament used these powers in 1875 to establish the SCC and the Exchequer Court. Chapter 3 discusses these and other developments in the court system and the judiciary. The SCC was supreme in name from the outset, but it was never truly supreme in this period. Litigants could bypass it entirely on the way to the JCPC, or appeal from the SCC to the JCPC. It took some decades before the court achieved the stature and respect within Canada that it grew to have later in the twentieth century. In part the authority of the court was diminished by its being not infrequently overturned by the JCPC in matters of constitutional law.

All Canadian courts were staffed by judges whose appointments were frequently partisan, promotion to the bench being a principal patronage tool available to the federal government. The final section of chapter 3 analyses this phenomenon. Chapter 3 also details the establishment of new court systems in the Prairie west in the 1870s, the integration of existing ones in British Columbia and Prince Edward Island into the federal system of appointments and remuneration, and developments internal to the provinces that, while not occurring in every province, were sufficiently ubiquitous to allow us to label them a national trend. These include principally the fusion of courts of common law and equity, the professionalization of the judiciary below the level of the superior courts, and the establishment of courts of appeal separate from those superior courts.

Chapters 4, 5, and 6 of part 1 examine the sources of the law in this period, both in Quebec and in the common law provinces. They remained statutes, including the *Civil Code of Lower Canada*, and case law, but both underwent transformations. Judges in common law provinces still looked to English law for governing principles – indeed they arguably did so more than they had before 1867. At the same time there was a limited, though discernible, move towards internal self-reliance, a willingness to create a distinctive Canadian jurisprudence responsive to local circumstances, to look for guidance not only to Westminster Hall but to provincial apex courts and the SCC. The trend to fashioning something that one could term Canadian law was most marked, however, in the plethora of provincial and federal statute law, which grew markedly in this period, in depth and breadth, as the Canadian state, writ large, expanded its reach into numerous areas of social and economic life. In doing so, it amended or replaced the common law on particular topics. Specific examples are dealt with in part 3; chapter 4 looks at this development only in outline. That outline featured two particular trends: the adjustment to their statute books required of all provinces that had been colonies to account for the fact that many provincial statutes as of 1867 dealt with subjects given to the national Parliament by the *BNA Act*, and the need to come to grips with the continuing influence on provincial law of received English statutes. As noted earlier, chapter 4 also analyses the impact of the *Civil Code of Lower Canada* and the continuing evolution of Quebec's mixed legal system.

Chapter 5 examines the feature of Canadian law that distinguished it from England itself and from most British settler colonies/dominions – the continued, indeed increased, importance of the civil law in the country's second-most populous province. The adoption of the *Civil Code of Lower Canada* in 1866 helped anchor the civil law in two ways: first, it tamed the luxuriant polyjurality of Lower Canadian law with its multiplicity of sources, presenting the main principles of the private law in a single document written in clear and relatively non-technical language. Second, it did so bilingually, so that the law was now accessible to those belonging to both of the province's main linguistic groups. The *Code* inspired substantial commentary, culminating in Pierre-Basile Mignault's *Le droit civil canadien* in nine volumes (1895–1917). But the interpretation of the civil law within a court hierarchy topped by the SCC and the JCPC with their mostly common law trained judges proved to be less than smooth, as noted earlier.

In Chapter 6 we turn to the legal professions, legal education, and legal literature. Lawyers were not slow to seize the new opportunities presented by the union of the British North American colonies, in politics, business, and civil society. The most noticeable trends were the emergence of 'large' law firms (five to 10 lawyers) to serve the needs of large corporations, the spread of university legal education on the US model everywhere except Ontario, and the adoption of the Ontario/

Quebec model of statutory self-governance for the legal profession across Canada, as well as in Newfoundland. Exuberant expansion of the profession in the post-Confederation period resulted in a 'golden age' of local legal services, but this trend reversed by the turn of the century as various tasks became routinized and less lucrative. Full-time law professors remained very rare in the new law schools, but a surprising amount of legal scholarship was written by practising lawyers and judges, supporting a small number of law journals and legal publishers. While provincial legal cultures, especially that of Quebec, retained some distinct features, increasing inter-provincial connections led to the creation of a national organization, the Canadian Bar Association/ Association du barreau canadien, by 1914. Meanwhile, in most provinces the profession reluctantly accepted a very few new entrants in the form of women and members of racial minorities, although women were excluded in Quebec, and British Columbia barred Asians and Indigenous candidates from becoming lawyers.

In part 2, chapters 7–10, the focus is largely on the relationship between the Canadian state and the Métis and Indigenous people, both those living in the original confederating provinces and those added to that state after 1870. Chapter 7 deals with the large geopolitical changes, principally occurring in the 1870s and 1880s. We begin with the acquisition by Canada of the territory between Ontario and British Columbia, which, in 1869 and 1870, resulted in the creation of Manitoba. The province was founded with the consent of its Métis inhabitants, despite Canada's initial attempts to ignore the need for such consent, which inspired Métis resistance. The *Manitoba Act* resolved the conflict and provided a foundation for a peaceful transition for the Métis people, a foundation that was not built upon, indeed was progressively dismantled, beginning almost as soon as it had been laid. We follow the founding of Manitoba with the numbered treaties of the 1870s, which also held out the prospect of lawful and peaceful adjustment of the relations between the Canadian state and the Indigenous people of the prairies. As in Manitoba, that prospect was not realized, and a combination of broken treaty promises and Métis grievances led to an unsuccessful armed rebellion. The most significant legal aspects of that rebellion were the measures taken after its military defeat to punish the participants, particularly the trial and execution of Louis Riel. We devote considerable space to this assertion of Canadian law, and highlight its substantive and procedural inadequacies as a legal proceeding. Chapter 7 also examines the relations between Canada, the new (1871) province of British Columbia, and Indigenous peoples' land rights on the Pacific coast. That British Columbia was able to deny the legal existence of those rights throughout this period, despite Ottawa's pressure to acknowledge them, is in some respects remarkable, particularly as the federal government acknowledged Indigenous title everywhere else in the West by signing the numbered treaties of the 1870s – a subject also dealt with in chapter 7. But in other respects it was not so remarkable, because it clearly indicated that when the imperatives of building a new country from coast to coast clashed with fidelity to the federal government's position on Indigenous rights enunciated in the 1870s, the former won out, and Ottawa gave up the struggle.

Chapters 8 and 9 move the focus from the integration of Indigenous peoples into the Canadian state to Canadian policies towards them. It can be summarized in one word – assimilation. Canada did not want Indigenous peoples to continue to be Indigenous, it wanted what it called a 'civilized' citizenry. Chapter 8 begins with the first federal statute devoted to Indigenous people, the 1869 *Enfranchisement Act*, which laid out a process whereby Indigenous people who were sufficiently 'advanced' could own their piece of reserve land in fee simple, bear a European name, and exercise the franchise like any other male holder of sufficient property. The enfranchisement provisions were incorporated into the first *Indian Act* of 1876, which became one of the longest and most detailed federal statutes, controlling all aspects of a reserve dweller's life, from inheritance to the choice of band leaders to where on the reserve a person could live. Although the *Indian Act* appeared to devolve authority to bands in the same way that municipal law did so to communities, almost every decision had to be approved by the minister in charge in Ottawa, the superintendent-general of Indians, while the minister's representatives, the Indian agents, kept a close eye and a tight leash on communities. In the 1880s and 1890s the attempt to control Indigenous life and societies was extended to some of their social and cultural ceremonial practices, criminal provisions being enacted that banned dancing and feasting in ways that disturbed white Canadian sensibilities – no matter how similar Indigenous rituals might have been to European ones, an irony not lost on the few white Canadians who opposed such laws.

Chapter 9 deals with one aspect of assimilation law and policy that has engaged the attention of the Canadian public in recent years to an extent that history rarely does – residential schools. It places the rise of residential schools from the mid-1880s in the context of education policy generally towards Indigenous children. While education was seen from the outset as a crucial policy tool to achieve assimilation, it was the failure of day schools to achieve this goal that caused the government to put its financial resources into residential schools. There was no better way to 'take the Indian out of the child' than by starting when Indigenous people were young and taking them away from family and community. Looking at it as we do from the vantage point of hindsight, we understand it to have been a flawed policy. It was also flawed in execution. To use a modern term, it was a 'public-private partnership' that went horribly wrong. Residential schools were entrusted to religious organizations because it was cheaper than a state system, the kind of system that prevailed, though not universally, for everybody else in Canada. Religious organizations were more than happy to take on the job, because it provided ideal conditions for the harvesting of souls. When Indigenous people resisted the often terrible physical conditions and the physical and psychological abuse, the government turned in the 1890s to legal coercion.

In spite of settler efforts to ignore or supplant Indigenous law, the subject of chapter 10, it continued to play a fundamental role in many Indigenous communities. Given the difficulty of generalizing about the Indigenous experience, some specific examples are singled out for examination: the Gitxsan, the Mohawk of Kahnawà:ke, the Six Nations of the Grand River, and the Métis. All faced the challenge of adapting to a new economy while also facing new pressures from settler society to conform to European legal and other norms, via the *Indian Act* and other mechanisms. For a variety of reasons the Métis had the most difficulty maintaining their traditional laws, not unconnected to the problems in securing their land base, as described later in chapter 14. In the other communities, Indigenous law displayed a certain resilience, even as compromises with settler demands were required on various issues.

Part 3 of this book, chapters 11 through 14, we have entitled 'Building the New Dominion: Capital, Labour and a Criminal Code.' It covers four areas of law that were of great significance in dealing with the challenges of a creating a new state in an era of nation-building, economic growth, and the settlement of the West by non-Indigenous peoples. Part 3 is also distinct from parts 1 and 2 in saying a lot about areas of law in provincial jurisdiction, with the exception of chapter 13 on criminal justice. Parts 1 and 2, apart from chapter 5 on the civil law, are largely about areas within federal jurisdiction. Dealing with multiple provincial jurisdictions made the task of presenting a succinct and coherent narrative especially challenging. Part 3 could have been organized differently, and our only claim is that we have tried to organize it in the least imperfect way.

We begin part 3 with chapter 11, topics in law and the economy, principally incorporation law and insolvency. Incorporation was a head of both federal and provincial jurisdiction, depending on whether the corporation was located in one province or more. But the principal development in this period, the rise of general incorporation by letters patent rather than incorporation by an act of the legislature, occurred in all jurisdictions, albeit at different times. The chapter also charts the very significant increase in the number of corporations operating in a rapidly industrializing dominion. Although general incorporation became available everywhere in the half-century after Confederation, special act corporations continued to be created by Parliament and provincial legislatures. This was mostly because general incorporation statutes excluded companies operating in certain sectors, notably railways and banking. But some incorporators also preferred to get a customized special act rather than incorporate using the standard letters patent model. The other major topic dealt with in chapter 11 is insolvency, which as it turns out was largely a topic of provincial jurisdiction. The federal government had jurisdiction over bankruptcy and passed a bankruptcy act in 1869. But it was repealed in 1880, after which provincial insolvency regimes, which included the increasingly less used remedy of imprisonment for debt, occupied the field. Chapter 11 also examines aspects of regulation of the economy, in the mining, banking, and railway sectors. In dealing with the last-named, the federal government laid the foundations of the twentieth-century regulatory state.

Chapter 12 on labour and employment law is set against the large transition of this period mentioned at the beginning of this chapter – the transformation of the economy by industrialization. This development saw the labour process greatly altered for many working people. Much more, and larger-scale, workplace conflict ensued, and the law was one of the major weapons used by employers in those conflicts. Many employment disputes continued to be dealt with through master and servant law, within which imprisonment greatly declined as an employer's remedy. But employers used the law in a number of other ways, especially in large-scale industrial conflicts where they were faced with increasing numbers of unions who did not have support from the law beyond no longer being illegal. The civil law torts related to interference with trade took the place of the criminal law, and judges mostly applied that law with rigour. A notable aspect of chapter 13 is the increasing, albeit often ineffective, legislative interference in workplace disputes, health and safety, and compensation for injuries to workers. Arbitration legislation was passed at both the federal and provincial levels, but because it was not mandatory to participate in and awards were not binding, arbitration was largely a dead letter. Health and safety laws were concerned primarily with child and female labour, not the safety of male factory workers, and were largely ineffective from lack of enforcement. The common law governing compensation for injuries was significantly altered by statute, perhaps the major advance for labour in this period. But injured workers or their families still had to go to court. Only in Ontario, and not until 1914, was a modern-day workers' compensation scheme introduced.

Chapter 13 examines the development of major aspects of criminal justice, principally the substantive criminal law, criminal courts and procedure, and punishment. We have already noted in our discussion of liberty and order the ways in which the enactment of the *Criminal Code* in 1892, the first section of chapter 13, reflected the latter more than the former, because the harshest available model was chosen. Yet in placing most of the law of crimes and punishments in one, albeit very long, statute, the Code made the law more easily accessible to all. Transparency about what is criminal and what is not, and in the available punishments, is a necessary if not sufficient contributor to liberty. At the same time, an equally distinctive break from the past was Canada's creation of a unique 'colonial' system of justice in the North-West Territories. By 'colonial' we mean that Britain and other colonial powers frequently 'adapted' criminal procedure to suit their untutored colonial subjects. They imbued magistrates with large summary powers, reduced the size of juries and ensured that subject peoples did not sit on them, and policed those same subjects with armed and mounted gendarmeries, which dramatically symbolized state authority. The Indigenous people of the Territories were dealt with in the same way as the non-white subjects of many parts of the empire, consistent with the theme running through part 2 of Indigenous people as Canada's colonial subjects.

Order rather than liberty is also emphasized in chapter 13's discussion of the creation and expansion of the federal penitentiary system and of two important intermediate prisons under provincial control in Ontario. It may seem trite to say that imprisonment is not about liberty, but there are gradations of order. In this period, penitentiaries were the embodiment of harsh and unremitting regimes of hard labour, and the discipline of solitary confinement and the silent system. If prisons were to rehabilitate, as they had been briefly imagined to do in the 1840s, they rehabilitated through these harsh regimes, and not through education, training, or much in the way of remission incentives. The final sections of chapter 13 examine the ultimate expression of state power, the death penalty. Although used only for those convicted of murder, with the exception of Louis Riel, it was still employed with vigour. About half of those sentenced to death were hanged rather than seeing their sentences commuted to long terms of imprisonment. At the same time there was in this period a pronounced tendency not to hang the small number of women convicted. Nor was there a clear bias against Indigenous defendants. Indeed, there was a willingness to take cultural differences into account, which spared from the noose some Indigenous people who, in taking life, had acted in line with the dictates of their own cultural beliefs. Pluralism played a very significant role in this small corner of the administration of the law.

The definition and allocation of property rights, the subject of chapter 14, is fundamental to any economy. The transformation of the great commons of western Canada with their seemingly limitless herds of bison to millions of surveyed rectangular fee simple plots where no bison roamed is a main theme of this chapter. The treaty and legislative measures taken to achieve this were noted above. To complete this survey of western developments, the chapter examines the complex issue of Métis land titles in Manitoba. It then follows the Prince Edward Island land question to its final resolution shortly after the Island joined Confederation, the expropriation of the remaining large proprietors, and the transformation of their tenants into fee simple holders. The remainder of the chapter examines the reaction against absolutist notions of property and environmental pollution through both the common law (the tort of nuisance and the invention of restrictive covenants) and legislation (the beginnings of municipal land use regulation and provincial legislation addressing water pollution). Protection of property remained a primordial function of the state, but increasingly it was called upon directly to protect some property owners against others as the limits of individualized adjudication were reached.

The changing legal status of women is noted in several chapters, but important developments in common law Canada (see chapter 5 for Quebec developments) are brought together in chapter 15, along with 'family law' generally. The most significant changes were those to married women's property. Some inroads on the doctrine of marital unity, whereby all a wife's property was either vested in or controlled by the husband, had been made prior to Confederation. They were expanded incrementally until by the end of the century married women everywhere outside Quebec could hold property independently of their husbands as if they were single. These reforms were motivated more by a desire to protect women and families than by an ideology of equal rights, even though they ended up giving propertied women virtually equal rights to their husbands in this sphere. The doctrine of marital unity was not abolished, only reformed in this area of the law. Both these points are evident in considering changes in custody law, where the position of mothers was much slower to change, either in case law or legislation, and where change was not predicated on any notion of spousal equality. The 'best interests of the child' test (accepted much earlier in Quebec) was largely accepted by the end of our period, but the slim resources for most married women meant that negotiation and litigation about custody did not occur on a level playing field.

Chapter 15 also considers the complex legal situation regarding divorce, a 'hot-button' topic where legislators feared to tread. Once slavery had been abolished in the United States, the next trope regarding the supposed superiority of Canadians to Americans revolved around divorce. The relatively high divorce rates there, and the seemingly frivolous grounds for divorce prevailing in some states, were a favourite topic of newspaper and other commentary. The extremely low divorce rates in Canada were constantly insisted upon as proving the superior moral tone of Canadians in general and of their family life in particular. Both English and French Canadians shared these attitudes, and as a result the federal Parliament did not exercise its constitutional power over divorce, leaving a patchwork of legal regimes in place across the country. Divorce by private act of Parliament remained the only means of ending a marriage in Ontario, Quebec and the Prairie west throughout the period. Pre-Confederation divorce courts in the Maritimes continued to function pursuant to section 129 of the *BNA Act*, and in British Columbia judicial divorce was available because the English *Divorce and Matrimonial Causes Act 1857*, instituting judicial divorce in England, was in force through the doctrine of reception.

The position of racial minorities in Canada, the topic of chapter 16, was unenviable, to put it mildly. In myriad ways federal and provincial legislation singled out Asians in particular, depriving them of the vote in British Columbia, and through discriminatory levies and labour restrictions aiming to oblige them to leave the province. The powerful labour movement in British Columbia saw the Chinese in particular as providing unfair competition. Widespread antipathy against them resulted in a major anti-Asian riot in Vancouver in 1907. While the levies and labour restrictions were either disallowed by Ottawa or struck down by the courts on division of powers grounds, the withholding of the franchise, which also entailed the right to enter some professions, was upheld. For a time the older generation of British Columbia judges struck down some of these measures on the broad ground that they offended equality under the law and amounted to 'a bill of indictment as against a race.' By the 1890s these judges were gone, however, and a more positivistic division of powers analysis prevailed thereafter, under the watchful eye of the JCPC. Meanwhile, the federal government, even as it disallowed many discriminatory British Columbia statutes, was taking its own measures to impede Asian immigration as much as possible. These included not only Chinese and Japanese nationals, but also non-white British subjects such as those from India, culminating in the notorious *Komagata Maru* confrontation of 1914. Elsewhere in Canada anti-Asian laws were not as wide-ranging as on the West Coast, being generally restricted to laws preventing Chinese restaurant owners from hiring white women in some provinces.

Blacks were generally not subjected to legislated discrimination, except for laws permitting segregated schools. Freedom of contract, however, provided a cover for the practice of discrimination in many areas of life, such as employment, accommodation, and entertainment. And in spite of repeated protestations by judges that justice was colourblind, Blacks did not fare well in the criminal justice system. Meanwhile, the federal government took steps to stem their immigration from the United States, ensuring that they remained a minuscule percentage of the population in 1914, under one-half of 1 *per cent*.

While all religions were theoretically on an equal footing, disputes over denominational schooling could turn into grave political controversies, with ethnocultural rivalries between English and French entangled with the religious dimension. The issue as it arose in Manitoba in the 1890s represented the gravest threat to national unity since the execution of Riel a decade earlier. The SCC affirmed the right to denominational schools based on the wording of the *Manitoba Act*, which was more expansive than the guarantees provided in the *BNA Act*, but the JCPC reversed, throwing the ball back into the political sphere. The Conservatives fumbled it badly and paid the price electorally when Wilfrid Laurier's Liberals prevailed in 1896. Laurier's compromise with the Manitoba government resolved the matter but the dispute had nonetheless shown how easily tensions could erupt between Canada's two largest cultural groups, and that a foreign court not aware of history and local circumstances was not a suitable decision-maker for such disputes.

PART ONE

The Law and Legal Institutions

2

The Constitution: Confederation, The *British North America Act*, and Post-1867 Developments

We begin this second volume of the history of law in Canada with the constitution, specifically the *British North America Act* (*BNA Act*). We will not devote much space to the events that led to three colonies coming together as four provinces to form the new dominion. Confederation was a political process bringing disparate colonies together into a new political arrangement. The general question of why this happened is well known from the extensive literature produced by generations of political historians, and here we provide only a brief summary of that process. Confederation also involved the melding of existing and new constitutional doctrines: the existing ones captured in the phrase of the preamble to the *BNA Act*, which stated that Canada would have 'a constitution similar in principle to that of the United Kingdom,' and the novel features in the body of the *BNA Act*. The content and structure of the *BNA Act*, and the elaboration of its meaning by the courts over the ensuing half-century, are matters of primary interest to the legal historian. The provisions that most concern us are sections 21 through 36, dealing with the Senate; sections 91 and 92, the division of powers; the judiciary provisions, sections 96–101; and sections 56 and 90, which together gave the federal government the power to disallow provincial legislation. When dealing with these topics we will not discuss Indigenous peoples, whose only role in the *BNA Act* is as a subject of jurisdiction in section 91 (24). As the title to the Confederation chapter in Peter Russell's recent constitutional history of Canada succinctly states,

'Aboriginal Canada Gets Left Out' of any participation in the constitutional arrangements of 1867.[1] Indigenous peoples will appear in many of the later chapters, especially chapters 7 through 10.

The first five sections of this chapter deal with the *BNA Act*, looking in turn at the Confederation process, the institutions of the new dominion, principally the Senate, the division of powers, the judiciary provisions, and disallowance. When dealing with the division of powers we will not discuss sections 93 and 94, on education and immigration, which are extensively dealt with in chapter 16. The next section examines the 'old' but continuing constitutional doctrines, principally those relating to the Crown, and the section thereafter the extent to which the new dominion was not truly 'independent,' remained subject to the UK government and without an autonomous role on the international stage. There follows an account of the addition of new provinces to the original four in the first half dozen years after 1867: British Columbia in 1871 and Prince Edward Island in 1873. Manitoba also joined in this period, in 1870, but we have reserved discussion of that to chapter 7, one of the chapters dealing with Indigenous peoples, because the fate of the Métis in the new constitutional structure was the crucial part of that story. This section also examines the entry of two more provinces into Confederation in the early twentieth century, Alberta and Saskatchewan, and the creation of the Yukon territory.

There follows a long section on the refashioning of the balance of power and jurisdiction between provinces and the federal government by judicial interpretations of sections 91 and 92 of the *BNA Act*, principally by the JCPC, between the 1870s and the early twentieth century. In this process what had been intended by many of the founders to be a constitution featuring a strong central government was remoulded into one with a more equal balance between the centre and the provinces. The final section examines the controversy over, and effective demise of, the federal government's power of disallowance in the late nineteenth century.

The Making of Confederation: A Very Brief Survey

Although we will not extensively discuss the general history of the making of Confederation, a few points need to be made here to provide a context for an examination of the provisions of the *BNA Act* most relevant to legal history.[2] First, while there was talk of union between the British North American colonies in the mid-1850s, and of a union of the Maritime provinces only, the serious business of constructing the federation did not begin until 1864 and was thus remarkably rapid.

Second, Confederation was essentially a process by which the unitary colony of the Province of Canada was split into two provinces, which were then joined by two other provinces from the Maritimes. As one historian has succinctly put it, 'Confederation originated as an agreement to federalize United Canada.'[3] Confederation was driven by the interests of what became Ontario and Quebec, which needed above all else to resolve the increasingly untenable constitutional structure of the *Act of Union* of 1840. Throughout the 1850s there were developing tensions within the Province of Canada, caused principally by the fact that the *Act of Union* gave Upper and Lower Canada equal representation in the assembly but the population balance changed in favour of Upper Canada from ca. 1850.[4] The response of many Upper Canadian politicians, especially reform leader George Brown, was to demand representation by population. They saw it as a way to legislate in accordance with their liberal, modern, low Protestant values, which were increasingly at odds with those of the conservatives, who more and more came to dominate Lower Canadian elections, in part because of the influence of a politically resurgent Catholic Church. In turn Lower Canadians became increasingly concerned at the effect that representation by population would have on the role of their bedrock institutions of the French language, civil law, and the Catholic Church. The legislative process became 'utterly dysfunctional,' and no solution could be arrived at until the 'grand coalition' between the conservative forces in Upper and Lower Canada, led respectively by John A. Macdonald and George-Étienne Cartier, formed a government with Brown for the purpose of dissolving the union and forming some form of federal system. Shortly before, in June 1864, a Province of Canada assembly committee on the constitution, chaired by Brown and with members from all parties, prepared a report stating that '[a] strong feeling was found to exist among members of the committee in favour of "a federative system,"' either within the Province of Canada or one involving British North America as a whole.[5]

Third, details of the new constitution were worked out in two intercolonial conferences, in Charlottetown in September 1864 and in Quebec City in October of the same year. The former was originally arranged to discuss Maritime union, but the Maritime premiers were persuaded by the Province of Canada's Governor General Viscount Monck to invite delegates from Upper and Lower Canada. In just six days Charlottetown produced unanimous agreement that, in Brown's words, 'federation of all the provinces [was] … highly desirable, if the terms of union could be made satisfactory.'[6] In advance of the Quebec conference the Canadian cabinet seized the initiative, drawing up a set of concrete proposals for a union. The 16-day Quebec conference, involving 33 delegates from four colonies drawn from both major political parties and attended also by two observers from Newfoundland, produced 72 resolutions, which largely formed the substance of the *BNA Act*. A subsequent conference in London in 1866 drafted the final language of the act but added very little of substance. Unlike the *Act of Union* of 1840, which was imposed on the Canadas, the 1867 constitution was very much a made-in-Canada document.

Fourth, in the end, the eastern provinces were somewhat reluctant adherents to the new arrangements. Two of them, Prince Edward Island and Newfoundland, did not join the federation in 1867, making it somewhat ironic that Charlottetown is often talked of as the cradle of Confederation. In addition, the New Brunswick assembly endorsed union in the summer of 1866 but did not vote on the specific terms. The Province of Canada assembly approved the Quebec Resolutions by a margin of 91–33, with much of the opposition coming from the Lower Canadian *rouge* party, the somewhat anticlerical grouping and the political descendants of the nationalist Louis-Joseph Papineau. But in May 1866 the Prince Edward Island assembly voted down the resolutions, and when the possibility of joining the pact was debated in St. John's it quickly became clear that there was little support, primarily because of the prospect of high tariffs to protect central Canadian industry, which would harm Newfoundland, whose markets were in Europe and the United States. In New Brunswick and Nova Scotia, Premiers Leonard Tilley and Charles Tupper soon found increasing opposition to the Quebec Resolutions, not to union as such but to specific aspects of the proposals. The result was that, after some twists and turns, both assemblies agreed to send delegates to the London conference to negotiate the final details, but neither voted on the principle of Confederation. Local politicians' desire, and perhaps ability, to join with central Canada was also augmented by the Province of Canada's agreement at the Quebec conference to fund a railway line from Quebec to Halifax. This became the Intercolonial Railway, seen by many in the Maritimes as necessary for the region's economic development.

Fifth, and finally, there were macro-level considerations favouring a united dominion. The one most stressed by Quebec historians is the need for unity to foster economic development, of which the intercolonial railway was a key element.[7] American expansionist continentalism, which had long lurked in the background of Anglo-American–British North American relations, also played a role. Concern about the United States in London was damped down in the early 1860s while the civil war raged, but the end of the conflict saw a revival of anxiety about American expansionism, exacerbated by Fenian (Irish nationalist) raids. The Fenians garnered much sympathy in the northern states, in part because Britain had favoured the Confederacy during the war. The belief that Britain's imperial position needed British North American unity was reflected in the preamble to the *BNA Act*, which included an assertion that the union would 'promote the Interests of the British Empire.' The local desire for union also coincided with Britain's concomitant desire to spend less on colonial defence and the support given by British capital to a union. Some $100 million in British capital had been invested in the Province of Canada in the 1850s, much of it in the troubled Grand Trunk Railway. Both Canadians and British investors believed that building the intercolonial railway would improve the position of the Grand Trunk and the British North American economy in general. Thus overall Canada did not have to fight for its independence; it pushed gently against an open door. In 1862 the colonial secretary stated that while the British government did not think it their place 'to initiate any movement towards ... union,' at the same time it had 'no wish to impede any well-considered scheme' that colonial politicians could arrange, 'assuming of course that it does not interfere with Imperial interests.'[8] If Britain had a position on the proposed federation, it was that the central authority was not strong enough; it wanted the provinces to be closer to municipalities and, with the myopia not untypical of empires, drew an analogy with the union between England and Scotland.

The *BNA Act*: The Senate, the Division of Powers, the Judiciary, and Disallowance

There was never any doubt that the constitution of the new dominion would be parliamentary, not presidential, and the number of members of Parliament in each province would be chosen on the basis of representation by population. Prince Edward Island delegates at Charlottetown argued for a House of Commons based on equal representation for each province, but that idea was quickly and firmly quashed by all other delegates.[9] But much still had to be worked out at the two 1864 conferences and thereafter. The principal issues were the Senate, the judiciary, the division of powers, and disallowance.[10]

The *BNA Act* section 17 established that legislative power would reside partly in an upper house, the Senate, which would take the place of the colonial legislative councils. Senators would represent the provinces, even though initially MPs from Ontario and Quebec could also simultaneously hold seats in the Commons and provincial legislatures. Ontario barred the practice in 1872 and the federal Parliament did so in 1873.[11] Sections 21 and 22 of the *BNA Act* set the number of senators at 72, representing three divisions – Ontario, Quebec, and the Maritime provinces – each division having 24. Nova Scotia and New Brunswick had 12 each. Senators had to be 30 years old and owners of freehold land, or its civil law equivalent tenure in *franc-alleu*, valued at $4,000; they were also required to own at least $4,000 in real and personal property, over and above all liabilities. Senators were to be appointed by the governor general, that is, the federal government, not elected, and held office for life. Sections 26 and 27 allowed for the addition of three to six senators, representing the three divisions equally, to a maximum of 78. The Senate provisions were thus in some respects a backward step. The property qualification was higher than it had been in some colonies, and there was no elective principle as there had been in the Province of Canada and Nova Scotia.[12] Finally, sections 146 and 147 dealt with the admission of new colonies into Confederation, providing that both Newfoundland and Prince Edward Island would have four senators each if they joined.[13] These numbers changed, of course, with the entry of other territories and provinces into Confederation in later decades; we have dealt here only with the *BNA Act* of 1867.

The composition of the upper house and the method of choosing its members were matters over which some time was spent at the Quebec conference, at which the upper house continued to be referred to as the legislative council. The delegates spent a week of 'fierce wrangling' on the issue, one that of all questions brought the conference 'closest to breakdown.'[14] Three points were debated. First, and most easily disposed of, how should seats be distributed among the provinces? All agreed that it should be done on the basis of 'equality,' but there was disagreement over whether that should be 'provincial equality' or 'sectional equality.' The latter, which as noted above was the formula adopted, was seen by central Canadian delegates as a generous concession to the Maritimes, which would have one-third of the seats but much less than one-third of the population. Nonetheless the premiers of

Nova Scotia and New Brunswick pushed hard for more before conceding the point. A more fundamental challenge was presented by Prince Edward Island, whose delegates advocated an American-style system, with all constituent units having equal representation. This proposal went nowhere,[15] but it did wring a small concession from central Canada that if Newfoundland, which sent two observers to Quebec, joined the Confederation pact, four senators for Newfoundland would be added. Newfoundland had initially been included in the Senate proposals as one of four 'lower provinces,' sharing the twenty-four senators allotted to that section. The composition of the Senate was also one of the few issues on which there was a change at the final London conference in December 1866. By then it was clear that Prince Edward Island would not be part of the new dominion, and Nova Scotia and New Brunswick successfully insisted that the allotment of twenty-four senators be retained for their section.

The second major issue at Quebec related to the Senate was the method of choosing senators. Whether they should be elected or appointed, and if the latter, who should appoint them, took up two days of the conference. Partially elected legislative councils had been in place in the Province of Canada since 1854 and Prince Edward Island since 1863, and the other colonies had approved the idea in principle, though they had not legislated it into practice.[16] Oliver Mowat, an Upper Canadian reformer and a minister in the Brown-Macdonald coalition, was the principal proponent of an elected upper house, while his party leader, George Brown, was its most vehement opponent. Brown's position was condemned by some as reactionary, a return to the colonial constitutions of the late eighteenth and early nineteenth centuries. But contemporaries who took this position failed to understand the reasoning of men like Brown and his fellow vocal advocate of appointment, Nova Scotian reformer Jonathan McCully. Brown had long opposed the undemocratic influence that an elected legislative council in the Province of Canada could wield, and his opposition to elected upper chambers was based on his bedrock belief in responsible government. An elective upper house would have real power and legitimacy and therefore be able to challenge the primacy of the Commons. In a speech he gave in Toronto after the Quebec conference, Brown argued that 'while the lower house controlled the government of the day and the government of the day appointed the members of the upper house, the people had full and efficient control over the public affairs.' But, he continued, '[t]he question ... [is] whether two elective chambers, both representing the people and both claiming to have control over the public finances, would act together with the harmony necessary to the right working of parliamentary government.'[17] These arguments convincingly won the day, and time has proved Brown, and Macdonald, right that the Senate would, with very few exceptions, be a body that considered and proposed amendments to legislation, not one that blocked it.

The third issue was related to the second. Given that senators would be appointed, who should appoint them? Once the appointive principle had been accepted, it did not prove that difficult to get unanimous agreement that the federal government would do so. This came with a rider that the initial set of senators would be a bipartisan group, appointed from all parties in proportion to their existing numbers in colonial legislative councils. There were suggestions of appointment by the provinces, but this was opposed, even by Maritime premiers Tilley and Tupper, for the same reason that they opposed election of senators. Senators chosen by provincial governments could call on their appointment as a source of legitimacy, which would embolden them to set themselves up against the democratic will. Men like Tilley and Tupper 'believed in parliamentary democracy ... more than they believed in a Senate that would be a voice for the regions.'[18]

The principal issue worked out between 1864 and 1867 was the precise division of powers, encapsulated largely in sections 91 and 92. There is broad but by no means universal agreement among historians that the scheme agreed on in the Quebec Resolutions, on which the *BNA Act* was largely based, was a centralist one, designed to create a strong national government.[19] As we will see later in this chapter, the primacy of the federal government was somewhat undermined in the decades after 1867 by judicial decisions, but this does not take away from the fact that the structure agreed upon in the 1860s was fundamentally centralist.

There was surprisingly little discussion of the heads of power in sections 91 and 92 at the Quebec conference, but one can see this centralist orientation both by a close examination of the text of the *BNA Act*, and by reference to the words of the founders. The heading of section 92 was 'exclusive powers of provincial legislatures,' that of section 91 'powers of the Parliament.' The powers of Parliament were not only the ones enumerated in section 91, while provincial powers were specifically enumerated, and limited only to the heads of jurisdiction listed in section 92. Residuary power rested in the federal Parliament, expressed partly through the preamble to section 91 that allowed the federal Parliament to legislate for the 'peace, order and good government' of the new dominion. Residuary power was also implicitly given in section 91 (29), which gave Parliament jurisdiction over 'such classes of subjects as are expressly excepted' in the descriptions of provincial powers under section 92, and went on to state that 'any matter coming within any of the classes of subjects enumerated in this section shall not be deemed to come within the class of matters of a local or private nature' assigned to the provinces. All of this was in substantial part a response to what was seen as the weakness of the federal government in the United States, where residuary power lay with the states and where states' rights had contributed to a bloody and costly civil war in the years immediately before Confederation. As a leading Prince Edward politician and its strongest pro-Confederation advocate, Thomas Heath Haviland stated, 'The basis of our scheme, so as to avoid difficulties of the United States, is to give limited powers to local Legislatures.'[20] Macdonald spoke at the Quebec conference to the same effect. The Americans' 'primary error' had been that 'each state reserved to itself all sovereign rights, save that portion delegated. We must reverse this process by strengthening the general government and conferring on the provincial bodies only such powers as may be required for local purposes.'[21]

The desire for a strong federal government can also be seen in other aspects of the *BNA Act*. The disallowance power, for example, discussed below, allowed the federal government to disallow provincial legislation that it thought trenched on federal power. Sections 94 and 95, on immigration and agriculture respectively, made both concurrent areas of jurisdiction but also provided that any provincial law in those areas 'shall have effect in and for the Province as long and as far only as it is not repugnant to any Act of the Parliament of Canada.' These two subjects were contentious in the 1860s. At the Quebec conference, voices were heard for both being local and concurrent powers, and the issue for both seems to have been settled by British North America's continuing need for immigrants. D'Arcy McGee, minister for agriculture in the Province of Canada government, observed that '[t]he General Government may draw attention to this country for settlement. The only permanent attraction we can offer is cheap land.' He therefore proposed that the local legislature 'should be bound to let immigrants have lands as hitherto. Immigrants should feel that they came to British America as a whole, and that they are free to choose lands as they like.'[22]

Most importantly, one can see the centralist ambition in the powers given to the federal Parliament. Those included the kinds of things that any national government had to have: control over the armed forces, the currency, and naturalization. But section 91 went much further. There would be a national criminal law, unlike in the United States, where criminal law was a state matter. 'It was admitted with one voice,' New Brunswick's John Hamilton Gray stated in his account of Confederation, 'that the criminal law must be the same throughout the whole, and that the Parliament of the General Government must form the criminal code.'[23] There would also be national jurisdiction over trade and commerce, national control of the banks, the fisheries, the post office, of laws relating to bankruptcy and insolvency, and much else required to give the central government the ability to manage and develop the national economy. Finally, as numerous treaties had been made between Indigenous peoples and the imperial Crown, the federal government also received jurisdiction over 'Indians, and lands reserved for Indians.'

The centralist orientation of sections 91 and 92 was reflected in contemporary debates and speeches at the Quebec conference and afterwards. No one was more emphatic on the point than Macdonald. He wanted the relations between the central government and the provinces to replicate those between the imperial Parliament and colonial legislatures.[24] At the same time, the provinces were clearly intended to be more than minor subordinate authorities controlling only insignificant matters. They received jurisdiction over education (via section 93),[25] civil (as opposed to criminal) law, court systems, the administration of justice generally (including police forces), municipalities, social services, the administration of public lands, and 'all matters of a local and private nature.' Provincial ability to raise revenue was limited to revenues from public lands, direct taxation, which at that time was of little import, and licensing fees. In recognition of this limited range of fiscal tools, federal subsidies of $2.5 million annually were provided.

This interpretation of Confederation as a centralist enterprise coupled with sufficient local powers to accommodate and sustain French-Canadian culture is a broadly accepted one, though not the universal view. Leading Quebec historian Eugénie Brouillet, for example, puts more emphasis on how much the colonies, especially Quebec, retained when they became provinces.[26] And almost since the day the new dominion came into being, some contemporaries and historians argued, and have continued to argue, that Confederation was a compact, an arrangement in which the provinces were intended to be equal partners with the federal government and sovereign within their own spheres. This argument will be taken up in more detail in the section below on the evolution of the division of powers after 1867. Before leaving this discussion of a centrally focused constitution, it is worth noting that at the time no politician considered Indigenous sovereignty to be part of the equation.

Within this broadly centralist framework, two closely related factors determined precisely what powers were given to the provinces and which to the national government. First, their respective powers broadly reflected the way that the union of the Canadas had worked in practice, almost from its inception. Increasingly over time the union legislature passed three different kinds of legislation: some acts were declared to operate throughout the Province of Canada, some to operate only within Upper Canada, and some only within Lower Canada. The most visible expressions of this practice were the three statutory consolidations produced between 1859 and 1861, one consolidating the laws applicable to Canada, the other two those applicable to Upper and Lower Canada respectively. There is a very close correlation between the subjects listed in sections 91–3 of the *BNA Act*, and those listed in these consolidations. The consolidations were in effect a blueprint for sections 91 and 92. Not only did central Canada drive the Confederation process, it also provided in large measure the details on what went in section 91 and what went in section 92.[27] Macdonald used the Province of Canada's experience with this form of quasi-federalism to justify the division of powers. 'We, in Canada, already know something of the advantages and disadvantages of a federal union,' he told the Province of Canada assembly in 1865, because 'since the union in 1841 we have had a federal union; that in matters affecting Upper Canada solely, members from that section claimed and generally exercised the right of exclusive legislation, while members from Lower Canada legislated in matters affecting only their own section. We have had a federal union in fact, though a legislative union in name.'[28]

Second, the content of sections 92 and 93 of the *BNA Act*, like the quasi-federal operation of the union after 1841, was intended to accommodate two distinct linguistic and cultural units. As noted above, by the 1860s the sectional equality of the Province of Canada was increasingly frustrating to the Upper Canadians, yet the Lower Canadians insisted on retaining it because it preserved their distinctive language, religion, civil law, and institutions legal, social, and cultural. Hence section 92 included in particular jurisdiction over local government ('municipal institutions in the province'), 'local works and undertakings,' property and civil rights, and the administration of justice. A separate section, 93, gave the provinces jurisdiction over education. The continuity with the union period, the need to protect certain aspects of Lower Canadian society and culture, and the extent to which the politicians from the Province of Canada drove the Confederation discussions, were all captured by John Rose, a friend and close confidant of Macdonald, speaking in the assembly in 1865: 'Those things have been carefully guarded which the minorities in the various sections required for their protection, and the regulation of which each province was not unnaturally desirous of retaining for itself.'[29] Antoine-Aimé Dorion, a sometime leading figure in the Lower Canadian *rouge*, or radical, party, and an anti-Confederate in the 1860s, stressed in the same year the need to retain what Lower Canada had long enjoyed within the Province of Canada. 'The people of Lower Canada are attached to their institutions in a manner that defies any attempt to change them in that way. They will not change their religious institutions, their laws or their language for any consideration whatever…. [You] will see the whole people of Lower Canada clinging together to resist, by all legal and constitutional means, [any] attempt at wresting from them those institutions that they now enjoy.'[30] George Brown, speaking at a dinner in Toronto before leaving for the Quebec conference, agreed. 'Education and the rights of property, and the civil law' were all given to local governments 'in order to afford that protection which the Lower Canadians claim for their language and their laws, and their peculiar institutions.'[31]

We move from the division of powers to the judiciary provisions, the *BNA Act*, sections 96–101. The most significant was section 96, which provided that the judges of the 'superior, county and district courts' of all provinces would be appointed by the governor general, meaning the federal government. The choice of 'Superior' Court in section 96 reflected the fact that the highest courts of common law and equity had different names in different colonies but, as holders of the jurisdiction of the royal courts at Westminster Hall, they had equivalent inherent jurisdiction. The inclusion of 'county and district courts' in section 96 was in effect a reference to Ontario, because when the *BNA Act* was passed it was the only province with such courts staffed by judges with legal training.[32] New Brunswick created professionally staffed county courts in June 1867, a few weeks before the Act came into force.[33] The significance of the inclusion of county and district courts, and most likely the reason why New Brunswick established county courts, was that section

100 of the *BNA Act* gave the federal government the responsibility for establishing and paying the 'salaries, allowances and pensions' of the judges of these courts.

Sections 97 and 98 ensured that the judges in the four original provinces had to be chosen from the bars of the respective province. Section 98 guaranteed that Quebec judges 'shall be selected from the bar of that province.' Section 97 dealt with New Brunswick, Nova Scotia, and Ontario and said the same thing, but with a proviso. Judges had to come from the local bar 'until the laws relative to property and civil rights' in the three provinces 'are made uniform.' Sections 97 and 98 applied to the four original provinces in 1867, not to any that were added in the future. As we shall see in chapter 3, most of the early judges appointed to the courts of Manitoba, the Northwest Territories, Alberta, and Saskatchewan were not residents of those regions before appointment to the bench, for the simple reason that there was not much of a local bar to provide them. But nor was John Hamilton Gray, appointed the third judge of the British Columbia Supreme Court in 1872, a 'local'; he was 'parachuted' in from New Brunswick.

Section 99 gave all Superior Court judges, but not those of the county and district courts, good behaviour tenure. This put the judges of New Brunswick, which did not have such tenure in 1867, on the same footing as those of the other confederating colonies, which did. Finally, section 101, the last of the judiciary provisions, gave the federal Parliament the power to create a 'general court of appeal for Canada' and to establish 'any additional courts for the better administration of the laws of Canada.' This provision will be more fully discussed in the next chapter, in relation to the establishment in 1875 of the SCC and the Exchequer Court.

Little has been written about the origins of the judiciary provisions. The only one that excited much debate in the 1860s was the requirement that judges be appointed from the bars of their own provinces. This section was related to section 94, which expressed the desirability of uniform laws for the common law provinces and gave the federal Parliament a permissive power to enact uniform laws but specified that any such legislation would not be in force until the local legislature agreed. Section 94's limitation to the common law provinces was obviously meant to ensure the continued survival of the Quebec civil law, but it has never amounted to anything, and all private law has remained provincial.[34] But even within the common law provinces there was a fear of Ontario judicial imperialism. In his account of the Confederation debates, John Hamilton Gray referred to this as 'a vague dread of the overawing power of Canada,' which 'led some of the delegates from the Maritime Provinces to fear that the courts of their Provinces might be filled with judges who were strangers to their laws, and whose traditions were with other lands.'[35] Gray did not refer to it, but there was likely also concern that local lawyers would miss out on desirable promotions to the bench.

As for the other judiciary provisions, it has been suggested that federal appointment was a form of quality control, an argument made by Edward Barron Chandler, a lawyer and a New Brunswick delegate at Charlottetown. Chandler reasoned that local legislatures would be deprived of much of their power after Confederation, and talented men, including talented lawyers, would therefore turn to federal politics. If judicial appointments were left in provincial hands, provincial governments would name their own lawyer supporters in local assemblies, by definition 'obscure and incompetent men who would excite the contempt ... of those practicing before them.' New Brunswick Premier Leonard Tilley 'warmly supported' this proposal for central appointment for the same reasons, as did the solicitor general for Lower Canada, Hector-Louis Langevin, in 1865.[36] A similar argument, that federal appointment was intended to make judges more independent of politics and patronage, is somewhat plausible, given the appointment scandals in the pre-Confederation era, especially the case of William Young, who, as premier of Nova Scotia, appointed himself chief justice in 1860.[37] Yet the argument is ultimately untenable. Section 96 did nothing to eliminate patronage, it merely centralized it.

Other explanations have included the argument that central appointment was an attempt to raise the status of the judiciary and, concomitantly, the rule of law, by making the latter a facet of national, not local, culture. It has also been suggested that the origin of section 96 resided in Macdonald's prescient desire to give future prime ministers, that is, himself, control over a raft of patronage appointments. This theory derives some support from the extent to which judicial appointments after 1867 were indeed heavily patronage based. It has also been argued that since provincial courts could hear cases involving the *BNA Act*, in contrast to US state courts, which could only rule on state law, contemporaries saw their judges as needing to be nationally appointed. A rather simpler answer is that while federal appointment was 'fortified' by a desire to retain plum patronage appointments in future federal politicians' hands, 'there is no evidence of any deep thinking about Canada's judicial system in the deliberations that produced the 1867 constitution.'[38]

Perhaps the most plausible explanation for why the federal government received the power of appointment was that it also got, in section 100, the responsibility of paying those judges' salaries. Judicial salaries had long been a non-trivial item in the very limited colonial budgets, and delegates may have well been willing to cede the appointment power if they could also be relieved of the payment responsibility. This argument is supported by one of Hector Langevin's speeches in the Province of Canada assembly in 1865. He reminded his audience that 'although it may be looked upon as a secondary consideration, yet it may as well be mentioned now, that by leaving the appointment of our judges to the Central Government, we are the gainers by one hundred thousand dollars, which will have to be paid for ... by the central power.'[39] The argument also draws circumstantial support from the actions of New Brunswick, noted above. About to lose the ability to appoint judges to its newly created county court, it knew it would come out ahead if the federal government, not the province, had to pay the salaries of the new court's judges.

Sections 56 and 90 of the *BNA Act* gave the federal government a power of disallowance over provincial legislation through the formal operation of the governor general's power, as the Crown's representative, to give or withhold royal assent to any legislation. Section 56 was a holdover from the pre-Confederation years when all colonial legislation had to be approved in London, a power that London used decreasingly after the colonies obtained responsible government. It applied to all federal legislation and provided that the governor general should send all legislation to which he gave royal assent to London, which then had two years to disallow it. Section 90 made section 56 applicable to provincial legislation. The lieutenant governors of the provinces would play the role of the governor general in section 56, and the governor general would play the role of the London authorities. A provincial act had to be disallowed within a year of its enactment. Here we will deal only with the largely uncontroversial origins and early use of the disallowance power.[40] Disallowance did not evoke strong emotions until the 1880s, when it was attacked by provincial rights advocates, and that part of the story requires an understanding of the provincial rights movement and the court battles over the division of powers. We will therefore pick up disallowance again in a later section of this chapter.

For some leading participants in the making of the *BNA Act* disallowance, proposed by Oliver Mowat and approved at the Quebec conference, it was a useful and necessary tool for protecting minorities against discriminatory provincial legislation. Judicial review of legislation was not well established, and was certainly not seen as a way of protecting minorities. Hence the resort to disallowance. John Rose, for example, a representative of the English minority in Canada East, saw it as a tool to safeguard his constituents' rights against a French and Catholic majority. George Brown agreed; minorities, or individuals, would have a way of avoiding 'unjust' legislation. Some Lower Canadian representatives in the Province of Canada assembly agreed that majorities within provinces might be prevented from controlling minorities, but opposed disallowance for that very reason. Henri-Gustave Joly, rouge party member for Lotbinière, worried that it would be used to undermine francophone control of Quebec out of solicitude for the English minority. Antoine-Aimé Dorion similarly voiced concern that local majorities would be overridden by the central authority. Although the evidence on why the disallowance power was included is thin, what there is supports the hypothesis that protection of minorities within provinces was the motivation.[41]

In fact disallowance was not used for such a purpose in the early years after 1867. In mid-1868 Macdonald himself (he was minister of justice as well as prime minister) told provincial governments that the federal authorities would use disallowance in only three circumstances: if provincial legislation was in whole or in part 'illegal or unconstitutional,' if provincial legislation clashed with national legislation in areas of concurrent jurisdiction, and in cases 'affecting the interests of the Dominion generally.' The first two categories clearly referred to provincial legislation that was ultra vires. The third category of disallowance was vague and open ended, but Macdonald also told his counterparts that provincial legislation should be disallowed 'as little as possible.' The power would be exercised 'with great caution' and 'only in cases where the law and the general interests of the Dominion imperatively demand it.' Moreover, if the federal government was considering acting, it would discuss the matter with the province first and give it the opportunity to rethink its position.[42] While a proponent of a strong central government, Macdonald sought to assure provincial leaders that he did not plan to use disallowance to override provincial autonomy in the fields included in section 92 of the *BNA Act*.

Macdonald was true to his announced guidelines. Between 1868, when it disallowed a Nova Scotia statute that conflicted with Parliament's criminal law power, and 1873, the federal government disallowed just five pieces of provincial legislation, all for reasons that came within the terms of Macdonald's 1868 letter.[43] This figure gives a somewhat false impression of the extent of federal government oversight, for on a number of occasions Ottawa asked provincial governments to amend or repeal legislation, and the province obliged. Most of the legislation considered in Ottawa was referred there by provincial lieutenant governors, who took it upon themselves to be concerned that it was outside provincial jurisdiction. But some legislation approved by the lieutenant governors was referred to the federal cabinet by the minister of justice, often with petitions from people in the relevant province, for consideration for disallowance. Ottawa refused disallowance in every such case, such as when local Catholics complained that New Brunswick's *Common Schools Act* would end the de facto denominational school system in the province.[44] Arguably this was a case where a minority sought to use disallowance to protect its rights. Conservative Timothy Anglin proclaimed in the Commons that the act 'outraged, insulted and deprived [Catholics] of their just rights and privileges.'[45] Macdonald did not disagree on the desirability of denominational education for minorities, but he insisted that the only issue was whether New Brunswick was within its jurisdiction in enacting the legislation. That question was resolved by the courts and is discussed in more detail in chapter 16. When disallowance did occur, it was not undertaken without substantial consultation, within Ottawa, between Ottawa and the provincial capitals, and between Ottawa and London, where the law officers of the Crown frequently contributed their opinion. On occasion, even when Macdonald had his doubts about a particular law, the federal government would let it stand. An 1870 Nova Scotia provision on the discharge of insolvent debtors 'may perhaps infringe on the jurisdiction of the Dominion Parliament,' concluded the federal cabinet, but 'the objection is not of sufficient importance to warrant … disallowance.'[46] Thus the disallowance provisions were used sparingly and not to protect provincial minorities. A similar approach was taken by the Mackenzie administration, which disallowed 18 acts in a comparable period. The increase was fuelled in large measure by the disallowance of statutes from the new provinces of British Columbia and Manitoba, which had seven and six statutes respectively disallowed. This legislation, dealing mainly with anti-Asian measures (British Columbia) and railway statutes contrary to dominion policy (Manitoba), is discussed in a later section of this chapter and in other chapters.

A Constitution Similar in Principle: Canadianizing the Crown

A constitution similar in principle to that of the United Kingdom meant a constitutional monarchy with a parliamentary form of government. Canada was also a federal state, which the United Kingdom emphatically was not, and federalism would require significant adjustments to both constitutional monarchy and parliamentary government. The *BNA Act* said much less about these principles than about federalism, ostensibly because the constitutional lore on these topics was well understood. But there was much less that could be said, or at least said succinctly, about these matters because so much of their development, both in the United Kingdom and in British North America, had occurred organically through convention rather than strict law. Thus, the key concept of responsible government was not explicitly mentioned in the act. Nor were political parties, or the office of prime minister. Nor was the cabinet, which appears only in the guise of 'the Queen's Privy Council of Canada,' of which it was (and is) a committee. Those actors who do appear frequently in the *BNA Act*, the Queen, the governor general, and the lieutenant governors, appear to have vast powers, whereas their exercise was heavily circumscribed by convention – though whether all these conventions applied in the new nation would become a matter of some debate. In this section we examine the position of the Crown, the role of conventions, and the nature of the new dominion.

Macdonald observed during the Confederation debates that 'not a single suggestion was made, that it could, by any possibility, be for the interest of the colonies, or for any section or portion of them, that there should be a severance of our connection' to the Crown.[47] Here was one topic on which Indigenous peoples, had they been consulted, and the settler population, with very few exceptions, could agree: the new state had to be a monarchy. Indigenous peoples had for centuries established relationships with the representatives of British monarchs, not with assemblies or other political bodies in settler society. Among the settler population, whether of British, French, or Irish extraction, the monarchy was familiar, it distinguished the northern nation from the United States, and it was associated with the rights and liberties that were thought to inhere in British subjects. Moreover, sovereignty in the new nation lay in the Crown in Parliament. Severing the monarchical connection would have required replacing the Queen with some other office or institution, and very few had any interest in doing so.

The British government tried to maintain Canada within the monarchical orbit by appointing one of Queen Victoria's sons-in-law as governor general in 1878 and her third son as governor general in 1911. Princess Louise Caroline Alberta was married to the Marquess of Lorne, who served as governor general from 1878 to 1883. A suffragist, feminist, and talented sculptor – all choices that horrified her mother – Princess Louise maintained her connection with Canada after returning to England.* Notably, on hearing of the 1885 Northwest Rebellion, she sent relief monies with the direction that they be distributed to relieve suffering on both sides. Her name was given to Lake Louise, the province of Alberta, and various other sites, while a Halifax battalion was renamed after her, the Princess Louise Fusiliers. Her brother Prince Arthur served as governor general from 1911 to 1916, the only royal ever to have done so. His first visit to Canada in 1869–70 was connected to his military duties, and he saw action as part of the force that repelled the Fenian raid at Eccles Hill, near Frelighsburg, Quebec, in May 1870. In 1869 he was made a chief of the Six Nations of Grand River, affirming their historic tie to the British monarchy. Arthur's daughter Patricia gave her name to a new regiment raised during the First World War, Princess Patricia's Canadian Light Infantry. The service of both royals during their vice-regal tenures demonstrated a performance of constitutional monarchy that was much appreciated in Canada. It also flattered Canadians' sense of importance by confirming the nation's role as pre-eminent among the dominions.[48]

Section 9 of the *BNA Act* stated that '[t]he Executive Government and Authority of and over Canada is hereby declared to continue and be vested in the Queen.' This provision, which may appear to accord the monarch a merely titular or symbolic role, was (and is) the cornerstone of Canadian government: it means that, constitutionally, the executive 'is not a creature of legislation but independent of it.'[49] Apart from the very few reserve powers of the monarch or her representative, prerogative powers could not, by the conventions of responsible government, be exercised other than on the advice of the prime minister or the cabinet. The cabinet was thus the inheritor of the residuum of inherent authority vested in the Crown known as the royal prerogative. The extent of these powers is evident from a partial codification of the prime minister's 'special prerogatives' contained in an Order in Council of 1896, which was itself issued under prerogative, not statutory, authority.

---

* Princess Louise was the first daughter of a monarch to wed a non-royal since 1515. The Marquess, later Duke of Argyll, belonged to the upper nobility but was not of royal blood.

They included the dissolution and convocation of Parliament, and the appointment, among others, of privy councillors, cabinet ministers, lieutenant governors, the speaker of the Senate, the chief justices of all courts, and senators. The list was not exhaustive, nor could it be: the full extent of prerogative power has never been categorically settled either in the United Kingdom or Canada, and 'its very imprecision confers on the Crown's advisers discretionary power of great breadth.'[50]

Debates in the early Confederation years centred on the extent to which the governor general was required to take the advice of cabinet before exercising the various powers vested in the office in the *BNA Act*. Some, such as the power of reservation in section 55 discussed above, were obviously to be exercised personally, but the situation with other powers was not always clear. In fact no new mandate was provided to the governor general in 1867; rather, the letters patent and instructions given to previous governors of the Province of Canada were simply recycled. This situation was rectified in 1878 when new 'permanent' letters patent and instructions were provided and various matters clarified – largely at the instigation of Minister of Justice Edward Blake – in favour of Canadian autonomy. Where the old instructions had set out eight topics on which reservation of a bill was obligatory, the new ones omitted this requirement and made the reservation of bills on any topic discretionary. The prerogative of mercy was now clearly stated to be exercisable by the governor general only after receiving the advice of the cabinet, and the possibility of his presiding over meetings of cabinet was removed.[51] On occasion, the intervention of a governor general enhanced rather than detracted from the practice of responsible government. After his defeat at the polls in June 1896, Prime Minister Sir Charles Tupper sought to fill some Senate positions and judgeships before handing over power to Laurier. Governor General Lord Aberdeen refused him, observing that he was not obliged to take advice on such matters from a defeated prime minister. Successive administrations did their best to prevent the governor general from intervening in the active business of government, and in this they largely succeeded by 1914.[52]

However, the governor general was a representative of the British government, chosen by it without consulting Canada. When the Marquess of Lorne neared the end of his term in 1883, he advised Macdonald of his desire to see the Canadian government consulted, to which Macdonald replied, 'The less we get involved in these matters the better.' As the appointment was made by the monarch on the advice of the British government, Macdonald's instincts were arguably correct. A practice did grow up later of consulting with the Canadian government to the extent of allowing it to negative a proposed appointment, but it was not until the 1926 Imperial Conference that it was declared that governors general of the dominions would no longer represent the British government.[53]

These developments are often referred to as 'Canadianizing the Crown,' but the most significant element of this process during this period was what might be called the federalizing of the Crown. This was an innovation in constitutional theory and practice that clashed with historic ideas regarding the so-called indivisibility of the Crown. There resulted a form of compound monarchy in which the lieutenant governors came to be seen as the Queen's representatives in their respective provinces, parallel to the role of the governor general in Ottawa. Such a conclusion was not obvious from the *BNA Act* itself, in which the power to appoint the lieutenant governors was vested in the governor general in council, that is, the federal government, pursuant to section 58, suggesting that such officers were meant to be protectors of federal interests in the provinces. Lieutenant governors could also be removed by the governor general 'for Cause assigned,' but there was no such check on the tenure of the governor general himself. Yet, in a series of decisions culminating in *Liquidators of the Maritime Bank of Canada v Receiver-General of New Brunswick* in 1892, the JCPC ruled that 'a lieutenant governor, when appointed, is as much a representative of Her Majesty, for all purposes of provincial government as the Governor General himself is, for all purposes of the Dominion government.'[54] In effect, the JCPC had reinvented federalism by giving provincial governments the full prerogative powers that accompanied all areas of their legislative jurisdiction under section 92. It was this, discussed in a section below, more than any expansive interpretation of the section 92 powers themselves, that elevated the provinces to the rank of co-ordinate authorities with the federal government.

Conversely, neither the North-West Territories nor the Yukon Territory, after its creation in 1898, discussed in a subsequent section, could claim to be a co-ordinate authority with the federal government. They remained in effect its protectorates because neither was constituted as a unit of a compound monarchy. The head of the government of the Territories held the title of lieutenant governor but was to 'administer the government under instructions given him from time to time by Order in Council, or by the Secretary of State of Canada,' while his Yukon Territory counterpart was styled a mere commissioner, with similarly limited powers.[55] After the creation of Alberta and Saskatchewan in 1905, the now much less populous North-West Territories lost its assembly, and its head of government would no longer be styled a lieutenant governor but rather a commissioner. All important decisions would be made in Ottawa.

The Meaning of Dominion:
Imperial and International Questions

Enough has been said here to show that the *BNA Act* can best be regarded as a constitutional sketch rather than a fully developed plan. In the British tradition, much remained to be worked out through convention and practice. Conventions are patterns of political behaviour that are considered binding by the actors in question but cannot be enforced by the courts, though their existence and content can be noted by them. Thus, the new constitution was a work in progress for some time. We will see in a subsequent section just how uncertain many basic principles of the new nation's constitution seemed to contemporaries. Even something as seemingly fundamental as whether the grant of 'exclusive' powers over certain matters to the federal authority was meant only in relation to the provinces, or whether it meant exclusive of the imperial Parliament, such that that body had surrendered these powers, was seriously debated in the 1870s. No less a figure than Chief Justice William Henry Draper of the Ontario Court of Appeal espoused the theory in an 1875 decision that the imperial Parliament could no longer legislate for Canada. Moreover, an 1872 copyright bill that contradicted imperial enactments on the subject was drafted on this basis. Governor General Lord Lisgar reserved the bill, and after examination in London it was left to expire. Even so, it took some time before the reference to exclusivity in section 91 was conclusively understood to envisage only provincial powers and not to override imperial authority. The *BNA Act* clearly did divide sovereignty, but not to the extent argued for in this debate.[56]

The *BNA Act* was devoted almost exclusively to domestic or inward-facing sovereignty, rather than outward-facing sovereignty in the international law sense. Canada in 1867 was not a fully fledged actor on the world stage. The governor general had no power to conclude international treaties in Canada's name; section 132 of the *BNA Act* empowered the Parliament and government of Canada only to take measures necessary 'for performing the Obligations of Canada … as Part of the British Empire, towards Foreign Countries, arising under Treaties between the Empire and such Foreign Countries.' Such treaties would be signed by British authorities but bind Canada and other British possessions. On some issues Canadians believed their interests were not sufficiently taken into account when Britain concluded treaties, creating a demand for more Canadian autonomy in this sphere. One such example arose during the Alaska Panhandle dispute. An old disagreement between Britain and Russia under an 1825 treaty over the boundary between Alaska and what would become British Columbia was revived after the Klondike gold rush of 1898, when Canada wanted the new Yukon Territory to have an outlet to the sea. After Russia sold Alaska to the US in 1867, it was Britain and the United States who entered a treaty setting up an arbitration tribunal to settle the boundary. The arbitration panel, featuring three Americans, two Canadians, and one British representative, settled the boundary in a fashion disadvantageous to Canada after a 4–2 vote, Baron Alverstone of Britain siding with the US members. Specialists have argued that the result was largely a correct interpretation of the treaty, but at the time Canada felt a keen sense of betrayal by Britain. Many believed that its interests had been sacrificed to British goals, which at the time included a push for détente with the United States.[57] Not long afterwards, when difficulties arose between Canada and the United States over problems of water flow and pollution in certain rivers on the border, Canada took matters more into its own hands. It essentially negotiated the International Boundary Waters Treaty of 1909 on its own account with the United States, albeit with British approval. The Canadian negotiator, lawyer George Gibbons, was adamant that such matters needed to be addressed by a permanent bi-national body with equal representation from each nation, rather than on an ad hoc basis, as the Americans initially wanted. This treaty created the International Joint Commission, to investigate, resolve, and prevent such disputes in future. It was arguably the most important bilateral treaty entered into by Canada prior to the North American Free Trade Agreement of 1988.[58]

Nationality was another realm in which Canada did not have full international legal personality. Prior to Confederation, residents born in the colonies were British subjects, and British subjects they remained after 1867; no new status of Canadian citizenship was created, nor would be until 1947. Nonetheless, in order to attract immigrants from non-British possessions, Canada wanted to be able to offer naturalization, as some colonies had done before 1867. A British act of 1870 confirmed that Canada could do so. The 1881 *Naturalization Act* set out very simple requirements: three years' residence, good character, an intention to settle in Canada, and taking the oath (or affirmation) of allegiance, with no language or literacy test. Such naturalization entitled one to all the rights and obligations of a British subject only within Canada, however, and had no extraterritorial effect. In other words, one became a subject of the Canadian Crown, but not of the British Crown. This act also adopted a deeply gendered definition of nationality by declaring that the nationality of a married woman followed that of her husband. A Canadian-born woman lost her British subject status if she married a foreigner (whether inside or outside Canada) and had no right to apply independently for naturalization. As a corollary, the wife and minor children of a man who was naturalized in Canada were automatically naturalized.

Dissatisfaction with the limited nature of this naturalization in both Britain and the dominions led to discussions about a 'common code' of British subject status that would have more than domestic effect. The content of this code was agreed upon at a 1911 imperial conference, creating a model law that each dominion was free to adopt or not, though all eventually did. Canada was the first to do so in its *Naturalization Act* of 1914, resulting in somewhat more demanding but still not arduous requirements for naturalization: five years' residence rather than three, as well as a language test to demonstrate an 'adequate knowledge' of spoken English or French. Instead of being issued pro forma by a judge, however, certificates of naturalization would now be issued by the secretary of state, who could refuse to do so for reasons of national security. This change effectively removed such decisions from any potential scrutiny by the courts. Britain had also conceded that the dominions could use immigration law to restrict the entry of non-whites, even those who were British subjects resident elsewhere in the empire, a matter discussed in detail in chapter 16. Most racialized British subjects would thus be unable to avail themselves of this 'imperial green card.' However, anyone naturalized under the 1914 law did have a 'portable' British subject status that would be recognized outside Canada itself.[59]

Extending Confederation: British Columbia, Prince Edward Island, Alberta, Saskatchewan, and the North

The new dominion's original four provinces were soon augmented to seven. The fifth province to join, in 1870, was Manitoba, but because the principal issues involving Manitoba's entry concerned the Métis people, we have put the discussion of Manitoba's accession in chapter 7, one of the chapters dealing with Indigenous peoples. Canada's sixth province was British Columbia, which from 1866 had been a colony incorporating both Vancouver Island and the mainland.[60] Discussions about British Columbia joining Confederation had begun in 1867, precipitated in part by the American acquisition of Alaska the same year. Indeed, section 146 of the *BNA Act* stated that British Columbia, Prince Edward Island, and Newfoundland could join the federation if their legislatures requested it.

The formal beginning of the local campaign to take British Columbia into Confederation was the formation of the Confederation League in May 1868, led by newspaper publishers Amor De Cosmos and John Robson. Robson, an Upper Canadian who had gone west with the gold rush, failed, and taken up journalism and politics, was one of the elected members of the colony's legislature, the legislative council. De Cosmos was one of the most colourful characters of nineteenth-century Canadian history. Born William Smith and raised in Nova Scotia, he left in 1852 for the California gold fields. He had some minor success as a gold miner but did better at other businesses, mostly photography. In 1854 he changed his name to the Latin for 'love of the universe'; his biographer is surely right to say that it 'would be more remarked upon and remembered than plain Bill Smith.' The league these men founded aimed not only to join Canada, but also to radically alter the colonial constitution, which was underdeveloped for a white settler colony. It was ruled by a British-appointed governor, and the executive councillors, his ministers, were not responsible to the legislature. The legislative council was not truly a representative body because only one-third of its members were elected. The majority of its appointed members and other senior officials were either British imports temporarily resident on the Pacific coast or senior employees of the Hudson's Bay Company, which had ruled the colony of Vancouver Island in the 1850s. James Douglas, who served as both HBC chief factor and British governor during that decade, stayed on as governor until 1864, when he was replaced by Frederick Seymour.

In the short period between 1867 and 1871 when the colony's future was debated, most white settlers saw De Cosmos as the leader who would put it on a sound political footing and en route to a stable economic future. They wanted to remain British, and joining a British dominion was a surer way to achieve that than being a neglected colony linked by geography only to American states. They needed a stable financial future, and Canada could pay off the colony's considerable debt. And they had to have land access to the central and eastern regions of the continent. Opposition to this program came from two sources: a small group of American-born residents who preferred annexation by the United States, and Seymour and his officials. The latter stood to lose their ample salaries, paid by London. When the Confederation League met in the fall of 1868, 37 resolutions were passed, almost all of them concerning the terms on which British Columbia would join Confederation. Canada should pay off the colony's debt, responsible government would be introduced, a wagon road would be built to provide an overland link to the east, and the province would control Indigenous affairs, immigration, land granting and settlement, and education. Seymour and his acolytes opposed a union with Canada, but events quickly overtook them. In 1869 Seymour died, and his replacement, Anthony Musgrave, supported union on the instructions of the Colonial Office. In 1870 Canada acquired the HBC territories, making possible the prospect of a dominion stretching from coast to coast, and also making feasible a transcontinental railroad. At the same time the colony was hit hard by an economic recession, strengthening the argument that being part of Canada would benefit the economy. Thus in the spring of 1870 the legislature agreed to enter Confederation, without responsible government, and a three-man delegation was dispatched to Ottawa to negotiate terms.

But there was little to negotiate, for the federal government gave the colony most of what it wanted. Canada agreed to take on British Columbia's debt, to pay an annual subsidy of $35,000 for the support of the government, and accepted, for the purposes of calculating a further grant from Ottawa that all other provinces had received, a white population of 60,000, far higher than the actual number of white settlers in the colony. Responsible government was not part of the Terms of Union, but it was accepted by all sides that it would be shortly implemented.[61] The principal colonial-era officials were pensioned off, the pensions to be paid by Ottawa and to start following 'political changes on the admission of British Columbia into the Dominion of Canada.' British Columbia was to be represented in Parliament by three senators and six members of Parliament. Most importantly, Canada committed to begin construction of a railway within two years 'from the Pacific towards the Rocky Mountains, and ... east of the Rocky Mountains, ... to connect the seaboard of British Columbia with the railway system of Canada.' This was accompanied by an agreement that British Columbia would sell Ottawa public land along the line within the province, to a maximum of 20 miles on each side. Finally, clause 14 of the Terms of Union stated, 'The charge of the Indians, and the trusteeship and management of the lands reserved for their use and benefit, shall be assumed by the Dominion Government, and a policy as liberal as that hitherto pursued by the British Columbia Government shall be continued by the Dominion Government after the Union.' A policy 'as liberal' as that of British Columbia has long been viewed as highly ironic, for as we will see in chapter 7, the legal and political disputes over lands and treaties between Ottawa, Victoria, and the Indigenous peoples themselves were a constant source of friction in the half-century after 1871, and beyond, caused by the illiberality of the province. The central condition of the deal, the railway, was not finished until 1885.

Six years after the *BNA Act*, Prince Edward Island also joined.[62] The Island began its path to Confederation by considering a union of the three Maritime colonies, the original subject of the 1864 Charlottetown conference. When the conference was joined by the central Canadian delegates, it quickly became apparent that Island representatives saw little benefit in joining a united British North America. The colony had a strong identity, a prosperous economy, and trade links with other Atlantic colonies and American states. The Island was nonetheless prepared to consider union and sent a delegate to the Quebec conference, but it was not persuaded. Most Island newspapers backed that decision, worrying that union would increase taxation, lead to conscription for Canadian wars, and bring an end to the local legislature. In 1866 Premier James Pope formally rejected the Quebec resolutions, and the Island took no further part in the events that culminated in July 1867. Economic considerations, however, almost immediately caused a reconsideration. The Reciprocity Agreement with the United States expired in 1866, but Island officials were unable to negotiate a new agreement without British permission. The abortive discussion nonetheless produced a reaction from Canada, concerned about the possible forging of ties between the Island and the United States; in 1869 it offered a deal to Charlottetown called 'Better Terms.' Canada would assume the Island's debts, fund a steamship service between it and the rest of the country, and pay $800,000 to buy absentee landlord holdings.[63] Premier Robert Haythorne declined the offer, partly because it would not resolve the land question, which he saw as requiring a deal with the British government, and partly because

Ottawa would not fund railways, which in his view were critical to economic development.

In 1871 the Island began to build a railway, believing it would improve the economy and increase tourism. But the project rapidly overspent its budget and racked up debt. By 1872 the colony was on the verge of economic collapse. In search of help, Haythorne went to Ottawa for discussions in February 1873 and put the resulting Confederation deal to voters in a general election. He lost, but to James Pope – who also backed Confederation, but on better terms. Pope reached a new deal with Ottawa, which the legislature approved. In it Canada took on the railway debt, agreed to provide a loan to enable the Island to buy the large holdings of absentee landlords, and promised to maintain a year-round communication link with the Island. Prince Edward Island joined Canada on 1 July 1873.[64] Pope joined the Macdonald government as fisheries minister.

The final two provinces to join Canada in this period were Alberta and Saskatchewan, in 1905. Before then, in 1882, the North-West Territories had been divided into four districts – Alberta, Athabasca, Assiniboia, and Saskatchewan. From approximately 50,000 white settlers in 1875, when Ottawa first organized the territorial government, the population grew to about 160,000 by 1900, and the large influx of immigrants in the early part of the twentieth century boosted it to close to half a million when the region entered Confederation as two provinces in 1905. From 1875 the Territories were governed by an Ottawa-appointed lieutenant governor and an appointed legislative council. Democratic elements were introduced between 1886 and 1888 in the form of four MPs and two senators in the federal Parliament, and the conversion of the legislative council into an elected assembly of 25 members. A decade later, in 1897, responsible government was conceded. Politics was non-partisan, despite the presence of parties, because all involved were largely concerned with promoting regional interests. The first and only territorial premier was Frederick Haultain, born in England and raised in southern Ontario, who moved west to practise law in Fort McLeod in 1884. He was nominally a Conservative but governed with the support of the Liberals.[65]

In the 1890s it became increasingly clear that the region needed its own sources of revenue and full local control over decision-making, rather than having Ottawa control the purse strings through annual grants. Calgary-based interests advocated provincial status from the early 1890s, and the first formal demand for provincehood by Haultain was made in 1900. Prime Minister Laurier turned it down at that time, but all concerned knew that the question was not if, but when. Haultain called a territorial election on the issue in 1902, winning handily. The question became partisan in the very early twentieth century, federal Conservative leader Robert Borden openly supporting provincial status while Laurier preferred to wait. The massive influx of settlers into the region in the first few years of the century forced Laurier's hand, and in January 1905 autonomy legislation was introduced in the Commons. The debate it provoked demonstrated that while territorial leaders may have agreed on the principle of provincehood, there was a divergence of views about how it should be done. Haultain wanted one large province, which he proposed to call Buffalo, Manitoba's Premier Rodmond Roblin also wanted one new province, but he wanted his western boundary extended substantially so that the two provinces between Ontario and British Columbia would be equal in size. Others wanted two new provinces, carved out of the northern and southern regions of the Territories. Laurier's two bills created what became Alberta and Saskatchewan, two provinces divided by a north-south boundary. Laurier feared that Haultain's idea would create a behemoth that, with ever increasing immigration, would upset the balance within Confederation. The autonomy bills maintained federal control of public lands, an issue discussed in more detail in chapter 14. The most contentious aspect of the bills was an attempt to confirm Catholic educational rights; it was eventually dropped after opposition objections so furious that it provoked the longest debate in Canadian parliamentary history. In turn that debate caused the date of provincehood to be deferred from 1 July to 1 September 1905.[66]

Events in the far north require us to return to the 1880s and 1890s. The islands in the high Arctic north of the HBC territories were on no one's mind during the Confederation debates. Section 146 of the *BNA Act* 1867 referred to the possible admission of Rupert's Land and the Northwest Territories to the union, but neither included the Arctic islands. Britain had a vague claim to the archipelago going back to Martin Frobisher's explorations in the sixteenth century, the ill-fated Franklin expedition of the 1840s, and some more recent forays. When a British subject and an American each inquired of the British Colonial Office in the 1870s if he could receive a land grant on eastern Baffin Island to carry on fishing and mining activities, the British asked whether Canada would be interested in taking over the territory. Canada was amenable though not enthusiastic, but no one knew whether the British claim was valid under international law, what the boundaries of this territory might be, or anything about the Indigenous inhabitants. Both governments at first wanted to accomplish the annexation via an imperial statute, but decided that exposure of all these uncertainties in parliamentary debate might be unwise. Arousing US interest in the region was especially to be avoided. Hence, the quiet route of an imperial Order in Council under the royal prerogative was taken in 1880. It contained a laughably vague definition of the territory in question, stating that from and after 1 September 1880, 'all British territories and possessions in North America, not already included within the Dominion of Canada, and all islands adjacent to any of such territories or possessions, shall (with the exception of the Colony of Newfoundland and its dependencies) become and be annexed to and form part of the said Dominion of Canada.' Britain was essentially giving Canada a quit-claim deed to the region. As one scholar has succinctly put it, 'The Imperial Government did not know what they were transferring, ... the Canadian government had no idea what they were receiving.'[67] The Inuit inhabitants were never mentioned in these negotiations, and in any case no one in Canada would have known where to find them.

Canada would not do much with this territory until 1895, when an Order in Council created the provisional districts of Ungava, Yukon, Mackenzie, and Franklin, the last-named including the Arctic archipelago. But the action would soon be in the western portion of this vast territory, not the east or the high Arctic. The Yukon gold rush 'is one of the few events in Canadian history ... that has entered into the collective memory of the entire world.' Prospectors had been seeking gold in the Yukon district for some years, but it was in August 1896 that George Washington Carmack, a US citizen, and his Indigenous partners, Keish (Skookum Jim) and Kaa Gox (Dawson Charlie) made the discovery at Rabbit Creek, quickly re-named Bonanza Creek, that triggered the gold rush of 1896–7. Thousands of people, including many Americans, flooded into the area, which at the time had 20 North-West Mounted Police (NWMP) stationed in the entire Yukon district. The Laurier government, elected barely two months earlier, was determined to ensure that British-style law and order would prevail, unlike the chaotic scenes that had accompanied earlier gold rushes in California and British Columbia. It has been argued that the institution of the miners' meeting, a type of self-governing assembly, was already keeping the peace remarkably well prior to the gold rush, and the NWMP presence was accepted with little resistance. By February 1898 the NWMP force had quintupled, and it would later rise to 300, presided over by the legendary Sam Steele. For almost two years they effectively governed the district, not only enforcing the law but serving as customs agents, recorders of mining claims and land titles, coroners, Indian agents, tax collectors, jailers, and guards for the Dawson banks, as well as running such postal service as there was. By 1898 the population of the district had swelled to some 40,000, such that some type of local government was warranted, leading to the transformation of the Yukon district into a territory separate from the North-West Territories in June of that year. The *Yukon Act* of 1898 put a commissioner at the head of the new government, assisted by an appointed council of up to six members, plus a territorial court with 'one or more' judges; three would be appointed by 1902. The executive had a limited power to make ordinances, but these were subject to disallowance, and in general the commissioner had to follow instructions given by the federal cabinet.[68] After 1900 the gold rush subsided and the population declined dramatically, down to about 4,000 by 1921, leaving the territorial government somewhat top-heavy.

In spite of the *BNA Act* containing a section on 'Provincial Constitutions,' the content or even existence of such constitutions was seldom alluded to during this period. This was in marked contrast to the United States, where state constitutions were an important part of the constitutional landscape from the outset. Another contrast lay in the preference for bicameralism in state legislatures (all but one being bicameral in the United States) versus unicameralism in the provincial legislatures. This aspect of provincial constitutions did attract some attention during this period. In 1867 only Ontario entered Confederation with a unicameral legislature, the other three provinces retaining their upper chambers. Vancouver Island had also had a legislative council, but the united colony of British Columbia entered Confederation in 1871 with a unicameral legislature, as did the new provinces of Alberta and Saskatchewan. Manitoba entered Confederation with an upper house, the only 'new' province to do so, but quickly abolished it in 1876 as a condition of receiving additional aid from Ottawa. The Maritime provinces began to restructure their legislatures in the 1890s. New Brunswick abolished its legislative council in 1891 with effect from 1892, while Prince Edward Island abolished both its chambers in 1893 and created a new unicameral legislature with two-member constituencies, one 'councillor' and one 'assemblyman' being named for each, and a property qualification being retained for those voting for councillors. Nova Scotia followed considerably later, in 1928, leaving Quebec as the only province with an upper house. Attempts were made to abolish it as early as 1878, but it would linger on until 1968. The reforms in the Maritimes were said to be motivated by a need for economy, but the main reason was that provincial administrations disliked having their legislation second-guessed, and possibly blocked, by the upper chamber. Few came to the defence of the upper houses as a necessary check on the power of majority governments, and here the logic of responsible government explains the contrast with the US experience. In the United States, where sovereignty lies with the people, constitutions aim to limit the power of the state through checks and balances, one being bicameralism. In Canada, sovereignty lies in the Crown-in-Parliament guided by the principles of responsible government. Under this model, the elected lower house is the principal and only legitimate source of authority, leading the upper house to be viewed either as an expensive luxury or an unnecessary constraint on the people's representatives.[69]

The Courts and the Remaking of the Division of Powers

In the first case decided by a Canadian Superior Court dealing with the division of powers in the *BNA Act*, Chief Justice William Johnstone Ritchie of New Brunswick was confident that the *BNA Act*'s words were abundantly clear about the relative jurisdiction to be exercised by the federal government and the provinces. 'It is difficult to conceive,' he stated, how 'the distribution of legislative power could have more clearly or more strongly secured, to the respective legislative bodies, the legislative jurisdiction they were respectively exclusively to follow.'[70] Ritchie, who was later named the second chief justice of Canada, could not have been more wrong. Over the ensuing half-century, and beyond, the meaning of sections 91 and 92 of the *BNA Act*, and thus the balance of power between the federal and the provincial governments, was the subject of considerable litigation in the courts – some 125 cases before 1900. That litigation involved the provincial courts of appeal, the SCC, and the JCPC. Some cases, especially those at the provincial courts of appeal level, were decided by the very men who had been part of the pre-1867 negotiations and taken a seat on the bench as reward for political service.

Arguments about the balance of the division of powers were not only made in courtrooms, they also surfaced in Parliament and provincial legislatures, and in the legal literature of the period.[71] Limitations of space prevent us from including much of this, and the emphasis here is therefore mostly on the cases. Many of the cases were the product of, and an aspect of, the political conflict known as the provincial rights movement, led by Oliver Mowat, Ontario premier from 1874 to 1897. Mowat, who personally argued some of the cases, saw that nothing would help his cause more than judicial decisions enlarging the scope of the provincial powers.[72] He told the Ontario legislature in 1882, 'I claim for the provinces the largest power which they can be given.... The provinces are not in any accurate sense subordinate to the Parliament of Canada; each body is independent and supreme within the limits of its own jurisdiction.'[73] Also key to the constitutional story were the politics of liquor prohibition and regulation. Prohibition was a major socio-political battleground throughout this period, and many of the leading cases concerned the relative powers of the federal and provincial governments to legislate in this area.[74]

The twists and turns of the case law are best analysed chronologically, dividing this period into three, delineated by whether judicial decisions tended to favour the dominion or the provincial governments.[75] Between 1867 and the early to mid-1880s the outcomes tended to favour the federal government. This does not mean that the federal government won all the cases; often it was not a party. But most of the cases in this period, whoever the litigants were, represented a victory for federal power. After 1883 and the JCPC decision in *Hodge v The Queen* there was a period of confusion, in which the courts were somewhat inconsistent in the thrust of their judgments and their reasoning.[76] From the early to mid-1890s, and especially after the 1895 decision of the JCPC in the *Local Prohibition Reference*,[77] the pendulum swung towards provincial power.

The legal arguments over the division of powers drew on two principal approaches to legal reasoning. One can loosely be labelled originalism; we say 'loosely' because originalism means different things to different people. We use it to mean simply the idea that the balance between sections 91 and 92 should be what the framers in 1867 believed it was. Such arguments were used by both sides and adopted by some judges before the mid-1880s. In the early years a variant of originalism was employed at the provincial court level by judges who engaged in what one author has called 'judicial statesmanship,' using their own experience of the pre-Confederation period and their views of what nation-building required to guide them.[78] Proponents of greater provincial power also employed a form of originalism, known as the compact theory of Confederation. There were two versions of the compact theory. Provincial compact theory held that the provinces came together and gave up some of the powers they had had as colonies, but not the power to regulate their own local affairs. In this view the provinces were the same polities they had been before 1867, not creations of the *BNA Act*, and compact proponents argued that the right approach was to look at what powers were exercised by the colonies before Confederation. The colonies had not been abolished as political units and then recreated as new polities subordinate to the federal government. Another version of compact theory was that Confederation was a compact between founding nations, French and English.

Compact theory was first extensively propounded by Thomas Jean-Jacques Loranger, a Quebec Superior Court judge, in the 1880s, as a central part of his argument that judicial interpretations of the constitution in the early years of the dominion had wrongly favoured the federal government.[79] The idea that Confederation was a compact is not only a historical artefact of this period, it has also been advanced by historians and constitutional scholars over many generations.[80] Its most prominent modern anglophone proponent argues that the origins of the compact can be traced to the *Constitutional Act* of 1791, which Quebec saw as a compact between the French-Canadian nation and the conqueror, and Ontario saw as a confirmation of its right to develop its own institutions rooted in the common law and British constitutional traditions. The 1867 arrangements and the subsequent debates and litigation over the meaning of the *BNA Act* were thus linked to the long pre-Confedation struggle for democratic self-government.

We do not find the compact theory persuasive as an explanation for the origins of Confederation, and in this we are in agreement with most historians, including most of those from Quebec.[81] Its 'long view' approach to 1867 requires large leaps to be made between the particular political struggles of much earlier decades – leaps for which the evidence for Upper Canada in particular is thin – and gives too little attention to the fact that Confederation was a remarkably rapid process because it was a response principally to short-term crises, particularly the dysfunction of the union from the 1850s. We also do not find it useful to argue about whether the courts in the later nineteenth century were 'right' or 'wrong,' whatever those terms mean. It is more useful for the historian to seek to uncover why the courts said what they said. But compact theory is important because in either of its two versions it played a role in the political and judicial struggle after 1867 to reshape Confederation. It made sense for those arguing for greater autonomy for the provinces to appeal to an understanding of Confederation that suited their arguments.

Arguments rooted in history were largely abandoned by both the federal government and the provinces in the 1880s, because the JCPC made it clear that the *BNA Act* should be viewed as an ordinary statute, to be interpreted according to the 'plain meaning' of the words, without reference to extrinsic considerations. This approach reflected an approach to legal reasoning in common law jurisdictions that is usefully called the emerging 'rule of law thought' of the later nineteenth century, which was underpinned in all areas of law by the idea that there were clearly delineated distinctions between law and politics and between different areas of the common (or civil) law. Rule of law thought, which will be discussed in more detail below, also reflected the ideology of liberal individualism.

Turning to the cases, the early decisions, all decided by provincial courts of appeal, demonstrated that judges both understood and accepted the new responsibility they had been given to review the constitutionality of legislative action.[82] Chief Justice Jean-François Duval of the Quebec Court of Queen's Bench (the province's appeal court) spoke for most of his judicial colleagues when he asked and answered a fundamental question: 'Can this Court interfere? I can have no hesitation in answering: Yes.' Judges similarly rejected arguments that the power of disallowance made judicial review unnecessary, and that the provinces were of equal status to the federal government. The federal government was the superior body, the provinces subordinate, of 'inferior rank and dignity,' even though their ability to legislate 'upon a wide range of subjects' contained in section 92 was 'absolute.' The courts also saw the opening words of section 91 – the peace, order and good government power – as a residual clause. Francis Johnson of the Quebec Superior Court stated that 'it must be clearly understood that there is nothing at all to prevent … [the federal Parliament] from legislating for the whole Dominion in matters not to be found in the list of those given to them, and not assigned to the provinces.' Chief Justice of the Ontario Court of Queen's Bench Robert Harrison stated similarly that 'unless a power be found clearly to have been conferred on the Provincial Legislatures by sec. 92, it remains an unenumerated power within the Legislature of the Dominion.'[83]

A series of very early decisions on prohibition of liquor, decided between 1875 and 1878, produced mixed results. The Nova Scotia and Ontario courts held that the provinces could enact prohibition, relying

Temperance was a major issue in Canadian politics in the late nineteenth century, and which level of government could regulate the liquor trade was correspondingly the subject of many major cases about the division of powers under the British North America Act.

Credit: *The Grip*, 6 June 1885.

on the power over property and civil rights contained in section 92 (13) (Nova Scotia) or the power over municipal institution in the province in section 92 (8) (Ontario).[84] In Ontario William Buell Richards looked to the context of pre-Confederation legislation. The municipalities had had the power to prohibit sales before 1867, and the participants in the conferences of the 1860s knew this. Richards also drew a distinction between retail and wholesale sales; the latter were 'quasi-national' and thus came under the trade and commerce power. New Brunswick and Quebec courts went the other way, holding that the federal power over trade and commerce prevailed and left no room for provincial prohibition.[85] Despite their differences over prohibition, all the courts allowed the provinces to regulate the retail liquor trade as a matter of purely local interest under section 92 (16). In the New Brunswick and Quebec cases, reference was also made to a provincial 'police power,' a term borrowed from the United States referring to the power of the states to regulate for the good order, public health, and morals of a local community, to support provincial regulation of liquor sales.

Another liquor-related issue in the same period concerned whether Ontario could raise revenue by licensing brewers and wholesalers. In an 1875 case, *R v Taylor*, the Ontario Court of Appeal found that the province could do so under the provincial licensing power in section 92 (9), which prevailed over the trade and commerce power.[86] More importantly, Justice Adam Wilson sounded a note of caution against the potentially limitless application of the property and civil rights power, which had also been argued in the case as supporting licensing to raise revenue. Property and civil rights were 'subjects of a very comprehensive range. Everything may be said to be encompassed within the generality of those terms.' Section 92 (13) must therefore 'be limited by the powers which are expressly or necessarily by implication vested in the Dominion Parliament.' Six years later Chief Justice of Ontario John Spragge similarly insisted that when the dominion legislated under one of its enumerated powers it could not by definition be 'an invasion of property and civil rights' and 'to hold otherwise would be to nullify the powers of Parliament.'[87] Spragge thus enunciated a generally pro-centralist position, in line with much of the early jurisprudence of the provincial courts.

In 1878 the recently established SCC decided its first case on the division of powers, *Severn v The Queen*, a case about whether Ontario could raise revenue by licensing brewers and wholesalers, the same issue that had been at stake in *Taylor*. The court held 4–2 that such licensing was a facet of the trade and commerce power.[88] Section 92 (9) was to be construed narrowly, as to do otherwise would be to conflict with trade and commerce, which must be given an expansive reading. Chief Justice Richards came to that conclusion by looking at pre-Confederation legislation, which he insisted was legitimate and necessary to 'enable us to be put in the position of those who framed the ... [BNA Act].' He continued, 'We can ... see very good reasons why these licences as to local and municipal matters should be under the control of the Local Legislatures, and equally good reasons why, as regards licences for such matters as would be likely to affect trade and commerce..., these latter affecting great and paramount interests, no express power was given to the Local Legislatures.' This was a signal victory for federal power, because it gave a broad scope to the trade and commerce power.

Severn also showed that a majority of the SCC judges believed that the *BNA Act* should be interpreted with its historical context in mind – an approach that favoured dominion power. Richards had used the same interpretive technique earlier in an Ontario decision, noted above, that validated provincial licensing, but here it produced a different result. He was aware of the alternative, using the technical rules of statutory interpretation, but firmly rejected it: 'It may be that I do not take a sufficiently technical view of the matter, that I look too much to the circumstances,' he said, but 'the power now claimed [by Ontario] to interfere with the paramount authority of the Dominion Parliament in matters of trade and commerce [is] so pregnant with evil, and so contrary to what appears to me to be the manifest intent of the framers' that the provincial claim had to be denied. The *Severn* court also rejected by implication Ontario's argument that provincial legislatures were 'sovereign, not subordinate, and had absolute and complete power within their jurisdiction.'[89] Perhaps because they could not conceive of both the dominion and the provinces being sovereign, the judges simply ignored the argument.

Five of the first six decisions of the SCC were, like *Severn*, victories for proponents of a strong central government. They included *Valin v Langlois*, in which the court upheld dominion legislation on contested federal elections. The case was an easy one, for section 41 of the *BNA Act* clearly gave the dominion jurisdiction, but the important thing about the decision was that the court firmly declared that Parliament could interfere with civil rights 'when necessary for the purpose of legislating generally and effectually in relation to matters confided to ... Parliament.'[90] Federal primacy, this time through an expansive interpretation of the trade and commerce power, was also confirmed in 1880 in *R v Fredericton*.[91] At issue was the *Canada Temperance Act* of 1878, the *Scott Act*, which was the Mackenzie government's response to the burgeoning prohibition movement. It established the local option nationally, allowing a majority of voters in any city or county to choose prohibition for their community by barring retail sales. The production and wholesale sale of liquor could continue, so long as the alcohol was transported immediately out of the prohibition community. The act was first challenged in New Brunswick, and in 1879 that province's Supreme Court, in a set of judgments that ranged widely over a variety of issues, declared it ultra vires. No single reason emerged from the court – prohibition was a moral reform and therefore local, it was local because of the local option, it was an element of property and civil rights. This decision was overturned by the SCC in 1880 by a 4–1 majority. Three of the SCC judges considered that the trade and commerce power was a broad grant of jurisdiction, easily capable of supporting the prohibition of any transaction. The fourth member of the majority, John Wellington Gwynne from Ontario, the most strongly centralist judge on the court, gave a wide-ranging judgment detailing the nature and underlying reasons for the division of powers. For the framers of 1867 the object had been to avoid the major mistake of the United States, the sovereignty of the states, and to create instead 'a quasi Imperial Sovereign power,' with powers 'as absolute, sovereign and plenary as consistently with its being a dependency of the British crown as it could be, in all matters whatsoever, save only in respect of matters of a purely municipal, local or private character.' From that it followed that the job of the courts was to look at the mutually exclusive powers listed in sections 91 and 92. Liquor sales were a matter of more than local concern, and not within section 92.

Two other early SCC decisions were also decisive victories for the federal government. *Lenoir v Ritchie* raised the question of whether the provinces could appoint Queen's counsels (QCs) through the prerogative power of the Crown as represented by the lieutenant governor.[92] Its significance lay not in the surface and picayune question of whether federally appointed QCs took precedence over provincially appointed ones, but in the fact that that issue turned on whether lieutenant governors, who were appointed by the federal government, were representatives of the Queen. If they were, then the provincial governments had the same status as the federal government. They were both constitutional monarchies, and both sovereign within the limits of their jurisdiction. If they were not, the provinces were creations of the *BNA Act*, subordinate to the national government. Two of the judges in the SCC did not rule on this constitutional question because they believed that the appeal could be disposed of without doing so, and Chief Justice Ritchie did not sit on the case because the lawyer involved was his brother. But the other three did answer the constitutional question, and decided against the provinces. William Alexander Henry held that provincial governments were 'simply the creatures of a statute [the *BNA Act*], and under it alone have they any legislative powers.' Henri-Elzéar Taschereau held that the *BNA Act* provided no support for the idea that the lieutenant governors exercised prerogative powers, and Gwynne, not surprisingly, agreed with both. *Lenoir* dealt with an issue 'of enormous consequences for the future of Canadian federalism' and did so decisively in Ottawa's favour, refuting a vital underpinning of the provincial rights movement, its contention that the provinces were of co-ordinate status to the national government.[93]

The only provincial 'win' in the early SCC cases was *Citizens' Insurance v Parsons*, which concerned Ontario legislation regulating the terms of insurance policies.[94] A unanimous Ontario Court of Appeal and a majority of the SCC both dismissed the constitutional challenge and held that the legislation came within property and civil rights. The SCC decision was arguably contradictory to the one it had given in *Fredericton*. Gwynne, in dissent, certainly read the majority decision this way. Taschereau also dissented, on the basis of the trade and commerce power: 'The words "regulation of trade and commerce" in sec. 91 of the British North America Act, mean "all regulations on all the branches of trade and commerce."' The apparent contradiction between *Fredericton* and *Parsons* has been persuasively explained as an attempt by the SCC in the latter to draw some line between the trade and commerce power, to that point so dominant, and property and civil rights.[95] An appeal was then taken to the JCPC, which gave its first substantial pronouncement on the division of powers. It was not the JCPC's first decision on the *BNA Act*, because an appeal could be taken directly to London from a provincial court, and cases about the division of powers from courts of appeal had been heard before and after the SCC was founded. Nor was it a case in which either level of government was a party, but that did not stop Ontario Premier Mowat from preparing a brief for Sir John Holker, a former British attorney-general and counsel for Parsons, who had challenged the legislation.[96]

There is not space here to discuss the history of the appeal to the JCPC, or the stature and personnel of that court.[97] But it is important to stress four general points relevant to what follows. First, the JCPC opted to hear a lot of Canadian cases – 103 appeals between 1879 and 1899, compared to 175 from all the other self-governing colonies. Second, of those 103, 36 were from the SCC, and the JCPC reversed Canada's highest court in half of them. Third, the JCPC gave only one judgment, formally because it was not a court as such but a body giving advice to the monarch, and practically because a single decision was seen to make the JCPC's pronouncements more authoritative. Fourth, from the outset the JCPC treated the interpretation of the *BNA Act* as a straightforward exercise in statutory interpretation. Its meaning was to be discerned from the words themselves, not from considerations of history and policy. This was presumably because the law lords had very little experience of federalism, and, as they not infrequently demonstrated, knew little or nothing about Canada. The meaning of words cannot be derived from the words themselves, but the fiction that it can was not infrequently a convenient device by which 'rules of statutory interpretation allowed the Judicial Committee to give a meaning to words of their own devising.' Indeed, the JCPC judgments, although apparently straightforward exercises in finding the plain meaning of words, often 'ranged far and wide in commenting on the objectives of Confederation, the structure of the *BNA Act*, and the proper determination of the scope of federal and provincial powers.'[98]

The JCPC dismissed the appeal in *Parsons*.[99] Sir Montagu Smith dealt with the particular issue before him with a narrow approach that recognized that there was no clear distinction between some of the section 91 powers and those contained in section 92, and disputes could not be resolved simply by saying that so long as a subject was within a section 91 head to some degree, then section 91 prevailed. The *BNA Act* could not stand for the proposition that 'powers exclusively assigned to the provincial legislature should be absorbed in those given to the Dominion Parliament.' Instead it was the job of the courts to determine to what degree, and to what extent, jurisdiction in a particular case lay with one level of government or the other. Sections had to be 'read together, and the language of one interpreted, and, where necessary, modified by that of the other' to get to a 'reasonable and practical construction of the language of the sections, so as to reconcile the respective powers they contain, and give effect to all of them.' Here Smith did not say anything very different from what the SCC had said. But he went further and suggested a broad approach to the meaning of property and civil rights, and a con-comitantly narrow one to trade and commerce. The former included all contracts, with the only exceptions being areas enumerated in section 91, such as bills of exchange and promissory notes, banking, and inter-est. Trade and commerce was otherwise limited to 'political arrange-ments in regard to trade requiring the sanction of Parliament, regulation of trade in matters of interprovincial concern, and [perhaps] … general regulation of trade affecting the whole Dominion.' But not the regula-tion of contracts in a particular business. Smith's remarks on trade and commerce became 'embedded' as precedent and 'had a deep and long-lasting effect on the federal power over trade and commerce.'[100]

Shortly after *Parsons* the JCPC heard another appeal from the SCC, *Russell v The Queen*.[101] At issue was the *Canada Temperance Act*. The New Brunswick Supreme Court held it constitutional on the author-ity of the SCC decision in *Fredericton*, and an appeal was taken directly to the JCPC by liquor interests who wished to see the act repealed or weakened. A leading temperance organization, the Dominion Alliance, led the defence of the act. The JCPC upheld it, principally under the peace, order, and good government provision. The *Canada Temperance Act*, stated Sir Montague Smith, dealt with 'the promotion of public order, safety or morals' and therefore came within the initial clause of section 91. Smith went on to say that the act also had 'direct relation to criminal law.' It was not an aspect of property and civil rights, because even 'though incidentally the free use of things in which men may have property is interfered with, that incidental interference does not alter the character of the law.' Laws 'designed for the promotion of public safety, order or morals … belong to the subject of public wrongs rather than to that of civil rights.' The JCPC also peremptorily rejected argu-ments that the act trenched on other section 92 heads of jurisdiction. In essence, the JCPC found that if the act did not fall under a section 92 head, then it was valid by the operation of the opening clause of section 91. This was a different approach to the SCC ruling in *Fredericton*, which had found the same act supported by the trade and commerce power. Smith had greatly reduced the trade and commerce power in *Parsons*, but now, somewhat confusingly, he went out of his way to say that in *Russell* the failure to discuss trade and commerce 'must not be under-stood as intimating any dissent' from the majority of the SCC judges who had decided *Fredericton*.

Russell provided the bookend to the first phase of the litigation about the division of powers, and by mid-1882 'the dominion position seemed powerful.... [It] seemed to have extensive powers over economic matters.'[102] Macdonald was very pleased with the ruling in *Russell*; he thought it 'a great protection to the Central Authority.'[103] But it would be an incomplete understanding of the period to 1882 to say that the triumph of the dominion was complete. In *Parsons* neither the SCC nor the JCPC believed that the trade and commerce power gave the federal Parliament carte blanche; the provinces had a power to regulate, if not to prohibit. The JCPC had been inconsistent. It had reduced the scope of trade and commerce substantially in *Parsons*, even if it was equivocal on the same issue in *Russell*. In addition, various provincial courts of appeal had issued judgments bucking the pro-centralist trend, and the SCC was rarely unanimous, even when it found for an expansive view of federal power.

From 1883 and the JCPC decision in *Hodge v The Queen*, the story became more complicated. *Hodge* concerned the validity of Ontario's 1876 *Liquor Licence Act (Crooks Act)*,[104] which had established provincially appointed Boards of Licence Commissioners to exercise the liquor licensing previously done by municipalities. The boards could also limit the number of licences issued. A challenge to the act was dismissed by both the Ontario Court of Appeal and the JCPC.[105] The challenge had little hope of succeeding because, as we have seen, the provincial power to regulate was well established, but what matters was not the result but the reasoning. George William Burton of the Court of Appeal, in responding to an argument that the province could not delegate lawmaking powers to the boards, gave an expansive view of provincial powers, asserting that provincial legislatures had 'plenary powers of legislation within their respective spheres as large and ample as the Imperial Parliament itself'; this was a statement that the provinces had an 'effective sovereignty.'[106] An argument that the act was ultra vires because of *Russell* might have been made, but neither the litigants nor the court knew about the *Russell* decision.[107]

The JCPC held that the *Crooks Act* was valid under section 92 (8) (municipal institutions) and as a matter of a local or private nature within the province (section 92 (16)). The jurisprudential significance of its decision was substantial and two-fold. First, it reiterated and confirmed the now very familiar 'double aspect' rule, first enunciated in *Parsons*: 'Subjects which in one aspect and for one purpose fall within sect. 92, may in another aspect and for another purpose fall within sect. 91.' The double aspect rule necessitates an inquiry into the purpose of the legislation. And in that regard the JCPC said that the powers contained in the act were those to make 'regulations in the nature of police or municipal regulations of a merely local character for the good government of taverns & licensed for the sale of liquors by retail, and such as are calculated to preserve, in the municipality, peace and public decency, and repress disorderly and riotous conduct.' As a result 'they cannot be said to interfere with the general regulation of trade and commerce.'[108] The second very significant part of the JCPC judgment was its statement about the nature of the provinces, for the London judges adopted the essence of Burton's reasoning on provincial sovereignty. This was a contention first made unsuccessfully by Ontario in *Severn*, and repeated in *Fredericton*, and in *Hodge* it was accepted. A few years later the JCPC amplified the point, stating that '[t]he object of [the *BNA Act*] was neither to weld the provinces into one, nor to subordinate provincial governments to a central authority, but to create a federal government in which they should all be represented, entrusted with the exclusive administration of affairs in which they had a common interest, each province retaining its independence and autonomy.'[109] The JCPC thus accepted the proposition that sections 91 and 92 delineated mutually exclusive spheres of power.

Although it can be seen in retrospect as a decisive decision, contemporaries, and many people since, found it hard to reconcile *Hodge* with *Russell*, decided very shortly before. *Russell* upheld federal prohibition, which suggested that liquor sales were a matter of federal jurisdiction, while *Hodge* permitted the provinces to regulate in the same field. The difference can be explained, and nowadays is explained, by the aspect rule, but at the time the aspect rule was relatively new. The confusion was not resolved by the next liquor case to go before the SCC and the JCPC, the *McCarthy Act Reference*.[110] It arose from the federal government's response to the *Crooks Act*, which Macdonald greatly resented because it gave the patronage opportunities afforded by liquor licensing to the province. The *McCarthy Act*, passed by the federal Parliament in 1883 after *Russell*, set up licensing requirements for liquor sales in hotels, saloons, ships, shops, and all wholesale transactions.[111] It was referred to the SCC, and both it and the JCPC held it to be ultra vires, except for the sections involving ships and wholesale licences, but neither gave reasons, as was the prevailing practice at the time in reference cases. Expressing frustration nonetheless with the overturning of some of the SCC's prior decisions, Justice Samuel Strong explained that the silence was also because 'our judgments will not make any difference there [at the JCPC]; as a matter of fact they never do. They do not appear to be read or considered there, and if they are alluded to it is only for the purpose of offensive criticism.' Strong had also shown his disdain for the JCPC in the five days of argument at the SCC, interjecting at one point that 'the expressions of the Privy Council increase the difficulty of construing the *[BNA]* Act because, first, we have to construe the Act, and then we have to construe the judgments of the Privy Council.'[112]

For the next decade Canadian courts continued to grapple with the problems caused by the inconsistencies between *Russell* and *Hodge*. The central issue in many of the cases continued to be liquor control, because the prohibition movement remained a significant factor in provincial and national politics. Canadian judges struggled over a variety of issues, but one in particular stood out: what was the relationship between the trade and commerce power and the provincial powers over property and civil rights, direct taxation within the province, municipal institutions, and matters of a local and private nature? There is not space here to provide a detailed account. Suffice it to say that decisions were rendered by courts in Nova Scotia, Ontario, and Quebec, and the collective results can be best summarized as 'confusion reigns.'[113] The general features of these cases were two differences in approach from the Canadian cases of the 1870s. One was that judgements frequently revolved around the JCPC decisions and their meaning, especially because those decisions were both authoritative and at times incoherent. The other, related, trend was that there was much less discussion than before about Confederation and history, those subjects being replaced by discussion of cases, especially JCPC cases. Justice Gwynne of the SCC was the notable exception; in *Huson v South Norwich* he wrote about Confederation as creating a powerful federal government.[114]

The JCPC rendered only one significant decision in the later 1880s, on the provincial taxing power in section 92 (2). In 1882 the Quebec government imposed a tax on all banks, insurance companies, and other corporations that did business in the province. The Quebec Court of Queen's Bench, by a 3–2 majority, found the Act intra vires the province based on section 92 (2), and an appeal went directly to London. The problem with the decision, as recognized by the dissenting judges, was that the tax to be paid by banks was a tax not simply on their place of business in Quebec but on their paid up capital, and thus a tax on individuals outside of Quebec and in violation of the section 91 power over banking. Nonetheless the JCPC upheld the lower court decision on the basis of the provincial taxation power. The argument that a tax on banks could be onerous enough to drive one out of business, and thus nullify the federal banking power, was dismissed with an assertion that the province would never do that. Most significantly, the argument that the tax interfered with trade and commerce was rejected by reaffirming the *Parsons* holding that the trade and commerce power had to be limited lest it trench on many powers in section 92. By this affirmation 'the ghost of the Canadian approach to trade and commerce was laid to rest.'[115]

The uncertainty of the later 1880s and early 1890s made it difficult to predict results in particular cases and modified the strongly pro-centralist orientation of the early SCC cases. In the last decade of the century, the third phase noted in the introduction to this section, the JCPC 'imposed a radically different template' on sections 91 and 92. That template was Lord Watson's, who, while claiming to deal only with the words of the *BNA Act*, 'indulged himself in wide-ranging conclusions and speculations about language, history, intentions and policy.'[116] Watson's first significant statement about the structure of the division of powers came in *The Liquidators of the Maritime Bank v The Receiver-General of Canada*[117] and was a confirmation that the lieutenant governors exercised the same prerogative powers as the Crown's representatives as they had before Confederation. This effectively overturned the position the SCC had taken on this issue in *Lenoir v Ritchie*. Watson went even farther down the road of provincial power when he asserted that the dominion had been given the powers necessary 'for the due performance of its constitutional functions,' with 'the remainder' of the powers 'retained by the provinces for the purpose of provincial government.' Section 92 powers were 'specially reserved for provincial legislation,' and that legislation 'continued to be free from the control of the Dominion, and as supreme as it was before the passing of the [*BNA*] Act.'[118] In this brief statement Watson gave all residual powers, those not enumerated in sections 91 or 92, to the provinces. In another decision the JCPC held that the fact that a power was contained in section 91 did not prevent a province from legislating in the area if it came within property and civil rights and the federal government had not itself legislated.[119] At issue was Ontario legislation providing relief to insolvent debtors by allowing them to make a voluntary assignment to creditors. Bankruptcy and insolvency were specific section 91 powers, and the federal Parliament, as discussed in chapter 11, had legislated in 1870 but repealed the act in 1880. The JCPC accepted that had there been a federal statute in existence the province would be 'precluded from interfering,' but a province was not so precluded when there was no federal legislation.

The major decision of the 1890s was yet another case about liquor regulation, the *Local Prohibition Reference*, which concerned an 1890 Ontario statute giving municipalities local option powers to prohibit liquor sales, which the *Canada Temperance Act*, declared intra vires in *Russell*, already did. The SCC held the statute unconstitutional by a 3–2 majority; the provinces had no power to prohibit liquor sales.[120] This did not resolve anything, however, because on the same day a slightly differently constituted Supreme Court released its judgment in *Huson v South Norwich*, another case on the same act, holding, also 3–2, that the province could prohibit on the basis of its jurisdiction over municipal matters.[121] When the case reached the JCPC it dealt largely with the question of whether the provinces could prohibit retail sales. The JCPC agreed with *Huson* that the provinces could do so, on the ground that it was a local and private matter.[122] In the process the trade and commerce power was further significantly narrowed, the JCPC stating that it did not encompass prohibition: 'A power to regulate naturally assumes ... the conservation of the thing which is to be made the subject of regulation.' More importantly, it reduced the peace, order, and good government power in section 91 to being applicable only in such matters 'as are unquestionably of Canadian interest and importance.' To give it more scope would 'destroy the autonomy of the provinces.'

The opening clause of section 91 was thus unequivocally no longer a residuary clause, encompassing anything that was not in section 92. This was a far cry from how it had been interpreted in *Russell*. But the JCPC nonetheless affirmed *Russell* by stating that it had been based on peace, order, and good government because there had been a national concern about liquor consumption at that time. The JCPC needed this fiction – the assertion was blatantly at odds with what the court had actually said in *Russell* – to justify the *Russell* holding while severely limiting the scope of the peace, order, and good government power on which it was based. Watson was thereby able 'to reconstruct Canadian federalism to his own satisfaction.'[123]

By the end of the nineteenth century the convoluted struggle over the meaning of sections 91 and 92 had been won by the provinces. The cumulative result of the cases was a 'triumph' for Oliver Mowat: 'The sovereignty of the provincial legislatures had been established; peace, order and good government ... seemed likely not to be interpreted expansively; section 91 (2) had been greatly restricted; [and] sections

92 (13) and 92 (16) had replaced it and had emerged as potentially large powers.'[124] Why the JCPC generally, and Lord Watson in particular, brought this about is not clear. It likely did not happen because the JCPC deliberately sought to fashion a decentralized country; there is no evidence for that, and in any event the JCPC was too ignorant of Canada to choose that course of action. Arguments have been made that Lord Watson simply got it 'right,' or alternatively that a decentralized federation made it easier for British capital to operate, or, in the further alternative, that the London judges acted out of 'institutional self-interest' by ensuring the continuance of transatlantic appeals and the judicial imperialism they represented.[125] Whether or not it provides the answer to the broader question of motive, a number of scholars have also pointed out that there was a congruence between decisions about the constitution in the 1890s and emergent ways of thinking about law, the 'rule of law thought' noted above.[126] The notion that all are equal under and subject to the rule of law was, of course, a long-standing feature of the British ideological world view. By the late nineteenth century this term had come to mean something more. Law was a science, and law was the best promoter and defender of individual liberty. The relations between the state and the individual were marked by clear boundaries within which each was sovereign in its own sphere. Those boundaries were to be delineated by courts, working objectively according to well understood and established principles. This movement of 'legal liberalism' began at mid-century in the English universities and spread to the United States and Canada; it also became reflected in the ideas of a broad range of lawyers and judges. It became firmly embedded in Canada at the same time as the provincial rights movement was gaining momentum, and by the time that the JCPC turned its attention seriously to the *BNA Act* it was a significant, if often unarticulated, underpinning of thinking about the law. In Canada nobody was identified more closely with this way of thinking than David Mills, variously an MP, a law professor, minister of justice under Laurier, and, in the 20 years after Confederation, one of the leading advocates of provincial rights.

Central to rule of law thought was the idea that law involved autonomous powers and sharp dividing lines between the holders of those powers. In the 1890s, and especially in the *Local Prohibition Reference*, the JCPC could not see the distinctions between sections 91 and 92 as fluid and dependent on context. Hence there was no analysis of the causes and meaning of Confederation. The only task of the court was to find the true meaning of the words in the *BNA Act* by looking at them in isolation, for their meaning was internally embedded. Not long after the *Local Prohibition Reference*, Canada's leading constitutional law scholar of the period, A.H.F. Lefroy, published his magnum opus, *The Law of Legislative Power in Canada*.[127] It cemented the view that the constitution could be understood by coherent rules about mutually exclusive powers, with overlaps reduced to a minimum and explained by the double aspect rule. Another crucial aspect of legal liberalism was a deep concern to vindicate private property rights as a central part of individual liberty. Watson, and some of his successors, saw the greatest threat to property rights coming from strong states, in Canada's case a strong central government.[128]

The Demise of Disallowance in the Era of Provincial Rights

As we saw in an earlier section of this chapter, disallowance was seldom used in the first decade after Confederation. When Macdonald returned to power in 1878 he made more use it than he had earlier, 41 provincial statutes being disallowed by his administration and those of his conservative successors between 1878 and 1896 (see table 2.1). The Laurier government disallowed a comparable number, taking into account that it was in office for fewer years than the conservatives had been. Overall disallowance was still used sparingly – two to three times a year. It was not employed evenly. Seventy-eight per cent of disallowances were of Manitoba and British Columbia statutes, and almost all of those disallowed fell into three categories: British Columbia anti-Asian statutes, which interfered with the federal powers over immigration or naturalization, discussed in chapter 16, the same province's attempts to appoint county court judges (chapter 3), and Manitoba railway incorporations, which interfered with national railway policy.

Disallowance became controversial when it was linked to the extended struggle for provincial rights, as happened when Ottawa disallowed Ontario's *Rivers and Streams Act* three times, the province having twice re-passed it after disallowance.[129] The legislation provided that everybody had a right to float logs down Ontario waterways and provided compensation for those who had invested time and money in improving their navigability. The statute was passed to resolve a dispute between a riparian landowner who had widened a tributary of the Ottawa River and a logger who had tried to use the waterway but been thwarted by the landowner. The landowner claimed that he had been deprived of property rights by the legislation and petitioned the federal government to disallow it. The dispute arose in 1881, when, as

Table 2.1. The Use of the disallowance power, 1878–1914

	Manitoba statutes	British Columbia statutes	Statutes from other provinces	Total statutes disallowed
Conservative administrations, 1878–96	19	13	9	41
Laurier administration, 1896–1911	3	21	6	30
Total	22	34	15	71

Source: G.V. La Forest, *Disallowance and Reservation of Provincial Legislation* (Ottawa: Government of Canada, 1965), 83–102.

we have just seen, there was much litigation between Ontario and the federal government over the division of powers. Macdonald became invested in the case, repeatedly disallowing the Ontario act, a radical departure from past practice because it was clearly within the property and civil rights power. Macdonald defended his action on the grounds that disallowance was in the national interest because the sanctity of property rights was part of the national interest. He told the Commons that '[w]e were protecting a man from a great wrong,… from a course which, if pursued, would destroy the confidence of the whole world in the law of the land. What property would be safe?… Would capitalists come to Canada if the rights of property were taken away?'[130] The argument backfired. It made the provincial rights advocates hostile to the very idea of disallowance, whereas for decades they had accepted it so long as it was used in the limited circumstances propounded in Macdonald's 1868 circular. Now Macdonald was claiming that it could be used at any time, for clearly valid provincial legislation, so long as the federal government believed that the national interest was at issue.

The rivers and streams dispute seemed to presage a new use of the disallowance power on the basis of the national interest. The *Manitoba* acts disallowed in the 1880s and early 1890s, for example, interfered with Ottawa's policy of building a national railway system, a policy at the heart of the Conservatives' vision for Canada. Laurier also invoked the national interest when he disallowed British Columbia immigration legislation because its covert anti-Japanese provisions affected Britain's foreign policy, especially its relations with Japan; foreign policy remained an area in which the dominion was still subservient to London. Although the disallowance power was used by both Conservative and Liberal administrations, it was seriously weakened in the 1880s and

1890s by the persistent attacks of the advocates of provincial rights. It was also undermined by the rise of rule of law thought and legal liberalism. The belief in separate and autonomous spheres of influence of legal actors, and in a sharp separation between law and politics, was easily translatable into the idea of the mutual exclusivity of federal and provincial jurisdiction. It was just as easily moulded to a conviction that disallowance was wholly illegitimate as an invasion of another's exclusive sphere of autonomous action. It was used only about once a year between the turn of the century and 1914, and only 13 times in the interwar period. Its last application was in 1943.

3

Creating the Dominion Court System

The half-century after Confederation was in many respects the zenith of the importance of courts and the largely private law they administered. Although court systems had been established in all colonies before 1867, the professional superior and intermediate courts examined in *Volume 1* operated alongside lay and very local courts in many places. Moreover, the vast expansion of the Canadian state following the purchase of the Hudson's Bay Company (HBC) lands in 1870 required the establishment of court systems in Manitoba, the North-West Territories, and, later, the Yukon Territory and the provinces of Alberta and Saskatchewan. The building of court systems in the region west of Ontario was a major exercise in nation-building, providing a significant aspect of the administrative infrastructure needed for settlers and asserting Canadian sovereignty in a tangible way. The existing British Columbia courts had also to be integrated into what after 1867 was in part a national system. Hence we begin this chapter with western Canada.

In subsequent sections we examine aspects of the transition from the pre-Confederation period, in which court systems had been exclusively colonial and local, to a hybrid of provincial and national. The 'constitution, maintenance and organization of provincial courts, both of civil and of criminal jurisdiction' were the preserve of the provinces under section 92 (14) of the *BNA Act*. But that Act's judiciary provisions introduced a national dimension. Section 96 gave the federal government the important power of appointment of all Superior Court judges and the concomitant responsibility of fixing and paying their salaries; both of these subjects are dealt with in later sections of this chapter, appointments extensively so. Two other sections of the *BNA Act* enhanced this national dimension. Section 99 gave all Superior Court judges good behaviour tenure, which the judges of the Superior Courts in New Brunswick, British Columbia, and Prince Edward Island did not have until they joined the Confederation pact in 1867, 1871, and 1873 respectively. Along with security of tenure, the *BNA Act* also provided in section 99 for removal of Superior Court judges for cause on a joint address of the Commons and Senate to the governor general. Section 101 empowered the federal government to create new courts, including a national Court of Appeal, which it did in 1875 with the establishment of the SCC. An important theme in our section on the SCC is its slow growth in stature; it took many decades for it to acquire the degree of respect within the legal community that matched its formal legal authority.

The development of a national court system is one of three large themes in this chapter. The second is the restructuring of provincial court systems, dealt with in a number of sections. This occurred at the Superior Court level with changes in the relationship between courts of common law and courts of equity and the introduction of separate courts of appeal in some provinces. It was also manifested in the creation and/or expansion of intermediate (county and district) courts – professionally staffed courts with a defined local geographical jurisdiction below the superior courts and above small claims courts.

The third major theme here, a series of sections that comprise most of the second half of the chapter, is judges, principally Superior Court judges. We first examine the related issues of judicial salaries and retirement pensions. Throughout this period there was, perhaps surprisingly, no uniformity in salaries across the country. Considerable space is given to the following section, on judicial appointments, which highlights the role played by political patronage, a perennial concern. In our final section we discuss the related issues of judicial scandals, and, to the extent to which one can assess it at this remove, the quality of the judiciary. This chapter is an institutional history of Canadian courts and their judges in the first half-century of the dominion, not a jurisprudential one nor a study of litigation. Jurisprudential issues are dealt with in many other chapters; one, the interpretation of the *BNA Act,* has already been discussed, in chapter 2.

Establishing and Integrating Court Systems in the West

The acquisition by Canada of the region west of Ontario and east of British Columbia in 1870 required court systems and judges to staff them. The *Manitoba Act* of 1870 made the *BNA Act* applicable to the province, and thus existing laws stayed in place – even if it was not always clear what those existing laws were.[1] The federal government created a court system not unlike those in the eastern provinces. The first lieutenant governor, Adams Archibald, appointed some 35 JPs, including 15 to preside in petty courts. The General Quarterly Court of Assiniboia had ceased to function during the Riel resistance, discussed in chapter 7, but the federal government reconstituted it and appointed as recorder a Quebec Superior Court judge, Francis Godschall Johnson. The Quarterly Court sat until a new Superior Court, briefly named the Supreme Court but very quickly renamed the Court of Queen's Bench, met for the first time in 1872.[2] It had inherent jurisdiction over all matters within the purview of the English courts of common law and equity. Its first four judges were all imports, not members of an existing local bar because there was none, as were a number of those appointed in the 1880s. This did not violate sections 97 and 98 of the *BNA Act* requiring judges to be appointed from local bars, because those sections applied only to the original four provinces.

The former HBC lands outside of Manitoba were in 1870 named the North-West Territories and posed larger problems in extending Canadian justice to them – a very small European population in a huge geographical area without judicial infrastructure. The region was ruled from Ottawa, initially directly and then indirectly through a lieutenant governor. The first federal regulation to set up new institutions of justice was an 1870 Order in Council, which authorized the appointment of JPs.[3] In succeeding years NWMP officers and Indian agents were all also made JPs. Three years later three federal statutes provided for, inter alia, the extension of several federal criminal statutes into the region, as well as Canadian criminal procedure, including summary justice. The most important of these statutes for our purposes was the 1875 *North-West Territories Act*, which established the system of stipendiary magistrates. A decade later those magistrates were given appellate authority over JPs. The magistrates were the equivalents of Superior Court judges in the provinces, the principal judicial officers of the territories, and again they were all imports. Three were appointed in 1876: James McLeod, former NWP commissioner;

Matthew Ryan, a Quebec lawyer; and Hugh Richardson, an employee of the Department of Justice. The Territories were divided into three judicial districts (Saskatchewan, Bow River, and Qu'Appelle), and each stipendiary was to hold court at circuit locations within each district – they all also had jurisdiction throughout the Territories. The magistrates had broad but not complete criminal law jurisdiction, detailed in chapter 13, and civil jurisdiction in tort up to $500 and debt or contract up to $1,000, with an appeal to the Manitoba Court of Queen's Bench.[4]

A major change occurred with the establishment of the Supreme Court of the North-West Territories (NWTSC), created by 1886 legislation but not formally inaugurated until 1887, after the trial of Louis Riel. Once the new court was operating, the stipendiary magistrates were abolished. The NWTSC had full original jurisdiction and was to apply English civil and criminal law as of 15 July 1870 insofar as the law had not been changed by imperial, national, or local statute. Its judges had to be current or former judges of a Superior Court in any province, or stipendiary magistrates in the Territories, or lawyers who had practised in Canada for at least 10 years.[5] Five judges were appointed, each with sole responsibility for one of five judicial districts, but there was no chief justice until 1902, when Thomas Maguire was appointed to that position. Three of the five initial appointees had been the stipendiary magistrates before 1886, and the other two were Thomas Maguire from Kingston, Ontario, and Edward Ludlow Wetmore from New Brunswick. The court was to sit en banc periodically in Regina, the territorial capital, to hear appeals on points of law raised by one of the judges. A further appeal could be taken to the SCC. The judges of the new court held office on good behaviour, unlike the stipendiary magistrates, and were non-voting members of the legislative council, there to provide legal advice as had invariably been the case in the late eighteenth and early nineteenth centuries in the eastern colonies. The Yukon was one of the five judicial districts created in 1886 but became a separate territory in 1898, and at the same time the Yukon Territorial Court was established, staffed by three judges by 1902. As in Manitoba and the North-West Territories, the early judges were mostly imported from central Canada.[6]

New courts were established when Alberta and Saskatchewan were made provinces in 1905. Initially the NWTSC continued as the Superior Court in each jurisdiction, but in 1907 the provincial legislatures created the Supreme Courts of Alberta and Saskatchewan, and the NWTSC was abolished. Half of the six judges of the NWTSC were appointed to the Supreme Court of Alberta, and the other half to that of Saskatchewan.

Both new courts initially comprised a chief justice and four puisne judges; in 1913 the Saskatchewan Supreme Court was expanded to include a fifth puisne judge. A district court system, the equivalent of county courts elsewhere, was also established in both provinces in 1907.[7]

Unlike the other western provinces, British Columbia was a colony with a court system when it joined Confederation in 1871.[8] That system had to be integrated with the Canadian one, a process complicated by the fact that the two Supreme Court judges in 1871, Chief Justice Matthew Baillie Begbie and puisne Justice Henry Pellew Crease, were very much part of the largely expatriate colonial establishment that held sway in the colony until Confederation and the introduction of responsible government. On some issues there was no difficulty. The federal government had agreed that the incumbent judges could keep their existing salaries, and this made Begbie the country's highest-paid judge.[9] It was also not difficult to have a third Supreme Court judge added, although the choice for the job, John Hamilton Gray, a leading New Brunswick Conservative who had seen his star fall in his home province, was not a popular one with the provincial leadership. Future premier George Walkem referred to him as an 'empty-headed favourite.'[10]

Other issues, however, caused considerable controversy in Victoria and Ottawa. The principal problem was the dispute over county courts, discussed below in the section on county courts. The county court imbroglio also involved a tripartite controversy between Ottawa, Victoria, and the Supreme Court judges, who believed that post-Confederation provincial governments sought to diminish their authority and status in a variety of ways, especially by increasing the jurisdiction of the county court judges. Doing so, complained Crease, when combined with federal legislation, which gave county courts everywhere jurisdiction in bankruptcy, reduced the BC Supreme Court to a 'mere shadow of its former self ... in nothing but its name supreme.'[11] Ottawa became involved over how many county court judges it wished to pay for, how much it wished to pay them, and what work they should do as officials funded by the federal government. It was unwilling to pay county court judges to carry out provincial administrative responsibilities, which the colonies had always done before Confederation.

The county court dispute also became one about the status of the Supreme Court, because in 1878 the provincial government's solution to the problem was to create two more Supreme Court judgeships and have the new judges preside in the county courts as well as the Supreme Court.[12] The existing judges saw this as an affront to the dignity of the court. Even more infuriating to the judges, especially the imperious Crease, the 1878 act required three of the five Supreme Court judges to reside on the mainland, not Vancouver Island. Crease thought it unconscionable that a judge should have to live among the 'nameless horrors of sight and sound' that prevailed in the interior mining camps, and saw the arrangement as a prime example of 'the unreasoning and levelling tendencies of *universal suffrage*.' Manhood suffrage had brought to power men 'entirely without any Education or Manners,' who sought to 'inaugurate a reign of terror' by moving the Supreme Court judges away from the capital because they 'stand between them [the provincial government] and absolute tyranny of the worst kind.'[13] Crease and his colleagues' attempts to persuade the federal government to disallow the legislation were unavailing. Indeed the legislature followed up the 1878 act with the *Judicial Districts Act* of 1879, which created four judicial districts and required a Supreme Court judge to reside in each of the three mainland districts.[14]

It is possible that one response of justices Begbie, Crease, and Gray to this 'tyranny' was their striking down of provincial anti-Chinese discriminatory legislation on the ground, among others, that it violated the rule of law, discussed in detail in chapter 16. In addition, in an 1882 case not directly related to any of these issues, the court ruled that it was not a 'provincial court' within the meaning of section 92 (14) of the *BNA Act*, but rather a 'national court,' because it predated Confederation. This meant that the provincial government's jurisdiction over the administration of justice in the province did not extend to the Supreme Court and local legislation affecting it, especially the *Judicial Districts Act* and the *Better Administration of Justice Act*, which had established two new judgeships, was ultra vires the province. Without giving reasons, the SCC overturned the British Columbia ruling.[15] After a number of years of seeing themselves as not bound by Canadian law or local politicians, the judges had been put in their place. While at one level the whole imbroglio amounted to 'very little' of significance, at another it 'marked the end of the colonial legal system,' an end that 'involved a painful ... adjustment to the realities of federalism and responsible government.'[16]

The Founding and Early Decades of
the Supreme Court of Canada

It took the federal government eight years to exercise the power given it by section 101 of the *BNA Act* to 'provide for the constitution, maintenance, and organization of a general court of appeal for Canada.'[17] From early in the new dominion both major parties supported the establishment of a Supreme Court, seeing it as a way of enhancing the credibility of the new dominion as a nation, as an instrument to achieve uniformity of laws among the common law provinces, and a body that could resolve disputes over federal and provincial jurisdiction. The Colonial Office agreed particularly with this last point, in 1869 suggesting, somewhat presciently, that 'a tribunal ... for the decision of all questions of constitutional law and conflict of jurisdiction' would be a good idea.[18] The first efforts to put these ideas into practice, however, foundered on disagreements about the court's jurisdiction. Macdonald introduced legislation in 1869 to establish the SCC that reflected his centralist vision for the country. It would hear appeals in all civil and criminal cases and have exclusive original jurisdiction to pronounce on the constitutionality of provincial, but not federal, legislation. Not surprisingly, Ontario Premier Oliver Mowat was strongly opposed; the power to decide the constitutionality of provincial statutes seemed unnecessary, given Ottawa's disallowance power. Macdonald brought in another very similar bill in 1870, which was equally unsuccessful; its critics saw it as 'designed to deal with an inferior level of government and to be used as an instrument of homogenization and centralization.' The bill was also withdrawn, and Macdonald, consumed with other matters, did not revisit the question.

A national Court of Appeal was on Alexander Mackenzie's campaign platform in the 1874 election and featured in his first speech from the throne. As we saw in chapter two, a small number of division of powers cases had already been decided by provincial courts, and Mackenzie saw a national Court of Appeal as 'essential to our system of jurisprudence and to the settlement of constitutional questions.'[19] In 1875 Minister of Justice Télesphore Fournier introduced what became the *Supreme and Exchequer Court Act* of that year.[20] It provided that the new court could hear appeals from the highest court in a province, be it a Court of Appeal or the highest Superior Court in those provinces that did not have a separate Court of Appeal. Indeed the SCC could initially hear appeals from any judgment of a court of original jurisdiction with the consent of both parties, but this provision was removed in 1879. The bill also contained recognition of a special status for the Quebec civil law: two of the six judges had to come from the bar of Quebec – a requirement that Macdonald's bills had not specified – and there could be civil appeals from Quebec only if the amount at issue was at least $2,000.[21]

The act took an approach that was different from Macdonald's on referring provincial statutes to the court. Section 52 gave the governor general the right to refer 'any matter whatsoever as he may think fit,' and the Court was required to hear the case and report its opinion, but not to give reasons. The SCC could be asked its opinion on the validity of any statute, provincial or federal, but only the governor general, not lieutenant governors, could make a reference. However, section 54 also gave the SCC jurisdiction over, inter alia, cases involving 'controversies' between the dominion and any province, or between provinces when two or more provinces had passed a similar statute, in actions in which the parties 'had raised a question of the validity an Act of the Parliament of Canada,' and in cases in which the parties had raised a similar question of the validity of a provincial statute. The SCC's jurisdiction in all these cases was predicated on the province passing legislation giving it jurisdiction to hear such cases, and most did so in short order.[22] The reference provisions in the 1875 act were little used over the next 15 years and often criticized as inadequate, because the Court was not required to allow interested parties to appear and make arguments, nor, as noted above, to give reasons. In a parliamentary debate on section 52 in 1890, Edward Blake called it 'extremely defective' for these reasons and the Court's answers the pronouncements of a 'Delphic oracle.' Macdonald agreed with him and promised an amendment the following session. In 1891 the *Supreme Court Act* was amended to provide for references on the constitutionality of any provincial or federal legislation and to require the SCC, and any dissenting judge, to give reasons. A contention that the reference power was unconstitutional as outside the proper functions of courts was rejected by the SCC and the JCPC in 1910–11. Despite the clear mandatory language of the statute, there were occasions in the twentieth century when the SCC either modified the question asked or refused to respond to it.[23]

There was some grumbling in Parliament over the cost of the Court, including the generosity of its judges' salaries, which were the highest in the country, but little discussion of the concept of judicial review. The major issues of contention were the effect of the new court on provincial powers, especially Quebec's, and appeals to the JCPC. Amendments to remove property and civil rights jurisdiction from the Court, and to require ratification of the bill by the Quebec legislature before it became law, were both defeated, as were attempts to limit the Court's jurisdiction to federal law so that it would not be able to pronounce on the civil law.[24] The only successful amendment was one proposed by Aemilius

Irving, Ontario Liberal MP and a future treasurer of the Law Society of Upper Canada. What became section 47 of the Act stated that '[t]he judgment of the Supreme Court shall in all cases be final and conclusive, and no appeal shall be brought ... to any Court of Appeal established by the Parliament of Great Britain..., by which appeals to Her Majesty in Council may be ordered to be heard.' To that point section 47 seems abundantly clear. But the section included a qualifier added by Irving: 'Saving any right which Her Majesty may be graciously pleased to exercise by virtue of her Royal Prerogative.' This last phrase made the meaning of the clause unclear. The JCPC was not a 'Court of Appeal established by the Parliament of Great Britain,' it was the body that advised the monarch on appeals made directly to her, and thus by making the SCC the 'final' Court of Appeal nothing changed. But the section could be interpreted as abolishing appeals to the JCPC if that body was included in British courts of appeal, even though not established by Parliament. The Colonial Office, uncertain about the meaning, ordered the governor general to withhold royal assent. Mackenzie was unwilling to bow to London's pressure and went ahead and established the Court and appointed judges while his justice minister, Edward Blake, went to London to resolve the issue. The resolution was to leave the section as it was, including Irving's amendment, and thus the right of appeal to the JCPC remained. In 1911 an Order in Council issued by London allowed appeals from any Superior Court in the empire to go to the monarch in council. Rules issued under this order allowed for two routes to appeal from Canada – via the SCC or directly from a provincial appeal court. This confirmed existing practice; a number of appeals directly from provincial courts had been heard before 1910.[25]

The 1875 act provided for a chief justice and five puisne judges, with at least two of the judges having to be from Quebec. The quorum was five, the same as it is today. The Mackenzie administration had no difficulty deciding where the initial members of the court should come from. The act required two from Quebec, and it was unthinkable that the most populous province should not have the same number. The small settler populations of the western provinces ruled out one of them supplying a judge, and there was no reason not to give both Nova Scotia and New Brunswick one each. Which men should serve was a more difficult issue. Mackenzie, presumably in an effort to ensure the new court's legitimacy, did not, as he did on 80 per cent of occasions (see below) and as all other prime ministers did, fill the bench with partisan appointments. William Johnstone Ritchie, the chief justice, had been a

Liberal MLA before becoming chief justice of New Brunswick in 1865, although he also had ties to New Brunswick Conservative leader Tilley. Two conservatives were appointed. Samuel Henry Strong from Ontario was a friend of Macdonald and had been instrumental in drafting his Supreme Court bills. Jean-Thomas Taschereau was a well-known and well-connected Quebec conservative. The only strongly avowed Liberal was Télesphore Fournier, a Quebec MP, minister of justice in Mackenzie's government, and the man responsible for taking the Supreme Court bill through Parliament. The other two, like Ritchie, were not strongly partisan. William Buell Richards had been a Reform Party MLA in the Province of Canada before appointment to the Court of Common Pleas in 1853, and thus had been a long time out of politics. William Alexander Henry had held a seat in the Nova Scotia assembly as both a Liberal and Conservative at different times, and run successfully as a Conservative candidate for the Commons in the 1867 general election, his choice of party deriving more from his strong pro-Confederation views than from political ideology.[26]

Two of the six initial appointees had many years of experience on provincial courts – Richards 22 and Ritchie 20 – while two others were seasoned but less long-serving – Taschereau 10 years and Strong six. Fournier and Henry had never been judges, and there is a consensus that Henry never should have been. He was considered to be 'a competent barrister, but no more than that,' who was likely chosen because by 1875 all Nova Scotia fathers of Confederation had received some kind of reward for their loyalty except him. The initial appointees did not include some men thought of by contemporaries as the best lawyers of their time, such as Edward Blake and Antoine Aimé Dorion. Even with all these caveats the Court's principal historians conclude that the Mackenzie government made reasonable selections in the circumstances, principally the fact that a number of eminent men did not want to move to Ottawa and/or preferred their present high-status positions in provincial judiciaries.[27]

The SCC's first two decades were not easy ones as it struggled to find and consolidate a national leadership role. To some extent its problems were the result of the controversies caused by the battles between the provinces and the federal government over the division of powers. In this area the SCC's problems were compounded by the fact that it was not in fact supreme, but subservient to the JCPC. There were other difficulties. In the early years the SCC had problems adapting to its role as a bilingual institution, in part for lack of resources. The *Supreme Court*

Reports, for example, published most reasons for judgment in the language in which they had been written, with no translation. Many of the non-constitutional cases on the docket dealt with minor civil and commercial law questions, so that its work was not something most lawyers paid attention to. The judges did not contribute to the Court's stature, in some cases by lengthy absences because they had no wish to be in Ottawa for any longer than they had to be. Jean-Thomas Taschereau was the most notable problem; he never moved his permanent residence from Quebec City, in violation of the *Supreme Court Act*'s residency requirement, and after much time lobbying unsuccessfully for an exemption resigned in 1878. Richards's ill-health, which caused him also to resign in 1878, meant that the Court lost two of its six judges within three years.

Although it was nine years before another judge had to be replaced, stability of personnel did not prevent continued erosion of the SCC's image. The problems were varied. Rural interests, especially those in Ontario, objected to the extra layer of courts in what they saw as a 'lawyer-ridden' society, and the expense. Legal establishments in many provinces, again especially in Ontario but also for obvious reasons in Quebec, found it incongruous that their highest court could be overruled by another comprising men mostly unfamiliar with provincial law. It was not just disagreement with decisions; professionals attacked some judges on the ground of competence, especially Henry. Among his critics was his colleague Strong, who in 1880 told Macdonald that Henry's most recent judgments were 'long, windy, incoherent, masses of verbiage, interspersed with ungrammatical expressions, slang, and the veriest legal platitudes inappropriately applied.'[28] This jeremiad was not atypical of Strong, and other judges, especially Ritchie, could be equally rude, publicly and privately. More mundanely, nobody liked having to travel to Ottawa to litigate, judges and lawyers found the plethora of dissenting and concurring opinions confusing, even though the practice had always marked the work of British and Canadian courts, and the SCC's early published reports were slow to appear, poorly edited, and too lengthy – this last despite the fact that it was the first court in Canada to publish its own judgments rather than have it done by private entities.

The largest difficulties the Court faced were over the conjoined problems of the legitimacy of judicial review and the judges' centralist view of the constitution. We have dealt with the latter in the previous chapter; the former reflected the fact that Canadians had been raised to believe in the supremacy of Parliament, with no role for a court to determine the constitutionality of legislation. Although it might seem obvious now that the court was intended to play a new role, the confusion caused was sufficient to draw a defence of its role from Ritchie himself. In *Valin v Langlois,* the first case in which the SCC confirmed that it did have power to review the content of legislation for its constitutionality, he noted the problems caused by 'the great diversity of judicial opinion' among provincial courts, which required 'authoritative declaration[s] of the law,' including 'the principles by which both federal and local legislation are governed.'[29]

Despite all these difficulties the SCC rendered decisions in an average of 72 cases a year between 1879 and 1892, and 87 annually in the following decade. It benefitted from the death of Henry in 1888, who was replaced by Christopher Patterson of the Ontario Court of Appeal. Shortly afterwards Robert Sedgwick, the deputy minister of justice in the federal government, replaced Ritchie, and George King of the New Brunswick Court of Appeal replaced Patterson, who died after serving only five years. The Sedgwick and King appointments strengthened the court, but the advanced age of other members, especially Fournier and John Wellington Gwynne, who had replaced Richards when he retired in 1878, and the irascibility and domineering personality of Strong, who had unwisely been promoted to chief justice on Ritchie's death in 1892, had a countervailing effect on morale. Fournier, Gwynne, and Strong were at various times encouraged, cajoled, and bribed with benefits to persuade them to retire, but they hung on for longer than they should have.[30] By the end of the century the Court had gained more respect among the profession from an overall improvement in the quality of its judges, especially the criminal law scholar Henri-Elzéar Taschereau, a relative of Jean-Thomas, appointed the first French-Canadian chief justice by Laurier in 1902, and Désiré Girouard, an 1894 appointee with no judicial experience but with a reputation for independence of thought and principled judgment, which he enhanced on the bench.[31]

The next decade, however, saw a decline in the performance and perception of the Court.[32] A major problem was the overtly patronage-based appointments made by Laurier.[33] Laurier made eleven appointments to the SCC between 1901 and 1911, nine of them of avowed Liberals, some of whom had devoted much more of their lives to politics than to law. Louis Henry Davies, for example, the only person from Prince Edward Island ever to serve on the court, practised law for just five years before becoming in turn a provincial assemblyman, premier, and attorney general, and then a federal MP and Laurier cabinet member. David Mills, although highly intelligent and scholarly, also practised

Henri-Elzéar Taschereau, the first French-Canadian Chief Justice of Canada.

Credit: Dictionary of Canadian Biography.

for about five years, after serving 19 years in the Commons and as both interior and justice minister. Wallace Nesbitt, appointed in 1903 from the Ontario bar, was an unusual appointment, for he had a sterling reputation as counsel and was a Conservative. But Nesbitt stayed only two years, supposedly resigning for health reasons, although he had a long and successful legal career in Toronto afterwards. While the legal ability of some other appointments made during this decade was lauded, all but Nesbitt were men who had served the Liberal party well. Charles Fitzpatrick, minister of justice under Laurier from 1902, effectively appointed himself to the SCC as chief justice in 1906. He had served both Laurier and the party well, and he owed Laurier not just loyalty but also $5,000![34] Although he was an experienced defence counsel, and his appointment received widespread approbation, the personal debt would surely shock our modern sensibilities, and may well have had the same effect in 1906 had it been known about.

The Court's problems in the immediate pre-war decade were not limited to personnel. Although its efficiency in dealing with its caseload increased, it was progressively undermined by the reversals it received in the JCPC, and even when its judgments were confirmed its status as not the highest court was emphasized. Its judges were also ever willing to be used by government on a broad variety of inquiries. At the end of our period many contemporaries remained unimpressed with the Court and saw it as having failed to carve out for itself a central place in the new dominion's governing structures. Nothing perhaps exemplifies this more than that between 1911 and 1917 there were rumours, and a failed Senate bill, of proposals to reduce its primary position – to divide it into two, one court for the east, one for the West, and to remove from its jurisdiction matters of property and civil rights and of a merely private and local nature.

Provincial Courts of Appeal

At Confederation only Ontario and Quebec had courts of appeal separate from the executive, established in 1848 and 1849 respectively.[35] As explained in *Volume 1*, Ontario's Court of Error and Appeal consisted of all nine members of the three provincial superior courts sitting *en banc*, as well as, from 1857, other judges appointed only to the appeal court who were retired judges of the superior courts.[36] Movement towards a Court of Appeal separate from the trial bench began in 1869, when no more than two of the judges who had presided over the trial were permitted to sit on an appeal. In 1874 the Mowat government changed the system more fundamentally. Henceforth the Court of Appeal would have a chief justice and three other full-time appeal judges, and would always sit as a panel of four.[37] Trial judges were prohibited from sitting on appeals of their own decisions. In 1878 the four-judge requirement was retained only for appeals from the superior courts; three was sufficient for appeals from lower courts. The new appeal court was largely but not entirely separate from the trial courts; Superior Court trial judges all retained ex officio appointments on the Court of Appeal and were used when needed to make a quorum. Similarly, and conversely, because the government thought there would not be enough work to occupy the appeal judges full time, they could preside over trials from time to time.

In subsequent decades the Ontario courts, including the Court of Appeal, went through a large number of reorganizations and name changes, too many to detail here, which created more separation, but never a complete one, between appeal and trial judges. The major change occurred in 1881, when the *Judicature Act* renamed the superior courts under the general title of the Supreme Court of Judicature. It was divided into two – the Appellate Division and the High Court of Justice, the latter being the trial division.[38] The 1881 Act also abolished the separate Court of Chancery, a matter discussed in the next section. The Appellate Division comprised the four judges of the existing Court of Appeal, but if pressure of business required, it could form itself into two divisions or panels, with the judges added to achieve this being selected by a vote of all the judges of the Appellate Division and of the High Court. The *Judicature Act* also added another level of appeal, the Divisional Court, comprising two or three judges of the High Court sitting to hear appeals from chambers rulings or other interlocutory matters. In 1897 the Appellate Division was increased to five judges, and in 1904 the jurisdiction of the Divisional Court was expanded; it could henceforth hear appeals from any decision of the High Court, as well as appeals from county courts and other lower courts.[39] Thus by 1914 there was still not a complete separation of trial and appeal judges. The judges of the first Appellate Division could still preside at trials when required, and those of the second Appellate Division were trial judges elected by their peers. Given that there were 14 judges of the High Court, there were potentially more appeal judges (the 10 judges of the two appellate divisions) than trial judges (the nine High Court judges remaining after five had been elected to the second Appellate Division).

Matters were more straightforward in Quebec. At Confederation the Court of Queen's Bench was the Court of Appeal and remained so throughout this period. It was staffed by a chief justice and four puisne judges before 1881, five thereafter. There was no complete separation between trial and appeal functions, because Queen's Bench was divided into the Criminal Court, which had original and appellate jurisdiction in all serious criminal matters, and the civil Court of Appeal, which heard only appeals from the civil trial court, the Superior Court.[40] The other two original confederating provinces did not have separate courts of appeal at Confederation, their respective Supreme Courts hearing appeals *en banc*, as did the Newfoundland Supreme Court. That did not change in this period in Nova Scotia, although in the late nineteenth and early twentieth centuries various proposals were made to move away from the old system. The province was the last in Canada to establish a stand-alone Court of Appeal in 1992. New Brunswick, conversely, split its Supreme Court into three divisions in 1913, one of which was an Appeal Division.[41]

In the early twentieth century two western provinces established separate courts of appeal.[42] Manitoba was the first to do so, in 1906. Appeals from Queen's/King's Bench rulings were previously heard by a panel of the judges sitting as a Court of Error and Appeal; one of the appeal judges could be the judge being appealed. In 1906 a separate four-person (five from 1912) Court of Appeal was established, initially comprising two King's Bench judges and two men appointed directly from the bar. As in other provinces, the appeal judges were ex officio judges of King's Bench, able to preside over any trials there.[43]

British Columbia's Court of Appeal was created a year after Manitoba's, in 1907, although the legislation was not proclaimed in force until 1909 and the Court first sat in 1910.[44] As elsewhere, appeals from Supreme Court judgments had previously been heard by the Court en banc, with appeals from county courts going to a single Supreme Court judge. The origins of a separate Court of Appeal can be found in part in pressure from the legal profession, which had argued for some years that separating trial and appellate functions would reduce delays in the court. Lawyers were also self-interested in the prospect of more judgeships. In fact appeals did not take up much of the Supreme Court's time, and for this reason Chief Justice Gordon Hunter told Laurier that adding a sixth judge to the Supreme Court would do much more to alleviate the workload problem.[45] In the short term an expanding economy, substantial population growth, the growth of a strong union movement, and the rise of radical political movements combined to create in the provincial elite an ever-increasing sense of a need to 'strengthen the province's institutional structures.' The Court of Appeal became part of an ambitious trend to endorse modernity that saw, among other things, new public buildings, including the Vancouver courthouse, and the endowment of a provincial university. The new court had a chief justice and three puisne judges. It could hear appeals from the Supreme Court and the county courts and was to alternate its sittings between Victoria and Vancouver. Two of the court's first four judges, Paulus Amelius Irving and Archer Martin, were promoted from the Supreme Court, while the other two, William Alfred Galliher and James Alexander Macdonald, came from the bar. Galliher and Macdonald were Laurier patronage appointments par excellence; before his elevation Macdonald was the leader of the provincial Liberal party. In 1913 a fifth judge was added, appointed by Borden – Albert Edward McPhillips, a provincial Conservative MLA and attorney general in the government of Richard McBride.[46]

The Fusion of Common Law and Equity

A significant theme in the nineteenth-century histories of all courts in jurisdictions deriving their law and legal systems from Britain was the fusion of common law and equity.[47] Fusion meant both the abolition of separate courts of Chancery and the transfer of those courts' jurisdiction to a Superior Court administering both common law and equity, with pleading and the rules of evidence identical whether a formerly equitable or common law remedy was sought. In the common law world these two changes, the institutional and the substantive, did not always go together, and Canada was no exception. In some jurisdictions partial reforms of procedure were enacted before Chancery was abolished as a separate court, meaning that some parts of equity were administered by common law courts, and vice versa. In others the abolition of Chancery as a separate court did not lead to substantive fusion; different 'sides' of a Superior Court dealt with equity and common law separately. And in some Canadian jurisdictions Chancery was not abolished as a separate court because no Chancery court was ever created; the sole Superior Court always operated with two 'sides.' The only British North American jurisdiction that had complete fusion in 1867, a single Supreme Court exercising both common law and equitable jurisdiction, was Newfoundland.[48] Thus in Canada we do not have just one history of fusion, but many. This section begins with Ontario, and then looks at the other common law provinces.

As we saw in *Volume 1*, Upper Canada was the last jurisdiction in British North America to establish a Court of Chancery, in 1837. The court was the subject of much criticism in the 1840s and 1850s, but it survived through internal reforms and by the elite legal profession hijacking the abolition movement and converting it to one for reorganization and modernization. The demand for abolition was revived after Confederation, and in contrast to Nova Scotia and New Brunswick in the 1850s, discussed in *Volume 1*, the debate over Chancery was not a very contentious one.[49] To some degree, reform demands were a response to a substantial increase in the Chancery caseload after Confederation; it went from 1,335 bills filed in 1867 to 2,071 in 1875.[50] This increased caseload was exacerbated by personnel problems – both a lack of administrators caused by government parsimony and the incompetence of the registrar, and later master, Andrew Norton Buell, who held his post for 20 years. In 1870 equity practitioners complained of 'the way in which the responsible duties ... [of] the various offices of the Court have been performed'; there were 'many needless delays and much consequent expense' for litigants, caused in substantial measure by 'the shortcomings of the officers.' These kinds of critiques mirrored those made of the English Court of Chancery in the same period.[51] Critics also complained of the rigidity of the separation between the two jurisdictions; litigants could not get equitable remedies from the common law courts, or common law remedies from Chancery. Legislative reform in 1856 had alleviated the problem to some extent; the *Common Law Procedure Act* of that year permitted Chancery to use some common law procedures, including the jury to find facts, and allowed the common law courts to issue injunctions and employ equitable defences in some cases.[52]

Ontario judges interpreted the 1856 Act narrowly, leading the *Canada Law Journal* to complain in 1872 that 'litigants have been prejudiced because courts of law and equity have not had co-ordinate jurisdiction.'[53] It was not until Oliver Mowat left the Chancery bench and became premier that same year that reform moved to the next stage, but Mowat did not wish to be hasty. The 1873 *Better Administration of Justice Act*, which he described as a 'transition scheme,' was designed to 'give us the advantage to be gained by absolute fusion, and prepare the way for that measure if it were thought desirable.'[54] The act's guiding principle was that '[t]he courts of law and equity shall be, as far as possible, auxiliary to one another …, for the more speedy, convenient and inexpensive administration of justice.' The most important section, 49, provided that '[n]o proceeding either at law or in equity shall be defeated by any formal objection,' which was a statement that achieving substantive justice prevailed over adhering to the technicalities of procedure and pleading.

With such clear direction from the legislature, augmented by an 1874 statute that allowed judges to sit in any of the three superior courts, no matter which one they had been appointed to,[55] the judges interpreted the 1873 legislation liberally. For example, in an 1874 case Chancery refused to grant an injunction to stop an action for specific performance launched in Queen's Bench. Vice-Chancellor Blake stated that 'the object of the Act … was to prevent the necessity of coming to this Court for the purpose of modifying or restraining proceedings at law. The power given to the common law courts enables them in such a case … to do complete justice … by making such an order … as this Court would grant.' Two years later Robert Harrison, chief justice of Queen's Bench, expressed much the same sentiments in referring to the 'spirit' of the 1873 act and insisting that his court could take jurisdiction over a case that he conceded was an equitable one. That did not matter, because under the act 'Courts of law and equity are made as far as possible auxiliary to one another for the more speedy, convenient, and inexpensive administration of justice.' 'Suitors,' he continued, 'when in the pursuit of simple justice, are no longer like shuttlecocks to be needlessly tossed from Courts of Law to Courts of Equity or vice versa. The spirit of modern legislation is as much as possible to enable each Court in the particular case to administer all the justice, called law or equity, which the case demands. Judges should, as far as in their power, consistently with rules of law, act in a similar spirit.'[56]

The enthusiasm with which Ontario judges embraced the 1873 Act was in marked contrast to the English judges, who greeted the full-fledged fusion introduced by the *Judicature Act* of 1873 with marked hostility.[57] Thus while Ontario's approach could be characterized as too cautious, incrementalism turned out to be wise, and by the time a bill to abolish Chancery was introduced in 1880 the leading voice of the legal profession, the *Canada Law Journal*, voiced consistent support for the measure, limiting its critique to suggestions for small and usually technical changes. A number of correspondents insisted that fusion was overdue; one of them referred to eliminating 'this blot on English jurisprudence' in the province. Another, writing after the act had come into force, noted that change was inevitable, because 'our two systems [were] gradually tending towards fusion, and the profession was gradually being prepared for some such measure as the present; and … it had to come to that sooner or later.'[58] When full fusion was legislated, in the *Judicature Act* of 1881, there was opposition from older and rural members of the profession, but not from the urban profession or from the general public.[59]

As we saw in the section on the Court of Appeal, the *Judicature Act* established a new court – the Supreme Court of Judicature – divided into two divisions, one of which was a trial court, the High Court of Justice, divided into three divisions. Despite the retention of traditional nomenclature each division had full legal and equitable jurisdiction. Henceforth any case that before 1881 had to go to Chancery could be initiated in any division of the High Court that the plaintiff chose, even though as a practical matter it was most likely to be started in the Chancery division. Similarly, any case that before 1881 had to be initiated in either common pleas or Queen's Bench could now be heard in the Chancery division. Every action in the future was to be begun by writ, thus abolishing the previous Chancery practice of bill and answer. Judges could be appointed to any division and could move from one division to any other. Any conflict between the two previously separate systems was resolved by section 17 (10) of the *Judicature Act*: 'Generally in all matters … in which there is any conflict or variance between the Rules of Equity and the Rules of the Common Law with reference to the same matter, the Rules of Equity shall prevail.' The county and district courts were excluded from the *Judicature Act*, but their judges became 'local judges of the High Court' for some purposes, and county and district courts were given the power to grant legal and equitable relief in all cases coming within their jurisdiction. The *Judicature Act* took most of its provisions from the English *Judicature Act*, a fact often approved of by legal commentators.[60]

Moving to other provinces, we saw in *Volume 1* that Nova Scotia and New Brunswick abolished their Chancery courts in the mid-1850s. Both provinces partially reversed this full fusion in later years. Nova Scotia created a judgeship on its Supreme Court called Judge in Equity in 1864, to handle cases that would, before 1855, have gone to the Chancery court. This was not a resurrection of Chancery but the creation of a division within the Supreme Court. James William Johnston was the first appointee, followed by five more in our period. New Brunswick also established a Judge in Equity on the Supreme Court, in 1879, to which Acalus Palmer was appointed, but then abolished the position when Palmer was forced to retire in 1894 in disgrace, as discussed later in this chapter. Both provinces passed *Judicature Acts*, in 1884 and 1909 respectively, which proclaimed the primacy of equity in language very similar to that used in Ontario. The New Brunswick *Judicature Act* also divided the Supreme Court into two divisions – the Chancery division, comprising two of the judges, and the King's Bench division, comprising the other four. When a separate appeal division was established in 1913 (see above) the Chancery division was retained, its judges being the three appeal division judges.[61] To complete the eastern picture, Prince Edward Island had a separate Court of Chancery at Confederation, which it retained until 1974, when it was abolished and its powers vested in the Supreme Court. It was the last Canadian province to fuse common law and equity, although there was some reform of procedure in 1884 that narrowed the practical distinction between the two courts. As discussed in *Volume 1*, Newfoundland never had a Chancery court, but it too passed a *Judicature Act*, in 1899, based on England's.[62]

None of the western provinces established Chancery courts.[63] Both British Columbia and Manitoba had an equity and a common law side to their respective superior courts. In British Columbia the former was dominated by Begbie, in part because he was the only judge of the court until Crease was appointed as sole puisne judge in 1870, and in part because he was a Chancery barrister who had trained at Lincoln's Inn. In both provinces the two divisions initially had different procedural rules, and one could not get an equitable remedy from the common law side. The procedural differences between common law and equity were eliminated in 1886 in Manitoba, but the two-division system remained until 1895, when the two divisions were abolished, procedural unity established, and a local *Judicature Act* passed. British Columbia did likewise in 1879, its *Judicature Act* stating that 'in every cause or matter commenced in the Supreme Court, law and equity shall be administered therein.' The Territories also passed fusion legislation when the territorial Supreme Court was established.

Professional County and District Courts, and Lower Courts and Specialized Courts

In 1867 the only confederating provinces with county courts were Ontario and New Brunswick, although Newfoundland and British Columbia had district and county courts respectively.[64] By 1914 all provinces except Quebec had them or the equivalent – intermediate courts below the level of superior courts but with a broader civil jurisdiction than magistrates' courts or some variant of what we would now call small claims courts. We refer here to civil jurisdiction of county courts, not criminal, because the latter is discussed in chapter 13. The Ontario county courts were so named in 1849, having previously been called district courts. Ontario also had a few district courts after 1849, for those areas of the province not yet included in counties, and they were renamed county courts when the region they served became a county. In 1867 there were 44 county court judges in the province; in 1914 there were 61 serving 37 counties and 13 district court judges serving 10 districts.[65] New Brunswick created its county court system as of June 1867, when it replaced one form of county court – inferior courts of common pleas presided over by lay judges – with a county court staffed by five legal professionals with jurisdiction over 14 counties. These intermediate judgeships were intended to provide cheaper, locally based access to civil justice than the superior courts on circuit could, while placing adjudicative power in the hands of legal professionals. The timing of this change in New Brunswick, as explained in *Volume 1*, was not accidental. By naming the courts as they did and staffing them with salaried lawyers two weeks before Confederation took effect, the province could add to its judicial machinery and have the central government cover most of the costs – the judges' salaries.[66]

Quebec did not have county courts. The judges of its Superior Court were assigned to and resided in judicial districts all over the province following the decentralization of 1857. Hence residents did not have to wait for judges to come on circuit from the provincial capital, and judges of the province's highest court were more accessible to litigants than in other provinces. Nonetheless, the province took steps to enhance this accessibility and also to counteract the problem that could arise with resident judges: the possibility that the local judge might be seen as biased against particular residents, whose only recourse was before him. To the former end the Circuit Court, comprising the Superior Court judges, had since 1857 conducted circuits to the smaller centres in their districts, where they heard cases to a maximum value of $100. In effect this made Superior Court judges take on the function of a county court, bringing justice in lower-value suits to the people. By the 1880s there was thought to be too much business for the Superior Court at Montreal, and in 1888 the province created an additional circuit court just for that city with jurisdiction at the lower end of the monetary limits for the Superior Court. The 1888 Act, however, gave the provincial government the power to appoint the judges, an obvious violation of section 96, and it was promptly disallowed. A new Circuit Court of the district of Montreal was established in 1893, with the federal government appointing its two judges. To try to combat the problem of familiarity leading to bias, a review process had been established in 1864; anyone dissatisfied with a Superior Court decision could have it reviewed by a panel of three judges of that court, of whom the trial judge could be one. Although this body was known informally as the court of revision, it was not really a separate court but merely another duty incumbent upon Superior Court judges, one that survived until 1920. This process served two goals: it was meant to be a safety valve against local prejudices, and was also in effect a cheaper form of appeal. The review panel's decisions could nonetheless be appealed to Queen's Bench.[67]

When British Columbia joined Confederation it already had a system of lower courts, named county courts from 1867, comprising six judges for six districts. These county court judges were stipendiary magistrates, not legally trained, and assigned to operate only within their own districts. They had civil jurisdiction over any dispute with a monetary limit of $500.[68] When British Columbia entered the union its county court system led to a variety of disputes between the federal government and the province, resulting in the disallowance of several provincial statutes by which the province tried to retain the ability to move county court judges around. Ottawa agreed to pay the salaries of the existing six stipendiary magistrates, 'so long as each of [them] … retains the office of county judge.' The province responded with legislation defining six county court districts. As noted earlier in this chapter, the act also expanded the county court's jurisdiction to include any case up to $1,000, all matters relating to wills and intestacy, probate, and the passing of executors' accounts, and the issuance of temporary injunctions. This brought the Supreme Court judges into the imbroglio. They fiercely resisted the expansion of jurisdiction as an insult to the dignity of the higher bench, and as an attempt to force out incumbent non-professional county court judges, political allies of the Supreme Court judges, by assigning them jurisdiction they were unqualified to exercise. Ottawa disallowed this act too, not in response to the Supreme Court judges but because of a provision that the incumbent county court judges should not be removed 'unless and until they received from the Dominion Government either suitable employment of at least equal value' or a pension of £332. As the incumbents were appointed at pleasure, this trenched on the governor general's prerogative of dismissing any at-pleasure appointee. The province's response was to add two men to the Supreme Court and have them serve as county court judges as well, discussed above.

The existing county court judges were finally retired and the new Supreme Court judges appointed in 1880. There followed the impasse described above over the constitutionality of all provincial legislation about the Supreme Court, during which time the judges continued to do county court work. They did so also after their defeat at the SCC, but only until 1883, when a new *County Court Act* divided the province into six districts. A seventh district was established in 1893. The county courts had a general jurisdictional limit of $1,000, and responsibility for the range of matters as per the 1877 act, plus concurrent jurisdiction with the Supreme Court in others. The earlier provision for having Supreme Court judges sit in the county courts was also retained. In 1884 Ottawa appointed the first professional county court judge for the province, Eli Harrison, to sit for the district of Cariboo.

In the 1870s three other provinces – Manitoba (1872), Prince Edward Island (1873), and Nova Scotia (1876) – also created county courts. In each case their proponents argued that they would provide more local, and in other ways more accessible, civil justice than the superior courts could for claims of a 'middling' amount. In each province these arguments were rebutted by critics who saw the new courts as unnecessarily providing jobs for lawyers and patronage opportunities for governments, through their allies in Ottawa. The debates of the 1870s replicated the arguments over intermediate professional civil justice that were first raised in Nova Scotia in the 1820s and continued to be voiced in other colonies through to Confederation.[69]

The Manitoba county courts displaced the previously existing petty sessions courts, had a jurisdictional limit of $100 in debt actions and one of $25 damages in petty assaults, met annually in each of the province's six counties, and were presided over by any Queen's Bench judge sitting with panels of local magistrates. County courts also functioned as a court of sessions for the first meeting each year, complete with grand juries, to conduct the local government affairs of the county. Thus Manitoba had county courts but no county court judges. In 1881 the province was divided into three judicial districts, and a county court judge was named for each, new appointees, not the Queen's Bench judges. Two men were appointed in 1882, a third in 1883. Over time more districts were created by dividing the original three, and more judges appointed, so that there were eight by 1907.[70]

Prince Edward Island, like New Brunswick six years before, created a county court system just in advance of joining Confederation.[71] The previous commissioners' courts (small debt courts) were abolished, and one court was established for each of the province's three counties, to be presided over by a barrister of at least seven years standing who held office on good behaviour. The courts performed circuits within their counties and had jurisdiction in contract and tort from a minimum of $35 to a maximum of $150. The timing suggests strongly that the legislation was enacted to ensure that Ottawa would pay the salaries. The most contentious issue was appointment. The original draft of the bill would have had the lieutenant governor appoint the initial judges before 1 July, with the federal government doing so thereafter. The opposition Liberals objected to this as a blatant attempt to secure the short-term advantage of three patronage appointments and also argued that it contravened the spirit of the Confederation arrangements. The government won this point, arguing that it would be unconstitutional for a bill passed before the colony joined Confederation to include a clause giving appointing power to the governor general. The initial appointees included Edward Palmer, a member of the Liberal opposition. A year later he was elevated to chief justice of the Island's Supreme Court by the Mackenzie government.

Nova Scotia established county courts in 1874, staffed by seven professional judges.[72] It was a hybrid system, between a county and a district court, because the federal government would not pay for a judge for each of 18 counties when those counties were far less populous than Ontario's. Instead the counties were grouped into seven districts. One district – Halifax – comprised the county of the same name, but the other six were made up of two counties in one case and three in all others. The county court judges, legal professionals as elsewhere, and with good behaviour tenure, performed circuits within their districts. They had jurisdiction over all contractual actions to the value of $400, and over tort claims up to $200. As with all other county courts, some actions were outside their jurisdiction, especially those where title to land was in issue and those where the validity of any devise or bequest was disputed. The presumption was that suits would be decided by the judge, not a jury, but the judge had discretion to use a jury for cases worth more than $80. If a jury was called, it was to be a five-man jury, '4 of whom, in case they cannot agree after two hours absence, may render a verdict.'

As elsewhere county courts were a response to demands for greater speed and accessibility than could be provided by the Supreme Court, which sat for extended terms in Halifax and left the capital only for annual or semi-annual circuits, which involved brief visits to a variety of communities. They relieved the Supreme Court of a substantial amount of its case load, which many agreed was unreasonably backlogged. As Liberal Attorney General William Smith put it in 1870, '[a] large amount of arrears … is to be found on the dockets, so that the temple of justice has been virtually closed against the assertion of the rights and the redress of the grievances of the people.' Despite this the measure took some time to pass the assembly; it was first mooted in 1870 and raised again in 1872, failing to pass both times, and finally succeeded in 1874, although it was not proclaimed in force until 1876. The Nova Scotia county courts were inferior to the local Supreme Court in more matters than jurisdiction. The judges had to retire at 80, and thus did not have life tenure. County court judges were, however, very much 'the pinnacle of local legal order,' and '[f]or many a provincial lawyer, an appointment as county court judge in one's home town was a long-cherished prize after a quarter century of practice.'[73]

While all county court judges except those in British Columbia held office on good behaviour, they did not do so by virtue of section 99 of the *BNA Act*, which guaranteed this status only for Superior Court judges. Provincial legislation before and after 1867 provided most county and district court judges that tenure, for by the 1860s it had become a convention to extend it to intermediate judges. In 1882 a federal statute confirmed this convention, to bring the British Columbia judges into the fold.[74] That the British Columbia county court judges had previously had at pleasure tenure was discussed in Ottawa as a possible ground for disallowance of the 1878 provincial legislation on county courts. Zebulon Lash, deputy minister of justice, somewhat disparagingly concluded that 'in the present state of the county courts ... of British Columbia, it is probably better that the judges should hold office during the pleasure of the Governor-General.'[75] On a related point, while the *BNA Act* provided that Superior Court judges could be removed by the governor general following a joint address by the Senate and the Commons, it said nothing about the removal of other judges. Only Ontario provided a method of removal before 1882, dating from 1857 when a Court of Impeachment had been established. It consisted of the chief justices of the two common law courts and the Court of Chancery, to which could be referred any complaint about a judge's 'inability or misbehaviour.' It was abolished by the same 1882 federal act which gave all county court judges good behaviour tenure and also provided that they could be removed for 'misbehaviour, or for incapacity or inability to perform his duties properly, on account of old age, ill health or any other cause.' The inquiry was to be conducted by one or more judges of the SCC or the provincial Superior Court.

County court judges were always seen as inferior to those on the superior courts, and promotions from county courts were extremely rare. Typical of the attitude to county court judges was federal Justice Minister Alexander Campbell's comment that Louis Arthur Prud'homme was 'respectable' and 'some say he knows enough law for the [Manitoba] county court.' James Emile Pierre Prendergast was an exception; he moved from the Manitoba county court to the NWTSC in 1902, was put on the Supreme Court of Saskatchewan in 1907, and later transferred back to Manitoba, as a Queen's Bench judge. William Henry Pope Clement similarly went from the British Columbia county court to the provincial Supreme Court in 1906. But these are two of a very small number of examples, and in 1906 Laurier observed that it was the 'almost ... invariable rule' that county court judges could not expect promotion.[76]

We conclude our review of the new dominion's courts with a brief examination of two other issues. First, there were civil courts below the level of county court. Before 1867 all colonies established courts, variously named, that filled the role of what can be termed small claims courts. These were generally continued after Confederation, with some name changes and, more importantly, small increases in jurisdiction due to inflation and the desire to make civil justice more accessible. Prince Edward Island was an exception; the legislation establishing county courts abolished the existing commissioners courts, although one pre-Confederation lower court, the Mayor's Court in Charlottetown, was retained. The Halifax City Court was also continued, despite the introduction of county courts, but lost some of its jurisdiction. There is not space here to detail all the changes to small claims court jurisdiction, but some examples will suffice to make the point that there was a continuing process of establishing such courts and incrementally expanding their jurisdiction. Nova Scotia and New Brunswick maintained the small debt jurisdiction of JPs, augmenting the monetary limits from time to time. In addition in 1876 New Brunswick set up 'parish courts' to be presided over by a commissioner, and in 1895 Nova Scotia established municipal courts with concurrent jurisdiction with the JPs. In 1895 British Columbia established small debt courts, two JPs sitting together with jurisdiction to try debt cases worth less than $100. In 1913 Saskatchewan gave single JPs jurisdiction to try civil claims up to $50. Quebec relied less on JPs, who had relatively little civil jurisdiction. Rather a variety of small claims courts operated: recorders' courts in some areas; district magistrates' courts, which had the same powers as courts consisting of two or more JPs; and commissioners courts, which were established in parishes on petition of 50 landholders of the parish and had jurisdiction over claims of $25 or less.[77]

Second, specialized courts exercised jurisdiction in particular areas. Some were well-established holdovers from the pre-Confederation period. Nova Scotia and New Brunswick, for example, had courts of divorce and matrimonial causes, discussed in chapter 15. Also in existence before 1867 were admiralty courts established by British statutes in Quebec City, Victoria, and Halifax. These were abolished in 1891 when the Exchequer Court was made the admiralty court along with its other responsibilities, with local judges sitting in six cities. One of those local judges, Joseph McDougall, sat in Toronto, having previously dealt with admiralty cases at the same location as a judge of the Maritime

Court of Ontario, established in 1877 to deal with admiralty law cases originating on the Great Lakes, but abolished in 1891.[78]

Judicial Numbers and Remuneration

In 1866 there were 53 Superior Court judges in the British North American colonies, one for every 65,000 inhabitants. The number of such judges on the now provincial courts almost tripled in the first half century of the new dominion, the result of expansion in the personnel of the Ontario and Quebec courts, the addition of new provinces, and the creation of two national courts.[79] As illustrated by table 3.1, by 1914 Canada had 137 Superior Court judges and 142 county and district court judges.[80] Quebec had by far the most Superior Court judges – 54 – but this is an anomaly because, as noted above, Quebec never established county courts. The Superior Court numbered 18 judges in 1867, and its complement grew to 40, one chief justice and 39 puisne judges, by 1914.

By section 100 of the *BNA Act* judicial salaries were to be both 'fixed and provided' by the federal Parliament. Salaries had varied from colony to colony before Confederation, and the first federal legislation on the topic, the *Civil List Act* of 1869, retained pre-Confederation differences for the original four provinces within and between courts.[81] Ontario and Quebec puisne judges were paid more ($4,000) than their Maritime brethren (approximately $3,200), and within each colony chief justices, including chief justices of the province and of individual courts within the province, were paid approximately $1,000 more than puisne judges. The salary received by Matthew Baillie Begbie, chief justice of British Columbia, was his pre-1871 salary and the highest in Canada – $5,820; as noted above this was in the Terms of Union. Begbie was unique among provincial judges in being paid more than those in Ontario and Quebec. His successor received $5,000, the same as chief justices in the Maritime provinces and the Prairies and $1,000 less than Ontario and Quebec. These differentials remained throughout this period. In the early twentieth centuries Ontario and Quebec chief justices were getting $8,000, and puisnes $7,000, while those in almost all other provinces were paid $1,000 less. There were two exceptions. From 1875 SCC judges received $1,000 more than anybody on the provincial courts, and thirty years later the gap had increased to $2,000. Despite their relatively elevated remuneration, the salaries have been described as 'clearly insufficient,' and most judges drew them in advance, despite the banks discounting their warrants.[82] At the other end of the scale,

Table 3.1. Superior, district, and county court judges, 1914

Jurisdiction	Superior Court judges	County and district court judges	Total judges
Alberta	9	11	20
British Columbia	10	13	23
Manitoba	10	8	18
Newfoundland	3	3	6
New Brunswick	7	6	13
Nova Scotia	7	7	14
Ontario	19	74	93
Prince Edward Island	3	3	6
Quebec	54	n/a	54
Saskatchewan	6	17	23
Yukon Territory	1	0	1
Federal courts (SCC and Exchequer)	8	–	8
Total	137	142	279

Prince Edward Island's judges were the lowest paid when that province joined Confederation, at just $3,000 for the chief justice and $2,500 for the puisnes, and they were still the lowest paid thirty years later.

Salary differentials could be expected to create considerable resentment among those less favoured, especially when the federal government was responsible for remuneration. The issue was raised publicly by the New Brunswick judges in the early 1870s, who complained that paying them less than their central Canadian counterparts made for an 'invidious distinction,' a violation of the principle of equal status for all provinces within Confederation. Ironically they also complained that it was wrong for judges in Manitoba and British Columbia, 'where the population is small, and the judicial work necessarily very limited' to be 'placed on an equality with the Judges of ... Nova Scotia and New Brunswick.'[83] Thus their proposal was not for uniformity but for higher salaries for themselves. The federal government bowed to the pressure for higher salaries for all provincial judges in 1873, but differential renumeration continued. There was a further round of across the board increases in 1905, but again no uniformity among judges from different provinces.

County court judges were paid somewhat less, and their remuneration also fluctuated from province to province, although less so than in the case of Superior Court judges. As of 1868 the only county and district court judges, in Ontario and New Brunswick, received just $2,000, and in Ontario this meant a reduction for some judges because they no longer received a mixture of salary and payments from a fee fund. The stipendiary magistrates appointed for the North-West Territories in 1875 were paid slightly more, $3,000. Over the next 30 years county court judges in various provinces got between $2,000 and $3,000, meaning that their salaries remained static for decades.[84]

The same 1868 federal legislation that set the first judicial salaries also provided for pensions for retired Superior Court judges, which some colonies had instituted before 1867 for all judges, while others relied upon ad hoc legislative or administrative provisions.[85] Pensions previously awarded to judges and other government officials were continued. For the future, pensions were provided after 15 years of service, or when a judge 'becomes afflicted with some permanent infirmity, disabling him from the due execution of his office,' and resigned.[86] The pension for all retiring judges was two-thirds of the salary the judge was receiving at the time of his resignation. The same provisions were applied to the SCC judges. The statutory provisions on pensions were permissive, not mandatory, throughout this period, and so one of the problems from the pre-Confederation days remained; it undermined judicial independence to have a judge know that his pension was a gift from the executive, even if he had good behaviour tenure. There is no evidence, however, that any judge was refused a pension. Much more significant was the lack of a mandatory retirement age until 1927. As we saw in the section above on the SCC, there were a number of examples of men clearly past their prime continuing in office, and the provision allowing retirement because of infirmity before 15 years' service had been completed was presumably designed to encourage it. The incentive was not sufficient to persuade Gwynne and Fournier to retire from the SCC in the 1890s when their irascibility and absence retarded the court's work, nor was a Commons motion permitting them to do so with a pension of 100 per cent salary. Prime Minister Charles Tupper threatened to legislate mandatory retirement, and his justice minister asked the registrar for information on attendance and cases delayed by the absence of the two oldest judges. The two eventually resigned under pressure from Chief Justice Strong, who made it clear that he would support a legislated mandatory retirement age of 80. In 1903 the Laurier government, faced with similar problems in various courts, increased the financial incentive to retire by legislating a pension amounting to full salary for older long-serving judges.[87]

In 1873 pensions were first enacted for New Brunswick and Ontario county court judges. They could be claimed by a judge who had 15 years' service and a 'permanent infirmity' preventing him from continuing in office. The pension was two-thirds of his salary. Over the years these terms were extended to judges of newly created county courts, and pensions were periodically improved. From 1874, for example, a county court judge could receive a pension after 25 years, even if he had not become incapable, and in 1877 the period of service required for an infirm judge to earn a pension was reduced to 10 years. In 1913 pensions for county court judges were raised to 100 per cent of salary for those with 30 years' service, and mandatory retirement at 75 was introduced.[88]

Judicial Appointments

Speaking at a Liberal rally in Ontario in 1877, Edward Blake, minister of justice in the Mackenzie administration, asserted that, given the importance of judicial posts, and given that judges were appointed on good behaviour and without a mandatory retirement age, it was 'a most sacred duty on the part of a Government' to appoint 'the very best men' to the bench. However, the meaning of 'the very best men' in this period was mercurial. John A. Macdonald did not find it so difficult to decide which kind of men were best. He told Timothy Anglin in 1871 that '[w]henever an office is vacant it belongs to the party supporting the Government.' Macdonald did make a nod to the need for the person appointed to be able – someone 'competent to perform the duties' – but beyond that it was crucial that the appointee be 'bona fide a friend of the Government at the time': 'My principle is, reward your friends and do not buy your enemies.' Macdonald was speaking of government appointments generally but his views included judges.[89] Some 20 years later he struck a rather different note, asserting that 'we don't allow political considerations to interfere'; only if the candidates were equally good was 'a political friend … preferred.'[90] Macdonald, as we shall see, was gilding the lily. Judicial appointments in the pre-Confederation era had long been, to a considerable degree, a reward for political service and made in the expectation of loyalty to governors and appointed councils. Hence the complaints about tory judges associated with governing elites in the Maritimes and the Canadas before mid-century. The advent of responsible government made appointments to the bench more politically partisan. Confederation shifted the judicial appointment power from colonial governments to the new federal one, a change that did not remove patronage from the appointment process.

In 1910 social critic Goldwin Smith expressed no doubt about the role of patronage in judicial, and other, official appointments. Writing about politics in Ottawa, he asserted that 'there was absolutely no political issue of any moment, nothing but a struggle for place carried on by intrigue and corruption, extending … to appointments. To serve a political purpose one who had not practiced law for twenty years was made Chief Justice. Of legal patronage generally party use was made, injurious to the independence both of Bench and Bar.'[91] Historians have not disagreed. Studies of post-Confederation politics that both Conservative and Liberal administrations extensively used their powers of appointment to the civil service and related positions, and of awarding contracts, to give jobs and favours to party supporters, and it is generally accepted that judicial appointments were made much the same way.[92] For all his insistence on his 'sacred duty,' Blake himself acknowledged that 'the Government must of course rely largely upon the advice of those of its friends who from local knowledge and intimate political connection have the best means of deciding upon the political aspect of the question.'[93] When Alexander Mackenzie lost the 1878 election, Blake appointed several 'midnight judges' the day before he handed over office, and Charles Tupper tried to do the same in 1896, but the governor general would not ratify his appointments.[94] When Nova Scotia created a county court system in 1876, the Liberal government in Ottawa filled every post with a party stalwart.[95] Lewis Wallbridge of Belleville, a friend of future Conservative prime minister Mackenzie Bowell and a frequent correspondent with Macdonald on the politics of rural Ontario, was made chief justice of Manitoba in 1882, despite never having been to the province or held a judicial post anywhere.[96] The exceptions were few. When Oliver Mowat resigned as Ontario's vice-chancellor in 1872 to become premier of the province, Macdonald appointed Edward Blake's younger brother and fellow Liberal Samuel Hume Blake to succeed him, albeit while admitting that 'had there been a good Conservative [equity] practitioner who could have done the duty as well, he would certainly have been preferred.'[97]

The consistently stated conclusion that patronage was a crucial part of the judicial appointment process after Confederation is based largely, with one exception to be discussed below, on evidence about individual appointments rather than on systematic statistical analyses.[98] In the tables that follow we provide a breakdown of Superior Court judicial appointments and promotions for all provinces and territories, and the Supreme and Exchequer Courts of Canada, from 1867 to 1914.[99] The tables do not include appointments to county and district courts, but it is reasonable to assume that the strong pattern of partisanship presented here was also reflected in those appointments.[100] There are separate tables for initial appointments to a Superior Court, including appointments directly to a provincial Court of Appeal and to the SCC (tables 3.2 and 3.3), and for promotions within provincial court systems to courts of appeal and chief justiceships, including chief justices of Canada (tables 3.4 and 3.5).

Each table categorizes the appointees in one of three ways.[101] The 'partisan' column includes active supporters of the appointing party – MPs, unsuccessful electoral candidates, election workers, and party officials. 'Partisan' also includes what might be termed 'passive' supporters of the appointing party, people who were known to identify with the Liberals or Conservatives but did not overtly involve themselves with the party. This column also includes judges appointed not as a result of their own affiliations but because the appointment was a way of rewarding a party supporter – the appointment was partisan, even if the appointee was not.[102] In the early period 'partisan' also includes appointments from the Maritime provinces of supporters of Confederation. In all three Maritime provinces, Confederation was a major issue of contention before and after 1867, with strong anti-confederate movements operating in New Brunswick and Nova Scotia, and the debate over joining the dominion was not resolved in Prince Edward Island until 1873. In all three jurisdictions Confederation divided people within parties, and some Liberals were appointed by Macdonald as a reward for supporting it. Appointments to the British Columbia courts defy easy characterization. Provincial politics were not fought along political party lines until the very end of the century. It is nonetheless possible to designate most British Columbia Supreme Court appointments in this period as partisan or otherwise by an analysis of the appointee's relations with federal administrations: was he a supporter of the Confederation movement, and/or was he inclined to take a conciliatory or adversarial stance with Ottawa on implementing the Terms of Union? John McCreight, for example, appointed in 1880 when two new positions on the court became available, was clearly Conservative in his politics, and a strong supporter of Confederation in 1871. Macdonald's appointment of him was partisan in both senses in which that term is used here; he was of conservative bent personally and a person who merited a reward for supporting the province joining Confederation.[103]

Table 3.2. Appointments to all superior courts by conservative administrations, 1867–1914

Administration	Partisan	Opponents	Non-partisan	Total
John A. Macdonald, 1867–73	19 (66%)	6 (20%)	4 (14%)	29
John A. Macdonald, 1878–91	60 (81%)	5 (7%)	9 (12%)	74
John Abbott, Mackenzie Bowell, John Thompson, and Charles Tupper, 1891–6	18 (95%)	0	1 (5%)	19
Robert Borden, 1911–14	24 (100%)	0	0	24
Total – Conservative administrations	121 (83%)	11 (7%)	14 (10%)	146

Table 3.3. Appointments to all superior courts by liberal administrations, 1867–1914

Administration	Partisan	Opponents	Non-partisan	Total
Alexander MacKenzie, 1873–8	24 (80%)	5 (17%)	1 (3%)	30
Wilfrid Laurier, 1896–1911	111 (90%)	6 (5%)	7 (5%)	124
Total – Liberal administrations	135 (88%)	11 (7%)	8 (5%)	154

The 'opponents' column includes all appointees who were active partisans or known supporters of the party not in power at the time the appointment was made. The 'non-partisan' column includes people who were known not to be partisans of either party and were thus likely appointed or promoted for their professional reputation as lawyers and jurists, as well as, in a very few cases, judges known to be politically neutral or simply disengaged from political partisanship, even if they did not have substantial legal reputations. We are not suggesting that only those appointees in this third column were excellent lawyers. Many of those in the first two columns were so as well, but they also had well-known and consistent party affiliations or their appointments can be classified as partisan for one of the other reasons given above. Tables 3.2 and 3.3 include almost all of the Superior Court judges appointed during these years; there were nine for whom we were unable to gather sufficient information.

Four conclusions are apparent from tables 3.2 and 3.3.[104] First, some 85 per cent of all initial appointments to Superior Court benches were partisan, as we have defined that term. In only 7 per cent of appointments did politicians choose someone clearly identified with the other party, and they chose a person based on his legal reputation, with no connection to politics, about the same number of times. Examples of 'opponents' being appointed, such as Mackenzie's naming of Robert Harrison, a committed Conservative and protégé of Macdonald, directly from the bar to the chief justiceship of the Ontario Court of Queen's Bench in 1875 were rare. Second, there was a non-trivial difference between the two parties, with the Liberals more likely to make partisan appointments, by a margin of 5 per cent, 88 to 83 per cent. This difference is largely attributable to the appointment practices of Sir Wilfrid Laurier, 90 per cent of whose 124 appointments were partisan. Yet to some extent the overall difference between parties is also attributable to the relatively low level of partisanship displayed by Macdonald in his first administration. His 66 per cent of partisan appointments in those years is the lowest for any administration in this period. Macdonald's approach may well have reflected his sense that he was engaged in making Confederation work and building on the gains made by the formation of the Grand Coalition with George Brown, discussed in the previous chapter. As soon as Confederation was achieved, Brown left the coalition and Macdonald fought to retain support among some members of his reform party, and patronage was one way to do so.[105] Macdonald was also less partisan in his second administration than his conservative successors, especially Robert Borden, who made relatively few appointments during the three and a half years he was in office during this period, but made them all on a partisan basis.

Third, and this is a related point, the links between party affiliation and judicial appointments became stronger, not weaker, over time. From 1867 until Macdonald's death in 1891, 103 of the 133 appointments made, 77 per cent, were partisan. Thereafter the figure rises to 92 per cent (153 of 167). The six prime ministers after Macdonald's death, Conservatives and Liberals, were all more likely to rely on patronage than the dominion's first two chief executives. We are not suggesting that political patronage is the only lens through which to look at judicial appointments. Many other factors were involved in the choice of individual to be appointed – a point we elaborate on below. But the relevance of other considerations does not negate the primacy of patronage; non-patronage consideration decisively affected the choice of which partisan appointment to make, not whether the appointment should be a partisan one.

Tables 3.4 and 3.5 analyse promotions within superior courts. Here the Liberal-Conservative difference in appointments was reversed, and there was less emphasis by liberal governments on rewarding party men or making otherwise partisan appointments. The Conservatives

Table 3.4. Promotions within superior courts by conservative administrations, 1867–1914

Administration	Partisan	Opponents	Non-partisan	Total
John A. Macdonald, 1867–73	4 (67%)	0	2 (33%)	6
John A. Macdonald, 1878–91	9 (69%)	1 (8%)	3 (23%)	13
John Abbott, Mackenzie Bowell, John Thompson, Charles Tupper, 1891–6	7 (100%)	0	0	7
Robert Borden, 1911–14	8 (73%)	2 (18%)	1 (9%)	11
Total – Conservative administrations	28 (76%)	3 (8%)	6 (16%)	37

Table 3.5. Promotions within superior courts by liberal administrations, 1867–1914

Administration	Partisan	Opponents	Non-partisan	Total
Alexander MacKenzie, 1873–8	4 (50%)	4 (50%)	0	8
Wilfrid Laurier, 1896–1911	19 (64%)	9 (32%)	1 (4%)	29
Total – Liberal administrations	23 (62%)	13 (35%)	1 (3%)	37

made partisan promotions slightly less often than they made partisan appointments, 76 compared with 83 per cent, although as with appointments there was a substantial difference between Macdonald and his successors. In stark contrast, Liberal administrations engaged in partisanship in promotions only 62 per cent of the time; most strikingly Laurier's 64 per cent partisan promotion rate was well below his 90 per cent partisan appointment rate. These figures on promotions should be treated with caution. They are based on the same evidence about a judge's politics as the appointment figures in tables 3.2 and 3.3, and that may be less useful when it comes to promotion. To what extent can a Conservative or Liberal judge on appointment be still considered a Conservative or Liberal, and his promotion partisan, when he had been on the bench for some years? One would expect experience and reputation to count for more when deciding chief justiceships or promotions to appeal courts than initial appointments.

A study of Laurier's promotions makes a similar but related point – Laurier filled the higher positions on courts by promotions from within 65 per cent of the time, rather than by 'parachuting' in outsiders from the bar. The relationship between promoting from within and partisanship in promotion is simple – the more one promotes from within, the less likely that partisanship will prevail, because the candidates for promotion are bound to include senior judges appointed by a different government. Laurier came to power with benches substantially staffed by Conservative government appointees over the previous eighteen years. He had a stark choice between rewarding seniority and experience or making partisan appointments from outside the existing judiciary.[106] An excellent example of Laurier's policy in this regard is the case of Charles Townshend, promoted to chief justice of Nova Scotia in 1907. Townshend had originally been appointed to the court by Macdonald in 1887, very much a partisan appointment, as he had been elected to both the Nova Scotia assembly and the Commons as a Conservative, and served as minister without portfolio in Simon Hugh Holmes's Nova Scotia Conservative cabinet. But when the chief justiceship came available in 1907, Laurier preferred him over the junior, and Liberal, puisne judge, Arthur Drysdale and went against the advice of Nova Scotia's cabinet representative, William Stevens Fielding, in doing so.[107]

The opposite factor might have accounted for Macdonald appearing to be more partisan than Laurier. Macdonald had to choose his chief justices from among judges mostly appointed by himself. The difference between Macdonald and his Conservative successors, and Laurier, also derived from the fact by the late nineteenth century there was 'an emerging convention' emphasizing seniority in promotion decisions.[108] This was certainly true for the SCC,[109] and the evidence from Borden's government supports the thesis. All of his twenty-four initial appointments were partisan, while three of his eleven promotions were not.[110]

The political backgrounds of appointees were clearly a major factor in their appointments and, less so, in promotions, but they were far from the only factor that determined whether a particular individual was appointed. A complex melange of other considerations went into the decision.[111] All prime ministers and all ministers of justice were lobbied on almost every appointment by men who thought they were worthy candidates, by their supporters and detractors, and by others plying different lines for or against candidates – the need to appoint Catholic judges, the need to represent provinces or regions of the country, the need to represent regions within provinces, and so on.[112] Lobbying came from many quarters – regional ministers, provincial politicians, members of the bench, leading lawyers, religious leaders, and others. Making an appointment involved not only satisfying these multiple demands, but also balancing 'professional ability and reputation, ... ethno-religious considerations, and the overall public interest in a bench characterized by impartiality, integrity, dignity and competence.' Another factor important for Laurier in Quebec was competition, not just for a seat on the bench but also for a prime location. Because the Superior Court was so much larger than other superior courts, and organized by regions, potential appointees preferred to sit in or near their place of residence, and the result was intensified lobbying. Laurier was also very concerned with the use of judicial appointments to advance his nation-building agenda. He sought 'to balance the dichotomies of English and French, Protestant and Catholic, East and West.' Thus he looked to maintain a French-Canadian presence on the Manitoba courts, but probably did not make Pierre-Amand Landry chief justice of New Brunswick in 1908 because he thought the majority English population not ready for an Acadian chief justice. He was sufficiently concerned to placate the strong 'Orange factor' in Ontario politics that his record of appointing Catholic judges was little better than the Conservatives. Finally, in Laurier's case, and for that of many of his predecessors, 'unforeseen events and the hazards of timing also played their role in the case of many an individual candidate.'

A few examples, out of many that could be offered, make the point that particular choices were the product of a multitude of factors.[113] When Arthur Sifton left his position as chief justice of Alberta in 1910 to be premier, Laurier received conflicting advice from two very influential men in the party, Frank Oliver, MP for Edmonton, and Senator Peter Talbot. He preferred Talbot's candidate, William Simmons, despite the fact that Oliver was Alberta's representative in the cabinet. Difficult personal considerations perhaps played a role in Horace Archambeault's appointment as the chief justice of the Quebec Court of King's Bench (and thus of Quebec) in 1911. Archambeault was a relatively junior judge of the court, appointed in 1908, and thus his appointment went against Laurier's tendency to promote by seniority. In choosing Archambeault Laurier turned down the claims of Joseph Lavergne, his former law partner, whose wife Émilie was generally assumed to be Laurier's mistress. Lavergne attributed Laurier's decision to the 'indépendence de mon fils,' Armand, who was a Liberal MP facing expulsion from the party because he was espousing views favourable to Laurier's political enemy, Henri Bourassa. The twist in the tale was that many thought Armand Lavergne was actually Laurier's biological son. Laurier did not reply to Lavergne's suggestion and told Archambeault, a former attorney general of Quebec, that he was 'le choix qui était indiqué par le barreau.'

Public Perceptions of the Judiciary and Judicial Scandals

We conclude this chapter with a necessarily brief excursus into public perceptions of, and attitudes towards, the judiciary. In his two years as minister of justice from 1875 to 1877 Edward Blake was beset by a litany of complaints about judicial 'imbecility, deafness, infirmity, partisanship, drunkenness, ignorance, fraud and pig-headedness,' and his predecessors and successors in the office received correspondence along the same lines throughout this period.[114] Given what we have said about the importance of patronage in judicial appointments to the superior courts, it is hardly surprising that there were accusations of partisanship after someone went on the bench. If judicial appointments were part of the currency of patronage, then critiques of partisanship were an inevitable accompaniment of receiving a plum post. For the same reason there were bound to be judges accused of not having the requisite legal knowledge and judicial judgment. As we saw above, there were times when some SCC judges were criticized by their colleagues and others for their lack of legal ability, with William Alexander Henry providing the best example. We cannot at this remove attempt to assess how true these accusations were, without a full understanding of the context of a case and the state of the law in a particular area. What matters is that complaints about partisanship and less than ideal legal talent were not infrequently made and presumably believed by enough people to enable us to conclude that the bench was not always held in high esteem in this period. This problem was not new. As we saw in *Volume 1*, judges in the first half of the nineteenth century were often active members of colonial establishments, and after mid-century and the shift of the appointment power from London to responsible colonial executives, appointments were frequently made on the basis of patronage. Confederation changed little in this regard, merely shifting the venue from what were now provincial capitals to Ottawa.

A good many of the other faults listed above were equally both true and the product of subjective assessments. Judges were often appointed after retiring from long careers in politics, and there was no retiring age, and thus physical infirmity in some was only to be expected. Again using the example of the SCC, we saw above that there were occasions when some SCC judges were criticized by their colleagues and others for having stayed too long. We cannot here recount and assess all the occasions when individual judges were complained of. Rather, we provide a brief overview of three occasions, from three different provinces, when problems on the bench went beyond being a concern of those in judicial and other elite circles and became public scandals.

This happened twice to the Quebec judiciary in the 1870s.[115] Quebec's Queen's Bench and Superior Court judges had been in the spotlight for a number of reasons from 1868, including accusations against Justice Aimé Lafontaine of embezzling large sums of money when he had been a Crown land agent before his appointment to the bench, and oft-repeated claim that Lewis Thomas Drummond was both a notorious drunkard and an insolvent and fraudulent debtor who used his position on the bench to prevent his effects being seized by his creditors. In 1873 the simmering resentment against the judiciary in general contributed to what was effectively a 'lawyers strike' by the bar against the behaviour of two recently appointed judges of Queen's Bench. They treated not only each other but also lawyers with great discourtesy. Worse, they prevented lawyers from doing their job. They refused to allow some to plead and gave rulings without hearing the parties. The Montreal bar responded with resolutions and petitions, and some refused to appear in Queen's Bench for an entire session. The leader of this campaign was bâtonnier and MP Antoine-Aimé Dorion. The scandal ended in a comprehensive victory for Dorion. The worst offenders among the judges resigned, and in 1874, with the Mackenzie government in power, Dorion was appointed a judge of Queen's Bench and chief justice of Quebec.

The second time that the Quebec bench had the public spotlight trained on it came a little later and largely concerned Justice Charles Mondelet of the Superior Court of the Montreal district.[116] A controversial figure throughout his career, Mondelet had successfully defended a number of *patriotes* accused of murder during the rebellions. Rehabilitated in the 1840s, he was appointed to the Montreal Superior Court in 1849, and it was he who ordered the Catholic Church to bury Joseph Guibord in consecrated ground, a case discussed further in chapter 5. He was once described by Macdonald as mad and by Quebec MP Luc-Hyacinthe Masson as 'a little out of [his] … head.' He caused considerable chaos in 1875 when he refused to sit on cases involving the federal *Insolvency Act* of 1875 or the *Dominion Election Act* of 1874, both of which he claimed were unconstitutional on the ground that they created more duties for the judiciary, a matter for the provincial, not the federal, government.[117] This, despite the fact that a court had ruled otherwise when the matter was litigated. The result was a substantial increase to the backlog in the Montreal court, which handled half the cases in the entire province. In turn this caused considerable public controversy, and the crisis was compounded by three other judges threatening to resign if something was not done about Mondelet, and by the bar holding meetings and passing resolutions. Minister of Justice Blake tried to persuade him to resign, and Mondelet used the opportunity to demand a pension of 100 per cent of his salary rather than the statutory two-thirds. We can only speculate on how the affair might have ended had not Mondelet died in December 1876.

If Mondelet provides an example of reckless disregard of judicial duty and of 'pig-headedness,' Acalus Lockwood Palmer and James A. Vanwart of the New Brunswick Supreme Court were poster children for dishonesty. Appointed judge in equity in 1879 despite a reputation for financial improprieties in his law practice, Palmer proved to be a skilled and very efficient judge, especially in dealing with the receivership cases that came under his jurisdiction. But the fact that his brother, son, and nephew were all at various times involved in many of the cases before him raised eyebrows. In 1893 accusations of nepotism were published by John Ellis, editor of the *Saint John Globe*, which also accused him of taking a bribe of $5,000 to rule one way in a case. The story was widely believed and turned out to be true, and a group of Saint John lawyers, alarmed that Palmer was lobbying for a vacant seat on the SCC, told Minister of Justice John Thompson that 'he is unfit to be the judge of any court, and … absolutely dishonest.' Palmer was the subject of an extensive debate in Parliament and, unable to brazen it out, resigned early in 1894 under threat of removal under section 99 of the *BNA Act*. He moved to the United States, from where he might have followed the career of the man who replaced him, Vanwart. An unremarkable man, other than the fact that he was always hard up, in 1900 he declared to the sheriff who was trying to seize property to satisfy an execution order that he had no assets. He was then subjected to examination as a judgment debtor, in the process of which it came out that he had 47 unsatisfied creditors and while in practice had several times misappropriated client funds. Like Palmer, with impeachment looming, he was allowed to retire, and like Palmer he decamped to the United States.[118]

Our third example comes from the end of our period and from the west coast.[119] Archer Martin was appointed to the British Columbia Supreme Court in 1898, at the remarkably young age of 33, the result of some years of devoted service to the Liberal party and of a sterling reputation as counsel. His first few years were uncontroversial, but when Gordon Hunter succeeded to the chief justiceship, a long hostility ensued. The lightning rod was new rules of court made in 1906 that gave Hunter increased power in deciding the schedules and case assignments of the other judges. The issue of who sat where had long been contentious in the province, as discussed earlier in this chapter, and in the early twentieth century each of the five judges took turns presiding over civil and criminal cases in Victoria and Vancouver and on assize circuits to the more remote areas. They also sat together periodically as the full court in Victoria to act as the de facto Court of Appeal before a separate one was established. Martin believed that the new arrangements threatened judicial independence by giving a chief justice the power to influence decisions by coercing judges with the threat of unpopular assignments. Martin was not entirely wrong. Hunter did impose last-minute schedule changes on him and prevented him from sitting on the full court by sending him on assize at the same time. But Martin's response was far over the line – he refused assignments, cancelled hearings, put himself into court sittings to which he had not been assigned, or failed to show up when doing so was needed for quorum. Lawyers in Victoria complained to Ottawa and asked for his removal because of the resulting chaos. The feud between Hunter and Martin lost some of its vigour when the latter was put on the newly created Court of Appeal in 1909, but Martin always seemed to find a reason to pepper his judicial and other disagreements with Court of Appeal colleagues and Supreme Court judges with personal invective. The press delighted in reporting every dispute. Martin was actually a very able lawyer and judge, and progressive in some of his views, but his biographer notes that in the lore of the British Columbia profession he is remembered more for his disputes than his judgments.

In a 1912 article in the *Canadian Law Times* the anonymous author argued that appeals to the JCPC should be abolished, and cited in support of that view the opinions of most of the country's leading newspapers[120] that Canada's court of last resort should be a Canadian institution, located in Canada and staffed by Canadians. Although such a development was more than three decades into the future, it is surely instructive that by the eve of the First World War many influential Canadians had a high regard for the country's superior courts. Although the SCC itself had had to struggle to achieve the respect of the political and judicial establishment, the senior judiciary was generally well regarded, seen as an institution Canadians should be proud of. This chapter has revealed imperfections in the court system after 50 years of dominion status, perhaps most notably the prevalence of partisanship in judicial appointments. Nonetheless that half-century had seen the extension of the system into all regions of the country, considerable innovation and modernization, and the integration into one national whole of disparate colonial systems. Provincial courts were properly so-called because their geographical jurisdiction was limited by provincial boundaries, not because they were entities entirely different from a system of federal courts, as in the United States.

4

Sources of Law:
Statutes, Codes, and Case Law

The sources of law after Confederation were what they were before 1867 and, with the obvious and notable exception of the *Charter of Rights*, what they are today – the constitution, international law, particularly treaties entered into by the United Kingdom on Canada's behalf, Indigenous law (discussed in chapter 10), statutes, the Quebec civil code, and case law. But this simple truism is deceptive for a variety of reasons when discussing the sources of law for this period. In the common law jurisdictions statutes – discussed in the first two sections of this chapter – grew in volume and importance as legislators in every province looked to alter common law rules in a wide and increasing number of areas. The substantive content of those changes is not dealt with here. Rather it is examined in most of the chapters to follow, especially chapters 11 through 16. Here we are interested in how statutory consolidations were conceptualized and organized, and in the extent to which statutes were borrowed by some jurisdictions from others.

The second section examines case law. There has long been a debate in the legal historiography of the common law provinces, and of the SCC, about the extent to which Canada was a legal colony of Britain in this period. Indeed, some have argued that it became more so after Confederation than in the colonial period, a proposition that we test here to the extent possible, concluding that, as in so many areas, the story is a complicated one. The third, fourth, and fifth sections look at the *Civil Code of Lower Canada*, which, while technically a statute, functioned effectively as the common law, or droit commun, of Quebec. It contained the fundamental rules and doctrines in all areas of private law. The treatment here relates not to its substantive content, which is examined in the next chapter, but to its organization, to a variety of general interpretive issues unique to it, and to its relationship to other sources of law. Also analysed is its reception in the legal community in the first half-century after its adoption.

Before looking at the various sources of law, we need to discuss the reception of law. Ontario, Quebec, the Maritime provinces, and Newfoundland had all established reception dates before 1867. The date for British Columbia was unclear then and remains contested. A proclamation of 1858 declared the law of the new mainland colony of British Columbia to be English law as of 19 November 1858. It was repealed and replaced by an 1867 ordinance that set the same reception date for the new united colony of British Columbia, which included Vancouver Island. But English law was in force on Vancouver Island from 1849, when a commission was issued to the governor, Richard Blanchard.[1] There was also uncertainty about the prairie region, which Canada acquired in 1869–70 in a three-way arrangement with Britain and the HBC, dealt with in chapter 7. Canadian statutes of 1869 and 1871 dealing with the North-West Territories did not address the question, because they provided only that the laws in force in Rupert's Land and the North-West Territories would continue in force when the region was admitted to the Union, and the *Manitoba Act* of 1870 was silent on reception.[2] However, when Manitoba established a Supreme Court it was given jurisdiction 'over all matters of Law and Equity, ... and such powers and authorities in relation to matters of Local and Provincial jurisdiction, as in England are distributed among the Superior Courts of Law and Equity, and of Probate.' This was an implicit reception of all common law and equity, much like the reception provisions of the Maritime colonies in the eighteenth century, which were contained in instructions to governors to establish courts. Nonetheless, Parliament passed two reception statutes for Manitoba and the Territories, in 1886 and 1888. The former, the statute establishing a Supreme Court in the Territories, provided that English laws as of 15 July 1870 – the date Manitoba and the Territories entered the Union – were in force in both 'in so far as they were applicable.' The latter was to the same effect for Manitoba and passed for 'the removal of doubts.' Those doubts derived from the fact that in 1886 the Court of Queen's Bench had declared the reception date to be 1670, the date of the HBC Charter, and the Court of

Appeal affirmed that ruling in 1888. Doubts as to the applicable law in Manitoba involved more than just the reception date for English law. In 1880 the first *Consolidated Statutes* of Manitoba had included some Laws of Assiniboia passed in the 1860s and considered still in force.[3]

A final topic that needs some attention in this introduction is the nature of the legislative process. Today most bills are public bills. They originate within government (or very occasionally with individual MPs or their provincial counterparts), relate to matters of public importance, and dominate the legislative agenda. Private bills, dealing with matters of a purely local or private nature, are much less common. To take a random example, in 2020 the Manitoba legislature passed 30 statutes, 28 of which were public acts and the remaining two private acts. One of the latter altered the way that property belonging to the United Church of Canada in Manitoba could be dealt with, and the other amended the statute, itself a private act, creating the Winnipeg Humane Society Foundation. In the nineteenth and well into the twentieth century this balance was reversed. Provincial legislatures sat on average only two months every year until the 1960s, with the majority of their business devoted to private, not public bills. During our period 60 per cent of bills passed related to local and private matters, and only 40 per cent were public acts. Individual members were active not only in seeking private acts for their constituents on various matters, but also with regard to public bills. Party discipline prior to the turn of the twentieth century was much looser than it later became. In Quebec's Assemblée, for example, prior to 1904, 46 per cent of public bills originated with individual members, both those in government and those in opposition. Moreover, governments with a majority often lost votes on bills they proposed, because their own members voted against them. And while the experience of other provinces was similar in this regard, Quebec governments also had to deal with the upper house, which regularly rejected government bills or amended them significantly in the decades after Confederation.[4]

After about 1900 provincial governments began to exert more control over the legislative process. Party discipline was strengthened, the role of individual members in initiating public bills was curtailed (though the proportion of private acts remained high), and the drafting of legislation gradually became more uniform and less scattershot in style and expression. In Quebec the legislative council became more docile, restricting its amendment function mostly to technical matters. In short, a legislative environment more familiar to modern eyes was emerging in the last decade or so of our period.

Federal and Provincial Statutory Consolidations

The increased role played by statutes in the half-century after Confederation can be simply and graphically illustrated. Table 4.1 shows the number of individual statutes in each statutory consolidation between Confederation and 1914, and includes Newfoundland, still a British colony. All provinces are represented except Prince Edward Island and Alberta, which did not bring out new editions of their statutes in this period. As table 4.1 reveals, some of these publications were called revisions and some consolidations, but both words meant the same thing to contemporaries, and we will refer to them all as statutory consolidations, except when we instance a particular title. The legislation establishing commissions to prepare new editions of a jurisdiction's statutes, and that instructing commissioners to add to their work by incorporating statutes passed since they had begun, invariably told them to 'revise, classify and consolidate' the statutes.[5] The only exception was British Columbia's *Revised Statutes* of 1897, discussed below. The revision commissioner, Chief Justice Davie, took pains to distinguish his work of revision from the 'mere' consolidation or collection of 1888.

A statutory consolidation was a publication of all statutes in force, each of which would consist of an original statute together with all amendments made since its passage or since the last consolidation that included it. The purpose was what it had been since statutory consolidations were first passed in various colonies starting in the eighteenth century – to make it easier to find the current law by obviating the need to go back and search through all amendments passed over the decades since the original statute was passed.[6] This rationale was only once explicitly stated in this period. New Brunswick consolidated its statutes in 1877, and more than 20 years later had not done so again. The preamble to a statute authorizing what became the *Revised Statutes* of 1903 noted that the passage of time had 'seriously impeded' the administration of justice and increased its cost.[7] For the same reason consolidations of particular statutes were also done on numerous occasions. The *Indian Act*, for example, which is reviewed in chapter 8, was first passed in 1876 and was itself a consolidation of four statutes relating to Indigenous people passed between 1868 and 1874, and it was consolidated again in 1880.[8]

The instructions to commissioners were largely the same, and stressed that they were not to alter the substance, to make new law. The commissioners for the New Brunswick consolidation of 1877, for example, were permitted to alter the language of statutes 'as may seem requisite to preserve a uniform mode of expression,' while those for the federal

Table 4.1. Federal, provincial, and colonial consolidated/revised statutes, 1867–1914*

Jurisdiction	1870s	1880s	1890s	1900s
Canada	—	RSC 1886 – 185	—	RSC 1906 – 155
Ontario	RSO 1877 – 224	RSO 1887 – 250	RSO 1897 – 342	RSO 1914 – 301
Quebec	—	RSQ 1888 – 71	—	RSQ 1909 – 74
Nova Scotia	RSNS 1873 – 114	RSNS 1884 – 128	RSNS 1900 – 187	—
New Brunswick	CSNB 1877 – 120	—	RSNB 1903 – 189	—
Newfoundland	CSN 1874 – 117	—	CSN 1896 – 145	—
British Columbia	Laws of British Columbia 1871 – 100 CSBC 1877 – 265	CSBC 1888 – 121	RSBC 1897 – 195	RSBC 1911 – 247
Manitoba	CSM 1880 – 96	RSM 1892 – 150	RSM 1902 – 178	RSM 1913 – 209
Saskatchewan	—	—	—	RSS 1909 – 153

* Table 4.1 does not include the North-West Territories. The Territorial Ordinances were consolidated in 1888 and 1898, but we have not included them because territorial law was a combination of federal statutes passed for the Territories and local ordinances, of which there were about 60 in the 1888 consolidation: *The Revised Ordinances of the North-West Territories* (Regina: Government Printer, 1888).

consolidation of 1906 contained an almost identical clause. The instructions invariably included an admonition to 'not alter the legal effect' of the original words. Commissioners could change the phraseology 'without altering the sense,' and any changes in wording were to be made 'without changing the legal effect of the statutes.'[9] Consolidations were therefore unambitious exercises. There was no talk of law reform, codification, or rationalization, and if commissioners thought that substantive changes should be made they were told that they could do no more than recommend amendments. More substantively reformist language did appear in instructions to commissioners for the 1897 revised statutes of British Columbia and Ontario, a matter to which we will return.

As table 4.1 demonstrates, all jurisdictions adopted a relatively uniform approach to how often they brought out new editions of the statutes. Ontario, British Columbia, and Manitoba each did so more or less every decade, Nova Scotia did so every decade until 1900, while the federal jurisdiction, Quebec, New Brunswick, and Newfoundland did so only twice in this period, once every two decades. In the case of Quebec, that was probably because so much of Quebec law was contained in the *Civil Code,* and as a result Quebec's consolidations contained far fewer statutes than any other jurisdiction. For Newfoundland one can reasonably assume a similar correlation between less frequent consolidations and relatively few statutes. New Brunswick and Nova Scotia were likely contemplating another edition in the 1910s, when war intervened.

In most provinces the number of statutes increased with every consolidation as the common law was amended, as some areas of common law were cast in statutory form, and as new areas of law such as business corporations emerged. The exceptions were Ontario between 1897 and 1914, the federal jurisdiction between 1886 and 1906, and British Columbia between 1877 and 1888. Despite the drop in the Ontario numbers it still had more statutes than any other jurisdiction at the end of our period. The real aberration for that province is the very large increase of almost 100 statutes between 1887 and 1897 because of the addition of English statutes and parts of English statutes, a matter discussed below. That there were almost 30 fewer statutes in the federal consolidation of 1906 than there had been in 1886 is accounted for by the passage of the *Criminal Code* of 1892, discussed in chapter 13. The 1886 *Revised Statutes* included more than 40 statutes on criminal law and procedure that were effectively reduced to one six years later. The startling change in British Columbia between 1877 and 1888 resulted from the fact that the 1877 consolidated statutes included 84 acts or ordinances passed by the various colonial legislatures before 1871. By the next consolidation of 1888 many colonial-era statutes had been repealed.

The consolidations differed from each other in how the statutes were arranged. The authorizing statutes always instructed the commissioners to 'classify' the statutes, but they did not say how to do so. All jurisdictions but Quebec numbered all the statutes consecutively. Beyond that, two principal arrangements were employed. Most jurisdictions, the four original confederating provinces and Newfoundland, arranged the statutes into 'titles,' between 15 and 35 of them, and fit each statute into the applicable title. This approach catered to legal professionals, who would have been able to find the right statute under 'domestic relations,' 'descent of property,' or 'mercantile law and contracts.' Even within this group, however, there was a subtle but significant difference. Four out of five of the Ontario consolidations had just 15 or 17 titles, so that each title had to be reasonably general, such as 'public departments, revenue and property' and 'laws affecting special classes of persons.' Conversely Nova Scotia and New Brunswick employed between 26 and 35 titles. New Brunswick's 1903 consolidation, for example, had 35 titles into which 108 statutes were slotted, five statutes per title, and having so many titles meant that each could be given a more particular name, one that was understandable to the non-legally trained – mines, public parks, railways, prisons, and public charities are examples. Quebec employed the fewest number of titles – 12 in both 1888 and 1909 – but it also had the fewest statutes, just over 70, so that each title had an average of only 6 statutes. Quebec was unique in one respect: the statute numbering started anew at chapter 1 within each title.

Other jurisdictions did not use titles. Manitoba and British Columbia (from 1887) arranged the statutes alphabetically, perhaps to make them more accessible to a lay reader. Manitoba, for example, started its 1902 and 1913 *Revised Statutes* with agriculture, aliens, and anatomy, ended volume 1 with lunatics, and concluded volume 2 with wolf bounty, workmen's liens, and workmen's compensation. These consolidated statutes thus resembled the alphabetical organization of magistrates' manuals and other legal guides produced for, or at least accessible to, a lay readership. The federal consolidations of 1886 and 1906 do not fit into either of these two principal categories. The statutes were simply numbered, although the numbering was not random; cognate statutes were grouped together, even if they were not arranged into titles. The same approach was taken with the Manitoba consolidation of 1880, before that province adopted an alphabetical arrangement from 1892. In only one instance, the British Columbia consolidation of 1877, were the statutes simply numbered without any discernible rhyme or reason to the order.

There was considerable variety in the numbers and status of men tasked with preparing the consolidations. For some – British Columbia in 1897 and Quebec in 1888 – there was only a single commissioner. Between two and four was common – two worked on British Columbia 1887, three on British Columbia 1877 and on four of the Maritime provinces' consolidations, while four men compiled the 1900 *Revised Statutes of Nova Scotia*. Ontario used a large group for all its consolidations – eight in 1877, 13 in 1887 and 1897, and 10 as well as some members of the executive council in 1914. Ontario used a substantial number of judges, members of the Court of Appeal, and all the trial courts. In 1887, for example, the 13 commissioners included three Court of Appeal judges, a judge from each of the three divisions of the High Court, the former chief justice and lieutenant governor of Manitoba Alexander Morris, and Oliver Mowat, premier and attorney general. The propriety of judges doing this work was discussed, albeit inconclusively, in the *Canada Law Journal* in 1903.[10] Presumably opinion in the Maritime provinces was against it, for they preferred eminent lawyers to judges on every occasion. British Columbia 'mixed and matched' for its first three revisions and then stipulated that no judge could be a commissioner for what became the 1914 revision. The Newfoundland commissioners in 1874 were both lawyers and assemblymen, because the consolidation was done by a select committee of the assembly. There were eight commissioners for the 1906 *Revised Statutes of Canada* – Sir Samuel Strong, who had recently retired as chief justice of Canada, Deputy Minister of Justice E.L. Newcombe, the Department of Justice Chief Clerk Augustus Power, the registrar of the SCC, E.R. Cameron, one lawyer from each of Ontario, Manitoba, and Nova Scotia, and a Quebec notary.[11]

The task of consolidation in a new country made up in part of long-established colonial jurisdictions was complicated by the fact that pre-Confederation legislation had to be integrated with statutes passed since 1867. This was especially a problem in the 1870s. The Ontario commissioners found this additionally difficult, noting that they were required to consolidate statutes passed since 1867 with 'a great measure of enactments passed under a constitution which no longer exists,' that of the Province of Canada. They were to some extent aided by the latter's statutory consolidations of 1859 and 1860, which divided the statutes into those applicable only to either Upper or Lower Canada and those applicable to the Province of Canada as a whole. The first two could be either all included, subject to whether provincial statutes had directly or indirectly repealed or amended them and to whether they were now under section 91, or all omitted. But the third group had to be dealt with case by case. Even if a Province of Canada statute was included, commissioners argued that they were 'justified in altering the form of most of these enactments so as to bring them into harmony with the new constitution of the province or the plain intention of the Legislature.' But not all, and in some cases they called for new legislation. When the statutes were published they included a schedule of colonial Acts repealed by the consolidation.[12] The British Columbia commissioners struggled with this problem as well, and that province's 1877 consolidation included 84 pre-1872 colonial statutes considered still in force while also listing as not applicable 295. Nova Scotia and New Brunswick did not have this difficulty to anything like the same extent, because they had consolidated their statutes in the 1850s and early 1860s, and their post-Confederation consolidations were largely continuations of the earlier ones. Quebec's commissioners were in the same position as Ontario's and responded with delay. An 1876 statute authorized a provincial consolidation, as did an almost identical 1880 statute, but the work was not completed until 1887.[13]

A greater difficulty for the provincial consolidations of the 1870s in particular was the division of powers. A host of colonial-era statutes dealt with subjects now under federal jurisdiction. Some topics were easily dealt with. It was simple, for example, to not include colonial statutes defining what constituted serious crimes and what penalties should be imposed. Criminal law was a federal matter, what constituted criminal law was relatively easy to decide in many instances, and, as we will see in chapter 13, Parliament very quickly occupied the field in the late 1860s. Indeed the federal government introduced legislation in the two to three years after Confederation in many areas of section 91 jurisdiction, including banking, bankruptcy, the currency, Indians, naturalization, and penitentiaries, and those statutes repealed, sometimes implicitly and sometimes expressly, colonial statutes.[14] But in the 1870s in particular federal and provincial officials were quite uncertain about exactly which subjects came under section 91 and 92, as evidenced by, among other things, the extensive correspondence over disallowance, already discussed in chapter 2 and to be discussed again in a number of later chapters.[15] The Ontario commissioners for the 1877 consolidation cited this problem as one of the factors that delayed their work. They hoped that the federal government would solve this problem by getting a consolidation out first, but the first federal consolidation did not appear until 1886. In what would be viewed by modern constitutional lawyers as a massive understatement, those same commissioners observed that 'it was a matter of some nicety to draw the line which separates' section 91 powers from others 'in relation to which the Provincial Legislature may exercise exclusive powers of legislation.'[16] As we saw in chapter 2, they could not look to the courts for much guidance; provincial courts of appeal were only beginning to grapple with how sections 91 and 92 fit together, and the SCC was not established until 1875.

Ultimately the Ontario commissioners included some statutes and parts of statutes, and omitted others, on the basis of 'the degree of doubt entertained with regard to them.' The same problem affected all the revisions of the 1870s. The *Revised Statutes of Nova Scotia* of 1873, for example, included an appendix of 'unrepealed legislation ... upon matters wholly or partially within the jurisdiction of the Parliament of Canada, or of doubtful jurisdiction,' and the 1877 *Consolidated Statutes* of New Brunswick also listed statutes that were now under federal jurisdiction or for which provincial jurisdiction was 'doubtful.' This problem never disappeared for statutory consolidators in this period; it was still an issue in British Columbia in the 1890s, according to sole consolidation commissioner Theodore Davie.[17]

Another problem for those tasked with preparing statutory consolidations was to determine which British statutes were in force. Reception doctrine holds that at the reception date all British statutes are in force in a colony, provided they are applicable to local circumstances, and remain in force until altered by local enactment. British statutes once received were still the law of a colony, even if they had been repealed in the United Kingdom.[18] Received statutes were not the only imperial statutes in force in Canada. Those that had been passed with specific application to Canada were also part of Canadian law *proprio vigore.** They serve as a reminder that from 1867 Canada was a dominion, still part of an empire, and that the Westminster Parliament was an imperial Parliament, able to legislate in certain matters affecting the whole or any part of the empire. The most obvious example of such a statute, included in all revisions of this period, was the *BNA Act* itself. Some consolidations also contained other British statutes relating to Canada, such as the *British North America Act 1871*, discussed in chapter 14, passed to validate the entry of Manitoba into Confederation, or acts dealing with provincial or international boundary disputes.

As we will see in later chapters, on a number of occasions courts had to rule on whether certain British statutes were in force in a province. Those preparing consolidations could never ignore the question, but only minimal attention was paid to it in the 1870s and 1880s. Most consolidations included some British statutes in their preliminary pages or appendices, but the issue did not become a major one until the late 1890s. It played a major role in the 1897 consolidations in both British Columbia and Ontario. In 1895 the statute authorizing a new consolidation for British Columbia instructed the commissioner to include 'the statute law of England, in force in and applicable to this Province.'[19] The sole commissioner was Theodore Davie, attorney general from 1889, premier from 1892 to 1895, and chief justice of the Supreme Court thereafter. A new consolidation was very close to his heart. He had introduced the authorizing statute, which became law in February 1895, and 10 days later resigned as premier so that he could do the work. A week later he was appointed commissioner, and two days afterwards he was sworn in as chief justice of the Supreme Court, only the second chief

----

* 'Of or by its own force independently.'

justice following the death nine months before of the iconic, and now to some notorious, Matthew Baillie Begbie.[20] Davie was not the only sole commissioner, but he was unique in being the only one who drafted his own authorizing statute and took on the job at the same time as being chief justice.

Most importantly, Davie was surely the only commissioner with a deep passion for and commitment to the enterprise. He did not intend simply to make it easier to find the law. In introducing the revision bill he stated that previous consolidations had been 'of a rather preliminary and perfunctory character' and that he was proposing 'something very different': 'a revision which shall be the result of carefully comparing one act with another, of taking up each section separately, and considering its bearings in relation to the common law and in relation to other provisions of the statutes.' It is telling that he called it a revision and not a consolidation, for he believed, unlike most people, that there was a difference, and the statute he shepherded through the assembly showed as much. It authorized the commissioner not just to omit expired and repealed Acts, but also to 'revise and alter the language…, not so as to change the sense, but so as to give better effect to the spirit and meaning of the law.' He could also 'frame and draw new provisions and suggestions for the improvement of the law.' This mandate was strikingly different from all other authorizing statutes, which told commissioners that they could change words but not 'alter the legal effect' or 'the sense' of the originals. Davie used some of the same language, stating that he could not 'change the sense' of any provision, but at the same time he undermined that injunction by requiring himself 'to give better effect to the spirit and meaning of the law.' He thus made a distinction between the 'legal sense' of words used and the 'spirit and meaning' of the law. An additional, and major, part of his mission was to improve the statute law by determining which British statutes were in force.

Davie worked remarkably quickly. He produced a first instalment of the statutes in January 1896, nine months after starting work, and the second instalment a year later. Between them the two instalments totalled nearly 2,000 pages and contained 198 statutes, over 70 more than in the *Consolidated Statutes* of 1888. Where applicable, British statutes and/or statutory sections were incorporated into his draft Acts. His report accompanying the first instalment made a mockery of his instructions in the statute that he had drafted. Many of his draft statutes, he proudly asserted, had been 're-drawn and re-arranged, objectionable features removed, and such changes introduced as experience, the altered conditions of the country, and judicial decisions show to be necessary.' His reports explaining his work show his 'supreme self-assurance, attention to detail, and zeal for rationalization.' His explanation in his first report of what comprised his proposed *Sheriffs Act* neatly captures how he had examined all relevant legislation, ancient and modern, UK and provincial, and come up with an amalgam of all: 'This is a condensation of the English law relative to Sheriffs, and of the British Columbia statutes upon the same subject. The Act sweeps away the old Statute Law of England ... and assimilates that law to that now existing in England, as modified and changed by Provincial Legislation.'

When Davie's first report and the accompanying draft statutes were debated in the assembly in 1896 they excited considerable controversy. Various members disagreed with particular changes to particular statutes, and a few of the draft statutes were passed with significant changes to Davie's drafts. When it looked as if discussing all the statutes would take up inordinate time and lead to many amendments, the attorney general asked the assembly if it wished to continue with the process or give the government the authority to proclaim into force all or some of the statutes. This proposal received very little support and the government withdrew all the other bills. The problem was obvious. In the words of Henry Helmcken, the son of British Columbia father of Confederation John Sebastian Helmcken, to adopt Davie's draft statutes without debate would be to let him 'legislate for the House.' The matter went into abeyance for the rest of the 1896 session while Davie wrote his second report. When that was completed the government took a different tack, submitting both reports and all the draft statutes to a commission consisting of Davie and two provincial Supreme Court judges, former premier George Walkem and Montague Tyrwhitt-Drake. It was remarkable that Davie was given the job of evaluating his own work, but surely no more remarkable than being given the job of sole commissioner, proceeding under a statute that he had drafted, in the first place.

In the event the addition of a level of review made no difference. The revised statutes became a government measure and support of and opposition to them a question of politics not principle. In May 1897, before the revised statutes had been presented to the assembly for approval, that body passed a statute providing a mechanism for bringing the revision into force.[21] Its preamble noted that Davie's draft was being examined by commissioners, and that it was 'expedient' to add to the draft the statutes passed in the 1897 session, since Davie had finished his work. This latter provision was ubiquitous, appearing in every provincial statute bringing into force a revision in this period, because revisions were always completed up to the end of one year and had to be brought into effect the next. What was not common was that this would all happen without legislative scrutiny. As one MLA stated in debate over the bill, the legislature was asked to pass a bill to 'make law a revision which had not yet been made … without ever seeing the revised version.' Yet that is what happened. The three-man commission worked through the rest of 1897 assessing Davie's 198 draft statutes against criteria laid down in section 3 of the *Revised Statutes Act* – criteria that were both nearly identical to those used in other provincial consolidation statutes and somewhat contradictory. On the one hand the commissioners' work should 'not depart or vary from the spirit of existing law nor change the sense of the same,' and any corrections made should only be of any 'contradiction or ambiguity' and not change the 'legal effect' of the existing statutes. On the other hand, changes in language were acceptable if they were needed 'to meet local circumstances' or 'preserve a uniform mode of expression,' so long as they did not, again, 'alter the legal effect.' But there was also a proviso to the last criterion that altered its meaning substantially: it was not 'a departure from the spirit of existing law, or a change in the sense of the law,' if a rewording gave effect to case law that had interpreted the statute.

Given the discretion the *Statute Revision Act* conferred, it is not surprising that the commissioners found that of the 195 statutes submitted to it, only 14 did not comply with section 3. Their report was filed on 31 December 1897, a follow-up report was issued on 10 February 1898, briefly describing the changes they had since made to the 14 statutes, a bill was introduced on 14 February, and on 4 March it received royal assent. In the interim, on 21 February, the entire remainder of the 181 statutes was proclaimed law, along with 10 British statutes that were not included in the main body of the revision but in a 'preliminary' section as in force in the province. They included *Magna Carta*, the *Habeas Corpus Act* and related statutes, *Quia Emptores*, the *Statute of Uses*, the *Grantees of Reversions Act*, and the *Real Property Act 1845*. Overall, 93 per cent of Davie's recommendations made it into the revised statutes.

No other jurisdiction did anything as far-reaching as British Columbia in 1897 or at any other time, but, presumably inspired by what Davie had done, Ontario gave much more attention to which British statutes were in force in its contemporaneous consolidation. Initially it appeared that Ontario's *Revised Statutes* of 1897 would be just like the 1877 and

THE

REVISED STATUTES

—OF—

BRITISH COLUMBIA

1897

BEING A CONSOLIDATION AND REVISION OF THE

STATUTES APPLICABLE TO BRITISH COLUMBIA, AND WITHIN THE
POWER OF THE LEGISLATURE TO ENACT.

VOLUME I.

Revised and Consolidated under and pursuant to the Acts 58 Victoria, Chap. 49,
and 60 Victoria, Chap. 41.

PUBLISHED BY AUTHORITY.

VICTORIA, B. C.:
Printed by RICHARD WOLFENDEN, Printer to the Queen's Most Excellent Majesty.
1897.

TABLES OF CONTENTS.

———:o:———

No. 1.—PRELIMINARY.

———

IMPERIAL ACTS.

PAGE.

MAGNA CHARTA.. xvii.

HABEAS CORPUS:

31 Car. II., c. 2:

An Act for the better securing the Liberty of the Subject, and for Prevention of Imprisonments beyond the Seas............. xxix.

1 & 2 Philip & Mary, c. 13:

An Act touching Bailment of Persons......................... xxxvi.

43 Geo. III., c. 140:

An Act to enable the Judges of His Majesty's Courts of Record at Westminster to award Writs of Habeas Corpus for bringing Persons detained in Gaol before Courts Martial, and the several Commissioners therein mentioned........................ xxxvi.

44 Geo. III., c. 102:

An Act for the more effectual Administration of Justice in those Parts of the United Kingdom of Great Britain and Ireland called England and Ireland, by the issuing of Writs of Habeas Corpus ad Testificandum in certain cases .... xxxvii.

56 Geo. III., c. 100:

An Act for more effectually securing the Liberty of the Subject xxxviii.

1 & 2 Vict., c. 45:

An Act to extend the Jurisdiction of the Judges of the Superior Courts of Common Law, and to provide for the taking of Special Bail in the absence of the Judges .... xli.

REAL PROPERTY:

18 Edw. I., St. 1, c. 1:

The Statute of Westminster the Third................ .... xliii.

27 Hen. VIII., c. 10:

An Act concerning Uses and Wills .... xlv.

32 Hen. VIII., c. 34:

Concerning Grantees of Reversions to take advantage of the conditions to be performed by the Lessees .... li.

8 & 9 Vict., c. 106:

An Act to amend the Law of Real Property .... liii.

The *Revised Statutes of British Columbia* 1897 (this page and opposite) included an extensive section on which English statutes were in force in the province, an issue which concerned many of the provincial and federal statutory consolidators of this period. Note that British Columbia revised statutes included English statutes going back to Magna Carta.

1887 versions. Thirteen appointed commissioners consolidated the statutes to the end of 1896 and were instructed to add those passed in the 1897 assembly session. Volumes 1 and 2 were completed, passed, and published in 1897, containing 17 titles and 321 statutes. Given what then transpired, somebody must have become aware of and interested in what British Columbia had done, and an elaborate process of compiling a third volume of English statutes still in force in the province was begun. The work was done by George Smith Holmested, senior registrar of the High Court, overseen by a five-person committee of leading judges. It took more than four years to complete and was published as volume 3 of the 1897 revised statutes in 1902.[22]

Volume 3 was divided into two principal sections. The first was a 37-page appendix itself divided into four parts: Constitutional Acts; certain imperial statutes of general practical utility in force in Ontario *ex proprio vigore*; *The Habeas Corpus Act*; and a table of imperial statutes in force in Canada at the end of 1901, *ex proprio vigore*. The first comprised seven statutes, three passed before the eighteenth century and four in the eighteenth and nineteenth centuries, including the *Quebec Act*, the *Constitutional Act* of 1791, and the *British North America Act 1871*.[23] The second consisted of British statutes about evidence law. Part 3 was self-explanatory, the *Habeas Corpus Act* of 1679, and part 4 was a listing of British statutes dating from 1552 – a statute prohibiting the buying and selling of offices – to just before Confederation, the vast majority being from the Victorian period. The second section was the most interesting, consisting of six additional titles to those in volumes 1 and 2. Distributed among the six new titles were twenty-one additional statutes. These were Ontario statutes in form, part of *RSO 1897*, but British statutes in substance. Three examples will serve to make our point. Chapter 330 of the 1897 *Revised Statutes*, *An Act Respecting Real Property*, had as section 1 the *Statute De Donis Conditionalibus* (1285) and as section 2 the *Statute Quia Emptores* (1290). Other sections reproduced British statutory provisions on, inter alia, rights of dower and curtesy. Chapter 331 of the 1897 *Revised Statutes* was *An Act Concerning Uses* and simply reproduced every word of the 1535 *Statute of Uses*. Finally, chapter 338 was *An Act for the Prevention of Frauds and Perjuries*, an exact reproduction of the 1677 *Statute of Frauds*. Theodore Davie had laboured mightily to integrate old British statutes with more modern ones. The Ontario draftsmen, if they can be called that, employed a scissors-and-paste method. The whole was praised by the *Canada Law Journal*, which wondered 'why the public and the profession were allowed to grope for over a hundred years in the dark' for a clear statement, in one place, of which British statutes were in force.[24] Yet some of the 21 additional statutes passed in 1902 dealt with areas of law already part of volumes 1 and 2. In title 22, Mercantile Law, there were two subheadings, one of which was 'Insurance 2.' The *Revised Statutes* already had two statutes on insurance companies. Somebody looking for the statute law on insurance would now have to look in two different places, reducing the utility of compiling revised statutes in the first place. Here and there among the additional 21 the drafters provided a reminder, a marginal annotation to also consult an earlier chapter of the revised statutes.

Federal and Provincial Statutes: Cross-Border Borrowings

It was not uncommon in the nineteenth century in federal states (and is not uncommon today) for jurisdictions to borrow from each other when enacting statutes that changed the common law or took the jurisdiction into an area of social and economic life not previously regulated. This was not surprising. Statutes are the expression of new ideas about socio-economic or political organization, and ideas are rarely constrained within boundaries. Once the seed of an idea was planted, it was only sensible to look for models from elsewhere about how to grow and nurture it. In post-Confederation Canada, in areas as discrete as family law reform, the collection of vital statistics, workplace regulation, inheritance law, forms of business enterprise, and many others there was much copying of statutes from one jurisdiction to another.

There is not space here to survey the whole gamut of such copying, and we will use just two examples. As we will see in chapter 15, all Canadian provinces enacted changes to the common law rules governing the property and civil rights of married women. These developments were far from uniform, some provinces changing the law more radically and earlier than others. When provinces with similar objectives legislated, entire sections were copied verbatim from another jurisdiction. For example, in 1872 Ontario provided that a married woman could hold, as property separate from her husband, all her 'wages and personal earnings,' including money made 'from any literary, artistic or scientific skill,' free from the 'debts or dispositions of the husband' as if she were not married. Exactly the same provision later appeared in a British Columbia statute of 1873, a federal statute passed for the Northwest Territories in 1875, and a Manitoba statute of 1881.[25] Similarly, an 1884 Ontario Act granted married women enhanced civil status – the right to contract, the right to sue and the responsibility of being sued on their contracts, and similar status with regard to torts. Over the next decade and a half an identical provision became the law of British Columbia, New Brunswick, Prince Edward Island, Nova Scotia, and Manitoba. Not all of the legal reforms in this area can be seen as enhancing women's rights. Some looked to enable married women to carry out their parental and domestic roles when the husband failed to do so by not supporting his family. The first such provision was passed in Upper Canada in 1859, allowing women to obtain a protection order and keep their earnings if one of a long list of circumstances prevented husbands from taking financial or other care of the family, or showed that they were unwilling to do so. Identical provisions, including the same list of circumstances, were later legislated for Manitoba, Nova Scotia, and Prince Edward Island.

Our second example comes from a very different area of law and involves not just the provinces but the federal jurisdiction. As we will see in chapter 11, a very significant development in company law after 1867 was the widespread adoption of general incorporation. The pre-Confederation system whereby a company wishing to incorporate had to obtain a private act from the legislature or be operating in a particular sector of the economy gave way to one in which any company, no matter what its field of enterprise, could apply for letters patent of incorporation. The federal jurisdiction was the first to enact such a regime, passing an 1869 statute that stated at the outset, 'The Governor in Council may, by letters patent under the Great Seal, grant a Charter to any number of persons, not less than five, who shall petition therefor, constituting such persons and others who may become shareholders in the company thereby created, a body corporate and politic, for any purposes or objects to which the legislative authority of the Parliament of Canada extends.'[26] An identical statement was contained in general incorporation legislation passed over the ensuing 20 years by Ontario (1874), Manitoba (1875), Quebec (1881), Nova Scotia (1883), New Brunswick (1885), the North-West Territories (1886), and Prince Edward Island (1888). The only difference was that, to use the example of Manitoba, the last phrase read 'to which the legislative authority of the Legislature of Manitoba extends.' Each of the general incorporation statutes also had a default limited liability clause in identical terms: 'The Shareholders of the Company shall not as such ... be responsible for any act, default or liability whatsoever, of the Company ... beyond the amount of their respective shares in the capital stock thereof.' Thus, the task of many legislative drafters in this period, over a wide range of areas, was alleviated by the ability to copy those who had gone before them. Given the small number of lawyers, or indeed staff in general, employed by governments at the time, it made sense for those drafting legislation to use what was already in circulation, rather than try to invent every clause anew.

Case Law

The half-century after Confederation saw several new trends in the use of case law by Canadian courts. First, the publication of case reports, commenced in Upper Canada, became much more widespread and regular. This meant that the case law of each province could be consulted by lawyers and judges in other provinces, supplementing the UK and US case law that was already available. Second, the role of provincial courts of appeal diminished somewhat; they were no longer the apex courts in their jurisdiction, as they had been when appeals to the JCPC were rare. After 1875 their decisions were subject to appeal both to the SCC and to the JCPC, placing them fairly far down in the hierarchy of courts. Appeals to the JCPC from the common law provinces were rare until the 1880s and did not really take off until the first decade of the twentieth century, as seen in table 4.2. Finally, the last quarter of the nineteenth century saw the doctrine of stare decisis being insisted upon more rigorously, both in Canada and in the United Kingdom. This trend witnessed attempts by UK courts to ensure that their decisions were followed by courts in the empire, and their disapproval of resort to US and other foreign sources of law. These moves were part of a larger trend, evident on both sides of the Atlantic, to re-imperialize Canadian law, but also inspired some resistance motivated by a desire to develop a distinctive domestic law suitable for Canadian circumstances.[27]

With these developments in mind, we will examine how the courts of the new dominion developed the common law, particularly the private law. Much of this discussion revolves around the relative influence of UK and US authorities, both case law and textual, in Canadian courts. Just as the relatively poor and underpopulated Canadian provinces had to import financial capital to build physical infrastructure and develop their economies, so too they had to import intellectual capital in the form of legal knowledge to complete their juridical infrastructure. English law had been received into all the colonies (albeit with some limits in Quebec) and of course remained highly influential. Prior

Table 4.2. JCPC appeals, Quebec and common law provinces, 1870–1919

Decade	Total appeals	Quebec appeals	Common law provinces	% Quebec: Other provinces
1870s	67	55	12	82:18
1880s	63	31	32	49:51
1890s	70	32	38	45:55
1900s	103	43	60	58:42
1910s	185	37	148	80:20

to Confederation, US authority, especially that of New York and Massachusetts, had also been looked upon positively and employed with some regularity for reasons of practicality and cultural affinity. After 1867 this began to change for a number of reasons, some involving an enhanced 'pull' towards UK law and others a greater 'push' away from US law, though the latter factor did not operate to the same extent in all the provinces.

To begin with the 'pull,' the simple fact that British jurists and the British Empire in general were at the height of their fame in the late nineteenth century had much to do with the enhanced appeal of UK decisions. One shared in the reflected glory of empire by citing decisions from the mother country that carried considerable weight and prestige because of the perceived high quality of their reasoning. This mimetic trend can be found in many areas of Canadian law and legal culture at the time in addition to case law, including major statutory reforms such as the *Judicature Acts*, the *Bills of Exchange Act* and the *Sale of Goods Act*, and those dealing with married women's property. Practical factors such as faster transportation links and the easier availability of English law books and case reports also had a role to play in the uptake of English decisions.[28] In this regard, the appearance of the first edition of *Halsbury's Laws of England*, in 31 volumes between 1907 and 1917, was a turning point. For guidance on any point of English law, one no longer had to consult myriad texts and cases; rather, the current authoritative view could be found under the appropriate topic heading in *Halsbury's*.

On the 'push' side, some factors made recourse to American law less desirable. After the Civil War, the number of published decisions from state courts became unmanageable, even for Americans. In this context, some Canadian judges adverted to their uncertainty about what US law was on a given point. Chief Justice William Young of Nova Scotia lamented in 1869 the 'utter inconsistency of the American decisions, which as their judges and text writers confess, it is ultimately impossible to reconcile with each other.' On the practical side, maintaining subscriptions to ever-proliferating series of US case reports became more than many Canadian law libraries could afford. US texts continued to be consulted, but some judges found their statements of law 'unsatisfactory, as we have in most cases no means of examining the authorities referred to.'[29] Probably the biggest 'push' factor, however, was that the UK courts themselves began to deprecate the citation of US authorities after earlier being reasonably receptive to them. In 1889, in remarks picked up in the legal press in Canada and the United States, Lord Halsbury observed bluntly that citing US cases as being on the same par as English cases was simply 'wrong,' while Fry LJ deplored the citation of American authorities as 'a waste of time.'[30]

The SCC seems to have shared in the general trend towards lessened dependence on US sources, especially after 1900.[31] In the provincial courts, there was regional variation regarding the use of US cases. Nova Scotia continued to use them the most, given its many historic links with the northeast, while their use dropped off in the 'loyalist' provinces of New Brunswick and Ontario. It is likely that jurists in the Prairie provinces continued to rely on US authorities more than in the East, given the many cross-border ties in the great plains, but there is no comprehensive study. In British Columbia, as discussed in chapter 16, the courts relied heavily on California and Oregon decisions in invalidating various statutes discriminating against the Chinese, but this was on a topic where no English precedents were available. Any pattern in other areas of law is not yet clear.

Enhanced attachment to UK decisions was also a function of the growing rigour of stare decisis. While the practice of lower courts having to follow the decisions of higher ones had been long ingrained in the common law, the position on courts of coordinate rank was not settled. Was a Court of Appeal bound by its own decisions? Was a trial judge of a Superior Court bound by decisions by fellow judges on the same point of law? In the 1890s the UK courts began to make much more categorical statements on these matters than they had before. In 1895 the Court of Appeal declared in a one-line decision that the trial judge in the instant case had correctly applied an existing Court of Appeal authority, as he was bound to do; hence the appeal had to be dismissed because the Court of Appeal had no power to overrule itself – end of story.[32] Three years later the House of Lords repeated this in more striking language:

'A decision of this House upon a question of law is conclusive and nothing but an Act of Parliament can set right that which is alleged to be wrong in a judgment of this House.' As the Lord Chancellor, Lord Herschel, delivered both these judgments, the message could not have come from a more authoritative source.[33]

The appeal of certainty in judicial decision-making reached new heights in Ontario, where the legislature felt compelled to intervene in 1895. In a move thought to be unique in the British world, the *Judicature Act* was amended to make decisions of the Court of Appeal binding on itself and on all lower courts, and to render High Court judges bound by all decisions of fellow judges in that Court brought to their attention. If a trial judge strongly believed a previous decision to be in error, however, the matter could be referred to a higher court for resolution. The Quebec Court of Appeal, by contrast, did not regard itself as bound by its own decisions at this time, though this stance was not met with universal approval.[34]

The SCC did not make a definitive pronouncement on this issue until 1909, in *Stuart v Bank of Montreal*. While the Court had never actually declined to follow one of its own majority decisions, there were scattered dicta from some of its judges indicating that it could do so. In *Stuart*, the issue was whether a wealthy married woman, who had agreed to stand as security for a large loan to her husband's business, should have received independent advice before entering the transaction. As no fraud or sharp dealing was alleged, the issue came down to whether the relationship of husband and wife was such that a presumption of undue influence arose under such circumstances, giving rise to a duty on the bank to ensure that the wife obtained such advice. A 1904 decision of the Court, *Cox v Adams*, had answered yes to this question, although there was disagreement on whether some judges in the majority had or had not based their grant of relief on the ground of fraud, which was not present in *Stuart*. Justice Anglin exhaustively reviewed the evolution of stare decisis in the United Kingdom and Canada, noting that 'in Ontario, this case is regarded as very important and it has been a subject of much speculation how far this court would deem itself bound to follow' it. Speaking for the Court, he concluded that 'unless perhaps in very exceptional circumstances, a previous deliberate and definite decision of this court will be held binding, if it is clear that it was not the result of some mere slip or inadvertence.' While stated slightly less categorically than in the UK cases, the decision conveyed that the court would consider itself henceforth as bound by its own decisions.[35] Somewhat ironically, given that stare decisis is not part of the civilian tradition, the court had earlier opined that it was bound by its own decisions in civil law matters from Quebec.[36]

These developments did not address directly the relationship of British to colonial courts in the context of stare decisis. It was accepted by all that decisions of the JCPC on Canadian appeals were binding on all Canadian courts, including the SCC. But did decisions of the English Court of Appeal or the House of Lords bind courts of equal or lower rank in Canada? In 1879 the JCPC addressed this issue in *Trimble v Hill*. This was an Australian appeal relating to the interpretation of the *Gaming Act*, an 1845 UK statute, which had been adopted in identical terms in New South Wales. The Supreme Court of New South Wales (equivalent to a provincial Court of Appeal in Canada) had declined to follow an English Court of Appeal decision on the interpretation of the act, as it conflicted with a local decision on the same point. The JCPC decided that 'in colonies where a like enactment has been passed by the Legislature, the Colonial Courts should also govern themselves by' the English Court of Appeal's interpretation of it, reversing the New South Wales decision. As to whether the SCC, in light of *Trimble v Hill*, would be bound by a decision of the English Court of Appeal, Anglin J said in *Stuart* only that 'the duty of this court would require most careful consideration.'[37]

The JCPC's pronouncement did not mean that Canadian courts were bound by all English Court of Appeal decisions, just those where a UK statute had been copied in a Canadian jurisdiction and the English Court of Appeal had interpreted one of its provisions. All in all, this was a modest demand. Nonetheless, it pointed to developing cracks in the facade of Canadian courts' deference to courts in the metropole, revealing a nascent nationalism in some quarters. Justice Frank Hodgins of the Ontario Court of Appeal noted in a 1923 article that *Trimble v Hill* 'met in some quarters with a cold response.'[38] He himself did not favour it, calculating that 14 judges across Canada had followed it while nine had not, the first in 1886. The statute of 1895 noted earlier made the issue moot in Ontario, as it obliged the province's judges to follow decisions of the Ontario Court of Appeal – implicitly, even if they conflicted with decisions of the English Court of Appeal. A later commentator, Bora Laskin, future chief justice of Canada, concluded that it was all a tempest in a teapot. UK decisions were generally followed, he opined, 'because they reflected agreeable propositions of law,' not because of any obligation to do so.[39] The fact that some Canadian judges objected to being forced to follow them, however, shows that characterizations of Canadian jurists as becoming uniformly deferential to English norms in the later nineteenth century are likely overdrawn.[40] Even in Ontario, the most anglophile in juridical matters of all the provinces, British hegemony was never complete. Resisters to it aimed to create a law suitable for Canadian conditions where these were understood to be distinctive. Moreover, the focus on the use of UK or US authority can also obscure another trend developing during these years: the tendency of provincial courts to start citing one another. In Nova Scotia, for example, Ontario emerged as a 'secondary legal metropolis' in the later nineteenth century.[41]

Perhaps more important in the end than whether legal rules enunciated in UK decisions were binding on Canadian courts is the question of form, method, and underlying values. Across the common law world, the idea of legal science was reaching its heyday. Jurists sought to make law similar to the natural sciences, restricting its sources to legislation and case law, and insisting on logic, close grammatical analysis, and abstract decontextualized reasoning as the only proper tools for legal analysis. Indeed, the phrase analogizing the law library to a laboratory was coined in the early 1870s by Christopher Columbus Langdell as he began his long term as dean of Harvard Law School.[42] History, culture, and emotion were correspondingly de-emphasized, as seen in chapter 2. The JCPC was particularly insistent on employing tools of positivist legal analysis, and its position at the summit of the empire's appeal structure ensured that its techniques would be taken up in all colonial courts. It could not have imposed these ideas, however, if they were not already circulating through the broader legal-cultural universe, via law schools, legal texts, and professional associations.

The *Civil Code of Lower Canada*

The *Civil Code of Lower Canada* of 1866 was not a revolutionary document. It was meant to be primarily a restatement of the existing law, with any alterations recommended by the commissioners clearly indicated as 'new law.' It aimed to distil the kaleidoscope of sources that characterized the law of Lower Canada, to modernize the law by infusing economic liberalism into property law and the law of obligations, and to render the law accessible in equally authoritative French and English versions. As historian Edmond Lareau said in 1889, 'Codification had as its goal the elimination of the conflicting origins of our laws and the creation of a homogeneous corpus of law that is entirely Canadian, one that makes us forget its diverse sources.' The codification enterprise thus had both a modernizing and a universalizing mission.[43]

For some, this was a problem. Jurist Maximilien Bibaud opined that a code would interfere with the organic evolution of the law, voicing a critique similar to that made by Friedrich von Savigny and followers of the historical school in Europe. Jean-Joseph Beauchamp regretted that the Code had made the study of the history of the civil law seem irrelevant, transforming lawyers from scholarly intellectuals into efficient technicians. 'We practice [law] more and study it less,' he lamented in 1895. Apart from these occasional reservations, however, the *Civil Code* quickly became a unifying document for all groups within the legal profession, from law students to judges. They also became quite protective of it, seeing it as 'their' Code. Many feared that untutored legislators (who nonetheless included many notaries and advocates) would mar its harmony and cohesiveness with poorly conceived amendments. In 1879 lawyer Édouard Lefebvre de Bellefeuille called for a process that would 'shelter the Code from legislative fantasies and put it out of the reach of members who sought to improve on Roman law or the doctrines of Pothier.' It quickly proved indispensable to all members of the profession and had the advantage of being conveniently portable. Its rational arrangement and clear expression became points of pride when compared to other legal traditions. Lawyers from both major cultural groups shared these views. As Montreal lawyer Robert Davidson McGibbon stated in 1905, that '[t]he superiority of the civil law to the common law as a scientific, philosophic system, is obvious.' Teaching the Code became by far the dominant element in legal education until after the Second World War, powerfully influencing the mentalité and indeed the identity of generations of Quebec lawyers and notaries.[44]

The Code inspired a substantial legal literature, especially in the form of multi-volume commentaries written by lawyers or judges who were often part-time professors of law as well. Despite the establishment of three faculties of law in the province by 1878, none had career professors until Frederick Parker Walton secured a full-time appointment as dean of McGill in 1897. The first major commentary was written by Thomas Jean-Jacques Loranger, but he was able to complete only the first two volumes, comprising an introduction and a treatment of the law of persons in Book One of the Code. For him, one great benefit of the codification was that it would popularize knowledge of the ancien droit, which it mostly preserved. In spite of his reverence for the past, however, Loranger advocated a more 'scientific' approach to legal research and regretted that existing scholarship was mostly limited to routine matters of practice. His view of legal science included both legal history and a law and society approach: to know the law, he observed, 'it is not sufficient to know its texts, one has to understand its application.'[45]

Towards the end of the century, the pace of doctrinal production quickened: L.-A. Jetté's *Cours de droit civil* (1880–4) was based on his lectures at Laval's Montreal campus, while François Langelier's *Cours de droit civil* in six volumes (1905–11) originated in his lectures at Laval's home campus in Quebec City. Over both of these towered Pierre-Basile Mignault's magisterial *Le droit civil canadien basé sur les «Répétitions écrites sur le Code Civil» de Frédéric Mourlon, avec revue de la jurisprudence de nos tribunaux* in nine volumes (1895–1916). These works, especially those of Jetté and Mignault, featured exposition more than analysis and, like Loranger, were concerned to demonstrate the continuity between the ancien droit and modern Quebec law as a means of legitimating their own positions. Mignault's work was explicitly based on the *Répétitions* of Frédéric Mourlon, a French doctrinal work from the 1840s, but in his later volumes he grew confident enough to jettison his model and compose his own work rather than annotate another's.[46] In some areas he attempted to come to grips with the challenges of modern society unknown in Mourlon's day, especially in the field of industrial accidents, as will be seen in the next chapter. Mignault's work was especially prized by lawyers and judges because it included extensive references and discussion of contemporary Quebec case law interpreting the Code. Langelier, a liberal whose views contrasted sharply with those of his ultramontane fellow jurists, was more prepared to advance bold interpretations of the Code, both as a legal writer and as a judge (1898–1911). Much less likely to refer to the older French writers or modern Quebec case law, he observed that 'not one in twenty students read the authors or cases cited to them.' In his insistence on scrutinizing closely the text of the Code, his views echoed those of the advocates of legal science in the common law world.[47]

Three extraordinary compilations, one centred on the Code and two on Quebec case law, also deserve mention. The *Bibliothèque du Code civil* was a 21-volume work by Charles-Chamilly de Lorimier and Charles-Albert Vilbon published between 1871 and 1890.[48] A work of reference rather than a commentary, it included the original text of the Code in

Pierre-Basile Mignault (1854–1945) authored a nine-volume treatise on Quebec civil law (1895–1916) that remains a key reference even today. During his time on the Supreme Court of Canada (1918–1929), he insisted strongly on the specificity and autonomy of Quebec's civil law, speaking out against a tendency to assimilate it to the common law.

Credit: Courtesy of Bibliothèque et archives nationales du Québec.

both English and French, the comments of the codification commissioners on each article, the full text of relevant passages from all works cited in the commissioners' final report as well as 'other authorities,' the full text of any judicial decisions interpreting a given provision, and a table of concordance comparing the *Civil Code of Lower Canada* with the French and Louisiana civil codes. In stressing the continuity between the ancien droit and the Code, jurists such as de Lorimier could ignore or gloss over the troublesome legacies of the French Revolution. He did concede, however, the 'limited utility' of the ancien droit to the resolution of various modern problems.[49]

Jean-Joseph Beauchamp undertook nothing less than a complete compilation of the principles derived from all known case law in Quebec from 1770 down to 1913, organized by subject matter – a Quebec version of the *Canadian Abridgment* avant la lettre. This Herculean task required nearly 5,500 pages spread over four volumes. It was complemented by the work of Justice Michel Mathieu, co-founder of the *Revue légale*, professor and then dean of Laval's law faculty in Montreal (1886–1915), and editor of the *Rapports judiciaires révisés de la province de Québec*, issued in 29 volumes between 1891 and 1905. Judicial decisions published in scattered sources between 1838 and 1891, prior to the standardization of Quebec law reporting in 1892, were collected in this series, making them much more readily accessible. Also included were decisions of the SCC and the JCPC dealing with Quebec civil law. Mathieu not only reproduced all these decisions but also annotated them, providing exact references to sources mentioned in the judgments and noting later statutory changes to matters discussed in past cases. Mathieu's contributions went beyond compilations, as he also produced an annotated version of the 1778 *Traité des substitutions fidéicommissaires* by the French writer Claude-François Thévenot d'Essaule de Savigny. The substitution was a device from the ancien droit for creating inter-generational settlements of property, abolished by the Revolution and hence no longer the subject of commentary in France. Mathieu displayed his deep learning by updating the law on this very complex topic as applied in Quebec. The efforts of Beauchamp and Mathieu demonstrate the extent to which the common law's reverence for case law had become part of Quebec's legal culture.[50]

If some of these authors displayed a certain ambiguity with regard to the modernizing mission of the Code, emphasizing its links to the ancien droit, they and other members of the profession were more forthright in veering away from the original universalist mission of the Code. Soon the Code was being seen as a monument to national pride, a locus of French-Canadian identity, and a bulwark of local autonomy. To some extent this was motivated by the fact that after 1875 the Quebec courts were part of a judicial hierarchy extending to Ottawa and ending in London, where civilian jurists were in a distinct minority. MP Désiré Girouard presented a bill in 1881 that would have deprived the SCC of jurisdiction in civil law matters, highlighting current anxieties in the Quebec legal professions. Mignault, speaking about the *Civil Code of Lower Canada* at a conference celebrating the centenary of the *Code Napoléon*, said not one word about the non-French sources of the Code, labelling it, with no little exaggeration, 'l'image du Code français.' He concluded his remarks by stating that his tributes were inspired by 'the beautiful motto of the province of Quebec, formerly New France: 'Je me souviens' – a phrase with a special resonance for French-Canadians. These currents of nationalist feeling did not seem to unduly alarm English-speaking members of the legal professions, who had come to share a certain pride in the civilian tradition fostered at McGill's Faculty of Law and noted earlier in the remarks of R.D. McGibbon. During and after the Great War, however, as political disagreements between English and French Canadians widened into a chasm, clerico-nationalist views would harden and focus more insistently on the *Civil Code* as a vehicle enshrining specifically French-Canadian values.[51]

Despite these ideological currents, when it came to the implementation of the *Civil Code* in the courts and at the level of day-to-day law, its mixed heritage was still very much apparent. Recourse to French authors remained more common among the judiciary than among the lawyers who wrote about developments in Quebec law, with no perceptible difference between judges of French or British origin in reliance on such authors. And judges did not rely only on the ancien droit, but also referred often to more modern French authors. Lawyers writing on Quebec law were more inclined to deal directly with the modern case law, though they did not ignore the ancien droit.[52] One may say that the Code tamed and managed the ancien droit without completely replacing it: indeed, article 2613 stated that all prior law not inconsistent with the Code continued in force.

Pre-1866 law had also included a certain quota of English law: testamentary freedom, the English form of wills, and certain aspects of commercial law among others – innovations that were continued in the *Civil Code*. How were they to be interpreted, once they were ensconced in a civil code? And more generally, what universe of legally relevant persuasive if not binding sources was thought to be available in the wake of codification? On the first question, Dean Walton was the first to offer clear guidance. He declared that articles of English origin should be interpreted according to English legal norms and authorities, while those of French origin should be interpreted according to those norms and authorities.[83] In this he probably restated an existing practice, but the use of English (including Anglo-Canadian and American) sources was not limited to the interpretation of articles of English origin, as will be seen in chapter 5. In part this practice was due to the role of the SCC and the JCPC in the judicial hierarchy, but judges and lawyers in Quebec from both cultural groups not infrequently invoked sources from common law jurisdictions.[54] In this they participated in a broader 'polyjurality' that characterized North American legal thought in the first two-thirds of the nineteenth century, when national/state/provincial borders were seen as more porous and the nature of law itself more fluid.

The rise of liberal legal positivism began to undermine this legal pantheism to some extent, and Quebec experienced this trend along with the rest of North America. With regard to the openness of Quebec jurists to legal ideas and sources from other jurisdictions, while there probably was some decline during this period, any shift to 'monojurality' is likely overstated.[55] Jean-Joseph Beauchamp opined in 1913 that 'our national law is in the process of formation.… One day we will have a homogenous corpus of national law probably composed of French, English and American law as well as our customs … [and] enlightened by our hallowed French ordonnances, upon which all the nations of Europe and America have drawn.'[56] Quebec litigants and their lawyers also had recourse to the JCPC far more frequently than their counterparts elsewhere in Canada, suggesting little hesitation in resorting to this 'foreign' body. Quebec appeals ranged from a high of 82 per cent of all Privy Council appeals from the provinces in the 1870s to 42 per cent in the 1900–10 decade, after which their frequency was more in line with Quebec's share of the Canadian population.

The *Civil Code of Lower Canada*: Structure and Scope, Reform and Amendment

The *Civil Code* was not intended to be a complete statement of all the private law, but it did cover the fundamentals in each area, presented in a logical and coherent manner. It was divided into four books, framed by some introductory and closing provisions, as set out table 4.3. Each of these books will be described briefly, and more will be said about the law within them in chapter 5. More attention will be devoted here to Book One because it dealt with a topic – the law of persons – considered fundamental in the civil law but not organized as a discrete area of law in common law theory. Book One dealt mostly with the civil status of natural persons but also contained a title on corporations not found in the *Code Napoléon*.[57] It began with the three fundamental divisions of personal status: British subjecthood, alienage, and civil death. The first possessed the full panoply of civil rights; the last, comprising those condemned to death and members of some religious communities, almost none; and aliens lay somewhere in between, possessing most

Table 4.3. The structure of the *Civil Code*

Title	Articles
Preliminary Title	17
Book 1: Persons	356
Book 2: Of Property, Ownership, and Its Different Modifications	209
Book 3: Of the Acquisition and Exercise of Rights of Property	1695
Book 4: Commercial Law	335
Final Provisions	3
Total	2615

civil rights, such as the right to own immoveables, but not all political rights. They could sit on juries, for example, but only in cases where a foreigner was a party and a jury de medietate was required (article 26).* Book One proceeded to direct how registers of civil status were to be kept, outlined the concept of domicile, and set out the rights of absentees (persons who had disappeared and not been heard from for five years) and their heirs. It then moved on to the law governing the status of persons at different points in the life cycle: marriage, filiation, legitimate versus illegitimate children, paternal authority, minority, and majority. It also provided regimes of protection via either tutors or curators for the vulnerable: minors, and those interdicted because suffering from 'an habitual state of imbecility, insanity or madness' or whose prodigality gave 'reason to fear that they will dissipate the whole of their property' (articles 325, 326).[58]

The 103 articles on marriage were at the heart of Book One, taking up almost one-third of it. They dealt with impediments to marriage, formalities, oppositions to marriage, annulment, the obligations of spouses, and separation from bed and board. The Code declared marriage indissoluble except by death, but the possibility of parliamentary divorce after Confederation soon provided another potential cause of dissolution, as will be explored in chapter 15. The *BNA Act* also gave marriage (other than the solemnization of marriage) to the federal government, thus permitting the eventual overriding of some of the Code's provisions relating to marriage prohibitions based on blood and affinity. The Code's prohibitions remained in place through section 129 of the

---

* The jury *de medietate* allowed for an accused from one linguistic group, a francophone for example, to be tried by a jury (in civil or criminal matters) comprising half francophones and half anglophones. See *Volume 1*, 222, 301.

BNA Act until 1882 when, in a bill promoted by Quebec MP Désiré Girouard, Parliament permitted marriage with a deceased wife's sister.[59]

Book 2 defined ownership and real rights less than ownership, while Book Three, comprising nearly two-thirds of the Code, covered the modes of acquiring property rights (finding, gift, succession, will, and sale), losing them (mainly through prescription), and creating security interests in them through hypothecs and pledges. It also dealt with the entire law of obligations, including nominate contracts and marriage covenants. Book Four on commercial law was something of an anomaly as it was, in the European tradition, considered a topic distinct from the civil law properly so called. In France there was a separate *Code de commerce* in addition to the *Code civil*, but the Quebec codifiers had been directed to include commercial law within the *Civil Code*. Most of the topics in Book Four, such as bills of exchange, merchant shipping, and the like, in any case fell within federal jurisdiction and hence were soon superseded by federal laws such as the *Bills of Exchange Act, 1890*.

It is often stated that the Code was long considered untouchable, in order for it to remain as a monument to fundamental French-Canadian values, but this statement requires considerable qualification. The legislature at first seemed interested in elevating the status of the Code. In 1868 it amended the *Interpretation Act* to state that 'no act or provision of the legislature in any way affects any article of the [*Civil Code* or the *Code of Civil Procedure*], unless such article is expressly designated for that purpose.' This provision, however, was effectively a dead letter. Legislation amending codal provisions, but without the above caveat, was sometimes passed but not incorporated within the Code itself for several years. This was the case with the trust, which was adopted in 1879 but not incorporated in the Code until 1888. And some legislation that should arguably have been incorporated never was. In the first half-century after 1866, however, amendments to the Code were relatively frequent. With the possible exception of the addition of the trust, they often amounted to tinkering rather than significant reform, but the likelihood of amendment depended very much on the area of law in question. Family law was indeed untouchable, with no substantive changes prior to 1914 and only relatively minor changes thereafter until the Quiet Revolution. And this was despite the fact that France offered a model for some improvements in the legal status of married women, for example, or the possibility of legal adoption – changes that were not enacted in Quebec until decades later. Patriarchal authority and ultramontanist views of the family would remain unshakeable until well into the twentieth century.[60]

The law of persons also remained mostly unchanged, though one would expect this area of the law to remain stable for long periods. In 1870 habitual drunkenness was added to the list of causes for which one could be interdicted, and in 1896 the use of certain drugs was added. In 1906 the Liberal government of Sir Lomer Gouin abolished civil death for those condemned to death and those in religious orders, a step taken in France decades before, in 1854. Civil death for members of religious orders was abolished outright, while for those condemned to death or to perpetual personal punishment (effectively restricted to life imprisonment) it was replaced by civil degradation. This status deprived those subject to it of all political and most civil rights and assimilated their legal position to those interdicted for insanity. The main difference with civil death was that forfeiture to the Crown of the property of those affected was no longer mandated. Confusingly, however, the new status of civil degradation was not added to the Code itself and remained marooned in the amending act of 1906.[61]

In other areas, by contrast, especially economic and commercial relations, the Code could be amended without undue controversy. Imprisonment for debt went in 1897, though these provisions were merely transferred to the new *Code of Civil Procedure* adopted in that year, and the regime of construction privileges was overhauled in stages with a view to better protecting suppliers and workers.[62] The regime of privileges over moveable property was also adjusted a number of times, while provisions for bulk sales were added directly to the Code in 1910.[63] Such reforms were not seen as threatening to the French-Canadian identity and were palatable because commercial law, while included in the Code, was not considered to be part of the core of civil law. Indeed, it was defined out of the civil law by the major commentators: Jetté, Langelier, and Mignault all excluded it from their voluminous works, and no independent treatment would be attempted until 1936.[64]

Although the *Civil Code* was in form a statute, it was conceived as a restatement of the common law, or droit commun, of Lower Canada. It did not occupy the same unchallenged place in Quebec's legal firmament as the *Code Napoléon* did in France, where the latter purported to abolish all pre-existing law and also aimed to reduce the role of judges in the legal order. The *Civil Code* co-existed with the ancien droit where it did not replace it, with a growing mass of provincial statutes, some of them dealing with topics covered in the Code, with federal statutes that in some cases rendered ineffective the Code's provisions, and with a proliferating corpus of case law. Moreover, after its early attempt to give the Code a quasi-constitutional status above that of other legislation, the Quebec state limited itself to publishing a sole official version of the Code in 1866 and leaving all later editions to private enterprise – with the inevitable accompaniment of textual errors, omissions, and inconsistencies. The Code was not part of the *Revised Statutes of Quebec 1888* or subsequent revisions.[65] The Quebec state did subsidize the *Bibliothèque du Code civil* project to the tune of $6,000, but this work clearly targeted a professional audience rather than the broader public.

Codification did, however, achieve two important goals. It went a long way to overcoming the problem of extreme diversity of sources for Quebec law by restating the fundamentals of the applicable private law in a single document, expressed for the most part in clear and non-technical language. And through its bilingual presentation it helped to bridge the two main cultural groups, English and French, although it ignored the possible role of Indigenous law in the province's legal order. Finally, although not a goal of codification itself, the existence of the *Civil Code of Lower Canada* provided the nucleus of a shared legal culture and identity across Quebec's legal professions.

5

Quebec Civil Law: A Mixed Legal System in Confederation

The 1866 *Civil Code of Lower Canada* enshrined a combination of economic liberalism and patriarchal family relations, but it was up to judges, advocates, and notaries to give life to its provisions, and to legislators to reform them if necessary. In doing so they would be influenced by the general economic, cultural, and socio-political climate prevailing in Quebec in the post-Confederation years, which will be briefly sketched here. The biggest change in the half-century after the adoption of the Code related to the economy. In 1866 agriculture was the principal way of life, whereas by the 1880s the Industrial Revolution had begun to transform the province, allowing the exploitation of its resources and the creation of wealth on a massive scale. By the early 1900s the Canadian Pacific Railway's Angus Works at Montreal was the largest railway workshop in the world, with a labour force that fluctuated between 4,000 and 8,000 workers, while the electricity generation works at Shawinigan (1898) was the second-largest in the world, after Niagara Falls. Montreal was the largest city in Canada and its financial capital, with 70 per cent of all stock trades handled on its stock exchange until Toronto's edged ahead in the 1920s.

While anglophones dominated the economy, a sizeable bourgeoisie of French-Canadian origin also emerged in this period, with Sir Rodolphe Forget, chair of the Montreal Stock Exchange from 1907 to 1909, generally considered the first French-Canadian millionaire.[1] Financial institutions such as the Banque d'Hochelaga, Crédit-Foncier

Franco-Canadien, and the Banque canadienne nationale had primarily francophone management and clientele, while caisses populaires (credit unions) emerged after 1901 to cater to working-class francophones and other groups. The wealth generated by all this economic activity would not be shared equally: it was mainly white men who directed the economy, while the legal capabilities of married women were highly circumscribed, workers' rights remained tenuous, and Indigenous peoples found themselves pushed to the sidelines in the interests of 'development.' The reserve at Kahnawà:ke was cut up by all manner of transportation infrastructure, while on Quebec's north shore, railway building, the creation of the Parc des Laurentides, and the reservation of huge tracts of land for private clubs pushed the Hurons of Lorette out of their traditional hunting grounds and obliged them to turn to outmigration, handicraft production, and urban labour.[2]

Culturally, the most prominent force in Quebec society was the Catholic Church, led by an increasingly ultramontane episcopate. Papal encyclicals that opposed liberalism, socialism, and modernity were eagerly embraced by Quebec's ecclesiastical hierarchy, and infused the curriculum of the collèges classiques that educated most of Quebec's legal professionals. Leo XIII's 1879 encyclical *Aeterni patris* called for a return to the philosophy of St. Thomas Aquinas as the basis of all intellectual inquiry, while his *Rerum novarum* in 1891 attempted to respond to the world created by the Industrial Revolution. It criticized both socialism and unbridled capitalism, called for just wages for the working classes, and supported the creation of trade unions to advance their interests within a structured, hierarchical society. Thomist philosophy, with its emphasis on immutable divine law and natural law as superior to positive law created by human authority, provided a ready tool for religious authorities to intervene in legislative and socio-political debates, though overt clerical interventions in elections would eventually be challenged in court and found sufficiently problematic in some cases for the election to be voided.[3]

In contrast to many societies where industrial transformation led to less fervent religiosity, Quebec saw the opposite trend. The dominance of the Catholic Church had begun in the wake of the rebellions, when a chastened bourgeoisie needed to form an alliance with the clergy to exercise political power. One part of the price was ceding control over education to the clergy, in contrast to the situation emerging everywhere else in North America. In 1853 11 per cent of the teachers in Catholic schools were clerics; by 1887 it was nearly half. The numbers of men and women in religious orders increased dramatically after 1840, such that virtually all parishes were well staffed in the post-Confederation years.[4] The church thus possessed adequate personnel to manage the faithful and try to ensure that its precepts were enforced. One measure of its success was the increasing proportion of parishioners in the diocese of Montreal who performed their Easter duty over the course of the nineteenth century: 30 per cent neglected to do so in 1839, falling to 10 per cent by Confederation and by 1910 only 1 per cent. Religion was a powerful force for social cohesion and conformity, with the clergy often working in concert with state legal personnel such as the clerk of the peace to ensure order in communities in a variety of ways outside the formal legal order.[5]

This is not to say that Quebec society was ideologically homogeneous. A form of liberalism challenging the dominance of the Catholic Church in the province, urging freer inquiry and receptive to modern views on a variety of issues, had begun to emerge prior to Confederation and grew in influence afterwards. The Institut Canadien in Montreal, founded in 1844 and the nerve centre of these ideas, found itself attacked by church authorities with such vehemence that it was eventually forced to close. Emblematic of this struggle was the Guibord affair. When one of the Institut's members, Joseph Guibord, was denied burial in the consecrated portion of the Notre-Dame-des-Neiges cemetery after his death in 1869, the conflict entered the legal sphere. The decision was challenged by Guibord's widow with the support of the Institut, culminating in a JCPC decision that overturned it. However, the first time Guibord's body was sought to be interred, in November 1875, a mob upset with the decision prevented it. The burial succeeded on the second attempt only with the assistance of hundreds of soldiers. In spite of the Institut's closure, its ideas lived on and were eventually espoused in a more moderate form by the Liberal Party of Wilfrid Laurier.[6]

While the church was seen as a mainstay of the Quebec nation, francophone nationalism was not as prevalent in the immediate post-Confederation years as it would later become. The provincial Conservatives had supported Confederation and remained in power with only brief interruptions from then until 1897, when the Liberals began a long reign lasting until 1944 with one short interruption. The hanging of Louis Riel in 1885 and Canadian participation in the Boer War (1899–1902) caused many francophones in Quebec to question their position in Canada and Canada's position in the British Empire, leading to a more assertive nationalism that would be further stoked by the First World War. Such nationalism led to a focus on the *Civil Code* as a monument to the Quebec nation in the interwar years, a trope that was clearly present, but not nearly as prominent, in the period under review. Three of the principal topics dealt with in the *Civil Code* will be the main focus of this chapter: family law, obligations, and property.[7]

Family Law

While ideas about the permanence of marriage and its role as the foundation of society were not substantially different between the inhabitants of Quebec and those of the other provinces, the *Civil Code* laid out the obligations of husbands and wives in stark language that had no precise counterpart in the common law.

- Article 173. Husbands and wives mutually owe each other fidelity, succor and assistance.
- Article 174. A husband owes protection to his wife; a wife obedience to her husband.
- Article 175. A wife is obliged to live with her husband and to follow him wherever he thinks fit to reside. The husband is obliged to receive her and to supply her with all the necessaries of life, according to his means and condition.

These were not mere precatory words: they represented legally enforceable obligations. When Dame Webster lost her suit seeking separation from bed and board from her husband Mr. Fisher and was given notice by him that she was to return home within 48 hours, Justice Pagnuelo upheld his right to do so. She was to return home within two weeks or lose all the advantages under her marriage contract. When a pregnant Dame Poulin left her tubercular husband to reside with her parents out of fear for her health, Mr. Lafontaine obtained an order obliging them to turn her out within two weeks in the expectation that she would have to return to him. However, husbands too had to live up to their obligations: a wife was justified in refusing to cohabit with her husband if he could provide no 'decent' place for them to live, even though the Code seemed to grant him plenary authority to decide this.[8]

The idea that marriage was a form of association that needed a singular 'head,' and that the husband was fitted by 'nature' to perform that role, was strongly held by the church and permeated popular and legal culture.[9] The obverse of the husband's empowerment was the legal disabling of the wife in property transactions, relations with third parties, and authority over the children of the marriage. In spite of these disabilities, at Confederation married women in Quebec were in a better economic position in some respects than their sisters in the common law provinces. Under the civil law, separation of property permitted women who owned property at the time of marriage to secure it from the claims of the husband and his creditors, even if the husband's consent was still needed for important transactions regarding that property. Women married in community of property were entitled to half of the community's assets upon surviving the husband, while a husband's testamentary freedom reigned virtually unconstrained outside Quebec. Moreover, customary dower under the civil law could be more generous than common law dower.

After Confederation, however, as will be seen in chapter 15, a series of legislative reforms in the common law provinces mandating complete separation of property for married women and affirming their legal autonomy (to make contracts and alienate property without marital consent, for example) began to make the position of Quebec wives look less enviable. Quebec wives who worked outside the home were not able to control their own salaries until 1931, and all wives lacked the capacity to contract or even to open a bank account without their husband's consent until 1964. Community of property still provided significant protections for widows, but at a cost: the husband was the sole head of the community during the marriage and he alone could enter into transactions regarding its property. Customary dower was not abolished but, in keeping with the new liberal ethos of property, could either be excluded entirely by marriage contract, or if not, was effective against third parties only if the right was registered against the immovables in which it was being sought. Conventional (contractual) dower could also be provided for in a marriage contract in place of customary dower but was again subject to registration. Ultimately, a right formerly provided by law was left to contractual negotiation, which usually meant it was left to the discretion of the husband-to-be.[10]

In Quebec a married woman's legal incapacity prevented her, with very few exceptions, from contracting or commencing a legal action without her husband's permission, though article 184 of the Code permitted her to make a will without her husband's consent. With her husband's authorization, a married woman could become a public trader (marchande publique). In such cases article 179 said she could 'obligate herself for all that relates to her commerce,' as well as bind her husband if community of property existed between them. Otherwise, her economic position and the extent of her legal capacity depended entirely on her matrimonial regime. Spouses could adopt separation of property by contract, or community of property, which, as the default regime, did not require a contract; the latter could also be adopted and to some extent customized by contract. While community of property had some advantages for wives, especially if they survived their husbands, it also severely limited their autonomy. Sarah McFarran found this out to her cost when she sued for injuries allegedly caused by the negligence of a railway company, joining her husband to authorize the suit. She succeeded at trial before a jury, but lost at all three levels of appeal. All held that any debt arising from the injury belonged to the community and that only the husband could take the action as its administrator. He could not authorize her suit because she was, in effect, suing for a debt that 'belonged' to someone else in the eyes of the law.[11]

Much of the case law interpreting codal provisions dealt with spouses married in separation of property, which had become the commonly used regime for both the British and French-Canadian bourgeoisie over the course of the nineteenth century. Separate property represented some security for a wife who had her own assets, as they would be protected from the husband's creditors, but it provided only a very weak form of legal autonomy, as most dealings with that property still needed the husband's consent. This regime also had its pitfalls. While articles 1384 to 1425 of the *Civil Code* provided for extensive freedom in the content of marriage contracts, even allowing certain types of clauses not permitted in other types of contract (such as gifts of future property), once entered into, marriage contracts could not be altered.[12] Moreover, no transfers of property between spouses, aside from 'customary presents,' were allowed after marriage in any matrimonial regime, in an effort to prevent both frauds on creditors and the possible exercise of undue pressure by the husband on his wife to transfer assets to him. In other words, while the rights of wives were limited by the husband's position as head of the family, the rights of both spouses were limited in the interests of supporting the institution of marriage itself, and of protecting third parties. Husbands sometimes sought to use their wives to hide assets from creditors, but when challenged in court the ban on interspousal transfers usually sufficed to declare the transaction invalid.[13]

The Code declared that both spouses had a responsibility to raise and maintain any children (article 165), but this could be and commonly was varied by marriage contract. In most contracts the husband alone took on these responsibilities, and here the ban on altering marriage contracts could work to a wife's advantage. If a husband had agreed to maintain the children of the marriage, even where a wife obtained custody after a judicial separation, he still had to pay full support, as the parties could not vary this by private arrangement.[14] Husbands also typically made promises to transfer property to their wives in marriage contracts. The details could vary considerably, and such promises could prove illusory when their wording was scrutinized in court. Thus, in a 1906 case, where a husband had promised his wife upon their marriage in 1894 all the furniture he currently owned plus all he would own at his death, should she survive him, upon his bankruptcy the creditors were entitled to seize all the furniture. Even the furniture he owned at the date of marriage was to be transferred to his wife only as a *gain de survie* should she survive him, not as a present gift *inter vivos*.[15] Fine distinctions could arise here, however. When Sarah Fox in 1907 claimed the sum of $5,000 that her marriage contract promised she could demand 'at any time,' though it would return to her husband if she did not survive him, she succeeded against his creditors. This was not a *gain de survie*, as it was specified that it would 'return' to him if he survived her; therefore, the property must have passed to her to begin with.[16] This narrow victory in the appellate court (by a majority of three to two) showed that reliance by wives on such promises in marriage contracts was always risky.[17]

The ban on spouses advantaging each other after marriage, however laudable its goals, could have unjust consequences. In 1908 Clara Paquette, an impecunious widow, married a well-off Montreal merchant, Godefroy Courville, who had an adult daughter, Marie Anne, from his first marriage. In spite of his wealth, Courville provided in their marriage contract that Clara would receive only $1,500 on his death, naming Marie Anne as his universal legatee. When he fell ill, Clara provided extraordinary nursing services – of the most unpleasant kind – to her husband. A grateful Courville had a cheque for $500 made out to Clara, which she cashed shortly before his death in 1911. An ungrateful Marie Anne succeeded in reclaiming the sum for Courville's estate, that is, for herself. As an interspousal transfer, the cheque could be justified neither as having spared Courville the expense of hiring a nurse, nor as payment to his wife for her services. Wives were expected to perform such actions gratuitously, yet another example of the wifely abnegation demanded by the Code. Courville should have made a codicil to his will if he wanted to give her an extra $500.[18]

Joseph De Sola and Amanda Esther Davis. In Quebec, judicial separation was seen as an acceptable alternative to divorce, especially by Catholics. For others it could be a prelude to divorce, as with the Jewish couple from Montreal shown in this 1880 photo. Amanda Esther Davis, daughter of wealthy cigar manufacturer Samuel Davis, married Joseph de Sola, son of the city's most prominent rabbi, in 1881. She secured a judicial separation based on Joseph's physical violence and adultery in 1883, and a parliamentary divorce in 1885.

Credit: Notman Collection, courtesy of McCord Museum, Montreal.

The law of succession also treated married women unfavourably in various ways, unless they were married in community of property. For those married in separation of property, a husband benefitted from freedom of testation over all his property aside from that promised to his wife in a marriage contract. Where the parties were married in community of property, the same freedom applied to all assets that did not fall within the community. Should a husband die intestate, however, all property that he could have willed would be transmitted to his blood relatives, children first, and in their absence parents, siblings, or more remote relatives, as far as the twelfth degree of consanguinity. Only in the absence of any such relatives would the widow inherit (article 636).[19] Moreover, such a succession was labelled 'irregular' by the Code: the widow was not, like 'regular' heirs, seized by law alone, but was required to be put judicially in possession of the inherited property (article 638). While favouring the lineage over the spouse was common in western society at the time, in few places did the widow occupy such a lowly position in the line of succession.[20] And consistent with the other legal disabilities under which she laboured, the married woman could not accept a succession (from a parent, for example) without the authorization of her husband or a court (article 643).

The *Civil Code* declared marriage to be dissoluble only through death (article 185), though this provision was subject to federal authority over divorce after 1867. The only real choice available to unhappy spouses during this period was judicial separation (séparation de corps, separation from bed and board). Divorce, theoretically available to Quebec residents but only through a private act of Parliament, was virtually unknown: on average, no more than one per year was granted to Quebec couples prior to 1915.[21] Annulments were even more rare and raised hugely controversial issues implicating the church–state relationship. While the Code itself permitted annulments under certain circumstances, the grounds for obtaining them were wider under canon law. The majority opinion among doctrinal writers and judges was that the ordinary courts had to recognize all ecclesiastical annulments fully, meaning that the parties were free to marry again. However, in a celebrated 1901 case where two Catholics had been married in Quebec by a Protestant minister, contrary to canon law but validly under the *Civil Code*, the Superior Court refused to recognize an ecclesiastical annulment of the marriage, one confirmed in Rome. In the eyes of state law, the parties were still married. This view was later confirmed by the SCC in 1912 in a reference regarding proposed amendments to the federal *Marriage Act*, and finally by the JCPC in *Despatie v Tremblay* in 1921. Both cases profoundly shocked Catholic sensibilities.[22]

Separation agreements were entered into by spouses who chose to live apart but were considered against public order and unenforceable if one party failed to observe the terms. Justice Carroll observed that '[i]t often happens among well-educated people that they try to hide difficulties arising in the family that might compromise its honour. Thus, they enter into arrangements that have no legal force, but to which the parties submit.'[23] In Montreal at least, judicial separation was an increasingly popular remedy after 1900, with the number of petitions doubling between 1900 and 1905 (from 34 to 71), and doubling again from 1910 to 1915 (71 to 141). Women made up over 80 per cent of petitioners, and the success rate for those petitions that did not end by abandonment or settlement (about 14 per cent) was high – 92 per cent. The procedure offered some advantages: it was much cheaper than divorce; a wife could request support on an interlocutory basis during the course of the proceedings, as well as the cost of the court fees; and the petition could be made *in forma pauperis*, which was how one-third of women petitioners began their claim.[24]

Most importantly, unlike divorce, which could be granted by Parliament only on proof of adultery, judicial separation was available for a wide range of causes. Article 189 declared that either spouse could demand separation from bed and board for 'outrage, ill-usage or grievous insult committed by one toward the other.' Article 190 left the sufficiency of such allegations to the discretion of the court, which was expressly directed to 'take into consideration the rank, condition and other circumstances of the parties.' Judges and authors were quick to take up this invitation. The most respected doctrinal writer of the period, Pierre-Basile Mignault, observed that an act justifying a judicial separation for 'a well brought-up person' might be only an act of 'rudeness' or a 'slap' for someone further down the social scale and hence not sufficient to maintain the action. A close consideration of the moral behaviour of the parties, especially the wife, and their class position was de rigueur in actions for judicial separation.[25]

This could work in favour of blameless wives, but hovering over such judgments was a concern by the judiciary to uphold the position of the husband as head of the family, even to the point of permitting the 'correction' of his wife by physical violence. Such discipline was thought to be justified by article 174, which provided that 'a wife [owed] obedience to her husband.' Thus, in an 1890 case that would be constantly cited thereafter, a unanimous five-judge bench of the Court of Revision stated that a wife could not obtain a judicial separation on the ground of her husband's physical maltreatment if she had provoked this reaction 'by the frivolity of her conduct and her disobedience to the legitimate orders of her husband.'[26] Needless to say, an adulterous wife received little mercy: she would lose all 'advantages' under her marriage contract automatically, and could forfeit any gifts therein at the judge's discretion (articles 208 and 211). If married in community of property, she was sometimes deprived of her share in the community even though there was no clear authority in the Code for doing so. It does not appear that adulterous husbands ran this risk. However, even an adulterous wife could claim support from her husband unless she began living with another man.[27]

If successful in her action for judicial separation, as the vast majority of women were, a wife was almost always granted custody of any minor children, in stark contrast to the common law rules on custody, which favoured the husband. She could also claim immediately any gifts and advantages granted by the marriage contract unless they were conditional on her surviving her husband. Separation from bed and board also led to a dissolution of the community of property if the spouses were married under that regime, thus providing the wife with some assets to begin her new independent life. She also recovered some, though by no means total, legal autonomy. No matter what her former regime, she could now administer all property in her own name and take legal action alone in that regard; but still she could not alienate an immovable without judicial consent. She would normally receive an alimentary pension for any minor children and herself as well, although this would end with her husband's death and did not bind his estate except for any arrears.[28]

Judicial decisions added a gloss on this area of the law that was favourable to the wife. If she could prove sufficient cause for separation from bed and board, such as domestic violence, she could set up a separate household and request an alimentary pension without pursuing an action for separation from bed and board. In spite of the increasing recourse to this action, it was still considered to bring shame and dishonour on the family. Thus Anastasie Lafleur, who fled her violent husband, sought only an alimentary pension and not separation from bed and board 'to avoid a scandal.'[29] Scandal was a double-edged sword, however. It was contrary to religious and social norms that one spouse joined in matrimony should request the ability to live apart from the other. The law could deal with this situation only by finding one party 'guilty' of not having lived up to his or her marital obligations. In many cases, however, mutual incompatibility was the real problem – but this was not a permissible cause for separation from bed and board. Nonetheless, where such incompatibility led to serious, escalating and public strife between spouses, scandal of a different kind reared its head. Such couples were not a good advertisement for marriage in general and threatened the institution itself. In such cases courts threw up their hands: 'The public interest and morality require imperatively that the parties not be required to resume a conjugal life that presents serious dangers for each of them and for the good order of society.'[30]

The 1866 Code set out a double standard on allegations of adultery in actions for judicial separation. Adultery alone on the part of the wife sufficed for the husband's success, whereas a wife had to prove that the husband kept his 'concubine' in the matrimonial home (article 188). However, an important step was taken in 1885 when the Superior Court declared, relying on French authority, that if the adultery was 'public,' such behaviour constituted a 'grievous insult' within the meaning of article 189. Thus, where the plaintiff could prove her husband consorted publicly with prostitutes, she was granted separation from bed and board even though no adultery took place in the home.[31] Adultery was alleged by wives in only a quarter of petitions, with physical violence being the main impetus to seeking a judicial separation. Nonetheless, the less rigorous interpretation of article 188, along with a certain heightening of expectations regarding male conduct, may have induced women to seek separation from bed and board more frequently in the early twentieth century.

Adultery might enter the law of domestic relations in another way, via an action in damages for alienation of affection. While open to wives, the action typically saw a husband suing the man who had seduced his wife. Article 1053, dealing with fault-based liability, was the basis for such actions. Actual adultery was not required, provided the third party had induced the one spouse to be morally unfaithful to the other, such as by leaving the matrimonial home.[32] In an 1874 case, Justice Routhier described the basis of the action (at least in cases involving actual adultery) as essentially an interference with the husband's property: 'For the married woman does not belong to herself, she belongs to her husband ... whose property the third party grievously harms.'[33] Such casual association of wives with property in the legal imagination was yet another example of the indignities to which married women were subject.

As head of the family, the husband also possessed paternal authority over the children of the marriage. A mother could exercise such authority only upon the death, incapacity, or absence of her husband, or as the result of a judicial separation. As noted in *Volume 1*, the codifiers had departed from French law on this topic by not reproducing the despotic powers given to French fathers by the *Code Napoléon*. The holder of paternal authority in Quebec had only a moderate right of correction over minor children, and both jurisprudence and juristic opinion agreed that the powers vested in the holder of paternal authority were provided only in order to further the best interests of the child – a concept that entered the common law relating to custody only in the late nineteenth century. Summarizing the law as long understood, Mignault states that '[p]aternal authority is no more than a tool given to mothers and fathers to help them successfully carry out the physical and moral education of their children.'[34] Moreover, such powers related only to the person of the child and not its property, which had to be administered by a tutor duly appointed, though a parent could be appointed tutor.

Given that paternal authority was already limited by the best interests of the child, an inherently fluid concept, it is difficult to discern patterns in the case law over time. The courts were adamant that paternal authority could not be surrendered by a mere private contract, Justice Monk labelling the very idea 'monstrous.' Any such contract entered into by a parent with a third party could be ignored and the child reclaimed from the person to whom it had been entrusted.[35] Where child custody was debated between spouses in the context of judicial separation proceedings, article 214 of the Code stated a default rule that custody would go to the party granted the separation, but authorized the court to grant custody to the other party or even to a third party, usually a relative or religious institution, if that would be for the 'greater advantage' of the child. Disputes over custody were usually framed, as in common law jurisdictions, as habeas corpus applications brought against the person detaining the child.

The cases dealing with interspousal custody conflicts reveal a slight tendency to favour the mother, possibly influenced by the rise of maternal feminism in the later nineteenth century, but these cases may also be interpreted as demonstrating a nascent awareness of the rights of the child.[36] In this respect, the common law and civil law approaches to custody began to converge, as we will see in chapter 15. The highwater mark along these lines was probably the 1900 decision of Justice Mathieu in *Daoust c Schiller*.[37] Victoria Schiller had left her husband, alleging maltreatment, and returned to live with her father, leaving her seven-year-old son with his father. No judicial separation was sought by either spouse. Two weeks after her departure, Dame Schiller went to her son's school and brought him home with her. The father by writ of habeas corpus claimed that she had deprived the child of his liberty and wanted him returned to the paternal home. Justice Mathieu interviewed the child, whom he found to be 'intelligent,' and who expressed a wish to remain with his mother. Under such circumstances, he found that the child could not be said to have been deprived of his liberty, hence the father's claim was dismissed. 'A child of seven years of age,' he observed, 'needs more often, perhaps, the care of his mother than that of his father.'[38] While a wife owed obedience to her husband and was under a duty to cohabit with him, according to the judge habeas corpus was not the proper way to enforce these duties.

The Quebec courts consistently refused to set an age below which a child's wishes were not to be considered, but also did not consider themselves bound by such wishes. Where the dispute was between the parents and a third party, the parents' wishes had to prevail, even where the child was as old as eighteen. Thus, where a young woman of that age had left the Catholic faith of her family, become a Protestant, and fled to a boarding school run by Baptists, her father was allowed to secure her return via habeas corpus, against her own wishes and those of the school.[39]

While the family was seen as the bedrock of society across Canada during these years, and both English and French Canadians shared a horror of divorce, the improvements to the legal status and capacities of married women in the common law provinces made no headway in Quebec. The reforms outside Quebec began to subtly undermine the legal status of the husband as head of the family, even though no statute expressly demoted him, making the position of spouses in common law Canada less unequal, even if still far from equal. The *Civil Code* saw no movement in this regard, and no widespread call for reform of matrimonial relations was evident in Quebec. The availability of separate property with its modest nod to wifely autonomy may have played the same role in Quebec that equitable separate property had in common law jurisdictions for centuries. By providing an option for the propertied that permitted some recognition of a wife's autonomous economic existence, systemic reform for all spouses was stymied. Some very modest improvements to the position of married women were accomplished through judicial interpretation, as with the reinterpretation of adultery in article 189 and the availability of 'freestanding' alimentary pensions in cases of de facto separation following serious marital conflict, but it was children more than married women who benefitted from such reform sentiment as existed prior to the First World War.

Obligations

The civil law treats the law of obligations as a unitary field, with two subcategories – contractual and extra-contractual (delictual) liability. Where the Code's treatment of contracts departed in some respects from the French model, the provisions on delict were, with one important exception, mostly copied from the *Code Napoléon*, these articles themselves being mostly restatements of the ancien droit.

The Code of 1866 elevated autonomy of the will to be the primary principle governing contractual relations, diverging from the ancien droit where this principle was held in balance with the protection of vulnerable parties from exploitation. In this it participated in the embrace of economic liberalism common to many Western countries in the later nineteenth century. Somewhat curiously, this basic principle was left implicit in the Code, contrary to the *Code Napoléon* with its lapidary formula that 'contracts legally formed take the place of law for the parties.'[40] Nor did the *Civil Code of Lower Canada* reproduce the French clause that contracts must be executed in good faith. Very few articles in the Code regulated contracts or forbade particular stipulations. Contractual freedom was subject only to the general proviso that no clause could contravene public order and good morals, which, itself, would be interpreted narrowly by the courts. Most provisions were suppletive or facultative, setting out default rules if the parties themselves had not addressed a particular issue, or providing basic rules of contract interpretation. Article 1024 did state that 'the obligation of a contract extends not only to what is expressed in it, but also to all the consequences which, by equity, usage or law, are incident to the contract, according to its nature,' but this reference to 'equity' would remain unremarked in the jurisprudence for over a century. In an effort to encourage contractual relations, the Code provided that most contracts needed no particular formalities, nor were there any linguistic requirements prior to a 1910 law discussed below. Finally, no power was granted to courts to revise contracts where unforeseen circumstances made performance significantly more onerous for one party than expected at the time of contract formation.[41]

The most significant divergence in contractual matters between the French and Lower Canadian codes related to lesion as a cause for contract rescission. Under the ancien droit, lesion referred to a situation where there was too great a disparity of value in certain exchanges. In such cases an abuse of contractual power was presumed, allowing the disadvantaged party to demand the termination of the contract and restoration of the status quo. The *Code Napoléon* narrowed the scope of lesion somewhat but allowed it to be pleaded in at least four situations. In the best-known of these, a contract for the sale of an immoveable could be set aside by the vendor where the price paid was less than seven-twelfths of the market value (known as lésion d'outre-moitié).[42] The *Civil Code of Lower Canada*, by contrast, abolished the doctrine of lesion completely between parties of the age of majority. It permitted only contracts by minors (whether for movables or immovables) to be set aside for 'simple lesion,' the necessary disparity in prestations being left to the discretion of the judge. The commissioners reasoned that immovables changed hands in Quebec more frequently than in France, making prices less stable and the protection contained in the French Code less applicable. Where lesion was alleged by a minor, however, the courts exercised broad discretion to grant relief, looking at the minor's subjective circumstances rather than, as in France, the objective disparity in value in what had changed hands. For example, in a 1906 case a minor working for an automotive company had subscribed for 20 shares of its stock at a price of $2,000. His father sued as tutor to set aside the contract, pleading that as the son had paid for only a quarter of the stock and had no funds to pay more, he was likely to lose all his investment. The company's defence, that it was in a flourishing state and hence no lesion existed at the time of the contract, was not accepted by the court.[43] This jurisprudence is of a piece with the emergent emphasis on the rights of the child seen in the previous section.

The reinforcement of freedom of contract was also evident in various other codal provisions. Articles 1057 and 1135 removed the power formerly available to the courts to reduce penalty clauses in contracts. Article 1025 effected the transfer of title to a defined object upon the conclusion of the contract of sale, subject to a few exceptions, without any need for a change in possession. In other cases, the protections for debtors mandated by the Code in certain transactions were effectively negated by court decisions allowing creditors to structure deals in ways that sidestepped these protections. Thus, where a person bought property on instalments but defaulted after having paid most of the purchase price, court decisions allowed the seller-lender to repossess the property while retaining the sums previously paid, even though articles 1538 and 1539 were supposed to prevent this abusive practice. Quebec judges on the SCC wrote the judgments upholding these manoeuvres, though the two of them were not always in agreement.[44]

One of the few examples where the Code seemed to restrict freedom of contract was article 1676, which stated that '[n]otices by carriers, of special conditions limiting their liability … [were not effective] whenever it is proved that the damage is caused by their fault or the fault of those for whom they are responsible.' The article was admittedly ambiguous – did 'notices' include actual contractual terms? – but the Quebec courts consistently interpreted it as preventing a carrier from excluding liability for their own negligence. In an 1897 case dealing with liability for goods damaged while being shipped by sea, however, the SCC exploited the ambiguity to overturn this line of authority. Justice Taschereau, writing for a unanimous court including Justice Girouard, decided that Quebec law needed to conform to the law elsewhere in Canada and the British Empire, where such clauses were permitted.[45]

Only two inroads on contractual freedom were made by the legislature prior to the Great War. The first, in 1906, was an amendment to article 1149 of the Code, which prohibited a court from ordering a debt to be paid in instalments without the consent of the creditor. The amendment allowed a court to order payment by instalments where the debt was 'made up of interest exceeding the legal rate, [which] seems to the court to be usurious.' This very modest move towards consumer protection was followed by another, more significant over the long term, in 1910. Amendments to article 1682 of the Code in that year provided that all contracts, including tickets and notices, with public utility, railway, and navigation companies had to be written in French and English. For some years, Quebec nationalist Armand Lavergne had been trying to get such a bill passed. His first attempt in 1906, while an MP, had failed in spite of being supported by a petition that he claimed contained 1.7 million signatures, including many from anglophones. Expelled from the federal Liberal Party in 1907, he was elected to the Assemblée Nationale in Quebec the following year. Railway companies and many large businesses lobbied against the bill when he presented it in 1909, causing it to fail in the legislative council, but the next year it succeeded. There was no administrative apparatus created to ensure compliance, merely a fine of up to $20 for contraventions. Any such fine was 'without prejudice to recourse for damages,' though it is not clear what kind of damages might have been contemplated.[46] Weak as it was, this was the first step taken towards the protection of the French language in Quebec.

Turning to extra-contractual liability, the relevant law was contained in articles 1053 to 1056. Where the common law of the period featured a law of torts, with each wrongful act such as defamation, trespass, battery, nuisance, etc., considered a separate tort with its own peculiarities, the civil law featured a unitary law of delict oriented to the concept of fault. The title of this chapter was 'Of Offences and Quasi-Offences,' where the former were understood as intentional wrongs and the latter as those arising from negligence, though both were types of fault. Article 1053 laid out the basic principle: 'Every person capable of discerning right from wrong is responsible for the damage caused by his fault to another, whether by positive act, imprudence, neglect or want of skill.' Article 1054 then imposed liability on an individual for damage caused by the fault of persons 'under his control and by things which he has under his care,' setting out various examples of this responsibility, such as parent–child, schoolmaster–pupil, and master–servant. Article 1055 dealt with the liability of owners of animals for damage caused by them, and owners of buildings for harm caused by lack of repair or defects in construction. Article 1056, dealing with liability for wrongful death, was exceptional in having no counterpart in the French Code. It would arouse the most controversy in the years ahead, as its origin was 'clouded in the most complete obscurity. No mention of its source was made by the commissioners, no mention in the project of the Code, nor in the amendments submitted to the Legislature; nor in the statute of 1865 containing such amendments.'[47]

While 'fault' was clearly the lynchpin of civil liability, the other two elements – harm and causation – also gave rise to interpretive debates. Given the very general wording of these provisions, judicial interpretation would determine their application. One strand of these debates raised the question of the relative influence of English versus French authorities in this context, especially with regard to the mysterious article 1056. Another asked how well codal provisions designed for an agricultural and commercial society would bear up in the context of a new industrial era. An employer's liability for industrial accidents would be the key issue in this regard and will be the focus of what follows.

The half-century after Confederation saw the rapid industrialization of Quebec, a phenomenon encouraged by a provincial state that saw this as the route to greater social prosperity as well as the means of stemming the tide of out-migration. Some 900,000 Quebeckers left the province between 1840 and 1930, mainly for the northeastern United States, though many eventually returned.[48] Railways, steam power, and new manufacturing processes boosted Quebec's GDP enormously but, as elsewhere, also created the potential for more, and more serious, injuries than had existed in a world dependent on energy derived from water, wind, and the muscle of humans and animals. Reported industrial accidents increased tenfold in the two decades after 1888, and even then all agreed such events were seriously under-reported.[49] Thus the civil liability provisions of the new Code would be interpreted largely through case law that emerged from the activities of railways (injuries to passengers, employees, and persons struck at crossings) and factories (industrial accidents). In all these cases, except those of non-passengers struck by trains, there was a contract between plaintiff and defendant, either for carriage or employment, but contract played a muted role in these actions unless the defendant raised an exonerative clause. Mignault and other writers agreed that such cases were properly brought in delict.[50]

Each of the elements of fault, harm, and causation gave rise to considerable controversy. What exactly constituted fault in an industrial setting, and what standard should employers have to meet in ensuring worker safety around dangerous machinery? Was non-pecuniary harm such as grief at the loss of a loved one (*solatium doloris*) a valid head of compensation? And who would bear the risk where the cause of an accident was unknown or obscure?

Turning first to the existence and proof of fault, it is perhaps surprising – when compared to the common law experience – that some Quebec judges found ways to lighten the burden of worker plaintiffs to ensure that they could recover – in stark contrast to the common law. First, the judges raised the standard of care. It did not suffice for an employer to adopt the usual safety standard in the industry if better precautions existed. The best available techniques had to be used, creating a legal incentive to continuously upgrade safety measures. Second, after the passage of the *Quebec Factories Act* of 1885, which obliged employers to adopt a variety of safety measures such as fencing machinery, a failure to do so raised a presumption that any accident was due to the fault of the employer, in effect shifting the burden of proof.[51] Third, after first allowing employer-imposed waiver clauses by which workers gave up their right to sue for injury, the courts changed course and said they didn't apply where the employer was guilty of faute lourde (gross negligence); and such clauses were not binding on widows and children where a worker was killed on the job.[52] Finally, there was an emerging current of jurisprudence that used article 1054, regarding liability for things under one's care, to effect a shift of the burden of proof from worker to employer where a piece of machinery malfunctioned.[53] Summing up these trends, legal writer J.C. Lamothe, a strong advocate for worker rights, declared in 1905 that 'through a humane fiction the courts ingeniously manage to find a fault [in the employer], or even to create one where it does not exist, in order to compensate the victims.'[54] McGill law dean Frederick Parker Walton, writing in 1910, saw in this case law a surreptitious adoption of the theory of 'professional risk,' then current in France, which suggested that when accidents arose, the person profiting from the carrying on of hazardous activities such as manufacturing should bear the risk in preference to the innocent employee.[55] Even Mignault, a strong defender of fault-based liability, agreed with the trend of the case law to find in favour of the injured worker even if he did not always approve of the analysis leading there.[56]

Judges were less likely to see railways as inherently dangerous, and passengers injured in accidents could lose because they could not point to any specific conduct of the railway company that constituted fault. In *Ranger c Cie du Grand Tronc*, the plaintiff was attempting to descend from the train as it slowed at a station but was thrown forcefully to the platform when it sped up again without warning. She sustained serious injuries and lost the baby she was carrying, but the Superior Court dismissed her action, the judge noting laconically that there was no more reason to presume the railway was at fault than that she was.[57] The Quebec courts were more generous to the injured passenger in *CPR v Chalifoux*; they found fault in a case where a twisted rail caused a derailment. But the SCC reversed, with the sole Quebec judge on the panel dissenting. The judges, citing mostly UK and US authority, noted that the rail had recently been inspected and was not shown to have been defective. They preferred to attribute the accident to the extreme variations in temperature around the time of the accident, rather than to any fault of the railway.[58]

Deciding what kinds of harm were compensable did not create many problems where physical injuries were concerned, though companies constantly contested the quantum of damages. To little avail: higher courts, after some hand-wringing, generally deferred to jury verdicts.* Damages for wrongful death, in particular compensation for grief, were in a different category. The issue here was legal, not factual: how to reconcile the conflicting approaches derived from English and French law? Unlike French law, the common law had not allowed recovery for wrongful death at all until the passage of *Lord Campbell's Act* in 1846, a statute copied in the Province of Canada the next year, and made applicable to both Upper

---

* Juries in civil matters, though not part of the Continental civil law tradition, were introduced by the British in 1764 and available continuously from 1791; see *Volume 1*, 221.

and Lower Canada.[59] The common law had also, again unlike French law, forbade recovery for mental anguish in a wide variety of situations, including grief resulting from the wrongful death of a loved one. In interpreting the 1847 statute, Lower Canadian judges in an 1857 case had, by a bare majority, allowed the French view to prevail, but the matter remained somewhat controversial and exposed certain cultural differences.[60]

The common law's fixation on pecuniary loss could require, at least in theory, a kind of cold calculation that many Quebec jurists found distasteful and downright immoral. In an 1891 case where damages for grief were sought by the parents of a child who died from ingesting a toxic drug provided by a negligent physician and pharmacist, counsel for the former argued that no compensable harm was suffered by the parents. Justice Louis Jetté observed heatedly that following this reasoning, 'if someone murders your aged father whom you are obliged to support, not only would you get no damages, but you would owe the killer thanks, since he relieved you of that burden,' calling this 'a barbaric principle that cannot be allowed.'[61] His confirmation of a jury award on this head of damages was nonetheless overturned by the Court of Queen's Bench, a majority of which found it imperative to establish 'a uniform jurisprudence upon this subject in the several provinces in the Dominion, and in Great Britain.'[62]

Such thinking also prevailed when a wrongful death suit launched by Agnes Robinson for the death of her husband, railway worker Patrick Flynn, went to the SCC not once but twice, and eventually to the JCPC. At the first trial Dame Robinson received $2,000 for herself and $1,000 for her minor daughter, the judge having directed the jury that they might 'consider the nature of the anguish and mental sufferings' of the plaintiff and her daughter. The SCC decided that this was a misdirection, such damages not being recoverable in law, and therefore a new trial was ordered. At the second trial damages for grief were nowhere claimed, but the jury made a much higher award, $4,500 for the widow and $2,000 for the child. CPR appealed this decision then raised an issue of prescription for the first time. The SCC agreed with CPR and reversed the trial decision, finding the limitation period had expired. Undaunted, Dame Robinson, with the aid of funds raised by the Conseil des métiers et du travail, an umbrella group of workers' organizations, took her case to the JCPC. There the court dismissed the prescription argument and restored the trial decision. It did not address the underlying issue of whether the SCC had been correct in denying the recoverability of damages for *solatium doloris*, but in their view article 1056 was quite different from its supposed English parent in several respects. This was at odds with the SCC's view, which regarded article 1056 as virtually a transcription of Lord Campbell's Act.[63]

In 1909 the SCC admitted that its own decision in *Robinson* on this point was 'shaken' by the JCPC's judgment in that case but declined to address the issue on the merits. In this case, *CPR v Lachance,* the court did not interfere with a jury award of $4,000 to the family of a deceased worker at CPR's Sherbrooke railyard, where the award included the loss of the husband's services at home, his care and protection of his wife and family, and his assistance in managing the family's resources.[64] Thus it appears that with a little creativity the ban on the recovery of loss for grief under article 1056 could be avoided.[65]

The JCPC also disagreed with the SCC on another aspect of article 1056. It had become common for railway companies to require employees to join and pay into company-established mutual benefit societies as a condition of employment, and to give up any claims against the company for injury or death suffered on the job. Article 1056 stated that a cause of action existed in the widow and certain other relations, provided that the deceased had not 'obtained indemnity or satisfaction.' In *Miller v Grand Trunk Railway,* the Quebec courts found, after a jury trial, that Dame Mary Miller was entitled to $6,000 and her four minor children to $1,000 each after Miller's husband, Richard Ramsden, was killed on the job. The SCC reversed, stating that a death benefit paid to Ramsden's estate was an 'indemnity' disentitling his heirs from taking any action against the company. The JCPC restored the trial judgment. It held, first, that Ramsden could not sign away the rights of his widow and children, who had an independent right of action under article 1056 for their own losses, as had already been decided in *Robinson.* Second, while the company paid into the accident insurance fund, it did not pay anything into the fund providing death benefits. This was structured as a mutual life insurance scheme funded entirely by the employees themselves, with benefits payable on death from any cause. Thus any 'indemnity' had been provided not by the company but by the deceased's own co-workers. A corollary of *Miller* was that the SCC's 1899 decision in *Reg v Grenier* was also overturned, as it too was based on the assumption that a benefit from such a plan could constitute an indemnity under article 1056.[66]

On the third element of the liability equation – causation – the Quebec courts were relatively generous in giving the benefit of the doubt to the plaintiff where it was uncertain whether the injuries were caused by the fault of the defendant or had some non-negligent origin, but the SCC flip-flopped on the issue. In a 1900 case it held that the family of a mine worker killed in an explosion could recover where the company had allowed a large quantity of dynamite to accumulate in a location where workers were in proximity, even though the exact cause of the explosion was unknown. In effect, a presumption of causation could arise when such negligent behaviour was proved.[67] In a similar case the next year involving the explosion of a machine that filled cartridges with powder and shot, the SCC overturned a jury award of $5,000 in favour of an injured worker that had been upheld unanimously by two levels of appeal court in Quebec, even though the exact cause of the explosion could not be determined. For the SCC this was fatal to Archibald McArthur's cause. He, aged only 18 at the time of the accident, appealed *in forma pauperis* (as had Mary Miller) to the JCPC, which restored the original award. Lord MacNaughten stated that '[exacting direct proof of cause] cannot be of universal application, or utter destruction would carry with it complete immunity for the employer.'[68] The JCPC was not known as a worker-friendly court, but on this and other issues it was prepared to uphold the view of the Quebec courts and part company with the SCC.

In addition to benefitting from a somewhat generous jurisprudence on the requirements for employer liability, workers in Quebec were also in a better legal position than those in the common law provinces with respect to the lessened availability of employer defences. The defence of common employment, a relatively recent judge-made creation in the common law (though being abolished in several provinces in the late nineteenth century, see chapter 12), had no counterpart in the civil law: the employer could be held liable when an employee's negligent act or omission harmed a co-worker. Contributory negligence by the employee, a complete defence to an action against the employer at common law, was also absent from the civil law, though the employee's negligence could reduce the damages available pursuant to the doctrine of comparative fault. And voluntary assumption of risk, though theoretically available, did not loom as large in the civil law jurisprudence as under the common law. Only experienced workers who could fully appreciate the risks inherent in particular acts might find this defence raised successfully against them.[69]

This account of a somewhat worker-friendly law of employer liability is reflected in the success rate of plaintiffs, at least in reported cases. In the 125 employer liability cases reported between 1876 and 1911, workers' success rate was 72 per cent in Superior Court, rising to 78 per cent in the Court of Queen's Bench.[70] At the SCC, however, it fell to 53 per cent, provoking J.C. Lamothe to observe that 'La Cour suprême est devenue le cauchemar des victimes d'accidents du travail.'[71] Indeed, it was thought that lawyers commonly advised workers to limit their claims to just under $2,000 where possible, the dollar limit for cases that could be appealed to the SCC.[72] That court, influenced largely by the common law, took a more stringent approach to the proof of employer fault and causation and was often sceptical of the innovations advanced by the Quebec courts. It did not accept, for example, that the provisions of the Quebec *Factories Act* could create a civil cause of action, characterizing them as mere 'police regulations,' contrary to the preponderance of opinion among Quebec judges.[73]

The Quebec courts, for their part, pushed back, as they had done on the issue of *solatium doloris*. A 1905 case featured a miner who was ordered to go into a pit known to be dangerous because recent dynamiting had partially dislodged a large rock, and had his leg crushed and amputated when the rock fell. Upholding the jury award, Chief Justice Routhier, speaking for the Court of Revision, took the opportunity to lament that the SCC was 'in the process of establishing on these questions a jurisprudence that I can only call unfortunate, and which seems to contradict the ideas that prevail today in all civilized countries.' He went on to accuse the Court of 'applying the pre-1880 English law' (before the *Employers' Liability Act* had been passed there) in a way that treated workers as tools or units or production rather than human beings.[74] Mignault also criticized the SCC for its refusal to follow Quebec opinion on the effect of the *Factories Act*, although the unanimous opinion of the court on this issue had been written by Justice Girouard of Quebec.[75] However, perhaps chastened by such critiques and by being overturned by the JCPC in *Robinson, McArthur*, and *Miller*, the SCC eventually came to restate the nature of the employer's duty regarding worker safety in Quebec in a serious and purposive way that would have met with the approval of Quebec jurists – just before the *Workmen's Compensation Act* superseded the existing law.[76]

Even assuming that the law itself was not completely unfavourable to workers, however, problems of access to justice could render the substantive law irrelevant. The estimates are that only one-quarter of injured workers ultimately received any compensation.[77] Many workers did not have the cultural or economic resources to sue their employer. Only 6 per cent of workers were unionized in Quebec by

1911, though fraternal and workers' associations could fund litigation in some instances, as they had done for Agnes Robinson, and no doubt provided some advice to injured workers. Lamothe advocated a legal aid scheme for injured workers to allow them to pursue their claims, to no avail. Even where a plaintiff was successful at law, problems arose. Appeals were frequent, meaning the payment of any award could be delayed for years. When paid, damages took the form of a lump sum. Contemporaries thought that lawyers often claimed a good part of such awards pursuant to informal contingency fee arrangements, while many workers were ill-equipped to invest a damages award that would generate an income stream for the future. It was also thought that poorly educated workers, unaware of their rights, were disposed to accept small settlements in return for giving up damages claims.[78]

If workers had good cause to complain of the problems inherent in an accident compensation regime based on liberal principles, private law, and plaintiff initiative, employers were also unhappy with the vagaries of what would later be called the 'forensic lottery.'[79] Employers did not object to paying accident compensation as such. Rather, the prospect of having to pay a large lump-sum award, even if somewhat remote, was always a cause for concern. Thus when reform began to be discussed, a main goal of employer groups was to ensure that a cap on damages was adopted, and in this they would be successful.

Although reform of employers' liability law in Quebec was driven by factors similar to those in the rest of North America – the widespread adoption of dangerous industrial machinery that caused increasing numbers of gruesome accidents and deaths – Quebec's reform was shaped by developments in France and the United Kingdom that treated the problem as one of private law. It did not involve the creation of an administrative body designed to supplant the courts by collecting insurance premiums from employers and providing benefits directly to injured workers or their estates, as with Ontario's 1914 Workmen's Compensation Board, discussed in chapter 12. Rather, the Quebec *Workmen's Compensation Act, 1909,* was in effect an amendment to the *Civil* Code's general provisions on civil liability in articles 1053–6.[80] The new act featured 'a frank acceptance of the new principle of "professional risk,"' a concept that appeared in the case law in the early twentieth century.[81] This principle recognized that many industrial accidents had no discoverable cause or were not actually due to anyone's negligence. Thus, those profiting from the activity – employers – should be responsible where innocent workers were harmed in the process. Payouts for workplace accidents were a cost of doing business that should ultimately be borne by consumers, not by the injured party or their family.

The adoption of this no-fault principle was undoubtedly an advance for workers. Those injured or killed in 'accidents happening by reason of or in the course of their work' in sectors covered by the act (those employed in agriculture and on sailing ships were expressly excluded, those employed in forest work included later pursuant to judicial interpretation) would no longer have to prove fault of the employer and were entitled to certain compensation as of right. Nor could employers contract out of the act. However, unequal participation of worker and employer groups in the process leading up to the 1909 act ensured that the latter managed to shape the legislation largely in their favour. When a reform bill introduced in 1904 encountered strong opposition from industry groups, the government created a commission to study the issue, chaired by lawyer Arthur Globensky. It studied international, mainly European, examples of reform for nearly two years, and most of its recommendations were adopted in the resulting 1909 act. Employer groups submitted many strong briefs, while those submitted by labour were few and weakly argued. While the resulting bill emulated both the French and UK legislation, it eliminated or reduced almost all the stronger labour-oriented provisions from both. Employers resisted compulsory insurance, and succeeded. Where the French legislation required a pension of 66 per cent of a workers' wages in cases of permanent and total incapacity, Quebec's was set at 50 per cent. In cases of temporary incapacity, the pension was payable commencing only where such incapacity lasted seven days after the injury, instead of four in France. Compensation for death or permanent disability was restricted to four years' wages, with an upper limit of $2,000 in all cases, where previous cases had awarded up to $4,000 or $5,000 in such situations.[82] Moreover, it was to be paid as a lump sum and not as a life pension, as in France. And unlike in the United Kingdom, where an employee had the choice to sue at common law, no such option existed under the Quebec act. Nor was compensation for industrial diseases provided for, upon which a start had been made in the UK act of 1906 and would be in Ontario's 1914 act. No claim could be commenced without permission of a Superior Court judge, which was to be granted pro forma except that the judge was authorized to 'use such means as he may think useful to bring about an understanding between the parties'; in other words, to act in a mediator-like capacity to reach a resolution.[83]

In short order the defects of an act framed within the parameters of private law would become evident: lack of security for pensions in case of employer insolvency; ongoing litigation over whether accidents were work-related; the unsuitability of lump sum payments; and the overall low level of compensation. The Trades and Labor Congress of Canada, which had played little role in the lead-up to the 1909 act, was calling for its repeal or significant amendment by 1910. But it would be decades before Quebec chose to follow the administrative board model adopted in other provinces, a matter taken up in *Volume 3*.

Property

The *Code Napoléon* had abolished feudalism and institutions of the ancien droit that had favoured the maintenance of property in noble families, such as the fideicommissary substitution (a form of inter-generational settlement) and the long lease known as emphyteusis, which could exist for up to 99 years and involved the lessee undertaking improvements to the property. The *Civil Code* of 1866 maintained these devices but in general hewed closely to the simplified, and somewhat rigid, regime of property found in the French Code. Indeed, in this area more than any other did the two codes resemble each other.[84] Each featured a small number of ways in which ownership could be broken down or limited, comprising the usufruct or life interest; the right of use and habitation (essentially a usufruct limited to the needs of the holder and his or her family); and servitudes over the land of others. Unlike the common law, where leases were effectively a hybrid of contract and property, under the civil law they were seen as exclusively contractual.

The Code of 1866 thus featured a concept of property in which the liberalizing reforms of the United Canada period came together, one more suitable for the capitalist society that was rapidly emerging in Quebec. Thomas Jean-Jacques Loranger, a prolific legal writer and Superior Court judge from 1863, was entirely in favour of these changes, noting that 'the concentration of wealth in the family may suit older nations. But it paralyzes the development of resources in a new country, still covered in forests, where the circulation of property is one of the primary needs of the population.'[85] Key to free circulation of property was a clear definition of ownership. Article 406 declared, 'Ownership is the right of enjoying and of disposing of things in the most absolute manner provided no use be made of them which is prohibited by law or by regulations.' The liberal nature of property was especially evident with immoveables, where most restraints oriented to keeping such property in the family line had been done away with. Dower was mostly reduced to a contractual benefit, as noted earlier. The retrait lignager, which aimed to keep inherited property within a family lineage, was gone, and so were the restrictions in the ancien droit on the giving or willing of assets to a second spouse (article 764). Article 599 directed that all property in a succession was to be treated as one fund for division among the heirs, without reference to its origin or nature, privileging economic value over family ties. The implementation of a registration system for immoveables had made titles more secure and alienable, and done away with most 'secret hypothecs' – liens on property that might exist without registration. Most importantly, seigneurial tenure had been abolished and all titles converted to free tenure (franc alleu roturier), first on the island of Montreal in 1840, and then across the province in 1854. There was nonetheless a certain deceptive quality to this abolition that will be dealt with below.

With regard to moveable property, a broad company law had been passed in 1864 making corporate shares a more common form of property in the province, while 1858 had seen the abolition of the usury law that formerly set the maximum rate of interest at 6 per cent. The 1858 Act stated that parties could 'stipulate for … any rate of interest or discount that may be agreed upon,' except for banks, which could not demand more than 7 per cent on money loaned out. The default rate of interest, if none were stipulated in a contract, would remain at 6 per cent.[86] After Confederation 'interest' was a topic given to the federal government, but while it kept banks to the 7 per cent cap on interest rates, it did not otherwise limit rates, with one exception. In 1906 the federal *Money-Lenders Act* attempted to set a limit of 12 per cent on loans of up to $500, but as the Act contained no definition of 'interest' it has been doubted whether it had much effect. It may, however, have provided a guideline for what constituted a 'usurious' rate of interest with regard to the amendment to article 1149 of the *Civil Code*, discussed earlier.[87]

Despite the centrality of liberal property to the Code, there remained aspects of the civil law that prevented the full exploitation of assets for business purposes, in particular with regard to the creation of security interests. Moveable property, for example, could not be hypothecated (article 2022): to secure a loan using such property as collateral, the debtor had to transfer possession of it to the creditor, hardly a solution for most businesses (articles 1968–78). The issue was addressed in two ways. First, many corporations had clauses inserted in their acts of incorporation that allowed them to issue bonds using all their property, moveable and immoveable, as security for bondholders. This solution was finally generalized in the 1914 *Special Corporate Powers Act*, modelled on statutes in common law jurisdictions, which allowed companies to create a general charge on all their assets, present and future.[88] This solution was no help to small businesses or partnerships that were not incorporated. The second solution relied on federalism to do an end run around the restrictions in the Code. Pursuant to the federal power over banking, the *Bank Act* was amended in 1890 allowing banks to take certain kinds of moveable property as security for loans, overriding the Code's restriction in this respect.[89]

The Act effecting the province-wide abolition of seigneurial tenure in 1854 in some ways accomplished the exact opposite of what was suggested by its title, *An act for the abolition of feudal rights and duties in Lower Canada*. For if the act did indeed abolish seigneurial tenure, the method adopted for compensating the former seigneurs ensured that the payment of seigneurial dues would continue in some form for over a century after its passage. A cadastre in several volumes was published in 1863 showing the sums to be paid to the owners of the 330 seigneuries enumerated in it.[90] This compensation came in two forms: the annual seigneurial dues (cens et rentes) owed by the former censitaires were converted into constituted rents and continued to be owed by them. All other rights, such as the mutation fee known as lods et ventes, were compensated from a state fund of some $10 million. In addition, each former seigneur was allowed to take all unconceded land in the seigneury as individual property instead of, for example, having it escheat to the province. For every lot a constituted rent was calculated, at 17 times the former cens et rentes. The lot owner could pay this capital sum and be discharged forever from any further payment, or could continue to pay an annual sum of 6 per cent of this capital sum in perpetuity. Should the owner decide to pay the capital sum later, the previous annual payments would not be deducted and the initial capital sum would always remain payable. However, there were no adjustments for inflation, such that the value of both sums declined over time. The notarial fees for drawing up the required documents, in addition to other administrative charges (frais de quittance), could be substantial, discouraging commutation. Finally, paying off the capital sum was not seen to add to the market value of the property, creating even less of an incentive to do so. Almost no former censitaires had commuted their dues after 1840 when a similar system was instituted on the island of Montreal, nor did many do so after 1854.[91]

For any given lot owner, the annual payment to the former seigneur might be quite small, but when these were aggregated the sums could be substantial. In the seigneury of Beauport, admittedly one of the oldest and most populous seigneuries, the capitalized dues amounted to almost $20,000 in 1859, which would be approximately $640,000 today. The compensation for the other rights lost and the value of the unconceded lands in the seigneury that now belonged to the former seigneur in free tenure amounted to another $13,000 payable from the state compensation fund, or $416,000, for a total of well over $1 million in today's money.

The constituted rents were financialized and themselves became commodities, as the 6 per cent return was considered a very good investment for the time. Companies such as Montreal Trust and Crédit Foncier Franco-Canadien bought out a number of seigneurs, such that Crédit Foncier owned the rights to 17 seigneuries at one point.[92] The ostensible 6 per cent return on these rents could in fact be much less once all the transaction costs of collecting them were factored in, including lawsuits against those reluctant to pay up and title searches to follow changes in ownership. Those entitled to the rents usually employed agents, who charged a commission and expenses to collect them from the lot owners. The way these agents portrayed themselves might make one doubt whether any 'abolition' of the seigneurial order had taken place. F.O.T. Lamarche, who collected rents due on a North Shore seigneury on behalf of Crédit Foncier Franco-Canadien, used a letterhead in the 1910s and after captioned 'Seigneurie de Lanoraie et d'Autray' with his name in Gothic lettering, his address prefaced with 'Bureau seigneuriale,' and his title as 'agent seigneurial.' It would take the stimulus of the Great Depression of the 1930s to open the next chapter in the saga of the 'abolition' of seigneurial tenure.

Despite the strong influence of French law on the property provisions of the Code, soon after its adoption new provisions were added regarding the trust, an institution that would cause no end of controversy in Quebec, both as to its origins and its juridical basis. The Code included two articles from the French law that made some reference to trust-like devices. The first, article 869, allowed testators to leave property for charitable 'or other lawful purposes' via three modes: to legatees who would be 'merely fiduciary or simply trustees,' to their testamentary executors, or to legatees charged with carrying out these purposes.

Article 964, referring to a 'legatee who is charged as a mere trustee,' complemented article 869 by directing that where the purpose contemplated by the testator had lapsed or become impossible, the property in question would pass to the heirs of the testator unless the will had specified that it was to remain with the legatee charged with the trust. In spite of the use of the word 'trust' in the English version, both of these articles reproduced specific provisions in French law that were not examples of some wider trust-like institution in the ancien droit.[93]

The British population, meanwhile, were familiar with the trust as understood under the common law and used it on occasion in their wills from at least the early nineteenth century. When the provisions in such wills were contested, the courts upheld the testator's intention and did not declare such clauses invalid, but the risk of continuing to rely on such judicial benevolence was clear. For example, the 1870 will of Hugh Fraser, by which he devised his entire residuary estate 'in trust' to trustees who were directed to incorporate a company to create and maintain a free public library and museum in Montreal to which the assets would be transferred, was held invalid by the Court of Queen's Bench. The JCPC upheld the will, but only on the basis of article 869, not through any importation of the English trust. Moreover, it opined that the Quebec law on this question was 'in an unsettled state,' clearly hinting that some legislative action was desirable.[94] An act to validate the creation of trusts in the context of gifts and wills (albeit not retroactively) was duly introduced as a private member's bill by Jonathan Wurtele, later a Superior Court judge, in 1879. Its provisions were added to the *Civil Code* in the 1888 revision of the Quebec statutes as articles 981a–n.[95] Although this trust was spoken of at the time, even by Mignault, as building on French antecedents, the better view is that it was new law unconnected to articles 869 or 964, adopted to legitimize the practices of the British population. How the dual ownership of the common law trust, with its separation of legal title in the trustee from equitable title in the beneficiary, could be reconciled with the unitary concept of ownership laid down in article 406 was not addressed in these new articles. Nor was it clear whether English authorities could or should be cited when these articles had to be interpreted by courts. Such challenges did not come before the courts for some time, and will be explored further in *Volume 3*.

Quebec's legal culture was always distinctive, but in the 50 years after Confederation that distinctiveness assumed its modern form. It was a mixed system, drawing on French, English, and now Canadian sources, but more disciplined, focused, and coherent than it had been in the colonial era. Much of that focus had to do with the *Civil Code* and the *Code of Civil Procedure*, especially the former, which served as the anchor for Quebec legal culture. It could do so because private law was still the centre of the legal universe, with the welfare state and the rise of public law yet to come. Quebec law was mixed, not just in its sources, but in its juridical infrastructure: a largely French-derived private law operated in an English-style court system in which the selection of judges, the practice of individualized judgments including dissents, the format of those judgments, the style of advocacy, and the role of case law in general were all recognizably Anglo-Canadian.

The great achievement of this period was that the advocates, notaries, and judges of both principal cultural groups made this system work. That they did so was largely because the Codes had fulfilled one of their principal goals: making the law accessible in French and English. Anglophone lawyers and judges not only became bilingual more often than in the past but came to appreciate the strengths of the civil law more fully. The bad old days of unilingual anglophone judges unsympathetic to the civil law were long gone. Francophone lawyers had an incentive to learn English to engage with business clients, many of whom were anglophone, and to argue before the SCC, which was not yet a bilingual institution. Pierre-Basile Mignault himself exemplified this linguistic duality. Born in Worcester, Massachusetts, to an anglophone mother and a Quebec-descended father, he spoke English as his first language but became fluent in French after moving with his family to Montreal as a boy, so fluent that he wrote all his major works in French. In this he prefigured the career of Louis St-Laurent, another fluently bilingual lawyer who began teaching law at Laval in 1914 and would go on to become prime minister. A growing legal literature, especially Mignault's soon-to-be-completed multi-volume work and Walton's *Scope and Interpretation of the Civil Code of Lower Canada* helped to define the contours of Quebec civil law and to legitimate its intellectual achievement. Indeed, Mignault remains a frequently cited author today. A measure of the growing confidence of Quebec jurists was their occasional calling out of the SCC for decisions that were seen as wrong-headed interpretations of the civil law embodying values alien to their legal and cultural traditions. Meanwhile, the JCPC was generally respectful of the autonomy of Quebec civil law.

This is not to say that all was rosy in Quebec's legal universe. With so much of the business world managed by anglophones, it was harder for francophone lawyers, even bilingual ones, to break into the more lucrative world of corporate law, though some did. The familiar trope of two solitudes was still the norm within legal practice, as in the culture at large. Even though the Code itself did not explicitly privilege Catholicism, many legal professionals and judges assumed that its interpretation should be consonant with Catholic values, leading to severe ideological conflicts with non-Catholic jurists, especially in the field of family law and women's rights. The attempts by Annie Macdonald Langstaff, McGill BCL 1914, to join the Quebec bar, denied by the Court of King's Bench in 1915, were a harbinger of things to come. During the interwar years, as will be seen in *Volume 3*, Quebec jurists doubled down on the need to maintain the traditional male-centred values enshrined in the 1866 Code, while also fending off what were seen as increasingly strident attempts by those elsewhere in Canada to make Canadian law more uniform by assimilating Quebec law, and to denigrate the French language and Quebec culture.[96]

6

The Legal Professions, Legal Education, and Legal Literature

Lawyers had played leading roles in politics, business, and society prior to Confederation, but mostly within the confines of their own province. Opportunities in all three spheres abounded in the much larger Dominion of Canada, and lawyers were not slow to take advantage of them, as increasingly extensive rail networks facilitated inter-provincial connections. Consider Benjamin Russell, who managed to combine practising law in Dartmouth, Nova Scotia, and a half-time position as professor at Dalhousie Law School with serving two terms as an MP between 1896 and 1904. When the House of Commons was in session Russell caught the train to Ottawa after his Friday class, arrived on Saturday at midnight, went to the Dominion Methodist Church on Sunday, attended to his constituents' business on Monday, and took the train late in the day, returning to Halifax in time for his Wednesday class.[1] Lawyers' self-employed status, their understanding of government, and their frequent appearances in courts and other public venues made them seem especially suited to serve as political representatives. And serve they did. In the governments of Canada, Ontario, and Quebec, there were only seven years between 1867 and 1914 in each jurisdiction when the prime minister or premier was not a lawyer. This was especially impressive in Quebec where, of the 13 premiers during these years, the only two non-lawyers were physicians. The proportion of lawyers in Parliament between 1867 and 1914 was never below one-quarter and sometimes reached one-third. Lawyers were also essential in private life during these years, which represented the heyday of private law and court-centred dispute resolution before the rise of the administrative state after the Great War.

If much of this story represented continuity with the pre-Confederation period, there was also significant change, especially from the 1880s. The most noticeable occurred with the emergence of the 'large' law firm practising corporate law, and the establishment of university legal education everywhere outside of Ontario. Also significant was the adoption of the Ontario/Quebec model of professional regulation via statutory delegation to a provincial law society in all provinces and Newfoundland, with Prince Edward Island the only exception. Little change occurred in the internal demographics of the profession, although this period did see the removal of barriers to the entry of women to the profession in most provinces, and the admission of a very few members of some religious, ethnic, and racial minorities.

The numbers of lawyers varied considerably over the period both within and between provinces, starting from a base of about 1,480 in British North America (including Prince Edward Island and British Columbia) in 1867. In general, following the surge in recruitment to the bar and the notariat in the 1850s and 1860s in central Canada, the late nineteenth century was 'a golden age of local legal services for smaller cities, towns, and villages.'[2] Recruitment to the bar had plummeted in the Maritimes prior to Confederation but recovered thereafter, leading to a similar pattern of lawyerly diffusion. The turn of the century, by contrast, saw a sharp and sudden contraction in recruitment to the bar and the notarial profession everywhere in central and eastern Canada: see table 6.1. In Ontario the growth rate of lawyers plunged to -2.5 per cent and -0.9 per cent in the first two decades of the twentieth century, respectively, while the 118 lawyers in Halifax in 1900 represented a peak that would not be exceeded for over half a century, even as the city's population tripled over that time. The notarial profession counted nearly 800 members in Quebec in 1870, but only 669 in 1900, even though the province's population had increased by some 37 per cent.[3]

The fact that similar trends can be observed in much of the contemporary United States suggests that continent-wide factors were at play. The principal explanatory variable is likely the 'systemic stabilization' that ensued after the growth of credit-rating agencies made lending a more secure enterprise. This in turn led to a marked decline in the routine debt litigation that had long been a staple of rural and small-town lawyers. The contraction of the profession in central and eastern Canada

Table 6.1. Lawyers in Canada, 1867–1911

Year	Population	Lawyers	Population per lawyer
1867	3,463,000	1,480	2,339
1881	4,325,000	1,234	3,504
1891	4,831,000	1,115	4,332
1901	5,371,000	1,081	4,968
1911	7,207,000	1,339	5,382

Source: Censuses of Canada, 1867–1911

led to a concentration of lawyers in the major cities, and a declining presence in smaller centres. Quebec, where the presence of village notaries remained widespread, was an exception. In the West, by contrast, the story was still one of growth and geographic diffusion, spurred both by immigration from central and eastern Canada, and later by locally born entrants. Internal lawyerly migration peaked around 1914: between 1905 and 1914, for example, at least 92 Nova Scotian lawyers went west, including leaders of the profession such as William Bruce Almon Ritchie, but their numbers declined rapidly thereafter. New Brunswicker, Dalhousie Law graduate, and future prime minister R.B. Bennett, who relocated to Calgary in 1897 to join the practice of Senator James Lougheed, well described the appeal of the West when he wrote to an Ontario lawyer in 1903: 'The fact is a young man with push and enterprise ... will make more money in a year by speculating in real estate and going in for life and fire insurance and a little law than he would make in five years in Ontario.'[4] Bennett's remarks also highlight the seamless connections between law and business in the world of the turn-of-the-century Canadian lawyer.

By the eve of the First World War the Canadian legal profession, while still featuring relatively distinctive provincial legal cultures, had achieved a significant level of national cohesion. This trend culminated in the founding of the Canadian Bar Association in 1914, while Quebec notaries would create their own voluntary association two years later. The ethos of the profession slowly changed during this period from 'Georgian professionalism,' centred on the idea of the gentleman-scholar or gentleman-statesman, to '"modern professionalism," in which formal qualifications based on demonstrated expertise replaced gentlemanly worth as the primary claim of the professional.' Part of this expertise could be demonstrated through legal writing of various kinds, which grew considerably during this period. Professional leaders also insisted on a broader cultural mission for anglophone lawyers, aiming to make them 'missionaries in service of a secularized trinity: law, Britishness and civilization.' The critical role of university legal education in facilitating this shift is evident, even if relatively few Canadian lawyers had in fact attended a university law school by 1914. This shift was less evident in the Quebec notarial profession, which took much longer to adapt to the socio-economic transformations consequent upon the industrialization and urbanization of the province.[5]

The Emergence of the 'Large' Law Firm

At least a dozen of Canada's largest law firms trace their beginnings to partnerships of two or three men, often related by blood or marriage, that coalesced in the 1850s through the 1880s. These firms took on work for, or themselves founded, the new railway companies, banks, insurance companies, and manufacturing concerns that were beginning to appear in British North America. The boost given to manufacturing by the National Policy soon led to the growth of corporations whose legal business could no longer be handled by two or three partners. This trend had begun a little earlier south of the border, but its growth in Canada was propelled by similar domestic circumstances and not direct importation of the model. Three things about these firms need to be stressed at the outset. The first is that while 'large' by the standards of the day, they were minuscule by modern standards, when firms of hundreds of lawyers no longer raise an eyebrow. The second is that the growth in size generated much larger rewards and a new division of labour and compensation within the firm. Third, the nature of the work of these larger law firms rapidly diverged from that done by solo practitioners or small partnerships, giving rise to a new form of stratification within the profession. Each will be examined in turn.[6]

Scholars have defined the 'large' firm during this period as one with five or more lawyers, a cut-off the Dominion Bureau of Statistics continued to use until 1950. In 1914 the average size of 27 major firms in the United States was still under nine lawyers; in Canada the average size of the 10 largest firms was almost identical, at 8.5. In 1882 there were only five Toronto firms with between five and nine lawyers, and none of that size anywhere else in Canada. Montreal and Halifax would join the 'five and over' club in the 1890s. By 1902 the three largest firms in Canada, all in Toronto, had 15, 13, and 11 lawyers respectively, and matters had not changed appreciably by 1914. Despite being the commercial capital of Canada during this period, Montreal's law firms did not rival the size of those in Toronto, the largest having seven lawyers.[7] These were the preserve of anglophone lawyers, aside from a few francophones such as George-Étienne Cartier and Antoine-Aimé Dorion, who were active in the corporate-commercial world in the mid- to late nineteenth century. Eugène Lafleur, the Protestant Montreal advocate often considered by contemporaries the best Canadian lawyer of his generation, was one of the very few who was equally at ease socially in both the city's French and English circles. In 1885 he founded the firm that would become Clarkson Tétrault a century later, before it merged with McCarthy's to become McCarthy Tétrault. It was one of over a dozen firms established in the 1860–90 period that survived and prospered to become interprovincial and transnational megafirms in recent times, firms such as Stewart McKelvey (founded Halifax, 1885), Bennett Jones (founded Calgary, 1882), Fasken (founded Toronto, 1863), Osler (founded Toronto, 1877), and Gowlings (founded Ottawa, 1887).[8]

The growth of firm size led almost inevitably to a distinction between partners who shared the net profits of the firm and other lawyers who were paid a salary. Daniel Thomson was the first such salaried lawyer at Beatty Chadwick and Biggar in the early 1870s, while in the Halifax firm Borden, Ritchie, Parker and Chisholm, founded in 1889, the two last-named men were on salary. It was assumed that all salaried lawyers would eventually proceed to become partners if they stayed with the firm, but the way in which this would occur was not uniform within or between firms. Nor did this assumption of eventual partnership lead to any strategic focus on recruiting, which long remained a surprisingly casual process. Ties of blood and marriage, along with social contacts that could prove useful in generating business, were generally critical factors. But a farm lad with no connections and a strong work ethic could also be taken on, as was David Fasken at the Beatty Blackstock firm in the early 1880s – the ancestor of the firm now known as Fasken. In these larger firms, partners shared the net profits unequally. Partnership agreements were constantly being revised to determine the respective share of profits of each partner, leading in some cases to acrimony.[9]

What were all these lawyers doing? The dominant trend in these larger firms was the transition 'from courtroom to boardroom.' Litigation was no longer such an important part of the time allocation, income, or identity of many of these lawyers, although the balance between litigation and corporate solicitor work varied from firm to firm. Advising corporations about business as much as legal matters, serving as financial advisors, and sometimes actually managing corporations now occupied substantial time – though law firms seldom followed the advice they gave to businesses in their own internal organization, which bordered on the chaotic. By the early 1890s, just over half the $120,000 annual gross income of McCarthy, Osler, Hoskin & Creelman of Toronto came from non-litigation files. This was not a one-way street, however: some firms, such as Beatty Blackstock of Toronto, down-sized their litigation departments at one point, only to restore them later on.[10]

Despite the shift away from litigation in the larger firms, there was one tribunal before which lawyers in such firms were eager to appear: the JCPC. In addition to the prestige and high fees that accompanied participating in such appeals, the social perks were considerable. Canadian counsel always tried to arrange their appeals for July 'so that they could combine business with pleasure.' The latter included leisurely Atlantic crossings by ocean liner, accommodation in the finest hotels, and the social whirl of summertime London. The Canadian high commissioner arranged for Canadian counsel to be admitted to the royal enclosure at Ascot and secured invitations to the annual garden party at Buckingham Palace, while the Inns of Court took turns feting the Canadians at a banquet each year. These occasions, where the top lawyers from across Canada mingled with the cream of the English bar and legal establishment, did much to maintain the dominant place of English legal forms and ideals in the mentalité of Canadian lawyers until after the Second World War and the end of JCPC appeals.[11]

The rewards available to the men who created these firms were staggering compared to those of their pre-Confederation confrères. John Abbott of Montreal, who would become Canada's third prime minister near the end of his life, counted among his clients railway magnate Sir Hugh Allan, brewer John Thomas Molson, the Bank of Montreal, the Canadian Pacific Railway, and the HBC. Thought to be the wealthiest advocate in the province in his heyday, he declined the chief justiceship of the province at least twice because accepting it would deprive him of four-fifths of his income, meaning he would have earned at least $30,000 per year, close to $1 million in current purchasing power. In addition to his professional earnings, Abbott invested wisely with knowledge gained from the circles in which he moved. On his 300-acre estate at Senneville on the west island of Montreal he built a baronial mansion, laid out farms, orchards, and gardens, and indulged his passion for

Britton Bath Osler, probably the leading trial lawyer of this period.
Among his many cases, he was the lead prosecutor of Louis Riel in 1885.

Credit: *Dictionary of Canadian Biography.*

orchid cultivation. Sir James Aikins of Winnipeg had a similar stable
of blue-chip clients. With the fortune he made from them and from real
estate speculation, he was free to devote considerable time to founding organizations such as the Canadian Bar Association (1914) and
the Conference of Governing Bodies of the Legal Profession (1925).[12]
The rewards earned by the corporate lawyer could come with a cost.
In 1899, at age 60, the last year before he ceased work due to 'nervous
prostration,' Britton Bath Osler had travelled 15,000 miles by train and
spent at least 118 days in court. The headline to his obituary read, 'Generally Believed Death Due to Overwork.'[13]

Corporate firms of the type pioneered by Abbott and others represented only a small proportion of the legal profession in any province.
The vast majority of lawyers continued to work as sole practitioners or

in small firms of two to four partners. Thus when Justice W.R. Riddell of the Ontario High Court declared before the Ontario Bar Association in 1907 that '[t]he old family lawyer … has become a thing of the past,' replaced 'by the business man, the acute pulse-feeler of the money market [who is] more in the world and less in his chambers,' he was guilty of some hyperbole.[14] The corporate lawyer had become an icon of the profession, but the 'old family lawyer' would continue to be an indispensable figure on the professional and social landscape, carrying out the usual tasks of conveyancing, drafting contracts and wills, administering estates, engaging in litigation in local courts, incorporating companies, recovering money for creditors, and doing occasional criminal defence work. The law office of 1914 probably did not look very different from that of 1867, except in two respects. Modern technology, in the form of the telephone and typewriter, would be evident in the latter office, while its support staff were now more likely to be female than male. Printed forms were also much more common, obviating the drudgery of endless copying that was the lot of the clerks or articling students employed in pre-Confederation law offices.

One should not draw too sharp a distinction between corporate law firms and more traditional firms, however. While the identity of their clients and the nature of their rewards differed, they shared an essentially commercial ethos. In this they were more similar to US lawyers than to the English legal professions, where barristers were obliged to practise alone and most solicitors preferred the more genteel work of conveyancing to corporate involvements. In smaller centres lawyers competed with lay providers of legal services such as JPs and lay conveyancers. They could not rely on the monopoly on conveyancing enjoyed by English solicitors and needed to be nimble in their efforts to attract clients and provide value-added services if they were to stay ahead of the competition. Some lawyers belonged to two or more firms in different centres, aiming to enlarge their client base. Others charged a finder's fee for referring business to other lawyers, a practice frowned on but not forbidden. As smaller centres grew and incorporated, acting as town or municipal solicitor became an attractive way of supplementing one's income, as did becoming an insurance agent. Lawyers did not hesitate to move from one town to another to seek out better opportunities and were proud of their ability to adapt and survive in a competitive market. An anonymous lawyer observed in 1897 that '[w]e need not fear serious competition here on the part of the expensively educated English solicitor, accustomed to a much higher scale of fees than ours, and generally incapable of adapting himself to Canadian methods.'[15]

Towards the end of the century local lawyers' associations began adopting fee tariffs and discouraging members from charging below scale. They did not address the issue of contingency fees, however, a US innovation that remained controversial. The English *Attorneys' and Solicitors' Act* of 1870 had legislated the customary ban on contingency fees. Considered to have been received into the western provinces, it was re-enacted in Ontario in 1909. Moreover, champerty and maintenance were believed to have been retained as common law crimes by a general provision in the *Criminal Code*. Manitoba was the first to break with this tradition, permitting contingency fees by a statute of 1890, the validity of which was upheld by the Manitoba Court of Appeal in 1910. The BC courts took the opposite view, striking down a similar law passed there in 1901 when it was challenged, but the legislative response was so weak that its strictures could easily be evaded. Even in Ontario, which long remained officially hostile to contingency fees, there is evidence that they were employed in the shadow of the law. Whether such practices increased access to justice in the Canadian context remains an open question.[16]

University Legal Education

As noted in *Volume 1*, university legal education had barely begun in Canada prior to Confederation. The two law schools at McGill and Laval, founded in 1848 and 1854 respectively, could boast only a few dozen graduates in total by 1867. The Law Society of Upper Canada, for its part, refused to recognize university law degrees from Ontario or elsewhere as abridging its own requirements. In this it mimicked English barristers and solicitors, for whom university legal education was anathema. Eventually, however, even it was affected by the North American movement towards university legal education. In 1889 it reorganized its own educational offerings in the form of the Osgoode Hall Law School, although its lectures were offered concurrently with articling. When its first principal, William Albert Reeve, died suddenly in 1894, lecturer John King, father of the future prime minister, was passed over as his replacement. The job went to Newman Wright Hoyles, a son of Chief Justice Sir Hugh Hoyles of Newfoundland, who would serve until 1923.

By 1867 many aspiring lawyers from the Maritimes had attended a university law school or obtained such a degree – in the United States.

Some 90 Maritimers are known to have attended Harvard Law School alone in the decades before 1880. Hence the momentum behind university legal education in Canada next shifted to the east, before skipping over central Canada and heading west at the very end of this period. Various attempts to create 'home' legal education in the Maritimes failed before two university law faculties were successfully founded: one at Dalhousie University in Halifax in 1883, and one affiliated with King's College, Windsor, Nova Scotia in 1892 but, for complex reasons, located in Saint John, New Brunswick. While these institutions invoked the rising law faculties of the US eastern seaboard as models, they did not have the financial or intellectual resources to occupy the august position occupied by the Ivy League schools. Nor did they possess anything like the autonomy of the latter. American university law schools had arisen at a time of professional disorganization, when bar associations were weak or non-existent. By the time the bar associations began to re-establish themselves at the end of the nineteenth century, the law faculties had staked out a highly influential role for themselves, one from which they could not be dislodged. In 1900 they created the Association of American Law Schools (AALS). When the American Bar Association proposed to the AALS its plan for the reintroduction of a mandatory clerkship after law school, the AALS refused to agree to it. The plan was dropped, and clerkship virtually disappeared from the US scene.[17]

In Canada, these roles were reversed, with the provincial bars much more powerful than the new law schools. In Ontario, the bar ran its own law school, as we have seen, and used its statutory monopoly over legal education to discourage the opening of university law schools. The Quebec bar initially allowed law faculties to determine their own curricula and did not oppose the creation of a new faculty by Laval in Montreal in 1878, one that would eventually be absorbed into the Université de Montréal. But in 1886 the bar secured an amendment to its own constitutive act allowing it to dictate not only the content of university law programs, but even the number of hours devoted to each course. The bar also stoutly resisted any attempt to interfere with apprenticeship as an independent mode of entering the legal profession, or to dispense with the *stage* (clerkship) required of those who possessed law degrees. In 1890 McGill persuaded Attorney General Thomas Chase Casgrain to introduce a bill permitting university law graduates to practise law without further qualification, but it did not pass. Given that most instructors in the Quebec law faculties were themselves practising lawyers, and often highly prominent ones at that, opinions on this proposal were mixed, even within the academy. The universities did succeed, however, in having a law passed in the same year that allowed any holder of a bachelor's degree to enter a university program in the liberal professions or start a legal apprenticeship, without the traditional entrance examination that had been administered by the Barreau or the Chambre des notaires.[18]

Aspiring notaries could enrol in the university law faculties, but few did so, as the latter were concerned exclusively with the preparation of advocates. Between 1856 and 1880 only 15 per cent of Laval law graduates became notaries. The Quebec notarial profession lobbied for a distinct notarial program within the law faculties, hoping that a university law degree would provide better preparation for candidates and enhance the prestige of their profession. McGill was finally persuaded to create a chair in notarial law in 1880, but Laval delayed until 1898, when it named two professors in the field. Nonetheless, entry via a five-year apprenticeship after completion of a course at a collège classique, rather than via a university law degree, long remained the main mode of entry into the profession. The university notarial courses themselves were long seen as inadequate to prepare candidates for the challenges of a more competitive business environment where banks, trust companies, and accountants were increasingly offering services that notaries had traditionally provided.[19]

The relationship between law schools in the Maritimes and western Canada and their respective bars was somewhat more collaborative, even if the law societies still held the upper hand. The much greater exposure of aspiring Maritime lawyers to the university law schools of the United States had led to 'perceptible enthusiasm for what was understood to be the American educational experiment.'[20] The more visionary among their bar leaders thought that Maritime lawyers would be disadvantaged when they faced better-trained lawyers from Ontario and Quebec in the new arena of Confederation and saw university legal education as a way to close the gap. The Dalhousie Law School was promoted by the indefatigable attorney general and future prime minister, John Thompson, and up-and-coming Halifax lawyers such as Robert Sedgwick and Wallace Graham. When philanthropist George Munro offered to endow a chair in constitutional and international law for the founding dean, a nearly bankrupt university gratefully accepted. The Nova Scotia Barristers' Society itself took a somewhat hands-off attitude at first, but later granted a 'degree privilege' to the law school, obliging its graduates to write only the examination in practice and procedure after completing service in articles, before being called to the bar. The reputation, heroic efforts, and long tenure of its first dean, Richard Chapman Weldon (1883–1914), and of his second-in-command, Benjamin Russell (1883–1921), helped the institution to survive its first difficult decades.[21]

The Saint John Law School, by contrast, came together with unseemly haste as ethical scandals tarnishing both judges and senior lawyers (see chapter 3) persuaded the New Brunswick bar that a law school would improve the profession's public image and perhaps the ethical standards of future lawyers.[22] What began as a feasibility study by the governors of the University of King's College in June 1892 ended with a law school in Saint John staffed by volunteer lecturers opening its doors in the first week of October. In 1901 the Barristers' Society secured an amendment to the law that enabled graduates of the Saint John Law School to be admitted as attorneys without further examination, although they too had to serve a period as articled clerks, similar to Dalhousie's degree privilege. Unlike Dalhousie, Saint John would not have a full-time dean, a large law library, its own premises on a university campus, or even very many degree students, for quite some time. Nonetheless, the vision of the law school as a community resource rather than a narrowly conceived professional school inspired loyalty and commitment from many quarters of the province. Both Dalhousie and Saint John admitted 'special students,' non-degree candidates of both sexes interested in the law for its own sake or for work-related purposes, in not inconsiderable numbers in their early decades.[23] The Ivy League law schools in the United States, by contrast, had been limiting their student body to degree candidates for some time in the name of enhancing legal professionalism.

University legal education in the Prairie provinces emerged virtually overnight in 1912–14. The University of Alberta Faculty of Law was founded in 1912 (initially a part-time program with concurrent articles), the Saskatchewan College of Law offered its first classes in 1913, and the University of Manitoba created its School of Law in 1914. The coincidence in timing obscures the differing influences at play in each province. In Manitoba the Law Society had offered its own lectures from time to time from 1877, and a regular series by 1908. Demands by students and key members of the elite bar coalesced to create the momentum for a university-affiliated law school, spurred on by the spectre of private law colleges arising in the province. A 1912 university extension bill 'would have permitted a private business to grant degrees by correspondence or instruction in the fields of "law and business."' Such institutions were well known in the United States (albeit disdained by the AALS), enabling a more diverse range of students access to legal education, but the Law Society of Manitoba was entirely opposed to the measure. What emerged in 1914 was a law school run as a sort of joint venture by the University of Manitoba and the Law Society, governed by a board of trustees with equal representation from each institution, but in which the Law Society really called the shots.[24]

The year 1913 saw Saskatchewan endowed with two law schools: a College of Law at the University of Saskatchewan in Saskatoon, and a law school run by the provincial Law Society in Regina. Arthur Moxon, a Rhodes scholar and practising lawyer, and Ira MacKay, a professor of classics and philosophy, provided the College of Law with serious academic heft. In Alberta the Law Society gave lectures in Calgary for a few years in the 1910s, but centralization of legal education in the provincial university in Edmonton won out. In British Columbia the advent of university legal education was impeded by the protracted birth and difficult early years of the University of British Columbia itself, which did not begin classes until 1915. The year before, in response to urgent pleas by articling students, the Law Society created 'law schools' in both Victoria and Vancouver. The Law Society of British Columbia would have preferred to work with UBC, but the university would long have other priorities.[25]

By 1914, then, virtually all Canadian provinces outside Ontario had initiated university legal education, and even the Osgoode Hall Law School, with respect to number of faculty and curriculum, was not so different from the university faculties. In Quebec the bar kept the academy on a very short leash, but elsewhere the law societies afforded the law faculties somewhat more autonomy. Everywhere they survived on a shoestring budget with at most two full-time professors, obliging them to rely on practising lawyers as adjunct professors. Even deans were mostly part-time. Weldon was the first full-time law dean in Canada, followed by Reeve at Osgoode in 1889, though styled 'principal' rather than dean, and Frederick Parker Walton at McGill the third in 1897, his position made possible by a $200,000 endowment provided in 1890 by tobacco magnate William MacDonald. The collective scholarly output of this small professorial cadre was necessarily modest, but occasionally a pearl of scholarship emerged, such as Walton's *Scope and Interpretation of the Civil Code of Lower Canada* (1907). The very existence of these institutions, however, marked a distinct break with the English experience, where law faculties had nothing to do with professional preparation. University legal education was now a North American phenomenon.[26]

Legal Literature

In chapter 4 we discussed the literature on the Quebec civil law. Here we examine writing about the common law and statutes, including the *BNA Act*, by authors from all provinces, including Quebec. The volume of such writing increased exponentially after Confederation, the result of the increase in the size of the profession, and the intrusion of state law into more and more areas of Canadian society. The growth in output was most marked in Ontario and manifest in both books and in journal articles. The great majority of what was produced was written for the practical use of a professional audience, very little for a scholarly community for the simple reason that, as we have seen, the legal professoriate was very small. In this section we will deal first with law books and then with law journals.

Before Confederation legal publishers produced little, mostly lightly annotated rules of court, statutes, and similar productions. While useful for the lawyer in practice, these were not so much written by their titular authors as compiled by them. Such material continued to be published throughout this period; indeed it formed the bulk of books about law. Examples include William Leggo, *Forms and Precedents of Pleadings, and Proceedings in the Court of Chancery for Ontario*, published first in Hamilton in 1872, with a second edition brought out in Toronto by Carswell in 1876. The preface stated that it was intended to cater to 'the practice in this Province,' with material relevant only to England 'carefully eliminated.' At over 1,000 pages it was certainly comprehensive, although its bulk was filled out by forms. Another example from the 1870s, the equivalent for Quebec, was Ivan Wotherspoon's *A Manual of the Practice and Procedure in the Several Courts Having Civil Jurisdiction in the Province of Quebec*.[27] Over time these were increasingly joined by books that were still written for the profession, and still based closely on the statutory or case law sources, but went beyond collation and reproduction to exposition of general principles. Cornelius Masten's book on corporate law published in 1901 and Robert B. Henderson and Peers Davidson's work on partnership are examples from the field of business law; the latter was a co-production by a Toronto and a

Montreal lawyer, and included a chapter on Quebec law.[28] The volume of such literature increased over time, as demonstrated by the business law example: there were four such books published in the 1880s, three in the 1890s, and 10 between 1900 and 1914.[29] They also became more geographically diverse. While nine of these 17 were brought out by Toronto publishers, including all four of those appearing in the 1880s, five were published in Montreal, and one in each of Ottawa, Vancouver, and Calgary. Although most of them devoted considerable space to incorporation under the federal *Incorporation Act*, they also dealt with provincial Acts, including the volume produced in Ottawa, which covered Quebec law.[30] We have used the example of the law relating to the formation and operation of types of business enterprises, but the same trends are evident in a variety of fields: insolvency, commercial law, banking, insurance, real estate transactions, and procedure, the last especially focused on the provincial *Judicature Acts* and the fusion of law and equity, discussed in chapter 3.

The growth in law book production was not limited to private law, economic activity, and procedure. Public law books were principally about municipal and criminal law, although a small literature on constitutional law also emerged. Books on municipal law were often aimed at municipal officials as much as lawyers.[31] As discussed in chapter 13, the federal government very quickly legislated a national criminal law after Confederation, and Samuel Robinson Clarke's *A Treatise on Criminal Law, as Applicable to the Dominion of Canada*, published in 1872, was the first response to this change in the legal landscape. It was followed by books written by judges, Henri-Elzéar Taschereau and George Wheelock Burbidge, in the 1870s and 1880s, the former describing itself modestly as 'hardly anything else but a compilation,' although each clause of a statute was followed by an explanation of its meaning and 'the rules of pleading, practice and evidence applicable to it.' After the *Criminal Code* was passed in 1892, Taschereau published a book on it, as did James Crankshaw shortly thereafter.[32] Constitutional law was represented by a small coterie of authors. As discussed in chapter 2, Quebec judge Thomas Jean-Jacques Loranger brought out his *Letters on the Interpretation of the Federal Constitution* in 1883, and a year later Jeremiah Travis of Saint John wrote to refute his arguments. Dennis O'Sullivan followed with his *Government in Canada* three years later, and William Henry Pope Clement published *The Law of the Canadian Constitution* in 1894. Unquestionably the major constitutional treatise, Augustus Henry Lefroy's *The Law of Legislative Power in Canada*, appeared in 1898.[33]

All the books mentioned to this point were about local law. In this period Canadian authors did not write texts about the pillars of Anglo-Canadian common law, contracts, property, and the still emerging field of tort law. Lawyers had to rely on the standard texts, mostly English but some American, sometimes augmented with Canadian cases, such as Fry's book on specific performance and Odgers on evidence.[34] No book on Canadian contract law was published until 1914, and even then the author and most of the cases were English.[35] The same was true for torts, still not a well-developed specialty even in England, and the first Canadian-authored publication in this period was Joseph MacDougall, *Law Lectures on the Subject of Torts and Negligence*, a slim volume of under 200 pages, published in 1882 and consisting of transcriptions of his lectures to students at Osgoode Hall Law School. He made it clear that there was no 'originality in the text,' as the lectures had been prepared 'in the midst of the duties demanded of a busy professional man' who had done no more than to 'select freely from well-known text writers.' A more substantial text on torts was published in 1908, although it was like the contracts volume noted above, an English book with Canadian cases.[36] Real property law was treated similarly. Some English classics with annotations to Canadian cases and statutes were produced, but the basic exposition was written by English authors for an English audience.[37] One exception in this area was title registration, where the local law was different, especially in provinces that had introduced the Torrens system, discussed in chapter 14. Some books in this area were published in the West, where Torrens was dominant.[38]

These authors were representative of a coterie of individuals who emerged in this period that we can legitimately call the lawyer-scholars of their time. Based mostly in Toronto and Montreal but also in Ottawa, Quebec City, Winnipeg, Victoria, Saint John, and Halifax, they practised law and also wrote seriously about both law and its practice.[39] They were not what we would now call interdisciplinary scholars, they did traditional internal legal scholarship, parsing the cases, thinking about where statutory reform of the common law was needed, offering critical analyses of judgments in light of precedent and principle, though seldom in light of policy, at least overtly. They not only wrote books, but also contributed articles to the law journals, few in number at Confederation but augmented by the addition in particular of the *Canadian Law Times* from 1881. Some of them also taught part-time at McGill, Laval, Manitoba, Dalhousie, and Osgoode Hall.

A typical example was Edward Douglas Armour. His *Treatise on the Investigation of Titles to Real Estate in Ontario, with a Precedent for an Abstract*, known as *Armour on Titles*, was written in 1887, 11 years after he was called to the bar. He practised for a few years with Alexander Leith, a leading authority on real estate who himself was an author, and then formed his own firm and quickly established a reputation as a leading practitioner in the field. *Armour on Titles* went through three further editions in 1894, 1903, and 1925. The last was published three years after his death, under the joint names of Armour and his son Archibald. *Armour on Titles* was, like the vast majority of law books published in this period, a text for somebody practising real estate transactions, a combination of descriptive explanations and a 'how to' manual, replete with case and statutory references. As the example of Archibald Armour suggests, not unlike other Canadian lawyers who wrote about law in this period he belonged to a multi-generational legal family, although he was more connected to the upper rungs of the legal establishment than many. His father was a lawyer, and his uncle was John Douglas Armour, the leading lawyer in eastern Ontario who was appointed to Queen's Bench in 1877, to chief justice of that Court in 1887, to the Court of Appeal as chief justice in 1900, and to the SCC in 1902. Edward Armour also had brothers and cousins and sons who were lawyers. He never ceased practising, and in addition to also writing books he founded the *Canadian Law Times*, which he edited for 19 years, and taught real property and constitutional law at Osgoode Hall Law School from its opening in 1889 until 1910. His teaching and writing earned him an honorary doctorate from his alma mater, Trinity College, in 1902.[40]

Another prominent legal family who also contributed to the burgeoning stock of Canadian law books was the Hodgins family, John George Hodgins, Egerton Ryerson's right-hand man in running the Ontario school system for decades, and his brother and two of his sons. John George was a lawyer who never practised, but he wrote about the law pertaining to schools. His brother Thomas penned two books, on election law and on bills of exchange. One son, William Egerton Hodgins, a lawyer with the Department of Justice who married Eleanor, daughter of Sir William Johnstone Ritchie, chief justice of Canada, was much more a compiler of sources than an original author. He put together a massive collection of documents related to disallowance and used throughout this book, as well as a *Synopsis of the Provisions of the [Federal] Companies Act Relating to the Incorporation of Joint Stock Companies.*

Another son, Frank Egerton Hodgins, who was appointed directly to the Court of Appeal from the bar in 1912, wrote books on life insurance contracts.[41]

The leading star in this firmament of lawyer-scholars was John Skirving Ewart. He has been aptly described as a minor player in the political history of this period but a 'formidable legal scholar.'[42] He was a nephew of Oliver Mowat, called to the bar in 1870. He practised in Toronto for a decade before moving to Winnipeg in 1881, where he became one of the leading counsel. Ewart represented the Catholics in the struggle for minority language educational rights, a subject discussed in detail in chapter 16. He moved back to Ottawa in 1904 and continued with his practice, but slowly allowed it to lapse while he concentrated on a campaign for greater Canadian independence from Britain, writing several books on that subject. He was also a regular contributor to the *Canadian Law Times* on subjects as varied as chattel mortgages and restrictive covenants.[43] In Winnipeg he founded the *Manitoba Law Journal* in 1884. The area in which he made his mark was the law of estoppel. He wrote a series of articles about it in the later 1890s and in 1900 produced a major book, *An Exposition of the Principles of Estoppel by Misrepresentation*.[44] It has been described as 'among the best legal scholarship done in Canada between Confederation and the 1920s,' the work of 'a powerful and insightful figure.' At the time estoppel 'was composed of inconsistent and incomplete fragments,' and Ewart was able to 'construct a coherent and unified structure from this jumble.' His work has been compared to, and placed alongside, the major English writers of the day who sought to impose unity and coherence on the common law, not by arguing for statutory reform of doctrine derived from cases but by organizing the cases around the underlying principles in what its proponents described as a scientific manner.[45]

Moving from law books to law journals, at Confederation there were only two legal journals published in the four confederating provinces. The Toronto-based *Canada Law Journal*, which had operated since 1855 as the *Upper Canada Law Journal* and changed its name in 1868 to mark the new political arrangements, published continuously until 1922 when it and the *Canadian Law Times*, discussed below, merged to become the *Canadian Bar Review*. It was devoted to legal news of all kinds and to case law, more than to sustained commentary or analysis on particular topics, though it did contain some articles of that nature. It published numerous short editorial notes, as many as 10 per monthly issue, on case law, legislative developments, changes in court personnel, and the like. Several times a year it devoted a section to a review of recent English cases in addition to its accounts of Canadian case law. The other substantial legal journal in the new dominion was *La Revue légale*, subtitled *Recueil de jurisprudence et d'arrêts*, a collection of jurisprudence and case law, published in Quebec. It was founded in Sorel just after Confederation, in 1869, and in its early years provided case reports from elsewhere in Canada on matters of federal law, as well as occasional French, American, and English cases, and short analytical notes on discrete topics. It soon became a more targeted publication, however, restricting itself mainly to Quebec cases. Its editor, Michel Mathieu, on the Superior Court from 1881, embellished these with lengthy footnotes that sometimes became almost parallel judgments, in the manner of French law professors. Even with a more local orientation, *La Revue* ceased publication in 1892, but was resurrected by Jean-Joseph Beauchamp as *La Revue Légale, nouvelle série*, in 1895. It repeated the cycle, starting off with a blend of case law and doctrinal analyses written by judges, advocates, and notaries, many by Beauchamp himself, before reverting to a pure collection of case law in 1907; in this form it survived until 2012. In 1898 a second law journal commenced publication, *La Revue du Notariat*, which has continued to the present.

During this period four new journals were launched with varying degrees of success. Three of these – the *Manitoba Law Journal*, its successor the *Western Law Times*, and the Toronto-based *Canadian Law Review* – were short-lived. Of much greater longevity and significance was the *Canadian Law Times*, founded in 1881 by Edward Douglas Armour and published by Carswell. Armour served as editor from the outset until 1900. More serious and with national and international, not just regional, content, the *Times* lasted for 41 years until the merger with the *Canada Law Journal*. In the 1880s Armour frequently editorialized on the need for a law school run by the Law Society, and when one was established in 1889 he became a principal lecturer, like all the faculty other than Principal William Albert Reeve on a part-time basis. The *Times* published 17 issues in its first year, but quickly went to monthly issues, and from 1908 until the end of our period it published 1,000 or more pages a year.

Each issue combined brief reports of cases from provincial courts across the country and from the SCC, as well as book reviews, law society news, announcements of judicial appointments and retirements, and correspondence. After a few years the final issue of each year was over 100 pages long and almost entirely comprised of news and cases from every province's courts, and occasionally from those of

Newfoundland. Most importantly, each volume also contained articles of various lengths, some substantial pieces of 20 or more pages, but most slightly fewer than 10. Some were more than 50 pages in total because longer pieces were published in multiple parts. Some were reprinted from other law journals, American and English. They were generally doctrinal analyses, sometimes extended case commentaries, very much in the vein of the scholarship that dominated law reviews until some 30 years ago and still regularly appears. The subject matter was extremely broad – all areas of public and private law, the legal profession, and some international law. A majority of the articles appeared as notes, unattributed, even some long and multi-part ones, but every issue had at least one or two attributed articles.

As one might expect, a number of the book authors already discussed contributed regularly to the *Times* and indeed may have written more than it appears because they might also have written unattributed notes. But counting only attributed pieces we find Frank Hodgins as the author of 15 articles and his uncle Thomas of 10. Ewart was a 19-time contributor, and George Smith Holmested, registrar of the Ontario Supreme Court,[46] and Lefroy composed six and five articles. Other major contributors among the book writers were Charles Morse (10 articles) who also published *Apices Juris and Other Legal Essays in Prose and Verse*, a collection of his previously published and unpublished essays about substantive law, legal history, and, perhaps a first in Canada, law and literature.[47] Only one of the people the *Times* published was definitely a woman, one Margaret Center Klinglesmith, but her contributions were reprints of articles she had written in American journals.[48] One of the two most prolific authors, with 28 attributed articles, was Silas Alward. A New Brunswicker, he studied at Acadia and Brown Universities, was called to the New Brunswick bar in 1866 and was elected mayor of Saint John 1866–9. He practised law in Saint John, represented that city in the provincial legislature from 1887 to 1889, and was on the faculty of the Saint John Law School. He turned to serious scholarship only as he was retiring from politics at almost 60 years of age. The first of his 28 articles in the *Times* was published in 1898, and he averaged two a year between then and 1914. He wrote about estoppel, expropriation, adverse possession, contributory negligence, trustees, and that was only in 1898 and 1899. Tort law was his principal interest – general principles, libel, nuisance, and *Rylands v Fletcher*. A little standard English legal history leavened the doctrine, as did articles on malice and impossible excuses. He deserves to be better known.[49]

Not surprisingly, given Edward Armour's dual roles as editor and lecturer, there was a strong link between the law school that started in Osgoode Hall in 1889 and the pages of the *Times*. Armour himself did not publish a single article under his name, though it is not unlikely that he contributed short anonymous notes. But others connected to the school did so. The first principal, William Albert Reeve, penned only two articles, one of which was his inauguration address, but his successor, Newman Hoyles, wrote 19 between 1896 and 1910. He wrote on legal education, not surprisingly, but also on receivers, lunatics' estates, the *Civil Code*, naturalization, labour law, estoppel, res judicata, and maintenance. John Delatre Falconbridge and Shirley Denison, who joined the faculty in 1910 and 1911 respectively, each wrote for the *Times* six times before and after they started at Osgoode Hall, and each also authored law books. Falconbridge taught at Osgoode for 44 years, later becoming dean. Neither Christopher Robinson nor Samuel Bradford, who joined in 1912 and 1913 respectively, wrote for the *Times* before their appointments or in the year or two afterwards, suggesting that publishing was not a route to law teaching or seen as a necessary activity once one became a law teacher.

It was, however, clearly a passion for the single most prolific contributor to the *Times*, Alfred Henry Marsh, who was on the Osgoode Hall staff from the founding of the school in 1889 until 1912. Before joining the faculty he practised law and regularly indulged his interests in writing about a wide range of subjects. Between 1881 and 1889 he published 18 articles in the *Times*, seven of them multi-part pieces. Eleven were about mortgages and real estate transactions, and three were on the division of powers and international law. In 1889 he was appointed equity lecturer at Osgoode, and henceforth he made that something of a specialty, writing a further 21 articles up to 1904. He wrote frequently about equity generally, and about mortgages, trusts, and perpetuities, but also branched out into the JCPC, company law, and the revised statutes of Ontario's treatment of English statutes in force. He also published his lectures on equity as a short book.[50] It is not known why he stopped publishing in the *Times* in 1904 but continued teaching for another eight years. No writer about the common law published as much as he did in the 1880s and 1890s, and of course he may have placed articles in other journals that we have not located. Canada has not generally been thought of as a place where significant legal scholarship on the common law took place in this period. There were notable exceptions in Ewart and Lefroy, who published major books. To their names we should perhaps add those of Alward and Marsh, whose work appeared in short articles, not books, and was doctrinal but still serious legal scholarship.

Professional Governance: The 'Canadian Model' Established

In 1867 law societies with statutory powers to compel membership and regulate members' conduct existed in only two provinces. By 1914 all provinces except Prince Edward Island, as well as Newfoundland, had adopted this model. It was a Canadian invention. The Incorporated Law Society in England (for solicitors) and state bar associations in the United States were voluntary societies to which a minority of the profession belonged. The Canadian model represented a transfer of authority from the courts, which had previously regulated both admission to the bar and discipline, to the bar itself. While the transfer was not total – courts still possessed some disciplinary authority over lawyers, and legislatures still occasionally admitted applicants by private act – the direction of the shift to self-regulation was unmistakeable.[51]

Unlike the situation with university legal education, it was the West that moved first, with the Maritimes and Newfoundland following some time later. Virtually all of Manitoba's early lawyers were from Ontario or advocates or notaries from Quebec, so it is not surprising that they reproduced the model they knew in the *Law Society Act* of 1877. Ontario likely also provided the model for the Law Society of British Columbia, which was incorporated by legislation in 1874 and its governance vested in five benchers, as well as a secretary and treasurer. Membership was effectively made compulsory in 1884, explicitly in 1895. An 1873 Act permitting anyone to appear as advocate for another in the inferior courts, as the result of a shortage of lawyers in less settled areas, presented a significant inroad on the Law Society's monopoly and long remained a cause of complaint. Lawyers from the United States and other provinces allegedly exploited this loophole to carry on practice in the hinterland without paying fees to the society or being subject to its rules.[52]

In the North-West Territories there were no real restrictions on practising law prior to the passage by the Territorial Council in 1885 of the first *Ordinance Respecting the Legal Profession*. It grand-parented existing practitioners and specified who was entitled to practise in the courts in future, both now labelled 'advocates.' Whether this reflected some Quebec influence is not clear, but the first person to enrol, in January

1886, was Quebec advocate Amédée Forget, who would become lieutenant governor of the North-West Territories in 1898. The ordinance, under which 186 men were admitted as advocates, did not endow the legal profession with any powers of self-regulation. That was left for an ordinance of 1898, passed after the Territories achieved responsible government the previous year. It incorporated the Law Society of the North-West Territories, provided that it would be governed by nine elected benchers, at least one to be drawn from each judicial district, made membership in the society mandatory, and specified the acts over which advocates possessed a monopoly. Its powers were similar to those of the Law Society of Upper Canada, save that discipline was left entirely with the courts except for a 1904 amendment authorizing the benchers to strike a convicted felon from the roll. On the eve of Alberta and Saskatchewan's provincehood the next year, there were some 300 lawyers enrolled with the society. *Legal Profession Acts* of 1907 endowed the two new provincial law societies with the same powers as the 1898 ordinance, with disciplinary power still left largely with the courts. Lawyerly nomenclature was now changed from 'advocate' to 'barrister and solicitor,' presumably to demonstrate affinity with the existing provinces.[53]

Despite having voluntary Barristers' Societies established as far back as 1825, Nova Scotia and New Brunswick were slow to transform them into statutory regulatory bodies. Resistance arose from rural-urban tensions, where 'country' lawyers did not wish to be taxed by a provincial body in return for the dubious privilege of being ruled by what they saw as an urban clique. Such tensions arose in Ontario as well, where a rural lawyer lamented in 1891, 'I object to pay a tax to maintain a library for Toronto lawyers, pay for lunches for benchers and dancing parties for Toronto swells, and get nothing for it.'[54] Both in Nova Scotia and Ontario, associations of lawyers arose to challenge the dominance of their law societies. The Provincial Barristers' Association in Nova Scotia disappeared early in the twentieth century, while the Ontario Bar Association survived by becoming a social and advocacy body for lawyers. In Nova Scotia, it was only the determination of Attorney General J.W. Longley, who had spent some time at Osgoode Hall early in his career, that ensured final passage of the 1899 statute giving the Barristers' Society authority over the entire bar. The society would be governed by 'councillors,' not 'benchers,' as would its New Brunswick counterpart. There, the same ethical scandals that motivated the creation of the law school in 1892 led the legislature to vest regulatory powers over all lawyers, including some disciplinary power, in the Barristers' Society in 1903. The change had come earlier in Newfoundland (1889), where the governors of the Law Society of Newfoundland were called 'benchers' individually and 'convocation' collectively, as in Ontario.[55]

These statutes at first gave law societies authority over admission, education, relations with external bodies, and management of the capital amassed from members' fees. Adding discipline to the list was a relatively late and incremental development. While the Law Society of Upper Canada had disbarred barristers as far back as the 1820s, it did not acquire statutory power over discipline until 1876 and shared it with the courts until the 1920s. British Columbia was precocious in giving disciplinary powers to its Law Society. In 1874 it was given 'full power' to discipline any barrister or attorney, up to and including disbarment, subject to an appeal to the Supreme Court of British Columbia, and the Quebec Barreau possessed similar powers. The Law Society of Newfoundland acquired similar powers in 1889, while in the Prairie provinces discipline would not be granted to the law societies until after 1914. In fact, even those law societies possessing such power, such as the Law Society of Upper Canada, were not enthusiastic about exercising it, usually did so only where client funds were misappropriated, and responded more often to complaints from other lawyers than from clients.[56] Those alleging negligence by their lawyers were always told to seek their remedy in court. The Law Society did not police standards of practice outside of actual dishonesty or conduct unbecoming the profession.

Members of the law societies' governing bodies were elected for terms of one to five years, but the oldest law society in Canada was the last to adopt representative democracy. Most Law Society of Upper Canada benchers had life appointments, and convocation itself selected their replacements, until legislation of 1871 finally forced elective governance upon the society. Thirty benchers at large would now serve five-year terms, but electoral governance did not necessarily do away with oligarchy. There was nothing to prevent corporate law firms from dominating law society councils, as they appear to have done in Ontario and Manitoba at least. In 1891, for example, nine out of 30 elected benchers in Ontario came from three large firms. In Manitoba, retiring presidents and those who had served five terms as benchers were awarded life bencherships; most of these came from large firms. In Nova Scotia, meanwhile, there was pushback against large firm dominance, a reaction to the long tenure of corporate lawyer (and future prime minister) Robert Borden as president from 1896 to 1903. At first country members challenged Halifax's ascendancy in society affairs: in 1904 council was doubled to 24 members, each county outside Halifax electing one member and Cape Breton two. In 1908 one legislative amendment limited a president to serving two consecutive one-year terms before sitting out two years, while another prohibited more than one member of any firm from being elected to any council position. As a result, unlike Ontario and Manitoba, large-firm representation remained in balance with that of sole practitioners and small partnerships for decades to come.[57]

The organization of the Quebec bar followed the generally decentralized mode of the Quebec courts, noted in chapter 3. There was a general corporation for the bar of Quebec, headed by the bâtonnier of the province of Quebec, but also regional sections (four at Confederation, six in 1888, seven by 1909), each constituted as a separate corporation with its own bâtonnier. The provincial-level council comprised all the regional bâtonniers as well as up to 10 other delegates from the sections. Each section held annual elections for its council members, who chose the delegates to the provincial council. With this arrangement there was perhaps less chance for the larger urban firms to dominate than in other provinces with a sole provincial governing body, whose members were elected at large. The eight-member council for Montreal's section, however, had to have one member representing the 'country districts' within its jurisdiction, suggesting some attempt to avoid such a monopoly of representation. The powers of the Quebec bar over admission, legal education, discipline, and fees were the most extensive of any provincial bar society, elaborately set out in its governing statute.[58]

While the spread of statutory self-governance for lawyers across Canada is an important theme in this period, the growth of county and local law associations, independent of the law societies, should not be ignored. Local associations attuned to local conditions could serve as 'sensitive antennae to ascertain and pass on problems to the [provincial] Governing Body.'[59] In Ontario, county law associations maintained local law libraries and promulgated minimum fee schedules. In British Columbia they emerged in the 1890s and passed on proposals for reform, such as a desire for the Torrens system of land registration. In Quebec, the local 'sections' of the Barreau may have served similar functions. More research into relations between these local associations and the provincial governing bodies is needed to understand how the Canadian model of self-government maintained its sway for so long.[60]

Where notaries were concerned, the decentralized system of three regional chambers created in 1847 did not prove successful. There was no unity of approach, and examinations were not administered rigorously. In 1870 a complete revision was undertaken, and a sole Chambre des notaires for the entire province was created. It tried to raise educational standards and advocated for more training in commercial matters and accountancy for notaries, given that they were now being called upon more often to act as financial advisors. The Chambre also tried to implement a system for inspecting notarial greffes, to ensure that crucial documents were being safely stored for the long term. Its record of success in these matters was mixed, as a tradition of notarial independence did not accord with the Chambre's attempts at regulation. The Chambre's efforts were also hampered by the relative poverty of large sections of the notariat. In 1898 one-quarter of its members refused to pay the $4 annual fee to the Chambre, further hampering its efforts to improve the state of the profession. Acceptance of remuneration far below the profession's fee schedule also led to a race to the bottom that changed direction only after the supply of notaries began to decline around the turn of the century.[61]

Towards Diversity?

The late nineteenth- and early twentieth-century bar was composed almost entirely of white males, but the barriers of gender, race, and ethnicity were finally breached, albeit barely. This period saw several 'firsts,' but the numbers of non-traditional lawyers in the Canadian bar by 1914 were still minuscule. Formal impediments to the entry of certain racial groups, such as Chinese, Japanese, and South Asians, would remain in place for decades in British Columbia and were mirrored in the increasing restrictiveness of Canadian immigration policy regarding non-white peoples in the early twentieth century, discussed in chapter 16. Meanwhile, the substandard education provided to most Indigenous students ensured that they were not able to pass the qualifying examinations to enter apprenticeships, which included a knowledge of Latin, while the fact that an Indigenous person would lose Indian status upon joining the legal profession was a powerful disincentive to those few who might have overcome such barriers. Some nonetheless did so, as we will see in chapter 8.

James Robinson Johnston, the first Black lawyer called
to the bar in Nova Scotia, in 1900.

Credit: *Dictionary of Canadian Biography.*

Black populations remained small in the dominion, but a few Black lawyers followed the lead of Jamaican immigrant Robert Sutherland, who had been called to the Ontario bar in 1855. Abraham Walker, descended from a Saint John Black Loyalist, obtained a law degree from the National University in Washington, DC, and was called to the New Brunswick bar in 1882. He would later be the first person to enrol in the new Saint John Law School, of which he spoke very highly. Delos Rogest Davis, son of an American slave who had escaped to Upper Canada via the underground railroad, was called to the bar of Ontario in 1886 and practised in Amherstburg until his retirement in 1909, while his son Frederick would be Ontario's next Black lawyer. And James Robinson Johnston of Halifax graduated from Dalhousie Law School in 1898 and was called to the bar of Nova Scotia in 1900. All encountered racism in

The second woman lawyer in Canada, Mabel French (1881–1955) battled authorities twice to secure bar admission, first in New Brunswick (1907) and then in British Columbia (1912). She practised law briefly in Vancouver before relocating to England in 1913, where she appears not to have continued her legal career and lived out her life in quiet obscurity.

Credit: *The Canadian Magazine* 39 (June 1912), 140.

various forms. Walker was pointedly excluded from a celebration of the centenary of the New Brunswick bar in 1885 and never obtained the QC that had been promised him by federal and provincial authorities. Davis required two acts of the legislature to get him admitted as a solicitor and barrister, given his inability to find a lawyer willing to act as his principal. He did eventually receive a KC, but only after he retired. Johnston benefitted from the support of elite white patrons, pursued a successful practice, and seems to have suffered least from racism, but his inspiring career was brought to an ignominious halt when he was murdered by his brother-in-law in 1915.[62]

A few Jewish lawyers followed the lead of the Hart family in Quebec, who had pioneered in this respect in the 1830s and 1840s. Early Jewish lawyers were Canadian born and highly educated, and mixed relatively easily in elite circles. Samuel Jacobs, who obtained law degrees from both McGill and Laval, was called to the bar of Quebec in 1894 and named a KC in 1908. In spite of widespread anti-Semitism he managed to become a leader in both the profession and the wider community, ultimately serving as MP for a Montreal riding from 1917 until his death in 1938. He formed practices with lawyers of both French and British descent, as well as other Jewish lawyers, over the course of his career. Jacobs also assisted Annie Macdonald Langstaff in her unsuccessful efforts to qualify for the Quebec bar after she graduated with a BCL from McGill in 1914. Solomon Hart Green, who was related to the Quebec Harts, graduated from the Saint John Law School and was called to the New Brunswick bar in 1906. He became the first Jewish lawyer in western Canada when he moved to Winnipeg, pursued a successful practice there, and sat in the legislative assembly from 1910 to 1914. Lionel Davis, descended from one of Toronto's oldest Jewish families, joined the prominent firm of Beatty Blackstock in 1904 as an articling student, then stayed as an associate until 1913 before launching his own firm. Several other Jewish lawyers called to the bar in Ontario between 1890 and 1914 also had a much easier time of it than would the children of poor Eastern European immigrants who arrived in Canada in the early twentieth century. In British Columbia, Samuel Davies Schultz became the first Jewish judge in Canada when named to the county court in 1914.[63]

Francophone lawyers of course dominated in Quebec, but elsewhere found entering the profession difficult. Pierre-Amand Landry was the first Acadian called to the bar in New Brunswick (1871), and although followed by eight more by 1900, the ratio of Acadian lawyers to the Acadian population was still highly unfavourable, 1:10,000 compared to 1:1100 in the anglophone areas of the province. Landry was appointed to the County Court in 1890, the Supreme Court in 1893, and as chief justice of King's Bench after the reorganization of the Supreme Court in 1913, but was still the sole Acadian on the bench at that point. In Ontario, francophone lawyers slowly emerged in Ottawa and French-speaking communities in the north and southwest. They seemed to have more success in western Canada, where some Quebec immigrants and local francophones secured leading roles. Marc-Amable Girard, for example, a notary from Quebec, became the first premier of Manitoba under responsible government in 1874, and three Quebec-born francophones featured prominently in its early judiciary.[64]

The entry of women into the legal profession was even more controversial than that of men of colour. Decades went by after the admission of Arabella Mansfield to the Iowa bar in 1869 as the first female lawyer in the United States, without any corresponding movement in Britain or the empire. Not until fifty years later would the *Sex Disqualification (Removal) Act* of 1919 open the legal professions to women in Britain.

As is so often the case, Canada occupied a middle position: when Clara Brett Martin was called to the bar of Ontario in 1897 she was the first woman lawyer in the empire. Legislation championed by Premier Oliver Mowat himself was required to force a reluctant Law Society to admit Martin first as a student-at-law and subsequently as a barrister. Four more women would be called to the bar of Ontario before 1914, while Mabel Penery French would be the first woman lawyer in New Brunswick (1907) and British Columbia (1912), only after a series of struggles similar to Martin's.[65] These women did not grace the pages of the law journals of the day, but both Martin and French wrote on legal issues affecting women in publications of the National Council of Women. And while Marie Lacoste Gérin-Lajoie, the daughter and wife of lawyers, could not join the profession in Quebec, she was an important popularizer of family law in that province. The 'apostolat juridique' of this self-taught jurist included treatises and articles on law aimed at a lay audience, and a variety of lectures and courses.

A trickle of women and minorities into the legal profession did little to alter the image of the ideal lawyer as a Christian (preferably Protestant) white (preferably northern European) male, while a focus on heroic 'firsts' ignores the plight of those who may have aspired to join the legal profession but were unable to because of racism, sexism, or economic barriers. Aside from Jewish lawyers, who began to join the profession in greater numbers after the war, the trickle of non-traditional lawyers would remain so for decades to come. The 'face' of the legal profession was changing, slowly and tentatively, in the decades around 1900. It would take many more decades before the nature of legal professionalism itself, based on centuries of white male practice, began to be unpacked, re-examined, and challenged.[66]

By 1914 the descendants of the colonial bars in the East were still marked by their distinct local legal cultures, but they, along with the new post-Confederation bars in the West, were beginning to coalesce as a national professional group. This was most evident in the formation of the Canadian Bar Association in that year, inspired in part by the existence of the American Bar Association, founded in 1878. While these lawyers participated in the development of a North American 'new professionalism,' characterized by an emphasis on legal science and university legal education, they departed significantly from both English and American models in their model of governance. As of 1914, only 30 per cent of US lawyers belonged to a local or state bar association, while roughly half of English solicitors belonged to the

Incorporated Law Society in 1900. Barristers were in theory governed through their Inns, but their powers were as obscure as the origins of the Inns themselves. In Canada and Newfoundland, all lawyers except those in Prince Edward Island had to belong to a statutorily created provincial law society if they wished to practice law.[67] As creatures of statute, these law societies were obliged to maintain good relations with their respective provincial governments and generally did so. The presence of the attorney general as an ex officio member of their governing bodies provided a potent reminder of the role of the public interest in law society deliberations.

This collective approach appealed to some US Progressive-era reformers who felt that the lack of effective governance of US lawyers was detrimental to the interests of lawyers, their clients, and the public. The most effective of these reformers was Herbert Harley, who founded the American Judicature Society in 1913. Harley visited the Law Society of Upper Canada and Ontario courts in that year, corresponded with bar societies in other provinces, and lobbied state lawmakers relentlessly to pass legislation creating integrated or unified bars on the Canadian model. He scored his first win with the Bar Society of North Dakota in 1921, whose constitutive law was modelled directly on Saskatchewan's, and many more states would follow in later years. Even so, relations between the legal profession and state governments were and would remain much more fraught in the United States than in Canada.[68]

In their daily practice of law, Canadian and American lawyers had much more in common than either had with English lawyers. In both countries, the business side of law surged ahead with the growth of the large corporate law firm in the late nineteenth century, and the golden age of the small-town law firm faded as the number of lawyers contracted (aside from western Canada) in the early twentieth. In professional education, too, Canada was becoming more like the United States. University law schools were still minor players in legal education in Canada in 1914, but they were poised to claim a larger place in the post-war world. For the moment, however, virtually all published legal scholarship was the product of scholarly minded lawyers and judges, not academics.

PART TWO

Indigenous Peoples and the New Dominion

7

Canadian Law and Indigenous Peoples I: The Métis, the Numbered Treaties, British Columbia, and the Rebellion

Canada's history of Indigenous-settler relations has been divided into three periods. Cooperation came first, before Confederation, and was followed first by coercion, starting in the half-century after 1867, and then by confrontation, in the second half of the twentieth century.[1] This alliterative chronology, like all such efforts, tends to downplay the extent to which change is always accompanied by continuity but is nonetheless apt for this period. In the period covered by this volume Indigenous peoples lost control of vast amounts of their land base and were subjected to sustained efforts by the new dominion to transform their economies, way of life, and cultural beliefs – efforts that utilized, among other things, the power of the law.

Canadian government policy in the first half-century after Confederation is discussed largely in the two chapters that follow this one. This chapter is about the establishment and consolidation of Canadian sovereignty in the Prairie West region, and the tensions between the federal government and British Columbia. The first section deals with the region known as Assiniboia or the Red River colony, which entered Confederation in 1870 as the country's fifth province, Manitoba. The second section principally examines the making of seven treaties, known as the numbered treaties, between 1871 and 1877, between Canada and many Indigenous nations living between the Ontario border and the Rocky Mountains, as well as Treaties 8 through 11, signed between 1899 and 1921, dealing with more northerly areas. The principal legal effect of these treaties for the Canadian government was the extinguishment of Indigenous title to most of the land. Where Indigenous title was extinguished, the land became Crown land and available to be granted to settlers of European origin. Where Indigenous title was not extinguished, the land remained, in Canadian law, subject to that title and set aside for, or reserved for, the Indigenous inhabitants. The third topic in this chapter also centrally concerns Indigenous title. When British Columbia, a colony of European settlement, joined Confederation in 1871, it had signed only a handful of treaties with the Indigenous inhabitants, all in the early 1850s and covering only a small part of Vancouver Island. Indigenous title had not been extinguished to the vast majority of the province, and after 1871 the provincial government did not accept that there was such a thing as Indigenous title in British Columbia. The result was a dispute between the provincial and federal governments that lasted not just throughout this period but until the Supreme Court of Canada's decision in *Calder v Attorney-General of British Columbia* in 1973. The final topic addressed in this chapter is the Northwest Rebellion of 1885, principally its legal aspects; we discuss the legal proceedings following the rebellion, principal among which was the trial and execution of Louis Riel.

The Métis, the Red River Resistance, and the Founding of Manitoba

Although Confederation did not include the West, section 146 of the *BNA Act* allowed for the future admission into the new dominion of British Columbia and Prince Edward Island and, on an address from Parliament to the Crown, of 'Rupert's Land and the North-western Territory, or either of them.'[2] In December 1867 a series of resolutions passed in the Commons in favour of the addition of Rupert's Land, in response to which Britain insisted that any transfer had to be negotiated with the HBC.[3] An agreement that the HBC would surrender its rights to Britain, which would then transfer the land to Canada, was made easier by the fact that Britain was as keen to divest itself of the region as Canada was to acquire it. Canada paid the company £300,000, and the HBC also received the land around HBC posts to a maximum of 50,000 acres and one-twentieth of the land in the 'fertile belt' where future white settlement was expected. In June 1869 Parliament legislated that the region would be known as the 'North-West Territories' and administered by a lieutenant governor and council.[4] The deed of transfer was signed in mid-November 1869 and intended to take effect very shortly afterwards. But it did not become effective until 15 July 1870, because of the events discussed here, which resulted from the fact that before 1870 none of the people living between Ontario and British Columbia took any part in the discussions. Macdonald himself recognized the problem for the inhabitants of Red River, telling Cartier that 'no explanation' had been given 'of the arrangement by which the country is handed over to the Queen.... All these poor people know is that Canada has bought the country from the Hudson's Bay Company and that they are handed over like a flock of sheep to us.'[5]

The inhabitants of the Red River region were not sheep. In 1867 they were some 12,000 people, 80 per cent of whom were Métis.[6] The origins and history of the Métis and the Red River colony were discussed in *Volume 1*;[7] what matters for current purposes is that by the 1860s they saw themselves as a distinct community, united by their mixed-race ethnic origin, culture, and attachment to place.* They believed they should be part of the process that brought the area into Confederation, and that the terms of any such union – for that is how they viewed the 'acquisition' of the territory – must include provincial status and protection for the French language and their land rights. In 1869 that view was not shared by the government of Canada or by the small number of settlers who since the early 1860s had been moving into Manitoba from the east, largely from Ontario. These 'Ontario expansionists' saw the HBC lands as their natural next frontier to conquer and held views about the future of the region diametrically opposed to those of the Métis. Known locally as the Canadian party, they wanted a new province settled by British and Ontario Protestant immigrants. Within Ontario they were supported by the Reform Party and the Orange Order, and its members were strongly, indeed as time would show, virulently, anti-French and anti-Catholic.

The lieutenant governor appointed under the 1869 Act was William McDougall, a Toronto lawyer and journalist and a somewhat inconsistent adherent to the Reform Party. He had been Upper Canada's commissioner of Crown lands in the early to mid-1860s, during which time he repossessed reserves on Manitoulin Island and developed his belief that Indigenous people stood in the way of 'progress.' A supporter of the Macdonald-Brown coalition, he was rewarded by being made minister of public works. He accompanied Cartier to London in 1868 to negotiate the deal with the HBC, took the lead in putting the resolutions through the Commons in late 1867 that called for the incorporation of

---

* A map of the Red River colony showing its parish divisions accompanies chapter 14.

the HBC lands into Canada, and was made lieutenant governor in September 1869. He was probably chosen because his cabinet colleagues preferred him to be out of Ottawa, and was a poor choice. Like many in Ontario he believed that before any power was given to local authorities, Manitoba needed a 'settled Canadian population,' that is, a white English Protestant one.

In the three months between McDougall's appointment and the end of 1869 the political situation in Red River was dramatically altered. There is not space here to recount this period in detail, but four events stand out. First, a team of surveyors led by Colonel John Dennis began to lay out survey lines in Red River, sent by McDougall while he was still minister of public works. The survey laid out square sections and cut through the Métis river lots, laid out running back from narrow river frontages. The Métis saw this as ignoring their rights in the land that they held by customary title, not Crown grant. Dennis resided with John Christian Schulz, the leader and vitriolic spokesman for the Canadian party, which did nothing to reassure the locals that it was not part of a wider scheme to take away their land and grant it to incoming settlers.

Second, Louis Riel, son of local Métis notable Jean-Louis Riel, emerged as the principal leader of Métis resistance to the incorporation of Manitoba without negotiations with the Métis and recognition of their rights. A native of Red River who had been educated in Quebec and worked in the law office of rouge notable Rodolphe Laflamme, he was just 24 when he returned to Red River in 1868. Having consolidated his leadership of the Métis against his rival William Dease, he formed the Métis National Committee, which interrupted the survey's work and told the surveyors to leave in October 1869. Riel was summoned before the Council of Assiniboia, the HBC appointed body, which, pending the transfer, was the government, to explain his actions, but ignored the demand. Third, McDougall journeyed west to take up his new post, reaching the US-Canada border at Pembina, Dakota territory, on 30 October 1869. He had received a message from Riel not to enter Red River until the Métis had negotiated with the Canadian government and had also been told the same by Joseph Howe, secretary of state for the provinces. He moved forward nonetheless, until he was met by a Métis force under Ambroise Lépine, Riel's right-hand man, and compelled to retreat.

Finally, and most importantly, in November and December Red River was essentially taken over by the Métis. On 2 November Riel led a force of some 400 Métis into the undefended Fort Garry, the HBC's principal trading post. Ignoring an order from HBC Governor William Mactavish to lay down their arms, the Métis debated extensively how best to proceed in a convention that met intermittently over a two-week period. In early December the convention passed a 14-item 'List of Rights,' which included representation in the Commons, a bilingual local legislature, and a bilingual judge for the 'Superior Court.' There was no specific mention of Métis land rights, but number 14 demanded that 'all privileges, customs and usages existing at the time of transfer be respected.'[8] This List of Rights, the first of four iterations, was a sophisticated political manifesto. It included provisions on who would pay certain costs as between the federal and provincial governments, for the protection of minority language rights, and on the construction of long-distance transportation networks – all like the *BNA Act* and the later BC Terms of Union. It was drawn up by Riel and supported by the anglophone mixed-race community. It was issued almost contemporaneously with the establishment of a provisional government and a 'Declaration of the People of Rupert's Land and the North West,' issued in the names of John Bruce, president of the National Committee of the Métis and of the convention, and Riel, the secretary of the convention.[9]

A central theme of the declaration was that the transfer of Red River to Canada from Britain was illegitimate without the inhabitants' consent. A government 'commands the obedience and respect of its subjects,' but 'a people, when it has no Government, is free to adopt one form of Government, in preference to another, to give or to refuse allegiance to that which is proposed.' The HBC had been acknowledged as the legitimate government until, 'contrary to the law of nations' it 'surrendered and transferred to Canada all the rights which it had … in this Territory, by transactions with which the people were considered unworthy to be made acquainted.' In these circumstances 'fundamental moral principles' provided that 'from the day on which the Government we had always respected abandoned us … the people of Rupert's Land and the North-West became free and exempt from all allegiance to the said Government.' The provisional government was 'the only and lawful authority now in existence in Rupert's Land and the North-West which claims the obedience and respect of the people.' The proclamation then shifted from the illegitimacy of the HBC's actions to Canada's, declaring that it 'refuse[d] to recognize the authority of Canada, which pretends to have a right to coerce us, and impose upon us a despotic form of government.' McDougall had been sent 'to rule us with the rod of despotism,' and his entry resisted 'conformably to that sacred right which commands every citizen to offer energetic opposition to prevent this country from being enslaved.' The proclamation ended on a conciliatory note. The provisional government was ready 'to enter in such negotiations with the Canadian Government as may be favourable for the good government and prosperity of this people.'

The declaration made a powerful case for the innate right of self-determination, founded on the 'Law of Nations,' and stressed the popular origins of the provisional government. It was not simply a Métis government, but one that enjoyed broad support among the inhabitants. It sidestepped the question of Britain's participation in recent events; it was the HBC that had purported to sell what it did not have, and Canada that wrongfully claimed authority. The only mention of Britain came as support for the condemnation of Canada for seeking to impose 'a despotic form of government … contrary to our rights and interests as British subjects.' The declaration avoided any direct break with the Crown and invoked the idea that 'British subjects' had certain inalienable rights. For all that it mirrored the American Declaration of Independence in talk of the right of self-determination, it did not do what that declaration had done – break decisively with the Crown.

The declaration was issued a week after McDougall's final and useless gesture. Ignoring a cable from Ottawa telling him not to enter Red River, he crossed the border in the dead of night and read a proclamation of the transfer of Rupert's Land to Canada to the empty night. Shortly afterwards he decamped to Ottawa, leading Macdonald to note that between them McDougall and Colonel Dennis 'had done their utmost to destroy our chances of an amicable settlement.'[10] The Canadian government was nonetheless hopeful that a settlement could be reached, and its immediate response was a proclamation issued by Governor-General Sir John Young on 6 December offering an amnesty for taking up arms and assuring those who had done so that all their 'civil and religious rights and privileges will be respected' and 'your properties secured to you.'[11]

In the first half of 1870 two parallel processes played out. First, in Red River the provisional government maintained control, despite protests and violence by the Canadian party, which included attempts to assassinate Riel. The most important incident, however, was an act of violence by the provisional government. Thomas Scott was one of about 50 men who joined with Schultz in the latter's fortified store and tried to set up a government opposed to Riel. The store was surrounded, its residents surrendered, and 56 men, including Scott, were taken prisoner. Scott and several others escaped and decamped to Portage La Prairie, a Canadian party enclave, from which they organized an expedition to free the other prisoners and capture Riel. In fact the prisoners were released by Riel at the request of senior HBC official Donald Smith, who was asked by Macdonald to calm matters down. The Portage La Prairie group nonetheless persisted in approaching Fort Garry, where they were captured without violence and confined in the fort. Scott did not quietly accept his situation, insulting and openly displaying his contempt for the Métis. In early March he was put on trial by the provisional government, convicted by an ad hoc tribunal presided over by Ambroise Lépine of 'insubordination' and striking his guards, and executed by firing squad. Allowing this to happen was the one large mistake Riel made. When the news reached Ontario the Canadian party supporters erupted in anger, led by the Orange Lodge, demanding revenge. Edward Blake's liberal provincial government put a $5,000 bounty on Riel's head and to appease Ontario Macdonald ordered a military force to go to Red River.

While all of this was going on, the Métis, francophone and anglophone, agreed at a February convention that they wanted to join Canada so long as their 'rights, properties, usages and customs be respected.'[12] The convention appointed three delegates to negotiate in Ottawa: John Black, an HBC employee and the last president of the General Quarterly Court of Assiniboia; Alfred Scott, a member of the English community in Red River; and Father Noel-Joseph Ritchtôt, a priest seen as a leader among the Métis. The delegation had with them the fourth List of Rights. The earlier clause that 'all privileges, customs and usages existing at the time of transfer be respected' now appeared in a more expansive form, as a demand that 'all properties, rights and privileges enjoyed by us up to this day be respected, and … the recognition of and settlement of customs, usages and privileges be left exclusively to the decision of the Local Legislature.' It also included a guarantee of denominational schooling and a franchise of all males 21 years old who were British subjects and 'possessed of a house.' Specifically excluded from the franchise were 'Indians' because they were 'neither civilized nor settled,' but another clause did require that treaties be concluded between Canada and Indigenous nations. The list did not include an amnesty, probably because it was believed that Young's proclamation would be honoured. But that had been issued before Scott's death, and henceforth Ottawa would not agree to one, given the political repercussions that would ensue in Ontario.

Fourth List of Rights
9 May 1870

1. That this province be governed:
1) By a Lieutenant-Governor, appointed by the Governor-General of Canada;
2) By a Senate;
3) By a Legislature chosen by the people with a responsible ministry.
2. That, until such time as the increase of the population in this country entitle us to a greater number, we have two representatives in the Senate and four in the Commons of Canada.
3. That in entering the Confederation the Province of the Northwest be completely free from the public debt of Canada; and if called upon to assume a part of the said debt of Canada, that it be only after having received from Canada the same amount for which the said Province of the Northwest should be held responsible.
4. That the annual sum of $80,000 be allotted by the Dominion of Canada to the Legislature of the Province of the Northwest.
5. That all properties, rights and privileges enjoyed by us up to this day be respected, and that the recognition and settlement of customs, usages and privileges be left exclusively to the decision of the Local Legislature.
6. That this country be submitted to no direct taxation except such as may be imposed by the local legislature for municipal or other local purposes.
7. That the schools be separate, and that the public money for schools be distributed among the different religious denominations in proportion to their respective populations according to the system of the Province of Quebec.
8. That the determination of the qualifications of members for the parliament of the province or for the parliament of Canada be left to the local legislature.
9. That in this province, with the exception of the Indians, who are neither civilized nor settled, every man having attained the age of 21 years, and every foreigner being a British subject, after having resided three years in this country, and being Possessed of a house, be entitled to vote at the elections for the members of the local legislature and of the Canadian Parliament, and that every foreigner other than a British subject, having resided here during the same period, and being proprietor of a house, be likewise entitled to vote on condition of taking the oath of allegiance. It is understood that this article is subject to amendment, by the local legislature exclusively.
10. That the bargain of the Hudson Bay Company with respect to the transfer of government of this country to the Dominion of Canada, never have in any case an effect prejudicial to the rights of Northwest.
11. That the Local Legislature of this Province have full control over all the lands of the Northwest.
12. That a commission of engineers appointed by Canada explore the various districts of the Northwest, and lay before the Local Legislature within the space of five years a report of the mineral wealth of the country.
13. That treaties be concluded between Canada and the different Indian tribes of the Northwest, at the request and with the co-operation of the Local Legislature.
14. That an uninterrupted steam communication from Lake Superior to Fort Garry be guaranteed to be completed within the space of five years, as well as the construction of a railroad connecting the American railway as soon as the latter reaches the international boundary.

15. That all public buildings and constructions be at the cost of the Canadian Exchequer.
16. That both the English and French languages be common in the Legislature and in the Courts; and that all public documents as well as the acts of the Legislature be published in both languages.
17. That the Lieutenant-Governor to be appointed for the province of the Northwest be familiar with both the English and French languages.
18. That the Judge of the Supreme Court speak the English and French languages.
19. That all debts contracted by the Provisional government of the territory of the Northwest, now called Assiniboia, in consequence of the illegal and inconsiderate measures adopted by Canadian officials to bring about a civil war in our midst, be paid out of the Dominion treasury, and that none of the Provisional government, or any of those acting under them, be in any way held liable or responsible with regard to the movement or any of the actions which led to the present negotiations.

Fourth List of Métis Rights (this page and opposite). The first List of Rights was drawn up principally by Louis Riel and accepted at a convention on 1 December 1869. The second amended list was agreed to by the convention of 40, 20 anglophones and 20 francophones, which met between 25 January and 10 February 1870. The third list was drafted in secret by the executive of the provisional government and given to the delegates who travelled to Ottawa on 22 March 1870. The principal delegate, Father Noel-Joseph Richtôt, carried the fourth list with him to Ottawa. The crucial difference between the first and second lists and the third and fourth was that the former referred to Red River as a territory of Canada; the latter demanded provincial status.

Credit: Lawrence J. Barkwell, "Métis List of Rights: The Evolution of the List from the First to Fourth Iteration," The Virtual Museum of Métis History and Culture.

The negotiations, conducted principally between Cartier and Ritchtôt, Macdonald being seriously ill, took only a few weeks, and the terms agreed were enacted in the *Manitoba Act*, introduced in the Commons on 4 May and receiving royal assent on 12 May.[13] It provided that Manitoba would enter Confederation as a province, with a bicameral legislature (elected assembly and appointed legislative council), French and English as official languages, and a guarantee of denominational schools. By section 30 control of all land was vested in the federal government, but sections 31 and 32 protected existing Métis land rights and provided for future grants to the Métis. The Manitoba that became part of Canada was much smaller than it would become later in the century, approximately 177 by 209 kilometres and known colloquially as the 'postage-stamp province.' The *Manitoba Act* appeared to be a 'win' for the Métis. We will see in later chapters that the guarantee of denominational schools proved illusory (chapter 16), and that Métis land rights were not respected (chapter 14). But this does not take away from the fact that in 1870 the Red River resistance was successful. The Canadian party fought a sustained rearguard action in the Commons over the act, proposing a series of amendments, which were all roundly defeated. The amendments sought to bring the region into Canada as one unit, the North-West Territories, rather than as two, to impose rule by governor and council, without an assembly, and to delete the land clauses. Prominent among the movers of these amendments was McDougall, now the Conservative member for Lanark North. Although the Commons sat until 3 a.m. on one occasion, and the debates were frequently fractious, the bill that was originally presented passed with no significant amendment.[14]

The government had little choice but to agree to Métis demands to ensure a peaceful transition. Yet it also acted inconsistently, to use a neutral term, in preparing and dispatching a military force led by Colonel Garnet Wolseley, a British regular army officer, to Red River while it was negotiating and legislating. It has been argued that sending a representative of the Canadian state was reasonable, that the military could consolidate Canadian authority and maintain order until civil authorities arrived to begin the transition to civilian government. That was how the force was depicted in Governor General Young's closing speech to the parliamentary session; the expedition was an 'errand of peace' and 'assurance to the inhabitants of the Red River settlement … that they … may rely upon the imperial protection of the British sceptre.'[15] Such a view also finds support in the fact that a new lieutenant governor, Adams George Archibald, scion of a prominent Nova Scotia legal and political family and a supporter of Confederation, also went to Red River, arriving only some 10 days after Wolseley issued a proclamation from what is now Thunder Bay promising 'equal protection to the lives and property of all races and all creeds.' But whatever the surface reasonableness of the decision to send troops, and the conciliatory messages to the Métis, Ottawa could not have been unaware of the fact that Wolseley's force of just over 1,000 consisted of some 400 British troops and the remainder volunteer militia from Ontario, the vast majority of them Orangemen. This suggests that the purpose was punitive, or at the very least that the government knew that violence would likely ensue and turned a blind eye to that inevitability. So too does the fact that almost as soon as Archibald arrived, Wolseley and the British regulars left, leaving the Orange militiamen as the occupying force.

Riel, having abandoned hope that news of an amnesty would arrive and persuaded that he would be treated harshly, imprisoned, or possibly worse, left Fort Garry before the army arrived, and a reign of terror was unleashed on the Métis population by the militia. Homes were broken into and searched, numerous Métis were harassed and assaulted, including André Nault, who had commanded the firing squad that shot Scott. He was kicked, stabbed, and left for dead. Two members of the tribunal that had convicted Scott were killed. Archibald refused to assist the Orangemen by issuing an arrest warrant for Riel, but he was also ineffective at controlling their extra-legal behaviour, although he was fully aware of the breakdown in order. 'Many of the Métis,' he told Macdonald, 'have been so beaten and outraged that they feel as if they were living in a state of slavery.'[16] Yet Archibald also sought, and was able to rely on, the assistance of Riel and Lépine in raising a force to oppose a Fenian uprising launched from the United States with the intent of annexing the territory. The Métis gave more to the Archibald administration than they received. Archibald proved to be an ineffective governor. He had difficulty putting together a strong cabinet and disliked and distrusted Schultz and his ilk but thought the Métis were a primitive people who would not, and should not, survive in the face of the advance of civilization. His heart was not in a job that he had taken only on the promise of a seat on the Nova Scotia Supreme Court.[17]

The final act of the Red River resistance was the rebellion of 1885, and that is the subject of the last section of this chapter. In the shorter term, Macdonald's government continued to refuse the promised amnesty, despite pressure from Quebec and a resolution in favour of one from the Manitoba assembly.[18] This refusal gave the Canadian party a legal weapon; an arrest warrant was issued against Riel and Lépine for the murder of Scott. Riel was not tried because he could not be apprehended, but Lépine was arrested in 1873 and tried and convicted in October 1874 before Manitoba Chief Justice Edmund Burke Wood, a Liberal appointee and a man with close connections to Schultz, from whom he had borrowed money as soon as he arrived to buy a palatial residence in Winnipeg.[19] The trial was a 'show trial' much more than it was a criminal proceeding. The question of jurisdiction was a serious one, the defence argument being that the HBC government had resigned in December 1869, and when it did so the law in force was British law. That law required capital felonies committed in Rupert's Land to be tried in the courts of Upper or Lower Canada, pursuant to two early nineteenth-century statutes.[20] When on 15 July 1870 the transfer to Canada was officially completed, Canadian law applied, but the *Manitoba Act* was not retroactive. Hence Lépine could not be tried by a Manitoba court for a capital offence allegedly committed in the interregnum. This was a persuasive argument, amply supported by the authorities, but Wood simply ignored the issue of jurisdiction.

When the trial moved from jurisdictional arguments to the evidence, the case for Lépine having any direct involvement in the murder of Scott proved flimsy in the extreme. The evidence as to whether he was present at Scott's execution was inconclusive, and there was no credible testimony at all to suggest that he was one of those who shot Scott. But the trial was not really about Lépine's culpability but Riel's, and about the legitimacy of the Métis resistance. The defence argued that the provisional government was de facto legitimate in the circumstances, a necessary expedient to keep the peace once the Council of Assiniboia was defunct and no legitimate authority had replaced it. Eight defence witnesses testified to this effect, four of them former members of the Council of Assiniboia. Their effect was muted because Wood refused to allow written evidence of the proceedings of the provisional government and of its correspondence with Ottawa. Wood's address to the jury was a summary of the prosecution case interspersed with denunciations of the provisional government. The jury found Lépine guilty after only a few minutes' deliberation, and the death sentence was automatic.

The Lépine verdict was not appealed, because the defence expected a political resolution, a pardon. and or a general amnesty. The Quebec assembly passed a unanimous resolution for a pardon in December 1874, and a huge number of petitions to the same effect poured into Ottawa, but as with so much else in this story, pressure from expansionist anti-Catholic forces in Ontario meant that the cabinet refused. Governor-General Dufferin, Young's successor, referred the matter to London, where the Privy Council advised that by international law a general amnesty was warranted. Colonial Secretary Carnavon agreed to a pardon for Lépine conditional on a prison sentence. This was an unusual proceeding, because, as discussed in chapter 13, after Confederation the royal prerogative of pardon was exercised by the governor general, not by London. It was both expedient – it saved the federal government involvement in the controversy – and strictly legal, because the events took place before the coming into force of the *Manitoba Act*, in what was therefore British territory. Ironically, therefore, London's pardon confirmed the illegitimacy for lack of jurisdiction of Lépine's conviction.

We end this section, fittingly, with Riel. He was never tried, and in an 1873 by-election won a seat in Parliament as the member for Provencher, Manitoba. He travelled to Hull, Quebec, but at the last minute declined to take his seat, afraid that once in Ontario he would be arrested, or perhaps assassinated. He ran again in the February 1874 general election and won. This time he went to Ottawa and signed the oath book as a member but was expelled on a motion by Conservative Mackenzie Bowell, seconded by Schultz, and supported by Liberal members whose numbers were augmented in the 1874 general election. With the encouragement of leading Quebec Conservatives he won the resulting by-election. He was finally given an amnesty in 1875, when Parliament passed a motion for one that stressed both the offers of amnesty and Riel's assistance against the Fenian incursion. The price was five years' banishment, which Riel accepted.[21] History has credited him with bringing Manitoba into Confederation in a way that respected the rightful claims of its pre-Confederation residents of full or partial European extraction. The federal government substantially accepted that those claims were indeed legitimate, but too often bowed to political expediency in allowing the Ontario expansionists, imbued with their deep-seated hatred of francophone Catholics, to disrupt what would otherwise have been an orderly transition.

The Numbered Treaties, 1871–1907

Less than a year after the *Manitoba Act*, Parliament legislated a form of government for the North-West Territories. A lieutenant governor would rule by ordinance, with the assistance of a council of seven to 15 persons (changed to 21 in 1873).[22] A necessary step before white settlement could begin was to make treaties with the Indigenous people of the region. For the federal government the principal purpose of these treaties was to extinguish the Indigenous title to most of the land, thus by English law freeing it up to be granted to settlers of European origin. Seven such treaties, the numbered treaties, were negotiated between 1871 and 1877, major landmarks in the relationship between the Canadian state and its Indigenous citizens. Ottawa's policy in this regard was determined both by the terms of the transfer of the HBC land to Canada, which talked of the need to compensate Indigenous people 'for lands required for purposes of settlement,' and by the pre-Confederation experience and policy of Upper Canada, which since the late eighteenth century had made many such treaties with Indigenous nations.[23] That experience was brought into the new federal Ministry of Justice, reflected in the views of Hewitt Bernard, brother-in-law of, and sometime private secretary to, Macdonald, and his choice for deputy minister of justice. 'There is not a shadow of doubt,' Bernard stated in 1875, still the deputy minister under Mackenzie, 'that from the earliest times, England has always felt it imperative to meet the Indians in council, and to obtain surrenders of tracts of Canada, as from time to time such were required for the purposes of settlements.' This principle had been confirmed by the Royal Proclamation of 1763 and 'has been followed to the present time' in the territories that were now part of Canada.'[24] Barnard was wrong. The policy had not always been followed outside Upper Canada, but it would be followed by the federal government in the newly acquired prairie region. At the same time, and as we will see in the next section, Indigenous title was consistently denied by the provincial government of British Columbia. Indeed Bernard's views quoted here were the reason for disallowing BC's *Crown Lands Act* because it did not recognize Indigenous title in unsurrendered lands.

Bernard was not sure exactly what the Indigenous interest in the land was and what rights it conferred. He referred on a number of occasions to 'territorial rights.' He did not know whether they were 'of a legal or equitable nature.' But he did know that Indigenous title 'must, of necessity, consist of some species of interest in the lands.' He believed that it was 'not a freehold in the soil' but was rather a 'usufruct, a right of occupation or possession of the same.' Bernard's uncertainty derived from the fact that no British or Canadian colonial court had stated what Indigenous title consisted of, although the US Supreme Court had done so in a series of cases from the 1820s. There would be no such Canadian statement until both the SCC and the JCPC ruled in the mid- to late 1880s in *St Catherines Milling and Lumber Company v The Queen* that Indigenous title was no more than a 'personal and usufructuary right, dependent upon the good will of the Sovereign.' *St Catherines Milling* arose out of a dispute between the federal government and Ontario over the ownership of the underlying title to land after it had been surrendered by treaty, and no Indigenous people or any advocate for them took part. The JCPC view of the content of Indigenous title was not that different from Bernard's, but the idea that it was not a right embedded in the common law but simply 'dependent upon the good will of the Sovereign' was different. It was emblematic of a broader change from seeing Indigenous people as rights holders in a pluralistic world to viewing them as dependent wards of the state. *St Catherines Milling* stood as the leading case until 1973, when in *Calder v Attorney-General for British Columbia* the SCC declared that Indigenous title was an inherent right predicated on historic possession.[25]

In the summer of 1871, very shortly after the *Northwest Territories Act* was passed, commissioners were west of Ontario negotiating the first of the numbered treaties of the 1870s. In six years the first seven numbered treaties were signed, covering the vast majority of the land between Ontario and the Rocky Mountains. In this section we deal principally with those seven treaties. They were settlement treaties, made to pave the way for extensive white settlement, and different from Treaties 8 through 11, signed between 1899 and 1921, covering land further north and focused on extinguishing title to make way for resource development. Canada had good reason to engage in treaty-making in the 1870s.[26] It was necessary because Indigenous people held a form of title to their lands recognized by British and Canadian law, and that title had to be extinguished before land could be granted to others. The dominion wanted not only to acquire the West, but also colonize it, and treaties were the way to make settlement a legal and peaceful process. As the Indian Affairs Branch *Annual Report* for 1873 put it, there would be both 'inconvenience and danger' in any attempt 'to pass over the territorial rights of numerous bands who might (had justice been withheld from them) have become formidable.'[27]

The *Annual Report* reflected both past experience and future difficulties if treaties were not signed. Treaty 1 was negotiated after the Saulteaux prevented some settlers from going past Portage La Prairie, and Treaty 3 was needed when the Ojibway demanded money for crossing the northwest angle through the northerly Ontario and Manitoba lakes. Alexander Morris, the chief negotiator for Treaty 5, the Lake Winnipeg treaty, insisted that 'Indian title to the territory in the vicinity of the Lake should be extinguished so that settlers and traders might have undisturbed access to its waters, shores, inlets and tributary streams.'[28] The transportation imperative included a railway across the prairie, necessary for white settlement and, as we saw in chapter 2, to fulfil the Terms of Union with British Columbia. It would be very difficult to build and run a railway through country consumed with conflicts with Indigenous peoples. Canada could observe the counter-example of the United States, which, after the Civil War, engaged in large-scale Indian wars costing $20 million a year, about the same as the entire annual budget of Canada's federal government.

On the other side of the equation the First Nations were also motivated to regulate their relationships with Canada through treaties. The buffalo population had been declining for some years, and the rate of decline increased in the later 1860s and through the 1870s.[29]* The challenge of food insecurity meant that many Indigenous leaders were searching for alternatives, and the most obvious source was agriculture. Those leaders wanted treaties that included both material assistance – seed, livestock, equipment, and the like – and agricultural instruction. The Cree leaders who signed Treaty 5 at Norway House in 1875 had a different if equally compelling economic incentive. Many of the Cree had been employed by the HBC as boatmen and lost those jobs with the advent of steamships on Lake Winnipeg. They wanted to move to agricultural land further west. Related to the desire for economic adaptation was a more general belief that increasing their knowledge of European ways was necessary to prosper in the very different world that was coming. Hence all of the numbered treaties included school provisions. Other pressures on First Nations included intertribal wars in the 1860s, especially between the Cree and the Blackfoot, a product of dwindling resources. A succession of smallpox epidemics in the 1860s and early 1870s also added to the pressure on Indigenous leaders to avoid conflicts with the Europeans. Overall, therefore, the plains peoples were not hostile to treaties. They were used to decades of trading interactions with the HBC and had their own deep-rooted traditions of treaty-making with other Indigenous nations. But they were insistent on protecting their rights when they could and in striking the most advantageous bargain. As one historian has aptly put it, the position of Indigenous people changed dramatically after mid-century: they went 'from being confident occupiers of a vast region with sufficient resources to facing an uncertain future they had not chosen.' Given this, 'they were determined to try to secure their survival and to have a role in shaping how that future would unfold.'[30]

---

* 'Buffalo' is the commonly used term for the North American bison, and we will use it here.

The fact that both sides had reasons to sign treaties does not mean that the treaty process was equitable. The Indigenous people and the Canadians had very different ideas of the nature of a treaty and what it included. The former believed that it was part of an ongoing relationship and comprised both the recorded text and the things said in negotiations, the latter that it was the end of bargaining, like a contract. The parties also understood the relationship between humans and the land very differently. The treaties purported to transfer title to the land from Indigenous nations to Canada. Yet Indigenous people did not believe that they owned the land in the sense that Europeans understood ownership and therefore did not believe that they could sell it. In signing treaties, Indigenous nations believed they were making agreements with the Crown to share the land with white settlers. We will discuss these incommensurable visions in more detail later in this section. Before doing so we will provide an overview of the treaties.

The first two treaties, Treaty 1, the Stone Fort Treaty, and Treaty 2, the Manitoba Post Treaty, were signed in August 1871 with the Saulteaux and Swampy Cree and the Chippewa and Cree peoples respectively.* Treaty 1 covered approximately 30,000 square miles of southeastern and south-central Manitoba, and Treaty 2 about 34,000 square miles in what is now central, west-central, and southwestern Manitoba and a part of what is today southeastern Saskatchewan. The chief government commissioner for these treaties was Archibald, performing double duty as treaty commissioner and lieutenant governor of Manitoba and the territories. Treaty 3, the North-West Angle Treaty, was signed in October 1873 with the Ojibway and covered roughly 34,000 square miles in what is now northwestern Ontario and parts of south-eastern Manitoba. It therefore included regions east of Manitoba, as did Treaty 5, the Lake Winnipeg Treaty, signed in September 1875 at Norway House with the Saulteaux and Swampy Cree peoples. It covered about 100,000 square miles in what is now central and northern Manitoba as well as those parts of northwestern Ontario not covered by Treaty 3. For Treaties 3 through 6 the government's chief treaty commissioner was Alexander Morris, who replaced Archibald as Manitoba's lieutenant governor. Treaties 4, 6, and 7 ceded to the Crown large parts of what is now Saskatchewan and Alberta. Treaty 4, the Qu'Appelle Treaty, approximately 50,000 square miles, was signed in September

---

* We have retained the names of the Indigenous groups that were used at the time of each treaty. Today the Ojibway, Saulteaux, and Chippewa are referred to as Anishinaabe.

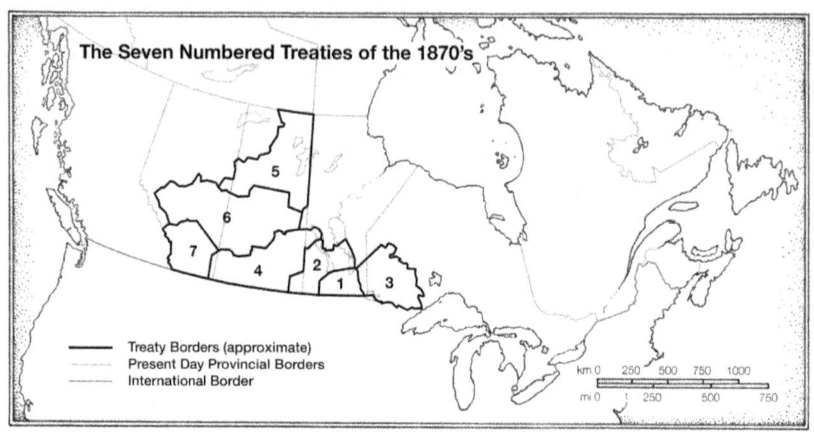

The numbered treaties of the 1870s.

Credit: Drawn by Christopher Hoyt.

1874 at Fort Qu'Appelle with the Assiniboine, the Cree and the Saul-teaux, whose traditional territories were in central and southern Sas-katchewan. Treaty 6, which never received another appellation, was signed in late August 1876 at Fort Carlton and in September at Fort Pitt with the Cree and Assiniboine of central Saskatchewan and central Alberta. By it the Crown acquired about 120,000 square miles. The final treaty of the 1870s, the Blackfoot Treaty or Treaty 7, covered roughly 35,000 square miles and was signed in September 1877 with the Black-foot, Blood, Stony, and Peigan peoples of southern Alberta. For Treaty 7 Ottawa was represented by David Laird, a Liberal MP from Prince Edward Island who was made lieutenant governor of the Territories in 1876 after the *North-West Territories Act* of 1875 established an adminis-tration separate from Manitoba.[31] For all treaties there were later adhe-sions, Indigenous bands in the relevant region agreeing to 'take treaty,' a process that began in the 1870s and continued for decades.

The treaties were all very similar and based on the Robinson Trea-ties of 1850 and 1851, discussed in *Volume 1*, which covered the Lake Superior and northern Lake Huron hinterlands.[32] They all began with a clause stating that the Queen wished to 'open up to settlement and immigration a tract of country' that was then described. Treaties 6 and 7 included this phrase but added after 'immigration' the phrase 'and such other purposes as to Her Majesty may seem fit [Treaty 6] or meet [Treaty 7].' This 'opening up for settlement' provision was followed by what we term the 'conveyancing clause.' In Treaties 1 and 2 it stated that the Indigenous nation 'do hereby cede, release, surrender and yield up' to 'Her Majesty the Queen and Her successors forever all the lands included' within certain boundaries. In the remaining treaties the wording was different; rather than simply ceding 'the land,' the Indigenous signatories ceded 'all their rights, titles and privileges whatsoever, to the lands.' This latter formulation more closely adhered to the English law of real property, in which the Crown owns all the land and all others own estates, the use of land for a time, as tenants of the Crown. Both forms of the clause were less elaborate and less a replication of standard common law conveyances, not referring to 'reversions and remainders' and the like as some of the Upper Canadian treaties of the late eighteenth and early nineteenth centuries had done.[33] From Treaty 3 onwards the Indigenous signatories not only ceded their specific local territories but also 'all their rights, titles and privileges whatsoever, to all other lands wherever situated in the North-West Territories, or in any other portion of the Dominion of Canada.'

The conveyancing clauses always included, as common law conveyancing documents did, a 'metes and bounds' description of the land being transferred. The 'metes and bounds' description of a parcel of real estate delineates the boundaries of the area being conveyed by reference to natural landmarks and directions from one such landmark to the next. For example, Treaty 1 described the area transferred to the Crown as follows:

> Beginning at the international boundary line near its junction with the Lake of the Woods, at a point due north from the centre of Roseau Lake; thence to run due north to the centre of Roseau Lake; thence northward to the centre of White Mouth Lake, otherwise called White Mud Lake; thence by the middle of the lake and the middle of the river issuing therefrom to the mouth thereof in Winnipeg River; thence by the Winnipeg River to its mouth; thence westwardly, including all the islands near the south end of the lake, across the lake to the mouth of Drunken River; thence westwardly to a point on Lake Manitoba half way between Oak Point and the mouth of Swan Creek; thence across Lake Manitoba in a line due west to its western shore; thence in a straight line to the crossing of the rapids on the Assiniboine; thence due south to the international boundary line; and thence eastwardly by the said line to the place of beginning.

Every treaty provided for reserves to be set aside. There were differences among the treaties on how this was to be done. Treaties 1 and 2 reserved land 'for the sole and exclusive use of the Indians,' the reserved land specified in the same kinds of metes and bounds definitions that delineated the land given to the Crown. In contrast Treaty 3 contained promises to set aside reserves for farming of land 'deemed most convenient and advantageous for each band' by the government, the selection of the land to be made 'after conference with the Indians.' Treaty 4 was to the same effect, but Treaty 5 returned to designating the areas reserved for each band with metes and bounds descriptions. Treaty 6 reverted to the government choosing the reserves after consultations with Indigenous bands, while Treaty 7 specified the areas reserved.

Common to all treaties, including those in which the reserve area was described, were limitations on the size of reserves according to population. Thus in those treaties that designated a tract of land, the tract was not the reserve but the land out of which reserves would be taken. Treaties 1 and 2 specified 160 acres per family of five, with the acreage proportionately adjusted for larger or smaller families. Treaties 3, 4, 6, and 7 provided for four times that amount, one square mile (640 acres) for a family of five, while Treaty 5 reverted to 160 acres. Specifying acreages by family size was a way of providing for successive generations; the larger the number of children the more likely it was that more land would be needed in the future. The increase to 640 acres in Treaty 3 has been ascribed to the fact that the land was not suitable for white settler farming, so that government negotiators easily conceded larger reserves. The larger per family allocations in the other treaties had a different cause – hard bargaining by Indigenous negotiators, which derived in part from understanding how much the government needed treaties. All treaties also included provisions protecting the 'rights' of any white settlers occupying land within the area reserved. In the words of Treaty 3, the Crown retained the right to 'deal with such settlers as [it] shall deem just.' But in every case this would be done 'so as not to diminish the extent of the land allotted to Indians.'

Hunting and fishing rights outside of reserves were not mentioned in Treaties 1 and 2 but were included in the others as part of what have come to be known as the 'taking up' clauses. As with other clauses, the language was almost identical each time, stating, as Treaty 4 did, that the Indigenous signatories had the 'right to pursue their avocations of hunting, trapping and fishing throughout the tract surrendered.' These rights were limited in every case by being 'subject to such regulations as may from time to time be made by the Government.' This proved to be a very significant limitation when governments began to legislate seasonal limits and quotas for all hunters. A more substantial limitation on hunting and fishing rights was that they would not in the future apply to 'such tracts as may be required or taken up from time to time for settlement, mining or other purposes.' Again these words are from Treaty 4; Treaties 3, 5, and 6 added 'lumbering' to the list, and Treaty 7 'trading.' The 'taking up' clauses applied to surrendered land, but they all also included a provision for altering what land was reserved by expropriation. Treaty 3, for example, provided that any reserve land that 'may at anytime be required for public works' or other buildings could be expropriated with compensation only for the value of improvements. Treaties 4 to 7 provided additional compensation in the form of 'an equivalent in land or money for the area of the reserve so appropriated.'

The treaties all provided cash payments, both immediate one-time payments and annuities, to all members of the Indigenous nation. Treaties 1 and 2 provided for a $3 immediate payment and a $3 annuity for each person, and in Treaty 3 this was increased to $12 and $5. Some of the treaties also provided for larger payments and/or annuities for chiefs and 'headmen,' and others for presents to notables of suits of clothing, horses, and wagons and, in Treaty 7 only, rifles. Additional common clauses were those banning the sale of intoxicants and those that responded to the signatories' desire for education to help in adaptation to the coming new world. There was a clause in every treaty providing for schools, never more than one sentence.

Also included to assist with the transition to a new socio-economic reality precipitated by the decline of the buffalo were, from Treaty 3 onwards, agricultural assistance and training clauses. During the negotiations for Treaty 4, Morris told the Indigenous leaders that '[w]hen fish are scarce and the buffalo are not plentiful she [the Crown] would like to help you put something in the land,' promising 'cattle to help you' and 'seed to plant.' Treaty 4 promised to any bands that had taken up farming or would do so in the future 'two hoes, one spade, one scythe and one axe for every family, … and enough seed wheat, barley, oats and potatoes to plant' the land broken. In addition, there was to be provided 'one plough and two harrows for every ten families … cultivating,' and to each chief for the band's use 'one yoke of oxen, one bull, four cows, a chest of ordinary carpenter's tools, five hand saws, five augers, one cross-cut saw, one pit-saw, the necessary files and one grindstone.' Morris told Ottawa after the signing of Treaty 6 that the Indigenous people 'saw buffalo, the only means of support, passing away,' and were 'anxious to learn to support themselves by agriculture.'[34] The treaty promised a similar list as in Treaty 4 of farm implements, seeds, and draught animals. It also included other things: money to the Indian agent for the purchase of ammunition for hunting and twine for fishing nets, and up to $1,000 to be spent by the agent 'in the purchase of provisions for the use of such members of the Band as are actually settled on the reserves and engaged in the cultivation of the soil, to assist and encourage them in such cultivation.' Most notably it included unique clauses providing the Indigenous people with government aid in the event of outbreaks of disease or famine:

> That in the event hereafter of the Indians comprised within this treaty being overtaken by any pestilence, or by a general famine, the Queen, on being satisfied and certified thereof by Her Indian Agent or Agents, will grant to the Indians assistance of such character and to such extent as Her Chief Superintendent of Indian Affairs shall deem necessary and sufficient to relieve the Indians from the calamity that shall have befallen them.... [A] a medicine chest shall be kept at the house of each Indian Agent for the use and benefit of the Indians at the direction of such agent.

Ottawa thought that Morris had given too much away in Treaty 6 and replaced him for Treaty 7 with Laird. But although Treaty 7 did not have the medicine chest or famine clauses, the Indigenous signatories were not willing to be fobbed off with an inferior treaty in other respects and wanted terms suited to the climate and soil of southern Alberta, which favoured stock raising. Thus the terms included $2,000 for ammunition for hunting, axes, saws, and other tools, and cattle, the number depending on the size of families, as well as a bull for every chief and sub-chief for the use of the band. Laird was perhaps worried that he too would receive Ottawa's disapproval and ensured his superiors that cattle were not only better for local conditions but also cheaper. The initial outlay might seem large, but 'when it is considered that cows can be readily purchased at Fort McLeod for twenty or twenty-five dollars per head, and their delivery to the Indians will cost an inconsiderable sum, the total ... expense of supplying the articles promised by this treaty will ... [be] less than those under either Treaty Number Four or Number Six.'[35]

While the Indigenous signatories were obviously different in each case, there was considerable continuity on the government side.[36] The chief commissioners were joined for each negotiation by one or two other commissioners, and a variety of other individuals were also involved on the government side – officials, interpreters, missionaries, the North-West Mounted Police (NWMP), HBC employees – and for some of the treaties the Métis played an important role as intermediaries. Various officials signed treaties as witnesses, as did a number of Métis for Treaty 4. Attesting witnesses for Treaty 3 also included at least one female relative of Morris, his daughter Christine, who travelled with the government party perhaps as a diversion from the fact that Morris's family found the time spent in Manitoba and the Territories 'an exile.'[37]

Many of the treaty negotiations were notable for their extensive use of protocol and rhetorical flourishes long used in Indigenous treaty-making by both Indigenous and European negotiators. Government envoys presented medals and uniforms on behalf of the Crown, and long speeches stressed that the treaties were being made with the Crown. These protocols went back to the eighteenth century and/or the fur trade era. Morris was the most adept at using symbolism and rhetoric, and played heavily on the image of the Crown as a source of bounty and benevolence, contrasting the Crown with the American government and its tendency to resort to warfare. Treaty 6 negotiations, for example, began with the pipe-stem ceremony, a sacred ritual that embodied the idea that commitments made were to be kept. Yet it is unclear how much the commissioners really understood about the meaning of such ceremonies; for Morris the pipe ceremony simply indicated 'friendship' with the Cree, a word with multiple nuanced meanings.[38]

The negotiations were often protracted because the Indigenous representatives were adept at driving the best bargain they could. Wemyss Simpson, assistant commissioner to Archibald, called the size of reserve demands for Treaty 1 'exorbitant,' but the Saulteaux would not be budged.[39] The Treaty 3 negotiations took longer than expected because the Cree wanted an agreement granting rights of way through their territory to the new province of Manitoba, not a land cession. The government had tried to make a treaty for the region in both 1871 and 1872 but was rebuffed and had to wait until 1873 for one. The government's persistence was the result of its desire to open a route to the West that did not involve going through the United States. It was ultimately able to effect an agreement because of internal divisions among the Indigenous nations and Métis intervention. The former arose because the more northerly bands were losing the employment opportunities they had had with the HBC and were therefore more willing to come to an agreement, whereas bands to the south continued to have access to seasonal employment and were less willing to treat. Even these internal dissensions might not have brought about an agreement but for the intervention of three Métis who persuaded the more reluctant bands to sign the treaty.

Treaty 4 was also difficult for the federal negotiators, in part because Indigenous leaders knew of the unfulfilled outside treaty promises in Treaties 1 and 2, discussed below, and were intent on getting everything they wanted into the treaty, and in part because the Indigenous leaders had difficulty comprehending the altered relationships between the HBC, Britain, and Canada. They wanted the HBC and its trade to remain and to secure compensation for the HBC having been paid for the land in 1869 – land that the Indigenous leaders thought was not the company's to sell. 'The Company have stolen our land,' they told Morris. Only when they were convinced that Morris either would not discuss the matter – the Indigenous view – or that he simply did not have the authority to do so – Morris's view – did they stop insisting on discussing it. Another matter that retarded negotiations was that Indigenous chiefs wanted the Métis included in the treaty as recipients of hunting rights. Morris again made it clear that he did not have the authority to do this, only promising that 'the Queen will deal justly with all her Children.'[40]

The most difficult treaty to negotiate for the Canadian officials was Treaty 6, which covered the largest area of any of the treaties.[41] The Cree people of the region had asked for a treaty as early as 1871 because of concerns about the decline of the buffalo, but the government refused at that time, preoccupied with negotiations over the entry of British Columbia into Confederation. By 1876 the government was forced to treat, because of threats to disrupt survey and telegraph crews in the region. There has long been a consensus that First Nations got better terms than they did in any preceding treaty, thanks to their leaders' tenacity, which was the result of a variety of factors: the decline of the buffalo continued, so there was more at stake; First Nations had much experience at negotiations, so they were more cautious about concessions and more 'hard-nosed'; and Canadian negotiators had to deal with the fact that there was disagreement on the other side, with older chiefs having to convince younger ones that food shortages left them no choice. In addition, the Indigenous participants hired their own interpreter for the first time, Peter Erasmus, the son of a Danish settler at Red River and his Métis wife. He enjoyed excellent relations with Cree leaders and in 1876 was hired by Mistawsis (Big Child) and Ahtahkakoop

(Star Blanket). He was reputed to be an 'accomplished linguist,... fluent in English and several Cree dialects, as well as Ojibwa, Stoney … and Blackfoot.'[42] The largest points of contention were the famine and medicine clauses, discussed above. They were strongly resisted by Morris, because he knew Ottawa would not approve, but he was forced to relent to get a deal. Even with these clauses included, there were two significant holdouts: Poundmaker and Big Bear.

We return to the issue raised before we described the treaty terms, that the fundamental problem with the treaties was that they did not represent a true meeting of minds. In recent decades there has been an outpouring of writing about the Indigenous view of the treaties, based on new research, much of it in the oral traditions of the Indigenous peoples, and on a greater understanding of Indigenous world views and laws.[43] This research has revealed four interrelated problems with the treaties: the written terms did not reflect what the Indigenous signatories believed had been agreed; many of the provisions of the treaties were not fulfilled; Indigenous people had a view of what a treaty was that was very different from those with European cultural understandings; and Indigenous signatories did not believe that they were ceding the land, or that they could do so – they believed that they were making agreements to share it. We will deal with these points in turn.

The first of these problems was very quickly manifested. Treaty 1 included a 'Memorandum of Things outside of the Treaty Which Were Promised,' signed by Archibald and three others. The promises covered agricultural stock and equipment and presents to Indigenous leaders as marks of respect. A journalist who witnessed the Treaty 1 negotiations later told the government that 'the Treaty was signed, the Commissioner meaning one thing, the Indians meaning the other.'[44] This list became a source of contention, because Ottawa initially refused to acknowledge liability for anything not written in the Treaty itself. In 1872, just a year after Treaties 1 and 2 had been concluded, Morris became aware that three of the Treaty 1 bands had refused to take their 1872 annuities because of the failure to deliver on these promises. Although Ottawa would not acknowledge that it had breached its obligations, in 1875 it accepted that the memorandum should be considered as part of Treaties 1 and 2 and thus provided the promised articles. But it would not accept the validity of any other outside promises, although it did, 'out of good feeling to the Indians and as a matter of benevolence,' agree to raise the annuity for both Treaties from $3 to $5 and to make additional one-time payments to chiefs. These increased payments were stated to be an abandonment of 'all claims whatever against the Government in connection with the so-called "outside promises"' other than those contained in the memorandum.[45] The government might have been willing to concede what was in the memorandum because among the other additional outside promises was one of more land further west for future generations.[46]

The Treaty 1 memorandum was the only such contemporary government document to acknowledge the fact that many of the understandings that the Indigenous negotiators thought they had come to did not find their way into the written texts. The remarkable similarity between the treaties was not the result of a consistent acceptance of the same terms by different Indigenous peoples, but of the Canadians bringing their standard form, discussing and agreeing on various details, and then ignoring those oral agreements. During the negotiations for Treaty 3, the only one of the treaties where there is a written record from both parties, the principal Indigenous negotiator, Chief Powassin, had notes taken by Joseph Nolin, a Métis from Red River. The notes surfaced in the early twentieth century and are now known as the Paypom Treaty. They documented a number of differences between the promises made by the commissioners and the official text. The agreed upon terms that were not in the text were that the Indigenous people would not be conscripted, that there was a right to harvest wild rice, and that any gold or silver found on treaty territory would be 'to the benefit of the Indians.' The evidence of Europeans in this instance strongly suggests that the 'final' written text was drafted in 1872 and simply omitted matters discussed in the negotiations of 1873.[47] Similarly, the Indigenous view of the Treaty 4 negotiations is manifested not by writing but by a different kind of material visual evidence, a pictograph made by Chief Joseph Pasqua, one of the signatories. Remarking on Treaty 6 but with words applicable to all the treaties, one commentator has argued that to understand that treaty one must consider 'both the actual treaty document and the recording of the discussions involved.' Oral communication is central to Indigenous culture, in which it is understood that 'men are literally bound by their words' and thus 'the verbal assurances and statements of the commissioners were accepted by the Indian people as part of the treaty agreements.'[48]

That the written text did not reflect the agreements made is also illustrated by the medicine chest clause in Treaty 6. The Indigenous signatories believed from representations made during the negotiations that the clause entitled them to free medical supplies and services. The federal government later refused to recognize a legal duty to provide these services, although it agreed to do so on 'moral or humanitarian grounds.' Other aspects of Treaty 6 present the same problem. Government negotiators thought they were providing for subsistence, the Indigenous leaders believed they were being promised prosperity. As a result the Indigenous negotiators believed they could choose how much land would be available to them and thus saw the advent of surveyors for the Canada Land Survey, discussed further in chapter 14, as a violation of the treaty. They believed that 'the needs of reserve farmers might increase or change as they shifted their attention towards agriculture and away from hunting,' and thus that the government had 'pledged itself to put them in the same position as the white man,' a goal that might well require adjustment of the terms over time. It took only a few years for the Treaty 6 signatories to complain about non-observance of the terms, both about specifics, such as the number of ploughs to be provided, and about a general failure to adhere to the 'spirit and intent' of the treaty.[49]

The opposite problem was also pervasive – things that were not discussed in the negotiations appeared in the treaties. This was especially true of the 'taking up' clauses. These clauses granted continued hunting and fishing rights on surrendered lands, but subject to limitations that were not part of the discussions. Ojibway oral histories, for example, show that for Treaty 3 the Ojibway agreed to a clause on hunting and other resource use rights that stated that they 'will be free as by the past for their hunting and rice harvest.' There was no agreement that the rights were subject to regulation, as Treaty 3 and every other treaty stated, or that they would not apply in land 'taken up' for settlement or other development.

Turning to the second problem identified above, the agricultural provisions did not produce prosperity because the government failed to provide all that was promised, and some of what was supplied was of inferior quality. Moreover, it quickly became clear that Ottawa preferred subsistence agriculture by peasant farmers rather than production for the market because the latter represented competition for white settlers, who themselves struggled with the climate, natural disasters, and a lack of knowledge, as we will see in chapter 14.[50] Along with these failures to live up to specific treaty promises went deeper and more pervasive problems: indifference to the starvation that afflicted a number of First Nations in the late 1870s and the 1880s and to the related poor medical conditions in many communities. The famine and medicine chest clauses were only written treaty terms in Treaty 6, but all treaty negotiations featured assurances of the Crown's concern for its Indigenous partners and promises that the Crown's bounty would be spent in taking care of them when needed.[51]

The third problem was in part the cause of the first two. The European negotiators saw treaties in contractual terms, agreements in which a final resolution was arrived at after bargaining and consisted only of what was written on paper. The Indigenous leaders saw the treaty process as being more about the beginning and the ongoing development of a relationship, not its conclusion. In some Indigenous languages there is no word that translates directly as 'treaty,' but Indigenous people nonetheless were well used to inter-societal agreements and considered them sacred covenants, establishing permanent peace and friendship relationships, even if specific terms might well change as circumstances did. Although government negotiators used many Indigenous symbols and practices, it is very unlikely that they fully understood the Indigenous world view. The problems of cross-cultural comprehension were acknowledged at the time by some Europeans, albeit through a culturally chauvinistic filter. Duncan Sinclair, a surveyor sent some years later to lay out the Treaty 5 reserves, lamented that '[g]reat allowance is to be made for the poor creatures because they have very dark ideas of our language and only slowly comprehend our bargains with them no matter how clearly we explain matters to them.'[52]

The lack of shared understandings had the largest impact in the land cession clauses. Indigenous nations had made numerous agreements among themselves about access to and the use of the land resource before the 1870s. They involved 'distinct processes for determining how lands and resources would be shared.' They were agreements, in the words of one elder, 'to protect our land' and to 'share this land and its resources with all newcomers.' It has been shown that the Indigenous protocols employed for Treaty 1 represented 'legal principles of non-interference in each other's affairs, [and] respect for each other's territory and jurisdiction.'[53] Letters written to Ottawa by Indigenous leaders within the first two decades after the signing of Treaty 3, and oral tradition evidence regarding Treaties 6 and 7, among other evidence, demonstrate that for the Indigenous participants the treaties were about land sharing and not land acquisition. The same holds true for all of the treaties. The 'conveyancing clauses' were 'agreed to' by nations that had no notion of the private ownership of land. They understood controls over the use of the land's resources, and they had a well-developed sense of territoriality, but that was centred on the idea of specific territory being for the occupation and use of specific nations. In this world view, land 'belonged' to the group, and the group included past and future generations as well as the present one. The land itself was, in common law terms, inalienable, and its 'sale' to the Crown by Indigenous people an impossibility; to employ a fundamental term in the common law of property, the treaties offended the principle of *nemo dat quod non habet*.*

We conclude this section with a very brief examination of the three other numbered treaties concluded in this period, between 1899 and 1907, which were all 'resource' more than 'settlement' treaties.† Treaty 8 was signed with the Woodland Cree, Beaver, and Chipewayn (now Dene) peoples at Grouard, Alberta, in July 1899, with a further eight adhesions added shortly afterwards and four more in 1900. It covered northern Alberta, northeastern British Columbia, southern parts of the Northwest Territories, and northwestern Saskatchewan, at approximately 325,000 square miles the largest land area of any treaty in this period. Treaty 9, the James Bay Treaty, was signed at various locations in 1905 and 1906 with the Cree and Ojibway peoples whose territory was in far northern Ontario and the Northwest Territories. It covered the land draining into Hudson and James Bays. There were later adhesions, very much later, in 1929 and 1930. Treaty 10 was signed at île-à-la-Crosse, Cane Lake, and Lac Brochet in 1906 and 1907 with Cree and Chipewyan people. It covered roughly 85,000 square miles of northern Saskatchewan and a small area of Manitoba.[54]

All three treaties were structured the same way as the 1870s treaties, with the important distinction that the initial 'opening up for settlement' clause included immigration and settlement but also 'trade, travel, mining, lumbering and such other purposes' as the government determined. They all contained conveyancing and reserve clauses, with the latter varying between 160 and 640 acres per family of five. Treaty 10 was unusual in providing, for the first time, for people who 'prefer to live apart from band reserves' to be allocated 160 acres in severalty, not alienable without the government's consent. One-time cash payments, annuities, and schools clauses were included. Treaties 8 and 10 contained promises of agricultural and hunting supplies, but Treaty 9 did not, presumably because agriculture was simply not suited to any part of the region. All treaties also had the same 'taking up' clause as the 1870s treaties,

---

* No one can give what they do not have.

† See map on p. 234. The final numbered treaty, Number 11, was concluded in 1922 with the Dene and Inuit peoples of what is now the Northwest Territories.

protecting hunting and fishing rights, which were nonetheless subject to regulation and inapplicable to tracts that 'may be required … from time to time for settlement, mining, lumbering, trading or other purposes.'

The Indigenous people of each of the treaty regions had asked for treaties for many years, in the case of Treaty 10 since 1879, because they saw their traditional economies increasingly subverted by incoming white hunters, prospectors, and lumbermen whose activities both reduced the animal population and reduced the habitat of fur-bearing and subsistence animals. A degree of protection for hunting and trapping rights would, they hoped, enable them to survive, and annuities would serve as a backstop in difficult times. The government deferred entering into treaties until the very late nineteenth and early twentieth centuries because it did not wish to incur the expense. It was brought to the table for Treaty 8 by an effective Indigenous blockade of the route to the Klondike goldfields, and for Treaty 10 when Saskatchewan and Alberta became provinces and Ottawa wanted to extinguish the Indigenous title to allow for mining and other forms of resource exploitation. The Treaty 8 commissioners had their work cut out, Indigenous negotiators refusing to sign the initial draft presented to them because it did not include enough protection for hunting, trapping, and fishing rights. Agreement was eventually achieved based on oral promises, including support for the elderly and medical care for all as needed, but these did not make their way into the written terms. There was much hard bargaining over these treaties, Treaty 9 especially, and the Indigenous leaders were able to extract significant concessions. But the written texts, pre-drafted and brought to the various meeting places, remained unchanged.

Treaty 9 was unusual in that significant aspects of it were negotiated between the federal and Ontario governments in the years immediately before 1905, a result of an agreement made between the two governments in 1894 that Ottawa would not make further treaties in Ontario without provincial consent. The agreement was the result of the JCPC decision in the *St Catherine's Milling* case, discussed above, which in holding that any Indigenous rights to the land were not inherent legal rights but favours from the Crown also held that the underlying title to Indigenous land belonged to the province as part of its jurisdiction over public lands in section 92 (5) of the *BNA Act*. Thus one of the treaty commissioners was, for the first time, a provincial appointee – Daniel McMartin, a mining specialist from Perth, Ontario. In addition one of the constraints on the commissioners insisted on by the Ontario government was that no site that could be exploited for the development of hydroelectric power could be included within any reserve.

British Columbia: Federal-Provincial
Disputes over Indigenous Title

As discussed in *Volume 1*, there were 14 treaties concluded between the Crown and Indigenous peoples in British Columbia between 1850 and 1854, covering only 3 per cent of Vancouver Island, and none thereafter. They are known as the Douglas treaties after the man who negotiated them, Vancouver Island's governor, James Douglas. Douglas remained governor until 1864, but his belief that the Indigenous inhabitants had rights in the land put him increasingly out of step with many other local leaders, formal and informal, in the colony. After Douglas's retirement, Joseph Trutch, chief commissioner of Crown lands, was effectively in charge of Indigenous land policy. Crutch became British Columbia's first lieutenant governor after Confederation and in that capacity insisted that the early 1850s agreements were acts of goodwill designed to maintain friendly relations and not acknowledgments of Indigenous title. Trutch shared with many settlers and provincial politicians a view of Indigenous people as 'lazy and ugly,' as 'savages' – judgments with both ethnocentric and economic origins, for part of what made them 'savage' was their lack of the accumulative ethic, which meant that they did not use land as productively as Europeans. In the 1860s local colonial policy towards the Indigenous inhabitants was, to put it mildly, ungenerous. On Trutch's initiative they were effectively barred from pre-empting land and unilaterally segregated on inadequate reserves of no more than 10 acres per family.[55] Clause 14 of the Terms of Union of 1871 contained what was therefore in effect an oxymoron: while the dominion took jurisdiction over reserves under section 91 (24) of the *BNA Act*, the clause went on to say that 'a policy as liberal as that hitherto pursued by the British Columbia Government shall be continued by the Dominion Government after the Union.' British Columbia's policy towards its Indigenous population had been as far from 'liberal' as could be imagined. The idea of a 'liberal' policy practised by the colony before 1871 was called 'little short of a mockery' in 1874 by David Laird, federal minister of the interior. In saying this he was criticizing those who had agreed to the Terms of Union: 'They could hardly have been aware of the marked contrast' between the province's past policies and those of Upper Canada and the Dominion, he remarked.[56]

For the ensuing half-century Ottawa sought to make the province accept that an Indigenous title existed, and to act accordingly by concluding treaties surrendering that title, but the latter steadfastly refused.

The difference between the governments' attitudes is captured by a coincidence of timing. British Columbia became part of Canada on 20 July 1871, and two weeks later, on 3 August, the Crown's representatives signed Treaty 1, extinguishing Indigenous title to a large part of southern Manitoba. The difference between the two governments was exacerbated by another problem. Jurisdiction over Indigenous land was effectively split. Section 91 (27) gave the federal government jurisdiction over reserves. But the province controlled Crown lands and mineral rights under sections 92 (5) and 109 of the *BNA Act*, which gave it the right to allocate reserves. While the Terms of Union required the province to transfer land to the dominion for the establishment of reserves, they did not specify how much land.

That this would create a problem became evident as early as 1872.[57] The federal government appointed Dr. Israel Wood Powell superintendent general of Indian affairs in the province and asked him to investigate and report. Powell had lived on Vancouver Island since 1862 and was a very successful doctor and a vocal advocate of Confederation. An assimilationist, he was nonetheless more sympathetic to Indigenous interests than the vast majority of his contemporaries and proved a consistent critic of the province's land policy.[58] He believed that an 'Indian war' had only been narrowly avoided because the Indigenous peoples were not united and organized. Their enmity, he warned, 'might become more disastrous than any calamity to which the colony is liable.' This was said at a time when Indigenous people greatly outnumbered settlers in the new province. In 1874 he reported on many meetings he had had with Indigenous leaders unhappy with past policies. A petition from 7 Secwepemc (Shuswap) chiefs, for example, stated that reserves were too small, the land on which they were located too rocky to cultivate and/or too difficult to irrigate, and the process of reserve allocation had been done without the agreement of the Indigenous people themselves. Powell agreed, telling Ottawa that '[t]he Indian Reserves ... are ... in a most unsatisfactory condition ... so small and insufficient ... as to occasion constant disputes as to their limits.' The Indigenous person 'looks with envy on the large possession of the Whites, and with discontent upon the small areas allowed to himself, as the primitive and original possessor of all, and to which his rights have been ignored by past Colonial Governments.' When the two governments first negotiated reserve size, Ottawa demanded 80 acres per family, the province wanted what was in place, 10 acres, and they compromised at 20, although the province insisted that this did not apply to existing reserves.

While there were voices in British Columbia supporting Powell, principally the missionary lobby, British Columbia's leading lights decidedly did not. Trutch ridiculed him for his lack of knowledge about Indigenous people and argued that Indigenous policy should be left to the local government. Provincial attorney general George Walkem told Ottawa that the cornerstone of that policy was that Indigenous people should 'mingle with and live amongst the white population with a view of weaning them by degrees from savage life, and of gradually leading them by example ... to adopt habits of peace, honesty and industry.' The charge of a lack of provincial spending on Indigenous peoples was refuted by citing the money spent on surveying, suppression of the illegal liquor trade, and aid for the sick and destitute, and by Indigenous peoples' exemptions from bridge tolls, direct taxes, and some customs duties. The inability to pre-empt land was offset by providing an example of one who had done so after petitioning the lieutenant governor and demonstrating that he could use the land 'intelligently.' Not recognizing Indigenous title was sound policy, because good land ought not to be 'left uncultivated in the hands of a nominal and irresponsible proprietary,' who were 'utter savages.'[59]

In the mid-1870s Ottawa came down firmly on Powell's side. In 1874 it disallowed the province's *Crown Lands Act* because it ignored Indigenous rights.[60] Hewitt Bernard's report on the Act, with which his minister Télesphore Fournier concurred, noted 'the known, existing and increasing dissatisfaction of the Indian tribes of British Columbia at the absence of adequate reservations of lands for their use,' which stood in marked contrast to 'the liberal appropriation for those in other parts of Canada upon surrender by treaty of their territorial rights.' The act rested on the assumption that public land in British Columbia was the 'absolute property' of the province, an assumption that 'completely ignores ... the honour and good faith' of the Crown. Moreover, while the *BNA Act* gave public lands and minerals to the provinces, it did so subject to trusts and other pre-existing interests, and that included Indigenous title, which must be 'some species of interest in the lands of British Columbia.' The same year Laird's *Annual Report* stated that the land question was 'a great obstacle in the way of the satisfactory administration of Indian affairs in that Province.' Reserves were 'utterly inadequate,' and Indigenous land rights 'are ignored and their claims subordinated to those of the white settlers.' David Mills, a lawyer and the minister of the interior in 1877, thought British Columbia's policy 'not only unwise and unjust, but illegal,' although he was prepared to ignore the illegality if larger reserves were set aside. Governor-General Lord Dufferin was convinced that the honour of the Crown was engaged. Canada must adopt 'just and humane dealings towards our fellow Indian citizens,' for a 'liberal policy' in this regard was a 'most sacred and important function' of the federal government.[61]

The federal government sought to resolve the matter by negotiation, probably because another dispute was brewing in which Ottawa was clearly at fault. Clause 11 of the Terms of Union obliged it to start building the Pacific railway within two years, and it had not done so. Whether it was a trade-off or not, in 1876 Ottawa and the province agreed to create a Joint Indian Reserve Commission. Mills admitted in his report on the establishment of the commission that 'the question of the rights of the Indians in all the lands in British Columbia in which their rights have not been extinguished by treaties between themselves and the Crown is still unsettled,' but he let it go for the present.[62] The commission comprised one member appointed by the province, Archibald McKinlay, and one by the dominion, Caulfield Anderson, who held federal appointments in the province. Anderson and McKinlay were both former HBC men, and the former generally sympathetic to Indigenous people; as we will see in chapter 10 he believed that they had inalienable rights to fish. The third member of the Joint Commission, and its chair, was Gilbert Sproat, appointed by agreement between the two governments. Sproat was equivocal on the question of whether there was an Indigenous title, but he believed that Indigenous people should be respected and had a right to a generous allocation of land to ensure their sufficiency and prosperity.[63]

The commissioners were to travel the province and decide on the number and size of reserves needed. They reflected a compromise between the positions held by the two levels of government; reserves could be larger than before, but the commissioners were not to concern themselves with the title question. Moreover, given that the commission might advocate reductions in reserve size in some cases, Ottawa passed an Order in Council exempting British Columbia from the surrender provisions of the *Indian Act*, discussed in the next chapter, which required Indigenous consent to land surrenders.[64] The commissioners were to be as generous as possible to the claims of Indigenous people without jeopardizing the interests of white settlers. In its two-year existence the commission attempted to 'fairly' adjudicate between white and Indigenous interests.[65] It travelled two circuits, one in the lower mainland and the other in the interior. On the first circuit the commissioners' small party would make camp and hold an initial meeting with the local groups at which Indigenous chiefs would speak. Thereafter rough censuses were taken and surveys done. Proceedings at each location were concluded by a meeting where decisions were explained, any small changes were addressed, and final speeches made. The commissioners were not bound to a formula for acreages or to the limits of prior reserves. They generally supported existing white claims whose legality rested on adherence to the provincial land-granting procedure, and also favoured 'industrious squatters' over the claims of Indigenous people, evincing no intention of relinquishing the space intended for white colonization. The first circuit allotted 25,000 acres of reserve land to 3,000 Indigenous people, giving to reserves only as much land as they thought could be spared from that needed for white settlers. Strong Indigenous attachments to specific village sites made it difficult for the commissioners to concentrate people in larger reserves, but the commissioners did recognize the traditional reliance of many Indigenous peoples on fishing, and allocated many small reserves around established fishing stations.[66] Generally Sproat was pleased with the results. But for all that it improved the position of the Indigenous inhabitants, the circuit revealed the commissioners' ethnocentric biases; they were there 'for the Indians good, which was to become more like white men,' and 'an assumed cultural superiority … characterized the ideological underpinnings of the circuit[s].'[67]

The second circuit turned out very differently. An Indigenous resistance by a Secwepemc confederation, organized by Chief Petit Louis at Kamloops, emerged to oppose reserve allocation and further white settlement. Diplomacy avoided a conflict, and some allocation took place, but the circuit was cut short. In early 1877 the provincial government asked Ottawa to disband the commission. Interior Minister Mills refused, instead asking Sproat to continue alone, which after some bargaining he did. By this time Sproat had become much more sympathetic to Indigenous interests. He still thought title to land was largely irrelevant, saw no need for treaties, and believed that Indigenous people should be 'civilized,' should adapt to and adopt Western values. He thought they would ultimately not survive as separate nations within Canada. But, his biographer insists, he 'was much more sensitive than his contemporaries were to the moral and legal ambiguities that the process involved,' and he comes off best among British Columbia officials in all accounts of the Indigenous land question. He thought that the 'civilization' process needed time, that it would be effected by the

Indigenous people themselves, and that resources were needed to make that happen. He laid out reserves that he believed would give Indigenous people sufficiency and the ability to participate in commerce, but would not prevent or hinder white settlement.[68] His mission was complicated by a number of distinct but related issues: the Pacific railway was planned to traverse many tracts of traditional land; the provincial government both complained to Ottawa that his reserve allocations were too large and kept on granting land to settlers without reference to his work; Indigenous groups were often threatened with alienation from sources of water, and every move he tried to make entangled him with settler property rights and prejudices. His relationship with the provincial government worsened as he made clear his support of both more generous land allocation for Indigenous peoples and substantial autonomy for them. He became not just a conduit for Indigenous views but an advocate, 'a defender of Native land rights against the pervasive encroachments of a settler society and its government, and an advocate of native management of their own local affairs.' Nothing exemplified his attitude to local self-government more than the meeting he had with the Nlaka'pamux at Lytton in 1878. The latter proposed a comprehensive system of local government predicated on a principle of autonomy, which Sproat largely accepted.[69]

Sproat went further than the federal government wanted and, faced with opposition from both levels of government, he resigned. The Joint Commission was a failure in derailing the long-standing provincial policy on land allocation to Indigenous peoples.[70] The province got its man as Sproat's successor, Peter O'Reilly, a member of the provincial establishment and Trutch's brother-in-law. His views on Indigenous people were the standard fare of most white British Columbians: they were lazy, dissolute, immoral, and dirty.[71] He stayed in the post from 1881 to 1898 and made 26 expeditions, during which he allocated more than 600 reserves. He believed that reserves should be laid out before white settlement, but often got to a location too late for that. Most of his time was spent travelling; he generally spent a day or less in inspection and allocation. His reserve allocations followed a standard formula. He talked with local Indigenous leaders to discover where the band's principal residence was, established what land in the area was not already granted to white settlers, and allocated fishing and village sites as well as some agricultural land. If there was no good agricultural land available, he assigned unproductive land to reserves. His work brought a litany of complaints from Indigenous leaders: reserve boundaries were drawn in the wrong places, reserves were allocated to the wrong people, and, most importantly, the good land in the area had already been granted to settlers. Indigenous complaints came in the form of passive resistance – invoking missionary support and petitions to Victoria, Ottawa, and London, all unheeded. When a delegation of Indigenous leaders met with Premier William Smithe in 1887 to demand a treaty like those made on the prairies, which other Indigenous people had read about in a book (presumably Morris's *Treaties of Canada*), Smithe told them that he had never seen such a book, and that 'there is no such law either English or Dominion' acknowledging Indigenous title.[72]

It was perhaps natural for British Columbia politicians to lie about this issue, but Macdonald knew otherwise and did not lie. He told the Commons in 1881, the year after he had appointed Trutch lieutenant governor of British Columbia, that he was 'strongly of the opinion that if the Government raised the question of the Indian title,' the courts were likely to 'maintain the right of the Indians and their title to the occupation of the soil until that right whatever it might amount to was extinguished.'[73] He was wrong about the British Columbia Supreme Court, because in 1886 Chief Justice Begbie ruled that Indigenous people in the province had no rights except those they were given by the 'grace and benevolence of the crown,' and that 'a long historical chain of authorities' could be marshalled to show 'the negation of all Indian rights to the land.'[74] The SCC might have disagreed, although after the late 1880s it would have had to get around the *St Catherine's Milling* judgment. In any event neither Macdonald nor his Conservative successors referred the matter to court. The strong lobby of British Columbia MPs mattered more to the federal government than either the Indigenous people or the DIA, which also opposed British Columbia's policy. Both major parties had believed in the 1870s that Indigenous people had a valid legal claim to rights in their land, and that those rights should be extinguished by treaties. But that required co-operation with the province, which was not forthcoming. Thwarted by a settler government, Macdonald was loath to make it a matter for the courts. A person motivated primarily by principle might have done so, but Macdonald was not that person; he was, to put it generously, more pragmatic.

In the later nineteenth and early twentieth centuries, disagreements between the dominion and the province over reserves and Indigenous title continued, and the issues moved slowly towards a confrontation in the courts. A small cadre of lawyers advocated for recognition of an Indigenous title, notably John Murray Clark, a Toronto lawyer and the leading Canadian expert on the land rights of Indigenous people, and Arthur O'Meara, a less able lawyer but a passionate believer in those rights. O'Meara was an Ontario lawyer turned missionary in the Yukon who relocated to British Columbia to advocate for the Indigenous cause.[75] Getting the matter into court was difficult, because of the doctrine of sovereign immunity from suit and because it was unclear if the federal government could take a reference to the SCC on an issue of provincial law (see chapter 3). The deadlock was almost broken in 1911. Two years earlier Laurier had commissioned an opinion from lawyer and poet T.R.E. (Tom) MacInnes on Indigenous title, and he produced one that effectively foreshadowed the SCC's judgment in *Calder v Attorney-General of British Columbia* some 60 years later.[76] It showed that an Indigenous title in British Columbia had been recognized in the 1850s by the British government, the HBC, and the colonial government, that such a title had been recognized earlier in other parts of the empire, and that neither the colony nor the province could derogate from it without the consent of the Indigenous occupants and the British government. In consequence the Laurier government prepared a test case, an action in ejectment against a white settler in the Exchequer Court. But Laurier lost the 1911 election over free trade with the United States, and the Borden Conservatives dropped the case.

In 1912 the matter was taken up by another federal-provincial reserve commission, the McKenna-McBride commission, chaired jointly by James McKenna, a long-standing and senior employee of the DIA and one of the negotiators of Treaty 8, and Richard McBride, the British Columbia premier.[77] Its terms of reference did not include Indigenous title, but it was charged with, among other things, achieving a more equitable distribution of reserve acreages. Hearings were heard throughout the province and were rife with misunderstandings caused by different languages and conceptual frameworks. When the issue of title arose it was brushed aside by the commissioners, as not within the scope of their inquiry. The commission recommended additions to some reserves and reductions in the size of others, known as cut-offs. More acreage was added than was cut off, but the value of the land lost to Indigenous nations was much greater than that added. Many Indigenous requests for more land were refused, the most common reason being that the land had already been alienated to white settlers.

The final act in this phase of the British Columbia Indigenous land question lies outside our period, the 1927 report of a joint committee of the Commons and the Senate inquiring into the land claims of the

Allied Tribes of the province. The joint committee concluded that no claim for Indigenous title had been established, and 'the matter should now be regarded as finally closed.' This was the end of the first phase of the British Columbia Indigenous land question. The second phase ended in 1973, when the SCC accepted the claim to title of the Nisga'a people in *Calder*. The third phase is still ongoing. But those are stories for *Volume 3*.

The 1885 Rebellion and the Criminal Law

A detailed account of the 1885 rebellion is beyond the scope of this volume. We deal here with the legal proceedings that followed, principally with the trial of Louis Riel, the most controversial trial in Canadian history. Before we do so we will briefly discuss the principal factors that led the Métis and a small number of Indigenous people to resort to an armed uprising, and the other trials that followed its suppression. The causes of the rebellion connect the Riel trial with the previous sections of this chapter on the Red River resistance and the numbered treaties. The numbered treaty provisions on agriculture did not bring food security in the short term, and many Indigenous bands suffered much privation in the 1880s. The land provided for reserves was not the best for agriculture, and bovine disease and poor harvests because of bad weather contributed to an insufficient food supply. The government was well aware of the problem and knowingly failed to fill the gap with provisions as promised in the treaty. The worst suffering was among Treaty 6 bands, those who had been promised, but were not given, famine assistance. It was principally the Cree bands led by Poundmaker and Wandering Spirit, signatories to Treaty 6, that joined the rebellion.[78]

The *Manitoba Act* was in the very short term a good result for the Métis, but there turned out to be little future in Manitoba for them. They ended up with very little land and were quickly swamped by white settlers, both subjects discussed in chapter 14. Many Métis moved west to new settlements in Saskatchewan, but after just a few years their tenure in their new land was threatened by the arrival of government surveyors laying out lots for white settlers. In 1884 the Métis persuaded Riel to return to Canada from Montana and spearhead a movement for the redress of grievances. How that movement, which began with a petition to Ottawa and a request that delegates be received there, as in 1869–70, descended into armed resistance is well known. The rebellion, which featured several battles and left over 100 Métis, Indigenous people, and settlers dead, lasted some seven weeks, after which Riel surrendered.

In the aftermath of the rebellion 85 people were charged.[79] The government fully expected to get a substantial number of convictions. Minister of Justice Alexander Campbell told the lawyers chosen to prosecute that '[t]he object of the Government would be accomplished by ... a certain number of convictions. I should expect to hear of thirty or forty leading [defendants] having been found guilty.'[80] He got well over that. Thirteen Indigenous people were tried for murder, of whom 12 were convicted of the full offence and one of manslaughter. Of those 12, eight were executed, and four had their sentences commuted to prison terms. Nineteen other Indigenous people were convicted of treason-felony (a term explained below) and received prison terms of two to three years in Manitoba's Stony Mountain penitentiary. In addition, 22 other Indigenous people were convicted of offences ranging from larceny to arson and received sentences ranging from six months to 14 years, most in the two- to six-year range, and a small number were convicted but got less than six months. Of the non-Indigenous defendants, 32 members of the council created during the rebellion and who pleaded guilty, almost all of them Métis, 14 were discharged. Eighteen were convicted, of whom 15 were given prison sentences ranging from one to seven years. Two anglophone white men were also tried, one of whom was Riel's secretary, William Henry Jackson. He was found insane and not fit to stand trial. The other man, Thomas Scott, who was in fact not white but an anglophone Métis, was acquitted of aiding and abetting the rebellion.[81]

The most important of these trials were those of Indigenous participants for murder held at Battleford, of whom eight were hanged, and those for treason-felony of 19 Indigenous leaders, of whom the best-known are Poundmaker and Big Bear, who received three-year sentences. The non-capital offence of treason-felony originated in 1848 British legislation to widen what could be charged as treasonous to include conspiracies as well as overt acts. It was a useful device to achieve convictions from juries reluctant to see someone sentenced to death, and to extract guilty pleas from those who might otherwise have contested the charge. A Canadian version of the Act was passed in 1868, and the Indigenous leaders were charged under section 5, which dealt with a person who 'compasses, imagines, invents, devises, or intents ... to levy war against Her Majesty ... in order by force or constraint to compel her ... to change her ... measures or counsels.' The penalty was two years to life in prison.[82] The decision not to pursue capital charges against a large number of defendants was a classic example of the judicious use of the law in a time of political turmoil, combining the terror of the death sentence in a small number of cases with forbearance in others. It avoided the law becoming an instrument of unmitigated terror and thus illegitimate.

The trials of the Indigenous defendants were marked by a failure of most to understand the proceedings, poor translation, and, with a few exceptions, no legal counsel. Even when counsel was made available, the lawyers took little time to prepare, failed to gather supporting witnesses, and did not challenge prosecution evidence or prevent their clients incriminating themselves. Even had the lawyers been effective, they faced the implacable hostility of two of the judges, stipendiary magistrates Charles-Borromée Rouleau at Battleford and Hugh Richardson at Regina. The former was a knowledgeable lawyer but had suffered much loss of property in the rebellion and conducted the murder trials with 'blinkered vengeance,' convinced, in his words, that the 'Indians should be taught a severe lesson.'[83] The latter, about whom more below, was keen to serve the government. The executions were the result of the government's desire 'to crush any remaining vestiges of First Nations autonomy,' and the limited involvement of a few leaders and bands provided the pretext. The proceedings were not justified as deterrents, for the vast majority of Indigenous people had not joined the rebellion. The lieutenant governor of the Territories, Edgar Dewdney, knew this and reported it to Macdonald, but Ottawa saw an opportunity to get rid of 'troublesome' Indian leaders and their 'nagging call for revision of the [numbered] treaties.'

The Trial and Execution of Louis Riel

In Riel's case the government worked implacably to secure a conviction for high treason with the intention from the outset of executing him. Since 1886 the trial has been both denounced as an unfair proceeding intended to convict, not just try, Riel, and defended as exactly the opposite. Equally subject to passionate scholarship on both sides has been the decision to execute Riel, not to commute the death sentence. For much of our history, opinions about the Riel trial and execution diverged along predictable fault lines, French/English and Métis/non-Métis, but in more recent decades many people of all ethnic and linguistic backgrounds have seen Riel's treatment by the legal system as a politically driven overreaction fuelled by prejudice.

With the military defeat of the rebellion the federal government had a decision to make about whether to put Riel on trial or settle for some lesser response, such as exile.[84] Ottawa quickly decided on a trial for treason, to be held in Regina. It was by modern, but not contemporary, standards a rapid proceeding. The presiding judge was Hugh Richardson. As we will discuss in more detail in chapter 13, he was one of three stipendiary magistrates with jurisdiction to hear all criminal cases in the Territories. When the trial began on 20 July 1885, nine lawyers were present, five for the prosecution and four for the defence. The former comprised three counsel brought in from Ontario – Britton Bath Osler, Christopher Robinson, and George Wheelock Burbridge – as well as Thomas Chase Casgrain and David Scott Lynch. Casgrain was born in Detroit, the son of French-Canadian parents, and educated in Quebec. He was a part-time professor at Laval law school and a Crown prosecutor brought in to have a French-Canadian on the prosecuting team. Lynch, like so many early Manitoba and territorial lawyers, was a recent (1882) immigrant from Ontario who was the mayor of Regina, where his practice included work as a Crown prosecutor. The prosecution team was headed by Burbidge, the federal deputy minister of justice, who, as we saw in chapter 3, was in 1887 rewarded for his service by being made the first judge appointed to the Exchequer Court. The lead courtroom lawyer was the tireless Osler, mentioned in chapter 6, whose legal practice had included a lot of work as a Crown prosecutor. He also had a large and very remunerative practice representing railway companies and a reputation as a formidable advocate. Robinson was the son of the most dominant legal figure in pre-Confederation Ontario, Sir John Beverley Robinson, and a very successful lawyer, his principal client being the federal government.[85]

On the other side were three lawyers from Quebec, not chosen by Riel but by the Ottawa-based Association Nationale pour la Défense des Prisonniers Métis, and one local, Thomas Cooke Johnstone, who was added in Regina to have someone experienced with the Territorial justice system. Thirty-six years old, he had moved to Regina from Ontario in 1882. He became an experienced criminal lawyer and was appointed to the first Supreme Court of Saskatchewan in 1907. François-Xavier Lemieux was the only one of the three who had practised criminal law extensively and successfully and he was also a prominent and well-known Liberal activist, having won a seat in the Quebec assembly in 1883. Charles Fitzpatrick was an anglophone Liberal from Quebec who later became minister of justice under Laurier and, in 1906, was appointed to the SCC as chief justice. James Greenshields, only 33, was plucked from practice with his brother in Montreal. Overall the defence team did not have the status or experience of the prosecutors.[86]

The trial took just seven days spread over two weeks.[87] The first two days were largely taken up with legal arguments about whether the court had jurisdiction, discussed below, following which the defence secured a week's adjournment to gather documentary evidence and find and persuade witnesses to appear. The trial resumed on 28 July and that and the next day were spent with the prosecution introducing many documents and calling 15 witnesses to testify to Riel's leadership of the rebellion. It was hardly difficult to establish that Riel had played a leading role in the events of 1885. The defence then took its turn on 30 July and concentrated on insanity as a defence, despite the fact that Riel did not want that. One day was nonetheless taken up with evidence from three people of Riel's erratic behaviour, and the testimony of four medical witnesses who gave opinions that his actions demonstrated insanity. The lay witnesses included two priests who testified to rapid changes in personality and of religious beliefs well outside the mainstream of Catholic, indeed Christian, doctrine. The medical witnesses included three superintendents of asylums: Dr. Francois Roy, of the Beauport asylum in Quebec; Dr. Daniel Clark, of the Toronto asylum; and Dr. James Wallace of the Hamilton asylum. The legal test for insanity in 1885 derived from the 1843 McNaghten decision of the House of Lords.[88] It was a specific and narrow test and not designed to find whether a person was insane in any general sense. A person could escape criminal culpability only if he or she could prove that at the time of the commission of the offence he or she had been 'labouring under such a defect of reason, from disease of the mind, as not to know the nature and quality of the act he was doing, or if he did know it, that he did not know what he was doing was wrong.' This test, which is still the law, was criticized by many in the nineteenth century, including by some of the medical witnesses at the Riel trial, but that had no impact on Richardson. In his charge to the jury he cited it verbatim. The medical witnesses also probably had little influence on the jurors. They were unpersuasive because they did not believe in the McNaghten test, and they were quite effectively cross-examined by Osler, who drew admissions that Riel's eccentric behaviour may have been a deception.

There followed reply evidence from the Crown, including its own medical witness, Dr. Augustus Jukes, the senior surgeon of the NWMP, who had spoken to Riel many times in jail, and other witnesses who had talked to him in prison. All testified that he spoke and behaved rationally. Fitzpatrick made a long speech for the defence, after which Riel addressed the jury. The entire defence case took up one day. On the next day, 31 July, both sides made closing arguments, and towards the end of the day presiding judge Richardson began his summing up, which he finished in short order on 1 August. The jury retired immediately and after an hour of deliberation returned with a guilty verdict and a recommendation of mercy. Riel spoke again when asked if he had anything to say before sentence. Richardson then pronounced the mandatory death sentence.

A number of aspects of the trial have long been the subject of controversy. Before we assess the trial we need to define our criteria. It must be judged against the standards of his time, not ours, which is true when writing any history. The principal modern defender of the trial has argued that the appropriate question to ask is not simply whether the standards of the 1880s were used, but also whether Riel 'was tried in the same way as would any other man who had committed similar actions in the same jurisdiction.'[89] We do not use that criterion because this was a unique trial for treason. No one else was tried for high treason in the wake of 1885, and no one else was tried for treason in a region of Canada that had a criminal justice system unlike any other part of the country. No one else was tried for treason who had aroused vituperative animosity in Protestant Ontario just over a decade previously. No one else has ever been hanged for treason in post-1867 Canada. No one would argue that Riel had not been responsible for an armed rebellion. But that very fact made this a political trial, and political trials are about much more than legal culpability. The government worked inexorably to produce a result that would send the right political message. Thus the more appropriate question is that posed by another commentator: 'What decisions did the government make ... in areas where it had options and is there a pattern to those decisions?'[90] The government made two large decisions of great significance, about the jurisdiction of trial and the exercise of the royal prerogative of mercy, both of which were adverse to Riel, and a number of smaller decisions, all to the same effect.

Trial venue was critically important. The decision to hold it in the North-West Territories appears on its face not only reasonable but correct, given that criminal trials were and are invariably conducted in the jurisdiction in which the alleged offence took place. But the Territories had a unique system of criminal justice, established in 1875, and discussed in detail in chapter 13. For our purposes the salient and unique features of territorial criminal justice in 1885 were the status of the trial judge and the composition of the jury. The presiding judge was a stipendiary magistrate, not a Superior Court judge. Stipendiary magistrates in the Territories did not have good behaviour tenure, the hallmark of judicial independence; they held at pleasure appointments. The government could have held the trial in Manitoba, or in the Territories by appointing a special commission of oyer and terminer presided over by a Superior Court judge, and discussed doing one of these things.* But it chose instead to hold it in the only region of Canada where the judiciary provisions of the *BNA Act* did not apply and where the presiding judge would not be independent. Moreover, the statute creating a Supreme Court for the Territories, staffed by judges with good behaviour tenure, received royal assent on 2 June 1886, before the Riel trial began, but did not come into force until 1 January 1887.[91] The government could have either delayed the trial six months or made the legislation immediately effective, and in either case the trial would have been presided over by an independent judge. There was no mention of a link between the Riel trial and judicial independence when the bill was debated in the Commons, but there was a discussion of judicial independence in general. Liberal justice critic Edward Blake asked if it was intended to give the judges of the new court good behaviour tenure, and when Justice Minister John Thompson said that it was Blake approved: 'Good behaviour … is the proper tenure for a judge.'[92]

The person chosen to preside was Hugh Richardson, who had qualified for the bar in Ontario in 1847, and practised there for over 20 years, including six as a Crown attorney. He was prominent in the militia and in 1872 was made chief clerk in the Department of Justice in Ottawa. His appointment as one of the stipendiary magistrates was thus a reward for service from a government that could dismiss him without reason. He was also the paid legal adviser to the lieutenant governor and an ex officio member of the council of the North-West Territories. He presided in other rebellion-related trials, including those for treason-felony of Poundmaker, Big Bear, and One Arrow. In 1887, a few months after Riel's trial, he was promoted, perhaps as a reward for his service in the Riel trial, to senior judge on the new NWTSC, effectively the chief justice for a court that did not have one. Thus the presiding judge was

---

* Literally 'to hear and determine.' Special commissions were issued when there was no court of competent jurisdiction in the region or, much more often, when the court was an itinerant, or circuit, court, which would not visit the jurisdiction for some time because it conducted circuits once or twice a year. The government could have named any Canadian judge or judges to preside.

someone without tenure, a member of the Territorial legal and political establishment, whose earlier law practice had been as a prosecutor, and he was soon after given a promotion. He spoke no French. He was impatient to get the case over with, constantly pushing to start earlier in the day or go a little later than planned. As we will see below, he was not very good on the law, although a recent study of his everyday work as a judge argues that he was generally fair and conscientious. He was not unqualified, and there is no overt evidence of bias towards Indigenous people or Métis. But he was, by one recent account, 'careless, lazy, and irresponsible' as well as being weak on the law. As one MP argued in the Commons in 1886, he was an 'unhappy choice.' His biographer praises him for his conduct of the trial, arguing that he gave Riel 'considerable latitude to speak in his own defence.' But that was not unusual in a capital case, and the same biographer is the most prominent defender of the fairness of the trial. A more recent account takes strong exception to this characterization, citing not just the Riel trial, but the many other rebellion-related trials over which he presided.[93]

The second important feature that resulted from its being held in the Territories was the composition of the jury. Richardson sat with Justice of the Peace Henry Le Jeune and a six-man jury. As discussed in more detail in chapter 13, the jury provision was designed to accommodate the fact that the region had a small and scattered European population (there were no Indigenous people on any jury), and it was considered to be an acceptable modification for 'routine' criminal trials. Had the trial been held anywhere else, of course, there would have been the time-honoured 12-man jury, doubling the chances of a hung jury. Although Riel was allowed to make his case in French,[94] the jurors were all anglophones: two merchants and four farmers. Had the trial been held in Manitoba there would have been francophone jurors among the 12. Had it been held anywhere else than in the Territories the jury pool would have been randomly selected, not chosen by the judge. In the Territories when jurors were required, the stipendiary magistrate summoned 'such male persons as he may think suitable' to form the jury pool from which the six jurors were chosen. The pool chosen by Richardson was 36 strong, all anglophone, with four merchants, 31 farmers, and one 'contractor.' It was likely that an array chosen by Richardson would not have been very different from one chosen randomly from people living in and around Regina, but that merely emphasizes the fact that the jurors were not Riel's peers. They were white anglophone settlers, with no sympathy for or understanding of Métis grievances. The defence team did not use all of its six peremptory challenges, only five, probably because one white settler farmer from Regina was much the same as another.

Riel's defence lawyers objected to the venue and the special procedures as soon as the trial began, on two grounds, one very technical and irrelevant to this account. The other was that a trial by jury in a capital case meant a trial before an independent judge with a 12-man jury, an ancient and hallowed right in the English constitution. In the course of making the argument about the lack of judicial independence Greenshields, while he insisted that he had the 'utmost respect for the court,' could not have endeared himself to Richardson by calling a stipendiary magistrate 'a servile creature,' especially as Richardson had objected to the word 'creature' to describe a judge who served at pleasure in another rebellion trial.[95] The issue of the court's capital case jurisdiction had been litigated and resolved adversely to the defence in the James Connor murder case of 1885, which took place in Moose Jaw. In that case the defence took the question of Territorial criminal procedure to the Manitoba Court of Queen's Bench, but lost.[96] In the Riel trial the prosecution responded to this argument by pointing out that the jurisdiction of magistrates in India was much the same, and that the defence contentions went to the very validity of the territorial justice system.[97] Richardson did not involve himself in the legal argument, making fewer than 10 one-sentence interventions. His most substantive comment made it clear that he was not going to brook any suggestion that there was anything wrong with the jury: 'Suit the jury to the occasion.' While the legal arguments failed at the time, the judicial independence and jury issues tainted the trial.

Another problem concerned the charges. It was not until the trial started that the defence knew which statute was being employed. Unlike in other parts of Canada, criminal procedure in the Territories did not involve the presentation of an indictment to a grand jury, the indictment including the relevant statute. The prosecution simply laid an information sworn by Alexander Stewart, the Hamilton, Ontario, police chief who was the chief investigator, before Richardson in July 1885. It was couched in the same language an indictment would have used, referring to many of the actions that were part of the law of treason, including levying war against the Crown, and stated in the standard words of an indictment that Riel's actions were 'against the form of the statute in such case made and provided.' But it did not name the statute. When the trial began the defence assumed the charges were being brought under the Canadian *Lawless Aggressions Act*, discussed below, but were told by Osler that the prosecution was proceeding under a 1352 English statute defining which acts constituted treason.

The 1352 statute was law in Canada in 1886, and it prescribed only one mandatory penalty on conviction, death, which was presumably why it was employed.[98]

Although the lack of pretrial disclosure of the applicable statute must have caused the defence lawyers some surprise, it did not change their tactics. They had come prepared to argue that the information was invalid and could still make that argument. The information contained six charges, in two nearly identical groups of three. One group charged Riel, 'being a subject of our Lady the Queen,' with levying war at Duck Lake, Fish Creek, and Batoche, the other group charged him with the same offence at the same places, but described him not as a subject but as a person 'then living within the Dominion of Canada and under the protection of … the Queen.' In short it charged him with committing the same offences as a subject and as not a subject, and on that ground Johnstone argued that the information was 'bad because it is double.' Richardson, who seems to have struggled to grasp this argument, shortly stated that there was nothing to it and told Riel to plead. But there was substance to the defence argument. Riel was not a subject. He had renounced his allegiance to Britain and taken out American citizenship. An American citizen could have been charged with a capital offence under the *Lawless Aggressions Act*, a Canadian statute passed in 1867 to deal with the Fenian threat. It created a capital offence similar to the 'levying war' offence under the *Treason Act*, but the accused had to be a citizen of another country.[99] The likelihood is that the government, which initially favoured proceeding this way, abandoned the idea because the act applied to people who had invaded the country, whereas Riel's entry was peaceful, and because it was concerned about the diplomatic repercussions from the United States from seeming making this an international incident.[100]

The problem of Riel's citizenship was solved by the second group of three counts in the information, which charged him not as a British subject but as a person owing local allegiance 'under the protection of our Sovereign Lady the Queen.' The doctrine of local allegiance can be traced back to the seventeenth century and the prominent writer on English criminal law Sir Matthew Hale, who argued that if an alien lived on British territory and enjoyed 'the benefit of the King's protection and commit a treason, he shall be judged and executed as a traitor, for he owes a local allegiance.'[101] A related doctrine of 'natural' or 'perpetual' allegiance applied to persons who had been British subjects but been naturalized in another jurisdiction. Both doctrines had caused problems after the American revolution, and both had been significantly undermined by naturalization legislation in Britain and the new dominion. If local allegiance was to be relied on, Riel would have to have lived in Canada long enough to be under the protection of the Crown, but that was highly unlikely, given how soon before the rebellion he returned and how short a time it lasted. The status of both doctrines of local and natural allegiance was unclear in 1885. The lack of clarity must have been known to the prosecutors, which is why they charged Riel both as a subject and not as a subject, and why they concealed the charging statute until the trial had started, giving the defence less time to prepare. In fact the defence team did not pursue these subjects, perhaps because for lack of preparation.

Some critics of the trial have also argued that it was flawed because there was no pretrial examination of whether Riel was fit to stand trial on the ground of insanity.[102] There was a provision requiring a pretrial examination in the 1869 consolidation of criminal procedure, discussed in chapter 13, which was later included in the first *Criminal Code* of 1892. But the 1869 provision was not part of territorial law because Canadian rules of criminal procedure had to be specifically extended to the Territories, and the statute had not been. It has been argued that the lack of such a hearing was a further reason for changing the venue. Yet one cannot read the transcript and not conclude that Riel was fit to stand trial. He was undoubtedly annoying to his lawyers and obtuse in refusing to answer the question of whether he wanted to defend himself or use counsel with a simple yes or no answer. But the obtuseness was the tactical response of someone insisting on his point and knowing that he would have to abandon it if he did so answer. His point was that his actions were justified in light of Métis grievances. Initially Lemieux tried to offer this defence but Osler shut him down. 'My learned friends have opened a case of treason, justified only by the insanity of the prisoner,' he complained, but 'they are now seeking to justify armed rebellion for the redress of … grievances.' Not only were the two defences inconsistent, but the latter was 'no justification at all.' It was 'not really any defence in law,' 'a counter-claim against the Government and that is not open to any person on trial for high treason.' Osler was quite correct. Yet the strategy might have worked with a differently constituted jury, one consisting of at least some Métis or Métis sympathizers, and if the defence had been able to present evidence to make their case, which they were not.[103]

Fitzpatrick's long speech to the jury on 30 July cleverly conflated Métis grievances and insanity. He argued that those grievances were valid, and that given the support Riel had received from the Métis, a sane and rational man would not have started an armed rebellion. He would 'lie low and continue fomenting this movement,' so that, in the long run, the people of the Territories would win their 'rights.' All Riel had to do was 'exercise the ordinary dictates of prudence and caution and common sense' to eventually achieve his ambition. Moreover, he understood the deep attachment between the Métis and their priests, and it made no sense for him to deny Catholic doctrine. A sane man 'would not have attempted, with a handful of half-breeds … to force Canada to grant him his rights … [and] he would not have … endeavoured to take the half-breeds … from their allegiance to their religion.' Riel's actions were 'entirely inconsistent with the possession of a sound mind.'

When Fitzpatrick was finished Riel addressed the jury, a long and rambling speech, going back and forth between the politics of the previous 15 years and God and Jesus Christ. We cannot make a judgment about Riel's sanity. All we will venture is that much of the later writing about it has concentrated on his beliefs, especially his religious beliefs, and the evidence that Riel's beliefs were inconsistent with established Christian doctrine, that he claimed to talk directly to God and saw visions, is highly persuasive.[104] That puts him in the same category as a host of people, including Jesus Christ, Joseph Smith, and a bevy of popular contemporary TV evangelists. Whether that makes him insane depends ultimately on one's view of religious belief.

When the jury found Riel guilty they recommended mercy, which Richardson promised to forward but did not say that he would support. The jury gave no reasons for the recommendation, because they were not required to, so we have to speculate about why six anglophone settlers did not wish to see Riel hang. A plausible explanation is that they thought that the rebellion was not justified but was 'understandable in view of the government's dilatory handling of settlers' grievances.' Evidence supporting this interpretation comes from remarks made later by a juror who said that the jury commented more than once on the need to have Macdonald himself in the witness box.[105]

There followed appeals, first to the Manitoba Court of Queen's Bench, with little hope of success. It was heard by three of the court's four judges, all anglophones, and all appointees of the Conservatives. The chief justice, Lewis Wallbridge, whose somewhat remarkable appointment is discussed in chapter 3, was viewed by many French-Canadian politicians as anti-French. Whatever his merits as a jurist, they did not include appreciation of judicial independence, for he had assisted the government in planning its trial strategy, although this fact did not become known for more than a century.[106] The court's only francophone judge, Joseph Dubuc, was deliberately absent. Dubuc, originally from Quebec, had long been a defender of Métis rights, and it was he who had persuaded Riel to run in the 1872 federal election for Provencher. But he increasingly distanced himself from Riel in the 1870s and declined to sit on the appeal because he thought Riel a heretic.[107] Kitzpatrick and Lemieux argued the appeal, assisted by leading Winnipeg lawyer John Skirving Ewart, whose legal stature was discussed in chapter 6 and whose advocacy of the educational rights of franco-Manitobans will be highlighted in chapter 16. They had nothing new and nothing (to the appeal court) compelling to offer. In addition to some technical objections, they replayed the issue of whether the trial should have been held in Regina and argued that the insanity plea should have been accepted.

The final act was a petition to the JCPC for leave to appeal. Riel's lawyers addressed the court, which did not call on the Crown. The JCPC very rarely agreed to hear a criminal case, and this was no exception. In a brief two-page decision denying leave it noted that the facts were clearly proved and undoubtedly supported the conviction for high treason. The defence had argued insanity, but the jury had 'negatived that defence.' The panel found only two arguments 'capable of plausible or, indeed, intelligible expression,' both of which had been disposed of by the Manitoba Court. One was that the governing statute required notes of the proceedings to be taken 'in full,' but shorthand had been used and the notes later written up. The JCPC gave this very short shrift. The other was that the legislation establishing the Territorial justice system was invalid because of its departures from common law. The JCPC roundly dismissed the argument, noting that Parliament could legislate for the Territories, that departures from aspects of the common law were hardly untypical to suit local circumstances, and that for it to hold otherwise 'would be of highly mischievous consequence,' invalidating the entire Territorial justice system.[108]

The final stage in Riel's story was the decision to let the sentence be carried out. As explained more fully in chapter 13, all death sentences received some consideration of whether the condemned person should be granted a commutation. Every commutation decision involved petitions for or against execution, and Riel's case was no different. Petitions demanding that the execution take place came from white settlers in the Territories and an Orange organization in Toronto, but they were greatly outnumbered by those that poured in with thousands of names attached from Quebec and Manitoba, from French-Canadians living in New York, from other locations in the United States, and from France. There were even a few from Ontario, from Ottawa and from Essex and Russell counties. The pro-Riel petitions variously deprecated Richardson's conduct of the trial and the lack of a true jury of Riel's peers, argued that Métis grievances were legitimate, asserted that Riel was insane, and stressed that his actions were political. Some mentioned more than one of these reasons, and many were couched in identical language, their text conveyed from one place to another. They were read and signed in many public meetings and demonstrations. At one of the latter Thomas Casgrain was hanged in effigy, although he was nonetheless able to win a seat in the Quebec assembly in the 1886 election as a conservative.[109]

It was all to no avail. The government was determined that Riel would hang. The politics of the rebellion demanded it. Riel had taken up arms, and many people had been killed. A week after the JCPC announced its decision the government appointed a three-man medical commission to assess whether Riel had become insane since the trial; to hang an insane man would clearly have been wrong.[110] To say that the government manipulated the membership and result of this commission is an understatement. None of the doctors were experienced with mental illness. One was Jukes, who had been recommended by Macdonald for the post of senior surgeon of the NWMP and in any event was hardly likely to be sympathetic to the rebellion. He expressed a personal aversion to capital punishment but insisted that after multiple visits he had found Riel's religious views 'peculiar' but was certain that on all other matters he was 'a sane, clear-headed and accountable being.' Another member, Michael Lavell, was a successful doctor and medical educator and a long-time friend and supporter of Macdonald. Before he reported, the prime minster sent him private instructions to find Riel sane. He obliged, writing that Riel was 'a vain, ambitious man, crafty and cunning, with powers in a marked degree to incite men to desperate deeds.' The third member, Dr. François-Xavier Valade, was not so obliging. He concluded that Riel was not 'an accountable being,' although he did agree that the jury had correctly found him guilty under the McNaghten rules. Macdonald's cabinet simply ignored this finding and ordered the execution. Moreover, when the issue was debated in the Commons, the government responded to a request for the medical reports by publishing a very misleading version of Valade's, consisting only of one long sentence.

This last action was consistent with many others. The government was determined from first to last to convict and execute Riel and thereby send the strongest message it could that the still fledgling Canadian state would not brook armed opposition. Riel was hanged inside Fort Battleford on 16 November 1885. Although public executions had been abolished in 1869, Macdonald ordered both that the scaffold be high enough that spectators could see the event and that local Indigenous notables be brought in to witness the event in 'an extraordinary orchestration of ritualised punishment.'[111]

8

Canadian Law and Indigenous Peoples II: The *Indian Act*, the Reserve System, and Assimilation

In 1867 there was a small body of colonial legislation dealing with Indigenous peoples, most of it focused on preventing settler intrusions on reserves. As we saw in *Volume 1*, the legislation was largely ineffective because of inadequate enforcement.[1] The federal government first exercised its jurisdiction over 'Indians and lands reserved for Indians,' section 91 (27) of the *BNA Act* in 1868, creating the office of secretary of state. The first incumbent was Hector Louis Langevin, and he was also appointed the superintendent general of Indian affairs (SG), with 'the control and management of the lands and property of the Indians in Canada.' The position of SG was shifted to the secretary of state for the provinces in 1869, over which former Nova Scotia Indian commissioner Joseph Howe presided until May 1873. Thereafter, until 1880, what was known as the 'Indian Affairs Branch' was a part of the Ministry of the Interior, and its head, David Laird, became the SG under Mackenzie's Liberal government. John A. Macdonald was SG between the return to power of the Conservatives in 1878 and 1883, during which period, in 1880, a separate Department of Indian Affairs (DIA) was established, over which the SG presided.[2] Despite this formal change, the DIA and the Ministry of the Interior were always closely linked. The same man headed both departments until 1936.

The chief bureaucrat was the deputy SG. In 1867 that was William Spragge, who had held a similar position in the Province of Canada since 1862. Spragge died in April 1874 and was replaced by Lawrence

Vankoughnet, who had also been an Indian Department employee under the Province of Canada and who held the post for almost 20 years, until 1893. In the 1890s a new breed of men held the post, people either lacking in knowledge of Indigenous peoples or who believed they knew enough to harbour contempt for them: Hayter Reed, 1893–7, retired soldier, Indian agent, and Indian commissioner for the Territories; James Smart, 1897–1903, who was deputy minister of the interior and got the DIA job when two positions were amalgamated; Frank Pedley, 1903–13, a Toronto lawyer; and Duncan Campbell Scott, 1913–32, poet and long-time employee of the DIA.[3]

The 1868 Act confirmed that lands and other property held in trust for Indigenous peoples before Confederation would continue to be held on the same terms, and established the first federally legislated surrender requirement for alienating reserve land.* It also provided the first post-Confederation definition of 'Indian' as a person of 'Indian blood,' or a person 'residing among' the latter who was 'descended on either side from Indians.' The statute did not exclude Indigenous women who married non-Indigenous men. It applied only to the original four provinces, and repealed the existing Nova Scotia and New Brunswick legislation, but not that of the Province of Canada. The chapter on 'Indians' in the 1859 *CSC* continued to apply in central Canada to the extent that it was not inconsistent with the 1868 statute. In the 1869 *Enfranchisement Act*, discussed in detail in the second section of this chapter, a 'blood quantum' was added to the definition for the purpose of distribution of annuity payments. A recipient had to be of at least 'one fourth Indian blood.' For the same reason a woman who married 'any other than an Indian' would 'cease to be an Indian … within the meaning of' the act, as would any children she had with a non-Indigenous man. The government justified this as a measure designed to stop white men getting their hands on a share of band revenues. In 1874 the 1868 act and other early federal statutes were made applicable to all provinces, albeit with exceptions and with a power given to the governor general to exempt Manitoba and British Columbia from all or any parts of the legislation.[4]

The first *Indian Act* of 1876 consolidated all existing legislation and established a legal regime to govern the tens of thousands of Indigenous people who lived in all regions of the Canadian state. It retained the definition of 'Indian,' although it provided that a woman marrying

---

* The surrender requirement is more fully discussed below, in the section on reserve lands.

out could keep her share of annuities and other interest payments payable to the band to which she formerly belonged. The definition also excluded any 'half-breed in Manitoba who has shared in the distribution of half-breed lands,' the 1.4-million-acre grant to the Métis in the *Manitoba Act*, although widows and persons of mixed ethnicity who had adhered to a treaty were included.[5]

Between 1879 and 1914 Parliament passed a further 23 statutes on Indigenous peoples. Seventeen amended the *Indian Act*, three consolidated and amended it, and three were separate from it. The *Indian Act*'s increasing reach into every aspect of Indigenous life can be measured both quantitatively and qualitatively. The original Act had exactly 100 sections, the revised statutes versions of 1886 and 1906 131 and 195 sections respectively. Over time the act covered an increasing range of issues: management of reserve lands; prohibition of alcohol sales; allocation of timber rights; strictures on sexual practices, co-habitation and 'illegitimacy'; Sabbath observance laws; bans on cultural practices; and many more aspects of social, economic, and cultural life. It was all aimed at the assimilation of Indigenous peoples with settler society through the extirpation of Indigenous social, religious, cultural, and economic values and their replacement by European settler ones. Federal government policy was one of assimilation, 'a policy designed to move Aboriginal communities from their "savage" state to that of "civilization" and thus to make in Canada but one community – a non-Aboriginal one.' Contemporaries only rarely called this assimilation, but the words they did use – civilization, advancement, improvement – meant precisely that. John A. Macdonald did use the word. The nation's goal, he told his cabinet in 1887, was 'to do away with the tribal system and assimilate the Indian people in all respects with the inhabitants of the Dominion, as speedily as they are fit to change.'[6]

While the goal of assimilation remained consistent, the way the state sought to achieve it varied. From Confederation to the mid-1880s Canadian policy aimed to remake Indigenous societies through persuasion and the voluntary adoption of westernization. Principal among these voluntary policies was enfranchisement, which entailed acceptance by Indigenous people of a wide range of European values, and with which this chapter begins. The early period also saw the establishment of the reserve system in the West, the subject of the second section of this chapter, with much emphasis placed on the protection of reserve lands from interference in, and acquisition by, white settlers. There was an inherent long-term conflict between reserve protection and enfranchisement, for one aim of enfranchisement was the conversion of reserves to land held individually, as common law fee simples. In turn that would have led to the alienation of those individual land holdings to others, to land previously occupied exclusively by Indigenous people being owned and occupied, to a greater or lesser degree, by non-Indigenous individuals. During this first period there were also attempts to persuade Indigenous people in central and eastern Canada to adopt western governance models, to choose their leaders by election rather than accepting leadership by traditional elites, discussed in the third section below. Education was also to the fore from the outset, and that subject is dealt with in the next chapter.

After the mid-1880s the federal government sought social and cultural change through an increasing degree of compulsion and coercion. The principal causes of the shift were twofold. By the 1880s there was ample evidence that enfranchisement and other policies were failures from the perspective of the federal government, and the DIA employed more aggressive measures to force Indigenous people to adopt Western values. In addition, the 1885 rebellion caused a general hardening of attitudes towards Indigenous peoples, who went from worthy but untutored inhabitants of Canada who deserved and would ultimately accept the benefits of 'civilization,' to ungrateful, potentially disloyal 'savages' who needed to be brought to heel as quickly as possible. They were seen as lacking sufficient ambition and intelligence to reform and advance themselves. Legislation was augmented by administrative measures such as the introduction of a pass system restricting Indigenous mobility in the Northwest Territories.[7]

This chapter examines four principal aspects of the assimilationist drive of the first half century of the new dominion – the three already discussed, as well as the outlawing of traditional religious and spiritual practices and ceremonies from the 1890s. These topics were the most important aspects of the *'Indian Act* regime,' which the 1997 *Royal Commission on Aboriginal Peoples* concluded imposed a 'legislative straitjacket' on Indigenous people, 'regulated almost every aspect of' their lives and 'recast [them] as ... dependent ward[s]' of the state.[8]

Enfranchisement

Enfranchisement was part of the 'civilization' movement, which had become a major aspect of colonial policy towards Indigenous people by mid-century. Enfranchisement meant something more than the right to vote, although it did entail that. For white Canadians before the introduction of manhood suffrage in the late nineteenth century, voting required not only being male but also a property owner. For

Indigenous men, enfranchisement was an affirmation that they lived, worked, spoke, and thought like a white person and had, and desired, private property. In the words of Hector Langevin, enfranchised Indigenous persons were those who 'by their education and knowledge of business, their intelligence and good conduct' were 'as well qualified as the whites to enjoy civil rights, and to be released from a state of tutelage.' Before Confederation enfranchisement was available under the Province of Canada's *Gradual Civilization Act* of 1857. The *Gradual Civilization Act* was continued in force for Ontario and Quebec in the first federal legislation of 1868, but the following year it was replaced by a new *Enfranchisement Act*.[9]

The principal provision of the *Enfranchisement Act* was section 13, which allowed the government to issue letters patent for a life estate to a portion of a reserve to 'any Indian' who 'from the degree of civilization to which he has attained, and the character for integrity and sobriety which he bears, appears to be a safe and suitable person for becoming a proprietor of land.' Thus 'civilization' was a qualification for private property ownership, which in turn was an affirmation that a person was 'civilized.' The land in which he was to have a life estate was 50 acres 'allotted to him within the Reserve.' Sections 1 and 29 of the *Enfranchisement Act* authorized surveys of reserves and provided that when a reserve had been surveyed and divided into lots, nobody would be lawfully in possession of a lot 'unless he or she has been or shall be located for the same' by order of the SG. This 'location' by the SG was a 'location title' and the document signifying which 50-acre plot was a 'location ticket.' The location ticket was 'the most important innovation' of this period, 'an essential feature of the civilization process and a necessity for enfranchisement' because 'it was a means by which the Indian could demonstrate that he had adopted the European concept of private property.'[10]

The *Enfranchisement Act* did more than make Indigenous men individual owners of reserve land. Section 16 provided that every man enfranchised had to choose a Christian name and surname 'by which he wishes to be enfranchised and thereafter known.' That name would appear on the letters patent granting the life estate. The enfranchisee's wife and children were also enfranchised. Most significantly, from the issuance of the letters patent all legal distinctions between an Indigenous person and white settlers would end. The former would 'no longer be deemed Indians within the meaning of the laws relating to Indians.' The only exception was that enfranchised

22   Cap. 6.   *Indians.*   32-33 Vict.

CAP VI.

An Act for the gradual enfranchisement of Indians, the better management of Indian affairs, and to extend the provisions of the Act 31st Victoria, Chapter 42.

[*Assented to 22nd June, 1869.*]

13. The Governor General in Council may on the report of the Superintendent General of Indian Affairs order the issue of Letters Patent granting to any Indian who from the degree of civilization to which he has attained, and the character for integrity and sobriety which he bears, appears to be a safe and suitable person for becoming a proprietor of land, a life estate in the land which has been or may be allotted to him within the Reserve belonging to the tribe band or body of which he is a member; and in such case such Indian shall have power to dispose of the same by will, to any of his children, and if he dies intestate as to any such lands, the same shall descend to his children according to the laws of that portion of the Dominion of Canada in which such lands are situate, and the said children to whom such land is so devised or descends shall have the fee simple thereof.

Life estates in lands may be granted in certain cases.

16. Every such Indian shall, before the issue of the letters patent mentioned in the thirteenth section of this Act, declare to the Superintendent General of Indian Affairs, the name and

Duties of Indians with respect to enfranchisement.

surname by which he wishes to be enfranchised and thereafter known, and on his receiving such letters patent, in such name and surname, he shall be held to be also enfranchised, and he shall thereafter be known by such name and surname, and his wife and minor unmarried children, shall be held to be enfranchised; and from the date of such letters patent, the provisions of any Act or law making any distinction between the legal rights and liabilities of Indians and those of Her Majesty's other subjects shall cease to apply to any Indian, his wife or minor children as aforesaid, so declared to be enfranchised, who shall no longer be deemed Indians within the meaning of the laws relating to Indians, except in so far as their right to participate in the annuities and interest money and rents, of the tribe, band, or body of Indians to which they belonged is concerned; except that the twelfth, thirteenth, and fourteenth sections of the Act thirty-first Victoria, chapter forty-two, and the eleventh section of this Act, shall apply to such Indian, his wife and children.

Effect of enfranchisement.

An Act for the Gradual Enfranchisement of Indians …, SC 1869, c. 6, ss. 13 and 16, laid out the conditions under which Indigenous people could be given individual title to a section of reserve land.

men and their families could still receive their shares of the band's treaty annuities, rents, and interest payments.* The life estate held by the enfranchisee was converted into a fee simple, but that process was deferred by a generation. His children would inherit a fee simple. The initial enfranchisee's only testamentary power over the remander in fee simple was the right to choose among his children. If he made no will, it would descend to them by the applicable provincial intestacy laws. If the holder of a life estate died without leaving any children, the land would escheat to the Crown 'for the benefit of the tribe'; it would again be part of the reserve. The act contained other restraints on alienation; the land held under a life estate could not be mortgaged or sold to satisfy a debt.

Initial enfranchisement and individual land ownership applied only to men, although, as noted above, women would also become enfranchised as wives or daughters of enfranchised men. An adult woman would likewise be enfranchised if she was the daughter of, and the chosen or intestate heir of, an enfranchised man, but she could not be enfranchised in her own right. Widows were excluded as heirs, both by the provision limiting a man's testamentary choices to his children and by sections 14 and 18, which dealt respectively with widows with and without children. The former provided that if an enfranchised man died without children but leaving a widow, she would only have a licence to occupy for life or until remarriage. At her death, or upon remarriage, the land would escheat to the Crown. Section 18 dealt similarly with a widow with minor children. She was entitled to 'reside on the land' left by her husband during the minority of the child, although only if 'she lives respectably.' White males who married Indigenous women were excluded from being located on a reserve.

The *Enfranchisement Act* excited little debate in Parliament, perhaps because it was not very different from the *Gradual Civilization Act.* According to Langevin in introducing the bill, it was 'another attempt in the direction of civilizing the Indians, a number of whom had already shown that they 'could be entrusted with the same privileges as white men' and deserved to be encouraged and protected in their efforts. The only issue raised by two Quebec Liberal MPs, Luther Holton and Antoine-Aimé Dorion, was that the provision barring white men who

---

* 'Bands' was the term used in this period, and as a result we will employ it also. Today 'bands' are called nations.

married Indigenous women would deter intermarriage. The MPs considered this bad policy because whites tended to make 'substantial improvements' to reserve land. The Act was extended to Manitoba and British Columbia in 1874.[11]

It very quickly became apparent that there was effectively no take-up of enfranchisement. When in 1873 the Commons asked for a return of all those who had done so it received a terse reply – none.[12] This response was not surprising, for three years earlier the Confederacy Council of the Six Nations had met at Grand River with some 100 delegates from principally Anishinaabe nations from across Ontario and Quebec to form a new political alliance to respond to the large change in white settler government, Confederation.[13] The delegates took slightly divergent attitudes towards the act. The Six Nations rejected it outright, while those from elsewhere were less adamant. Most did not object to the idea of losing their legal disabilities, but they, and the Six Nations, resisted giving the government power over reserve land. The same Indigenous nations met again in 1874 to respond to a request from David Laird, SG and minister of the interior in the new Mackenzie government, for consultations on the legislation that would become the first *Indian Act*. There was a similar divergence of views. The vast majority of the Six Nations delegates rejected enfranchisement entirely, insisting that converting reserve land into fee simples would break up the reserves and 'deprive us of our rights and leave us disinherited.' Six Nations' views crossed the divide within the community between Christians and followers of the Longhouse religion.

The fact that no Indigenous person had opted for enfranchisement led to a rethinking by the government about the process. There was broad agreement that Indigenous people should have full rights to individual landed property and that this should be a prerequisite to full citizenship. But Laird advocated an evolutionary approach, arguing that they 'cannot all at once get rid of [their] … inheritance,' that it would take time for them 'to understand the motives and acquire the habits of the white man, who labours to accumulate wealth.' As a result the first *Indian Act* laid down a four-stage process for enfranchisement. First, a man or married woman had to be 21 and to have 'obtained the consent of the band of which he or she is a member to become enfranchised.' The inclusion of married women reflected a change in the statutory definition of 'Indian,' which now included 'any woman who is or was lawfully married to … any male person of Indian blood.' Unmarried women were not included in the definition of 'Indian' in the Act, nor could they become enfranchised. Second, an aspiring enfranchisee had to have been 'assigned a suitable allotment for that purpose' by the band. This was a change from the *Enfranchisement Act*, which had given the power to locate a person to the SG. It was an adoption of one of the requests made by the Anishinaabe delegates in 1874. This provision on location should be read in conjunction with sections 6 and 7 of the Act, in the part dealing with reserves, which provided that on a reserve that had been subdivided into lots, 'no Indian shall be deemed to be lawfully in possession of' a lot unless he or she had been 'located for the same by the band, with the approval of the Superintendent-General.' Third, once these steps had been taken, the SG was to appoint somebody to report on 'whether the applicant is an Indian who, from the degree of civilization to which he or she has attained, and the character for integrity, morality and sobriety which he or she bears, appears to be qualified to become a proprietor of land in fee simple.' This language was very similar to what had been in the *Enfranchisement Act*, with the word 'morality' added. If the report was favourable, the Indigenous person became a 'probationary Indian.' After three years, if the probationer's conduct was deemed 'satisfactory' by the SG, he would be issued letters patent granting the land in fee simple. The provisions in the *Enfranchisement Act* for new European names being chosen, and for the end of legal distinctions, were retained.[14]

The *Indian Act* thus altered the law on enfranchisement in three significant ways: married women were potential enfranchisees, the one-generation delay to obtain a fee simple was eliminated, and bands were given some control over the process by predicating an individual's right to apply for enfranchisement on being located by the band on a plot of reserve land. While the government saw enfranchisement as highly desirable, and in some respects made the process of achieving it and fee simple ownership quicker, it also required band consent. Consent was included because officials saw Indigenous people as divided between those more 'advanced' and those less so, with the former only needing enhanced opportunities for enfranchisement. Laird insisted that enfranchisement would contribute to lifting the 'red man out of his condition of tutelage and dependence,' and that it was Canada's duty 'to prepare him for a higher civilization by encouraging him to assume the privileges and responsibilities of full citizenship.' This attitude explains section 93 of the Act, which allowed a band council to decide 'to allow every member of the band who chooses, and who may be found qualified, to become enfranchised.' Other provisions augmented inheritance rights for the families of 'probationary Indians,' so that reserve land was less likely to be returned to the band when an enfranchisee died. The only Indigenous persons enfranchised without the band's consent were the highly educated – doctors, lawyers, Christian ministers, and anybody with a university degree – who were 'ipso facto … enfranchised.' The enfranchisement provisions did not apply to British Columbia, Manitoba, or the Territories unless the government included them by proclamation. It did not do this until 1886, and then only minimally, having them apply to three bands in Manitoba and the Territories.[15]

When the Act was debated in the Commons, Laird insisted that experience with the *Enfranchisement Act* showed that band consent was necessary if enfranchisement was to be accepted. Hector Langevin agreed that consent was a necessary protection for people who were 'like children to a great extent,' but he also, presciently, argued that it would make enfranchisement difficult to achieve for those individuals who wanted it when the band did not agree. Liberal member Gavin Fleming of the North Riding of Brant thought the government should decide if its policy was 'one of preservation or one of absorption.' He preferred placing Indigenous people on 'precisely the same footing with whites' and would have included more inducements to enfranchise. His Liberal colleague from Brant South riding, William Paterson, also favoured making enfranchisement easier because 'the endeavour to perpetuate the Indian in the Canadian nation was an anomaly.' Thus two MPs from the same area, presumably with experience of the Six Nations, proposed ignoring the one thing that recent experience had shown the Six Nations to be most desirous of retaining – their sense of national identity reflected in their reserve homeland. Conversely Macdonald, now in opposition, did not believe that full legal equality was beneficial if it included 'the right to absolute disposal' of land, for that would allow 'land sharks to get hold of their estates.'[16]

It bears notice that while the federal government tinkered with the mechanism by which Indigenous people could become holders of land rights in severalty through enfranchisement, other provisions of the *Indian Act* expressly prevented them from doing so through the homestead provisions of the *Dominion Lands Act* of 1872. That Act is discussed in chapter 14. Suffice it to note here that it provided a mechanism for white settlers to acquire for free land freed up for settlement by the numbered treaties. Section 70 of the *Indian Act* provided that no Indigenous people in Manitoba and the Territories 'shall be held capable [of] … acquiring a homestead … right to any portion of land.' In part this was because the land was set aside for non-Indigenous settlers in much larger amounts – 160 acres, not 50. But in part it was because turning Indigenous people into owners in severalty was only part of the objective; the government wanted them to be owners in severalty of reserve land, thus bringing about the eventual demise of the reserve system.

Deputy SG Vankoughnet believed that more people would wish to be enfranchised than before, and the reaction of at least some Ontario bands must have bolstered this belief. The Grand Council met in the summer of 1876, without any Six Nations delegates, and voted 66 to one in favour of the new enfranchisement provisions. The vice-president, William Wananosh, chief of the Sarnia Band of Chippewas, proposed a motion, which passed unanimously, to thank Laird and to express the 'hope' that the 'Indians of Canada [would be] elevated and benefitted by the enfranchisement' provisions, which he had 'no doubt many of our people will avail themselves of.'[17]

Despite this apparent enthusiasm, enfranchisement had a very low 'take-up' rate in the next two to three decades. When in the late 1870s the government was again asked to provide a list of those who had been enfranchised, the questioner, Simon Dawson, Conservative MP for Algoma, was 'confident' that the list would not be long. The *Indian Act* provisions, he lamented, 'had been conceived in a spirit opposed to the customs most cherished by the Indians,' were designed 'to break up the tribal system,' a system 'endeared to the Indians by many associations, and … the last remaining protection which they had against the rapacity of the white man.'[18] The only significant use of enfranchisement was by a small band of about 70, the Wyandot of Anderdon, Essex County, whose reserve was on the Detroit River, consisted of large farms, and was one of the most prosperous in Ontario. All members applied for enfranchisement in 1877 and completed the three-year probation in 1880. Since they all received fee simple titles to their lots, the reserve disappeared. They probably chose this route because they were a small band of refugees from the Huron-Wendat confederacy who had been defeated in earlier wars and then migrated, first to Quebec, then to Kansas, then to the Windsor area. They had no larger nation with which to affiliate and were in any event well integrated into the surrounding settler society. One member, Solomon White, son of a hereditary chief, was fluent in English and French, had been called to the bar in 1865, and in 1878 was elected to the Ontario legislature as a Conservative. The only other person to enfranchise in the 1870s was John Norton, from the Moravians of the Thames Band, a 300 or so strong community of refugees from Pennsylvania during the Revolutionary War who were granted what is now the Moravian reserve at Orford, Ontario. He applied in 1878 and received his fee simple of 50 acres in 1883.[19]

As in the early 1870s the lack of applications for enfranchisement was the result of resistance by band councils to the subdivision of reserves into individually owned lots. Macdonald thought this a 'strange aversion,' since it gave individuals 'a better title to their respective holdings than they previously possessed.' But he was missing the point. Indigenous people knew full well that enfranchisement meant the long-term loss of community and culture that would inevitably follow loss of the reserve base. It also entailed the abrogation of their treaty relationships with the Crown that would follow absorption into the Canadian body politic. The government responded to the 'problem' of a lack of enthusiasm by an 1884 change to the *Indian Act* designed to limit the control that the band exercised. Henceforth if an individual wished to be enfranchised, and the SG approved, the band council had 30 days to provide reasons 'of a personal character' why the person should not be enfranchised. If no such reasons were forthcoming, or if they were and the SG decided that the applicant was nonetheless suitable, he could grant a location ticket to the probationary enfranchisee for three years. Macdonald saw the amendment as necessary because there was little sign of 'the much-to-be-desired demand for enfranchisement' and the cause was band councils standing in the way of individuals who showed an 'inclination for further enlightenment,' indeed who were 'anxious for this step.'[20]

Indigenous peoples felt differently. In 1884 the Grand Council met at the Cape Croker reserve on Georgian Bay, and while most of the delegates, predominantly Anishinaabe, were in favour of being granted the vote, they objected to the idea that an Indigenous person would be 'obliged to sever his connection with his people,' that the 'tribal union' that they were 'anxious to retain' would be broken up. There was some disagreement between the Christians from southern Ontario and the northern Indigenous people. The former wanted their young people to become citizens, but without giving up their First Nations connections. The latter simply did not want, in the words of Chief Shingwauk of the Garden River Band, to become 'like a white man.' Both groups nonetheless agreed on their disapproval of the new power given to the SG to override the band's wishes on enfranchisement. The response of individuals was not different. Only seven Anishinaabe men and women are known to have been enfranchised between the mid-1880s and 1900. Two, like the above-discussed John Norton, were members of the Moravians of the Thames Band. One of them, George Tobias, was described by the Indian agent as 'one half white' with a white wife. A few more individuals from Anishinaabe bands applied to their band councils to support their applications and to be granted a location ticket, but were refused. According to the Indian agent, one was told that when enfranchised 'he will become a white man and we don't want any white man living on the Reserve.' The reply is instructive; bands were applying their own citizenship laws to govern who was a member of the community at the same time that they were protecting their reserve's land base. The same resistance may have thwarted Moravian band member Jamieson Lewis in the early twentieth century, and an act of Parliament enfranchised him. The few other successful applicants were all from the Chippewas of Sarnia and Mississaugas of Alnwick bands, and were all exceptional in being Methodist ministers or the wives or sons of Methodist ministers.[21] Fewer than 100 people became enfranchised before 1900, most of them wives and children of male applicants, and only slightly more than 250 by 1920.[22]

In 1885 some Indigenous people were given the vote in federal elections without becoming enfranchised. Before then the federal franchise was available only to those on the provincial electoral rolls, and Indigenous people were excluded either indirectly by the property qualification or directly by discriminatory provisions in the legislation.[23] Macdonald's *Federal Franchise Act* was not principally about Indigenous people but about electoral politics in general, providing that returning officers, who decided who made it onto the electoral lists, would be selected by the Conservative government in Ottawa and not the Liberal government of Ontario.[24] But Macdonald also believed that his Ontario electoral prospects would be enhanced by Indigenous voters because they were more likely to vote Conservative. He argued that they deserved the vote because they had been military allies and considered themselves 'proud to call themselves British subjects as well as allies' and ought therefore to have 'the same rights as the white man.'[25] The Act gave the federal vote to Indigenous people living off reserve in central and eastern Canada if they met the same property qualification as anybody else, and those living on reserve who were 'in possession … of a separate and distinct tract of land in such reserve.' That is, an Indigenous man who lived on a sub-divided reserve pursuant to a location ticket could vote without completing the enfranchisement process. Some Indigenous men did vote in the ensuing decade, and they did more often support Conservatives rather than Liberals, although this tendency was far from monolithic. As a result a Liberal-controlled Parliament repealed the *Federal Franchise Act* in 1898.[26] In the mid-1880s the government believed that a by-product of being granted the vote was that more Indigenous would take up enfranchisement. But this hope was not realized. For those who since the very early years of the new dominion had looked to enfranchisement as a major contributor to the assimilation of Indigenous peoples it was a remarkable failure prior to 1914.

The Law and Practice of Reserve Protection and Reduction

Before Confederation, Indigenous reserve land was under the jurisdiction of the colonial governments, and in 1867 it became the responsibility of the federal government. The principal plank of colonial policy had been the preservation of reserves against settler intrusion, and reserve preservation remained a legislative ideal, indeed a 'sacred trust,' throughout the first half century of the new dominion. Early dominion legislation, including the *Indian Act*, provided that reserves would be held by the federal government for the benefit of Indigenous people. It also laid out the 'surrender requirement' for reserve lands; land could not be alienated to private parties 'until … released or surrendered to the Crown' first. From 1868 a surrender had to be agreed to by the chief of the band, or if there was more than one chief by a majority of them. That assent had to be given at a band meeting, summoned for that purpose and attended only by persons permitted to vote. A government representative had also to attend. When John White, MP for the East Riding of Hastings, Ontario, asked the government to sell a portion of the Tyendinaga reserve in 1872, Macdonald was adamant that this could not be done without consent. The assent had to be certified on oath before a Superior Court judge, and then transmitted to Ottawa. The surrender requirement was slightly modified in the 1876 *Indian Act*, chiefly consent being replaced by assent of a majority of the adult male members.[27]

The *Indian Act* was the first statute to define 'reserve,' as 'any tract or tracts of lands set apart by treaty or otherwise for the use or benefit of or granted to a particular band of Indians, of which the legal title is in the Crown.' Other provisions barred squatters and protected reserve land resources. No non-Indigenous person, except a wife, could 'settle, reside upon or occupy' any reserve, and nobody could remove timber or any other produce of the land without a licence. As before 1867, the government made efforts to remove white squatters.[28] All mortgages, leases, contracts, and the like purporting to give someone a right to reside on reserve land were declared to be void, and reserve lands were exempted from seizure by legal process. There were likely many violations of these provisions, some of which led to successful court actions. In 1876, for example, one Black got a writ of possession from Justice Betournay of the Manitoba Court of Queen's Bench for land against which he had given a mortgage. When the sheriff, one Kennedy, went to execute the writ he found that the land was on the St. Peter's reserve and refused to do so. Black applied for an order of mandamus to require him to do so, but Chief Justice Wood held the mortgage 'absolutely void' and the entire court proceeding 'of necessity equally void,' citing the *Indian Act*.[29]

The only exception to the prohibition on the occupation and use of reserve land was for railways, roads, or public works The legislation required that compensation be paid for any damages 'in the same manner as is provided with respect to the lands or rights of other persons.' The federal *Railway Act* of 1868 contained the same provision and also stipulated that if the price could not be agreed and the issue had to be arbitrated, with both parties choosing an arbitrator, the secretary of state was to select one 'on behalf of the Indians.'[30] These provisions were used on a number of occasions. In the late 1880s, for example, the CPR acquired part of the Kitsilano reserve in Vancouver for its West Coast terminus operations.[31]

Reserve 'protection' always involved a contradiction. On the one hand reserves were seen as places where Indigenous people could be sequestered and 'protected' from the deleterious effects of exploitation by white settlers. On the other hand a variety of policies, including enfranchisement, sought to transform Indigenous people into 'civilized' nations that would no longer need reserves. More importantly, the legislation did not prevent the alienation of reserve land, it prevented its alienation directly to private parties and provided a method by which it could be alienated, by surrender to the

Crown. Although treaties concluded in Ontario before Confederation and the numbered treaties of the 1870s ceded millions of acres to the Crown, the ceded land was not enough to meet the incessant demand for land for settlement and transportation and other infrastructure projects. Over time the reserve system was increasingly viewed as the principal impediment to such development. Until the 1890s Ottawa principally used informal pressure on Indian bands to agree to additional surrenders; beginning in the 1890s various amendments to the *Indian Act* gave the government coercive legal power to achieve this end.

In the early 1870s the demand for land surrenders came very largely from Ontario. Sometimes it involved a complete relocation to free up 'prime' areas for white settlement, and such proposals were disapproved of by Spragge because they involved Indigenous peoples being moved from land they had 'long occupied and regarded as their permanent homes,' the effect of which was to 'depress them [Indigenous people] and retard their progress.' Such proposals also violated 'solemn treaty' obligations and were regarded by those targeted as 'harassing and prejudicial' and showing 'an intolerance of Indians as a race.' Spragge had less objection to partial surrenders – sections only of reserves being sold. In 1875 the Chippewas of Sarnia surrendered land bordering on Sarnia, agreeing to do so 'to put stop to the complaints of their White neighbours that they were retarding the growth of the town.' Other surrenders took place for similar reasons the same year, including parts of Selkirk, Manitoba, because it was expected that the Pacific railway would run through that section of town. Similar surrenders of land close to towns were recorded in most other years in the 1870s. Spragge's successor Vankoughnet defended them because the land was then leased out, whereas before it was used by 'designing persons, living in the neighbourhood' who paid 'a merely nominal rental.'[32]

For the remainder of this period, surrenders continued to be made, over 700,000 acres between 1896 and 1907. They were often the result of pressure from Indian agents, which was constant, even if sometimes not successful. In the late nineteenth century, for example, Ottawa decided it wanted 40,000 acres of the Blood Agency reserve in what is now southern Alberta. Chief Crop-Eared Wolf resisted pressure from Indian agents for many years, with the help of a Fort MacLeod–based lawyer. Indian Agent R.N. Wilson was infuriated by this lack of 'co-operation' and tried four times to depose the chief, under the statutory provisions for doing so discussed in the next section. The DIA saw through the subterfuges and refused to accept the recommendations that Crop-Eared Wolf be deposed. It called the attempt to use the deposition power to force a surrender an 'objectionable practice' because it was coercive, a violation of the principle that surrender required consent. This incident in many ways was typical of the DIA in the 1890s, under Clifford Sifton. It supported and encouraged surrenders, even pressing chiefs to consent to them, but at the same time there were limits to the pressure it exerted and it insisted on the formal legalities. Sifton defended his attitude in the Commons, telling a critic that 'whatever may be deemed desirable or otherwise, the fact of the matter is that the Indians own these lands,' just as any fellow MP 'owns any piece of land for which he has a title in fee simple.' It was perhaps not coincidental that after many years of pressure and legal disputes the St. Peter's Reserve band in Manitoba agreed to a surrender in 1907, after Frank Oliver, as discussed below, a more aggressive advocate of surrenders, had taken charge of the DIA. Manitoba Court of Appeal Judge Hector Howell opined that the government had 'cheaply got out of a nasty tangle,' but a year later the surrender was repudiated by a substantial number of band members, who also said they had been promised money by the DIA, which they never received.[33]

Amendments to the *Indian Act* in the 1890s greatly facilitated settlers' ability to acquire reserve land by making the surrender requirement inapplicable to some transactions. In 1894 and 1895 the SG was given the power to lease reserve land for the 'benefit' of the Indigenous occupant, without first taking a surrender, and, similarly, to lease land 'for the benefit of Indians engaged in occupations which interfere with their cultivating land on the reserve.' In both cases land could be leased to non-Indigenous persons without the band's consent, the individual receiving some or all of the rent.[34] These measures were justified as necessary to promote economic growth, to which reserves were increasingly viewed as an impediment. Other amendments provided incentives for agreeing to surrender. One passed in 1898 allowed the government to distribute in cash to the band 10 per cent of the value of any land surrendered. The money could be used, with the SG's approval, for compensation for any improvements previously made to the land, or for reserve infrastructure. Previously any money made from land sales following surrenders went into a band's trust account, and only the interest was made available and then only if the SG approved the purpose for which it was to be put. This became an even greater incentive in 1906, when the amount that could be disbursed was raised to 50 per cent of the sale price. This was at the initiative of SG Frank Oliver, an Edmonton MP who brought to official Ottawa the attitudes to Indigenous people and their land of many in the West. There were six surrenders between 1897 and 1904, but 18 during Oliver's term in office. When he was asked about surrenders in the Commons, he admitted that the DIA was exerting itself to get what he termed 'surplus' reserve land, stating that 'if it becomes a question between the Indians and the whites, the interests of the whites will have to be provided for.'[35]

A 1911 amendment to the *Indian Act*, known as the Oliver Act, went further, making reserve land subject to expropriation, for one of two reasons. Any corporation or local authority that had statutory expropriating power could take 'a reserve or part thereof' for a railway, road, public work, or 'any public utility.' The expropriating authority had one more hurdle to surmount than in all other expropriation cases – obtaining the federal government's consent – but otherwise the procedure was the one normally followed in an expropriation, including the payment of compensation. Oliver, in defending this provision and the one discussed in the next paragraph concerning reserve relocation, was aware that the statute was a breach of treaty rights, but stated that 'there are certain circumstances and conditions in which the Indian by standing on his treaty rights does himself an ultimate injury as well as does an injury to the white people, whose interests are brought into immediate conjunction with the ... Indians.'[36]

The 1911 amendment also allowed reserves to be moved. A reserve had to adjoin, or be wholly or partly within, an urban centre with a population of at least 8,000. The SG could refer a case to the Exchequer Court to determine 'whether it is expedient, having regard to the interest of the public and of the Indians of the band ..., that the Indians should be removed from the reserve.' The presiding judge was required to assign counsel to represent Indigenous people who objected. Assuming the judge found in the SG's favour, Parliament had to adopt his findings by resolution before removal could go ahead. The band would receive the money from a sale or lease of the reserve land, which was to be given to individuals who sustained losses to buildings or other improvements, for the purchase of a new reserve, and the costs of

1-2 GEORGE V.

CHAP. 14.

An Act to amend the Indian Act.

[Assented to 19th May, 1911.]

HIS Majesty, by and with the advice and consent of the Senate and House of Commons of Canada, enacts as follows :—

1. Subsection 1 of section 46 of *The Indian Act*, chapter 81 of the Revised Statutes, 1906, is repealed, and the following is substituted therefor :— R.S., c. 81, s. 46 amended.

"**46.** No portion of any reserve shall be taken for the purpose of any railway, road, public work, or work designed for any public utility without the consent of the Governor in Council, but any company or municipal or local authority having statutory power, either Dominion or provincial, for taking or using lands or any interest in lands without the consent of the owner may, with the consent of the Governor in Council as aforesaid, and subject to the terms and conditions imposed by such consent, exercise such statutory power with respect to any reserve or portion of a reserve; and in any such case compensation shall be made therefor to the Indians of the band, and the exercise of such power, and the taking of the lands or interest therein and the determination and payment of the compensation shall, unless otherwise provided by the order in council evidencing the consent of the Governor in Council, be governed by the requirements applicable to the like proceedings by such company, municipal or local authority in ordinary cases." Compensation for lands taken for public purposes.

2. The said Act is amended by inserting the following section immediately after section 49 thereof :— Section added.

"**49A.** In the case of an Indian reserve which adjoins or is situated wholly or partly within an incorporated town or city having a population of not less than eight thousand, and which reserve has not been released or surrendered by the Indians, the Governor Inquiry and report by Exchequer Court as to removal of Indians.

187

An Act to amend the Indian Act, SC 1911, c. 14, ss 1 and 2 (this page and opposite), were amendments giving companies and municipalities power to expropriate reserve lands, and empowering municipalities of at least 8,000 people to move reserves situated wholly or partly with municipal boundaries.

providing the Indians with such other assistance as the Superintendent General may consider advisable; and the balance of the proceeds, if any, shall be placed to the credit of the Indians: Provided that the Government shall not cause the Indians to be removed, or disturb their possession, until a suitable reserve has been obtained and set apart for them in lieu of the reserve from which the expediency of removing the Indians is so established as aforesaid.

"7. For the purpose of selecting, appropriating and acquiring the lands necessary to be taken, or which it may be deemed expedient to take, for any new reserve to be acquired for the Indians as authorized by the last preceding sub-section, whether they are Crown lands or not, the Superintendent General shall have all the powers conferred upon the Minister by *The Expropriation Act*, and such new reserve shall, for the purposes aforesaid, be deemed to be a public work within the definition of that expression in *The Expropriation Act*; and all the provisions of *The Expropriation Act*, in so far as applicable and not inconsistent with this Act, shall apply in respect of the proceedings for the selection, survey, ascertainment and acquisition of the lands required and the determination and payment of the compensation therefor: Provided, however, that the Superintendent General shall not exercise the power of expropriation unless authorized by the Governor in Council."

[marginal notes: Proviso. New reserve. Expropriation of lands for new reserve. R.S., c. 143.]

relocation. No removal could take place until a suitable new reserve had been set aside for the band. The provision was drafted with certain urban centres that had reserves within their boundaries in mind, notably Sarnia and Victoria. In the latter case the Act legalized the purchase of the Songhee reserve, which had been bought by British Columbia just weeks before, a purchase that was illegal because it did not involve a surrender to the Crown. The reserve was then moved outside of Victoria and the land given over to urban expansion. For greater certainty, Parliament also passed a statute specifically validating the purchase. The provision on moving reserves was used a number of times and not repealed until 1951.[37]

Governance of Indigenous Bands and Reserves

Changing the way Indigenous peoples and reserves were governed was another *Indian Act* policy designed to advance assimilation. Indigenous leadership structures varied widely, but what they had in common was that they were not the elective system that determined who held political office in settler Canada. Some were hereditary systems, others involved chiefs being selected by consensus. In the Mohawk nation, male leaders were chosen for life by clan mothers, while among the Anishinaabe a clan system based on alliances among extended families prevailed. Some systems included aspects similar to Western-style electoral processes. Former chiefs Loran Pyke and Thomas White of the St. Regis Mohawk band, for example, told Deputy SG Hayter Reed in 1894 that all band members met when there was a vacancy for chief, nominations were received, and, if necessary, an election was held, the winner serving for life.[38]

Federal government policy was aimed at changing traditional leadership models to 'modern' Western ones. Traditional leaders were often considered an impediment to progress, and at the same time changes in governance contributed to the broader assimilationist project by adding democracy to individual property ownership. As Macdonald put it in 1881, an elective system 'will have the effect of accustoming the Indians to the modes of government prevalent in the white communities surrounding them, and … will thus tend to prepare them for earlier amalgamation with the general population of the country.'[39] The elective principle was also linked to the creation of a municipal government–like structure on reserves, with powers being delegated over a wide variety of local matters.

The introduction of the elective principle came as early as the *Enfranchisement Act*, the targets being the Six Nations and other Indigenous bands who supposedly already had experience with European democratic values. The idea was that 'intelligent, educated men, recognized as chiefs, should carry out the wishes of the male members of mature years in each band.' The legislation would establish a 'responsible' in place of the existing 'irresponsible' system, which the government believed was the desire of 'educated Indians … chafing under the authority of irremovable chiefs.' Section 10 provided that the government 'may order' that chiefs would henceforth be elected by all adult men, and those elected would serve for three years, unless 'deposed' by the government for 'dishonesty, intemperance, or immorality.' The same section also legislated limits on the number of elected chiefs and provided for a transition period for incumbent life chiefs. If elections were introduced a band could have only one 'head chief' and two 'second chiefs' for every 200 people; smaller bands, those of at least 30 people, could have one chief. The transition provision allowed incumbent life chiefs to stay in office even if elections were introduced, until death, resignation, or removal on the same grounds as above. These provisions were extended to Manitoba and British Columbia in 1874. The limitation of voters to men was not simply a reflection of Canadian suffrage law but also an attempt to undermine the matrifocal traditions of some Indigenous nations in Ontario and Quebec.[40]

The legislation did not require bands to introduce elections, and while Ottawa obviously believed the elective principle to be desirable, it did not impose elections until the 1890s. Before then it was left to bands to choose, and few did so. The reason, Spragge believed, was that 'the Indian mind is in general slow to accept improvements' and that Indigenous people were 'backward in perceiving the privileges which it confers.' The reluctance to adopt elections was, for Ottawa, most striking in the community they most expected to embrace it, the Six Nations. That band maintained its opposition for decades, although a faction within the community petitioned for an elected band council in 1873 and the issue still divided the community in the 1890s. Spragge attributed the resistance to there being too many hereditary chiefs whose power had for long been 'exercised uncontrolled' allowing them to keep their people 'in subjection.' But the time would come, he insisted, when 'a very large majority would be in favour of an elective Council.' But the principal reason for Six Nations' objections was that they had their own laws and resented any dominion interference with them, whether it was over citizenship (enfranchisement), band decision-making, or inheritance practices.[41]

This regime was largely carried into sections 61 and 62 of the 1876 *Indian Act*, which also stipulated that the election be held in the presence of the SG or his agent, an attempt to impose some oversight. It also changed the nomenclature. Head chiefs remained, but 'second chiefs' became 'second chiefs or councillors,' the use of councillors aping the term generally used for municipal elected officials. In addition the grounds for deposing life chiefs were broadened by the inclusion of 'incompetency,' an open-ended ground undefined in the Act, which gave bureaucrats more scope for depositions. The election provisions applied to all provinces, although it was generally considered for about two decades that western Indigenous people were not 'advanced' enough for them. A few bands in Ontario and Quebec did introduce elections after 1876. The Mississaugas who occupied land on the Six Nations reserve did so in 1877, as did a band on Manitoulin Island in 1878, and on the St. Regis reserve in Quebec some 200 members petitioned for an elected chief after splitting off from another band in the late 1870s. But these were exceptions. The DIA assumed that the obvious superiority of elections would manifest itself in time to 'civilized' people, but this line of thinking failed to appreciate both that the elective provisions of the *Indian Act* did not appeal to people who saw themselves as nations, not simply residents of reserves, and thus did not wish to be managed by Canada.[42]

By 1880 Ottawa believed that it needed stronger legislation, and in the *Indian Act* consolidation passed in May of that year the language of the operative section – 'may order' – was changed slightly but significantly to state that the government could do so whenever it 'deems it advisable for the good government of a band.' That year's *Annual Report* argued that elections were needed because hereditary chiefs 'may or may not fairly represent the intelligence of the band.' By definition, an 'intelligent' Indigenous person was one who preferred elective democracy over traditional leadership. Consistent with this thinking was a change to the status of hereditary chiefs when elections were ordered. The 1880 Act provided that if elections were held, the life chiefs could no longer carry out chiefly functions unless they had also been elected. They were thereby reduced to ceremonial figureheads. The legislation brought little change in the take-up of elections. That same year the DIA sent a circular asking agents to report whether the bands under their jurisdiction were 'sufficiently enlightened' to have an electoral system imposed on them. Most replied in the negative. Israel Powell, Indian superintendent for British Columbia, agreed that most bands were not ready but argued that the DIA should move ahead because younger, 'more advanced' men would be chosen as councillors and thereby exert 'a vigorous civilizing power,' which would not only 'stamp out hereditary chiefship' but also the 'ancient ignorance and barbarism' of the traditional chiefs. SG Macdonald applied the new *Indian Act* provisions to the bands that were favourably reported on, and in the early 1880s elections were held on at least three Manitoba reserves, and on seven in Ontario. Macdonald summarized the variations in reserve governance when addressing the Commons in 1884: 'In some of the tribes there are hereditary, in others elective chiefs, in others hereditary and elective chiefs combined. There are great varieties of organizations in the different bands.'[43]

In addition to changing the way chiefs were selected there was always a secondary plank to federal policy – providing chiefs and band councils with delegated administrative powers, similar to those wielded by local government in settler society. The purpose was to 'train' Indigenous people for the responsibilities of government. The *Enfranchisement Act* listed seven areas in which band councils could pass regulations, subject to confirmation by the government. The *Indian Act* added one more, and in 1886 eleven areas of jurisdiction were listed.[44] They included the power to impose fines or short periods of imprisonment on those who transgressed band regulations, and the power to make regulations about 'the attendance of school children' between six and fourteen. A number of bands used the local government powers to pass detailed codes on a wide range of matters. They included the Moravians of the Thames, who enacted 30 pages of by-laws mostly concerning construction on reserves. The Mississauga band of the Grand River passed a compilation of 20 sections and more than 50 subsections of regulations in 1885, all under the power to regulate schools, which went well beyond attendance to include the election and duties of school trustees, the curriculum, teachers' duties, prizes, and other matters.[45]

Band governance was the subject of new legislation passed in 1884, the *Indian Advancement Act*, which was a statute separate from the *Indian Act*. Its full title revealed its purpose: *An Act for Conferring Certain Privileges on the More Advanced Bands of the Indians of Canada, with the View of Training Them for the Exercise of Municipal Powers*.[46] Macdonald saw the legislation as providing 'quasi municipal privileges' for the 'more civilized' bands, and in introducing the bill in the Commons he made the analogy directly. The person elected chief councillor by his fellow councillors 'would be called a reeve among the white communities in Ontario.'[47] The act dealt with elections, band council structure, and by-law-making power and was to apply whenever a band was 'considered fit' for it by Ottawa. It applied throughout the country. Its principal innovations included extending elections from chiefs only to band councillors, who would then meet and select a chief councillor, not a 'chief,' a highly symbolic change that emphasized the link to municipalities. The act also laid out new rules for the timing and organization of elections; they were to be annual, not triennial, as under the *Indian Act*. Reserves were to be divided into 'sections,' in effect wards, between two and six for each reserve, with equal populations of eligible voters. The *Indian Advancement Act* also contained a list of delegated powers wider than those in the *Indian Act*, including powers to appoint constables and designate 'lock-ups,' to subdivide a reserve as a prelude to granting location tickets, to effect the 'removal and punishment of persons trespassing upon the reserve, or frequenting it for improper purposes,' and to impose a tax on land held by enfranchisees and those with a location ticket.

A great deal of control was given to the Indian agents over elections and council meetings, which was not congruent with municipal government. They were to preside at the election and tally the votes, and had 'full power' to determine whether someone was qualified to be an elector. They also fixed the date on which the councillors met to elect the chief councillor, and the frequency and timing of council meetings (between four and twelve a year), and presided at them. Presiding was more than chairing: the agents were to advise and guide, to tell councillors their powers, and adjourn meetings when they thought it appropriate. The obvious paradox in all this was that legislation designed to educate Indigenous people in the practices and principles of local self-government subjected them to the direction of the Indian agent in minute detail. This paradox received some parliamentary attention in a debate on band governance in 1890. A number of MPs, including opposition leader Laurier, decried the continuing supervision, arguing that many Indigenous people were quite able to govern themselves and were the equal of whites in this regard. Indigenous MP Samuel Burdett, a lawyer and the Liberal member for Hastings East, went further, noting that Indigenous people had never been conquered and thus had never lost their right to self-government.[48]

There were wider disqualification provisions than under the *Indian Act*, which also gave Indian agents even greater control. The grounds for removal were being a 'habitual drunkard,' 'living in immorality,' accepting a bribe, or being 'guilty of dishonesty or malfeasance of office of any kind.' These faults were to be proved 'to the satisfaction of' the SG. Nobody else but the Indian agent, however, was likely to be able to 'prove' such things to the SG. When this section was debated in Parliament it brought a wry observation from Edward Blake about intemperance, in which he suggested that such a provision ought to apply to white politicians. It seems probable that Blake meant the barb for Macdonald, notorious for his bouts of excessive drinking, but the prime minister turned it back, saying that he agreed with the principle but was concerned that its application would reduce the opposition benches.[49]

From 1884 there was therefore a two-track scheme for band governance. The *Indian Advancement Act* stayed on the statute book with minor amendments until the *Revised Statutes* of 1906, when it became Part II of the *Indian Act*. As with the *Indian Act*, very few bands chose elections under it. The DIA continued with its general policy of not imposing elections without consent until the mid-1890s, although it did so in a few cases, including on the Kahnawà:ke reserve in Quebec in 1889. The Misissaugas of the Credit adopted the act, but the Six Nations remained a holdout.[50] Following the appointment as deputy SG of Hayter Reed in 1893, the DIA changed its policy and from 1895 imposed elections much more frequently. Reed was a legally trained retired soldier who began working for the DIA in 1881, when he was made the Indian agent in Battleford. There he developed a low opinion of Indigenous peoples. In short order he was appointed to the territorial council and made assistant Indian Commissioner for the Territories. After the 1885 rebellion he advocated for the introduction of the pass system and various retributory measures, and in 1888 was promoted to Indian commissioner for Manitoba and the Territories. Under Reed the DIA imposed elections under either the *Indian Act* or the *Indian Advancement Act* on almost all the bands in Ontario, Quebec, and the Maritime provinces. Exempted were the Treaty 3 bands in northwestern Ontario, local agents advising that they were not sufficiently 'advanced.'[51]

The transition to elective democracy did not go smoothly. Many bands were divided by internal political rivalries and factional differences as well as by disagreements over the desirability of elections. A common response to the imposition of the electoral system was to elect traditional leaders, and the government reacted to this 'passive disobedience' by invoking its power to remove chiefs. Ironically Ottawa soon came to believe that an elective system was not the right solution, because Indigenous politicians behaved just like those of European origin, constructing campaign platforms to win votes. Often these platforms involved the presentation of grievances against the DIA. Reed recognized this almost immediately. Elective systems, he complained in 1895, 'are much worse than ... hereditary' ones, because elected politicians and candidates for office 'find it necessary ... to instigate or countenance opposition to the Department.' Ewan McColl, inspector of Indian agencies for Manitoba, agreed: 'The candidates for the position indulge in denunciations of the Government's treatment of them in order to influence the prejudices of the Indians against the Department and thus secure the necessary votes for their elections.'[52]

The policy of compulsion inaugurated in 1895 did not include the West, because western bands were not considered to be sufficiently well 'advanced' and because Reed's experience in the west convinced him that chiefs were an impediment to the DIA, elected or otherwise. In 1891 he had told Dewdney that he was persuaded of the 'desirability of abolishing the office altogether,' doing so being 'one of the strongest aids towards the destruction of communism and the creation of individuality.'[53] Four bands on the prairies displayed interest in being brought under the *Indian Advancement Act* in the late 1880s, but only two, the File Hills and Cowessess bands in the Saskatchewan district, actually did so. In the other cases the Indian agent demurred, arguing that they were not ready, and in yet others the band wanted the act without some clauses, was told it was all or nothing, and withdrew their assent. The *Indian Advancement Act* was used more often in British Columbia. The Cowichan band took it up in 1886, followed by three other bands by 1894.

Overall the DIA's policy regarding chiefs in the West was a melange of approaches, some of them not in accord with the statutory scheme. Administrative expediency prevailed. For example, the Cowessess band held elections every three years until 1903, but none between 1903 and 1911, those elected in 1903 serving for eight years. In a number of other cases the DIA allowed bands to hold elections under their customary rules, albeit supervised by the Indian agent. In yet other cases the DIA simply recognized existing chiefs, some of whom had been the signatories of the numbered treaties, which helped to buttress the treaties' legitimacy. Where it could not find chiefs to recognize, the DIA simply appointed chiefs or councillors, often for an indefinite term. The policy of indefinite terms was formalized in 1905 but was not applied consistently. These chiefs were clearly intended by Ottawa to be not so much representatives of their people as agents of the DIA. They had to sign an oath promising to obey all Canadian laws and to report all infractions of those laws, and to 'strive to advance the interests of all the Indians of my band morally and financially.' Thus they promised to adhere to the *Indian Act* and pursue 'advancement.'

The DIA also sought to effectively control chiefs by the use of the deposition power. One notorious and long drawn-out dispute involving the St. Regis band of Quebec provides an apt illustration. In 1887 internal differences led to a request to the DIA for deposition of three hereditary chiefs who had misappropriated band funds. The DIA deposed them on grounds of both dishonesty and incompetence, and also imposed elections, at the same time recommending that two other life chiefs, not involved in the defalcation of funds, retain their rank. The five men elected in 1891, and two of the men elected in 1892 in their stead, were also deposed, the former for election irregularities, the latter for other illegal actions. By the mid-1890s the Mohawks were requesting a return to the hereditary system, denied by the DIA, and on more than one occasion used civil disobedience and/or violence to prevent an election going ahead. The dispute over elections festered through the 1910s, two decades after it had started, with the protagonists being the DIA and different factions within the band.[54]

The deposition power was used frequently in the West, on 57 occasions between 1896 and 1911. More than half of these were for 'incompetency,' which more often than not meant not being ad idem with the Indian agent and/or DIA policy. Chief 'Tom' of the Mouse Mountain agency in Saskatchewan was removed in 1897 for bringing up his children 'to think that anything in the way of work at farming, cattle-keeping or schools is not good for Indians' – for Ottawa a clear indication that he retarded 'progress.' Perhaps the most notable deposition was of Star Blanket (Achuchwahauhhatohapit), a signatory to Treaty 4 who in the late 1870s and early 1880s was persistent in the demand for better terms than were in the treaty, which he claimed did not reflect the agreements made. He also resisted sending the band's children to residential schools and would not co-operate in attempts to stop performances of the ghost and thirst dances (see immediately below). He was labelled a 'malcontent,' deposed in 1893, and reinstated in 1895 when his people still followed his advice. He obtained reinstatement in part by agreeing to send children to the Regina industrial school, but this was not a complete climb-down, because he extracted a promise that the boys' hair would not be cut. The deposition power was also employed negatively, by refusing to depose chiefs that a band wanted removed but the DIA preferred. In 1909, for example, members of the James Smith Band petitioned for the removal of their chief, but the Indian agent strongly advised against it, because he thought the chief 'a good sensible man, willing to help the Agent and the Farmer.'[55]

Finally, in some communities, chiefs and councillors were simply dispensed with, making the Indian agent formally, as well as effectively, the person in control. The DIA thought this desirable because, when deprived of a chief, bands were more malleable to the 'advice' of Indian agents. To similar effect many Indian agents objected to holding elections at all, for a familiar reason: they would produce chiefs

and councillors who would agitate against DIA policies. For the Onion
Lake Band in Saskatchewan it was not present or future politics that
rendered having a chief unsuitable, it was the now-distant past. When
the band petitioned for chiefs and councillors in 1912 the DIA refused
'on account of their participation in the rebellion of 1885,' which had
caused them to lose their treaty right to chiefs in the first place.[56] As with
enfranchisement, an elaborate scheme conceived on the Ottawa drawing board to assimilate Indigenous peoples to western values, those of
elective democracy, foundered on the ground.

The Criminalization of Cultural and Religious Practices

In this final section we examine the use of the criminal law against
Indigenous religious and cultural practices. Large numbers of Indigenous inhabitants of the eastern provinces had been converted to Christianity during the centuries of contact before Confederation, and thus
it was western Canadian nations, a smaller percentage of whom had
converted, who bore the brunt of this turn to the coercive power of the
state. The principal target was the potlatch, or feast, a deep-rooted ceremony among west coast Indigenous nations. In 1883 a proclamation
declared that the Queen does 'enjoin, recommend and earnestly urge'
Indigenous people to 'abandon' and give it up. The following year the
potlatch and the Tamanawas dance were outlawed in an amendment
to the *Indian Act* that made it a misdemeanour to participate in either,
punishable, without the option of a fine, by imprisonment for between
two and six months. Those who assisted or encouraged an Indigenous
person or persons, directly or indirectly, 'to get up such a festival or
dance, or to celebrate the same,' were subject to the same punishment.[57]

The potlatch and the related Tamanawas dance were both important
aspects of west coast Indigenous culture.[58] A potlatch – the word simply means 'to give' – was a ceremony hosted by a family or extended
family, usually on special occasions such as births, marriages, and
deaths. Because guests who attended one incurred a social debt, other
potlatches were held to meet that social obligation. Dancing, singing,
and the relation of genealogies, accompanied by drinking, lasted many
hours, and at the end the host would distribute gifts to the guests. The
potlatch was a mechanism for social integration, both confirming who
belonged to the group and the relative status of people within it. Gifts,
for example, were distributed according to status. The potlatch changed
as a result of European contact and trade. Although its social meaning

remained the same, the advent of consumer goods altered what was given away, in nature and extent, a result of Indigenous people participating increasingly in the settler economy. By the later nineteenth century woollen blankets had become the chief items of exchange, and in addition more substantial and expensive items were distributed. In 1870, for example, Arthur Wellington Clah, a Tsimshian chief, invited 50 other chiefs to his house to celebrate the birth of his son, where they ate, drank large amounts of liquor, and watched a performance in which a group of young men dressed as 'Yankee' soldiers and armed with rifles performed military exercises. In 1876 Israel Powell reported on a potlatch involving 3,000 people and involving the distribution of $15,000 worth of goods. The Tamanawas dance was part of the potlatch, an initiation rite for young Kwakiutl men. It was variously referred to as *clokwana*, the wolf dance, and *hamatsa*, although the last word was also used to describe any secret society. Long prior to the arrival of Europeans it had involved acts of violence but by the time settlers arrived these had become largely symbolic. After a period of time in the forest the initiate was brought to a winter festival where he gnashed his teeth and pretended to bite people present. He was pacified by rattles shaken at him by healers, and ultimately tamed. What made the ceremony so objectionable to nineteenth-century British Columbians was the evocation of cannibalism.[59]

Few Europeans understood the meaning of either ceremony, but officials and missionaries were certain that they were highly undesirable. They were pagan rites, their continued practice made more offensive by the fact that many people who had converted to Christianity took a syncretic view of religion, continuing to observe the old ways. The aforementioned Arthur Clah, for example, was a convert to Christianity, who built several houses in the 1870s and 1880s, all of the completions being marked by feasts – sometimes called Christmas feasts, sometimes more traditional feasts, including a potlatch. There are many adverse references to the potlatch in Powell's long and detailed reports in the 1870s designed to bring Ottawa up to speed on the local Indigenous people. In 1875, for example, he deprecated the ceremony for the 'large amount of property … given away or destroyed,' and the 'continual round of feasting,' both of which were 'destructive to any settled habit of labour or industry.'[60]

Powell's reports reflected the principal critiques of the potlatch prevailing among the missionaries and the Indian agents, which were expressed in thousands of pages of often emotional reports to Ottawa.

Not only was it pagan, it had features that offended their sensibilities more than other non-Christian religious belief systems. Its wild excesses of drinking and feasting were 'symbolic of the savagery and depravity' of Indigenous peoples. It also represented a denial of the economic foundations of 'civilization.' Indigenous people were supposed to be learning the value not just of the acquisition of enough property to sustain life but also of its accumulation. The potlatch was the converse – it seemed 'wasteful and excessive – the antithesis to the twin pillars of the Protestant work ethic, industry and sobriety.' In addition the participants engaged in 'immoral practices,' including supposedly prostituting their female family members to raise the funds to participate. Missionary Cornelius Bryant complained that at potlatches people gave away almost everything they possessed, and 'reduce themselves to beggary and distress' in an orgy of debauchery. In 1879 Gilbert Sproat argued that it was 'not possible … that Indians can acquire property, or become industrious … while under the influence of this mania.'[61] We could fill many pages with similar comments, which said much more about critics' reactions than about potlatches and displayed no understanding of their social significance. The Tamanawas dance attracted much less discussion, but when it was talked about it drew the same kinds of comments. Remarking on the 1884 amendment that banned both ceremonies, Macdonald called it a 'heathenish dance' that 'is attended with much that is disgusting and degrading to the Indians.'[62]

White opponents of the potlatch were joined by a small cohort of Indigenous people who had converted to Christianity, but they were in a distinct minority, even though some were prominent. Peter Kelly, chair of the principal Indigenous political organization the Allied Tribes, supported a ban, as did Jane Cook, the only woman on that body's executive. Cook was very vocal, alleging that the potlatch harmed women and impoverished families. Opponents first tried persuasion but in the late 1870s turned to the federal government to outlaw the practice. A Catholic missionary, Gustave Dockele, for example, insisted that 'stringent measures' were needed to put an end to a 'heathen practice.'[63] The lobbying for a ban bore fruit with the 1884 amendment to the *Indian Act*, during the debate on which Macdonald called it 'debauchery of the worst kind' involving 'all kinds of orgies' and 'the cause of a great deal of misery and demoralization.' From the opposition benches Edward Blake echoed the sentiment, deprecating the 'insane exuberance of generosity,' which had a 'very demoralizing tendency.'[64] Indigenous people defended the potlatch as 'a custom prevalent among our people for many generations,' as 'the oldest and best of our festivals.' They pointed out its social and economic functions, such as public payment of debts, and the contribution that the purchase of items to give as gifts made to the provincial economy. Tellingly they also contrasted their customs to those of the settlers: 'The White man gives feasts to his friends and goes to theatres; we have only our potlatches and dances for amusements.' Like whites, 'we work for our money and like to spend it as we please, in gathering our friends together and giving them food to eat, … [and] dance and sing.'[65] Indigenous people not only condemned but defied the law. When they did so they found a provincial government unwilling to meet the expense of enforcement, which required breaking up groups of hundreds of people gathered for a ceremony.

Indian agents like Reginald Pidcock of the Kkewlth Agency were prepared to act and in 1889 effected the arrest of one Hamasack. He was tried by Pidcock, who like all Indian agents was also a JP, convicted, and sentenced to six months in prison. It was the only conviction obtained under the 1884 amendment and illegal because a JP did not have the jurisdiction to try indictable offences. The case went to the BC Supreme Court, likely on a writ of habeas corpus, where Chief Justice Begbie released Hamasack and also opined that the statute was too vague. Criminal law prohibits specific acts, but the law barred participating in a potlatch. 'It is by no means clear,' Begbie argued, 'what the Statute forbids.' The Act 'should have set out what acts constitute the forbidden festival,' but did not, and Begbie thought that lacunae meant 'that there would be some difficulty in convicting at all under the statute.'[66] It took a perhaps surprising six years to remedy the legal defect. In 1895 another amendment to the *Indian Act* recreated the offence, this time with a description of prohibited actions. It was made illegal to participate in or assist others to participate in 'any Indian festival, dance or other ceremony of which the giving away or paying or giving back of money, goods or articles takes place before, at or after the celebration of the same.' The amendment also criminalized the Tamanawas, making it an offence to engage in, or assist others in engaging in, 'any celebration or dance of which the wounding or mutilation of the dead or living body of a human being or animal forms a part or is a feature of.' These were indictable offences, the penalty a minimum of two and a maximum of six months' imprisonment.[67]

Although the offences were now better defined, few Indian agents in the later nineteenth and early twentieth centuries were prepared to take action because of the unrest that most believed would result. They were encouraged in this approach by the superintendent for Indian affairs in BC from 1899, Arthur Vowell, who thought the custom a harmless one. Agents were aware that many in the lower judiciary were unwilling to convict and, if they did so, handed out suspended sentences. If prosecutions failed, or resulted only in suspended sentences, officials believed that disrespect for the law generally would be the result. Moreover, quite a few in the BC settler community outside missionary circles opposed criminalization. Whites echoed Indigenous arguments in comparing the potlatch to Christmas, with its family gatherings, feasting, and gift-giving. The elaborate masks and costumes of the potlatch regalia were likened to fancy dress balls. More prosaically, merchants in regions where the potlatch was popular appreciated the significant increase in business from those who bought large quantities of blankets, bolts of cloth, sacks of flour, and other goods for gift-giving. Anthropologist Edward Sapir told Deputy SG Duncan Campbell Scott in 1915 that '[t]he economic argument is naturally the weightiest' against the prohibition of the potlatch.[68] There was some change in DIA policy after 1910, because Vowell's successor as superintendent, William Ditchburn, took a much more condemnatory view of potlatching, and he was supported by William Halliday, the agent for the Kwakiutl people who were its most ardent practitioners. Halliday enforced the law among the Kwakiutl, but the result was still not enough for those who wanted a vigorous state response. There were only 17 indictments preferred between 1895 and 1918, and only one successful prosecution prior to 1914. The turn to criminal law to enforce prohibition of a cultural practice never well understood by Europeans was a failure. The potlatch ban stayed on the statute books until 1951, although the ceremony declined for other reasons.

The other forms of Indigenous cultural practices prohibited in this period were the various ceremonial dances practised by the peoples of the plains.[69] Such dances went by European names such as sun dance, grass dance, and thirst dance, and many involved the giving away of gifts. Like the potlatch the dances were an integral part of many First Nations' culture, performed at large community gatherings, which also involved storytelling and other ceremonies. They were, among other things, a means of celebrating and appeasing the Great Spirit. The same 1895 amendment to the *Indian Act* that banned the potlatch applied to dances. The legislation contained a proviso that it not be 'construed to prevent the holding of any agricultural shows or exhibition or the giving of prizes for exhibits' at such a show, obviously designed to shield white settlers from prosecution. Prairie dances were seen by critics as part of a broader Indigenous culture that had to go as part of the 'civilization' process. The giving away of gifts, as with the potlatch, was profligate, and the dances represented a continuing attachment to traditional spirituality, which stood in the way of full adhesion to Christianity. They also displayed and/or induced 'mental instability' as participants worked themselves into 'a complete frenzy.'[70] Today, of course, many would say the same about aspects of Pentecostalism.

A number of prosecutions for dancing were successfully launched, although we do not know exactly how many. The convictions were all followed by prison sentences of two to three months.[71] Some of the prosecutions were for dancing done on reserve, others resulted from Indigenous dancers being invited to entertain the crowds at summer fairs in settler communities. The latter included the prosecution of Wanduta, a Dakota chief who performed with others at the Rapid City, Manitoba, July fair in 1902. When news of the event reached David Laird, Indian commissioner for Manitoba and the Territories who believed that such dances were 'foolish practices' and 'vestiges of a savage life,' he encouraged the Indian agent to prosecute. Wanduta received a four-month sentence, which he served in the Brandon jail. The fact that Wanduta's group had appeared at Rapid City only at the invitation of the fair's organizers, and that people in the settler community tried to intervene with Ottawa for a pardon and early release, shows that, as with the potlatch, many Europeans did not agree with the official policy of criminalization.[72] There is ample evidence that, despite the prosecutions, the dances continued, a fact also attested to by a further 1914 amendment to the *Indian Act* that required Indigenous persons in the West to obtain permission from the SG or an Indian agent before performing any dance off reserve or participating in any sort of show in cultural costume. Those who contravened this provision and those who employed Indigenous people who contravened this provision were liable to a fine of $25 or one month's imprisonment, or both.[73]

9

Canadian Law and Indigenous Peoples III: Education and Assimilation: The Origins and Expansion of Residential Schools

The education of Indigenous children was a central pillar of the dominion's assimilationist policies, a carry-over from the emphasis on Western-style education that had been one aspect of the policy of 'civilization' put in place in the Canadas from the 1840s.[1] The ministers responsible for Indigenous affairs in the 1870s frequently touted the importance of what Joseph Howe called the 'mental development' of his charges. Education went hand-in-hand with enfranchisement, given that the latter required fluency in English or French, and an appreciation of the superior accomplishments of white settlers' technology and governmental structures. Education was similarly tied to the goals of conversion to Christianity and the adoption of Western economic models – farming and selling skills in the labour market. SG Edgar Dewdney succinctly put it in 1891 that '[t]here are three tests which especially mark the advance of Indians towards civilization, viz, the adoption of the dress of the white man, engaging in agriculture, and the education of their children.' To achieve the necessary level of education it would be 'highly desirable' to 'obtain [the] entire possession of all Indian children.'[2]

While there was some continuity in education policy for Indigenous people before and after 1867, there was also dramatic change, in two related respects. First, as shown by table 9.1, the number of schools for Indigenous children expanded exponentially, from approximately 60 in 1867 to over 330 by 1914. By 1914 just over half of the schools for Indigenous children were in the West. Second, there was a dramatic

Table 9.1. Schools for Indigenous children in 1914

Province	Day schools	Residential schools	Total schools
Ontario	82	11	93
Quebec	29	0	29
Maritimes provinces	28	0	28
Manitoba	43	9	52
Saskatchewan	19	15	34
Alberta	4	20	24
British Columbia	45	18	63
Northwest and Yukon Territories	6	4	10
Total schools	256	77	333
Total enrolment	7,638	4,076	11,714

Source: *Annual Report*, 1914.

change in the types of schools provided. Only two residential schools operated in the original confederating provinces in 1867, and six more in the HBC territories and British Columbia, with the remainder being day schools situated on or near a reserve. By 1914 almost a quarter (23 per cent) of all schools for Indigenous children were residential schools, with 35 per cent of the Indigenous children in school in a residential establishment. Equally important, 67 of the 77 residential schools operating in 1914 were located in the West. The other 11 were in Ontario and comprised only 12 per cent of that province's 93 schools for Indigenous children.

Law played a significant role in these developments only from the mid-1890s, when legislation was passed to compel attendance at residential schools. Yet the silence of law looms large throughout any analysis of how residential schools operated. The absence of regulation and state oversight were crucial contributors to the myriad problems that plagued the system. We begin with a brief review of the school system for Indigenous children at Confederation, including an examination of what the federal government and Indigenous leaders saw as the principal goals of education in the 1870s and early 1880s. There follows an account of when, why, and how residential schools came to the fore in the early 1880s, and the subsequent growth in their numbers down to the turn of the century. We then review how the residential school system operated. The final section examines the period of disillusionment with residential schools from the turn of the century to 1914.

The School System for Indigenous People, 1867–1883

In 1867 there were 38 schools for Indigenous children in Ontario, a dozen in Quebec, fewer than 10 in British Columbia, at least four in the HBC territories, and none in the Maritime provinces.[3] The schools were almost all run by missionary societies. Twenty-four of the Ontario schools, for example, were operated by the Wesleyan Methodist Society or the New England Company, a non-denominational Protestant mission. Included in this total of around 60 schools were eight residential institutions: two in Ontario, two in the Territories, and four in British Columbia. The Ontario residential schools were the Mohawk Institute in Brantford serving the Six Nations and the Mount Elgin Institution at Muncey Town on the Carradoc reserve in southwestern Ontario. Both had operated since the 1830s and early 1840s, both were run by Protestant mission societies, and both were voluntary boarding schools to which some Indigenous parents from the locality sent their children to be taught to read and write and to acquire marketable skills. At the Mohawk Institute the boys were taught trades such as carpentry and blacksmithing, at Mount Elgin boys were taught 'trades and farming' and girls 'housewifery and tailoring.' The six residential schools operating in British Columbia and the HBC territories in 1867 were also mission-run, by the Methodist, Presbyterian, and Roman Catholic Churches.[4]

Mission-run schools for Indigenous children had received grants in aid from colonial governments, and the federal government continued that policy after 1867. In 1877, for example, grants totalling a little under $1,000 were made to day schools in Manitoba and the Territories. Government supported the schools because it saw education as an integral part of the assimilationist policies we examined in the previous chapter. Education would change Indigenous peoples' culture and belief systems to conform to white settler values. In the words of SG Hector Langevin, Indigenous people needed to acquire 'the education necessary to enable them hereafter to share the blessings of civilization.' This was seen as especially necessary for the people of western Canada. Deputy SG Spragge asserted in 1872 that the Indigenous people of British Columbia were 'cruel and intractable savages' whom education would turn into 'orderly and useful members of society.' He believed that Indigenous people were not 'savages' by nature, but from a lack of enlightenment. They were redeemable: education would teach them 'the useful employments of civilized life' and 'train them for occupations for which their natural ingenuity eminently fits them.' He was also aware that the government's ambitions dovetailed well with the churches' understanding of their Christian duty. The acquisition of the West, he believed, 'awakened an increased interest ... from all sections of the Dominion' among those who saw it as their Christian duty to direct their 'philanthropic efforts ... to the welfare of the aborigines.' Spragge's successor, Vankoughnet, identified the same goal and stressed the necessity of making education its linchpin: 'Give me the children and you may have the parents,' he wrote to Macdonald, and you will also solve 'that most difficult problem – the intellectual emancipation of the Indian.' Vankoughnet also believed that there was a good case for making education compulsory. David Mills, SG and the minister of the interior in 1876, similarly believed that Canada's duty was 'to prepare him [the Indian] for a higher civilization through education and other means, such as enfranchisement.'[5]

In the 1870s and early 1880s these goals underlay a substantial expansion in the number of schools for Indigenous children, principally in western Canada, from around 60 to about 140 by 1883. The prairies contained 37 of these schools by 1883, 18 in Manitoba and 19 in the Territories. The increase was almost all in on-reserve day schools. Ontario's 2 residential schools in the pre-Confederation period became 4 in the 1870s with the addition of the Wikwemikong Industrial School on Manitoulin Island and Shingwauk Home, a boys' institution that also operated a counterpart for girls, Wawanosh House, both at Sault Ste. Marie.[6] Only 3 residential schools were established in the Territories before 1883, 4 in British Columbia, and 1 in Manitoba. To continue receiving the government grant, schools had to achieve a certain average attendance, and on occasion they failed to do so, leading to closures.[7] In addition to education being a policy tool of the politicians and bureaucrats who wanted to 'civilize' Indigenous people, it was also something desired by many Indigenous leaders, as exemplified by the demands for school provisions in the numbered treaties, discussed in chapter 7. The Shingwauk Home, for example, was requested by the Garden River reserve's leadership, who wanted European schooling so that their children could 'make a successful adjustment to dramatic change that was coming into their lives with the arrival of large numbers of non-Native immigrants.' This was a sentiment shared by many Indigenous leaders; as one historian has aptly put it, they wanted education 'as a tool of cultural revitalization, as a means of mediating between themselves and the White communities.'[8] Indigenous leaders, however, did not envisage, and could not have envisaged, the large-scale move to residential schools and the results of that transformation. As is evident from their response to enfranchisement, they did not wish to see the destruction of their culture, the loss of their languages and identities as distinct and distinctive communities.

The Origins and Growth of the
Residential School System to 1900

In the 1880s and 1890s the number of schools for Indigenous children grew substantially. There were 287 such schools in 1900, double the number in 1883. The greatest growth took place between the mid-1880s and 1894, by which date there were actually 291 schools, more than in 1900, and in the West, especially on the prairies, where 49 schools in 1883 became 181 in 1894. More importantly, there was a dramatic augmentation in the number of residential schools. The 10 residential schools in 1883 became 43 in 1894 and 61 in 1900. As a percentage of all schools for Indigenous children, residential schools went from 7 per cent in 1885 to 14 per cent in 1894 and to 21 per cent in 1900. Again, the picture changed most dramatically in the West; the 37 residential schools in 1894 and the 55 in 1900 represented 84 and 90 per cent of all residential schools.

Although we have used the term 'residential schools' and will continue to do so, this was not the term used by contemporaries. They were known as industrial schools or boarding schools.[9] Both kinds of institutions were residential, not only teaching but also housing their pupils. There were two principal differences between boarding and industrial schools, one a matter of educational theory and the other of a more practical nature. Industrial schools were first established in the United States and Britain in the 1850s as mostly residential institutions, which served a variety of purposes. At different times and places they were used for children who refused to attend school, thereby segregating 'difficult' children from the majority, for deviant children who had not yet committed crimes that would put them in reformatories but were considered at risk of doing so, and as a form of juvenile reformatory. Some were voluntary, with children placed there by their parents or guardians, others were children committed by magistrates.[10] Ontario used industrial schools to discipline refractory children and to teach basic literacy and trade skills, and other provinces introduced them after Confederation. Their general purpose was to 'civilize' those who did not conform to 'respectable' values. The Mohawk Institute was Ontario's first industrial school and was continually praised in DIA reports for its success at teaching Six Nations children the values of white settler life.

Boarding schools and industrial schools were different. The former were designed to concentrate more on the basics of reading and writing, and to provide a less-advanced curriculum, teaching only elementary agricultural skills, whatever was necessary for their graduates to be smallholder farmers. In fact the curricular difference between the two was often more theoretical than real, especially for girls, whose education in either kind of school was largely learning domestic skills. It was also not so different for boys because, as detailed below, male pupils at both kinds of school were often put to work at agricultural tasks that, whatever their educational value may have been, were valued by school administrators as a way to save money by supplying food for the residents. A more significant difference between the two was that boarding schools tended to be smaller and often located on or near reserves. In 1910, for example, four of the nine boarding schools in Manitoba were on reserves and another four were 'adjoining,' 'near,' or a quarter of a mile away from reserves. In Saskatchewan five of the 13 boarding schools were on reserve, four were 'adjoining,' and one was three miles from a reserve.[11] Industrial schools had larger enrolments and were established in or near urban centres, well away from the children's home communities, in cities like Battleford and Regina.

The major causes of the turn to residential schools were twofold. The virtual disappearance of the buffalo by the late 1870s convinced Ottawa that the transition to an agricultural economy needed to be rapid. The *Annual Reports* in the late 1870s are replete with references to this problem. Dominion policy was 'a mixture of altruism and cynicism,' exemplified by David Laird's 1878 comment that the government's choices were 'to help the Indians to farm and raise stock, to feed them, or to fight them.'[12] Teaching Indigenous children to be sedentary farmers was best done through residential schools. Adults would be taught by farm instructors on reserve, but children could be more quickly converted if they were separated, to a greater or lesser degree, from their reserves and communities. More importantly for current purposes, the 1880s saw a significant change in thinking about Indigenous people, especially those of the Prairie West. They were increasingly seen as incapable of absorbing the benefits of 'civilization' in an evolutionary process and therefore needed to be quickly coerced into change. Politicians and bureaucrats consistently referred to the duty of the Canadian state to 'elevate the Indian from his condition of savagery,' from a state of 'ignorance, superstition and helplessness.'[13]

This quotation post-dates 1885, and although similar statements appeared before then, they became more frequent and more strident following the rebellion. Thus while the goal did not change from assimilation, the preferred methodology altered. When children lived with their families and communities the kind of education policymakers wanted, one that made Indigenous children more like white children, was not possible, certainly not quickly possible.

These goals were considered not achievable through day schools because of inconsistent attendance. The *Annual Reports* of the 1870s and early 1880s frequently referred to, and always published statistics on, the substantial gap between enrolment and attendance. The problem was blamed on parents wanting to continue to employ their children in family- and community-based economic activity, and on what Vankoughnet referred to in 1876 as Indigenous peoples' 'indifference to educational advantages.' Officials conceded that other factors, such as the difficulty of travelling a few miles to a reserve school in winter, were also a problem. But the paramount problem was the 'indifference [to education] and nomadic habits of the parents.' Schools 'which are not of an industrial character, and which do not possess the power of isolating for a time the young Indian from the irregular habits and nomadic pursuits incident to wild life in the canoe and the wigwam,' would not succeed. As SG Edgar Dewdney put it in 1890, the residential school 'disassociates the Indian child from the deleterious home influences to which he would otherwise be subjected. It reclaims him from the uncivilized state in which he has been brought up.'[14] On this issue officials in Ottawa were of equal minds with the missionary and other church-affiliated groups that operated the vast majority of the schools – day and residential. To take but one example, the Oblates of Mary Immaculate, who ran many of the Catholic schools, had been operating in the Duck Lake area of Saskatchewan from the mid-nineteenth century. In 20 years Father Vital Fourmond had no more than 60 or so converts to his credit and was frustrated by parents keeping their children away from his order's schools, mainly because they did not want them baptized. In the early 1890s he readily agreed with the Indian agent, Robert Mackenzie, that a boarding school at Duck Lake was needed; Cree children 'should be separated from their families, in order to bring them up as we desire.'[15]

For the DIA, and for the missionaries in the field, even good attendance would not have made day schools effective instruments of assimilation. It would take generations to effect evolutionary change – change that in any event would likely result in Indigenous people who were literate and trained for a changing economy, but still Indigenous in culture and belief systems. They wanted revolutionary change, the rapid eradication of all distinctions between Indigenous people and Europeans. They wanted, to quote Thomas Babington Macaulay, an earlier exemplar of the British imperial mission referring to the education of another kind of 'Indian,' to produce a class of persons 'Indian in blood and colour, but English in taste, in opinions, in morals, and in intellect.'[16] The best way to achieve this was to remove children from the social and cultural influences of family and community. As early as 1873 Spragge had recommended industrial schools as the best way for Canada's newest Indigenous people, those living in British Columbia, to learn 'the useful employments of civilized life.' Israel Powell similarly consistently reiterated his belief that residential schools would do the job of assimilation much better than day schools. It was manifestly true, he asserted in 1876, that 'barbarism can only be cured by education,' and equally true that industrial schools, though they would cost more, were 'more prudent and economical' in the long run. By the late 1870s opinion among both department officials and the church groups who actually ran the schools was strongly in favour of a school system that would separate children from the cultural influences of parents and communities. In his capacity as SG Macdonald put it forcefully in 1880: 'The Indian youth, to enable him to cope successfully with his brother of white origin, must be disassociated from the prejudicial influences by which he is surrounded on the reserve of his band. And the necessity for the establishment more generally of institutions, whereat Indian children, besides being instructed in the usual branches of education, will be lodged, fed, clothed, kept separate from home influences, taught trades and interested in agriculture, is becoming every year more apparent.'[17]

The shift to a preference for residential schools is often referred to the publication in 1879 of a report by Nicholas Flood Davin, a defeated Tory candidate in the election of 1878 who had been rewarded by Macdonald with an assignment to investigate industrial schools in the United States and to advise on whether they should be introduced in the Territories. Davin strongly recommended an industrial school system. Yet he was only reflecting a broader consensus, and indeed his detailed plan for the establishment of industrial schools said very little about the links between such schools and the underlying policy of assimilation. Presciently, if to no avail, Davin recommended against allowing religious denominations to run an industrial school system, because they tended not to feed the children adequately.[18]

In July 1883 Ottawa moved from expressing a preference for residential schools to building and funding them. An Order in Council established three industrial schools 'for the instruction of Indian children in mechanical arts and in agriculture, as well as in the ordinary branches of education' at Battleford, Qu'Appelle, and High River. Two were to be run by the Catholic Church and one by the Anglicans, and $44,000 was provided for them. The children were to be taught agricultural skills and some trades, principally those of carpenter and blacksmith. And of course they would be 'civilized' by the experience. The *Report* from the DIA that proclaimed this innovation also praised the Mohawk Institute for the fact that it 'annually turns out pupils sufficiently advanced to take their place in a civilized community.' Macdonald was aware that Indigenous people did and would 'show a reluctance to have their children separated from them,' but he rather blithely assumed that 'doubtless time will overcome this obstacle.' The government could begin with 'orphans and children who have no natural protectors,' and from such a start 'we must count upon the judicious treatment of these children by the principals and teachers of the institutions eventually to do away with the objections of the Indian parents to their children being placed under their charge.' The three new schools were operational within a year, and in reporting on that fact Macdonald also indicated that he wanted to see others established in Manitoba.[19]

The Operation of Residential Schools

The residential school system was funded by the government but run by a variety of religious denominations, principally the Roman Catholic and Anglican Churches – see table 9.2. The Catholic Church operated slightly over half the schools, the Anglicans just under a quarter. Government exercised a broad supervision, through Indian agents and a small inspectorate. But like many bureaucracies in this period, the DIA was understaffed and underfunded. The government's principal role was to fund the system. The churches contributed money from subscriptions raised by their members, but the bulk of the funding came from annual government grants. In the decade after 1883 these were block grants per school. Residential schools cost Ottawa much more than day schools,

Table 9.2. Denominations operating residential schools, 1912

Denomination	Boarding schools	Industrial schools	Total residential schools (%)
Roman Catholic	30	9	39 (53)
Anglican	13	4	17 (23)
Methodist	4	4	8 (11)
Presbyterian	8	0	8 (11)
Non-denominational	0	2	2 (2)
Total	55	19	74

Source: *Annual Report*, 1912.

which were financed by a more even balance of government and church funds, and industrial schools much more than boarding schools. In 1886, for example, the government spent approximately $145,000 on industrial schools, $45,000 on boarding schools, and $26,500 on day schools in Manitoba and the Territories. The cost was resented by some in Ottawa, especially by a DIA overseen by the parsimonious Vankoughnet, a man for whom 'fiscal considerations came ahead of human ones.'[20]

Feeling the financial pinch, Ottawa changed the funding formula in 1892 to one in which it provided a per capita grant based on student enrolment, up to an enrolment limit. The 'management' – that is, the churches – had to make up any shortfall in operating funds. The Order in Council establishing the new scheme provided comparative figures for per capita expenditures in 1891 three industrial schools. In 1890–1 each child at Qu'Appelle had cost $134, at Battleford $175, and at High River $185. Under the new system the per capita grants would be $115, $140, and $130 respectively. In the interests of economy the government knowingly underfunded the system, trusting those running the schools to 'make more effort in the way of economizing.'[21]

A reader of DIA *Annual Reports* would have been struck by the unrelenting optimism they espoused, especially before ca. 1900. Starting in 1896, the *Reports* also invariably included at least one graphic representation of progress and transformation. The pictures below are of Thomas Moore, a Blackfoot boy, 'before and after tuition,' that is, 'as he appeared when admitted to the Regina Industrial School' and 'after tuition.' The first depicts him dressed in buffalo robes, festooned with beads and his hair in pigtails, the second in suit and tie with hair cut short. It is an accurate representation of the physical transformation that residential schools produced, and implicitly of the cultural change that they were intended to bring about.[22]

Thomas Moore, before and after "tuition." Two pictures of an Indigenous boy – one in pigtails and wearing Indigenous clothing, the other with short hair and wearing a suit – before and after time at the Regina Industrial School.

Credit: *Annual Report of the Department of Indian Affairs*, 1896.

Today we are all very well aware of the reality that these images concealed, and of consequent condemnations of the theory and practice of the residential school system voiced by Indigenous communities and others. Most of our contemporary knowledge of that system and the problems it caused derives from the work of the Truth and Reconciliation Commission, which, because it highlighted the experiences of those still alive, and of the immediately preceding generations, is largely based on evidence about the system in the twentieth century.[23] Yet many of the problems go back to the early decades of residential schools, and they were not unknown to the government at the time. For the most part white Canadians did not reject the objective of assimilation. But by the turn of the century significant numbers of those connected with the system came to see that it was badly run and, from their perspective, ineffective. In this section we briefly summarize the many problems encountered by those who attended residential schools. Four principal ones were clearly manifested from the outset and became more serious through the 1890s:[24] conditions in the schools; the physical and psychological treatment of the children; attendance problems; and financial difficulties for the operators of the schools. We have separated them for the purpose of this account, but they were related, serving as cause and effect. Collectively they engendered a reduced faith in residential schools.

While conditions at residential schools varied, the evidence is overwhelming that problems were legion. Food was inadequate, in both quality and quantity, many schools were overcrowded, heating in the winter months was often inadequate, and children were worked hard at physical labour, which detracted from the educational return. From the 1890s the schools frequently employed what became known as the 'outing system,' whereby children were hired out to work to nearby farms, especially during harvest season. It was, noted Deputy SG Hayter Reed in 1896, 'one of the marked features of industrial institutions,' the 'hiring out of the children ... in any direction in which employment can be found.' And there was always work to be had: 'During the harvesting season, the demand for boys cannot nearly be met, and at all times more girls could be placed as servants if the numbers ... permitted.'[25] Exacerbating the harsh conditions, and also a result of them, there was widespread sickness and mortality among the children. We will discuss this in more detail below in relation to Dr. Peter Bryce's revelations in the early twentieth century, but the problem was endemic from the outset. We now know that many deaths went unrecorded other than in the minds and hearts of parents who never saw their children again, not even their corpses. At the time of writing we do not know whether the unmarked graves at Kamloops and Cowessess derive from this period, but we can say that if they did then the people who ran the schools and interred the bodies, in addition to perhaps being legally liable in other respects, certainly violated provincial and/or territorial laws on the duty to report deaths. Legislation on the collection of vital statistics was passed in every province and the Territories in the 1870s, and, among other things, required all householders to report deaths that occurred on their premises, and persons in loco parentis, ministers who performed funeral services, and anybody with knowledge of a death to do likewise.[26]

Both residential schools and reserve day schools were often staffed by poorly qualified and badly paid teachers. Many were young and inexperienced men and women who took jobs in remote locations only because they could not find other work. Vankoughnet could not have been the only bureaucrat to know this, lamenting in 1892 with reference to reserve schools that 'the salaries which the Department finds itself able to offer are totally inadequate to induce well qualified and certificated teachers to undergo the hardships and deprivations' involved. Only those who received a salary supplement from the church had a reasonable income.[27]

Although we know much less about physical and sexual abuse in the residential schools of the later nineteenth century than about later decades, some teachers and administrators compounded their educational inadequacies in this way. Residential schools were run by systems of order and discipline, not unlike prisons and reformatories, and maintaining discipline in all such institutions meant resort to physical force. Although it was common for school and other officials to refer to the use of corporal punishment as occurring only exceptionally, in 'extreme cases,' such words take their meaning from the context, and there is evidence that it was not a rare occurrence. In 1892 parents withdrew children from the Middlechurch boarding school in Manitoba because two students had had their 'clothes taken up' and 'been whipped.' Seven years later David Laird carried out an inquiry into the same school and concluded that children had been 'too severely punished.' The principal's use of bare back floggings was 'suggestive of the old system of flogging criminals.'[28]

On only one occasion that we know of did this problem reach a court. On 7 August 1913 Ruth Miller, her sister Hazel, and two other girls ran away from the Mohawk Institute. Ruth was 13, the others 11 or 12. They claimed they hated the food, having seen worms in the porridge and flies in the bread; indeed, the institute was commonly known as the mush hole for its over-reliance on unappetizing porridge. The Miller girls' father was a local man, Chief George Miller, who had sent them there because his wife had died, and he was unable to care for the girls on his own. All the girls were severely punished, but Ruth had the worst of it as the perceived ringleader – confined in a dark empty room three feet by six feet for three days, where she was fed on bread and water. After Ruth and Hazel ran away a second time and were caught, Ruth was whipped by the school governess, and the girls were discharged from the school. SG Duncan Campbell Scott believed the punishments were 'too severe' but refused to carry out the investigation demanded by the Six Nations council. Chief Miller then launched a civil suit on behalf of his daughters against the principal of the institute, Nelles Ashton, for $5,000. The case, heard in the Brantford High Court in April 1914, aroused great local interest. Of four heads of damages, the (presumably all-white) jury awarded damages in two: $100 for Ruth's solitary confinement, and $390 for being whipped on the back with a rawhide. The decision was not appealed and did not lead to systemic change.[29]

The contemporary sources contain even fewer references to sexual abuse than to physical maltreatment.[30] The experience of recent decades has shown that many kinds of residential institutions have done everything in their power to discourage and indeed punish people who complained, and to hide accusations from the public gaze when they are made. We know so much about such scandals nowadays largely from the revelations of living survivors, not available to the historian of the more distant past. We have glimpses from this period both of the existence of sexual abuse and of institutional responses to it. Jean L'Heureux worked at Oblate missions in the 1860s but was asked to leave the mission at Lac la Biche for making sexual advances to young boys and abusing at least one. He spent many years among the Blackfoot and served as a translator during the Treaty 7 negotiations. He was hired by the DIA in 1881 as a translator and later became a recruiter of young children for the High River industrial school, run by the Oblates, which included taking children into his home to 'prepare' them. In 1886 an Anglican missionary told Hayter Reed that he had his suspicions about L'Heureux, and in 1891 he was accused of abusing the boys in his home by Blackfoot Chief White Pup. The DIA's response was to force his resignation: Vankoughnet noted that it was not 'necessary' to 'state the cause.' Both the Oblates and the DIA, therefore, preferred to bury the accusations; the former even retained his services despite their knowledge of his history. The above-noted principal of the Middlechurch school in Manitoba was also the subject of complaints for his attentions to the girls in his charge, which he vigorously denied. A DIA official thought there was more than a grain of truth in the allegations but that no action should be taken because, while they were 'imprudent,' they were 'free of any criminal intention.' He was finally dismissed two years later after further accusations and another inquiry, at which his 'defence' included the assertion that he had not kissed any of the girls 'more than twelve times.'[31]

Moving from physical abuse to psychological damage, Indigenous people also objected to the assimilationist ideology with which the educational system was imbued. They wanted education in modern skills, but not the entire package of acculturation. Parents and children deeply resented the latter being made to speak English or French rather than their own languages. They also deprecated the distances the children had to travel to industrial schools, many of which were located in urban centres. Officials were quite aware that Indigenous parents did not want their children separated from family and community, and equally aware that it was a cruel and unnatural policy. Their response was to deflect such critiques by labelling them the price of 'advancement,' a necessary consequence of the progress that residential schooling brought. Some bands were able to avoid the worst of the problems by negotiating the terms on which schools were established. The Ojibwa of Shoal Lake in northwestern Ontario, for example, asked the Presbyterians for a school in the late 1890s. They got one, the Cecilia Jeffrey boarding school at Kenora, but as much on their own terms as the church's. Their contract with the church specified protections for some traditional ways, limited both proselytization and how much work the children would have to do, guaranteed that the children would be released from school to take part in traditional ceremonies, and stipulated that the police would not be used to apprehend runaways. The final article of the contract stated that 'a number of children shall be sent now and if they are well treated more shall be sent.'[32]

In part the school conditions and the assimilationist ideology were the cause of the attendance problems. DIA reports often stated that bands were keen to send their children to the schools. In 1889, for example, SG Dewdney reported that '[t]he lodging capacity of the industrial institutions in Ontario was tested to the utmost' in the previous year, and two years later Vankoughnet reported on an increase in attendance at residential schools. Statements like these, however, must be set against complaints about the difficulties of securing enough pupils. In the same report in which Vankoughnet talked of an increase in attendance, for example, he also advocated caution in building new schools: 'It is … better to fill the institutions already in operation.'[33] Indigenous parents' reluctance to send children derived in part from the school conditions and physical and psychological damage just described, knowledge of which did not take long to reach Indigenous communities. In the minds of the bureaucracy, Indigenous reluctance to have their children enrolled, and to maintain a regular attendance if they did, derived from the same causes that had discredited day schools in the eyes of bureaucrats in the 1870s and early 1880s – the fact that children took part in the full range of community pursuits, including hunting expeditions. This problem and the efforts to make western Indigenous people wholly dependent on farming led to Parliament giving the executive the power to declare the game laws of the North-West Territories and Manitoba applicable to Indigenous people.[34] The attendance issue also highlighted the distinction between boarding and industrial schools. Boarding schools, because they were on or near reserves, were more palatable to Indigenous leaders, parents, and children than the faraway industrial schools because children could make frequent visits home.

Resistance to sending children resulted in proposals that schooling be made compulsory. This idea gathered strength in the 1880s among church organizations, and SG Dewdney advocated it in his 1890 *Annual Report*, employing a somewhat perverse logic. A law making attendance compulsory, he asserted, would cause those schools 'to become more popular with the Indians than they are at present' – an admission that they were far from universally popular. The reason for the increased popularity was that the parents, freed from having to look after their children, would 'be at liberty to go where they pleased.' This of course contradicted the common complaint among officials that children took part in activities with their families and that was why they did not attend school. For some years, however, the government was reluctant to go so far. Some officials worried that it might bring conflict with Indigenous communities and would in any event be difficult to enforce. One of these was the then Indian commissioner for the North-West Territories, Hayter Reed. He was initially opposed to enforcing attendance, as a policy 'likely to irritate the Indians' that should be 'avoided as much as possible.' Many officials likewise preferred persuasion short of legal compulsion. For example, Cree chief Star Blanket was deposed as chief in 1893 for killing cattle to feed his band, despite the DIA having told him not to. In 1895, after the passage of legislation making it possible to compel parents to send their children to school, discussed below, he was told by the DIA that he would be reinstated if he persuaded some band members to send their children to residential schools. Star Blanket was well known as an opponent of residential schooling; in 1891 he was complained about by the Indian agent, along with his councillors, for not permitting band children to go to school.[35]

Ultimately the advocates of compulsion won the day, and in 1894 the *Indian Act* was amended to give the executive the power to regulate, generally or in relation to any province or band, 'to secure the compulsory attendance of [Indigenous] children at school.'[36] The regulations could provide for 'the arrest and conveyance to school, and detention there, of truant children and of children who are prevented by their parents or guardians from attending,' and for the punishment by fine or imprisonment of such offending parents and guardians. Most importantly, JPs and Indian agents were empowered to commit 'children of Indian blood under the age of 16 years' to a residential school until they turned 18. The legislation evoked very little debate, and almost all of what was said were complaints about the cost of residential schools. Only John Charlton, Liberal MP for Norfolk North and an impassioned advocate for the rights of women and children, referred to the essence of the amendment, asking Indian Affairs Minister T. Mayne Daly if the law was necessary and received the firm reply that it was, 'very much so,' because '[p]arents have interfered and taken boys away just when they were beginning to learn a trade.'[37]

The regulations made pursuant to the act gave officials sweeping powers to commit children to residential schools.[38] Sections 1 through 7 made it mandatory for all Indigenous children between seven and sixteen to attend a reserve day school. Section 9 was the residential schools provision:

> An Indian Agent or Justice of the Peace, on being satisfied that any Indian child between six and sixteen years of age, is not being properly cared for or educated, and that the parent, guardian or other person having the charge or control of such child, is unfit or unwilling to provide for the child's education, may issue a warrant authorizing the person named therein to search for and take such child and place it in an industrial or boarding school, ... and a child so placed in an industrial or boarding school, may be retained until the age of eighteen years of age is reached.

There was a notice requirement to the parents and an appeal, but the former did not apply to the Territories and the latter was hollow, given that if a parent objected an inquiry would be made by the Indian agent, the official who could initiate the proceeding in the first place. Other sections dealt with children who left the residential school, including giving various officers, including Indian agents, powers of arrest and search and seizure. The regulations removed from Indigenous parents any choice about whether and where children should attend school, but it did protect the rights of one stakeholder in the residential school system – the churches. Section 14 provided that 'no Protestant child shall be placed in a Roman Catholic School, or in a school conducted under

Roman Catholic auspices; and no Roman Catholic shall be placed in a Protestant School or in a school conducted under Protestant auspices.'

The move to compulsion was proof that the residential school system was not working as intended. Yet the DIA was officially reluctant to use its powers in this period.[39] In 1898 Deputy SG James Smart insisted that 'the Department's policy is as long as possible to refrain from compulsory measures, and try the effect of moral suasion and an appeal to self-interest.' He gave as a salutary example the case of a chief in Saskatchewan who had long been opposed to sending children away but had recently allowed two to go to the Qu'Appelle industrial school. But clearly persuasion could be very close to effective coercion. In 1897 Indian Agent Robert McKenzie, whom we cited earlier as an advocate of opening a residential school near one of his reserves, was convinced that the adopted son of Plains Man needed to be sent away: 'This boy is between 10 and 11 years of age, and if properly handled I think would grow up a good boy, but left on the reserve he will be a very bad boy,' he reported to his superior, Amédée Forget, Indian commissioner of the Territories. He was told that he should first try 'other measures' and only if they were unsuccessful resort to compulsion. McKenzie went to Plains Man's house with an NWMP officer and a warrant, and 'used all the persuasive power I could bring to bear,' to no avail. He gave the warrant to the police officer, and when Plains Man saw what was inevitable 'he gave in and gladly signed the papers rather than have the boy taken by the police.' McKenzie filled out an application form for the Duck Lake boarding school and delivered the boy there personally the same evening. The boy was not dragged away by a policeman, was not put under restraint, and Plains Man did not try to prevent his going. But if this was persuasion, it was as close to coercion as one could come without resorting to forced apprehension, and one very much doubts that Plains Man 'gladly' signed the paperwork. A little later, when Mackenzie was trying to have some local children sent further away to the Qu'Appelle industrial school, he again encountered parental resistance, which he overcame by threats to cut rations, a tactic that merits the oxymoronic label of coercive persuasion.[40]

Not until 1920 was legislation passed to strengthen compulsory attendance at residential schools, a subject we will return to in *Volume 3*. But in the 1890s, given all of their problems, doubts emerged in official quarters by the mid-1890s about the advisability and efficacy of residential schools. Two distinct arguments – that efforts to 'civilize' Indigenous people should not be made, and that whether or not they should it was pointless to try – were often conflated and can to some degree be traced to the coming to power in Ottawa in 1896 of Laurier's Liberal administration, and, more particularly as a result, of the rise to influence in Ottawa of men from the prairies, such as Clifford Sifton, a former Manitoba premier who became SG in 1896. Sifton and his successors took the 'settler view' of Indigenous people. The *Manitoba Free Press* greeted the news of his appointment by observing that 'nothing … will add greater lustre to Mr. Sifton's administration than the solving of the problem of teaching the Northwest Indians to live like human beings.' Although he initially believed that the residential school system needed to be continued but run more economically, Sifton soon changed his tune, arguing that Indigenous people could not be 'civilized,' and thus that residential schools served no attainable purpose. 'The Indian cannot go out from school, making his own way and compete with the white man,' he told the Commons in 1904. An Indigenous person 'has not the physical, mental or moral get-up to enable him to compete.'[41] The change in orientation was reflected in a remarkable piece of revisionist history written by Duncan Campbell Scott, superintendent of Indian education in 1910. 'It was never the policy … to transform an Indian into a white man,' he blithely asserted, but rather to 'develop the great natural intelligence of the race and to fit the Indian for civilized life in his own environment.' He went on to explain that Indigenous people had been, and should be, given 'instruction in the means of gaining a livelihood from the soil or as a member of an industrial and mercantile community.' It had not proved possible to effect a complete transformation – 'the Indian has not been changed into a white man' – but Indigenous people did have their own 'admirable characteristics,' more so 'than many white men.'[42]

Doubts about the advisability of the mission of residential schools were linked to concerns about the cost of the system. One response was greater emphasis on boarding schools over industrial schools. Industrial schools were the flagships, exemplars of full assimilation, which could not be achieved; boarding schools, with their less ambitious curricula, were more 'successful' simply because they attempted less. Boarding schools were also much cheaper to run. In 1895 there were 23 boarding schools and 14 industrial schools in the western provinces and territories, and by 1900 the respective numbers were 39, an increase of 16, and 17, an increase of only three. There were still only 17 industrial schools in the West in 1908, and 53 boarding schools. Hence almost all of the expansion after the mid-1890s was in the smaller type of residential school. Sifton took responsibility for this change. 'The system of industrial schools as I found it in operation when I took office, is not the best, or the most effective, or the most economic way of improving the condition of the Indians,' he told the Commons in 1904. Instead he had instituted a 'less elaborate system … of … boarding schools where a larger number of children can for a shorter time be educated more economically and generally more effectively.' In 1914 the new approach was reflected in an *Indian Act* provision allowing the government to 'declare any school or institution where children are provided with board and lodging as well as instruction, … to be an industrial school or boarding school.' Although both kinds of residential school were mentioned, the underlying purpose was to increase the number of boarding schools at the expense of industrial schools. This change in orientation did not prevent the residential school system from continuing to grow, albeit not as rapidly as before. Sixty-one residential schools operated in 1900, and 77 in 1914, a slower rate of increase than in the decade and a half between 1885 and 1900. This figure conceals a decline in the number of industrial schools in the West, to just 16 by 1914, while boarding school numbers grew to 61 – see table 9.1. The number of day schools also increased in the early part of the twentieth century, from 226 to 256, so that by 1914 residential schools were about the same percentage of all government schools for Indigenous people as they had been in 1900.[43]

The Revelations of Dr. Peter Bryce

None of these changes could do anything to ameliorate the deep-seated problems that plagued the system. Indeed they became more pronounced with every passing year. A clear sign that the DIA was aware that conditions in the schools left a great deal to be desired was the appointment in 1904 of the department's first medical inspector for residential schools, Dr. Peter Henderson Bryce. An expert on public health and an accomplished statistician, he served for 22 years as secretary to the Ontario Board of Health and was president of the American Public Health Association in 1900. Like most people of his day he believed in the civilizing mission and praised the work of Christian missionaries, whose 'heroic devotion' had been instrumental in 'transforming the Indian aborigines' from 'savages' into 'members of a civilized society.' In 1904 he moved from the Ontario government to the federal, appointed by Sifton as chief medical officer of his two departments, Interior and the DIA. An expert on tuberculosis, he was influential in developing medical standards for prospective immigrants in his work for Interior.[44]

In 1907 Bryce travelled to 35 industrial and boarding schools in Manitoba and the Territories. He did not examine the children but inspected the school premises and attendance and medical records. Two-thirds of his resulting report was taken up with a history of the system and with financial and attendance statistics. In just seven further pages he produced a sweeping critique of sanitary conditions in the schools and the health status of present and former pupils. Most had water supplied by wells, which were in a number of cases described as 'bad,' 'all bad,' 'not very satisfactory,' 'insufficient,' and 'inadequate.' Ventilation and sanitation systems were similarly criticized; his inspections of the former showed that, with two or three exceptions, 'no serious attempt at the ventilation of dormitories or school-rooms has hitherto been made.' These conditions were intimately linked to the health of the children, especially the very high rates of 'scrofula' and tuberculosis.[*] Bryce attributed high rates of infection to the difficulty of maintaining the required numbers to obtain the full grant, which in turn made the schools willing to take in infected children. Once there, 'the defective sanitary conditions of many schools, especially in the matter of ventilation, have been the *foci* from which disease, especially tubercular, has spread.' The problem was exacerbated by the ignorance of staff and the very few medical officers: 'Principals and teachers and even physicians were at times inclined to question or minimize the dangers of infection ... and nothing less than peremptory instructions as to how to deal with cases of disease ... will eliminate this ever-present danger of infection.'

Bryce thus drew clear links between the spread of infection, undernourished children, and poor sanitation and ventilation. Fully one-quarter of the children who had entered residential schools and for which he had records had died of tuberculosis in the institution or after they had left. At one school, File Hills in Saskatchewan, 69 per cent of former pupils had died. There was 'an intimate relationship between the health of the pupils while in school and ... their early death subsequent to discharge.' 'We have created a situation so dangerous to health,' he said, that his only surprise in analysing the results was that they 'were not even worse than they have been shown statistically to be.' He blamed the ignorance of those running the schools and debunked the theory

---

[*] Scrofula is also called cervical tuberculous lymphadenitis and is a form of tuberculosis infection caused by the same bacterium that causes pulmonary tuberculosis (TB).

clung to by some that high rates of tuberculosis among Indigenous people were the result of ethnic susceptibility to the disease.[45]

Bryce's report was printed but stayed largely within the DIA and was not publicized. It was briefly mentioned in the department's *Annual Report* for 1907, one paragraph in Bryce's report on all the work of his unit for the year. One Ottawa newspaper reported on it under the headline 'School Aids White Plague – Startling Death Rolls Revealed among Indians – Absolute Inattention to the Bare Necessities of Health.'[46] Some DIA bureaucrats did not object to the publicity because it supported arguments for closing industrial schools. Others with a stake in the system, such as Father George Hallam, were angered by the report, dismissing Bryce's ideas as 'new fangled' and arguing that he could not expect 'palaces for children.' Bryce's recommendations included having the government take over the schools, both because it had promised to do so in treaties and because the existing per capita funding system compelled the churches to increase enrolment and cut costs, including the money spent on feeding children.

Bryce stayed on with the DIA, and two years later, when southern Alberta schools were found to have high rates of tuberculosis, he recommended not only better ventilation and improved diet, but also medical supervision without any interference from the churches. His recommendations were accepted to a limited extent when in 1910 the DIA and the churches agreed on an overhaul of the system. There would be more government funding and inspection, living conditions would be improved, and more emphasis would be placed on improved day schools. Greater government regulation included a requirement that schools provide facilities for isolating the sick and standards for air space in classrooms and dormitories. But the superintendent of education at the DIA, Duncan Campbell Scott, tellingly thought ideas for institutional reform 'quite inapplicable to the system under which these schools are conducted.' In other words, there would be no diminution in the role played by religious denominations. Scott became the deputy SG in 1913, and Bryce never forgot his resistance to reform. His report concentrated on the ignorance of school administrators, a failure in training. But Scott could not pretend ignorance. His was a deeper moral failure.

Bryce was pensioned off from the civil service in 1921 and in 1922 published *The Story of a National Crime, Being an Appeal for Justice to the Indians of Canada*, much of which detailed the findings of his report and subsequent investigations into tuberculosis, and his dealings with Scott. He singled Scott out as responsible for the deaths of children after he had reported in 1907. Bryce was as much an assimilationist as most of his contemporaries, wanting, for example, school curricula to be the same as offered in the relevant provincial school systems because the goal should be for all Indigenous people to become enfranchised and 'enter into the common life and duties of a Canadian community.' But he blamed Scott for an 'active opposition' to his proposals, which included working behind the scenes to prevent the 1907 report being discussed at the annual meeting of the National Tuberculosis Association. Scott had shown a 'criminal disregard' for treaty promises to take care of the welfare of Indigenous people and was responsible for a 'trail of disease and death' going on 'unchecked' by the DIA.[47] Given the greatly increased interest in the relations between the state and Indigenous peoples among Canadian historians in recent decades, it is fitting that Bryce was one of the founders of the Canadian Historical Association in 1922.

Why Were Residential Schools
Not Abolished or Drastically Reformed?

Given the consensus that had coalesced by the early twentieth century about residential schools, and the revelations brought to light by Peter Bryce, one might ask why the residential school system did not die as a failed experiment two to three decades after it had been founded. Historians differ about who bears primary responsibility for a system that not only failed in its objectives but created so much human suffering and death – the churches that ran the schools day to day or the government that inadequately funded the system but never properly regulated it. There was clearly responsibility enough and more to go around, but we would tentatively stress the role of the churches, for two principal reasons. First, the churches were not only ardent advocates of assimilation, they were also continually involved in an internecine struggle for converts. Ends can always justify the means when the ultimate end is salvation. The harvesting of souls was the first priority, the physical well-being of the bodies the souls inhabited invariably less important. Second, the interdenominational rivalry that affected many aspects of Canadian politics also made the problems of residential schools more difficult to deal with. Even had they seriously wanted to, it was not possible for politicians to radically change the system and cut out the churches, given the centrality of religion to late nineteenth- and early twentieth-century settler Canadian life, culture, and politics. Politicians did not want to be accused of being opposed to one denomination or the other, with the consequent loss of electoral support. The disillusionment of many in the DIA could never be translated into fundamental policy change in such circumstances.

Much responsibility also lay with the state. Its inadequate funding system meant that the schools were chronically short of money, a problem they dealt with in part by reducing rations and fuel in winter, and in part by making the children work harder to produce food and thereby reduce the cost of supplies. The worsening conditions led to more parents resisting by not sending their children to the schools, which meant that the churches did not meet their enrolment targets and saw their grants reduced. In order not to lose children and therefore financial support, schools kept those who were sick in overcrowded and unhealthy conditions. Peter Bryce's findings revealed the result of a 'perfect storm.' As everybody knows, residential schools continued well into the later part of the twentieth century, but that is a subject for the next volume.

10

Indigenous Law and European Law: Adaptation, Resistance, Avoidance

The half-century after Confederation witnessed a sea change in settler state attitudes towards Indigenous law. Signs of this change were evident as far back as the 1840s, but prior to Confederation the colonial states had generally been content to allow Indigenous peoples to govern their internal affairs according to their own legal orders and pursuant to their traditional structures of authority. Only where Indigenous and settler interests directly conflicted, usually in connection with resource exploitation, did the colonial states intervene in a more intrusive way.

The immediately preceding chapters outlined how the dominion government used legislation, primarily the *Indian Act* and related statutes, to try to reshape Indigenous societies, even as it was entering treaties that promised coexistence with them and the ability to maintain their traditional ways of life. This chapter analyses the effect of those processes on Indigenous law. What impact did dominion measures have at the local level? What strategies did Indigenous peoples adopt to deal with this new interventionist stance by the state? Resistance, adaptation, and avoidance were all pursued to varying degrees by the communities examined here: the Gitxsan of northern British Columbia, the Mohawk of Kahnawà:ke, the Six Nations of the Grand River, and the Métis. They adopted these strategies at a time when the very idea of Indigenous law was being transformed in settler society, from a legitimate phenomenon understood in the context of eighteenth-century legal pluralism, to a set of folkloric practices or customs that did not 'count' as law. This occurred in spite of the fact that Indigenous authors such as Peter Jones (Kahkewaquonaby) and George Copway (Kahgegagahbouwh), both of them Mississaugas and Methodist missionaries, were beginning to write in English about the history and law of their own people.[1]

The rise of legal positivism, a philosophy that viewed legislation and judicial decisions as the only legitimate sources of law, led to the very idea of Indigenous law being considered an oxymoron. Nonetheless, there was a gap between the formal exclusion of Indigenous legality from the domain of law in settler legal theory, and its continued existence in Indigenous communities. And even within the settler legal order, Indigenous law was never entirely excluded. Sometimes it survived in the interstices of law and executive action, as when an Indigenous person convicted of murder might be spared the death penalty or given a relatively light sentence because of a 'cultural defence' related to justification for the killing under Indigenous law; this phenomenon will be discussed in chapter 13. At other times it appeared more openly, as in various family law contexts.[2]

Before examining these specific examples, it should be remembered that the most transformative event affecting Indigenous law in this period was the dramatic diminution of the lands subject to it, following the signing of the numbered treaties and, in British Columbia, the assertion of Canadian sovereignty and concomitant European settlement almost entirely in the absence of treaties. As the areas of direct Indigenous control shrank dramatically in the 1870s, the advent of the railway permitted an influx of settlers. Many of them took up Crown grants on the lands surrendered by the original inhabitants, a process examined in chapter 14. Nonetheless, it took some time for the demographics to shift in favour of settlers. Indigenous people in British Columbia, even after the terrible toll of epidemics earlier in the century, still outnumbered non-Indigenous inhabitants until the 1880s.[3]

State intervention was not uniform across all areas of law during this period. The dominion was concerned mostly with issues relating to land tenure, governance, and membership, along with certain institutions such as the potlatch that it believed to be detrimental to Indigenous communities and to the assimilation agenda. It was less concerned with family relations and succession, except as they sometimes intersected with the definition of membership or the shoring up of monogamy. Nor were all inhabitants of Indigenous communities opposed to these dominion measures. The reform of traditional governance structures in particular gave rise to differing views: younger men with some education in European ways and values were sometimes attracted to electoral modes of choosing leaders, while elders and matriarchs were not. Every society experiences differences of opinion at some point, and such dissent within Indigenous communities should not be interpreted as either inherently pathological or a full embrace of western values by younger members. What did become highly problematic was the emergence of a state of affairs such as that at Kahnawà:ke, where 'Canadian colonialism was neither total, nor completed, nor effective: it undermined the customary law of Kahnawà:ke and the equilibrium of the community without replacing them in any functional way.'[4] This could lead to a vacuum of authority, obliging individuals to resolve disputes as best they could on their own.

The Gitxsan

Of the polities examined here, the Gitxsan had encountered Europeans most recently. Tsimshian speakers, they are related to the Coast Tsimshian and the Nisga'a and have close relationships with their neighbours to the south, the Athapaskan-speaking Wet'suwet'en. They occupied, and continue to occupy, an area of the northwestern interior of British Columbia that includes the headwaters of the Nass and Skeena Rivers, a region that saw few resident Europeans until the Omineca gold rush in 1869. In the later nineteenth century, the Gitxsan population of about 2,000 occupied seven winter villages, where they lived in traditional longhouses. The relative inaccessibility of the area ensured that the Gitxsan were able to maintain their traditional laws and modes of governance, and oblige colonial authorities to respect their *xsiisxw*, or dispute-resolution norms, better than many other Indigenous communities. Evidence on the implementation of these norms is derived primarily from accounts of interactions between settlers and the Gitxsan where the latter sought to assert their own law.[5]

Disputes with Europeans arose out of employment relationships and incidents involving property damage or personal violence. The earliest European traders in the region relied on the Gitxsan to transport goods by canoe to interior locations, where mining or lumbering was carried on. When a Gitxsan man drowned by accident while so employed in the early 1870s, his relatives successfully obliged the employer to pay substantial compensation, even though no liability would have existed under the common law. Gitxsan law followed a rule of strict liability under such circumstances. It also followed a rule of collective responsibility in cases of criminal or tortious conduct. In 1872 the village of Gitsegukla burned to the ground, causing $6,000 worth of damage, likely the result of two Europeans having taken insufficient care to extinguish their campfire near the settlement. The local chiefs barricaded the Skeena River in anger, calling for a response from the colonial authorities. In due course, Lieutenant Governor Trutch arrived in a ship of war at Metlakatla near the mouth of the Skeena, where five chiefs from Gitsegukla joined him. Trutch advised that the blockage of the river would be 'forgiven,' that $600 would be given to the chiefs, and that in future any complaints against whites should be taken to him. Importantly, food, tobacco, and clay pipes were distributed to the chiefs and their followers, and the ship's guns were fired as a gesture towards spectacle, not intimidation. The chiefs responded with a song and a dance. The essential elements of dispute resolution within the context of a feast had been observed, satisfying the Gitxsan that their law had been respected, even if Trutch's party saw the money payment as an act of grace rather than an admission of liability, and the surrounding ceremonial as a means of reducing tensions rather than a legal obligation.[6]

The first murder of a settler by a Gitxsan on Gitxsan territory to be dealt with through English rather than Indigenous law was that of Amos Youmans by Haatq in 1884, discussed in more detail in chapter 13. Haatq's son had drowned by accident while in Youmans's employ but, contrary to Gitxsan law, Youmans had not informed the boy's family or offered the customary present and condolences. When Haatq discovered the truth he killed Youmans, whose own wife was Gitxsan. Haatq was tried for murder in Victoria and sentenced to death; his sentence was commuted to 10 years' hard labour but he died in prison before serving it out. Petitions from Gitxsan communities arguing for clemency based on Haatq's good character and adherence to tribal custom likely had some impact on the sentence.[7] They sought to educate the settler state about their law, stating that '[a]ll we want is that in case of a death of a Kiticksean while employed from any white man that his friends are told at once and that a small present is made to the relations of the dead man to show that there is no ill feeling between the parties.'[8] While the Gitxsan implicitly recognized that killings of settlers by Indigenous people would henceforth fall under the umbrella of English law, they expected, as Chief Geddum-Cal-Doe observed, that 'all of the circumstances of the case would be taken into consideration': in other words, that a combination of English and Gitxsan law would be applied.[9] Efforts by the colonial government to extend the reach of English criminal law included appointing some Gitxsan chiefs as special constables from at least 1888, perhaps earlier. While the chiefs were content with this recognition, community members did not always agree that their leaders should participate in enforcing the Queen's law.[10]

At what point the settler state extended its authority to deal with intra-Indigenous killings or other personal violence in northern British Columbia is unclear, but such matters were not uppermost in the minds of the Gitxsan. What mattered much more to them was authority over their lands and, especially, fisheries. Most Indigenous peoples west of the Rockies were not hunter-gatherers, but managers of marine and riverine animal and plant resources – mainly fish, but also shellfish and marine mammals such as seals. Indeed, 'the single most productive fisheries ... were in the interior at particular locations along the Fraser, Skeena, and Nass Rivers' – the latter two in Gitxsan and Nisga'a territory.[11] Salmon runs along these rivers attracted settler industry in the form of canneries in the 1870s, creating the potential for conflict over this highly valuable resource.

The early Douglas treaties on Vancouver Island recognized that the Indigenous parties 'were at liberty ... to carry on their fisheries with the same freedom as when they were the sole occupants of the country,' indicating an expansive recognition of Indigenous law. This view was also held by the first inspector of fisheries in the province, Alexander Caulfield Anderson, after the federal *Fisheries Act* was proclaimed there in 1877, followed by the *Salmon Fishing Regulations for the Province of British Columbia* in 1878. Anderson opined that 'the exercise of the aboriginal fishing rights cannot be legally interfered with, [because such] legitimate and hereditary rights [were] inalienably secured to the Indians, both on grounds of abstract justice, and of formal concession by the Crown.'[12] This view did not prevail, however, and by the later 1880s fisheries inspectors were attempting to enforce licensing requirements on Indigenous fishers. The Gitxsan at Hazelton asserted in 1888 that they would not apply for licences and would fish as they had always done. Their laws, they said, divided land between clans, and non-clan members could use them only 'with the permission of the clan chief and in the company of members of the clan who owned the lands.'[13] Eventually, however, with more state enforcement, they reluctantly began to apply for licences.

New regulations in 1888 introduced the concept of the 'native food fishery,' stating that 'Indians shall, at all times, have liberty to fish for the purpose of providing food for themselves but not for sale.' This limitation had no basis in Indigenous law whatsoever, the Gitxsan having always sold fish to neighbouring peoples and to HBC traders when they came on the scene. Even this limited access to the fisheries came to be 'interpreted down' by officials in the 1890s as a matter of grace by the Crown, rather than a right flowing from Gitxsan law and historic use.[14] The Indian reserve commissioners, discussed in chapter 7, themselves recognized the importance of fisheries to Indigenous peoples when allotting reserves, noting it specifically when the reserve at Hazelton was allocated to the Gitxsan.[15] The 'food fishery' construct was invented as an analogy to the land reserve on the prairies. It allowed a small portion of the resource to continue under Indigenous control, but opened the rest for settler use, in the case of fisheries to the canning industry.

These federal interventions were justified by the *BNA Act* grant of authority over 'sea coast and inland fisheries' in section 91 (12), but British Columbia also began to assert an authority to regulate commercial fisheries and canneries. It passed its own *Fisheries Act* in 1901 but delayed proclaiming it in force until 1907. Part of its motivation was to implement a colour bar. In 1913 provincial officials revoked the licence of a Prince Rupert cannery that had applied for independent licences under the federal regulations for 30 Indigenous fishers on the basis that 'only white fishermen and only white labour would be employed in connection with the cannery.' As will be seen in chapter 16, this was but one of a plethora of discriminatory laws against Indigenous people and Asian immigrants passed by British Columbia in many fields of political and economic life. After losing several court cases that confirmed that most authority over fisheries fell under federal jurisdiction, the province accepted in 1916 that it could not interfere with the granting of licences in this way.[16]

Elsewhere in British Columbia, Indigenous communities fought back against these restrictions, sometimes achieving success in settler courts, though it is not yet clear whether the Gitxsan engaged in such actions. They did become actively involved in the commercial fishery that developed in the later nineteenth century, working in the canneries and on the boats as employees, and occasionally securing commercial fishing licences themselves. This did not represent an abandonment of their traditional way of life, however, but rather a means of supplementing it and ensuring its continuance in what has been called a 'moditional' (modern and traditional) economy.[17]

With respect to land rights, mining activities and some agricultural settlement began to interfere with traditional activities in the 1880s. Contrary to the practice of the 1860s, when the building of the Collins overland telegraph was negotiated with the Gitxsan, work often began on new infrastructure without consultation or compensation. The Gitxsan resented these incursions, and the chiefs left the authorities in no doubt about their own claims. The 'chiefs and principal men of Kitwanga' advised the provincial government in 1884 that their territory was 'not held unitedly by all the members of the tribe but is portioned out among the several families, and no family has a right to trespass on another's grounds.' In the same year a chief advised the authorities that the 'exclusive right we claim to hunt, fish and gather fruit in any particular place is a hereditary right enjoyed by us before the white man came among us. It is a right most vigorously upheld by all our tribes without exception.' Gitxsan protests and direct action aimed at curbing further incompatible land use led to enhanced anxiety among settlers and the creation of the Babine Agency with a resident Indian agent at Hazelton in 1889. This was the prelude to a greater presence of the federal government, as it sought to establish the first reserve in the area in 1891, and to stamp out the potlatch under pressure from local missionaries – both measures very much opposed by the Gitxsan. The Gitxsan adopted some cosmetic changes to the feast, but it continued to operate as a critical institution in Gitxsan society. Among other functions, it involved the transmission of names and hence the territories that went with them. And while some settler activities were opposed, down to about 1900 the Gitxsan were able to pursue their traditional sustenance activities according to their laws of territorial allocation and land use with relatively little interference.[18]

After 1900, an increase in agricultural settlement and road and railway construction led to more conflict and more resistance, with the Gitxsan and other Indigenous groups exploring different tactics – legal and extra-legal. The province passed a game law in 1905 that prohibited beaver hunting, but the northern Indigenous peoples were able to secure an exemption until the end of 1911. The construction through Gitxsan territory of the Grand Trunk Railway, meant to link Winnipeg and Edmonton with the Pacific via the new settlement of Prince Rupert, was particularly troubling. Commenced in 1907 and completed in 1914, construction required up to 7,000 men to work in the Nass and Skeena Valleys, bringing all the ills that attend large numbers of unattached young men in an isolated location. The Gitxsan sought to protect their

Thee committee of Skeena River

We the committee here assembled, at
 Andimaul Skeena River on the 9th, day
of March 1910.

1.st. We decided that we do not want our
land reserved, we want the reserves to be taken
away.

2.nd   That our land to be given us back again, as
it belonged to our forefathers.

3d
Also we are pleased to know that King George's
act. which ordained on October 4th. 1763, has not
been changed

4th   Also that each family or tribe should still
held possicion of the land which is theirs by
inheritance.

Do hereby undersigned, under the hand of the
chief committee and people of nine Villages
of Skeena River.

Chiefs of kispiox B.C.   Stephen Morgen President
            on Skeena
(Sign) chief Walter Kaal × kilimkuldo
    "   Charles Smith   ×
    "   Paul Clarkaksck   ×
    "   Alexander Dairy   ×

Chiefs of Glen vawell on Skeena B.C.
sig Paul Dalagymoak
    " Sam Barlow +
Paul Green ×
Mark Green ×
Peter Brown ×

Petition from "Committee of Skeena River," 9 March 1910. Increasing incursions into their territory for railway construction and mining generated strong reactions by the Gitxsan of the Skeena River valley in British Columbia, as shown in this 1910 petition. Notable is the use of the Royal Proclamation of 1763 to bolster their claims for the return of their lands.

Credit: Simon Fraser University Native Land Claims Letters collection (summit.sfu.ca).

lands and women through occasional episodes of physical violence and intimidation of settlers, one of whom was murdered after being threatened by local Indigenous men.[19] They also joined the Indigenous organizational efforts that occurred in British Columbia in the early twentieth century, discussed in chapter 7, which included raising $700 to send three Gitxsan to Ottawa in 1908 as part of a larger delegation to meet with Prime Minister Laurier. Their demands, which invoked the Royal Proclamation of 1763 as protection for their land rights, included asking the government 'to pay them for all lands occupied by white men and to turn over to them all unalienated lands.' The completion of the railway and the war, however, followed by the rejection by the Canadian Parliament of any concept of Indigenous title in British Columbia in the 1920s, led to a marked reduction in such lobbying efforts in later years.[20]

Kahnawà:ke

Land, along with governance, was also a major issue at Kahnawà:ke during this period. In *Volume 1* we explained how the seigneury of Sault Saint-Louis was granted to the Jesuits in 1680 to hold for the benefit of the Mohawks. After the British conquest, Thomas Gage as governor of Montreal negated the rights of the Jesuits and awarded the seigneury to the Mohawks themselves, subject to the underlying title of the Crown. As seigneurs, the Mohawks conceded some land to Canadien farmers, as had the Jesuits, and collected seigneurial dues thereon. The abolition of seigneurial tenure in 1854 led to the two-thirds of the seigneury that had been conceded to non-Indigenous farmers being rendered private property and separated from what came to be known as the 'reserve.' The latter part was and remains about 12,000 acres. As noted in chapter 5, the 'abolition' of seigneurial tenure did not include the abolition of seigneurial dues, which were turned into a capital sum that former censitaires were obliged to pay off in the form of 'constituted rents,' often over a long period of time. These dues had been an important source of revenue for the chiefs, but after 1854 the Indian agents did not collect the rental payments with any assiduity, such that no one was paying them at Kahnawà:ke by the 1890s. The chiefs were supposed to be compensated for the expropriation of their rights, as were other seigneurs, but only one-tenth the sum of $100,000 allocated for this purpose was ever paid, and the claim is still being pursued.[21]

The second issue of concern was the continued carving up of the reserve with transportation infrastructure such as the CPR bridge, given

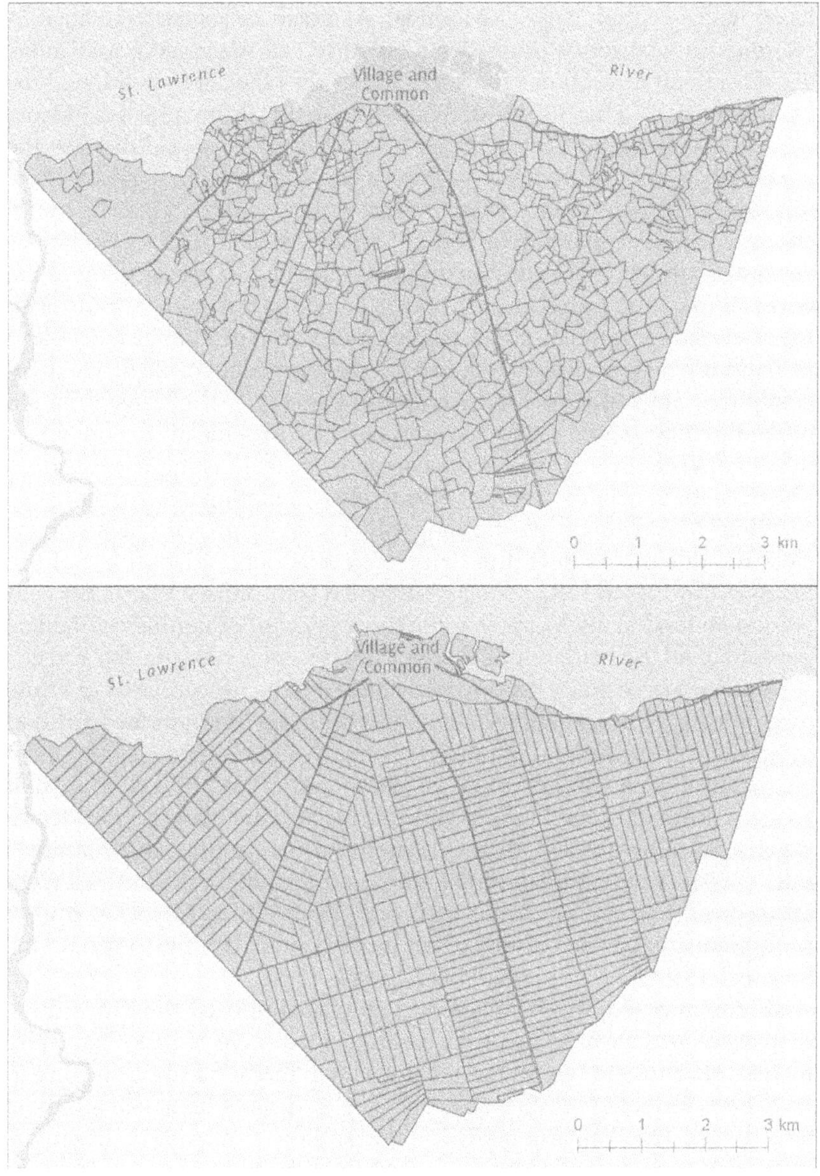

These "before" and "after" images illustrate the aim of the 1880s Walbank Survey: to transform Kahnawà:ke's organic land ownership pattern into one similar to a surveyed settler township. Impractical from the outset, it was never implemented.

Credit: Courtesy of Daniel Rück and Louis-Jean Faucher.

its strategic location close to Montreal. As noted in *Volume 1*, in an 1863 referendum a majority of residents voted to sell the reserve and move elsewhere, but this did not come to pass. In 1875 the chiefs petitioned the DIA, again asking for the sale of the reserve so that its members could join the Cherokees in the United States. The department would not pay the asking price, and the planned departure was stymied once again.[22] There followed the most ambitious and totalizing plan aimed at replacing Indigenous land tenure ever attempted in Canada: William McLea Walbank's survey of 1880–7. It aimed at nothing less than a total revamping of the boundaries of and rights in every parcel of land in the reserve, transforming the existing irregular-sized lots into a uniform grid pattern of 30-acre rectangles whose occupiers would have the equivalent of exclusive ownership (see the Walbank Survey maps on page 337). The transformation of landholding patterns and land tenure rules was meant to convert its inhabitants into the equivalent of yeoman farmers indistinguishable from their Canadien neighbours, thus effectively eliminating the reserve.[23]

While the average landholding of 31.9 acres at Kahnawà:ke was close to Walbank's target, the figure concealed large disparities: of 610 heads of families in 1884, 56 per cent owned some land while 44 per cent owned no land at all. Moreover, the top 5 per cent of families owned 24 per cent of all the land, with the largest landowners holding 255 and 261 acres each. These major landowners tended to be descendants of white men married to Indigenous women, whose descendants in turn had often married mixed-race spouses. Some Mohawk families, however, also controlled outsized holdings. These disparities, and a sense that white and mixed-race families did not respect the customs and traditions of Kahnawà:ke, led to violent attempts to intimidate these families into leaving. Arson, threatening letters, and the killing of livestock were all resorted to, resulting in at least one death. Osias Meloche, from a prominent mixed-race family, died in 1878 while trying to rescue his livestock from a barn that had been torched.[24]

If implemented, the Walbank survey was supposed to reduce these disparities in landholdings, but it might well have led to even more inequality. Those to whom land was given in the redistribution were to have been indebted for its value, possibly leading them to sell to others able to pay. The Walbank plan would also have eliminated Indigenous use-rights that were directed at communal benefit rather than individual enrichment. Mohawk land tenure laws aimed to provide land to all families who wished to practise small-scale agriculture. One was not supposed to occupy more land than one could farm personally with the help of family members, and anyone was free to settle on unoccupied land to this extent. A village common also afforded residents rights of pasturage. Another Mohawk principle related to the timber resource: everyone had free access to firewood for personal use, no matter where the trees stood. The sole exception was for sugar maples, which were treated as the property of those on whose land they grew. Thus, A could cut down trees other than maples on B's land and B could not stop it, provided the cutting was for personal use and not for sale. However, this key tenet of Mohawk law was undermined by a January 1876 Order in Council that declared all trees to be the property of the landowner and forbade logging on the property of others. The chiefs protested strongly, as this change would make landless families dependent on the purchase of firewood formerly available for free. Logging for sale off-reserve continued unabated in spite of the new edict, and DIA officials displayed neither the will nor the ability to stop it.[25]

The chiefs were reluctantly drawn into the Walbank process, having no real choice in the matter. But the DIA had no ability to determine all questions themselves, as the chiefs' advice was needed to determine who 'owned' existing lots, to create the 'before' picture on which the 'after' grid of 30-acre lots would be superimposed. A tribunal comprising four chiefs, the Indian agent, and Walbank himself considered 611 applications from persons claiming ownership of existing lots. Application of Indigenous laws of succession and membership often clashed with *Indian Act* provisions and DIA policy. For example, Mohawk law recognized that someone who had cared for an ailing landowner in their last illness had a better claim to the land than family members who did not assist the deceased. While many of these disputes resulted in the application of the DIA's preferred solution, in other cases the chiefs' views were accepted (though they were not unanimous on all issues). This example shows some grudging acceptance of Indigenous law by the DIA into the 1880s, in a process where the chiefs' participation was more than tokenistic though not equal.[26]

Ultimately, the plan came to an impasse. Money was the obstacle. Imposing Walbank's survey would have required compensating all those who lost land in order to create the ideal 30-acre lots, and this the department was not prepared to do. In the end, two legal orders continued to coexist uneasily at Kahnawà:ke: that of the white and mixed-race families who tended to use written conveyances and follow European-style norms of property transmission and use, and that of Mohawk families who relied on oral transfers and followed traditional patterns of transmission and use. The latter are more difficult to discern in the historical record because of their informality but are thought to have continued into the twentieth century.[27]

The participation of the traditional chiefs in the Walbank survey tribunal was their last known appearance before the band council system was instituted at Kahnawà:ke in 1889. The traditional governance structure featured a council of seven – one chief from each clan – based on two principles: decision-making within the clan, and equality of clans. Clan matriarchs played an important role in choosing the chiefs, who usually had life tenure once selected. In the 1870s some discontent emerged among younger men, who alleged incompetent leadership and began to push for an elected council. The DIA began refusing to confirm new chiefs when incumbents died or resigned, such that there were only three elderly chiefs in place by the later 1880s. As we saw in chapter 8, the *Indian Act* at first permitted bands to choose their leaders under their own rules, including life tenure, or to opt for the 'new rules,' which included a maximum of six chiefs being elected for three-year terms. Kahnawà:ke chose to retain its own rules in 1878. In 1884 the *Indian Advancement Act* provided for a different governance structure for more 'advanced' tribes, instituting a model overtly based on municipal councils, with one-year terms for ward-based councillors, the councillors choosing one of their number as 'chief councillor.' Both the *Indian Act* and the *Indian Advancement Act* expressly disenfranchised women, who had always played an important role in governance. In March 1889 the *Advancement Act* system was introduced by Order in Council, even though support for it in the community was far from widespread.[28]

Almost immediately, in 1890, seven women from the Bear Clan and 122 men from Kahnawà:ke petitioned the governor general for a return to the traditional chiefly system, the latter stating that 'we [want to] control our own rights and properties without asking somebody to control it for us [and] to retain and preserve our nationality as Ro-di-no-Shiou-ni [Haudenosaunee] until the Lord comes.'[29] In 1897, 88 women petitioned SG Clifford Sifton to the same effect, and similar petitions were also sent in 1901 and 1905. All received the same reply, that a return to the old system was not possible. Differences within the community were then transferred to the band council, where some members were prepared to work with the DIA while others were more oppositional, and yet a third group wanted to get rid of the band council entirely. Sometimes the community reacted by refusing to select councillors at all, as in 1898, and sometimes oppositional councillors refused to attend council meetings, so that no business could be transacted. While there were certainly undesirable consequences of this dysfunctional system, it is also likely that the confusion arising from it allowed some Kahnawa'kehró:non to go about their lives in their accustomed manner, while adapting to new technologies and challenges. On many matters the DIA could not impose its will either through the band council or through its own agents. Indian Agent Brosseau observed, in frustration in connection with a land dispute in 1900, that 'it is necessary to follow the custom of the reserve, which is contrary to law.'[30]

The Six Nations

While the Six Nations of the Grand River also experienced some discontent with traditional modes of governance, particularly among younger men, the *Indian Act* band council system was not imposed there until 1924. Hence the confederacy council retained authority over most aspects of the Six Nations' internal affairs during the period covered by this book. The later nineteenth century was a period of prosperity and lively associationalism for the Six Nations, who occupied a very large reserve of some 46,000 acres, although this represented only a tiny part of what was supposed to have been conveyed to them under the Haldimand Grant, as outlined in *Volume 1*. The population grew from about 3,000 at Confederation to some 4,700 by 1914. Families had been settled on 100-acre lots after the consolidation of the reserve in 1847, sufficient land to ensure a decent living. There were three longhouse 'congregations,' one each for the Seneca, Onondaga, and Cayuga nations, as well as Baptist and Anglican churches. An Orange Lodge, a temperance society, and a Six Nations Agricultural Society also emerged at this time.[31]

Education was one topic taken very seriously by the Six Nations Council and by most members of the community. By the 1870s there were 12 day schools on the reserve, as well as the Mohawk Institute industrial school on its edge. The council itself ran one of the day schools, the Thomas School, while the rest were under the supervision of the Six Nations School Board (SNSB). Established in 1878, the board was created as a result of disagreements between the council and the New England Company over funding of the schools. Composed of a representative from the DIA, three representatives of the chiefs, three from the New England Company, and one Wesleyan missionary, it was the first school board in the province in which Indigenous people had a significant role. As a result, a number of teachers in the day schools (and even some in the Mohawk Institute) came from the Six Nations, and they taught Indigenous language and history as well as the Western-oriented curriculum. The SNSB lobbied to have their schools use the Ontario Curriculum of Studies rather than the less challenging curriculum designed for Indian schools, and succeeded in 1908. Clearly, they wanted Six Nations children to have the best of both worlds.[32]

The council attempted to adhere to the spirit of the Great Law in its dispute-resolution function, while also navigating around the newly imposed strictures of the *Indian Act* after 1876.* Disputes over land boundaries, succession, and membership were resolved by the council, apparently without the intervention of lawyers on either side, though the Indian agent had the benefit of government legal advice if he chose to seek it.[33] On succession issues, the council was content to use the *Indian Act*'s provisions on intestacy as a framework, as they were believed to accord with traditional Haudenosaunee practices. Nonetheless, they did adjust them and at times overrode them entirely. Thus, while widows under the common law and *Indian Act* provisions were entitled to one-third of their deceased spouse's personal estate and a life estate in one-third of their realty and lost their share if living in adultery at the time of the spouse's death, the council also applied these provisions to widowers. They also followed their own customs in preferring a claimant who had cared for a dying person in their last illness to the relatives of the deceased who had neglected to do so, as occurred also at Kahnawà:ke. Thus, when Festus Johnson died intestate in 1886, the council awarded his entire estate to non-kin who had cared for him in his last year of life, excluding his adult children. Determining responsibilities as well as rights was a key aspect of the council's authority under the Great Law; those who did not carry out their responsibilities could not expect to see their rights respected. When people died without heirs, council would sometimes keep their property and lease it out, or in other cases sell it and add the proceeds to the Six Nations trust fund. The council exercised the power to confirm wills, with the DIA exercising only an appellate function. However, towards the end of the period, in 1912, the DIA began to assert the authority to confirm wills in the first instance, arousing protest and resistance from the chiefs.[34]

---

* The Great Law of Peace resulted from the fifteenth-century accord that ended the warring of the Indigenous peoples in the lower Great Lakes and created the Five (later Six) Nations Confederacy. It prescribed their governance mechanisms and kinship rules, laid out the rights and responsibilities of groups and individuals, and set out how disputes were to be resolved. See Kayanesenh Paul Williams, *Kayanerenkó:wa: The Great Law of Peace* (Winnipeg: University of Manitoba Press, 2018).

The council was often called upon to decide matrimonial disputes, leading to what the common law and the civil law would call judicial separation. To this end it would appoint a committee to look into the matter, mediate between the spouses if possible, and then make recommendations to council. Like settler courts, the council took a fault-based approach in such cases, typically awarding custody of minor children and some property to the 'innocent' party. The spouse determined to be at fault might see his or her personal annuity payments directed to the other spouse to assist in caring for children. There was, however, a second-chance doctrine, whereby an errant spouse could be given the opportunity to make amends and avoid a finding of 'guilt.' Again, a rights-based framework gave way to one where responsibilities to children and spouses were taken seriously.[35]

Marriage also gave rise to membership issues. Council eventually had to accept the 1869 federal statute providing that women who married non-Indigenous men forfeited their Indian status, because the DIA would cut off annuity payments for that person. If council continued to pay such women from their funds, they would in effect be reducing payments to everyone else. If a Six Nations woman married a man from another Indigenous community, she could be transferred to that band, but if the marriage did not work out and she wished to return, she would generally be allowed to do so.[36]

Despite the strictures of the *Indian Act*, the Six Nations managed to remain largely self-governing. With a secure land base, relative prosperity, and increasing levels of education, they were in a much better position than many Indigenous communities, able to resist DIA measures they disagreed with and secure a large measure of autonomy. The council adopted some of the trappings of decision-making in settler society, such as recording minutes of their meetings in English, but conducted their affairs in their own languages and resolved local disputes as much as possible within the framework of the Great Law.

The Métis

The Métis of western Canada had a very different experience from that of the Indigenous peoples discussed so far. Their emergence as a people in the late eighteenth and early nineteenth century was associated with a dependence on the buffalo, so numerous at that time on the plains. Efficient hunting of these animals required a highly structured and disciplined approach with broad communal buy-in. The Métis had thus developed a detailed legal framework to regulate this complex collective enterprise of the buffalo hunt, complete with sanctions for those who flouted it. They faced severe challenges with the decline of the buffalo and the fur trade and their consequent shift to agricultural pursuits. The legal structures of the seasonal buffalo hunt were not appropriate for more settled communities. In 1871 the Métis wintering at the mission of St. Laurent on the South Saskatchewan River, for example, 'all agree[d] that it was desirable in the interests of their families to change their nomadic life and have a fixed habitation and home.' This shift resulted in the creation of a new code designed to continue the self-governing traditions of the Métis in a more settled context. These codes drew on the customary law of the Plains Cree and other Indigenous groups and may also have been influenced by the communal traditions of the Hebridean and Orcadian Scots who worked for the HBC and intermarried with local Indigenous women.[37]

The code adopted at St. Laurent in 1873 provided for a president and council to be the executive and judicial authority for the community, accountable to a general assembly of all male adults. Gabriel Dumont, who would be Louis Riel's second-in-command in 1885, was elected president, and three of the eight council members were Dumont family members. The council was to sit on the first Monday of the month to hear petitions and render judgment thereon. Article XVIIII of the code provided that any decision of the council 'shall never be appealed by any of the parties before any other tribunal when the government of Canada shall have placed its regular magistrates in the country.' After a decision was made, the parties had 10 days to come to an arrangement if they wished, otherwise the council's original order would be 'forcibly executed.' The few substantive law provisions of the 1873 code dealt with injury to reputation (fines would be levied for defamation) and virtue (a fine would be levied on a man who 'shall dishonour a young girl and afterwards refuse to marry her'). Article XVIII provided that any contract was valid whether written in French, English, or 'Indian characters,' and could be proven without witnesses if the plaintiff 'testifie[d] on oath to the correctness of his account or contract.' Further 'Resolutions of St Laurent, passed by public assembly at the winter camp of the Métis' in December 1873 dealt with boundary issues and limits on tree cutting on common woodland, and declared that no one could claim more land than he could work personally.[38] It was also agreed that a tax in support of a school would be levied on each household.

The code was expressly stated to be temporary, the St. Laurent community being anxious to state that 'in forming these laws, they acknowledge themselves as loyal and faithful subjects of Canada, and are ready to abandon their own organization and to submit to the laws of the Dominion as soon as Canada shall have established amongst them regular magistrates [able] to uphold in the country the authority of the law.' Dumont wrote to other Métis communities near Edmonton and in the Qu'Appelle Valley, suggesting that they follow the lead of St. Laurent, but apparently none did. Further regulations were adopted in 1874 and 1875, including some related to the buffalo hunt. One of these declared that any party of Métis in the neighbourhood of the 'great caravan,' even though they claimed to be independent, should be bound in their hunting by the decisions of the 'council of the great camp' and would be 'obliged by force' to accept its decisions if they did not submit. It was this provision that led to conflict in the summer of 1875 and to the undoing of the 'little republic' that had arisen at St. Laurent.

That summer, when Dumont's party was preparing to embark on their hunt, they learned that a group containing English and French Métis, including some from St. Laurent itself, under the leadership of Peter Ballendine, a former Hudson's Bay Company employee, had earlier set out for the destination chosen by the main St. Laurent group, in violation of custom. Dumont conveyed a message to them urging them to join his party or face the consequences. The Ballendine group ignored the warning and when later confronted by Dumont's party, were fined by him and had some belongings taken equal to the amount of the fines levied. When Ballendine complained about this action to Lawrence Clarke, a Hudson's Bay factor at Fort Carlton and recently appointed a JP for the Territories, Clarke treated the matter as tantamount to sedition and notified higher authorities. It eventually came to the attention of Minister of Justice Edward Blake and even Colonial Secretary Lord Carnarvon. The commander of the Canadian militia, who happened to be on the prairies, and the commissioner of the NWMP, were sent to investigate and a NWMP inspector, Leif Crozier, met with Dumont at St. Laurent. There Dumont explained how their local government worked, stated they had no intention of doing wrong, and had only made their own laws because no other government existed. All parties accepted that Dumont and the Métis had simply been enforcing local custom and that Clarke had wildly over-reacted. Lord Carnarvon himself observed equably that 'it would be difficult to take strong exception to the acts of a community which appears to have honestly endeavoured to maintain order by the best means in its power.'[39]

In spite of this vindication, the laws of St. Laurent were effectively delegitimized by this incident. In any case, the laws were always understood to be provisional, adopted in view of the vacuum of authority on the prairies. Already in 1875 a NWMP district headquarters was established at Battleford, while Fort Battleford, erected in 1877, would become the capital of the North-West Territories. Treaty 6, signed in 1876, covered this area and was a prelude to the establishment of further structures of settler authority. The council of St. Laurent ceased to be active, but community meetings, often chaired by Dumont, continued to be held at which new issues were discussed, especially the building of a school, representation on the council of the North-West Territories, and the question of securing proper titles to the lands the Métis cultivated around St. Laurent. With self-taxation no longer feasible, the Métis petitioned Ottawa repeatedly for assistance in erecting a school. Success came in 1880, when grants in aid of constructing and furnishing schoolhouses anywhere in the North-West Territories were approved, along with a proportion of teacher salaries. A Métis member of the council of the North-West Territories had been appointed in 1872, but the person chosen, Pascal Bréland, had not supported Riel in 1869–70 and was not widely trusted by the Métis. The upper house of the Manitoba legislature had some Métis representation, but it was abolished in 1876, as noted in chapter 2.[40]

These successes paled, however, beside the lack of resolution of the land question, a critical spark that helped set off the flame in 1885. The French Métis preferred long, narrow, river-front lots along the great rivers of Saskatchewan and arranged their land-holdings accordingly. When the land came to be surveyed by the dominion, the grid system prevailed. Even though the *Dominion Lands Act*, discussed in chapter 14, allowed its provisions to be waived or altered in order to satisfy Métis claims, no such accommodation was forthcoming. Further, some blocks laid out were reserved for the HBC, others for schools. Métis who had occupied lands other than these could secure them as homesteads under the Act, but those less fortunate who occupied the reserved blocks found themselves obliged to purchase them or give them up. There followed more migrations, with Métis commonly settling along road allowances and any marginal land where they believed they might escape being disturbed. In 1896, at the urging of the Catholic Church, the dominion government set aside four townships of land in the Alberta District for a Métis colony where some of these displaced people could be settled. The plan was similar to that for residential schools: to educate the Métis for a productive life as agriculturalists. In effect, St. Paul des Métis aimed to be an open-air residential school for adults as well as children. The church ran the colony along very paternalistic lines, even retaining ownership of the land out of concern that the 'improvident' Métis would sell their lots if given title. This set-up eventually alienated the inhabitants, who preferred a life of hunting, fishing, and occupational pluralism to an exclusive devotion to agriculture. When most of them moved elsewhere, the church opened the colony to general settlement in 1909, upon which it turned into a French-Canadian parish almost overnight.[41]

The laws of the buffalo hunt were bound to disappear along with the buffalo herds. The Métis then tried to reinvent themselves as an agricultural people, using law as a touchstone of identity. But the promise of the St. Laurent model of law and governance, which might have been elaborated and spread across the prairies had Métis land rights been secured, was stillborn, and after 1885, impossible even to think of resurrecting. So crucial to the peaceful expansion of Canada across the prairies in 1869–70, the Métis became 'Canada's forgotten people.'[42]

Indigenous law faced many challenges as the settler nation sought to extend its control over land and governance from coast to coast to coast. While the numbered treaties seemed to contemplate a continued role for Indigenous law, the *Indian Act* aimed to supplant it in many areas. It is difficult to generalize about how this collision played out in the many and varied Indigenous communities. In comparatively well-resourced communities such as Kahnawà:ke and the Six Nations, the maintenance of traditional laws was more easily accomplished. In more remote communities, the DIA did not have the ability to enforce its will and there too Indigenous law could be more easily maintained. All the examples in this chapter illustrate that the partial integration of Indigenous individuals into the settler economy after the end of the fur trade – whether via commercial fishing, agriculture, or high steel work – did not indicate an abandonment of their traditional laws among themselves. They sought to continue to live by them for the most part, resisting DIA pressure or at least forcing compromises in some areas. In fact, the DIA had little choice but to recognize and try to understand Indigenous law even as they sought to make it irrelevant, as seen during the Walbank survey process. In other areas, such as marriage according to Indigenous custom (discussed in chapter 15), it served settler purposes to continue such recognition. The critical issue was how knowledge of traditional laws would be passed on, and this was connected to two things: customary practices of leadership including knowledge-keeping, and the vitality of Indigenous languages. The *Indian Act* threatened the first, the spread of residential schools the second. The full impact of these developments would not be felt until after the Great War and will be taken up in *Volume 3*.

PART THREE

Building the New Dominion:
Capital, Labour, and a Criminal Code

11

Law and Economy: Corporate and Commercial Law and Regulation

The Canadian economy underwent a substantial transition in the half-century after Confederation.[1] Gross national product (GNP) stood at just over $385 million in 1870 and had increased more than sixfold by 1914. Economic expansion was particularly marked from the mid-1890s onwards; in 1896 the GNP was $634 million, less than double what it had been in 1870. Between then and 1914 it almost quadrupled to $2.4 billion. The years from 1896 to the First World War 'encompassed the most rapid growth of real output that the Canadian economy ever experienced.'[2] There is a lively debate among economic historians on whether the principal cause of rapid growth was the wheat boom and the white settlement of the prairies, in effect the National Policy, but that question is not germane to this chapter.

Accompanying this overall economic expansion were large demographic increases, as we saw in the introduction, and a structural transformation of the economy. Urbanization and industrialization advanced at considerable pace, with manufacturing both expanding rapidly and diversifying. By about 1914 the disparate regions of the country were linked by almost 50,000 kilometres of railway lines, 14 times the approximately 3,600 miles at Confederation. In 1895 the number had stood at roughly 25,600, thus it doubled between then and 1914.[3] By the end of our period Canada was still a country in which more people lived in rural areas than in urban, but much less so than it had been. The censuses of 1871 and 1881 did not provide figures for rural and urban dwellers, and when the census first did so, in 1891, 68 per cent of the country's roughly 4.8 million people were classified as rural. Two decades later that percentage stood at 55, and fully 3.27 million people were classified as urban. The national rural-urban balance was made up of distinct regions where one or the other predominated. Urban dwellers were a majority of the population only in Ontario and British Columbia, but they also made up over 48 per cent of the population of Quebec. Rural dwellers were a substantial majority in the Maritime and Prairie provinces – 72 and 65 per cent respectively. The shift in population balances was both cause and result of a diversifying economy. Agriculture, forestry, hunting, and fisheries had contributed 39 per cent of the national GNP in 1870, and in 1914, driven primarily by the wheat boom, they still contributed a very healthy 21 per cent, or about $530 million. Manufacturing made up approximately 20 per cent of GNP in both 1870 and 1914, but with every other facet of the economy growing in absolute terms manufacturing's consistent roughly 20 per cent meant an increase from $76.9 million in 1870 to $447 million in 1914. Other related sectors of the economy – mining, construction, transportation, electric light and power – were 20 per cent of GNP in 1914, twice what they had been in 1870 (11 per cent).[4]

Accompanying these economic transformations were equally significant legal developments. The first two sections of this chapter analyse post-Confederation incorporation law, starting with general incorporation statutes enacted by all jurisdictions – federal and provincial. General incorporation meant that the vast majority of companies no longer needed to obtain a special act of incorporation from a legislature, making obtaining corporate status and its accompanying advantages, especially limited liability, quicker and cheaper. Our second section deals with the continuing use of special act incorporations, both by companies not permitted to use general incorporation acts, and by those that were but chose to apply for a special act. Our third section examines insolvency law and provides something of a contrast to general incorporation. General incorporation took hold nationally, even if it was adopted earlier in some jurisdictions than others. The principal modern legal regime to deal with insolvency – bankruptcy – was legislated nationally very early in our period, but was always contentious, and the federal legislation was repealed after a decade. Thereafter Canada operated for some 35 years without a national bankruptcy law, and because bankruptcy was an area of exclusive federal jurisdiction there were no provincial bankruptcy regimes.

A theme common to these first three sections is of statute law as a facilitative instrument in economic organization and development. But as in the vast majority of advanced economies, the law had long played a regulatory role in the economy, constraining the freedom of action of individuals in the interest of the common good. Before Confederation all colonial legislatures passed numerous statutes regulating economic actors in a host of ways. After 1867 this colonial legislation remained in force in the original provinces and was joined by much statutory regulation in the West. It was also enhanced by the very substantial legislative output of the new federal Parliament. Hence we devote our fourth and final section to public regulation of the economy, examining banking, a federal matter, mining, a provincial one, and railways, subject to regulation by both levels of government, depending on whether a particular railway was an intra-provincial or an inter-provincial/ international work. Public regulation in this period became something more than statute law, which determined weights and measures or qualifications for surveyors and the like. It represented the beginnings of the regulatory state, a development that was marked in the 1890s by the creation of the country's first modern-style administrative agency established to set and enforce standards and adjudicate disputes, the Board of Railway Commissioners.

Corporation Law: General Incorporation

Although the majority of business enterprises were carried on by sole proprietors or partnerships, this chapter does not deal with those forms of business enterprise, which required no special procedure to establish and were governed, as were many other areas of economic activity, by a mixture of the common law and provincial statutes. Sole proprietorships and partnerships were not distinguishable in law from the individuals who owned and ran them, and thus were distinct from corporations legally in being fully liable for all debts, as well as being generally much less well capitalized. There were exceptions, of course, perhaps the most notable being John Booth, who ran the largest lumber operation in the world and kept it as a sole proprietorship until the 1920s.[5] But corporations grew in number, because they allowed for the aggregation of capital and limited the liability of shareholders to their investment in the corporation.[6] In 1881 Montreal lawyer Charles Stephens justified the publication of another book on the subject by reference to 'the vast amount of money annually invested' in them, and in the following decade one of the leading corporate law texts prosaically but tellingly described them as 'common' – an observation amply borne out by the statistics presented below.[7]

Both as cause and effect of the expanding use of the corporate form, the most notable development in the law relating to incorporation was the rise of general incorporation, and the consequent decline in the need for, and use of, special acts of incorporation. By 'general incorporation' we mean incorporation under a statutory regime in which a company formed for any purpose could become a corporation by adhering to certain filing requirements and being certified as having the status of a legal person. General incorporation legislation was first enacted for the federal jurisdiction in 1869, with the last province to do so being Prince Edward Island, in 1888. General incorporation, however, was never applicable to all companies. In every jurisdiction, companies operating in certain sectors, notably railways, were required to obtain a special act to incorporate, as they had before Confederation.

Before Confederation, incorporation was governed by each colony. After 1867 it was a matter of both federal and provincial jurisdiction.[8] Section 92 (11) of the *BNA Act* gave the provinces jurisdiction over 'the incorporation of companies with provincial objects.' Thus a province could not incorporate a company to operate outside its own geographical jurisdiction. This limitation was assumed by contemporaries and confirmed by the Privy Council in 1881. This constitutional limitation was expressed in all the general incorporation legislation detailed below; the Ontario act, for example, stated that a company could incorporate in Ontario 'for any purposes or objects to which the Legislative authority of … Ontario extends.' Provincially incorporated companies frequently transacted business outside provincial borders, but they had to be headquartered and have their principal place of business within the province.[9] Section 91 contained no mention of incorporation, but it was assumed by both federal and provincial politicians that the federal Parliament had the exclusive power to incorporate companies operating within one of Parliament's enumerated powers, or operating inter-provincially with offices located in more than one province. These were principally banking and inter-provincial transport and communications.[10]

The development of incorporation law after 1867 was complicated by two factors. First, no provincial jurisdiction was a tabula rasa. As shown in *Volume 1* all colonies passed what we termed sectoral incorporation acts – legislation that allowed only companies operating in specific sectors of the economy to become incorporated by registration, whereas other companies had to obtain a special act. These sectoral incorporation statutes largely stayed in place after 1867. The principal difference between general incorporation and sectoral incorporation was that to incorporate under the former, a company had to apply to the provincial secretary, while to incorporate under the latter the application had to be approved by some lower authority, such as a municipality or a county official. We cannot detail all such legislation here, which was passed in every province, and will use just the example of Ontario. Ontario enacted general incorporation in 1874, and the 1874 statute was obviously still in force when the provincial statutes were revised in 1877. Also in force were eight sectoral incorporation statutes enacted by the Province of Canada allowing companies formed for, inter alia, the construction of roads, piers, wharves, docks, harbours, timber slides, and exhibition buildings to incorporate by registering with the country registrar. In 1879 another sectoral statute was passed, for companies supplying steam, heating, or electricity.[11]

Second, Ontario and Quebec entered Confederation with what we would term a de facto general incorporation statute. This was sectoral incorporation that was very broad, not applicable to just one sector, so that most, but not all, companies could incorporate under it. This originated in an 1850 statute for Upper Canada that permitted companies operating in the manufacturing, mining, mechanical, chemical, and shipbuilding sectors to incorporate by registering with the relevant county registrar and the provincial secretary, receiving letters patent from the latter. Other sectors were added in 1860 and in 1864, and in the latter year it was made applicable to Lower Canada. Thus although neither Ontario nor Quebec had general incorporation in 1867, their legislation made incorporation available to a very wide range of enterprises. This Province of Canada legislation also became the Canadian statute law in 1867 but was repealed when the federal Parliament passed its de jure general incorporation legislation in 1869, the first in Canada. In marked contrast to the Province of Canada, the sectoral incorporation statutes in the Maritimes were limited in scope. New Brunswick and Nova Scotia permitted incorporation other than by special act to any five or more persons; the former was only for 'mining or manufacturing purposes,' the latter more restrictive still, limiting general incorporation to any purposes except 'banking, insurance, or ordinary mercantile and commercial business.' It was little used because it was intended only to facilitate the incorporation of gold-mining companies, and in 1873

Chief Justice William Young doubted 'the wisdom leaving it upon the statute book.'[12]

Because it was the first, and because all subsequent provincial general incorporation statutes were largely replications of it, we will use the 1869 federal act as exemplary of all such legislation.[13] The incorporation process was not elaborate. A company with at least five shareholders could apply to the secretary of state to incorporate, after giving at least one month's notice of the intention to apply. Applications were reviewed by the Departments of Justice and Finance before being returned to the secretary of state for the issuing of letters patent. The application had to include the proposed name, the corporate objects, where operations would be carried on, the amount of capital stock and the number and value of shares, and the proposed by-laws. The names and addresses of the directors had also to be supplied; there had to be between three and nine of them, and a majority had to be both residents of Canada and British subjects. The amount of stock subscribed for by the applicants had also to be specified and had to be at least half of the total. The amount of stock actually taken up had similarly to be disclosed, and had to be at least 10 per cent of the total if that total was less than $500,000, 2 per cent if it was more than that. All these requirements were designed to weed out applicants not prepared to put a significant amount of their own money into the enterprise. The secretary of state was given the discretion to refuse the application if he was not satisfied that the applicants, 'especially' the directors, were 'persons of sufficient reputed means to warrant' granting the application.

The act also regulated how the corporation had to operate. Many provisions covered directors – their relationships with shareholders, term limits, powers to make contracts and hire and fire employees. Other provisions dealt with company stock – increases or decreases to the capital, stock transfers, and when stock subscribed had actually to be paid for. The public interest was protected by provisions for the keeping of certain records and for making stock records available to shareholders and creditors; a failure to keep books open for inspection could lead to forfeiture of corporate status. Sections 48 and 49 of the relatively short, 57-section act conferred limited liability on all companies incorporating under its provisions – an issue we will discuss in more detail later. To ensure that limited liability was known to those dealing with the company, section 48 made directors jointly and severally liable on every company contract that did not have 'limited' or 'limited liability' 'distinctly written or printed after the name of the Company where first occurring in such contract.' The requirement for notice of limited liability was expanded in 1877. Henceforth each corporation had to include the word 'limited' after its name in a notice 'in a conspicuous position' on the outside of all its offices, 'in letters easily legible,' and all company publications, cheques, promissory notes, and the like had likewise to include the word.[14]

The first province to pass a general incorporation statute was Ontario, in 1874, followed by New Brunswick and Manitoba in 1875, Quebec in 1881, Nova Scotia in 1883, and Prince Edward Island in 1888. The North-West Territories did so in 1886.[15] Ontario and Quebec waited some years after the federal act was passed because, as noted above, their law was the de facto general incorporation statute of the Province of Canada. In 1868 Quebec passed a similar and equally wide-ranging sectoral incorporation statute of its own.[16] As in other areas of law, in most provinces statutory draftsmen copied earlier acts. The Ontario, Manitoba, Nova Scotia, and Territorial statutes were essentially the same, for example, as the federal Act, with many sections identical and the differences in wording or section numbering, not substance. In addition to these general incorporation acts, most jurisdictions at some point passed statutes providing processes by which companies incorporated under other provinces' or countries' laws could register and be allowed to operate in the jurisdiction. The federal jurisdiction did not pass such legislation, but in 1902 it allowed foreign companies to incorporate federally, in large part in response to the fact that American companies were operating in Canada anyway. When introducing the act, Secretary of State Richard Scott gave the examples of mining companies in the Yukon and the North-West Territories and of insurance companies nationwide. He claimed that fully one-third of insurance companies operating in Canada were American.[17]

All but one of the general incorporation statutes provided for incorporation by letters patent, meaning that once applications had received the approval of the secretary of state or provincial secretary, the governor general or lieutenant governor would issue letters patent making the company a separate legal person.[18] In this respect Canada differed from both British and American jurisdictions, and to some extent with its colonial past. The United States, the United Kingdom, and most British North American colonies employed certificates issued by some official, often called the registrar of joint stock companies.[19] The letters patent method was chosen because it was more elaborate and formal than registration with a government department. It provided a greater level of scrutiny than that afforded by a mid-level bureaucrat because letters patent were issued by the governor general or a lieutenant governor, in effect the federal or provincial government.

Four jurisdictions are missing from this analysis. Newfoundland did not enact a general incorporation statute until 1899. Prior to that, the law was a broad sectoral act of 1856, based on the 1844 UK Act. The 1892 statute was a replica of the 1862 UK *Companies Act*, each of its sections referencing the corresponding section of the UK legislation. This made it structurally distinct from and much longer than the Canadian federal and provincial acts. It also employed the UK registration system, not letters patent. After they became provinces, Alberta and Saskatchewan continued to operate under the 1886 North-West Territories ordinance until the end of our period, so that all territorial corporations continued as provincially incorporated entities, provided their head offices were in the relevant province.[20]

British Columbia's incorporation law history was the most complicated of any province, largely for reasons discussed in chapter 4's section on statutory revisions. Its first incorporation law was the UK *Companies Act* of 1844, a broad sectoral incorporation statute stated by an ordinance of 1859 to apply to the new mainland colony. A further ordinance of 1865 adopted the 1862 UK Act – a general incorporation statute – and this was subsequently extended to the united colony. That law remained the only regime in place until 1878, when the province passed a *Corporations Act* that was sectoral but very broad. A decade later this broad sectoral approach was replaced by general incorporation; a two-section statute simply substituted 'corporations for any lawful purpose' for the former broad list of purposes. The statutory consolidation of 1888 incorporated the 1862 English Act 'as far as practicable.' When the statutes were consolidated in the *Revised Statutes* of 1897 there was uncertainty about which law(s) were in force, whether later statutes had repealed earlier ones, and if so which ones. The incorporation chapter in the 1897 *Revised Statutes* acknowledged that 'there are now several systems whereunder ... Companies ... can be incorporated' and declared that it was 'expedient ... to enact an exclusive and comprehensive law' for incorporation. The operative provisions of the 1897 act simply stated that 'associations of persons for the acquisition of gain by any lawful means ... may be formed according to the provisions of this Act,' provided a mechanism for all existing corporations to be registered under the new act, and declared that henceforth 'any five or more persons associated for any lawful purpose' could subscribe to a memorandum of association and form an incorporated company. The company had to register with the registrar of joint stock companies and received a certificate of incorporation. British Columbia therefore did not use the letters patent system.[21]

All of these general incorporation statutes excluded certain kinds of companies. Every province and the federal jurisdiction excluded railway companies; uniquely Nova Scotia removed them from the excluded category in 1900.[22] In addition, in 1912, perhaps for greater certainty on whether they were part of the general exclusion of railways, street railways were required to get a private act in Ontario. Railways were excluded, according to one contemporary, because they were 'enterprises, in which the public are largely and specially interested.' For the same reason they had been excluded from all sectoral incorporation legislation before Confederation.[23] Another excluded area was banking. In the federal act and in the Nova Scotia and Newfoundland statutes of 1883 and 1889 banks were excluded specifically. In all the other provincial jurisdictions banking was simply not mentioned, it presumably being unnecessary because of the limitation contained in all provincial statutes to matters within the legislative authority of the province. A third common exclusion was insurance, although the law here was more complicated. The federal jurisdiction and almost all provinces excluded companies established to sell insurance, but Nova Scotia did not do so until 1900, while Ontario did so for some of this period, going back and forth on the issue. In addition in Ontario and Quebec pre-Confederation sectoral incorporation legislation allowing for the incorporation of mutual insurance companies – those in which there were no shareholders and the owners of the company and the policyholders were the same people – continued in force after 1867.[24]

Other exclusions were limited to one or two jurisdictions and/or to only part of this period. Loan companies were not excluded in the 1869 federal act but were added to the list of exclusions in 1902 along with companies for the construction and operation of telegraph or telephone lines. Ontario also excluded loan companies, but only from 1897, while Nova Scotia excluded them in its initial general incorporation statute of 1883 and broadened the exclusion in 1900 to loan and trust companies. Close to the end of our period, trust companies were also excluded in Manitoba and Saskatchewan. One exclusion applied only in Manitoba – companies established for the buying and selling of land. This was done to make it more difficult for land speculators to combine to buy up land that both federal and provincial governments wanted to be taken up and retained by homesteaders – a topic dealt with in chapter 14. The need for land companies to obtain a special act was removed in 1902, by which year most of the land available for homesteading in the province was taken. British Columbia excluded tramways and telephone and telegraph companies until 1895. To the opposite effect Alberta added telephone and telegraph companies to its exclusions from 1907. New Brunswick and Prince Edward Island also excluded companies created for 'the management of trades unions, friendly societies, building societies or other associations of like character.'[25]

The post-Confederation general incorporation statutes all granted limited liability. Section 42 of the 1869 federal act, for example, reproduced in all other statutes, provided that 'each shareholder, until the whole amount of his stock has been paid up, shall be individually liable to the creditors of the company, to an amount equal to that not paid up thereon.' Shareholders' liability was thus limited to their investment in the company, and not beyond. Directors enjoyed the same general immunity in their capacity as shareholders, but they were personally liable as directors in three circumstances. First, they were jointly and severally liable to company and shareholders if they declared and paid a dividend when the company was insolvent, or if the payment of the dividend made it insolvent. Second, they were similarly liable for one year's wages for employees if the company had been sued and was unable to satisfy the judgment. Third, in some jurisdictions, including the federal, they were also jointly and severally liable on contracts that did not include 'limited' or 'limited liability' 'distinctly written or printed after the name of the Company.' This last provision, a form of creditor protection, was not included in some provinces' initial general incorporation Acts but was added later. Ontario, for example, added it in 1889, the amendment including not just the clause from the 1869 federal Act but also an additional one added to that Act in 1877 – that companies were required to prominently display their limited liability status on signage outside their offices, and in advertisements, company publications, promissory notes, and the like. The only province that never legislated any kind of public notice requirement was Prince Edward Island.[26]

While the 1869 act passed through Parliament without any controversy over general incorporation, in the legislative chambers or among the public,[27] limited liability was a different matter. We saw in *Volume 1* that limited liability was a controversial issue in some colonial jurisdictions, and although it was much less debated after Confederation, concerns about it did not entirely go away. In Parliament most of its critics were MPs from Nova Scotia, where limited liability had long enjoyed less support than in central Canada and the principle that a person should be responsible for their obligations still carried considerable weight. Indeed prior to the passage of the 1883 Nova Scotia general incorporation act, the pre-Confederation legislation remained in force and specified unlimited liability for all corporations formed under its very limited general incorporation regime. A shareholder was liable for the company's obligations 'as a partner to the same extent as if no corporation existed,' and the only way to oust this was by a special act of incorporation.[28] In the Senate Robert Dickey of Nova Scotia pointed out that limited liability, which he and others referred to as single liability, had never been adopted in the Maritime provinces before Confederation, for good reason.[29] Nova Scotia preferred double liability – shareholder responsibility for the corporation's debts to twice the value of their shareholding. Alexander Campbell, government leader in the Senate and the man who had introduced the bill, claimed that no company in either England or the Canadian provinces, other than banks, had double liability. He insisted on the importance of limited liability for attracting investment: 'The object of a single liability clause is to provide that capitalists may be induced to carry on business of importance to the country; that capital may be brought together without the shareholders being liable beyond their stock in any concern.' Speakers from the Maritimes nevertheless preferred double liability. Lemuel Wilmot of New Brunswick, which had limited liability from 1862,[30] thought that limited liability companies tended to act more recklessly, while Jonathan McCully of Nova Scotia pointed out that his province had extended single liability only to mining companies. McCully considered that while single liability had done well in encouraging investment, it had also caused creditors to lose their money by investing in poorly run companies. For all the conservatism expressed by Maritimers on this issue in 1869, however, the region's general incorporation legislation all had the same limited liability clause as the federal act and the other provinces.

There were numerous amendments to all the original general incorporation statutes. The principal ones involved increased protections for creditors and investors, and a streamlining of the federal incorporation process. Among the former was an 1876 Quebec statute that required incorporated companies, wherever and however incorporated, to deposit with the Superior Court a declaration of where its principal place of business was 'to increase the facilities for the institution of actions,' that is, to make it easier to sue a corporation.[31] In the mid-1880s Quebec also passed an act to protect investors, strengthening reporting requirements and prohibiting 'the practice commonly known as watering of stock,' the capitalization of surplus earnings, and 'every form and manner of fictitious capitalization of stock.' The same statute also regulated the payment of dividends and imposed personal liability on directors for actions that contravened the act. Anti-stock-watering provisions were also included in other provincial regimes, either by amending legislation, or, in the case of Prince Edward Island, by inclusion in the first general incorporation act passed.[32]

The principal amendments to the federal act, in 1902, were designed to make the incorporation process quicker and easier. The statute did away with the need to have applications vetted by various government departments, eliminated the notice period of an intention to apply, very substantially reduced the amount of stock needing to be subscribed before letters patent were issued from 50 per cent of the total to just one share per applicant, and removed the need for 10 per cent of the capital to be actually paid in. In addition, a majority of the directors were henceforth not required to be residents of Canada. The requirements eliminated were said by Secretary of State Scott to be 'tedious' and 'vexatious' and the cause of 'frequent delays.' The change was apparently 'heartily commended and ... appreciated by the commercial world.' The amendments clearly reduced the protections for anybody dealing with the corporation, and some senators objected to this. James McMullen, a director of the Grand Trunk and other railways, as well as of the Dominion Life Insurance Company, somewhat ironically declaimed against the 'enormous power' that companies had by being able to bring together substantial amounts of capital, and argued that the public should at least know in advance of an application so that dissenters would have ample time to make their voices heard. Perhaps influenced by a desire to keep his Wellington County, Ontario, residence separate from the city, he cited a rather modernistic example. Many manufacturers were significant contributors to pollution and to peoples' quality of life, and without a notice period, despoiling operations could begin without any community awareness. To other critics the changed provisions on paid-up share capital risked businesses being started with insufficient capital by operators prepared to cut corners and to borrow to make up the shortfall.[33]

Table 11.1. Incorporations under federal and Ontario statutes, 1874–1914, sample years

Year	Federal	Ontario
1874	12	57
1880	18	59
1886	43	90
1891	50	152
1896	90	154
1901	54	516
1905	293	762
1911	370	1,211
1913	812	1,179
1914	939	1,031

Sources: *Annual Reports* of the secretary of state, in Canada, *Sessional Papers*, and *Annual Reports* of the secretary and registrar of the Province of Ontario, in Ontario, *Sessional Papers.* The 1914 number given here for Ontario is actually for 1913, the 1914 numbers being unavailable.

We turn from the legal structure of incorporation to corporations' increasing presence on the country's economic landscape. Writing in 1881 the author of the first Canadian treatise on corporate law justified his publication by noting the great increase in the number of corporations, the 'vast amount of money annually invested in joint stock enterprise and the vast number of joint stock concerns which are annually chartered.' Table 11.1 provides evidence of this from the federal jurisdiction and Ontario, for both of which the statistics are easily accessible, although it also indicates that exponential growth in incorporations was still two decades into the future when these words were written.[34] The number of companies using the general incorporation acts of each jurisdiction increased markedly over time, although it took some years for those involved in business enterprises to adapt to the new regime. Between 1874 and 1879 inclusive only 64 companies were issued letters patent under the federal act, an average of just 10 a year. The number of incorporations under the federal act grew steadily if hardly spectacularly in the 1880s and 1890s, reaching a high of 90 in 1896, fell off for a few years, and then leaped up in the first years of the twentieth century to reach almost 300 in 1905. The streamlining of the process in 1902 contributed to the rise from 54 in 1901 to 293 in 1905. The largest annual increases came at the end of our period; by 1914 almost 1,000 new corporations were created each year. The Ontario numbers were higher than for the federal jurisdiction throughout this period, likely attributable to Ontario having had de facto general incorporation from 1850, to the growth and rise to dominance of the Ontario economy in this period, and to companies not needing to incorporate federally if they were not operating outside the province.

Three caveats should be borne in mind when dealing with these numbers. First, they are for all corporations that received letters patent, so that if a company incorporated, then either failed to get off the ground or existed for some time and then was wound up and replaced by another, it is included twice. One of many examples of failure and later reincorporation was the Sunlight Gas Company Limited of Montreal, incorporated federally in March 1902 with its corporate objects being 'to acquire, manufacture, use, lease and dispose of ... all kinds of apparatus and supplies relating and applicable to and for the production of acetylene gas, and for the purposes of heating, lighting and power.' It had a capital stock of $50,000, and was a reincorporation, a 'former company of the same name being insolvent.'[35] Second, the Ontario numbers include both new Ontario corporations and corporations formed elsewhere and given a licence to operate in Ontario. We have included them in the table because they were new corporations in Ontario, even if they were not newly created. Third, table 11.1 does not include companies incorporated under the sectoral incorporation statutes discussed above, which obtained their status by registering with county registrars. It therefore undercounts the total number of incorporations, probably quite substantially.

While providing extensive details about the kinds of companies using the federal act is beyond the scope of this chapter, we can say that they were varied considerably in purpose and size. Of the 18 companies issued letters patent in 1880, for example, 8 were capitalized at $25,000 or less, 7 between $25,000 and $200,000, and the most wealthy were the Canadian Telephone Company and the Sourie Coal and Fuel Company, both at $300,000, and Imperial Oil, at $500,000. In addition to the purposes encompassed by these examples, the 18 included the Montreal Milk Company, the Montreal News Company, the British and Northwest Colonization Company, the Desoronto Navigation Company, and the Niagara District Fruit Growers Stock Company. Almost all were to operate in Ontario and Quebec, and most were headquartered in Montreal.[36] In 1902, the first year in which more than 100 companies were incorporated under the federal Act, 42 of the 104 companies were in manufacturing, of items as varied as boilers, cigars, casting machines, and windmills. Retailing accounted for 10 companies, and lumbering and natural products for 17. Montreal had always been the country's commercial and financial centre, and 63, or almost two-thirds of the companies federally incorporated, were headquartered there. Toronto was a very distant second, with just four, fewer than other Ontario municipalities with 10, and than Winnipeg, with five. Ten companies were headquartered in Nova Scotia towns, none in Halifax; most were in the shipping industry, although they also included the Truro Knitting Mills Company, owned by the Stanfield family and with a capital stock of $300,000. Only four companies were headquartered in the Territories, one in Charlottetown, and none in British Columbia or New Brunswick. The capital stock of these 104 companies ranged from $12 million – the Mexican Light and Power Company – to $2,000 – the Hantsport Graving Dock Company, ship repairers – with 60 of them at $100,000 or less.[37]

The companies incorporated under the Ontario Act at roughly the same time were less heavily capitalized. Of the 177 incorporations in 1895, 137 (77 per cent) had an initial capital stock of $50,000 or less, with fully 56 (32 per cent) at $20,000 or less. No company was incorporated in Ontario that year with more than $1 million in capital stock. A wide variety of small- and medium-scale manufacturers show up – furniture, electric lights, brewing, batteries, bicycles, boots and shoes, typewriters, and leather goods – as do numerous service providers – transportation, electric light, advertising, and general delivery. These companies were dispersed across the province – 48 communities other than Toronto, Hamilton, and Ottawa were represented, accounting for 63 companies. The aforementioned three major cities were headquarters for 52 companies, with Toronto not surprisingly appearing most often, with 39, or one-third of the total.[38]

Corporation Law: Special Act Incorporations

General incorporation did not mean the end of special act corporations. The exclusions meant that some companies were still required to obtain one throughout this period. In addition, some companies that could have employed general incorporation chose not to. Bills to incorporate a company were always private member's bills. The incorporators had to find an MP or member of the provincial legislature to introduce it. This was never a problem in Parliament, and nor was there any difficulty in getting the act passed. Of a sample of seven private bills introduced in the Commons between 1871 and 1909, none spurred any debate at all, and all take up less than one page in *Hansard* for all three readings. This admittedly limited evidence suggests that it was no more difficult to have an act pass through Parliament than to register with the secretary of state.[39]

Corporations created by special acts were not subject to the requirements of the general incorporation acts. But they were regulated by companies clauses acts, which prescribed standard clauses for all special act corporations unless the special act specifically excluded a section or sections. This legislation predated Confederation in central and eastern Canada, and the first companies clauses acts after Confederation were the Quebec and federal statutes passed in 1868 and 1869 respectively. Some other provinces followed suit with similar legislation in the 1870s and 1880s, others relied for some of this period on pre-Confederation legislation, and in a number of jurisdictions, including the federal, the general incorporation and companies clauses legislation were at some point consolidated into the same statute.[40]

The congruence between general incorporation and companies clauses statutes extended to limited liability. The clauses on liability in the federal companies clauses act, for example, limited shareholder liability to the amount of stock invested in the company, providing the stock was fully paid up. A similar limited liability clause was also included in some regulatory statutes. Section 18 of the 1868 federal *Railway Act*, for example, specified that shareholders' liability to the corporation's creditors extended only to their stock.[41] The liability regime for special act incorporations could be varied by the special act itself, but none did except in Nova Scotia. Between 1867 and 1883, the year the province's general incorporation act was passed, the province's incorporation statute specified unlimited liability as the default regime. As table 11.2 demonstrates, in that period the assembly passed 286 special act incorporations, 211 of them (74 per cent) with limited liability, 70 (24 per cent) with double liability. Five operated with unlimited liability. Thus prior to 1884, for the vast majority of incorporators, obtaining a special act brought a very significant benefit. From 1884 on, all special act corporations had limited liability, as did corporations created under the general incorporation act of 1883. We were unable to discern any difference in the type of company that was granted limited liability as opposed to double liability, but there was a difference between the 1870s and the preceding and succeeding years. In the 1870s 78 per cent of special Acts included double liability, compared to the years before and after, when only 7.5 per cent did so. Clearly the views expressed above by Nova Scotians in Ottawa were shared by their counterparts in Halifax.

Table 11.2. Private act incorporations and liability clauses, Nova Scotia, 1867–1883

Period	Limited liability	Double liability	Unlimited liability
1867–70	90	8	3
1871–9	76	59	1
1880–3	45	3	1
Total	211	70	5

Source: Annual statutes.

Table 11.3. Special act incorporations, federal jurisdiction, 1867–1914

Purpose	Total
Railways	411
Banks	74
Insurance companies	156
Other excluded purposes	22
Not excluded purposes	283
Total	946

Source: Annual statutes.

Special act incorporations continued to be a significant part of the corporate law landscape generally after Confederation, even if not as much as before. Table 11.3 shows the number of special act incorporations passed by the federal Parliament before and after 1900. The first four rows are companies excluded from general incorporation by the 1850 Province of Canada statute, in force from 1867 to 1869, or by the 1869 federal act. The fifth row consists of companies that were not excluded from either statute. The largest single category was railway companies, 43 per cent of the total. As with the figures for general incorporations discussed above, the number given here is not the number for extant companies in 1914, because many never got off the ground, or failed, or merged. It is simply the number of special acts passed. But we are confident that it is an accurate reflection of relative numbers; there is no reason to suppose that these things happened to special act corporations any more or less than they happened to companies incorporated under the general incorporation regime. Perhaps the most noteworthy point from table 11.3 is that the second-largest category of special act incorporations were those pursuing purposes not excluded from general incorporation – companies that could have used that legislation but opted to have a special act passed. There were 283 of them, or 30 per cent, of the total. The largest group within this category were bridge and tunnel companies, and the second-largest trust, loan, and investment companies, but it also included, among others, printing, freighting, and warehousing, and manufacturing companies.

One might have expected that once it became possible for companies to incorporate without a special act they would choose what was surely the less cumbersome method. Contemporary writers offer us very little assistance on why they did not. None of the treatises on corporate law published in this period dealt with special act incorporations, and the only indirect evidence we have comes from William E. Hodgins, whose documentary collection on disallowance is often used in this book and who is discussed in chapter 4 as one of the cohort of lawyer/authors after Confederation. He worked for the Department of Justice in the 1880s and reviewed incorporation applications. He wrote a manual on incorporation under the federal act, in which he lamented that the applications he reviewed were 'frequently defective in point of form' and the statutory requirements 'not complied with.'[42] But this shows only that incorporators and/or their lawyers did not fully understand the process. On the one hand it seems unlikely that those same incorporators/ lawyers would prefer to sponsor a special act, a presumably more time-consuming and expensive process. Yet, on the other hand, the evidence from the debate over the 1902 changes to the general incorporation act is that general incorporation was considered an onerous process. That the 1902 changes made a difference is also suggested by the fact that use of the special act procedure declined after the turn of the century: 218 of the 283 special acts were passed before 1900, only 65 thereafter. The question of why special acts were used so often before 1900 and less so thereafter cannot yet be satisfactorily answered and requires further research. For our purposes what matters most is that the introduction of the 1869 general incorporation did not result in a wholesale alteration in practice.

The same phenomenon of the continuing use of special act incorporations was manifested in provincial statute books, as shown in tables 11.4 and 11.5. These tables are less precise than table 11.3 in distinguishing between companies excluded from using general incorporation legislation and those not so excluded, for two reasons. First, for each province the count of special act incorporations begins when the province joined Confederation, and in some cases, particularly Nova Scotia and Prince Edward Island, a number of years passed before general incorporation was introduced. Second, as discussed above, the exclusions from general incorporation varied from province to province.

Table 11.4. Special act incorporations by province to 1900

Province	Railways	Insurance companies	Others	Total
Quebec	91	7	134	232
Ontario	198	20	71	289
Manitoba	47	11	25	83
British Columbia	77	4	28	109
Nova Scotia	59	18	547	624
New Brunswick	74	12	156	242
Prince Edward Island	0	10	54	64
Total	546	82	1,015	1,645

Source: Annual statutes.
Note: The North-West Territories are not included in tables 11.4 and 11.5. Between the passage of the general incorporation act in that jurisdiction in 1886 and 1905, after which no ordinances were issued until 1922, only 13 companies were incorporated by special ordinance. Three were for municipal utilities in Calgary and Lethbridge, three were of stock growers' associations, and the remainder were principally of trust and investment companies.

Table 11.5. Special act incorporations by province to 1901–1914

Province	Railways	Insurance companies	Others	Total	TOTAL 1867–1914
Quebec	52	22	62	136	368
Ontario	90	1	19	110	399
Manitoba	21	24	43	88	171
British Columbia	70	10	15	95	204
Nova Scotia	33	2	155	190	814
New Brunswick	26	1	52	79	321
Prince Edward Island	0	1	134	135	199
Alberta	48	8	9	65	65
Saskatchewan	15	5	32	52	52
Total	355	74	521	950	2,595

Source: Annual statutes.

They all excluded railways and insurance companies for almost all of this period, therefore we have separated them from all other special Act incorporations. But a small number of the special acts in the 'other' columns were incorporations of companies excluded from the general incorporation legislation. Despite these limitations we believe that the tables provide a useful picture of the number of special act incorporations and, more importantly, of the ratio of special acts obtained by companies excluded from general incorporation legislation to those not excluded.

Tables 11.4 and 11.5 show the continuing importance provincially of special act incorporations. Almost 2,600 of them were provincially created in this period. In some respects the provincial figures follow the same trends as the federal numbers in table 11.3. Railway companies, including street railways and lines built to access mining or other resource extraction sites, were the single largest category, 901 of the total of 2,595, 35 per cent of the total. As with the federal jurisdiction, the use of special act incorporations declined over time. After 1900 only slightly more than half were created than in the period between Confederation and the turn of the century. We appreciate that we are comparing a 33-year period with one of only 14, and that therefore the annual averages of special acts were quite similar. But factoring in the population growth discussed in the introduction and the economic growth outlined at the start of this chapter, there was a substantial real decline in the role played by special act corporations.

The most striking feature of tables 11.4 and 11.5, of course, is the variation among provinces. All three Maritime provinces passed a disproportionate number, given their populations, with Nova Scotia especially an outlier, having more than Ontario and Quebec combined in both periods. Between 1867 and 1883, 301 special acts of incorporation were enacted, nearly 20 per cent of all legislation. The lack of general incorporation and limited liability before 1883 was not the cause; 323 special act incorporations were passed between 1884 and 1900, and 155 between 1901 and 1914. The numbers only dropped to fewer than 10 a year in 1907. Nor can exclusions from general incorporation explain the numbers, for overall the province had fewer exclusions than any other jurisdiction. A good part of the explanation lies in economic growth. The province did benefit substantially from the National Policy in the later nineteenth century. Its per capita industrial growth was higher than Ontario's in the 1880s, its overall industrial output increased by 66 per cent, a major iron and steel industry was established, and many of the special act incorporations were for manufacturing companies. A major boom industry was mining: 86 gold-mining companies and 101 other mining companies were incorporated by special act between 1867 and 1900. At the same time the 1880s and 1890s saw a relatively high number of business failures, with the result that there was a constant stream of new entrants, at least some of them incorporating by special act. But while all of this explains why so many corporations were formed, it does not explain why so many obtained special acts. Much more research would be needed to answer that question, especially given that there seems to have been a consensus in the assembly in 1883 that general incorporation was needed to bring the law into line with the rest of the country and to save legislative time and resources. In its absence we would suggest that culture must have influenced decisions. Nova Scotian promoters and investors preferred the more public nature of a special act to general incorporation.[43]

Maritime distinctiveness is also evidenced by the numbers for New Brunswick and Prince Edward Island. The former legislature created not that many fewer special act corporations than Quebec and Ontario, while the latter had almost as many as British Columbia. There was nothing distinctive about the New Brunswick incorporation patterns, beyond the prevalence of numerous railways, presumably many abortive or short lived. Prince Edward Island's high numbers are attributable to the prevalence of natural products manufacturing operations and, especially, fox fur companies – almost 70 in 1913 and 1914 alone. There is much work still to be done to fully understand all the figures presented here on special act incorporations.

<h3 style="text-align:center">Debtor Creditor Law: Imprisonment
for Debt, Bankruptcy, and Insolvency</h3>

Before Confederation the British North American colonies had a variety of approaches to govern relations between creditors and debtors who were unable to pay their debts. The principal common law remedy for creditors was imprisonment for debt, although all colonies enacted legislation to limit its application or ameliorate its effects. Some colonies also introduced bankruptcy laws, establishing mechanisms through which some insolvent persons could settle with their creditors and receive a fresh start in return.[44] After 1867 debtor-creditor law was a subject of bifurcated jurisdiction. The provinces had jurisdiction under section 92 (13) of the *BNA Act*, the property and civil rights power, while the federal government could legislate for bankruptcy and insolvency under section 91 (21). The difference between bankruptcy and insolvency, then and now, was that the latter simply meant that a person was unable to pay his or her debts, while the former was a formal legal proceeding in which an insolvent person's assets were distributed pro rata among his or her creditors, and the bankrupt was given a discharge, effective forgiveness of the still unpaid debt and the opportunity to make a fresh start. After Confederation the terms bankruptcy and insolvency were often used interchangeably, and thus one must look to the substance of legislation to ascertain whether an *Insolvent Act* was actually a bankruptcy measure.[45]

After 1867 imprisonment for debt remained part of debtor-creditor law. A creditor could apply for a warrant for the debtor's arrest before trial if he or she could show that the debtor had left the province or was likely to abscond.[46] More importantly, to the end of our period it also remained possible in every province but Alberta for a judgment creditor who was unable to make good on an execution against the debtor's property to have the debtor imprisoned until the debt was paid or compromised. The pre-Confederation ameliorative measures that substantially reduced its availability and made release easier when it was used were augmented in this period. They reflected concerns that imprisonment was ineffective and inefficient, the debtor denied the opportunity to earn money to repay the debt, as well as an increasing belief that it was inappropriate to employ what was effectively a criminal sanction for commercial failure. The requirements for release varied, and we do not have space to detail every provincial scheme. We will use the typical example of Nova Scotia.

In 1867 relief for imprisoned debtors in Nova Scotia required the debtor to petition a Supreme Court judge, or two commissioners, with a schedule of all his or her property and all debts. The adjudicator would then summon the creditor to 'show cause why such prisoner should not be discharged.' If the creditor was not able to do so – and principally that meant being able to argue that the debtor had given a false account – the debtor would be released after assigning his property to the creditor in trust for the payment of the debt. This did not constitute a discharge, because all property of the debtor discovered or acquired after release was liable for any remaining debt. In the 1880s the Act was amended to require creditors to show cause, even if the debtor was reluctant to apply for release. The ameliorative trend continued in 1890, when imprisonment became not the standard remedy for the judgment creditor but one for which a special order had to be granted by a court. The statute drew a sharp distinction between the 'innocent' or 'unfortunate' debtor and the dishonest one seeking to avoid paying. The judgment creditor had to show that the debtor was dishonest – that is, about to leave the province 'with intent to defraud his creditors generally,' or had the means to pay but was refusing to do so, or that the debt had been fraudulently incurred. If the creditor passed this hurdle, he or she could have the debtor examined in court, after which the judge, if satisfied that one of these grounds applied, could order imprisonment but only for a maximum of 12 months and only as one of two possible remedies, the other being an order for instalment payments. These provisions were retained in the 1894 *Collection Act*, a consolidation of existing legislation, which stayed in force throughout the rest of this period. Thus after Confederation there were more procedures involved in imprisoning a judgment debtor, some alternative to prison in the form of an order for instalment payments, and a limit on how long the debtor could remain in custody.[47]

Imprisonment for debt remained part of the law in all provinces but one. Only in Alberta was it abolished. In 1907 the Supreme Court of the North-West Territories ruled that the 1869 UK *Debtors Act*, which had consolidated much prior statute law, had been among the UK statutes received in the Territories in 1870. This meant that imprisonment for debt was part of the law inherited by Alberta and Saskatchewan, a fact that clearly came as an unwelcome surprise to local legislators. Alberta responded immediately with a 1908 statute declaring that the 1869 UK Act was not in force and followed this up a year later with another statute declaring that neither was any of the pre-1869 UK legislation.[48]

The dominant issue of insolvency law after Confederation was not imprisonment for debt, but bankruptcy.[49] Bankruptcy was always controversial, so much so that although a national law was enacted in the late 1860s it lasted only a decade or so. Early in Macdonald's first administration a Commons select committee recommended a federal act, but financier and MP John Abbott, entrusted by Macdonald with the task, was unable to get it through Parliament in 1868. The bill did pass the following year, by a narrow margin. It had a four-year sunset clause and thus had to be renewed in 1873 and again in 1874. It was amended in 1875 and finally repealed in 1880, having survived 10 repeal bills before that. For almost four decades thereafter there was no federal statute, and the provinces regulated insolvency until a federal *Bankruptcy Act* was passed in 1919.[50]

Section 2 of the 1869 Act provided that 'any debtor unable to meet his engagements' and any debtor 'who is required to make an assignment' of his assets had to make that assignment to a local official assignee. The assignee's job was to prepare a statement of the insolvent's affairs and make an assessment of the debts owing. Those debts would then be paid on a pro rata basis, and the insolvent could request a discharge of the remaining debt, which would allow him or her to resume economic activity unencumbered. A discharge required the consent of a majority of the creditors who between them held at least three-quarters of the debt. Even if the creditors agreed, a court could still refuse the discharge if it found that the debtor had committed fraud, made a preferential payment (paid one creditor separately and more than the creditor's pro rata share), induced a creditor in some way to vote for a discharge, or hidden assets. Courts also had a general discretion, absent these considerations, to suspend the discharge for five years. Conversely, the courts also had discretion to grant a discharge even if the creditors did not agree, although the debtor had to wait a year to apply for that, and creditors could oppose the application. Discharges could be of two kinds: first and second class. The former was for 'honest' debtors, those in trouble from misfortune. The latter could be granted to an insolvent who had been guilty of poor business management, extravagance, recklessness, carrying on a trade when it was clear that the business was insolvent, or committed other faults. Judges, who generally interpreted the *Insolvent Act* in debtors' favour, very rarely granted a second-class discharge. The 1875 amending statute gave the court an additional ground for discretionary refusal of a discharge – if the debtor's assets could only pay less than one-third of the debt. It was predicated on the belief that some debtors continued to spend too much, even after they were aware of the financial trouble they were in. Legislators were persuaded that the one-third requirement was an insufficient disincentive, and it was raised to one-half in 1877.[51]

The legislative regime was thus shot through with the need to make moral judgments, reflecting the fact that bankruptcy, before and after Confederation, posed fundamental questions of commercial morality. Many believed simply that debts should be paid, that nobody should be able to renege on their obligations. Alexander Mackenzie thought the legislation 'eminently conducive to public immorality,' for paying debts was more than fulfilling contracts, it was a moral duty that tested the individual's character. On the other side were people who drew a distinction between honest and fraudulent debtors and believed that the former were victims of unfortunate circumstances and deserved forgiveness and relief from a lifetime millstone of debt and harassment by creditors, and of having no recourse but to flee the jurisdiction. Parliamentary debates were complicated by the fact that Nova Scotia and New Brunswick had no bankruptcy law before Confederation, whereas the Province of Canada had one. Peter Mitchell, a senator from New Brunswick who was also minister of marine and fisheries, complained that 'hundreds of men of ability, talent and enterprise' in the Maritimes had had to leave the region because they had been 'unfortunate in business,' the alternative being imprisonment for debt, which his provincial colleague Lemuel Wilmot called a 'relic of barbarism.'[52] To these humanitarian arguments in favour of the discharge were added practical ones: a perpetual debtor was no good to the community and his or her discharge was in the public interest, and the only effective action debtors could take if they could not get a discharge was to flee the country, which did not help creditors. In fact discharged bankrupts did sometimes leave the country anyway because of the stigma of bankruptcy. Opponents of the discharge had a simple answer: – let them go, the community was better off without them. The idea that business was about character, trustworthiness, and honesty, and not simply about the accumulation of wealth, was still prevalent in the immediate post-Confederation period, even if receding in importance.[53]

The commercial morality question dominated debates over the early post-Confederation legislation. The government's first bill in 1868 drew opposition from both parties because it allowed a broad group of people to use bankruptcy, while the second bill succeeded, albeit with much resistance, in part because it allowed only 'traders,' which courts generally defined as people making their living by buying and selling, to claim a discharge. Such people might well be subject to the unfortunate vagaries of the trade cycle, more so than farmers, professionals, and others who were better able to control their indebtedness. The 1869 act also came under attack because it established two ways for a person to be declared bankrupt. Creditors could bring it about if they could prove that the debtor had committed one of 13 'acts of bankruptcy,' or the debtor could voluntarily file for bankruptcy. The vast majority of bankruptcies, between 75 and 90 per cent between 1869 and 1874, were voluntary, a fact resented by opponents of bankruptcy, and thus when the act was amended in 1875 it was to remove voluntary bankruptcies.[54] In fact judges were lenient towards debtors in applying the legislation. They rarely enforced the one-half rule to deny discharges, because with the abolition of the voluntary discharge it was creditors who forced hopelessly insolvent people into bankruptcy.

While commercial morality was a constant underlying concern throughout this period, other more particular and interrelated issues combined to bring about repeal and ensure that there was no bankruptcy law after 1880. One early problem was that different courts included different categories of people within the umbrella term 'traders,' which was not defined in the legislation. As a result the 1875 amendment specifically excluded farmers and labourers. But this in turn provoked reactions from farmer interests, who argued that farmers bought and sold and operated in a world of credit – they gave their grain to a miller, for example, and waited to be paid until the grain was ground, which might not happen if the miller became insolvent. The miller was a trader and could seek a discharge, while the farmer was not, and if the miller's insolvency precipitated that of the farmer the latter had no recourse. The definitional problem overlapped with a divergence in attitudes about bankruptcy between local interests and regional and national ones, a point that can be illustrated by again considering the farmer. Farmers tended to support repeal of the act, as did other small-town businessmen, because the common law gave them an advantage. The first creditor to sue could get the whole of the debt satisfied, or at least as much of it as the debtor's assets would meet. Canada was still very much an agricultural society in which local economies mattered more than distant networks. Creditors were not just from the same area as their debtors, many were family members, and both preferred to deal locally and essentially privately with problems. In *Re Jones*, an 1868 case, the defendant paid a significant debt to his mother at the same time that he was involved in proceedings with his other creditors.[55] In addition, farming interests were used to 'seasonal insolvency' caused by poor crop years. They could wait out the temporary crisis, but not if a creditor forced them into bankruptcy. It is also likely that the commercial morality discussed above was stronger in rural areas, adding to the weight of opinion against a bankruptcy law.

Conversely, those doing business at a distance wanted a bankruptcy regime so that they could get at least a share of the debtor's assets through a pro rata distribution. The problem of distance creditors became more pronounced in the 1870s, with western Canada joining Confederation. Support for the *Insolvent Act* and pro rata distribution was voiced in the 1870s by powerful lobbyists like the Montreal Board of Trade, which represented manufacturers and others doing business with the West. The Dominion Board of Trade also voiced opinions but was conflicted because its members included the boards of trade of smaller municipalities who sided with local creditors. When the Dominion Board recommended reform of the 1875 Act, the vote was 10:9, with the 9 favouring repeal.

Another problem that became evident when the act was operative in the 1870s was its uneven application. Assignees' qualifications and practices were far from uniform, and they were in a constant conflict of interest, owing a statutory duty to creditors and a personal loyalty to debtors out of whose estates their fees were paid. Some even colluded with debtors, going so far as to take bribes to hide assets. According to one critic an assignee considered himself 'retained by the debtor, whom he regards in the light of a client or customer.'[56] Even able and conscientious ones had trouble doing their job when they confronted preferential payments – payments of debts to some creditors but not others. Preferential payments were prohibited under the *Insolvent Act* and under some of the provincial statutes that regulated insolvency after the mid-1880s, discussed below. Assignees and their later provincial equivalents could void preferential payments made 'in contemplation of' bankruptcy or insolvency, but they were difficult to prevent and equally difficult to deal with after the fact. Those who made preferential payments often also absconded, having sold what they could and paid off family members. Assignees had trouble tracking down absconding debtors, and when they could locate them it was difficult to prove the intent required by the phrase 'in contemplation of.' In *Pineo v Gavazza et al*, for example, an 1885 Nova Scotia case, the assignee was able to void a payment made by an insolvent but was helped by the fact that the transaction was one between uncle and nephew and the uncle had not filed a claim under the legislation.[57]

More often preferential payments survived scrutiny by the courts, which tended to uphold them on the basis of what one judge referred to as the avoidance of 'technical rules as a test of fraud' in order to 'assist mercantile convenience.' In that case a preferential payment had prevented a debtor from having to shut down a productive business. In *McCrae v White* the SCC held in 1883 that the debtor could not have made a preferential payment 'in contemplation of' insolvency because he expected to be able to remain profitable by making the payment. In a number of cases in the 1870s the courts followed the 'pressure' doctrine – pressure to pay from a creditor negated the intent to make the payment 'in contemplation of.' This doctrine was disavowed in *Davidson v Ross* in 1876 on the ground that it went against the principle of pro rata distribution; henceforth the courts should not look for a subjective intent to prefer, merely at whether a preferential payment had been received. Courts found exceptions to *Davidson v Ross*, and the SCC overruled it in 1883. Adding to all these complications was the fact that the 1873 to 1879 period was one of economic depression in Canada and elsewhere, leading to a doubling of bank and business failures, which many commentators blamed on the availability of bankruptcy.

Bankruptcy was never a party issue. It divided both parties. Although the Conservatives were in power when the 1869 Act was passed, in a debate on it in 1872 George-Étienne Cartier made it clear that that 'did not make it a Government Question.' A Liberal government was in office when the 1875 Act passed, and Justice Minister Edward Blake was adamant that 'leading Members on both sides of the House have entertained conflicting views on the question,' which 'has been one on which political lines have never been drawn.' When the vote to repeal the act was taken in 1879, 76 Conservatives, 23 Liberals, and eight others made up the strong majority for repeal, while 30 Conservatives, 15 Liberals, and 10 others voted to retain the law.[58] Between 1880 and 1903 20 insolvency bills were introduced in the federal Parliament, only two of them by the government of the day, but none passed.

Insolvency law was affected by developments in federalism jurisprudence, in particular the fact that the JCPC adopted an increasingly pro-provincial stance, making the property and civil rights power the dominant residual clause in the *BNA Act*. In *Cushing v Dupuy* in 1880 the JCPC upheld the *Insolvent Act* as intra vires the federal Parliament. But the decision also implied that provincial insolvency legislation was constitutional as well under property and civil rights, as the hallmark of bankruptcy was the discharge, not insolvency. The first provincial insolvency statute was passed by Ontario in 1880, although it was not proclaimed in force until 1884, because the province waited to see if the federal government would pass another statute. Other provinces followed suit, although the statutes were far from uniform.[59] Henceforth, for the rest of our period, insolvency law was provincial and concerned solely with priorities among creditors. No discharge could be obtained.

The commercial lobby was consistently dissatisfied with this state of affairs, as evidenced by the fact that most of the bankruptcy bills introduced in the 1880s and 1890s were private member's bills sponsored by boards of trade. They were concerned with the differences between the provincial statutes and the fact that no provincial law prevented preferential payments. Pro-bankruptcy lobbyists supported unsuccessful court challenges to provincial legislation, which, if successful, would have left the provinces with the common law and forced the federal Parliament to fill the gap. They also advocated a constitutional amendment to give the provinces bankruptcy jurisdiction. The latter strategy went nowhere. The former muddied the waters for a while, but in 1894 the JCPC ruled that provincial legislation that gave an assignment of debts for the benefit of creditors priority over all other execution judgments was intra vires the provinces.

The debate over whether there should be a national bankruptcy law broadly reflected the demographic and structural economic changes outlined in the introduction to this chapter. More national and retail businesses emerged and more investors from the United States, the United Kingdom, and elsewhere put their money in Canadian enterprises, and all these new players added to the lobby in favour of a federal law. But consolidation and internationalization did not entirely or even substantially displace locally based businesses and locally oriented economies. The discharge remained controversial, with the same arguments for and against that had been voiced in the 1870s. Moral concerns dominated opponents' objections, and, increasingly, practical ones were voiced by those in favour of it. As the economy grew and the trade cycle produced its inevitable winners and losers, flight to the US was increasingly resorted to by debtors. The debate over bankruptcy lost some of its vigour after the turn of the century, when the post-1896 economic boom resulted in fewer business failures. It was revived immediately prior to the war, as a recession set in from 1913, in which business failures doubled over the previous year. When Canada emerged from the First World War, the cumulative effects of the slow transition to a more national and integrated economy, and the rural-urban balance finally tipping in favour of the urban, the urban creditor lobby dominated the debate and in 1919 a new federal bankruptcy act was passed. But that is a story for another volume.

The Regulatory State: Banking, Mining, Railways

In 1867 the common law and the free market values on which it was predicated were the dominant modes of thinking about the relationship between the law and the economy. The common law was predicated on the idea that it should protect and enhance a sphere of individual autonomy within which economic actors were free to pursue their personal self-interest without interference from the state. In turn society would be better off, both morally and economically. The collective good was defined as the sum of all individual goods. This vision was never a totalizing one in Western nations in the nineteenth century, and perhaps even less so in Canada than it was in the United States and Britain. Regulation, 'the imposition of rules by a government, backed by the use of penalties, that are intended specifically to modify the economic behaviour of individuals and firms in the private sector,' had a long history in pre-Confederation Canada.[60] Its use grew substantially after 1867, and this book is replete with examples. The organization of Indian reserves (chapter 8), legislation on occupational health and safety (chapter 12), and municipal by-laws on land use (chapter 14) are just a few. Regulation varied in intensity and form in different contexts and included active government intervention through what we would now call public-private partnerships, such as the Intercolonial and Canadian Pacific Railways, as well as public ownership, a prime example of which is the creation of a public power authority in Ontario in the late nineteenth century.[61] Regulation could also involve wholesale replacement of the courts and the common law, such as with the introduction of workers compensation, discussed in chapter 12. A similar intervention in the free enterprise economy was the *Anti-Combines Act* of 1889, testament to the recognition that free enterprise was not a panacea, despite the existence of common law doctrines on restraint of trade.[62]

Dealing fully with this topic would require much more than one section in one chapter, and here we deal only with three areas of major importance to the national economy and in which there was substantial government regulation: banking, mining, and railways. The last also allows us to examine the beginning of the regulatory state, the creation of government agencies to perform certain tasks at arm's length from the government.[63] These agencies not only made rules about the market but also adjudicated disputes among the entities involved and between those entities and governments. They were distinct from inspectors of factories or schools and the like, which were parts of the executive branch directly accountable to departmental superiors. We associate this kind of agency with a later period, but the first Canadian one was established in 1903, the federal Board of Railway Commissioners (BRC).

The *BNA Act* assigned legislative responsibility for banking and monetary policy to the federal government, principally in section 91 (14), banking, incorporation of banks, and paper money, but also through sections 91 (1), (4), (15), (16), and (18–20).[64] Central government control ensured that Canadian banking avoided some of the problems that bedevilled the sector in the United States, where a lack of central control produced considerable instability and calls for stronger regulation in the 1860s.[65] Immediately after Confederation there was a short-lived banking crisis when the Kingston-based Commercial Bank of the Midland District ran into financial difficulty and asked the federal government for help. The government refused and instead brokered a deal with the Merchants' Bank of Montreal to assume the Commercial Bank's assets and liabilities. It also legislated to extend existing bank charters and to allow banks established in one province to operate across Canada.[66]

Most importantly, a comprehensive *Bank Act* was passed in 1870, which laid out what became a highly durable system of regulation.[67] Banks had to be incorporated federally by special acts of Parliament, and federally incorporated banks could operate branches in all parts of the country. They were allowed to use deposits made in one part of the country to finance loans in areas where capital was more in demand. Capital and reserve requirements, and rules regarding the internal affairs of banks, such as eligibility requirements for directors, were established. An annual audit and the filing of various forms with the government were also required. However, there was no review of these documents, approval by the banks' directors being sufficient. The government left banking to the bankers, but that approach contributed to occasional failures of small banks, such as when an Ontario bank founded in 1904 to provide credit in rural communities, the Farmers Bank, failed in 1910 and depositors lost approximately $1 million.[68]

The banks nonetheless generally did well under this system. In 1870 there were 34, and four years later the number had risen to 51. The numbers dropped thereafter, the result of amalgamations, discussed below. In 1900 there were 36, and by 1914 just 22. English Canadians, including the English Quebec elite, controlled much of the banking system, although a modest number of banks were operated by francophones. Many banks expanded across the country and internationally. The Bank of Nova Scotia, for example, had 98 branches in 1910–44 in the Maritimes, 34 in other parts of Canada, and 20 outside of Canada, mostly in the Caribbean, Mexico, and Central and South America.[69] There was also a modest system of public banks. Government savings banks had existed in New Brunswick and Nova Scotia before Confederation, and Ottawa took them over and renamed them Dominion Banks. They formed a public system along with Post Office savings banks, which allowed individuals to make small deposits. Private banks criticized the public banks because they drew away deposits, but the federal government was not persuaded by this simple appeal to anti-competitiveness by wealthy financiers, and retained them because they offered a way for the federal government to raise capital to fund the construction of infrastructure projects, including the CPR, encouraged saving by working families, and provided opportunities to make patronage appointments.

The legislation permitted amalgamations, leading to criticisms that Canada had an oligopolistic banking sector. The federal government had to approve bank mergers and acquisitions, but most were allowed. Revisions to the *Bank Act* in 1900 removed the necessity of parliamentary approval of them. Instead, all that was required was a proposal of purchase, the consent of two-thirds of shareholders of the selling bank, and the approval of the Treasury Board.[70] Bank mergers were part of the corporate consolidation movement of the late nineteenth and early twentieth centuries and probably helped ensure stability in the sector, as at-risk banks were sometimes merged with larger institutions that could accommodate bad loans. Canada's most influential bank, the Bank of Montreal, expanded its operations by acquiring the Exchange Bank of Yarmouth in 1903, the Peoples Bank of Halifax in 1905, the Ontario Bank in 1906, and the Peoples Bank of New Brunswick in 1907.[71] One result was to heighten regional disparity. The Maritime provinces lost control over access to capital when head offices of their banks moved to central Canada.

The federal legislation provided that all bank charters expired every 10 years, unless extended. As a result banks and the federal government undertook decennial reviews, following which regulations were updated. An example of such a reform was the 1880 decision to give the holders of banknotes the first charge on the bank's assets, putting them ahead of other creditors. Another was the creation in 1890 of a bank circulation redemption fund, a form of deposit insurance. Chartered banks paid into the fund, and if any bank had to suspend redemption of their notes or deposits, the fund would pay the redemptions. Opposition to this fund by some banks led to the creation of the Canadian Bankers Association (CBA) in 1891, to represent the interests of the banks to the federal government. It soon received a bigger role, being empowered to oversee the bank circulation redemption fund. In 1900 the CBA was incorporated and given the power to regulate a national bank clearinghouse, although the Treasury Board had to approve the regulations.[72]

This period also witnessed disputes over the currency, especially banknotes. The federal government began to issue its own coins in 1870, initially produced in Britain. Canada established a mint in 1908, which manufactured domestic coins in small denominations, British sovereigns, and coins for Newfoundland. Coins from other jurisdictions, however, often circulated and were accepted in Canada. These foreign coins were assigned a value by the federal government and were legal tender. Banknotes were another matter. Advocates of a central bank wanted it to have a monopoly over the issuing of notes, which many banks objected to. The compromise was that both the chartered banks and Dominion did so. Dominion notes were either small denominations because banks could not issue notes valued at less than $4, or very large denominations for banks to use, with values as high as $50,000. During the gold standard period from the mid-1850s to the beginning of the Great War, chartered bank notes and deposits were receivable for gold or Dominion notes, which were also receivable for gold, though only at government offices. Little gold circulated domestically, but the gold standard limited the ability of banks or the federal government to increase the money supply, and when the country had a negative balance of payments in its international trade, gold flowed out of the country, shrinking the money supply. The national government had limited means of controlling monetary policy, except by using tariffs to shape trade. As of 1914, the minister of finance had to keep at least 25 per cent of the outstanding value of notes in gold. This reserve requirement placed a limit on the amount of federal spending, unless Canada acquired additional gold reserves. Although the Bank of Canada was not created until the 1930s, there was therefore a system for regulating the money supply, albeit one driven by the financial interests of the major banks and by international trade.[73]

The legislation encouraged uniformity in the banking sector, but there were provincial differences. Some provinces had usury laws before Confederation, and the dominion continued those caps on interest by passing province-specific legislation. In addition 'near banks' regulated by the provinces emerged, including credit unions, especially in Quebec, as discussed in chapter 5. The first caisse populaire was organized in Lévis at the turn of the century, and Quebec passed legislation in 1906 to regulate such institutions, which, as co-operatives, were designed to provide savings and credit services to members. They were designed 'to study, protect and defend the economic interests of the labouring classes,' but did not become a feature of banking outside Quebec until the Great Depression of the 1930s.[74]

While Canadian banking was marked by relative stability, Newfoundland suffered a major banking crisis in 1894, leading to a Canadian takeover of much of the sector. In December 1894 the two private banks, the Commercial Bank and the Union Bank, closed suddenly, leaving only the government-run Savings Bank in operation. The crisis stemmed in part from questionable lending practices. In the 1880s an oversupply of saltfish on the international market resulted in merchants and fishers taking on more debt. Many of the merchants who borrowed money from the banks also sat on their boards. As the banks depleted their reserves, they borrowed heavily from the Savings Bank and London banks. The failure of the Newfoundland banks shook the small dominion's economy. Some businesses collapsed, families lost savings, and the failure undermined Newfoundland's currency. Canadian banks stepped in and began to operate on Newfoundland in late 1894, helping ease the financial crisis.[75]

The currency and banking laws passed immediately after Confederation had major long-term impacts on the financial sector, public trust in banking institutions, and availability of credit. Canada suffered some bank failures but few widespread panics. The national branch systems ensured that depositors had some protection, as large banks' viability was not tied to the economic health of a single community. Banking law was thus a key part of nation-building, laying the foundations for 'oligopoly, branch banking, and relative stability.'[76]

In 1871 mining in Canada contributed some $4.4 million to the gross national product, just 1 per cent of the total. By 1913 its contribution had risen nearly twentyfold, to nearly $81.9 million, over 3 per cent of GNP. Much of the growth in the sector had come about from the mid-1890s.[77] Government intervention in the mining industry came in the form of encouragement – legal and financial – and regulation. The industry can be broadly divided into coal and mineral mining, the latter including the precious metals, gold and silver, as well as others that were extremely remunerative, especially nickel. Different kinds of mining were significant in different provinces. The country's most populous provinces, Ontario and Quebec, had no coal mines; the coal-mining industry was concentrated in Nova Scotia and Alberta, with a lesser role being played by British Columbia. Gold and silver mining was an important part of the economies of Ontario and British Columbia, and the Yukon Territory after the gold discoveries of the Klondike in 1896, with a much smaller contribution coming from Nova Scotia. The most important non-precious metal mining was northern Ontario's nickel industry.[78] The different histories of mining in various provinces included distinct regulatory goals and patterns. We will deal here with two examples, coal in Nova Scotia and nickel in Ontario, chosen because both were highly important enterprises in their provinces and each presented provincial governments with very different regulatory challenges. In Nova Scotia the issue was miner safety, in Ontario it was government revenue, because the Province of Canada bequeathed to Ontario an industry that contributed nothing to the public purse.

Coal mining had long been an important part of the Nova Scotia economy, and in this period it became even more so as demand for it for railways, steam-driven industrial machinery, and steel making increased exponentially. In the early 1880s the mines in Pictou and Cumberland Counties and on Cape Breton Island produced 1.365 million tons annually, five times more than its nearest rival, British Columbia, and output doubled in the next decade and doubled again in the 1890s. By 1896 royalties paid by coal companies accounted for 32 per cent of provincial revenues. By that time there were diminishing numbers of companies, as Dominion Coal, owned by American entrepreneur Henry Melville Whitney, began consolidating the 30 or so companies operating in 1893 – a process that led to Dominion controlling 70 per cent of the province's output by 1914. At the end of our period some 30,000 men and boys were employed in the industry. Much labour conflict marked the history of the coal industry in Nova Scotia, discussed in the next chapter.

Legislation on the coal industry predated Confederation and continued in force until 1873. All mines, from coal to gold, were under the *Mines and Minerals Act*, by which authority a chief commissioner of mines and inspector of mines were appointed. Coal-mining companies worked on long-term leases and were required to compensate landowners for damage to the surface. Royalties of 10 cents were payable on every ton of coal extracted, and companies had to submit annual reports detailing the number of shafts and levels in their mines, the amount of coal extracted, the kinds of machinery used, and total output. Leases would be forfeited if they had been abandoned or, in the opinion of the commissioner, not effectively worked, although the commissioner's decision could be appealed to a court. The regulatory scheme was designed to encourage active production, to keep the government informed about all aspects of the industry, and to ensure that the public purse benefitted, not just private operators.[79] Absent from the act was anything about miners' safety, and absent from its administration was a properly trained and technically competent commissioner and inspector with power to enforce even its minimal requirements. This despite the ample evidence of dangerous conditions, which led to frequent fires, explosions, roof collapses, and floods, with substantial resultant injury and considerable loss of life. Part of the problem was that when deaths occurred, coroners' juries comprised non-miners, who did not understand the technical reasons why tragedies had occurred.[80]

In 1871 Henry Poole was appointed to the vacant post of inspector of mines. He was a highly qualified mining engineer with experience in underground management and with enough of a conscience to find the high levels of 'accidents' disturbing. He persuaded the government to act, and in the 1873 statutory consolidation the *Mines and Minerals Act* was retained largely unchanged, but a new statute was added, the *Mines Regulation Act*. The former was much as it had been before Confederation, although it required more frequent, quarterly, returns. The latter, based on 1872 British legislation, included some sections that had been in the previous *Mines and Minerals Act*, but added many more to do with mine safety and working conditions.[81] It limited child labour: no boy under 10 could work in a mine, boys over 10 were restricted to the kinds of machinery they could operate, and there were daily and weekly hours limits for boys under sixteen. As we will see in chapter 12, this was a decade and a half before other provinces legislated restrictions on child labour in workplaces generally. Many other safety rules were instituted, including a prohibition on operating single-shaft mines because there needed to be alternate means of egress, as well as ventilation standards, and the attorney general was authorized to seek injunctions from the Supreme Court to close mines that violated any of the rules. The inspector's powers were broadened to include the right to make new regulations not in the act. Other sections of the act made contraventions by owners and managers offences, and increased the amount and frequency of reporting on all aspects of a mine's construction, expansion, and operation.

Poole's regulatory zeal was, however, short-lived and founded on the wrong premises. He believed that the vast majority of 'accidents' were caused by worker ignorance or carelessness. Mine managers were competent and careful, and needed only to be obeyed. Hence the *Mines Regulation Act* also included provisions giving managers the right to propose additional rules for a particular mine that, if agreed to by the commissioner, had the force of law. In addition, managers could lay charges against miners, but the reverse was not provided for.

The 1873 legislation remained unchanged until 1881, when two developments that began in 1879 bore fruit. The first was that Poole left his post to become general manager of the Acadia Coal Company. He was replaced by Edward Gilpin, an innovative mining engineer who persuaded and cajoled mine owners and managers to adopt new techniques and equipment that increased both productivity and safety. More important in effecting legislative change was the establishment of what became a strong miners' union, the Provincial Workmen's Association. Through sustained and effective lobbying it made mine safety an issue legislators could not ignore. The *Mines Regulation Act* was amended to provide for additional inspectors, for two-man miners' committees at each mine to be able to carry out regular inspections, for compulsory licensing of underground overseers, and for more representative coroners' juries. Further reforms followed in 1884, 1885, and 1890, strengthening the certification process for underground mine officials. Following the Springhill disaster of 1891, in which 125 men and boys died in an underground fire, miners became able to initiate prosecutions for infractions of the act, and, most importantly, the use of gunpowder to blast coal from the coal face was banned for three months if gas had been detected for three days running.[82] None of these measures came close to eliminating the dangers of mining, but they did reduce them. Further legislation of the later 1890s and the early twentieth century saw continual tinkering with safety regulations, but no fundamental change. Coal mining was at root an inherently dangerous activity.

Ontario's mining legislation was much less about safety than the balance between the public and private interest in the benefits flowing from mineral exploitation.[83] Ontario inherited gold mining legislation of 1864 from the Province of Canada that did away with the traditional common law reservation to the Crown of mineral rights when Crown land was sold to private buyers. Instead the Act provided for the outright sale of gold-bearing land at $2 an acre. Soon after provincehood a new *Gold and Silver Mining Act* was passed, embodying the same terms for all minerals. It contained a royalty clause, but vigorous and vociferous objections from the mining lobby led to its repeal and replacement with a *General Mining Act* in 1869, with no royalty clause. Under it anybody could stake a claim on Crown land and survey it, register that claim with the Department of Crown Lands, and receive full rights to whatever was beneath surface, at $1 an acre. All public interest was subsumed in the need to develop the province's resources, especially given that all its mineral resources were in the underpopulated north.[84] Over the ensuing 30 years mining operators, the majority American, took $33 million worth of gold, silver, and nickel from the Canadian Shield without contributing anything to the public purse.

Silver mining was the mainstay of the Ontario mining industry for two decades after Confederation and remained important thereafter. In the early twentieth century, gold and silver mining expanded exponentially after the discovery of the world's richest silver deposits at Cobalt and gold finds at Kirkland Lake and Porcupine. But the largest mining sector from the 1880s was nickel, a huge deposit being discovered in 1883 on the CPR right of way near Sudbury. American companies were again the principal players. Nickel mining was immensely successful, primarily because it was central to the production of an alloy that was widely used for armour-plating and for armour-piercing shells in a period of technological development in munitions. But by the mid- to late 1880s the Oliver Mowat–led provincial government became concerned about the lack of benefit to the public weal from the burgeoning mining industry and established a royal commission on mineral resources. Its report advocated the status quo; government's role should be simply in education and promotion, not regulation or revenue raising. It recommended the establishment of a Bureau of Mines to collect and publish data, and to advertise to investors. But there should be no safety regulations and no changes to the legal structure of the industry – freehold sales without mineral reservations should continue, and royalties should not be charged.

The commissioners were out of step with public opinion and the government. Mowat's government effectively ignored the commission's principal recommendations and in 1891 changed both legal pillars of the industry. Henceforth royalties of 3 per cent were to be charged on nickel, copper, and silver, and Crown lands could be leased for 10-year terms rather than sold, which meant that mineral rights stayed with the Crown. The latter provision was not retroactive and thus made little difference to the nickel industry, which had already bought very large acreages. Protests from both companies and the miners made passing the legislation difficult and was responsible for weakening both principal provisions. Although leases were to be the norm, it was possible for lessees to buy the land in fee simple after a period of time. More importantly, 'to assure speedy development' of mining, royalties were not to be collected for seven years after a patent or lease had been issued. An exception to this last provision was made for 'mines known to be rich in nickel,' for which the delay was only for four years. The Act also established a Bureau of Mines, headed by a director of mines, 'to aid in promoting the mining interests in the Province.'[85]

The Mowat government's reformist impulse also caused it to pass the first safety regulations for mines. Like the early factory acts discussed in chapter 12, the act principally concerned child labour. No girls or women could work in a mine, and no boy under 15 could work underground. Boys between 15 and 17 could be underground for only eight hours a day, 48 hours a week, and young men under 20 were barred from certain tasks. Mine owners had to report death or injury, close up or fence off abandoned shafts, provide adequate ventilation, and follow guidelines on the storage of explosives. The safety regulations in the 25-section act were not nearly as extensive as those for Nova Scotia coal mines, and nobody could prosecute an owner or a manger for infractions other than the newly created inspector of mines or a county attorney. Tellingly, the list of rules in the Act were to be followed 'as far as may be reasonably practicable,' a very significant limitation. In 1892 the *Mines Regulation Act* and the *General Mining Act* were consolidated in a new *Mines Act*.[86]

Mowat's royalty policy lasted less than a decade. When George William Ross became premier in 1899 he made development of the north a priority, commissioning an extensive survey of the region and promoting immigration and settlement, including establishing a Bureau of Colonization. With the province in good financial shape he also gave subsidies for railway construction. As part of his policy of northern development his government abolished all royalties on minerals and rescinded reservations in future land sales. Mining law and policy in Ontario put a priority on attracting investment and developing the region, with public interest considerations playing a minor and short-lived role.[87]

We conclude this section on regulation with railways. Regulations governing the construction and operation of railways, and fixing rates, had been passed in all colonies since the mid-nineteenth century, and after 1867 this colonial legislation stayed in force and was frequently augmented. As in other areas, the Province of Canada legislation became that of the dominion in 1867 and effectively remained so after the federal Parliament passed a *Railway Act* in 1868 because it was largely identical to the pre-Confederation act.[88] The federal and the Ontario acts dealt with the incorporation of railway companies, and with topics as varied as the expropriation of land, how much fencing was necessary, and the size and grade of bridges. Although railways could set their own rates, they had to be approved by the respective governments. The acts also included a series of safety regulations dealing with, inter alia, the carrying of dangerous goods and warning devices. All the rules were to be enforced by inspectors. The administration of both *Railway Acts* was overseen by railway committees of the respective cabinets until the early twentieth century.[89] Although the legislative schemes were essentially the same, the federal legislation and the committee of the federal cabinet were more important because they dealt with the most significant railroads of the period – those that operated across provincial borders. This included the railway system that was a crucial cog of Macdonald's National Policy, transporting the produce of western Canada east and the manufactured goods of eastern Canada west. We will therefore devote our discussion to the federal regime.[90]

Disputes between railways, and between railways and government officials, were common and became increasingly so from the early 1880s and the ever-growing expansion of western populations and railway mileage. Disputes arose out of conflicts between cities and provinces, between manufacturers and farmers, and between those who shipped and those who consumed the products of both. They were very often about freight rates[91] and they were taken to either the railway committee or the common law courts, the latter dealing with them by interpreting the terms of a corporation's charter against common law tests of reasonableness and non-discrimination. These were uncertain terms, and non-discrimination was difficult to establish, giving the railways an advantage in court, along with the ability of all well-heeled litigants to prolong litigation and drive up the cost. As a result there was increasing criticism of the power of the railways, particularly in western Canada, and of the railway committee and the courts. In 1897 *Globe* editor and devoted Laurier supporter John Stephen Willison asserted that 'in regulating rates, in preventing discriminations, in protecting the individual shipper, or the individual community against the calculated injustice or the insidious aggression of railway managers, [the railway committee] … is inert and impotent, a farce and a failure.' He also noted 'the strong feeling of antagonism to the Canadian Pacific Railway which finds voice in Western Canada.'[92]

In short order Laurier's new government embarked on a rethinking of its approach to railway regulation. The idea of an independent tribunal had been in play for over a decade, and increasingly informed opinion favoured such a move, often citing the example of the American Interstate Commerce Commission founded in 1887.[93] In 1898 Laurier appointed a young academic, Simon J. MacLean, to look into railway regulations and rates. He produced two reports, in 1899 and 1902, the second of which was more comprehensive and proposed a new system, which the government adopted. He argued that regulation was necessary, but also that the cabinet committee system did not work well precisely because it combined political and administrative roles. Although he did not define the difference between the two with great precision, he was clear that proper regulation of railways was an 'administrative' task and that it required attributes that politicians could not be guaranteed to have – experience, technical knowledge, and independence, the last protected by security of tenure. Hence the *Railway Act* of 1903 provided for 10-year renewable appointments to the BRC with removal only for cause.[94]

McLean went further, wanting the superior courts to have no role in reviewing a commission, because while a commission needed to be non-political, it did need to concern itself with policy, and courts were largely 'oblivious' to policy. On this point, however, the common law ideology that the rule of law always required some recourse to the courts prevailed, and section 44 of the act provided a right of appeal on questions of law and jurisdiction to the SCC, although in the former case an appeal was available only if the board itself agreed that the issue was a question of law and gave leave to appeal, and in the latter the SCC had to grant leave. The board itself could refer an issue to the SCC through a stated case, and there was also a provision for review of its decisions by the cabinet. In sum, 'the result was a distinctive institution which combined the "independent" regulatory agency and ultimate direct political control.' In subsequent decades many other agencies were created, and although there were differences in form, this was the 'dominant model.' Three years later Ontario copied the federal example, passing an almost identical act establishing the Ontario Railway and Municipal Board.[95]

The BRC dealt with all aspects of railway regulation, but its most important function was fixing rates to be charged for carrying passengers and, principally, freight, an area of decision-making in which it had almost unlimited power. It was greeted with approval by the legal community, largely because it was court-like in structure and personnel, although the *Canada Law Journal*, for one, recognized its dual nature: it would 'have to stand between … gigantic and influential [railway] companies and the public, and will see the necessity of protecting the latter and the individuals therein, from the greed and overbearance too often characteristic of rich and powerful corporations.'[96]

The composition of the BRC was a matter of contention. McLean advocated the American model of one person from the railway sector, one businessman, and one lawyer, but the act simply said three persons appointed by the governor general. The first chief commissioner was Andrew Blair, lawyer, long-serving premier of New Brunswick, and minister of railways and canals in Laurier's government after he made the switch to federal politics. There was much lobbying over who else should be appointed, and from which sector he should come, and probably for this reason the board was later expanded to six to accommodate different interests. James Mills, formerly principal of the Ontario School of Agriculture and Experimental Farm, was appointed in 1904 to represent the farmer interest, and he stayed until 1914. There were continual demands, to some extent successful, for a strong representation from the West. Opinion was invariably divided but rarely tepidly expressed on how much legal expertise there should be. The most prominent lawyer was Albert Clements Killam, put on the SCC in 1903 but very unusually staying there only briefly before being named chief commissioner, replacing Blair, in 1905. His appointment caused a hotly contested change to the chief commissioners' status and emoluments. Henceforth any judge appointed chief commissioner kept the tenure and pension provisions of his judgeship.[97]

The BRC was designated as a court of record and its decisions were published in a dedicated reporter, the *Canadian Railway Cases*. The appeal to the SCC brought another area of judicial review to that court, beyond determining the boundaries of sections 91 and 92 of the *BNA Act*. Before the First World War the SCC heard very few cases from the BRC, and in those that were heard it displayed no great hostility to regulation as such. When cases did come before it, the SCC observed the limits of judicial review, interpreting the governing statute to determine the board's powers and avoiding second-guessing policy decisions. In *Ingersoll Telephone Company v Bell Telephone Company*, for example, a 1916 case, it dismissed an appeal by a local phone company of a board decision on the rates to be paid for the use of Bell's long distance lines. The court did not consider whether the rate was the correct one but was satisfied that 'it was the purpose of Parliament to entrust to the Board the widest discretion, not merely as to the amount of the compensation,… but also as to the elements which should be taken into account in fixing it.'[98]

In taking this approach the SCC was very much in line with the provincial superior courts when they exercised review of provincial agencies. This perhaps surprising level of deference resulted in part from the ideology of the courts as neutral bodies administering a neutral common law. But it also resulted, it has been suggested, from the same

lack of hostility to state intervention in the economy that was manifest in other realms of public life and distinguished Canadian courts
from those in the United States and the United Kingdom. In addition,
and this is a derivative point, it has similarly been argued that business
interests were not averse to state intervention in and regulation of the
economy. One would expect elite judges to generally embrace, if they
did not articulate, the values of elite businessmen. If business saw regulation as sometimes being for their benefit – a notable example, workers compensation, is discussed in chapter 12 – then it is not surprising
that the courts were not hostile to regulation in general.[99] Nor were the
politicians. The appeal to the cabinet was rarely invoked, principally
because, it was widely believed, that would defeat the purpose of an
independent agency. It was also useful to politicians to have some body
to which to delegate these very contentious issues so they were not
being constantly lobbied by those with an interest.

12

Labour and Employment Law

The law relating to employment covered both individual employment (hereafter employment law or master and servant law) and collective employment (hereafter labour law). While substantial numbers of people worked alone or with only family members in the agricultural sector, not employed by another person, most people worked for somebody else. They worked as construction labourers, on production lines in factories, as domestic servants, clerks in offices, sailors, and many other occupations in a host of areas of the economy. Before Confederation almost all work was legally regulated by the law of master and servant, or what we would now call the common law of employment, and master and servant law continued to play a very significant role after 1867. We discuss it in the first section of this chapter.

A variety of developments in the half-century after Confederation reshaped the legal relations between employers and employees. The second and third sections of this chapter examine the law on collective action by workers, what we now call labour law. Whether trade unions and the ends they pursued were legal in the pre- and immediately post-Confederation period was unclear, but federal legislation in the early 1870s resolved that issue in unions' favour. Legislation of the early 1870s was federal because its substance was criminal law, but generally provincial governments had jurisdiction in labour and employment law, although the matter was not litigated until after the end of our period. But legalization of collective action did not make it desirable or acceptable to many in society, and in succeeding decades provincial law impaired the effectiveness of collective action. It did so when judges used the common law to undermine the effectiveness of workers' collective action through injunctions. Employers were able to invoke common law rules to obtain injunctions against actions taken by unions because no province established a legal framework that required employers to recognize the people chosen by workers to negotiate on their behalf as legitimate representatives who had to be bargained with in good faith. The law treated workers and employers as juridical equals, not compensating for the fact that their unequal economic power made workers very much not the equals of employers. Even hours of work were unregulated except in British Columbia, where an eight-hour day was legislated in some mining sectors in the early twentieth century.[1] In the late nineteenth and early twentieth centuries both federal and provincial governments did legislate in relation to workplace disputes, making some of them subject to arbitration and conciliation. But what is usually termed industrial legality, the modern, largely post-1945 system regulating workplace conflict, was not a feature of this period.

The fourth and fifth sections of this chapter examine other aspects of the law governing the employment relationship – the safety of the workplace and compensation for injuries suffered at work. In these areas there was a greater degree of state intervention than in workplace conflict. Safety regulations benefitted all workers, but they protected women and children more and were motivated in part by a concern to maintain and strengthen the family unit. Legislation on compensation for injuries was likewise motivated by a desire to mitigate the damage done by dangerous employment conditions and a concomitant wish to reduce the costs to employers once they began to lose cases in court.

Employment Law: Master and Servant

As detailed in *Volume 1*, except in Quebec, at Confederation master and servant law was a mixture of common law and statute.[2] The former saw the employment relationship as contractual. It defined the principal duties of employee and employer to respectively provide faithful and obedient service and to pay wages. The common law remedy for both parties was a civil suit seeking damages; it would not order an employment contract to be specifically performed. Colonial legislation did not much alter the substantive law. It provided a summary action before a JP for either party, avoiding the costs and delays of an action in provincial superior courts. It also provided remedies beyond damages. Employees could obtain a discharge from their contractual obligations, while employers could prosecute workers for refusal to work, making a criminal offence punishable by fine or imprisonment. These criminal sanctions had been repealed in Nova Scotia and New Brunswick before Confederation for most workers and were applicable only to apprentices and merchant seamen.[3] But in 1867 they still applied in Ontario, parts of Quebec, Prince Edward Island, and British Columbia, the last by virtue of continuing colonial legislation. Criminal sanctions were also made applicable to Manitoba and the Territories in the 1870s.[4] By this indirect route specific performance of employment contracts was available to employers; in practice the criminal sanctions were rarely used, for JPs invariably gave workers the option of returning to work.

In 1877 federal legislation effected a sea change in some provinces. The *Breaches of Contract Act* of that year enunciated two broad principles.[5] First, that breaches of contract, 'whether of service or otherwise, are in general civil wrongs only, and not criminal in nature,' and should therefore be treated 'like other breaches of contract, as civil wrongs.' Another section retained criminal sanctions, a fine of up to $100 or imprisonment of up to three months, for any person who, inter alia, 'wilfully and maliciously breaks any contract' knowing that doing so would 'endanger human life' or 'cause serious bodily injury' or 'expose valuable property ... to destruction or serious injury.' The same section also itemized particular actions that were to be criminal breaches of employment contracts – provisions derived from an 1850s Province of Canada statute passed specifically for railway companies. These latter provisions were not repealed until 1914. Otherwise the Act repealed the Ontario and PEI pre-Confederation legislation. The federal government brought it in in part because of the lobbying of the emergent trade union movement (about which more below), to which Prime Minister Mackenzie succumbed because he was under attack for his alleged mishandling of a strike by Grand Trunk Railway employees. The Ontario *Master and Servant Act* had been used by employers in this and other strikes, with strike leaders being taken to court, and in some cases imprisoned, for refusing to work.[6]

The act left the law in a confused state, because it did not repeal the Manitoba, British Columbia, or Territorial legislation making employee breaches criminal. Imprisonment for employee breaches was abolished in Manitoba in 1883, reinstated in 1891, and was still the law at the end of this period.[7] After 1905 the Territorial law became the law in

Alberta and Saskatchewan. In Quebec the law varied, depending on time and location. The *Breaches of Contract Act* repealed the pre-Confederation Lower Canadian statute for many areas, but it did not repeal the Montreal municipal by-laws dealing with masters and servants, which stayed in force until the 1930s and prescribed criminal penalties for breaches by employees. In addition in 1881 Quebec passed a new master and servant act for rural areas, which imposed fines on both employees and employers, the former for mistreating employees and non-payment of wages, the latter for 'ill-behaviour, refractory conduct, or idleness, or ... deserting from his service or duties, or absenting himself ... from his ... service' and other faults. In 1894 new legislation made a fine of $20 the standard penalty for all master and servant breaches in the province, 'all by-laws to the contrary notwithstanding.' But this had no effect on by-law application, and when Montreal's City Charter was consolidated in 1899 the city's authority to regulate servants and to enforce its regulations with fines and imprisonment was confirmed.[8] All of this was a result of the boundaries between sections 91 and 92 jurisdiction being unclear on some issues in the half-century after Confederation, as discussed in chapter 2.

Suits were brought under the various master and servant acts and city by-laws in lower courts, for which in most jurisdictions records have not survived consistently.[9] But limited research shows that the legislation was used mostly by workers for the recovery of unpaid wages. In Winnipeg, for example, in 11 months spanning 1909 and 1910 the police court heard 138 master and servant cases, all but four of them for unpaid wages. In Belleville, Ontario, between 1874 and 1877 the police court heard just 76 master and servant cases, 87 per cent brought against employers for wages and the rest, fewer than 10, against employees for desertion or disobedience. There were very few master and servant cases brought to the British Columbia courts for or against white workers, and in those that were, almost all involved wage recovery suits instituted by merchant seamen. But in the 1870s cannery owners in New Westminster used the provincial law to compel Indigenous people on the Fraser River to keep working, with courts obliging by handing down prison sentences. In Montreal employers took workers to the Recorder's Court in 'significant numbers,' although the rate of conviction fluctuated with the differing attitudes of recorders about whether breaches of employment contracts should indeed be treated as civil wrongs only. In Ontario the pre-Confederation *Master and Servant Act* continued to be employed until 1877, but convictions of employees for desertion and similar offences were very rare – fewer than 1 per cent of all summary prosecutions across a range of counties. Imprisonment was used sparingly, even when a conviction was achieved. Cases were commonly settled by a promise to return to work. This was also the usual practice in the Territories in the 1880s. Fifty workers were taken to court for infractions, most of them for desertion, but only two were ordered to be imprisoned without the option of a fine. The vast majority of cases were dismissed upon the employee agreeing to return to work. On the whole the penal provisions in master and servant legislation were more symbolic and ideological than an effective regulator of the labour market. The 'occasional and exemplary prosecution' was a telling reminder of unequal class relations, expressed by 'an employment regime that could curtail liberty for insubordination, ... lend legitimacy to employer authority,' and implicitly 'sanction employer self-help.'

Labour Law: Trade Unions and Workplace Dispute Resolution

The first trade unions in what is now Canada were formed in the early nineteenth century and operated as craft guilds more than modern trade unions. Workers, those in unions and those not, occasionally went on strike before 1850, and increasingly thereafter as workplaces grew larger and more impersonal.[10] There is an extensive but inconclusive debate in the historical literature about whether unions were illegal at common law as criminal conspiracies to restrain trade.[11] Because the answer to that question was as unclear to contemporaries as it is to historians, at Confederation unions occupied an 'indefinite area of toleration,' considered by some to be illegal but widely permitted to operate, indeed often enjoying co-operative relationships with employers. When such relationships broke down, employers could use the master and servant legislation; a striking worker breached his contract.[12] But generally employers accepted that unions were here to stay, an inevitable aspect of industrialization and larger workforces. The *Upper Canada Law Journal* made this point in 1867, arguing that 'as capital is generally represented by the few who are powerful, and labour by the many who are without the power of wealth, co-operation, or combination on the part of the latter, has been found necessary.'[13]

Three other considerations affected the debate over the legality of trade unions in the 1860s and 1870s. First, many politicians believed that legal repression would be a disincentive to the immigration of skilled labour immigration from Britain. Second, invoking the law was an uncertain strategy because a suit for criminal conspiracy required a jury – 12 men of backgrounds somewhat similar to those charged. Third, the 1860s saw the increasing use of associations of employers to try to control wage costs, making it difficult to insist that workers' combinations alone were criminal conspiracies. One employer prepared to use the law of criminal conspiracy was George Brown, publisher of the Toronto *Globe*, against printers who went on strike to raise wages in April 1872. Armed with a published legal opinion from Robert Harrison, a leading Toronto lawyer, Conservative MP for Toronto West and future chief justice of Queen's Bench, Brown had the printers charged with criminal conspiracy. The information laid against the printers not only charged them with conspiring to shorten working hours, it also laid nine other charges of using threats, intimidation, and molestation, and of inducement to breach employment contracts. It thus attacked not only the purpose of the strike but also the means allegedly used to achieve that purpose. This secondary legal assault was based on the common law and on English statutes copied in many Canadian colonies, often liberally interpreted by judges, criminalizing such activities.

Brown's actions precipitated a heated public and parliamentary debate, and the printers' strike became a short-lived cause célèbre. In June Parliament passed two statutes, the *Trades Union Act* and the *Criminal Law Amendment Act* [*CLAA*]. Section 2 of the former provided that 'the purposes of any trade union shall not, by reason merely that they are in restraint of trade, be deemed to be unlawful, so as to render any member of such trade union liable to criminal prosecution for conspiracy or otherwise.' Other provisions made agreements among union members for things like paying subscriptions unenforceable in court but not unlawful, and provided for the first registry of trade unions. But the statute said nothing about the means used to effect a union's purposes. Moreover, the *CLAA* undermined the *Trades Union Act* by creating offences that applied only to the means used when a union became involved in a dispute. Section 1 made it a summary conviction offence, punishable by a maximum of three months' imprisonment, to use violence against persons or property, or to threaten, intimidate, molest, or obstruct any person with the object of, inter alia, coercing a person to quit a job or not to return to work. It also provided very broad definitions of 'molest or obstruct,' including persistently following a person about, hiding tools and clothes, and 'watching and besetting' a residence. Because these statutes were an exercise of the federal criminal law power, they were constitutionally valid and national in effect.

These Acts were modelled on British legislation of 1871, and Macdonald's stated reason for introducing them was to harmonize Canadian and British law and thus not discourage the immigration of skilled workers. He also saw electoral advantage from pro-labour legislation. Although the Liberals did not oppose the bills, anti-union sentiment was inevitably attributed to the party because Brown, the long-time most prominent Ontario reformer/Liberal, was at the centre of events. But while Macdonald may have received kudos for the *Trade Union Act*, workers' organizations criticized the *CLAA*. They labelled it 'unnecessarily harsh and oppressive,' a tool that could be easily used by employers to repress union activities. It also gave them the 'legal image' of associations 'prone to criminal behaviour.' Labour groups' repeal campaign gathered momentum after 1874 and the accession of a Liberal government keen to secure working-class votes. In 1876 Justice Minister Edward Blake put through Parliament an amending statute that removed the language of employer and employee and simply referred to things done 'to compel any other person to abstain from doing anything which he had a legal right to do, or to do anything from which he had a legal right to abstain.' It also removed picketing for the purpose of providing information from what constituted 'watching and besetting,' and limited the meaning of intimidation to threats of using violence against persons or property. Labour preferred complete repeal, but it got a lot of what it wanted. In fact the act had rarely been used in the intervening four years, even during strikes, and it was similarly little employed after 1876.[14]

In less than a decade after Confederation much had changed in the laws governing labour and capital. The combined effect of the *Breaches of Contracts Act*, the *Trade Unions Act*, and the *CLAA* of 1876 had much reduced the availability of the criminal law to discipline workers. In part this was testament to the growing strength of the labour interest, and in part it was a triumph for liberalism, for the principle that individuals should be treated equally. Robert Harrison, George Brown's erstwhile lawyer, was chief justice of Queen's Bench in 1877, and in charging the grand jury at Hamilton, in the midst of a strike by workers on the Grand Trunk Railway, he sounded a clarion call for liberal values: 'There would always be fights between capital and labour,' he stated, and that was 'much to be deplored.' But the fact was that 'no man in this country is a slave ... [n]o man need work at a lower rate than he has bargained for, ... [and a] man has a perfect right to strike if he chooses.' On the other hand, 'every man is bound to fulfil the contract he has entered into,' and 'no man should interfere with another who chooses to do so.'[15]

For labour advocates the problem with the legal developments of the 1870s, and the liberalism that underpinned them, was what they did not achieve. They legalized trade unions, but they did not confer a right to join a union. They softened the criminal law governing union activities, but they did not impose a duty on employers to bargain with unions and to not engage in what we now call unfair labour practices, including dismissal of strikers and the hiring of replacement workers. Labour relations in the last quarter of the nineteenth century and the early years of the twentieth were marked by a form of industrial legality that has been described as 'liberal voluntarism.' The dominant feature of labour law was still 'the individual contract of employment operating within a system that left most terms and conditions to be determined according to the labour market.'[16] The state, the federal government, and the provinces did not establish regimes delineating and protecting the rights and obligations of employers and employees until sometime after the end of our period. The state did intervene in the areas of health and safety and workers' compensation, the subjects of the next two sections of this chapter, but was less active in labour conflicts over terms and conditions of work. When it did intervene, through the agencies of law enforcement and the courts, it was often on the side of employers. The one glaring exception was the British Columbia government's willingness to pass legislation to discriminate against Asian workers and thus protect the white working man from competition. This major departure from liberal individualism will be discussed at length in chapter 16. Operators often flouted this prohibition, hiring Chinese labour, much to the annoyance of white workers. James Dunsmuir, the largest mine owner, challenged the restrictions on division of powers grounds, and the JCPC struck down the legislation. The decision allowed Dunsmuir to continue employing Chinese at low wages, and he attempted to deduct pay from each of his Chinese mine employees to cover the cost of the case.[17]

The rest of this section analyses ways in which employers were able to use the courts and law enforcement to their advantage and also examines some limited, tentative, and largely ineffective state interventions in industrial conflict in the form of conciliation and arbitration schemes. This account of the legal history of workplace disputes after about 1880 must be set against a background of the major non-legal developments of the same period. In the ensuing three decades, workers' organizations, especially unions, grew substantially and workplace conflicts, most notably strikes, became a regular feature of the landscape. As noted in chapter 11, the period from the mid-1890s is dubbed Canada's second industrial revolution by economic historians, and increased production and industrial employment brought with them a substantial upsurge in conflicts as workers sought to improve working conditions and pay. Between 1891 and 1910 alone there were over 2,000 strikes involving over 300,000 workers, and in the ensuing decade those numbers grew to over 2,300 and 521,000 respectively.[18] These workplace disruptions affected almost all sectors of the economy, from steel and textile mills to mines and railway construction, and all regions of the country. Unions struck not only for better wages and working conditions, but also to enforce the closed shop. When they did so they employed the full arsenal of tactics, especially picketing designed to discourage the use of replacement workers but also consumer and trades boycotts against buying the struck employers' products and supplying the same with the materials needed to make those products. Employers, individually and collectively through bodies like the Canadian Manufacturers' Association (CMA) and local boards of trade, responded with their own measures, especially the use of replacement workers. Employers also made full use of the law enforcement resources available to them, inducing local authorities to deploy the police whenever an argument could be made that disorder had followed or would follow a strike. They also routinely hired private security and detective agencies to protect their private property rights and infiltrate and disrupt union organization.

Less often, but generally with telling effect, employers were able to invoke state military force 'in aid of the civil power.' The American owner of the London Street Railway did so in 1899 to combat strikes by members of the Amalgamated Association of Street Railway Employees in London and Cleveland, Ohio. In both places the community supported the strikes, boycotting the streetcars for months, and, in Cleveland particularly, resorting to violence against the company's property and intimidation of scab drivers. In both places the police were ineffective and the mayors called in the military, and both strikes collapsed. The owner suffered steep losses during the strike year but more than made up for them. Thus the state was willing at times to protect property and freedom of contract by using coercion. 'Soldiers, not police or judges' decided the issue.[19]

The principal legal issue in all this workplace conflict was the validity of the means used by strikers, in particular picketing, to make strikes effective. The provisions of the *CLAA* stayed in force until the enactment of the 1892 *Criminal Code,* which amended the law in one very significant respect: the exclusion of peaceful picketing from the 'watching and besetting' clause was dropped.[20] This enabled employers to obtain injunctions, discussed in more detail below, from pliant judges who were prepared to depict peaceful picketing as a common law nuisance, which they would not have been able to do had the exemption for communicating information been retained. In one case Justice Thomas Mathers of the Manitoba Court of Queen's Bench enjoined picketing that was neither violent nor intimidatory, setting an almost impossible standard to make it permissible: 'The persuasion, to be legal, must be such as to leave it to the absolutely free and untrammeled will of the workman as to whether or not' he would join the strike. Mathers further held that this test was not met in the case because of the 'coercive machinery and power' of a union over its members. Mathers represents an important feature of the legal battles of this period – what the union movement at the time, and many labour historians since, have seen as the anti-unionism of most judges, from police court magistrates to judges of appeal. Mathers was in fact not especially ideologically predisposed to prefer capital over labour compared to some of his contemporaries, but he did chair two commissions of inquiry into labour disputes in Manitoba before the First World War and criticized unions in both reports. He was also firmly committed to liberal values of free will and freedom of contract, as the quotation makes clear, and equally opposed to unions' belief that the collective pointed the way towards social and economic progress. Collectivism was by definition, and using his own word, 'coercive.'[21]

Employers frequently used the law to undermine picketing: the civil law and, after the exemption for informational picketing was left out of the *Criminal Code*, the criminal law. Picketers were charged with watching and besetting on a number of high-profile occasions and convicted, and the criminal activity was then used to support the imposition of an injunction. Magistrate George Denison of the Toronto Police Court, a Conservative martinet who intensely disliked unions, convicted workers on various occasions of criminal watching and besetting for following and name-calling replacement workers. Some had used the word 'scab,' and that was enough to constitute intimidation in his court. An aspect of this use of both civil and criminal law that irked the labour movement was that not infrequently the same lawyer acted as Crown prosecutor in a criminal case and the employer's lawyer in an injunction application based on the same facts. This clearly undermined the idea that the Crown prosecutor's role was to act as a 'minister of justice,' to lay the facts and the law before the court in an even-handed way, not to be an aggressive seeker of convictions. Because criminal cases brought against picketers were heard in magistrates' courts, without juries, and often if not invariably by judges like Denison who were notoriously anti-labour, many in the labour movement came to see the legal system as inherently stacked against them. The Canadian Trades and Labour Congress (TLC) lobbied without success to have the watching and besetting provision removed from the Code; they were able, in 1905, to achieve a lesser object, an amendment to allow those charged with such offences to elect trial by jury.[22]

The criminal law was useful to employers, but less important than the civil law. In the late nineteenth century the English courts invented new economic torts to aid employers in strikes, principally the tort of interfering with contractual relations, both existing contracts and contemplated new ones.[23] Canadian judges adopted these without demur. Civil litigation by employers based on these torts did not need to be ultimately successful, because interlocutory (interim) injunctions to prevent picketing, no matter how peaceful, were frequently granted pending a decision on the merits. The procedure was that when a prima facie case of illegality was made out, and harm to the applicant for the injunction was shown to be possible, an interlocutory injunction could be obtained to temporarily halt the activity pending a full trial on the issues. Applications for such injunctions could be brought ex parte (without the other side present in court). The legal test revolved upon whether the 'balance of convenience' favoured the temporary measure. Such a test worked well enough for both parties in commercial disputes and the like, but in labour disputes broadly worded injunctions meant that the effectiveness of the strike could be rapidly and radically reduced, and striking workers forced to settle.

Employers obtained at least 19 such injunctions between 1900 and 1914; they included the Massey-Harris Company in Ontario, the Grand Trunk Railway, and Dominion Coal in Glace Bay, Nova Scotia.[24] Most enjoined picketing, and some also prohibited calls for consumer boycotts and other sympathy action by non-striking workers. In a 1902 strike against a foundry in Toronto, even a labour newspaper that promoted the boycott was enjoined. Most of the injunctions were obtained against craft unions representing skilled trades, who in this period fought an often losing battle to maintain the closed shop. When they went on strike to defend their position an injunction against any picketing made it practically impossible for them to persuade replacement workers not to enter the workplace.

A related tactic used by employers was a civil action against the union and/or its officers for damages caused by the strike and picketing. These actions took place in a legal grey zone, uncertainty about whether unions could be sued at all. Unions were not legal persons but unincorporated associations. Some judges nonetheless found them liable, others found the union's officers liable, with the result that employers had a potent weapon to not only defeat a particular strike but also to extract substantial damages awards and thereby break the union. A notable example was an early twentieth-century miners' strike in the Kootenay region of British Columbia that pitted mining companies against the Western Federation of Miners. The companies brought in replacement workers, and the union picketed the railway station to try to persuade them not to break the strike. One company was successful in enjoining this, and the strike failed. The company and other employers went further, suing the union for damages and winning a very substantial award of $12,500. The union was forced into receivership as a result. Ultimately the labour movement, which was a powerful force in provincial politics, prevailed on this issue and had legislation enacted in 1902 to prevent unions and their leaders from being sued for damages unless the union authorized a 'wrongful act.'[25] Section 2 of the Act provided that trade unions were not subject to injunctions or liable for communicating facts or persuading by fair or reasonable argument. Section 3 offered immunity for publishing information about a strike or urging people not to purchase or consume the employer's products. Other provinces did not follow the lead of British Columbia, and after our period the BC Court of Appeal interpreted them narrowly and upheld restrictions on picketing.[26]

Many of the court battles involved not only union liability but also the related issue of whether picketing and/or the encouragement of secondary supporting boycotts were tortious. Illustrative of the intertwining of these legal issues was an Ontario case that went up and down the provincial court system and eventually all the way to the JCPC, *Metallic Roofing Company v Amalgamated Sheet Metal Workers International, Local Union No. 30.*[27] When the union went on strike in 1902 to try to get a closed shop agreement the company filed suit against the international union, the local, and officers of the local union, who were named as defendants in their own right and as representatives of the union defendants. The company quickly obtained an interlocutory injunction to stop the union advocating a boycott of the company's products and from picketing, and partly as a result the strike was quickly settled. But the company, with the financial support of the CMA, wanted to pursue litigation to make the union legally and thus financially liable for the actions of its members. The CMA had already started lobbying for legislation to make unions corporations, which would have made it possible to sue them, but was also prepared to go ahead now.

In the words of Justice Osler of the Ontario Court of Appeal, the suit was a tort action for 'conspiring to injure the plaintiffs in their business by calling out their workmen on strike.' The union filed motions arguing that it could not be sued, lost on some points and won on others, both sides appealed, and the proceedings continued through 1903 and 1904, with the Court of Appeal ruling on the case in early 1905. Osler's judgment held that neither the parent nor the local union were corporations or 'quasi-corporate' bodies, they were 'simply voluntary associations united for the purposes of promoting the interest of the members in relation to their employment.' The legal status of the members 'is more like that of the members of an incorporated club than anything else.' Thus a union could not be sued in its own name, and it could also not be sued by serving one of its members, 'no matter how exalted the position or high-sounding the title he bears.' However, Osler J.A. went on to hold that the company could take a representative action under the civil procedure rules; all the union members could be joined as individuals by suing one of them as a representative defendant. He followed recent English cases in finding the particular rule applicable to tort actions and to trade unions, both because the authority was English and because 'it would be a most deplorable result if a plaintiff should be found to be practically without remedy in a case of this kind.'

With these issues resolved, the case went to trial in the High Court in October 1905 before a special jury, a body of better-off citizens than sat on regular juries. Having been told by trial judge Hugh McMahon that the employees had been 'coerced' into going on strike by the union, by majority verdicts the jury found that the union had 'wrongfully and maliciously coerced' the employees to stop work, and that it had used 'threats and intimidation' to induce the company's customers not to buy the company's goods. The threats and intimidation consisted of letters to those customers, most of whom employed union men, informing them that those men would not handle Metallica's goods. Ten of the twelve jurors assessed the damages at $7,500. The union appealed to the Divisional Court, arguing that there had been no compulsion by the union and that the letters to the company's customers were 'a mere warning that the [company was] … unfair to organized labour.' Chancellor John Alexander Boyd roundly rejected these arguments, peppering his short judgment with classic liberal assertions about the fact that the employees' individual choices had been undercut by the collective; they had been 'content and satisfied with their situations, with their wages and hours of work,' indeed 'were passive until set in motion by the active procurement of the union.' He concluded that the withdrawal of labour was 'oppressive and unfair' to the company and that this unfairness was 'enhanced and [made] … affirmatively spiteful' when the letters were sent to customers. The Divisional Court was upheld by the Court of Appeal in a short judgment, and the case eventually reached the JCPC, which did not resolve the issue. It allowed the union's appeal but sent the case back for a new trial on the ground that there had been a misdirection by the trial judge that might have left the jury with the belief that it was a wrong in itself for the union to call the strike. At that stage both parties agreed to give up and settled the case without costs. But the significance of such suits was that unions and their leaders could be sued and that picketing and the invocation of secondary boycotts were tortious.

State Intervention in Labour Law: Arbitration and Conciliation

Running parallel to the industrial turmoil and legal battles of the late nineteenth and early twentieth centuries was experimentation with other ways of settling workplace disputes, with the state becoming involved in arbitration, mediation, and conciliation. These terms did not have the same technical meanings that they do today. What all such schemes had in common was the idea of resolving employer-employee conflicts without strikes or lockouts and by agreements facilitated by government-appointed intermediaries. The first such scheme was legislated by the government of Oliver Mowat in Ontario in 1873, modelled on the British *Councils of Conciliation Act* of 1867. Its effectiveness was limited because the act established voluntary arbitration and thus required both parties to agree to participate and to accept what the board of arbitration decided. It was simply an adaptation of the arbitration long available to parties in any commercial dispute. Mowat and most other politicians were not interested in compulsory arbitration because they believed in the free market, in this case facilitated by state intervention to assist in obtaining negotiated agreements. Disputes could be and should be resolved by 'the honour, good faith and sense of expediency' of the parties. Mowat put forward the legislation because he wanted to appear friendly to the labour vote and, a staple of all political issues in the period, to have a few more patronage appointments to make before the upcoming election.[28]

The usefulness of the boards of arbitration established under the Ontario act was also severely limited by the fact that while their decisions were binding they did not have jurisdiction over wages. They could only adjudicate disputes over employer-imposed fines and deductions from wages. Given this limitation it is not surprising that the act was hardly ever used. The federal Royal Commission on the Relations of Labour and Capital of 1886 revealed that labour wanted more wide-ranging and compulsory arbitration, and employers neither of these, preferring the market to settle disputes. The commission's reports recommended arbitration, but different forms of it, neither of which was adopted. The 1873 act was amended in 1890, but only by giving boards the power to fix future wages if both parties specified that they could do so. Another amendment in 1894 implemented a more complex regime of conciliation, discussed below, and arbitration, established permanent councils of both, and gave both the jurisdiction to rule on, inter alia, 'the price to be paid for work done, or in the course of being done.' But the councils could not decide the price for work in the future and, most importantly, their decisions were enforceable only if both parties had agreed in writing beforehand to be bound. The 1894 act was very similar to British Columbia legislation passed the previous year under pressure from the powerful labour movement in the province, but it, the 1894 Ontario act, and an almost identical Quebec act of 1901 were all ineffective, and as a result little used.[29] Overall voluntary arbitration made hardly any impact in Canada over the more than 20 years that it was on the statute books of some provinces.

The 1894 Ontario *Trade Disputes Act* also established councils of conciliation. It did not define conciliation, but the term had been in use for some time and essentially meant mediation, a process of bringing the parties together and assisting them to come to a negotiated settlement. The Ontario act was the first such legislation in Canada. It provided for any workplace dispute to be referred by the parties to either a council of arbitration or one of conciliation, or both sequentially. A council of conciliation was an ad hoc body appointed whenever both parties to a dispute asked the registrar of councils of conciliation to appoint one. Each council would comprise four people, two chosen by each side. When, as noted in the previous paragraph, Quebec copied the 1894 legislation in 1901, it too had a council of conciliation. As with arbitration, conciliation was little used; employers did not want state intervention, and employees did not want intervention that the employer could ignore. Ontario's final arbitration legislation in this period was contained in the 1906 major reform to railway regulation discussed in chapter 11. The act establishing the Railway and Municipal Board had provisions for both arbitration and conciliation in disputes between railways and their employees, and yet again participation was voluntary.[30]

Nationally compulsory intervention in workplace disputes also had little impact. Labour organizations had begun advocating compulsory arbitration in the 1870s, when the newly formed Canadian Labour Union (CLU) endorsed it in its inaugural constitution in 1873. Its principal rival, the Knights of Labour, also did so in 1881.[31] When these two organizations merged to form the Trades and Labour Congress of Canada (TLC) in 1898 compulsory arbitration was one of its major planks. Although the labour movement was strongest in Ontario, Quebec, and British Columbia in the 1880s and 1890s, the only province to institute compulsory arbitration was Nova Scotia, in the *Mines Arbitration Act* of 1888.[32] Major miners' strikes in the late 1870s and 1880s had led to the formation of the Provincial Miners' Association in 1879, which became the Provincial Workmen's Association (PWA) in 1881.[33] The PWA's first serious attempt to have compulsory arbitration legislated came in 1887, on the heels of an 1886 strike against the Acadia Coal Company over wage cuts. The union, a local of the PWA, asked for mandatory arbitration, which the company would not agree to unless the union first agreed to the wage cuts. After the strike had continued for some months, the government introduced an arbitration bill in April 1887. Management representatives lobbied aggressively against the bill, arguing that it violated free market principles. Their arguments prevailed and the bill was lost shortly before the strike ended with the defeat of the union.

A year later a substantially similar bill did pass. It provided that when a dispute over wages arose, 'the employer shall not dismiss or lock out the employed, nor shall the employed strike or abandon work,' until the commissioner of mines had been informed. The commissioner was given the discretion to decide whether the dispute should be referred to arbitration. If he decided to do so, a five-person board would be appointed – two chosen by the government, one chosen by each party, and a fifth chosen by the two party nominees. If the parties could not agree on the fifth person, a Supreme Court judge would make the appointment. The arbitrators were given access to the company's books and could impose a binding wage settlement. The act was used in a number of disputes, although employers resisted employing it when they could. In 1889, for example, the PWA applied for arbitration of a dispute at the Springhill mine but failed when the company went to the provincial Supreme Court and won on an argument that the commissioner of mines had not given it adequate notice and thus lacked jurisdiction. After this decision the company hired replacement workers, which in turn precipitated a strike by miners and maintenance workers. The dispute was resolved through government intervention. Another high-profile conflict the following year involved the Dominion Coal Company and whether wages should increase with a rise in coal prices, and the arbitrators sided with the company.

In part because compulsory arbitration had not been introduced anywhere else, and even in Nova Scotia had not been a success for labour, the TLC abandoned compulsory arbitration as a goal in the early twentieth century. With workplace conflict on the increase and with labour issues seen increasingly as an important aspect of national development, the federal government became involved. Laurier was also persuaded to do so because his Liberal Party was keen to increase its share of the labour vote.[34] Any federal legislation involving labour ran the risk of being unconstitutional as an infringement on the property and civil rights power in section 92 (13) of the *BNA Act*. Mindful of the constitutional problem, the federal legislation initially eschewed any form of compulsion. A *Conciliation Act* of 1900 allowed the government to appoint a conciliator or arbitrator 'where a difference exists or is apprehended between an employer … and workmen, or between different classes of workmen.' The aim was to intervene to facilitate voluntary negotiated settlements through conciliation or voluntary arbitration – to help the parties come to an 'amicable settlement,' to 'remove causes of friction,' and to 'promote good feeling.'[35] The federal government also created a Department of Labour in 1900, effectively run by Deputy Minister William Lyon Mackenzie King, who was an enthusiastic promoter of ideas to resolve labour conflicts. The act was used on a few occasions, with mixed success. King tried to work out compromises. Indeed with no power to impose settlements he could not do otherwise. He wanted to be able to intervene more effectively, but both employer and employee groups opposed compulsion. The government did go a little further than the *Conciliation Act* with legislation passed in 1903 after consultation with railway unions providing for non-binding arbitration of disputes on railways, including street railways. The act was used only once, in a 1904 strike by Grand Trunk telegraph operators.[36]

In 1906 a lengthy strike in the Alberta coal mines, which King was unable to resolve, combined with pressure from some labour leaders who looked favourably on effective government intervention, persuaded the Laurier administration to bring in the *Industrial Disputes Investigation Act* of 1907 (IDIA).[37] It applied to a broad swathe of industries crucial to urban development and western expansion – mines and an undefined but very broad category of 'industries connected with public utilities.' It banned strikes or lockouts unless the dispute was first submitted to a three-person board of conciliation and investigation. The act was administered by the Department of Labour, presided over by King after he won a seat in the Commons in a by-election in 1908. He believed that the delay in calling a strike or ordering a lockout that the act effectively caused would force compromises because neither side would want the adverse publicity. He was wrong. The act disadvantaged unions by making strikes illegal until the board had completed its work and by giving employers a breathing period during which they could recruit strike-breakers and/or fire union leaders. There were no sanctions for such activities and nothing to compel employers to bargain in good faith. In short, 'the IDIA functioned primarily to maintain production on capital's terms, while allowing the state to present itself as the impartial mediator facilitating industrial peace while favouring neither side.' Although the TLC had initially supported the IDIA, by 1911 it was demanding repeal. The act stayed in force until held unconstitutional in 1925 as trenching on the provinces' property and civil rights power.[38]

Workplace Health and Safety

By the end of our period some half a million Canadians worked in what the 1911 census described as 'manufacturing' industries, just under 20 per cent of all persons employed. Most of them – respectively about 230,000 and 142,000 – were in Ontario and Quebec. Many tens of thousands of others built and operated railways or toiled in mines or pulp and paper mills and the like. A slight majority of the Canadian population was still rural, although not in Ontario or British Columbia and barely so in Quebec, and many of the increasing numbers of urban dwellers worked in factories, large and small. When a person worked with, indeed often at the dictates of, a machine and the non-human power needed to drive one, injuries to the human body were the inevitable result. One response to the increased prevalence of workplace 'accidents' was a profound change in the law regulating compensation for those injuries, and that phenomenon is discussed in the final section of this chapter. Another response was an attempt to use the law to prevent injuries by making workplaces safer, and that is the subject of this section.

Some safety regulations had been in place before Confederation in particular industries, notably mining and railways, and after 1867 they were retained and augmented. Nova Scotia's mining safety regime, for example, has been discussed in the preceding chapter. To similar effect British Columbia's *Coal Mines Regulation Act* of 1877 banned the employment of boys under 12, required the appointment of certified managers, and provided for mine inspections.[39] Safety was also a concern in predominantly agricultural provinces, as exemplified by an 1877 Manitoba statute about threshing machine safety.[40] But Ontario was the first province to regulate working conditions more broadly, in factories, passing legislation in 1884 that was not proclaimed in force until 1886.[41] It was precipitated by failed attempts to legislate federally over child labour. In the 1870s a nascent 'child-saving' movement among social reformers had become increasingly concerned about the use of child labour, and they were supported by the labour movement, which objected to the competition it represented. A number of private member's bills regulating child labour were introduced in the Commons from 1879 on by Dr. Darby Bergin, MP for the textile mill town of Cornwall. The fact that he did so shows, yet again, the uncertain state of the law on the division of powers. More immediately, Macdonald's government responded to the public pressure by establishing a Royal Commission on Mills and Factories, which, despite its title, was actually about child labour. The commission reported that the use of such labour was increasing and that the hours worked and the nature of work were too great a strain on young persons and impaired their schooling.[42] The federal government brought in bills in 1882, 1883, and 1884 but they were all withdrawn, partly because of doubts over jurisdiction.

At this point, keen to court working-class votes as the labour movement increased in numbers following the end of the depression of the 1870s, Mowat's Ontario government brought in a bill that was both a child labour and a general health and safety measure. The Ontario act applied to 'factories,' defined as buildings listed on a schedule and any other buildings in which steam or other power was used, or in which manual labour was done, where 20 or more people worked. It set the minimum age for working in such establishments at 12 for boys and 14 for girls, and limited working hours for women and children to 60. Many of its provisions were specific to women and children, including a prohibition on employing them in ways that would result in their health being 'permanently injured' or in a variety of tasks such as cleaning machinery in motion. Provisions applicable to all workers mandated standards of cleanliness and ventilation, limited overcrowding, required guards on dangerous machinery, and stated that generally workplaces could not be in a condition whereby 'the safety of any person employed therein is likely to be endangered, or … the health of any person therein … permanently injured.' Factory inspectors were given broad powers of entry, investigation, and prosecution; their presence in the act is testament to a declining faith in the ability of the market to determine the best interests of society. In 1889 the legislation was made applicable to workplaces with five or more employees, not 20.[43]

The minimum age for children working was raised twice in the 1890s. In 1891 legislation raised the school-leaving age to 14 and provided that no child could perform any employment during school hours. This limited the daytime hours that boys aged 12 could work, although school attendance was only mandatory in the fall term. In 1895 the *Factories Act* itself was amended to bar all children, girls and boys, 14 and under, from working in factories.[44] The emphasis on protecting women and children reflected concerns about the effect of industrialization on the traditional family. Factories represented a separation of home and family because they took men from local artisanal work and relocated them to more distant workplaces and more routinized work tasks, often at lower rates of pay, while at the same time inducing women and children to take on unskilled low-wage labour to supplement family incomes. If women and children could not be prevented from working outside the home, they could be protected by the state from undue exploitation, a task previously the preserve of the male head of household. The *Factories Act* was followed shortly afterwards by legislation regulating child labour in shops and introducing protections for women and children employed in other businesses not covered by it.[45]

As in other areas of law discussed in this book, Ontario's lead was followed by other provinces with very similar legislation, sometimes with many identically worded sections. Factory acts were passed in Quebec in 1885, and in Manitoba, Nova Scotia, New Brunswick, British

Columbia, and Saskatchewan in the first decade of the twentieth century.[46] Ontario's *Shop Regulation Act* was also largely reproduced in other provinces, although in British Columbia, Manitoba, and Saskatchewan some of the 'protection' provided was later augmented to include 'protection' from working for Chinese employers, a subject taken up in more detail in chapter 16.[47] In addition, many provinces continued to enact separate health and safety legislation specific to railways and mining, sectors not covered by factory acts. For example, an 1890 Ontario statute regulated the use of explosives and how the walls and roofs of mining shafts should be supported. As with so much other safety legislation, it also prohibited child labour and limited the working hours of young people.[48] In largely similar vein, this period also saw legislation on such disparate matters as fire prevention in hotels and other public buildings.[49]

As with all regulatory regimes, the impact of legislation depended less on the words of the act than on the effectiveness of enforcement. The TLC recognized this in 1886, passing a resolution stating that legislation 'will fail in attaining the end sought if the inspector or inspectors appointed to secure its enforcement do not possess the confidence' of the workers, which would come only from effective enforcement.[50] The TLC was referring to the Ontario act, which was about to be proclaimed in force, the only one for which enforcement has been seriously studied. The early signs were not promising for labour. Nothing was done to appoint inspectors until mid-1877, six months after the Act had been proclaimed, and only three were appointed for three districts. Of those three, the one responsible for the most heavily industrialized district was Robert Barber, a manufacturer. The other two inspectors, one a well-known labour activist, James Brown, were Liberal Party supporters and their appointments therefore based to some degree on patronage. From the outset the inspectors preferred to persuade and occasionally cajole employers, not to prosecute infractions. This was especially true for Barber and the third inspector, O.A. Roque, a former Ottawa alderman. Between 1880 and 1900 Barber initiated three prosecutions, and Roque just one. Brown prosecuted 31 times, but that was less than three a year and all but two were for violations of the rules governing the employment of women and children and hours of work in bake shops. Obviously Brown was more proactive than his colleagues, but he could hardly have been less so. Tellingly, there were 207 reported workplace deaths and 2,632 reported accidents in the same period, and in none of these cases was the employer prosecuted. The ineffectiveness of enforcement can be attributed primarily to a combination of a lack of resources and a policy choice about how to spend what resources there were. The extension of coverage in 1889 to workplaces of five or more exacerbated the problem, adding thousands of workplaces to those already not inspected. Even though a fourth, female, inspector was added in 1895 with a jurisdiction limited to child and female labour, in 1901 the four inspectors were responsible for 6,543 workplaces. The lack of personnel meant that many inspections were 'walk throughs' taking less than half an hour. This was what government wanted, telling inspectors that they should be 'reasonable' and should enforce the Act 'with as little friction and annoyance as possible.' Therefore safety legislation brought in by the government to appease some interest groups achieved little because that same government wanted neither to spend money on effective enforcement nor to antagonize another and more important interest group, employers.

Compensation for Workplace Injuries

The law governing liability for workplace injuries changed significantly in this period, especially in Ontario where a full-fledged no-fault compensation scheme was introduced.[51] At Confederation the common law, in particular tort law, determined if a worker injured on the job would be compensated by the employer, and tort law did not favour workers. In addition to the financial impediments to going to court that all less-than-wealthy aspiring litigants had to overcome, the law of negligence favoured employer defendants in workplace injury cases because the worker had to show that the employer had actual knowledge of the unsafe conditions that led to the injury. In addition tort plaintiffs were denied any recovery if the defendant could show any degree of contributory negligence, which was a complete defence. Also a powerful defence was voluntary assumption of risk, in which an injured person had voluntarily assumed any risks associated with the activity. These doctrines reflected the mid- to late nineteenth-century subservience of common law to individualistic values of laissez-faire – free will and responsibility for one's own fate.

There was one further and very significant obstacle for an injured worker – the fellow servant rule. Usually traced to *Priestly v Fowler,* an 1837 English case, and to *Farwell v Boston and Worcester Railroad Corporation,* an 1842 Massachusetts case,[52] it was firmly established in English, American, and Canadian tort law. Its essence was that an employer was not liable for injuries to employees caused by the negligence of other employees. It has been persuasively argued that the rule was invented by the courts to shield the nascent and developing industries of the nineteenth century from liability for the costs of the damage caused.[53] It was a potent weapon in an employer's legal arsenal. Of the 16 reported cases on workplace injuries from Ontario courts between 1865 and 1880, almost all of them resulted in wins for the defendant, with eight decided in the employer's favour by application of the fellow servant rule.[54] In an 1866 decision Justice John Hagarty of the Court of Queen's Bench expressed 'great compassion' for a widow whose husband had been killed working on the Grand Trunk, but insisted that he could not 'abrogate the doctrine laid down in the numerous cases that follow *Priestley v Fowler*' and was inflexible in holding that it was 'a well settled legal principle' that an employee could not recover for an injury caused by 'his fellow servants' neglect.'[55]

Another case concerned an 1884 explosion at the Hamilton Powder Company in the village of Cumminsville, Halton County, that killed six men and injured many others. The company had received an urgent order for powder from the CPR, and in late September the owner directed that production had to increase from 250 barrels a day to 360. This meant that the equipment did not have sufficient time to cool down and became much more dangerous. A coroner's inquest laid the blame for the explosion on the company. One of the widows sued and won a $2,000 award. The company had this decision reversed by the Court of Appeal because the owner had ordered certain equipment to be repaired but left the carrying out of this order to his manager. The court held that as long as the employer had hired a competent manager, he did not need to follow up and ensure the work had been done. The manager was negligent, and thus the case was governed by the fellow servant rule. The families might have sued the manager, but he very likely did not have enough money to make it worth doing so.[56] As we saw in chapter 5, the civil law of Quebec included none of these employer defences, and successes achieved in the Quebec courts were not overturned by the JCPC, which was more respectful of the civil law in this area than the SCC.

As Canada became more urban and more industrialized, served by more railroads, and witnessed a growth in mining and manufacturing industries, criticisms of the consequent increase in injuries to workers and others evoked legislative responses. Such responses included the safety regulations we have just discussed, but also legislation to make recovery for injuries easier. Ontario was again the first province to act through the *Workmen's Compensation for Injuries Act* of 1886, the principal thrust of which was to do away with the fellow servant rule. It provided that if injury or death was caused to a workman by, inter alia, the 'act or omission of any person in the service of the employer done or made in obedience to the rules or by-laws of the employer, or in obedience to … instructions given by any person delegated with the authority of the employer,' the workman or his heirs would have 'the same right of compensation and remedies against the employer as if the workman had not been' in the employer's service.[57] Thus had the Cumminsville explosion happened two years later the result would likely have been very different. Another provision greatly limited the employer's ability to make an employee contract out of the act's provisions. The employer had the onus of showing that any such contract was indeed a genuine bargain made for real consideration. The act therefore not only undermined a common law rule, it also undercut the very basis of the common law's freedom of contract ideology by implicitly recognizing that such agreements were effectively coerced by the much greater bargaining power of the employer. The employer did get something in the act – a limitation of damages to three years' earnings.

The 1886 Act was followed by further legislation three years later similarly undermining the common law doctrine of voluntary assumption of risk. Henceforth an injured worker suing for compensation 'shall not, by reason only of his continuing' in his employment 'with knowledge of the defect, negligence, act or omission which caused the injury, be deemed to have voluntarily incurred the risk of the injury.' Other common law provinces followed Ontario's lead over the next two decades, most of them not only copying the substance of the Ontario legislation but passing word-for-word replicas of it.[58]

Our knowledge of the effect of the acts abolishing the fellow servant rule is limited to Ontario, but in that jurisdiction workers won more cases than they lost in jury trials, and more appeals than they lost when cases were taken to the Divisional Court or the Court of Appeal. This was in marked contrast to the period prior to 1886, when there had been very few cases brought by workers and almost all of them were lost. From the late 1880s the courts had a 'small but significant preference for workers,' a phenomenon attributed in part to jurors' dislike of large corporations having too much power, in part to judges' respect for jury verdicts and their inchoate sense of fairness, and in part to changing attitudes towards workplace injuries. The 1886 act was a complicated piece of legislation and left open much space for legal argument, but a complex act that allowed some workers to prevail was a world different from a simple common law rule that precluded success in almost all cases.[59] As the discussion of similar litigation in Quebec in chapter 5 makes clear, the more plaintiff-friendly civil law enabled a substantially higher percentage of injured workers to prevail.

In the very late nineteenth and early twentieth centuries a new idea began to be mooted in a number of provinces – compensation regardless of fault. Schemes to this effect were introduced in Germany and Britain in 1884 and 1897, and in a number of US states between 1908 and 1911.[60] The English Act of 1897 established a hybrid scheme. Injured workers could use the courts and the common law, and if they did there was no limit on damages if they could establish liability. Alternatively they could opt to use the act, which guaranteed compensation without a need to prove fault, but it applied only to certain industries – railways, factories, mining, quarrying, and laundry work – and awards were significantly less than a common law court would have given. Funding was provided by the employer.[61] This model was adopted in all four western provinces, Nova Scotia and Quebec, and the colony of Newfoundland, between 1902 and 1911.[62] None of the Canadian statutes applied to all workers, and there were variations among them in which industries were included. But in the words of the British Columbia act, they all required employers to pay compensation for injuries arising 'in the course of employment' and provided that the injured worker 'may, at his option, either claim compensation under this Act or take the same proceedings as were open to him' before its passage. Only Quebec did not allow the option of suing outside the act.

Ontario opted for a different and revolutionary direction, establishing the first modern workers' compensation scheme in 1914.[63] It differed from the legislation just discussed in two related ways. It did away altogether with the option of using the courts, requiring all injured employees to take their cases to a new tribunal, the Workmen's Compensation Board. It also established a compensation fund to which all employers and employees were required to contribute. Its origins can be traced to proposals in the waning years of the nineteenth century that some variant of the British model be adopted in the province, but nothing came of that and not until the coming to office of the Conservatives under James P. Whitney in 1905 was the issue taken up seriously, albeit only in Whitney's second term and after he came under increasing pressure from labour interests to tackle the question. Whitney was a new broom in Ontario politics, a believer in government intervention and regulation in the public interest. Most notably he pushed through public power and urban railway regulation against strong opposition from private interests.[64] In 1910 he appointed his one-time Conservative Party mentor William Ralph Meredith, then chief justice of Common Pleas, to be a commission of inquiry into workers' compensation. Meredith was a former leader, from 1878, of the provincial Conservatives whose years in politics were all spent in opposition while Oliver Mowat's Liberals won six consecutive elections. He left politics for the bench in 1894. As a politician he espoused social legislation and the cause of labour generally, and he carried his attitudes with him onto the bench, although in line with the formalist thinking of his age he drew a sharp line between law and politics and proclaimed himself to be able to do no more than to apply, not make, the law. In one exchange during the commission hearings he told a worker giving evidence and complaining about judicial class bias that a court was 'confined to administering justice according to law' and that any 'fault' in the system of compensation was 'not in the administration of justice' but in the law.' If change was desired 'you must change your law. It is the law that is at fault.'[65]

Meredith held 27 sessions of public hearings between 1911 and 1913, mostly in Toronto but some in London, Hamilton, Berlin (today Kitchener), and Cobalt. Many witnesses from both sides of the employer/ employee divide appeared, along with a few experts, principally from the insurance business. In March 1912 Meredith issued an interim report in which he described the existing law as 'entirely inadequate' and noted that all parties were agreed that a compensation scheme should be established. The following year he produced both his final report and a draft bill, and the latter, with few amendments, became the 1914 act. It provided that compensation would be given for both accidents and industrial diseases, in the form of periodic payments of 55 per cent of salary. The payments would last as long as the worker was disabled, and on his or her death dependants got a pension. Almost all sectors of the economy were included, the notable exceptions being agriculture and domestic employment; excluding the latter, of course, meant excluding large numbers of female workers. All common law claims were barred, as were both appeals and applications for judicial review. All payments were to come from a compensation fund, and all employers were required to pay proportionately into that fund. The scheme would be run by a government agency, the Workmen's Compensation

Board. Thus the act established what has been succinctly called 'mutual insurance administered by the state.'[66]

The 1914 act was highly significant. It was Canada's first legislation creating social insurance. With regard to labour and the law, it represented a sea change, greeted enthusiastically at the time by the *Industrial Banner*, a labour paper, as 'real social legislation' and 'the most far-reaching legislation that has ever been enacted by any government in Canada in the interests of the workers.'[67] Some employers likewise saw it as 'social,' condemning it as socialist legislation. For the legal historian the act confirmed and expanded changing attitudes to the relative roles of the state and individuals, the common law and legislation. Three other provinces shortly followed suit and enacted similar regimes during the First World War: Nova Scotia in 1915, Manitoba in 1916, and New Brunswick in 1918.[68] All other provinces did so later in the twentieth century and will be discussed in *Volume 3*, in which we will examine the rise of the welfare state more generally.

13

Criminal Justice: Criminal Law, Criminal Procedure, and Punishment

In the half-century after Confederation the criminal justice system underwent a profound transformation. In 1867 each colony had its own criminal justice system – criminal law, courts with criminal jurisdiction, policing and prosecutorial mechanisms, prisons, and governors who exercised the prerogative power of pardon. The only exception was that Upper and Lower Canada had separate criminal court systems, but the law governing crimes and punishments and criminal procedure was the same. Sections 91 (27) and (28) of the *BNA Act* gave jurisdiction to the federal Parliament over criminal law and procedure, and penitentiaries. Because the governor general of Canada was the principal representative of the Queen, he exercised the prerogative power of the royal pardon, meaning that the disposition of those sentenced to death was decided in Ottawa. The federal government therefore had jurisdiction over the substantive criminal law and criminal procedure and the two principal forms of punishment for serious offences. The provinces retained some of the criminal justice jurisdiction they had had in the colonial period, in relation to minor offences, under section 92 (15), 'the imposition of punishment by fine, penalty, or imprisonment' for breaches of regulatory offences connected to any other head of provincial jurisdiction. They also had jurisdiction over the administration of justice under section 92 (14), and 'public and reformatory prisons' under section 92 (6).

This chapter analyses the three principal aspects of criminal justice – substantive criminal law, criminal procedure, and punishment. The first section examines the legislation passed to create a national criminal law, which culminated in the enactment of the first *Criminal Code* in 1892. We then survey criminal procedure in three sections, the most notable development being legislation to streamline the criminal process for all but the most serious of offences. By dramatically reducing the use of juries the state made criminal justice quicker and cheaper, but also a bureaucratic routine in which accused persons were effectively cajoled into giving up their rights to trial by jury. Criminal prosecution generally, juries, and appeal rights are also discussed in these sections. Our fifth section looks at imprisonment for the more serious crimes other than capital offences, which before Confederation had become imprisonment with the abolition, or increasingly reduced use, of physical punishments other than death. Because the most important form of imprisonment, the penitentiary, was a federal head of power, the jurisdictional divide between penitentiary and other forms of prisons had to be sorted out. This was not difficult to do, but the federal government then had to construct a national penitentiary network. Our final two sections deal with capital punishment, looking in turn at the law and practice of execution and commutation generally, and then at the discretionary decision-making that decided who among those sentenced to death would die and who would be spared. The death penalty was the punishment for very few offences in the colonies by 1867 and was, with the exception of Louis Riel, used in this period only for those convicted of murder. But capital punishment retained an importance well beyond the small numbers of those subjected to the ultimate sanction. It represented state power at its utmost and needed to be managed through the prerogative of mercy. Deciding who should die was the preserve of the federal cabinet, whose decisions were opaque and discretionary in equal measure.

Legislation provided the framework for Canada's criminal justice system, but analyses of it must go beyond statutes and other forms of formal law, and examine its operation in application. Our final section, also on capital punishment, consists in part of an examination of cases involving women and Indigenous people who were sentenced to death. Through these lenses we are able to analyse the ways in which law, justice, gender, race, and culture interacted. Discretion lay at the heart of the everyday operation of criminal justice. Victims, police, prosecutors, juries, judges, prison officials, and the federal cabinet all could and did exercise discretion over who should be apprehended, prosecuted, convicted, imprisoned, and executed, and that discretion was exercised according to individuals' sense of justice, which was in turn sometimes shaped by their attitudes towards the accused, the victim(s), and the purposes of the criminal law.

Two related caveats are necessary here. First, there is not complete agreement among historians of criminal justice about the boundaries of the subject. Some would argue that criminal justice should encompass not only crimes of violence or property crimes, but every infraction of any law that brought a person into conflict with an agent of the state. Others studies look only at the more serious offences against the state, persons, or property.[1] For the purposes of one chapter in a book surveying many types of law in a federal state over a half century, we must inevitably concentrate on serious crimes rather than regulatory offences, on judges not JPs, and on capital punishment and long prison sentences rather than short terms of incarceration and fines. Our decision to do so is not solely the product of lack of space. Criminal justice is about the most visible manifestations of the state's coercive power, and those were the gallows and the penitentiary. Second, the boundaries between the subjects discussed here and other aspects of social regulation, such as youth reformatories, industrial schools, the formal and informal 'policing' of behaviour both by the police and other state and non-stage agents, are both fluid and malleable. Again because of a lack of space we cannot discuss provincial prisons or everyday urban policing.

Making a National Criminal Law

In 1866 there was some variation in criminal law among the seven British North American colonies, although the general principles were common to all. Nova Scotia, New Brunswick, and Prince Edward Island each had their own criminal statutes, the criminal law – also local and statutory – was uniform in Upper and Lower Canada, and both Newfoundland and British Columbia had adopted the English criminal law, the former as of 1837 and the latter as of 1858. Despite the broad similarities among the colonies, there was never any doubt in the Confederation debates that the criminal law should be national and thus uniform across the country.[2] Indeed, that it was a matter for the states in the US Constitution was one of many reasons that a strong central government was desired by those who crafted the division of powers, as discussed in chapter 2. Making the criminal law uniform was an immediate priority for the new federal government. In 1868 Parliament passed three statutes, relating to riots, accessories, and political offences. The bulk of the criminal law legislation was also supposed to become law in 1868 but was delayed in the Senate for reasons that are not important. It was passed in 1869, 11 statutes on almost all aspects of substantive criminal law, and a further seven on criminal procedure, including two dealing with juvenile offenders. The two principal statutes on the criminal law covered offences against the person and against property, while five more particular ones dealt with forgery, perjury, counterfeiting, offences related to military discipline, and malicious injuries to property. A further set of four statutes dealt with particular locations (public works, military and naval stores) or with more minor offences (vagrancy and cruelty to animals).[3]

The two principal statutes and four others were very close reproductions of English legislation of 1861, the *Criminal Law Consolidation Acts*, colloquially known as *Greaves' Acts* after parliamentary draftsman Charles Greaves. They were therefore not so much drafted as simply renamed and, to a small extent, reorganized, by Gustavus Wicksteed, law clerk to the Commons, and Hewitt Bernard, Macdonald's private secretary and the deputy minister of Justice, both assisted in the latter stages by James Gowan, a legal scholar, long-time judge of the Simcoe County court, and close confidant of and legal adviser to John A. Macdonald when he had been attorney general of Canada West.[4] The federal statutes, like their English originals, were verbose, especially compared to the statutory revisions of New Brunswick and Nova Scotia passed in the 1850s and 1860s. They also included many offences particular to England that had never been offences in the pre-Confederation colonies, such as the game laws.[5] Their most serious defect was that they presupposed a knowledge of the definitions of offences at common law. Nowhere in the English *Larceny Act*, for example, was larceny defined, and the same was true for the Canadian statute, even though many other terms were defined in section 1. But copying had the advantages of not adopting the law of any particular province and of not undertaking the lengthy process of drawing up a criminal code anew. Accompanying these enactments was the repeal by Parliament of the criminal statutes of the four original provinces.[6]

Five offences were made capital in these statutes – murder, treason, rape, statutory rape, and attempted murder.[7] The number of capital offences in the original four provinces was thus increased, although statutory rape and attempted murder were made non-capital in 1877. Rape remained a capital offence, but from 1873 the penalty could be either death or imprisonment. One of the principal reasons for including rape among the capital offences was Macdonald's belief that it was necessary to deter Black men's supposed propensity to sexually assault. 'We ... have maintained the punishment of death for rape,' he told New Brunswick Chief Justice William Johnston Ritchie, because of 'the frequency of rape committed by negroes, of whom we have too many in Upper Canada. They are very prone to felonious assaults on white women.'[8] Although 26 men were sentenced to death for rape or statutory rape in the first decade after Confederation, none was executed; indeed nobody was ever executed for rape even though it remained nominally capital until 1956.[9] This was a remarkable contrast with the United States, where anxiety over Black male sexuality ensured that rape remained capital until 1972, and that between 1930 and 1972 455 men were executed for rape, 89 per cent of them Black.[10]

Between 1870 and 1878 25 statutes were passed amending and/or supplementing the criminal statutes of the late 1860s. Partly for this reason two treatises on criminal law were published in the 1870s, designed to summarize and explain the increasing volume of statute law.[11] By the late 1870s there emerged a movement to do more than collate the statute law for professional use, but to codify the criminal law in comprehensive legislation, part of a more general belief that the entire statute law of the dominion should be codified. A great deal has been written on the meaning of codification, and there is disagreement among historians about exactly what the term means and to what extent legislation on different subjects meets the requirements to be called a code. In the common law world, codification originated in the early nineteenth century with the utilitarian philosopher Jeremy Bentham. Central to Bentham's thought, and that of many of his followers, was a critique of the common law as disorganized, unsystematic, obscurantist, and far too dependent on discretionary judicial interpretation. A code, in contrast, should be rational, ordered, scientific, and broadly accessible in plain language. Codification was widely, if not universally adopted in the United States in the antebellum period, but never taken up in Britain. It did, however, inspire criminal codes in many parts of the empire.[12]

Canadians who advocated criminal law codification made two specific arguments: that the criminal law, more than any other branch of the law, should be rendered more accessible, and that it seemed in the 1870s that Britain was about to embark on criminal law codification and Canada should therefore follow that lead. The high-water mark of English enthusiasm for reform came in 1877, when it looked as if the draft code of criminal law prepared by Sir James Stephen might become law.[13] Minister of Justice Edward Blake had $8,000 appropriated for a Canadian equivalent, but the initiative came to nothing when the Mackenzie government fell and Macdonald, newly returned to power, concentrated on the National Policy and the Pacific railway. In the event also the codification movement across the Atlantic petered out; Britain has never enacted a criminal code. Only consolidation was achieved, as in all areas of federal statute law, with the enactment of the first *Revised Statutes of Canada* in 1886; criminal law and procedure comprised 49 chapters out of 185 and replaced more than 150 federal statutes. But it was not a code, complete in itself, a single coherent whole that defined offences, arranged them systematically under categories, and was written in a way that made the law accessible to non-lawyers.

The Canadian *Criminal Code* passed in 1892 was not the product of a campaign by any single individual championing the idea over a period of time.[14] There was a small coterie of men who proposed reform of some kind, including Gowan and future SCC judge Henry-Elzéar Taschereau, but they were consolidators, not even minimally codifiers, and Taschereau wanted his name attached to a ground-breaking statute. The man most responsible for the code, its titular father and the political force who saw it through, was Justice Minister Sir John Thompson, a highly accomplished lawyer, former premier of Nova Scotia, former judge of that province's Supreme Court, and a believer in systemization. A staunch Conservative who had been persuaded by Macdonald in 1885 to give up his judicial seat to run for Parliament, he decided in the late 1880s that a code was a desirable reform. He engaged two other Maritimers to supervise the drafting done by C.H. Masters, reporter for the SCC. One was George Burbidge, who published a digest of the criminal law in 1890 based very largely on, and identically entitled to, Stephen's earlier work.[15] As deputy minister he had headed the prosecution team in the trial of Louis Riel, discussed in chapter 7. The other was Burbidge's successor as deputy minister, Robert Sedgwick, whom Thompson had brought to Ottawa from Halifax to replace Burbidge. In choosing these men Thompson rejected an offer to draft a code from Taschereau, who took the rebuff personally, severely criticizing the Code after 1892.[16] It is hard to fault Thompson for thinking that a sitting SCC judge was not the right person for the job, especially one whose 1874 book was a collection of Canadian statutes peppered with extracts from English authors and cases. Ironically Taschereau and Sedgwick were soon colleagues, Thompson appointing the latter to the SCC in 1893.

George Wheelock Burbidge: judge of the Exchequer Court, prosecutor of Louis Riel, and principal drafter of the first *Criminal Code*.

Credit: Federal Court of Canada.

Burbidge and colleagues drafted the Code in a year while doing their other full-time jobs. It was introduced in the Commons in 1891 and at the same time circulated to some 2,000 people for comment – Superior Court judges, attorneys general, and leading lawyers. Their replies ran to hundreds of letters, most of them favourable but almost all of them indicating that the writers had no sense that a code, a significant departure from past practice, was being contemplated. They saw the 1891 bill as another consolidation. A revised version passed both houses in 1892, more easily getting through the Commons than the Senate, and was proclaimed in force in July 1893.[17] It was divided into 10 Titles, the most important of which were Titles 2 through 6, dealing with different kinds of offences (against the person, property, public order, etc.), and Titles 7 and 8, dealing with procedure and post-conviction issues. It was not a revolutionary document, relying substantially on the existing federal statutes and the *Digests* previously produced by Burbidge and Stephen. In largely reproducing Stephen's draft code, it has been argued, Canadians chose a more authoritarian code than another one produced in Britain for other colonies by Robert Wright.[18] But it did make some large changes to the criminal law, including doing away with the distinctions between felonies and misdemeanours and principals and accessories and, as we will see below, introducing entirely new rights of appeal. In addition the word 'malice' was left out of the definition of homicide, provocation was statutorily defined, and lighter punishments for juvenile offenders were instituted. But generally it did what Thompson, speaking in the Commons, said it did – eliminated technicalities, archaisms, and obscure language. Most of all, it put all the important parts of criminal law and procedure in one statute, cutting Canada off from the imperial legacy of a criminal law contained in hundreds of different statutes. Newman Hoyles, principal of Osgoode Hall Law School, lauded this achievement a decade later.[19]

The Code has been generally viewed by historians as a disappointment for its failure to propound a broad set of principles of what constitutes a crime and the purposes and efficacy of different punishments. But this is to condemn it for not being something it was never intended to be. It has been aptly described as 'a perfect example of Canadian reformist conservatism.' The very idea of a code was fiercely and successfully resisted in the United Kingdom, with the judges to the fore. But nor was it the idealist version of a complete, unified, free-standing code, accessible to all, championed initially by Bentham. Sedgwick's view of such a code was that it was 'right in theory' but not 'possible in practice.'[20] There was little change in the fundamental principles of the criminal law after 1892. The Code was amended many times in this period, 65 changes being introduced in one act in 1900, but these were responses to problems revealed by judicial interpretations or introduced as a result of lobbying by interest groups in pursuit of their own moral reform agendas. Antipathy towards the Chinese, for example, which we will examine in detail in chapter 16, led to amendments to outlaw opium consumption in 1909.[21]

Criminal Procedure: Introduction
and the Northwest Territories

At Confederation the essential elements of the prosecution and trial process were not substantially different from English criminal procedure or what had existed in the colonies for many decades.[22] Anybody who believed that a crime had been committed – usually the victim, but if the allegation was one of homicide then the victim's family or neighbours – took a complaint to a JP (magistrate), who recorded depositions and, if satisfied that there was a sufficient case, ordered a constable to apprehend the suspect for questioning. In most cases, and certainly in almost all serious cases, the suspect would be kept in custody in the local jail to await trial. As we saw in *Volume 1*, during the colonial period there had been some innovations to this part of the process. In urban areas the JPs, often referred to as police magistrates and invariably stipendiaries – paid full-time professionals who were increasingly likely to be lawyers – established 'police offices,' to which suspects could be brought rather than having this done in the JP's home, which still happened in rural areas. In addition, by mid-century this initial examination of the accused person had begun to evolve into a preliminary inquiry, held publicly with sworn testimony. No statutes brought about this change, which was more advanced in Upper Canada than elsewhere, and more typical of an urban police office than a rural magistrate's parlour. It was simply increasingly seen as desirable to have the administration of justice more open and more efficient.

Assuming the magistrate found enough evidence to move to the next stage, the suspect would be jailed until the appropriate court met. Which court that was depended on the seriousness of the allegation. If the alleged crime was minor – a petty assault or larceny – the accused would be tried summarily (without a jury) by one, two, or three JPs in rural areas, the number depending on local statutory law, or by an urban court, often called a police court or police magistrates' court, again summarily. If it was a serious offence – robbery, burglary, rape, murder, and the like – the matter was one for a Superior Court, such as the Nova Scotia Supreme Court or the Quebec Superior Court. In all colonies but Quebec these were itinerant courts, the judges going on regular, if not frequent, circuits around the province, sometimes called the assizes. People accused of serious offences could languish for months in jail in some cases, waiting for the next visit of the assize judge. In all provinces there was an intermediate level of court in non-urban areas and some cities, usually called a court of sessions or some variant. It was a county-based court and met more often than the Superior Court in any given county, though never more than quarterly. Most sessions court judges were not lawyers, but JPs for the county chosen for their general 'worthiness.' This line between lower courts and intermediate courts had been redrawn in the Province of Canada in the 1850s, as we will see below, but for current purposes this description will suffice.

Whichever of the two higher-level courts an accused was slated to be tried in, the first stage of the trial process was an appearance before the grand jury, a body of at least 12 men, usually between 12 and 23, which met at the beginning of the court session and ruled on the indictments presented to it. At Confederation in every province but Ontario these indictments were prepared by the clerk of the peace for the county, using the depositions taken by the JP to formulate the charge. The grand jury met in secret and heard only evidence for the prosecution to decide if there was a case to go to trial. It needed at least 12 grand jurors, and a majority of all of them, to take the case forward, to find what was called 'a true bill.' Not surprisingly grand juries found 90 per cent or more of indictments to be true bills. There was a difference in the grand jury procedure between Ontario and the other provinces. As we saw in *Volume 1*, in 1857 Ontario established a system of county attorneys, salaried full-time legally trained men, one of whose jobs was to draw up indictments and present them and the evidence to the grand jury. This was an innovation; no other Canadian colony had established such a system before Confederation, and nor had England, although Scotland had long had a system of paid public prosecutors. In 1875 Manitoba became the second province to establish a system of county attorneys, on much the same conditions and with the same duties as those in Ontario.[23] County attorneys not only shepherded cases through the grand jury, they then presented the prosecution's case at trial. This was a marked departure from English practice, where prosecution at trial had long been private, a task to be performed by the victim or his or her family, and remained so until well into the twentieth century, although any private prosecutor could choose to hire a lawyer.[24] In other Canadian colonies/provinces lawyers generally prosecuted in court on an ad hoc fee-for-service basis, the fees paid from the public purse.

The final stage was, of course, the trial itself, presided over by a judge and with a jury of 12 in both the superior courts and what we have termed intermediate courts. As we saw in *Volume 1*, from the 1830s defendants had the right to make full answer and defence by counsel, but they were not competent witnesses and could not give sworn testimony at their trial. Much of the system just described had changed by the end of our period. In what follows in this section we deal with these changes thematically. We examine first the unique criminal justice system that was established in the North-West Territories. We then analyse the ultimately unsuccessful movement to abolish the grand jury. Next we look at the much more successful measures taken to reduce the use of trial juries. The trial jury, of course, was never abolished, and nor did anybody suggest that it should be. But its use was very considerably curtailed, beginning in the early 1870s. Finally in this section we deal with developments in the rights of an accused, in particular legislation to make him or her a competent witness and to provide a right of appeal.

Criminal justice systems were easy to establish in Manitoba and British Columbia. Both were provinces, and the latter already had a court system and criminal procedure based on the same English principles from which criminal justice in central and eastern Canada were derived. Manitoba received the substantive criminal law enacted by the federal Parliament in two federal statutes of 1871,[25] and the province passed local statutes between 1871 and 1873 that established JPs, the Court of Queen's Bench (initially named the Supreme Court), county courts, and county government by grand juries. The county courts were civil courts for all but the first meeting of the year, but they had summary criminal jurisdiction over 'petty assaults and batteries.' For that first session they were to 'open as a Court of Sessions,' with the grand jury in attendance, but only to transact county business, not to hold criminal trials. Most criminal offences were thus to be tried in Queen's Bench with both kinds of juries operating, and the clerk of the county serving as clerk of the peace.[26]

The Northwest Territories, however, was not a province, and, as we saw in chapter 7 in the discussion of the Riel trial, Parliament established a unique system of criminal procedure for the region in a series of statutes in the 1870s and 1880s. A key element of the system of criminal justice in the Territories was the North-West Mounted Police (NWMP), established in the same 1873 statute that inaugurated a system of stipendiary magistrates as the principal criminal court judges of the region.[27] The story of the establishment of the NWMP to counter the activities of American whisky traders in the Cypress Hills is well known and need not be retold here. It was conceived of and became a paramilitary police force, a gendarmerie modelled on other British colonial police forces, principally the Royal Irish Constabulary. Armed, mounted, with military-style uniforms, ranks, and discipline, its officers were spread across the prairie to assert Canadian sovereignty as much as to maintain law and order, which were to many minds the same thing. Although the stipendiary magistrates were the principal criminal court judges, the NWMP had 'almost complete responsibility' for all other aspects of criminal justice.[28] They were the surveillance arm of the state, patrolling, preserving the peace, and apprehending offenders. They served the stipendiary magistrates and other JPs, executed warrants, and escorted convicted persons to their place of incarceration (often the NWMP guardhouse). In addition, the commissioner and all superintendents were made JPs by the 1873 legislation giving them jurisdiction to try minor offences, so that the force was police, prosecutor, and judge rolled into one. Although there were other JPs on the prairies, most of the minor criminal cases that came before JPs were tried by NWMP officers, including those of individuals they or their men had apprehended. The NWMP was the active and visible arm of the Canadian state, enforcing the system of segregating Indigenous peoples on reserves, including the notorious pass system.

The same 1873 statute that established the NWMP also created the office of stipendiary magistrate, although none were actually appointed until 1876. One of the three appointed was James MacLeod, until then the NWMP commissioner. The stipendiary magistrates were given jurisdiction to summarily try a number of offences, all of which carried a maximum penalty of less than two years. More serious offences, those carrying a maximum penalty of up to seven years, could also be tried summarily before a judge of the Manitoba Court of Queen's Bench and any two stipendiary magistrates, with any penitentiary sentence to be served in the newly established Manitoba penitentiary, discussed in a subsequent section. Any offence for which the death penalty was available had to be tried in Manitoba by a Queen's Bench judge and a jury. In 1875 the system was modified, with any offence for which the penalty was up to five years' imprisonment being triable summarily before a judge of the Manitoba Queen's Bench and a local stipendiary as an associate. If the penalty was more than five years but not death, the same two men would preside but the accused had the option of a trial by jury. If he or she opted for that, it would be a six-man jury chosen by the judge or the stipendiary magistrate. Offences carrying the possibility of a death sentence had to be tried by a Manitoba judge and a jury, this time of eight and again chosen by the judge. The reason for these marked departures from procedure elsewhere in the dominion were the difficulties of finding enough men to serve of the right 'quality' in a sparsely settled region. For the same reason no grand juries sat in the Territories, although this was formally justified by the grand jury being a county-level institution and the Territories having no counties.[29]

In 1877 the criminal jurisdiction of the stipendiary magistrates was augmented. They became able to try capital offences with two JPs presiding with them and six-man juries. In default of any locally enacted jury ordinance the jurors were again to be chosen by the stipendiary 'from among such male persons as he may think suitable.' Accused persons were for the first time allowed peremptory challenges, no more than six, and could challenge for cause under the 1869 *Criminal Procedure Act*. In 1880 the need for two JPs as assistant judges was reduced to one, and the range of offences that could be tried was broadened yet again. This system stayed in place until the North-West Territories Supreme Court was created in 1886, which meant only the abolition of the stipendiary magistrates – the six-man jury remained. In the same year the newly created North-West Territories council enacted a jury selection ordinance, under which the sheriff made up the jury list of local residents and drew from a hat the names of those who would actually sit on cases. A considerable degree of official control remained, however. The sheriff was to place on the jury list only men 'qualified by their station and intelligence to serve as jurors.' When the ordinances were revised two years later this phrase was removed, although the sheriff still drew up the list of those called to a court session.[30] The result of all this legislation was a criminal process unique in Canada, always justified by the sparse population, but of course the population as a whole was not that limited. The white settler population was small, and the much more numerous Indigenous people were to play no role in this important state process other than that of defendant. The jury ordinance did not exclude Indigenous people explicitly; the only qualifications formally required were to be 21, under 60, not otherwise exempt, and resident within 20 miles of where the court sat. But sheriffs knew well, without having to be told in legislation, not to put women or Indigenous people on the lists. The stipendiary magistrate system was re-enacted in 1905 for the new North-West Territories shorn of the provinces of Alberta and Saskatchewan. The stipendiaries were given the criminal jurisdiction of the former NWTSC, that is, the power to try any offence, including murder.[31]

Criminal Procedure: The Decline of Juries

The size of the criminal trial jury was not changed anywhere else in Canada, but this period was marked by 'the decline of the jury.'[32] The decline occurred in the use of both grand and trial juries in the criminal process after 1867, and that diminution in use had multiple causes, some pragmatic but some more fundamental, including a loss of faith in both kinds of juries. We will deal first with the grand jury. Well before Confederation appointed grand juries had lost their role as local government bodies everywhere in Ontario to elected bodies, and the same had happened in many other parts of the country through municipal incorporation. The trend continued after Confederation through county incorporation in Nova Scotia and because grand juries were not established as the local government body in the Territories.[33] They retained their place in the criminal prosecution process everywhere except the Territories, even though it was less convenient than in the days when a grand jury would be called together to transact county business and review indictments at the same time. That very reduction in convenience was one of the reasons behind a movement to abolish the grand jury. It was costly for the government, and many people resented having to serve because it meant time away from the business of making a living, time spent getting to and from the place where the court sat, as well as time spent serving as a juror.

Disinclination to serve had long been a problem, but there were other, more deep-rooted reasons behind the abolition movement. The effective leader of that movement was Ontario district and county court judge James Gowan, who makes a number of appearances in this book. Gowan converted his long-time friend Macdonald to his view in the 1870s, but when Macdonald floated the idea of abolition Ontario argued that the grand jury was an aspect of the constitution of the courts, not a mere question of procedure, and thus within provincial jurisdiction. It was initially agreed to refer the question to the SCC, but then Premier Mowat changed his mind and refused consent. The constitutional issue remained unresolved, and Gowan continued his campaign against the institution. From 1883 and his retirement from the bench and appointment to the Senate, he had a national forum in which to propound his views. Those views, shared by others advocating abolition, were laid out in a long speech he made in the Senate in February 1889.[34]

Gowan began by conceding the longevity of the grand jury in England, but insisted, as he did with other matters, that ancient tradition should count for little and 'the common sense test of utility and fitness' for much in assessing whether any institution should be retained. From that he compared the system used in Scotland favourably to the English, throwing in for good measure assertions that Ontario magistrates were more than competent to do the job of deciding whether to commit somebody for trial. The growth in the use of stipendiary magistrates over the previous three to four decades meant that many JPs were 'able and experienced lawyers,' and those JPs who were not stipendiaries and therefore not legally trained were nonetheless 'competent to commit an alleged offender to gaol to await his trial.' Gowan also referred, albeit indirectly, to the fact that by that time the initial role of the magistrate had become what we now call a preliminary inquiry, held in public. In such a system grand juries were not just unnecessary – inexperienced, comprising men not legally trained, and a 'sham' – they were also an 'evil' and 'mischievous.' They were secret, 'practically irresponsible,' and had no place in a system which should be open to public scrutiny. He insisted that he had never known a case where the grand jury stopped an unwarranted prosecution, because any such attempt would not get past the magistrate in the first place. Conversely, he was 'strongly of opinion' that justifiable and necessary prosecutions had been stopped by grand juries through ignorance, prejudice, and favouritism. Even absent such problems, the grand jury simply did not have the expertise and experience to examine witnesses.

These were perhaps the worst defects of grand juries, but there were others. They met infrequently, so that a person committed by a magistrate might have to wait months before a trial. There was no procedure for challenging grand jurors, and thus people connected to either the accused or the victim could sit, as could those with a pecuniary interest in the outcome and those who had publicly expressed views about the case. These defects were exacerbated by the fact that a grand jury made its decisions by majority vote, so that all somebody with a strong opinion had to do was to persuade some but not all of his colleagues. Having made all these points early in his speech, Gowan recounted numerous anecdotes, none involving the names of any cases or individuals but all designed to disparage the institution. Perhaps someone told him to get on with it, for he moved to other substantive arguments – grand juries cost money, they were an affront to democracy, and while they may once have stood as bulwarks of liberty in 'the dark days of England's history' where monarchs wielded 'arbitrary power,' that was no longer the case. He also pointed out that since the advent of the speedy trial legislation of the 1870s, a subject discussed later in this section, only the most serious offences were now prosecuted on indictment.

Gowan was opposed principally by the Liberal leader in the upper chamber, former secretary of state Richard Scott, an Ottawa lawyer, who denied that the judiciary was divided on the question and argued that 'a very large number' of Ontario judges favoured retaining the grand jury. He also professed to know that 90 per cent of Ontarians were also in favour. The only speaker from the Maritimes who spoke in what had become an argument among Ontarians was Henry Kaulbach of Lunenburg, Nova Scotia, a Crown counsel, who conceded that the grand jury might be said to be outmoded and no longer necessary, but wanted to know what alternative system the government would propose. François-Xavier Trudel, a Quebec lawyer with deeply conservative and religious views, reminded senators that there were constitutional difficulties involved and also criticized both the grand jury and the lack of a public prosecutor in his province. To rely on private initiative, to expect 'the individual who is wronged' to bear the responsibility and the costs of prosecution 'places such a burden upon his shoulders that in many instances it is a denial of justice.'

The response of Minister of Justice Thompson was to ask all judges who presided over criminal cases, and all provincial attorneys general, for their views. He received only three replies from attorneys general – Mowat of Ontario, Theodore Davie of British Columbia, and James W. Longley of Nova Scotia – but 98 from superior and county court judges from every province, the SCC, and the Territorial Supreme Court. The result was thoroughly indecisive. Forty-eight people were in favour of abolition, including both SCC judges, 41 against it, and 12 'doubtful.' The three attorneys general were split, one in each of the three camps, and Gowan must have been disappointed to discover that of the Ontario judges who responded, exactly as many favoured abolition (23) as were either opposed (17) or doubtful (six). At the same time he might have taken some solace from the fact that his fellow county court judges preferred abolition by a substantial majority of 21 to nine, with five doubtful.[35] (We will discuss shortly the role of county court judges in criminal trials.) In these circumstances nothing was done, and indeed the grand jury continued to be used, albeit with decreasing frequency, well into the twentieth century. John Thompson did include abolition of the grand jury in the first draft of the *Criminal Code* submitted to Parliament in 1891, but likely as a red herring, an issue he knew would divert the opposition, give them a 'win' when he dropped it, and thereby mollify any opposition to the larger question of codification.[36]

The grand jury survived the frontal attacks on it, but the trial jury lost more significance in this period, not through any suggestion that it be abolished but by legislation making it decreasingly available and decreasingly likely to be used when defendants had a choice between a jury trial and a summary proceeding.[37] Two 1869 federal statutes were crucial to the process. One, the *Summary Proceedings Act*, was based on a Province of Canada statute of the same name, indeed was in many respects a replica of it.[38] It provided that a 'competent magistrate' could summarily try a range of offences substantially broader than JPs alone or in pairs had previously been able to try. They included a number of property offences where the value was under $10, some quite serious assaults, and offences related to bawdy houses. The effect was to substantially increase the summary jurisdiction of magistrates. A 'competent magistrate' was defined broadly to include a number of different kinds of magistrates, urban and rural, stipendiary and otherwise. The prerequisite for magistrates being able to exercise this broader jurisdiction was that the accused had to consent to it. The magistrate had to personally ask the accused whether he or she did so consent. If there was consent, the trial would take place more or less immediately, and if the result was a guilty plea or a conviction a maximum six-month sentence could be imposed.

The other 1869 statute was much more important. The *Speedy Trials Act* applied only to Ontario and Quebec and dealt with charges not covered by the *Summary Proceedings Act*, that is, with charges that 'may be tried at a Court of General Sessions of the Peace.'[39] Persons so charged could elect to be tried summarily by a judge – any county court judge, junior county court judge, or deputy county court judge in Ontario, and in Quebec by either a judge of sessions, or a district magistrate, or a sheriff, depending on which kind of person presided at the intermediate court in that district.[40] As with the *Summary Proceedings Act* the judge had to put the remanded person to his or her election, and if he or she chose a summary trial, the judge had to appoint 'an early day' for the proceeding. Section 3 stated what the purpose was: a person who elected trial by jury would 'remain untried' until either the court of sessions or the appropriate Superior Court next sat in the county or district. Because at common law the Quarter Sessions had jurisdiction over all criminal offences, although in practice serious charges had long been reserved for trial by jury in a Superior Court three other statutes passed in the same session limited the jurisdiction of the sessions. Offences punishable by death, those involving explosives, and a number of different frauds were all exempted.[41]

The *Speedy Trials Act* was a very large change in criminal procedure. Two decades later Gowan referred indirectly to it as one of the reasons for the grand jury being unnecessary. The county judges' criminal court in Ontario, he said, with just a hint of exaggeration, 'possesses a jurisdiction embracing for trial by judge alone without a jury, nearly every offence known to the law, except capital felonies.'[42] In the years between the passage of the act and Gowan's speech it was extended in two different ways. In 1875 it was made applicable to Manitoba, and the judges who could conduct a speedy trial in Ontario were broadened to include police and stipendiary magistrates. The act was further extended geographically in the 1880s, to British Columbia in 1884 and to the Maritime provinces in 1889. The delay in the extension to British Columbia had much to do with the disputes between the province and the federal government in the 1870s and 1880s over county courts, discussed in chapter 3. If speedy trial jurisdiction could not be given to county courts, the provincial Supreme Court judges were reluctant to take it, although in fact it was conferred on them.[43]

The frequently and publicly stated purpose of all this was to save the provinces the expense of convening juries and paying jurors, and of keeping accused persons in custody awaiting trial. The initial 1869 act was actually introduced in the Commons by John Sandfield Macdonald, the first premier of Ontario who also had a seat in Ottawa, which was permitted until 1872. He told his fellow MPs that the act would be 'the best means of cheapening the administration of justice.' More than twenty years later David Mills remembered that rationale, stating in a debate over the *Criminal Code* that Macdonald had brought in the act 'to get rid of the expense of maintaining a prisoner for a long term in goal, or keeping an innocent party ... for a long period before his trial began.'[44] Economy was a most desirable end, even if it meant forgoing the traditional trial by jury.

There were also non-financial reasons for the *Speedy Trials Acts*. There was less faith in the jury than was once the case. Both civil and criminal trial juries were increasingly criticized as 'ignorant' bodies that reached 'unpredictable verdicts.' They could also be 'more easily tampered with than professional judges.'[45] The acts reflected a growing belief that juries' lack of expertise was inconsistent with the spirit of the age, which stressed training, education, and competence as the qualifications for jobs. Yet here was an institution making very important decisions about the liberty of the subject with absolutely no professional experience. In short, the same kinds of critiques that Gowan and his ilk made of grand jurors could be made, and were made, of the men who sat on trial juries. The new procedure was also seen as beneficial to defendants. They could now proceed to trial quickly, a clear advantage in a system in which bail was rarely available and the wait for a trial could involve months in jail. Worse still was when the trial produced an acquittal or a conviction with a sentence the same as, or less than, the time spent on remand.

The legislation of the 1870s and 1880s certainly had the intended effect on the number of jury trials held across the country, which declined steadily, even as the number of people charged with offences rose. Whether or not the legislation was passed to measure the effect of the *Speedy Trials Acts*, the federal government started collecting and publishing criminal statistics pursuant to the *Criminal Statistics Act* of 1876,[46] and they amply bear out the success of the new system. In 1885, for example, there were 5,446 indictable offences tried, 1,107 of them, or 20 per cent, involving jury trials. Twenty years later the comparable numbers were 10,899 and 712; jury trials thus made up just 6.5 per cent of all trials of indictable offences.[47] One study of Nova Scotia shows that the Supreme Court had far fewer criminal cases to deal with, and as a result civil trials could be prioritized in a way they had not been before. Before 1889 the Supreme Court on circuit often had time to hear only criminal cases in their short visits to circuit towns, and civil ones were either relegated to the next circuit or, if it was possible, an additional session had to be held. After the *Speedy Trials Act* civil trials almost always dominated the docket. In Victoria County, for example, there were only 13 criminal trials between 1891 and 1924. In the more populous Colchester County there were only three years after 1890 when there were more criminal trials than civil.[48]

Criminal Procedure: Trial and Appeal Rights

We conclude this account of criminal procedure with a brief examination of the trial process itself. Along with the substantive criminal law acts of the late 1860s and early 1870s, Parliament also enacted a *Criminal Procedure Act*, based on a chapter of the 1859 *Consolidated Statutes* of the Province of Canada. It included the standard aspects of the trial process. The accused had the right to make a full defence by counsel, which, as we saw in *Volume 1*, had been conferred only in the 1830s and 1840s. He or she could see copies of all indictments and pretrial depositions and could challenge some jurors peremptorily (20 in cases carrying a death sentence, 12 in others) and others for cause (unlimited). The prosecution had fewer peremptory challenges, four in all cases. The right to a jury de mediatate linguae (see chapter 4) was confirmed, but not for aliens. In one respect an accused person's rights were reduced from the pre-Confederation period. Upper Canada had allowed an appeal on a question of law to its Court of Error and Appeal, but this was abolished, although all defendants could apply for a writ of error on the face of the record, a largely toothless right because there was no 'record' in a criminal proceeding, just a verdict. In 1876 the requirement for witnesses in criminal cases to appear was strengthened by a statute making them subject to fines or imprisonment if they did not appear – a measure that, while it could benefit both sides, likely worked more to the Crown's advantage.[49]

Two things were absent from an accused's rights that we now think of as standard and natural: the accused was not a competent witness, and thus could not give sworn testimony in his or her own defence, and there was no right of appeal. The former rule was of ancient lineage and initially applied to all parties in all cases, civil and criminal, on the grounds that parties were interested witnesses.[50] It was changed in mid-nineteenth-century England for parties in civil cases, and the same reform was enacted in many Canadian jurisdictions in the 1870s. But an accused in a criminal trial was not allowed to testify under oath in Canada until 1893, five years before the rule was changed in the United Kingdom.[51] The rule was justified on the somewhat contradictory grounds that an accused was likely to commit perjury knowing what was at stake, and in testifying he or she would be subjected to vigorous cross-examination, which could lead to self-incrimination. This latter argument rested on the same premise that conservative judges in both the United Kingdom and British North America had used to oppose the prisoners' counsel acts a half century earlier – that the judge was the best protector of an accused person. For this reason Canadian reform bills of the 1880s and early 1890s, many proposed by Liberal MP Malcolm Cameron, who wanted to make the accused not only competent but also compellable, were consistently opposed by the legal profession and were passed in the Commons but defeated in the Senate. On one occasion, appealing to the same notions of common sense and utility that Gowan had used, Cameron put it that '[a] person accused of a crime desires to give evidence in his own behalf. He desires to place his own oath against the oath of the prosecutor. He desires to explain the special circumstances that tell against him…. The answer of common sense, reason and justice is that he should be able to do so. The answer of the law is that he cannot do so; his mouth must be closed…. I say that position is neither reasonable, nor is it logical.'[52]

Ultimately legislation making the accused competent was another John Thompson product, introduced the same year as the *Criminal Code* and passed the following year. Like Cameron he wanted to make both accuseds and their spouses both competent and compellable, arguing that a criminal trial should be as thorough a search for the truth as possible. But a majority of MPs would not go so far; compellability smacked of the French inquisitorial system.[53] It is likely that Thompson floated the trial balloon of compellability in order to make competence easier to accept at a time when England had not gone that far. The act made accuseds and their spouses competent, although neither could 'disclose any communication made … [by the other] during their marriage.'

The other major procedural innovation of this period was the establishment of a right of appeal in criminal cases.[54] It was contained in part 52 of the 1892 *Criminal Code,* and was a significant innovation, ending a long tradition in Anglo-Canadian law of not allowing appeals from criminal trial verdicts and enacted some 15 years before the establishment of the UK Court of Criminal Appeals. Part 52 was taken more or less verbatim from James Stephen's draft code, which, as we saw in the first section of this chapter, never became law in England. Yet for such an important measure we know remarkably little about why it was enacted when it was. Here we will first describe and analyse the *Criminal Code* provisions, which necessarily involves examining what recourse was available to convicted persons before 1892, and then offer some explanations for the introduction of appeals.

Two sections of part 52 were particularly important. Section 743 (2) provided that at any point during or after the trial, a trial judge could 'reserve any question of law' that had arisen during the trial or during pre- or post-trial proceedings 'for the opinion of the Court of Appeal.' Subsection 3 went on to give the prosecutor or the accused the right to ask the judge to reserve such a question and, if he refused to do so, he nonetheless had to make a note of the objection. Subsection 6 then required that the judge had to state a case on any question that had been reserved, that is, to provide some account of what had brought the question into play. The reference to reserving a question was to the existing, in England and Canada, limited avenue for appeal. Prior to 1848, although civil appeals were well developed, the only way to challenge a verdict in a criminal case was to apply for a writ of error, to allege some mistake in the trial proceeding. The problem was that it had to be an error on the face of the record, and the 'record' in a criminal trial was extremely limited – the indictment, the jury list, and the forms that recorded the plea, the verdict, and the sentence. James Stephen put the problem bluntly when he said that 'the record takes no notice either of the evidence or of the direction given by the judge to the jury,' and thus 'the grossest errors of fact or of law may occur without being in any way brought upon the record.'[55] The inadequacy of the writ of error was recognized in the United Kingdom by the mid-nineteenth century, and the Court of Crown Cases Reserved was created in response. Henceforth after a conviction, a trial judge was permitted to 'reserve any question of law' for the consideration of the royal judges (the judges of King's Bench, Common Pleas, and Exchequer). This was still a very limited appeal, invocable by the judge, not the defendant, and it did not confer the power to grant a new trial. Versions of this legislation were passed in the colonies before Confederation and stayed in force after 1867. Thus reservation of a case by the judge was the only avenue of 'appeal' between Confederation and 1892.[56]

The significance of section 743, therefore, was threefold. It expanded, albeit in a limited way, the options for having a case reserved for consideration by an appeal court. Sections 744 and 745 added to an accused's appeal rights under section 743. They allowed the prosecution or the defence to appeal a trial judge's refusal to reserve a case to a Court of Appeal, with leave of the attorney general. More importantly, section 745 provided that if the appeal court took the case it could require the trial judge to provide his notes and any other evidence or, if it found the material supplied 'defective,' 'refer to such other evidence of what took place at the trial as it may think fit.' This was still a long way from modern rights of appeal, but it was also an equally long way from having the trial judge be the only person who could decide whether to reserve a case and having a grossly inadequate record on which the appeal court could rule. The other novel aspect of section 743 was that it allowed the prosecution to appeal an acquittal. Why this provision was included was never explained in Parliament, and historians have not found an explanation. The subject merits further study, especially the links between it and the distrust of juries and jurors discussed above.

The second highly significant innovation in part 52 was section 747, which allowed a convicted person to appeal on the ground that 'the verdict was against the weight of evidence.' The trial judge had to give leave, but if the appeal court agreed with the defendant's argument a new trial could be ordered. This was an appeal on findings of fact, available only to the defendant, unlike the appeal on law, which the prosecution could also invoke. The need for the trial judge to give leave was a significant limitation, but opening the door to an appeal on the facts was a major change. In addition, section 748 allowed an application to be made to the minister of justice if the trial judge did refuse leave. The minister could then order a new trial if he 'entertains a doubt whether [the defendant] … ought to have been convicted.' In short, this was an avenue by which wrongful convictions could be overturned. This has been termed a form of 'jury control,' reducing the discretionary authority of prejudiced or irrational decision-making by laymen.

The question of why these provisions were included in the Code has not been definitively addressed. The likely answer is that there had long been dissatisfaction in the legal community with the substantial disjuncture between civil and criminal appeal rights and the ability to obtain a new trial. There might also have been dissatisfaction with the limited criminal appeal powers given to the SCC when it was established in 1875. Any convicted person whose conviction had been affirmed by the court of last resort in a province could appeal 'against the affirmation of such a conviction.' This was a very limited appeal. The highest provincial court had to have affirmed the conviction, and it could do that only if the trial judge had reserved the case. Moreover, the *Supreme Court Act* permitted an appeal only where the provincial court was not unanimous.[57] The court heard only 13 criminal appeals between 1876 and 1892. After 1892 the SCC could hear more cases on more grounds; indeed the Code sought to make it a genuine court of last resort by prohibiting criminal appeals to the JCPC. The only 'real' criminal appeal before the 1892 *Criminal Code* was one included in the 1889 *Combines Act*, which allowed somebody convicted under that act the right to appeal 'upon all issues of law and fact.' This provision, evoking a tenderness towards monopolistic businessmen or corporations, was not in the original act but was added in the Senate.[58]

An effective right to appeal in criminal cases was an idea whose time had come, and that time was the opportunity presented by the decision to enact a code that was comprehensive, that dealt with both substantive criminal law and procedure. The fairness embedded in the very idea of appeal would have appealed to a man like Thompson, and there was no powerful lobby against criminal appeals as there was in England, where the judges were strongly averse to any change. Instead, a substantial body of legal opinion in Canada was prepared to ditch tradition in favour of utilitarian reform, as we saw in the debates over the grand jury. It was not powerful enough to get its way on that issue, but appeals were different. The appeal provisions were very little discussed in the Commons, and much of the debate concerned a proposal that was dropped, that jurors be required to answer written questions as part of the record.[59]

Imprisonment: The Federal Penitentiary System and Intermediate Prisons

By 1867 imprisonment had become the standard punishment for anybody not sentenced to death. The sentence of standing in the pillory had been abolished in some colonies and was declared inapplicable nationally in the *Criminal Procedure Act* of 1869. Whipping was retained for some offences throughout this period, but only as a discretionary adjunct to a prison sentence for those convicted of three offences, including attempts to sexually assault young girls, and it could be carried out only in prison.[60] Jurisdiction over penal institutions was shared between the federal government and the provinces in the *BNA Act*. The distinction between 'penitentiaries' and 'public and reformatory prisons' had its origins in penal practice of the Province of Canada, which by the 1840s was sending people sentenced to two years or more to Kingston Penitentiary, and the others to local jails or, where they existed, youth institutions. The new dominion maintained this practice, Kingston continuing to serve as the penitentiary for both Ontario and Quebec and the Halifax and Saint John penitentiaries becoming federally run institutions.[61] Only once during this period was there any suggestion of changing the 'two-year' line of demarcation. In 1887 Quebec proposed that the federal government assume all the costs of the prison system, which it thought too burdensome for the provinces, a rare example of a province suggesting its jurisdiction be reduced, and perhaps as a result the proposal went nowhere.[62] For the reasons given in the introduction, we will not, with two exceptions, deal with provincial prisons. There was a large number of them, and they performed multiple functions in the legal system – holding prisoners on remand and those confined for debt, incarcerating those sentenced to prison terms under two years, providing the place for executions, and even 'sheltering' society's most unfortunates in the winter – vagrants, prostitutes, the destitute. This very multiplicity of functions would require a whole chapter devoted to them, especially given that there were numerous differences among provinces.

The first *Penitentiary Act* of 1868 established the position of director of penitentiaries, although as many as three men could have that title, one of whom would be the chair. The directors were to 'have the control and management of all the Penitentiaries in Canada.' Although they could decide which 'system of discipline' should be used and determine the balance between punishment and reformation, the role of prison labour, the systems of rewards and punishments, and the degree of communication between inmates, many of these things were mandated in the act. It required that all prisoners 'shall be kept constantly at hard labour' for 10 hours a day.[63] It also mandated the silent system during work hours: 'No convict shall be permitted to speak to another convict upon any pretence whatever, nor to any officer or guard, ... except with respect to the work at which he is employed, and then only in the fewest words and in a respectful manner.' When prisoners were not working, separate – that is, solitary – confinement in non-working hours, night or day, was the rule. In other sections the act allowed prisoners to be moved from one penitentiary to another at any time, permitted the infliction of corporal punishment for infractions of prison rules, at the discretion of the warden, and required that male and female prisoners be kept separate. The women's wing of Kingston was the only penitentiary for women in Canada in this period. Sentence reductions of no more than five days a month for 'good behaviour, diligence and industry' which had to be 'exemplary,' were permitted. This system of incentives and rewards had been partially implemented at Kingston before 1867 and was known as the Crofton system after Irish prison administrator Walter Crofton, who had first employed it. Earned remission remained throughout this period and was extended in 1883; it has been called 'the outstanding achievement of late nineteenth century penal reform,' but that does not mean much, given that there were few or no other achievements.

In 1875 the 1868 act was repealed, penitentiaries were placed under the Ministry of Justice, and the three-director system replaced by a new post, the inspector of penitentiaries. This single individual was given two assistants, for Manitoba and British Columbia, the following year. In most other respects the substance of the Act remained as it had been, except that St. Vincent de Paul in Laval, Quebec, opened in 1873, was added to the list of established penitentiaries. Quebec prisoners housed in Kingston were transferred there. The two major changes were to the prison labour and punishment regimes. Section 35 divided labour into two kinds: obligatory, which had to be performed as before, and voluntary, extra hours of work at any job that convicts of 'exemplary conduct' could perform for remuneration, the money either being sent to their families or credited and paid on release. This voluntary labour could be contracted out to private employers. Section 67 provided also for earned remission for the same good conduct, a maximum of five days a month served. Section 37 required that a surgeon certify that any prisoner was in physical condition to receive corporal punishment, that the surgeon be present, and that whipping be limited to 60 strokes.[64]

The *Penitentiary Acts* allowed the federal government to designate 'any tract of land within the Dominion' as a penitentiary, and by 1880 three more had been established: the Manitoba penitentiary (1877, later renamed Stony Mountain); New Westminster in British Columbia (1878); and Dorchester in New Brunswick (1880). When Dorchester opened, the Saint John and Halifax penitentiaries became provincial institutions. They had been condemned by federal officials who visited them in the late 1860s as little better than common jails, overcrowded and with prisoners living in deplorable conditions, and a few years later things had only become worse. There were many more prisoners than cells, with the result that prisoners 'full of sores and loathsome diseases' lay on 'make-shift bunks, packed side by side,' in an open space.[65] The final penitentiaries established in this period, in 1903 and 1911, were the Alberta penitentiary in Edmonton and the Saskatchewan penitentiary at Prince Albert. Prisons in the Territories were also a federal responsibility before 1905, although no penitentiary was built in the Territories other than Edmonton.

The statutory regime for penitentiaries remained largely the same as established by the 1875 act. There were major consolidations of the act in 1883 and 1906, but they consisted mostly of the same sections reproduced. The remission provisions were altered over time, with the number of days off the sentence augmented. From 1906 convict labour could not be let out on contract, the result of objections from the labour movement. From the same date, solitary confinement in cells was limited to night-time, not during non-working hours during the day. This hardly meant much leisure in the company of others; working hours were 10 a day.[66]

Throughout this period officials formally saw the purposes of penitentiary imprisonment as twofold: punishment and reformation. The reformist optimism of the 1830s and 1840s, the belief that prisons' principal purpose was to rehabilitate the offender, was long gone. But reformation was always touted as an ambition, even though it was never said to be of greater importance than punishment and deterrence and in practice was invariably very much a secondary goal. The *Penitentiary Acts* placed the two objectives on a par and measured them in relation to the method of prison discipline employed. In discussing separate confinement, for example, section 32 of the 1875 act stated that 'no system of discipline in a penitentiary can be effectual for punishment, or for reformation of the criminal, unless it be combined with strict separate confinement during some period of time of his imprisonment.' Overall the Canadian penitentiary system was marked by 'institutional rigidities and punitive policies' that always put punishment, security, and discipline at the forefront of guiding policies and everyday administration. This was the 'enduring reality' of the penitentiary until at least the middle of the twentieth century.[67] The silent system and solitary confinement at night were always mandated. The use of whipping to enforce discipline was endemic, and prison labour, mainly stone-breaking, was pointless and demoralizing.

Some prison professionals, wardens, and penitentiary inspectors advocated better staff training, an improvement in prison conditions, specialized institutions, less use of the lash, and greater use of the Crofton system. The most notable was James George Moylan, who held the post of inspector from 1875 to 1895, John Creighton, warden of Kingston from 1870 until 1885, and Samuel Bedson, warden of Stony Mountain. But the reforms they were able to make were minimal. Over time a reduction in corporal punishment was achieved, through greater use of punishments such as solitary confinement in a small dark cell and hosing down with jets of cold water. The verdict of historians on Kingston and other institutions is unanimous: the 'repressive' Canadian penitentiary system of the pre-Confederation period 'simply lurched forward into the twentieth century,' the 'traditional punitive structures' playing out their 'grim role, continuing to ensure that convict life must be filled with all but unrelieved pain and suffering.'

Most prison officials saw their charges as hardened and unreformable criminals who needed most of all to be kept in subjection and submission. Some civil society organizations – churches, labour organisations, the Ontario Prisoners' Aid Association, founded in 1874, which later became the John Howard Society – proposed prison reforms but they had little influence on policy. Politicians were essentially uninterested in penitentiaries as anything other than sites of punishment and warehouses for society's most undesirable members. Macdonald, a native of Kingston, expressed this attitude very clearly during his first administration: 'Happiness and punishment cannot and ought not to go together. There is such a thing as making a prison too comfortable and the prisoners too happy.'[68] Penitentiaries caught the public's attention only when the anger and frustration of the inmates led to prison riots and other forms of protest, which on occasion were put down with the use of the armed forces. Three times during this period the armed forces were called to Kingston, the first in 1868.[69]

The only significant innovation in this period was the introduction in 1899 of parole, legislated in the *Ticket of Leave Act*.[70] It allowed any convict to be granted 'a licence to be at large in Canada,' or in any part of the country designated in the licence. The Act contained no specifications regarding if and when a convict could apply, and no criteria for granting a conditional release. It was all left to the discretion of the warden and penitentiary branch officials. A parolee had to report to the police after changing locations, and male parolees also had to report their presence monthly. It is fitting that we end this section with the only federal investigation into the penitentiary system in this period, the 1914 Royal Commission on Penitentiaries. It was misnamed, for it only investigated Kingston, which had experienced a significant disturbance the year before. The commissioners visited many American institutions but no other Canadian penitentiary. Its importance was reflected in the fact that the chairman was George Milnes Macdonnell, a Kingston lawyer, and the other members were prominent Kingston doctor and later dean of the medical school, Frederick Etherington, and Joseph Downey of Orillia, journalist and sometime provincial assemblyman who was the superintendent of the Ontario Asylum for Idiots.[71] Its 45-page report contained 23 recommendations, ranging from things very unlikely to be carried out (new prisons for first offenders), to more of the same (constant labour), to pious hopes ('in the employment of guards more regards [should] be had to the character and education of the applicant'). It did recommend an end to hosing and the dark cell, but this proposal was not adopted. Prison historians are agreed that only in the second half of the twentieth century, following the Fauteux report of 1956, which for the first time talked of 'treatment,' did any significant reform occur.

As noted in the introduction to this section, in addition to federal penitentiaries, we will also briefly discuss two unique carceral institutions, both established in Ontario. The Ontario Central Prison was the only provincial prison designed to operate like a penitentiary, while the Mercer Reformatory was the only free-standing women's prison, and one run and staffed by women. Both were promoted by John Langmuir, Ontario's inspector of prisons, asylums, and public charities from 1868 to 1882,[72] who was an indefatigable reformer and a tireless administrator. The Central Prison, located at the intersection of King and Strachan Streets in Toronto, was opened in 1874 as a provincial version of a penitentiary.[73] It was designed to solve the problem of a lack of work for convicts sentenced to serve their time with hard labour in provincial prisons that had no facilities to provide any kind of work. It was intended to be an 'industrial prison' for those serving less than two years who would rehabilitate through labour. The prisoners would work for private manufacturers who contracted with the provincial government, and the prison would turn a profit. What has been nicely termed 'capitalism's ... brilliant meeting with confinement' was, of course, a failure. It did not make money for the government, the initial major contractor went bankrupt, leading to an investigation by a provincial royal commission, prisoners engaged in myriad acts of rebellion against monotonous employment (or complete lack of employment), there were no training programs, recidivism rates were high, and harsh physical punishments were meted out for violations of the rules by the alcoholic strict disciplinarian warden, former Toronto police chief William Stratton Prince. It was rumoured that Prince carried out clandestine night-time burials. His successor, James Massie, a provincial MLA, was little better. The provincial government established a royal commission in 1885 to investigate charges of 'cruelty, partiality and mismanagement' against him, which concluded that the complaints were not well-founded. Despite all its problems, the central remained in operation until the First World War.

The Mercer Reformatory for Women, as its name implies, was a very different institution.[74] It was Canada's first separate women's prison, built in 1879–80 with $106,000 the government received through the law of escheat, Toronto businessman Andrew Mercer having died intestate with no heirs.[75] But this was a coincidence, and the reformatory's origins went rather deeper, a response to concerns of social reformers about what they believed to be the breakdown of the social and moral order caused by increasing urbanization and industrialization. It was also inspired by the influential women's prison movement in the United States. Langmuir insisted in 1878 that 'the very highest authorities in the specialty of women's prison administration' in that country favoured separate prisons for women. The Mercer was to rescue women gone wrong through some of the techniques that had been unsuccessful in the case of men – work and a disciplined regimen. In

Langmuir's words, it was to be 'an industrial reformatory for women.' But there was also a fundamental difference between the Mercer and men's prisons like the Central Prison. Corporal and other harsh punishments would not be used, and the institution was to be staffed only by women. It would be a maternal prison, one aspect of the middle- and upper-middle-class women's reform movement that also campaigned for temperance and protection against predatory male sexual violence.

Most of the women sent to the Mercer had been convicted of petty morals offences, prostitution, vagrancy, and drunkenness, and the hope was that the good examples and kindliness of respectable and God-fearing female prison officials would reclaim 'the criminal and fallen of their sex.' The sincerity of the women who ran the institution is undoubted, as was the class gulf between them and the inmates. Most of those sent to the Mercer had been convicted many times, and while incarceration gave them a respite from their lives as outcasts and occupants of the lowest rungs on the socio-economic scale, and while a small number secured 'respectable' employment as domestic servants and factory workers after release, most were already doomed to life on the margins. Recidivism rates were high, and while it has been argued that the Mercer was a success in maintaining its own regime internally, it effected little 'reformation.'

Capital Punishment: General

Apart from Louis Riel, the only people hanged in this period were those convicted of murder. A total of 272 people suffered the ultimate fate, 4 of them women.[76] They were not all convicted of murder, despite the fact that death was the mandatory sentence. Between sentence and the gallows lay the possibility of a pardon, commutation of the sentence. Capital punishment as the sentence for murder was never seriously questioned in this period. Liberal backbencher Robert Bickerdike, a wealthy businessman and an ardent defender of civil and minority rights, waged a one-man campaign to abolish the death penalty in the 1910s and introduced private member's abolition bills from 1914, but he was simply ignored. Indeed the possibility of a pardon was used by most commentators as part of their defence of capital punishment; generally people deserved to die if they had taken another's life, and those who did not had a way to have their sentences commuted.[77]

Before Confederation the royal prerogative of mercy was the preserve of colonial governors, and in the Quebec Resolutions, discussed in chapter 2, it had been proposed that it reside in future with the provincial lieutenant governors. But this was a provision that London would not accept. A prerogative power could be exercised only by the Queen's direct representative, and since lieutenant governors were appointed by Ottawa, only the governor general, appointed by the Queen, could issue a pardon. Although the status of lieutenant governors later became a much contested issue in division of powers jurisprudence, and although one of the many cases the provinces won on this question concerned an 1888 Ontario statute that asserted the lieutenant governor's right to commute sentences for infractions of provincial laws, Ottawa's sole power to commute death sentences was never questioned.[78] Moving the seat of decision from provincial capitals was not a major change for central Canada, and it does not seem to have troubled people in the Maritimes, but it did cause consternation for British Columbians after 1871, because officials there lost control of an important tool used to cow the Indigenous population at a time when it was still larger than the white one and, as we saw in chapter 7, the province was resisting attempts by Ottawa to change its policy of unilaterally establishing inadequate reserves. Between 1864 and 1871 26 people were hanged in the colony, all but three of them Indigenous. Between 1872 and 1880 nine Indigenous people and two whites were sentenced to death. Both whites and two of the nine Indigenous people were executed, seven having their sentences commuted in Ottawa.[79] Confederation thus wrought a substantial change to British Columbia's execution landscape.

The executive's review of death sentences was codified in the 1869 *Criminal Procedure Act* and later in the *Criminal Code*. The former provided that it was not necessary for a judge who pronounced the death sentence to submit a report before it was carried out, although he could do so if he believed that the convict was a candidate for mercy, or if an unresolved point of law had come up in the trial, or if there was any other cause to delay the execution. In the interim he had the power to issue a reprieve for enough time to allow for consideration of the case by Ottawa. A reprieved prisoner was to be isolated from the other prisoners. Judges' reports and trial transcripts became formally required in section 1063 of the *Criminal Code*. The 1869 criminal procedure statute also abolished public hangings. Henceforth executions were to take place within the prison, although people could, and did, apply for tickets to be allowed in as observers. More importantly, as we saw with the Louis Riel execution in chapter 7, the height of the prison walls, not the law, determined whether a hanging was visible to the public. There were numerous other cases in which something similar happened. When eight Indigenous participants in the 1885 rebellion were hanged for murder in 1886 at Battleford, Macdonald required the scaffold to be built high enough to permit viewing from outside. Reminiscent of the traditional use of public executions to instil terror, he also ordered that many other Indigenous people be brought to Battleford to witness the event. Executions took place in local jails in this period, and other notorious cases brought in large crowds, including that of Reginald Birchall, hanged in Woodstock, Ontario, in 1890 for shooting Frederick Benwell, and Joseph Thibault, hanged in Annapolis, Nova Scotia, for murdering a female pauper entrusted to his care. On the latter occasion the crowd simply pulled down the prison walls to witness the dispatch of the locally notorious killer.[80]

We know a good deal about the formal outlines of the decision-making process in capital case reviews.[81] Very shortly after Confederation the government established internal bureaucratic procedures for case reviews, which, whatever the statute said, included a requirement for the judge to write a report on every death sentence pronounced. In addition to summarizing the evidence at trial, the judge had to answer the key question: did he think the death penalty was appropriate? Although this and other material went formally to the secretary of state as the minister who nominally represented the governor general, the file was always reviewed in the Remissions Branch of the Department of Justice. For much of this period the chief remissions officer was the aptly named Augustus Power, a lawyer who joined the branch in 1875, became its head in 1879, and held that post for 34 years. The chief remissions officer made a recommendation to the minister of justice, who generally accepted it and presented it to cabinet. Nothing attests more strongly to the symbolic and political significance of the death penalty than that every death sentence was discussed by the cabinet. Governors general may have intervened more often than is known, but they mostly rubber-stamped what the cabinet had decided. In the best-known case in which this did not happen, that of Valentine Shortis, on whose behalf Lord and Lady Aberdeen used their influence to get the sentence commuted, the fact became known and caused much discomfort in Ottawa.[82]

Moving beyond formal procedures, some general points can be made about the results of the case review process. Although attempted murder and statutory rape were capital offences until the late 1870s,

The hanging of Louis Riel.

Credit: *Louis Riel, Martyr du Nord-Ouest Sa vie, son procès, sa mort* (anonymous author, Project Gutenberg, 2006)

and rape carried the death penalty as an optional sentence through-out this period and beyond, all death sentences for anything other than murder were commuted.[83] More importantly almost half (254, or 48 per cent) of the 529 people sentenced to death for murder had their sentences commuted, invariably to life imprisonment, or had a new trial ordered. A further seven people died before their cases were resolved, and the result is unknown in five cases, meaning that known executions totalled 272, or 51 per cent of those sentenced to death for murder. The question asked by many historians of capital punishment across many periods and jurisdictions is what made the difference in any given case between whether individuals were among the half who saw their lives ended or the half who lived on, for life or otherwise, in prison? That question cannot be conclusively answered, principally because the decision-making process, for all we know about its formal aspects, was opaque: no reasons were given and we do not have access to what was said in the cabinet room, let alone to what went on in men's minds or in private conversations.

It is not difficult to explain individual cases. That of Angelina Napolitano, for example, a poor recent Italian immigrant living in Sault Ste. Marie who killed her sleeping and much abusive husband with an axe in 1911, precipitated a massive international campaign for clemency. Over 100,000 people in Canada, the United States, and Europe wrote to Ottawa and/or signed petitions on her behalf. She came to epitomize concerns in the women's movement about spousal violence, female honour, and maternal virtue, for her husband had also tried to make her prostitute herself.[84] She was spared, but neither the volume of support nor abusive victims guaranteed a commutation. Louis Riel's case is evidence of the former, and that of Elizabeth Workman, hanged in 1873 after killing an abusive and drunken husband, demonstrates the latter.[85] All cases considered by the executive prompted members of the public to write or sign letters or petitions in support of a pardon or, rather less often, to demand that the convicted person hang, and the amount of paper generated varied greatly from case to case, but with no correlation to the result. The influence that powerful people could bring to bear did make a difference, positively or negatively, in some well-known cases, such as that of Valentine Shortis, discussed above, or of Hilda Blake, discussed below, but this factor was determinative in only a few cases that we know about. And very few of those sentenced to death were influential people or had influential connections. Class status meant that a case was unlikely to get to the commutation stage; the better off had access to the kind of defence counsel that could produce an acquittal or a conviction on a lesser charge. We also know that men who killed in the commission of sexual assaults were more likely than the average murderer to be hanged.[86]

It has been argued that a jury's recommendation of mercy tilted the balance in favour of commutation, a judge's even more so, and there is evidence to support that contention.[87] Of the 18 New Brunswick cases in which we know what the judge's recommendation was, the cabinet followed it in 14 cases. The comparable figures for Quebec between 1867 and 1890 are 23 and 19. But that only raises the question of why judges and juries did or did not make such recommendations. A judge would recommend commutation if he had doubts about the verdict based on the evidence, and judges and juries did so if they thought there were extenuating circumstances. But exactly what were 'extenuating circumstances,' and why did the cabinet agree or not agree with the recommendation? Statistical studies of the cases from the 1920s to the 1950s have amply demonstrated that, in the aggregate, inequalities of class and ethnicity mattered, and there is evidence for that in this period – some discussed below in the discussion of Indigenous people, and some provided by the numbers for Asians (Chinese, Japanese, and South Asians), 57 per cent of whom were hanged.[88] But this is only slightly different from the sample as a whole, and there was no difference in the case of Blacks. Probably 19 of the men sentenced to death for murder were Black.[89] Ten were hanged and nine had their sentences commuted, effectively the same rate of commutation as for the sample as a whole. As we will see in chapter 16, Canadians in this period were deeply prejudiced against Blacks, who suffered great inequality in myriad aspects of social and economic life. But the formal law did not draw overt distinctions between Black and white. Indeed, in public and political discussions of these cases commentators, including presiding judges, often used them to trumpet the merits of British justice and the rule of law in comparison to the United States, especially the increasingly Jim Crow southern states.

There were some differences related to time and place, although nobody has seriously examined why regional differences in the origin of cases would affect decision-making in Ottawa. The commutation rate for cases from Ontario up to 1880, for example, was 61 per cent, but for Quebec in the same period it was 44 per cent. But this did not mean that overall Ontario residents were advantaged. From 1881 to 1914 more of them were hanged than pardoned, and for the entire period exactly as many Ontario cases resulted in hanging as in commutation (76) with two people also receiving a new trial. The provinces/regions that did show a substantially greater number of hangings than pardons were New Brunswick, British Columbia, and the North-West and Yukon Territories, and that was largely the result of a greater than the overall average number of Indigenous and Asian people hanged. All of this is admittedly inconclusive, and that is our point. With the exceptions of cases involving women and Indigenous people discussed in the following section, in no case could the result have been predicted with a high degree of confidence. Aggregate statistics never explain any particular decision in a particular case. Hence the commutation process has been described as a 'lottery'; we turn to an examination of how cases involving two types of offenders were treated in this 'lottery.'

Capital Punishment: Women and Indigenous People

The most striking feature of the results of the executive capital case review process in this period was the extremely high rate of commutation for convicted women murderers. Women made up only a very small percentage of those convicted of murder and sentenced to death in this period, only 22 out of 529, 4 per cent, and of those 22 only 4 were hanged: 2 in the 1870s and 2 in the late 1890s. That there were so few convicted female murderers presumably explains to some extent why only 4 were executed; women's crimes simply did not pose a threat to social order. Beyond this, the men who decided these cases did not think it was appropriate to hang members of the 'weaker sex.' It has been argued that there was a de facto moratorium on executing women after 1899, which lasted a little over twenty years, a product of an effective and vocal women's movement that took up the cause after the Napolitano case, but that cannot account for the pronounced reluctance to execute women prior to 1900.[90] The circumstances of many of the crimes are revealing; at least 8 women killed children, usually their own and often illegitimate, and none were hanged. There is much evidence from this and other periods to suggest that women who killed their illegitimate infants were unlikely to be prosecuted, or if prosecuted acquitted or convicted of a lesser included offence, or, as we see here, if convicted then pardoned. Prosecutors, jurors, and the cabinet acted this way in part because these women killed from desperation at the social ruin that faced them, which was punishment enough, and in part because they were hardly likely to kill any other person.[91] In addition, one of the convictions was of a woman who was charged with her husband of murder after an abortion they performed led to the death of the woman, and Angelina Napolitano, and likely others, killed abusive husbands.[92]

We can look at this issue from the other direction, and ask why four women were hanged. Cordelia Viau was an accomplice with her lover, Samuel Parslow, in brutally getting her husband out of the way of their alliance, and they were both executed. Hilda Blake, the only woman sentenced to death in Manitoba over this nearly 50-year period, confessed that she had shot Mary Lane, the wife of her wealthy employer, and refused defence counsel. Shortly before her execution she said that she had been enticed to kill by Mary's husband, Robert, and a book-length account of the case argues that the prominent cabinet minister and Laurier loyalist Clifford Sifton had good reason to see her die and her and the whole matter buried. As noted above, Elizabeth Workman killed an abusive and drunken husband, and for all we know Phoebe Campbell, who took an axe to her spouse two years earlier, may have done the same thing.[93] We are not arguing that any of these killings were somehow justified; that would be a pointless and ahistorical contention. We are simply noting that the women who were hanged generally seemed to have stepped out of their submissive roles and, at the same time, how their actions were perceived could vary from person to person, so that even in the area where we have very strong evidence from aggregate statistics, there was always an element of chance in how the executive would decide the case.

Finally, we consider the cases of the 61 Indigenous people sentenced to death in this period. Between 1920 and 1957 62 per cent of Indigenous people convicted of murdering other Indigenous people were executed, and the rate rose to 96 per cent if the victim was white. In this period the numbers were somewhat different. Thirty-six of the Indigenous people sentenced to death, or 59 per cent, were hanged. Yet this total was made up of very different kinds of cases. As noted in chapter 7, eight Cree men were hanged at Battleford for killing white settlers during the 1885 rebellion, and only two had their sentences commuted, and if these 10 were removed from the sample, the execution rate for Indigenous people would be 50 per cent, the same for the sample as a whole. The application of the death penalty to Indigenous people was influenced by a variety of factors. On the one hand, there seems little doubt that at the moment of greatest crisis to the stability of the Canadian state – the 1885 rebellion – it was used as a blunt instrument of state power to cow those who had dared, or might in future dare, to challenge Canadian sovereignty. On the other side of the coin, the state had some qualms about executing people according to the strict dictates of Anglo-Canadian law when their own law would not have prescribed that penalty and Canadian law and values had only very minimally influenced many Indigenous societies.

The case discussed in chapter 10 of Haatq, or Ha-at, a Gitxsan man who killed white trader Amos Youmans in northern British Columbia in 1884, illustrates how this issue was sometimes handled. Haatq was tried in Victoria and defended by court-appointed counsel, leading barrister, and later BC Supreme Court judge Montague Tyrwhitt Drake.

He presented what is today called a cultural defence. Haatq had acted according to the dictates of Gitxsan law, which in the circumstances obligated him to exact revenge in blood. Drake called witnesses to show that Youmans knew Gitxsan law and indeed had been involved in compensation transactions in previous years. Drake did not believe he would or should secure an acquittal, telling the jury, 'I do not put forward these considerations to blind you as to the law of the case, that is clear and if it were a white man I should not think of it. But there are extraordinary circumstances which may well plead in the mitigation of the offence.' Presiding judge Henry Pellew Crease would have none of this. Gitxsan law was 'external to the case' and the jury was to ignore it, which they dutifully did and convicted Haatq of murder. Drake pursued his cultural defence in other fora, letters to provincial and federal authorities, and he was joined in his petitioning by local Gitxsan chiefs. Drake and his colleagues argued that a man should not be hanged for obeying the requirements of his own cultural understandings. Publicly no heed was taken to this claim by Lieutenant Governor John Robson, who insisted in a letter to the Gitxsan that not only was Canadian law now the law of the land, but in any event 'the Queen's law is better than yours.' As it turned out Crease only partially agreed with that. Although he had said at trial that Gitxsan law was irrelevant on the question of liability, he told Ottawa that 'it would be very unwise for the pardoning power not to consider' it and recommended that the death sentence be commuted. Ottawa accepted that recommendation, substituting 10 years in the New Westminster penitentiary. Haatq died in jail. Thus the state dealt with a challenge to the supremacy of its law by upholding its formal application, but exercising its discretion in the most discretionary area of the criminal law, the pardon process.[94]

Other cases were dealt with in a similar way when they arose in the North-West Territories and the outlying regions of British Columbia, including cases in which Indigenous people killed other Indigenous people because they believed them to be windigos (or wendigos), evil spirits that possessed human beings and caused them to kill other people and, in some traditions, eat them. There had been cases of Indigenous people convicted of killing windigos and not executed before Confederation.[95] In April 1885, Riskeyak (She Wins), an old Cree woman who believed herself to be a windigo and had asked to be killed, was dispatched by three Cree men near Fort Pitt, in the Saskatchewan district of the Territories.[96] At the time Fort Pitt was in the hands of a group of Cree warriors under Mistahimawaska who a few days earlier had captured the HBC trading post and base for a detachment of 24 NWMP officers. Prior to that they had taken Frog Lake, a nearby trading post and Catholic mission, killing nine of the 12 white settlers there. The policeman had all escaped except for one who was killed in the brief fighting, but 28 white and Métis civilians remained behind as captives. After Fort Pitt had been retaken in June, the Cree – Charles Ducharme (85), Wawasehowein (65), and Wahsahgamass (18) – who had had nothing to do with the rebellion were tried for the murder of Riskeyak in Battleford, before Charles Rouleau, one of the three stipendiary magistrates, and Pierre Chrysologue Pambrun, a Métis JP, sitting as an assistant judge by the provisions of the *North-West Territories Act*, discussed above. W. Prescott Sharpe was sent to Battleford to prosecute, but no defence counsel represented the accused men. The killing had been witnessed by dozens of the whites and Métis held captive by the Cree.

Sharpe went out of his way to negate a cultural defence because he believed, with good reason, that many settlers knew about the Cree belief in windigos and knew that killing them was considered not only justifiable but necessary. Instead it was magistrate Rouleau who drew a sharp distinction between killing settlers in a rebellion and the removal of a windigo, suggesting to the jury that it was open to them to bring in a verdict of manslaughter. The defendants needed to have killed with 'actual malice' (intention to kill) to be guilty of murder, and if they had thought themselves to be acting in self-defence it would be manslaughter. The jury were not quite so obliging, bringing in verdicts of guilty of murder for the two older men, but finding 18-year-old Wahsahgamass guilty of manslaughter. It is at least feasible that they returned the murder verdicts because they wanted to help stamp out belief in windigos. Rouleau could do nothing but sentence them both to death, but he also told Ottawa that he thought the murder verdict was wrong because they were doing what was right by their own lights: 'Taking into consideration their degree of civilization; the impression under which they were, that they ... were in duty bound to do away with their victim, the degree of malice was not sufficient to justify ... a verdict of murder.'

Justice Minister Thompson was initially not impressed. He correctly criticized Rouleau's use of the word 'malice' as requiring some form of malevolence when all it meant was intention to kill; recall that it was removed from the 1892 Code because of its tendency to confuse. For him the case was simple: a 'very cruel and deliberate murder of an inoffensive old woman,' which called for 'exemplary punishment.' But after further correspondence with both Rouleau and Sharpe he understood the fear that windigos produced and that killing them was considered a commendable act in many Indigenous communities. The death sentences were commuted. Ducharme died in the Stony Mountain penitentiary in 1890, but Wawasehowein and Wahsahgamass were released in 1899. In many respects what was unusual about this case was that the two men were tried and convicted of murder in the first place. In other windigo cases in the far North in the very late nineteenth and early twentieth centuries the authorities either did not bring charges, or if they did, charged manslaughter, or if a murder charge was preferred, the jury found a lesser verdict.[97]

14

Property Law

In this and other periods property law determined what resources people could command to subsist or do better, to accumulate wealth and prosper. Real property law, what for convenience lawyers call land law, also was frequently linked to community, culture, and identity. Previous chapters of this book have dealt with property law in various guises – chapter 5 on the distinctive nature of civil law concepts of and rights to property, chapter 7 on the British Columbia Indigenous title question and the land surrenders and reserve creation effected by the numbered treaties, chapter 8 on the links between land ownership and enfranchisement, and chapter 10 on Indigenous laws of land use rights and succession. In chapter 15 we will examine the intimate relations between property and marriage by charting the evolution of married women's rights to property in common law provinces. The lack of change in the civil law in this regard was noted in chapter 5. This chapter provides accounts of a variety of other property law matters. Some of these involved large issues that fundamentally shaped particular regions of Canada. Others were national in scope, affecting the lives of every resident of the new dominion in large and small ways.

The first main theme in this chapter is the spread of a particular package of rights in land across vast areas of western Canada, largely replacing the complex blend of common, family, and individual property rights known to Indigenous peoples for millennia. This process aimed to vest ownership, or fee simple, rights to land in an owner-occupier (ideally white and male, though some exceptions existed) who was assumed to be best placed to exploit it and thereby contribute to the national economy. Thus we begin with the fate of Métis land rights in Manitoba guaranteed by the *Manitoba Act* of 1870, picking up the story of the province's adhesion to Confederation begun in chapter 7. Next comes the closely related topic of the 1872 *Dominion Lands Act*, which allocated to white settlers rights to the western lands ceded by the numbered treaties, and the adoption of a new system of title registration that aimed to guarantee the land rights that had just been redistributed. The owner-occupier model was already implanted in eastern Canada, with the exception of Prince Edward Island with its large tenant population. The next section deals with the transformation of these tenants into fee simple owners.

While it was assumed that the largest possible autonomy regarding use and disposition should be recognized in land owners, the second theme of this chapter examines the reaction against such extensive powers when their exercise was seen to lead to socially undesirable results. Problems arising from unfettered land use were more evident in the urban areas that were growing quickly in the later decades of our period, and their immediate hinterland. Hence the latter parts of this chapter deal with the growth of municipal and provincial land use regulation, the judicial recognition of restrictive covenants that aimed to preserve certain urban areas from incompatible economic development, and the role of nuisance law in settling disputes arising from the environmental consequences of new industries and technologies. The free disposition of one's property on death also began to be restricted in some respects, partly as a result of the improved legal position of married women, and partly in order to prevent impecunious family members from becoming public charges. Finally, a section is devoted to the law of expropriation, a key feature of state power permitting the construction of transportation and other infrastructure necessary for communication and travel across Canada's vast spaces and for economic growth.

Métis Land Rights in Manitoba

The *Manitoba Act* of 1870, which formed the constitution of the new province, included provisions for land for the Métis. As we saw in chapter 7, the federal government agreed to the *Manitoba Act* in order to achieve a peaceful entry of the new province into Confederation, and not necessarily out of enthusiasm for ensuring to the Métis a stable and significant role in the province's future. The *Manitoba Act* included two principal provisions relating to Métis land. Section 31 began by stating that it was 'expedient, towards the extinguishment of the Indian title to the lands in the Province, to appropriate … one million four hundred thousand acres … for the benefit of the families of the half-breed residents.' Later the section provided that 'under regulations to be made … by the Governor-General' the lieutenant governor of Manitoba 'shall select such lots or tracts in such parts of the Province as he may deem expedient, … and divide the same among the children of the half-breeds of families residing in the Province at the time of the said transfer to Canada, and the same shall be granted to the said children.'

The reference to extinguishment in the opening phrase of the first sentence of section 31 confused contemporaries and later historians. The opposition Liberals insisted that, in Alexander Mackenzie's words, the Métis were 'either Indian or white,' and if the former, had an 'Indian title' extinguishable only by treaty, not by statute. The Macdonald government knew this was true with regard to Indigenous people, as we saw in chapter 7. It also must have known that had this been an act of extinguishment it would have included a reservation of land to a nation, not a grant to be divided among individuals in severalty. In fact the origin of section 31 was likely not the common law of Indigenous title. Rather, section 31 was one aspect of the political compromise needed to persuade the Métis to end their resistance to incorporation into Canada. Métis demands in the negotiations included control of public lands in the new province, which the original four confederating provinces had under section 92 (5) of the *BNA Act*. The federal government would not agree to that but offered the 1.4 million acre grant (the Métis grant) instead. The *Manitoba Act* received a rough ride in the Commons, which would have been rougher had the government been defending the grant as a concession to the Métis. The Métis grant was therefore 'sold' as necessary to extinguish Indigenous title, with the wording carefully and misleadingly chosen. It was only 'towards' an extinguishment of title, whatever that meant, and it was 'expedient,' not a legal obligation. Macdonald likened it to land being set aside for the settlement of loyalists in the late eighteenth century, and he later acknowledged that section 31 was 'a question of policy,' a way to 'make a Province at all … and assert the sovereignty of the Dominion.'[1] Section 32, which we will discuss later in this section, did not involve the allocation of new land to the Métis, but the protection of their existing land rights.

Section 30 of the *Manitoba Act* gave the central government jurisdiction over all 'ungranted or waste lands' in the new province and thus over the administration of the Métis grant.[2] Shortly after he arrived in Manitoba Lieutenant Governor Archibald proposed that the provincial government take on the task, but his suggestion was roundly rejected by Ottawa. Secretary of State for the Provinces Joseph Howe told Archibald to 'leave the land department and the Dominion Government to carry out their policy without interference.' To this effect early in 1871 the government established a Dominion Lands Branch in the office of Secretary of State James Cox Aikins to administer land granting in Manitoba and the Territories.[3] Ottawa quickly decided that the Métis land grant would come from the land immediately adjacent to the existing areas of Métis settlement in the Red River colony along the banks of the Red and the Assiniboine Rivers. This decision was formally enunciated in a March 1871 Privy Council 'Memorandum on the Subject of the Public Lands in the Province of Manitoba.'[4] Long before 1870 this region had been divided into 24 parishes, 14 bordering the Red River from St. Peters in the north to Ste. Agathe in the south, and nine strung out east-west along the Assiniboine River, from St. Charles in the east, at the intersection of the Red and the Assiniboine, to Portage La Prairie in the west. One more parish, St. Laurent, was to the north, on the shores of Lake Manitoba. Eleven of the parishes were populated by francophone Métis, the others by anglophones, mostly Métis but also white settlers. According to a census taken in 1870 in order to divide the new province into 24 electoral districts for the first assembly elections, the province had about 10,000 Métis, just over 6,000 francophones, and just under 4,000 anglophones.[5] There were also about 2,000 white settlers, either descendants of the Scottish settlers brought to the colony by Lord Selkirk in the early nineteenth century or retired HBC employees.

In the scheme of distribution decided in 1871 francophones and anglophones would be given land adjacent to their respective parishes along the Red and Assiniboine Rivers (see map).[6] The decision to consolidate the Métis population in this way was made because it was what most, if not all, of the Métis leaders wanted, and because the Métis were not farmers growing crops on widely dispersed family farms but combined subsistence agriculture with seasonal occupations including the buffalo hunt and employment with the HBC – employment that took them away from Red River for significant parts of the year. Consolidating Métis settlement also enabled the government to pursue its policy of populating the rest of Manitoba with white settlers from Ontario and other parts of Canada and Europe, who would form the backbone of a social economy of white yeoman farmers.

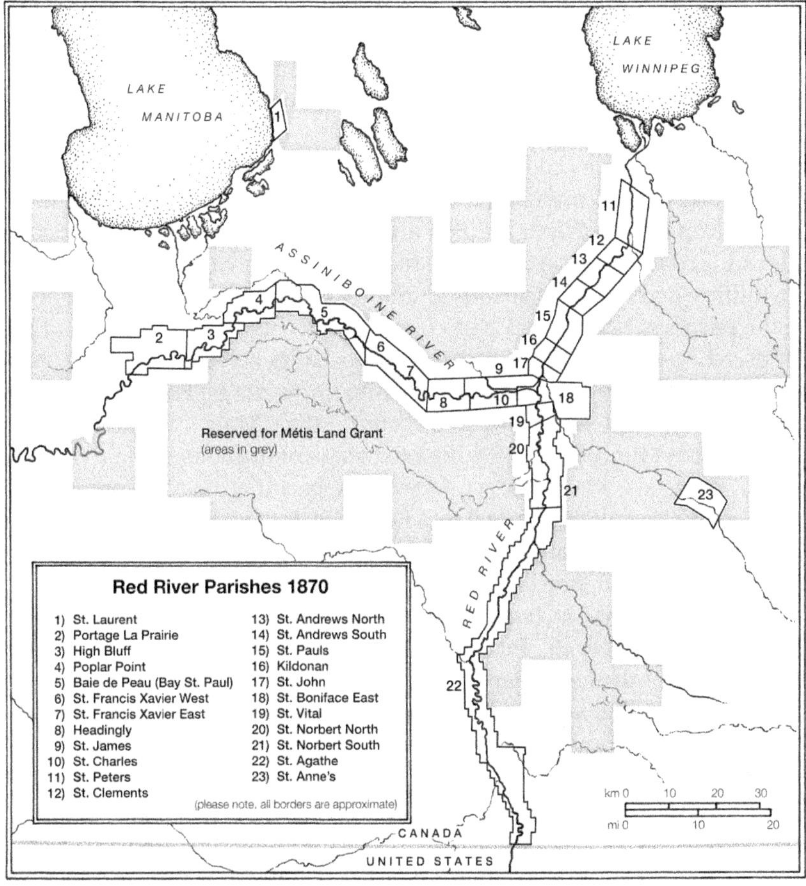

Red River region and adjoining parts of Manitoba in the early 1870s.
The map shows the location of the parishes which made up the Red River
colony before 1870, and of the adjacent land reserved for distribution
of the 1.4 million acre grant to the Métis.

Credit: Drawn by Christopher Hoyt.

The next stage of administering the Métis land grant was the reservation of specific areas in which grants would be made. This could not be done until the Dominion Land Survey, begun in 1871 and progressing east to west, had been completed for Red River. The survey divided the new western territories into grids consisting of townships. Each township was six square miles, or 3,840 acres. Archibald was given the task of selecting which townships would have land reserved within them for the Métis land grant. In 1872 and early 1873 he and his successor, Alexander Morris, reserved more than enough townships to enable the 1.4 million acres to be distributed among those living roughly adjacent to the parishes.* Archibald had committed to honour the choices of the Métis whenever possible, and township lands selected by them were withdrawn from that available for white immigrants. For the most part this process went well, and in February 1873 Morris began drawing lots for individual allotments, the next stage of implementing the grant.

This next stage was, however, subject to substantial delay. Before individual allocations could be made it was necessary to decide how many people were to share in the grant, which in turn would determine how many acres each person would get. The number of eligible Métis, and hence the size of individual grants, changed on more than one occasion; the acreage to be distributed was finite, and individual grants fluctuated with changes in the eligible population. After some disputes over whether it was heads of families or children who were envisaged by section 31,[7] in early 1873 the Macdonald government first passed an Order in Council and then enacted a statute, the *Construction Act*, which confirmed that the distribution would be to individuals who had been under the age of majority in 1870.[8] Section 31 granted land to children, not adults, because the Métis delegates in the 1869–70 negotiations had wanted a guarantee of sufficient land for the future as the population grew. Heads of Métis families in 1870 had the use of land adjacent to the banks of the Red and Assiniboine Rivers, and their rights to that land were protected by section 32 of the *Manitoba Act*, discussed below. According to contemporary estimates the *Construction Act* reduced the number of those eligible to share in the 1.4 million acres from about 10,000 to about 7,000 and increased the acreage per individual from 140 to 190. As a result, the drawing of lots to allocate land to individuals was temporarily halted. Further delay ensued, due to surveying errors, lengthy

---

* Before Manitoba was expanded in 1881 – see chapter 2 – it was much smaller, colloquially known as the 'postage stamp province,' and 1.4 million acres was approximately one-sixth of the province.

examination of claims, and recalculation of the numbers of those eligible.[9] The delays frustrated not only the Métis but also leading figures in Manitoba and Ottawa, who saw the tying up of land and its being kept back from homesteaders as, in the words of Manitoba Queen's Bench Chief Justice Edmund Burke Wood, a 'curse,' and a 'tremendous obstacle to the speedy settlement of the region.'[10] Not until 1876 did the government finally settle the question of who was entitled to share in the Métis grant – just over 6,000 children of Métis families resident in Manitoba in 1870. Individual allotments began again, now of 240 acres each. Over the next few years a total of 1,448,160 acres was allotted, and by 1880 the vast majority of allottees had received patents for fee simples.

A parallel development to the process of allotment was that Lieutenant Governor Morris persuaded Ottawa that Métis heads of families should be given something even though they were not part of the 1.4 million acre grant. The *Appropriation Act* of 1874, a federal statute, provided that heads of families were entitled to either a land grant of 160 acres or scrip to the value of $160, which could be used to buy land under the *Dominion Lands Act*.[11] Which of the two individuals would receive was left to executive discretion. Scrip is any substitute for legal tender, a form of personal property, and had been given to people of mixed ethnicity in treaties between Indigenous nations and the United States from the early 1850s. The value of the scrip in this case was derived from the fact that $160 was the cost of a quarter-section, 160 acres, for those who wished to buy land under the *Dominion Lands Act* rather than take advantage of that *Act*'s homestead provisions, discussed in the next section. A little over $500,000 of scrip was issued to Métis heads of families in 1870 or their descendants. An additional approximately 1,000 children of Métis in 1870 received scrip for 240 acres each in the later 1870s, because satisfying the claims of the roughly 6,000 used up all of – and more than – the 1.4 million acres.[12]

Thus, despite numerous delays, all of the land promised in the *Manitoba Act* was granted to Métis. As noted above, historians have sparred over who was responsible for the delays. They have also disagreed over who was to blame for the next part of this complicated story, which is that relatively little of the 1.4 million acres actually ended up being owned and occupied by Métis. It was sold to white speculators and eventually to white settlers, and many of the Métis living in Manitoba in 1870 relocated to Saskatchewan. Almost from the outset of the long process described thus far, some Métis sold their 'expectations' to white land speculators. That is, they sold the right to enforce the contract for sale of the land when the Métis vendor became entitled to a patent for a fee simple. Scrip was also bought up from heads of families who had received it. Macdonald bore witness in 1885 to what had happened in the previous decade and more, telling the Commons that '[t]he claims of the half-breeds in Manitoba were bought up by speculators. It was an unfortunate thing for those poor people.... The scrip was bought up; the lands were bought up by white speculators.'[13] The devices used were assignments, powers of attorney, and mortgages on the parental land of child grantees, and the 'vendors' were both children and heads of families who had been eligible for allotments between 1871 and 1873. Whether or not these transactions were fraudulent, in the sense of forged, or exploitative of illiterate people, or good bargains for putative grantees who did not want the land, or a mixture of all three will likely never be definitively established.

In the early 1870s members of the Manitoba assembly thought these dealings undesirable, to put it neutrally. Some advocated legislation to make entitlements to a share in the 1.4 million acre grant inalienable, but were unsuccessful. They did, however, succeed in having legislation passed in 1873 to make the contracts unenforceable. The preamble to the *Half-Breed Land Grant Protection Act*[14] [*Protection Act*] stated the problem: 'In consequence of the condition of surveys in the Province not permitting the distribution of [section 31 lands] ... very many persons entitled to participate in the ... grant in evident ignorance of the value of their individual shares have agreed ... to sell their right to the same to speculators, receiving therefor only a trifling consideration.' The *Protection Act* sought to 'discourage the traffic now going on in such rights' by making all transactions prior to the issue of fee simple patents unenforceable. The act also stipulated that if such a transaction had taken place, any money paid to the Métis was a debt owing by him or her to the speculator/purchaser, recoverable in the usual way. The right to the title to the land would remain with the Métis 'vendor' unless the judgment debt for the money paid could not be satisfied and the land had to be sold pursuant to a court order, as with any other unsatisfied debt claim proved in court.

The act was the work of Métis members and the strong settler francophone lobby in the assembly. The latter were Quebecers who had been encouraged to move to Manitoba and work to preserve the French language and the Catholic religion in the new province.[15] It created a dilemma for Morris, who was the head of the executive branch before the province moved to responsible government in 1874, and who reserved the act and recommended that Ottawa disallow it. Morris had 'no sympathy' for people who had bought up land claims for less than the market price 'or in an unfair manner.' But he objected to the *Protection Act*'s retroactivity and was also concerned that it 'opens a fruitful door for litigation' should purchasers seek to recover the price paid to the Métis vendors under contracts now rendered unenforceable. Federal Minister of Justice Antoine Aimé Dorion refused disallowance. His report emphasized the inadequacy of the bargains made but noted that the *Protection Act* did not ban such transactions. Thus they continued, despite the federal government's disapproval.[16] By the mid-1870s Manitoba and Ottawa were seriously at odds over this issue, the provincial assembly, increasingly dominated by representatives of new white settlers, repealing the *Protection Act* in 1875 and providing that so long as the agreement to sell future land rights was in writing it was valid. Ottawa disallowed that statute, but Manitoba repealed the *Protection Act* again in 1877, and this time Ottawa did not intervene. Minister of Justice Rudolph Laflamme noted that in the seven years that had passed since the passage of the *Manitoba Act*, the Métis must, 'as a general rule,' have become 'well acquainted with the value of their interests in land.' Thus they did not need the *Protection Act*. From the late 1870s through to 1885 Manitoba passed legislation progressively making it easier for those under 21 to sell land rights and retroactively validating past sales. The nadir was the 1885 *Titles of Half-Breed Lands Act*, which provided that 'in all cases where lands … belonging to infant Half-Breeds … have been sold … such conveyance shall be, and shall always be deemed to have always … been sufficient to vest in the grantee or grantees … all of the estate thereby purported to be granted.'[17]

Critics of the federal government have blamed Ottawa for not protecting the Métis from exploitation by whites or, more, conniving with private actors and allowing the Métis to be dispossessed as part of a broader scheme to make Manitoba a white settler province. Others have argued that when the Métis sold their land entitlements they did so by choice and struck largely beneficial bargains. They were no more 'exploited' than anybody else operating in a market economy, and their movement west was a choice they made motivated by a desire to stay together as a community and to continue to follow traditional economic pursuits, especially the declining and westward migrating buffalo hunt. These scholars do not dispute that there were instances of fraud but argue that the Métis were rational economic actors. The work of Gerhard Ens is especially valuable here for placing Métis history in the 1870s in a broader context of economic adaptation and migration going back to the 1830s.[18] This is not a historiographical debate that will ever be 'resolved'; few such debates are, because evidence must always be interpreted.

We turn to section 32 of the *Manitoba Act*, which dealt not with future land grants to the Métis but with the existing land rights of all non-indigenous people, Métis and others, settled in the Red River colony before 1870.[19] Section 32 was said to be 'for the quieting of titles, and assuring to the settlers in the Province the peaceable possession of the lands now held by them.' There were five subsections, but only the first four are important to our account. They dealt with rights to land that predated the *Manitoba Act* and were not derived from English law but from the 'custom of the country' – various laws that operated, formally or informally, under the HBC. Subsections 1 and 2 were the most straightforward, stating that all grants made by the HBC prior to 9 March 1869, whether in freehold or less than freehold, would be confirmed by a Crown grant. These grantees were mostly white settlers and some Métis who had been granted freehold or leasehold riverfront land in the Red River settlement by the HBC. All such grants were recorded in HBC registers, had been surveyed by the HBC, and comprised riverside farm lots of narrow frontage running back two miles from the river.[20]

Subsections 3 and 4 dealt with land rights in the Red River settlement not derived from grants from the HBC but held by Métis who were, under English law, squatters. There were two classes of such squatters:

3) All titles by occupancy with the sanction and under the licence and authority of the Hudson's Bay Company up to the eighth day of March aforesaid, of land in that part of the Province in which the Indian title has been extinguished, shall, if required by the owner, be converted into an estate in freehold by grant from the Crown.
4) All persons in peaceable possession of tracts of land at the time of the transfer to Canada, in those parts of the Province in which the Indian Title has not been extinguished, shall have the right of pre-emption of the same, on such terms and conditions as may be determined by the Governor in Council.

The references to extinguishment of Indigenous title in subsections 3 and 4 were to the Peguis Treaty of 1817, made by Lord Selkirk with Chief Peguis of the Saulteaux people and extinguished the Indigenous title to the land running two miles back from both banks of the Red and Assiniboine Rivers. The reference to 'occupancy with the sanction and under the licence and authority' of the HBC in subsection 3 was to laws passed by the Council of Assiniboia recognizing common pasturing and hay-cutting rights in what was known as the 'outer two miles' adjoining riverfront lots. Their recognition necessarily implied HBC recognition of the right to occupy the 'inner' two miles, the riverfront lots. Subsection 3 therefore recognized the 'custom of the country' and promised confirmation of such customary rights by a grant from the Crown. Subsection 4 dealt with a different class of person, those who occupied land within the Red River colony but outside the area conceded by the Peguis Treaty. Protection of existing land entitlements inside and outside of the treaty area was consistently part of Métis demands in 1869–70, present in every iteration of the 'lists of rights.' Equally importantly, the Métis were assured on a number of occasions before the passage of the *Manitoba Act* that, in the words of Joseph Howe, 'all their properties, rights and equities of every kind, as enjoyed under the government of the Hudson's Bay Company, will be continued them.' Howe's statement clearly encompassed subsection 4 as well as subsection 3 rights, and Macdonald similarly stated in January 1870 that 'all titles to land held by residents in peaceable possession will be confirmed.' Cartier told two of the Métis delegates in May 1870 that those with subsection 4 claims would receive confirmation of their rights 'as soon as the government can grant the necessary titles.' Moreover, the subsection 4 squatters' pre-emptive right would be more than a first right to purchase, it would be a free grant: 'No payment shall be required from any of the persons mentioned [in subsection 4].' Rather 'they shall be placed upon the same footing as the persons mentioned in the three preceding paragraphs.'[21] There could not have been a clearer commitment that rights to land based on pre-1870 laws, whether one calls them laws or customs, would be respected. Two years later, after Treaty 1 had extinguished the Indigenous title outside the Peguis Treaty area, the federal cabinet confirmed these promises in an Order in Council stating that those who applied under subsection 4 would be dealt with 'on the same terms' as the class of settlers described in subsection 3, entitling them to Crown grants.[22]

As with section 31, the federal government was slow to implement section 32, but by the fall of 1873 a process was in place by which claims were submitted to the local branch of the Dominion Lands Office in Winnipeg, ruled upon, and sent to Ottawa for confirmation and the issuing of the patent. People claiming under subsections 1 and 2 fared well in this process. They could rely on the HBC register and, if necessary, on affidavits showing a chain of title from the name in the register to the current applicant. Most of such claimants were successful, although in some cases not until 1878 and in many cases their acreage was reduced by provincial road allowance legislation.[23] Subsection

3 and 4 claims fared very differently, principally because of a change to the wording of the *Manitoba Act* by two statutes, the already discussed *Appropriation Act* of 1874 and another *Appropriation Act* of 1875.[24] Between them they provided a common definition of who could claim a fee simple title under subsections 3 and 4. They were 'persons satisfactorily establishing undisturbed occupancy of any lands within the Province prior to, and being ... in actual peaceable possession thereof, on 15 July 1870.' This changed subsection 3 by removing 'titles by occupancy with the sanction and under the licence and authority' of the HBC and substituting 'undisturbed occupancy,' and also by changing the date from 8 March 1869 to 15 July 1870. It changed subsection 4 by changing 'peaceable possession' to 'undisturbed occupancy ... and being in actual peaceable possession' of land. The acts also did away with the distinction between subsections 3 and 4 on the result of proving a claim; all would now receive a fee simple grant, not, as had been the case with subsection 4, a right of pre-emption only.

We have not found much evidence of why these changes were made, and thus what we have to say is admittedly speculative. The only aspect of them discussed in Parliament in 1874 was the upgrading of a right of pre-emption to a fee simple. But in 1875 Interior Minister Laird adverted to the limited way in which claims had been staked, and, more importantly, to the fact that some inhabitants had made no improvements.[25] This latter point was important, because it does indicate that the purpose of the statutory amendments was to impose a test for establishing a claim that was different from that laid down in the *Manitoba Act*. The new test incorporated elements of the common law of possession that were more stringent than the requirements embodied in the pre-1870 customary law. It was surely not coincidental that these changes were made shortly after the passage of the *Dominion Lands Act* in 1872, discussed in the next section of this chapter. Central to the homestead policy formalized in that act was the idea that settlers were given land for free on a probationary basis and could obtain the fee simple only after a period of residence, cultivation, and making improvements on the land. The *Appropriation Acts* were broadly to the same effect, applying similar criteria to section 32 (3) and (4) claims. The purpose of section 32, however, was to confirm existing customary methods of establishing rights to use and occupy land along the Red River long before 1870. As the *Manitoba Act* stated, section 32 was passed 'for the quieting of titles, and assuring to the settlers in the Province the peaceable possession of the lands now held by them.' The *Manitoba Act* made no reference to any further requirements of the common law. Doctrines drawn from the common law of first possession were inapplicable for the reasons already given. Doctrines drawn from the common law of adverse possession were equally inapplicable because pre-1870 Manitoba settlers, Métis, and others were not seeking to dispossess another title holder. The standards applied under *Dominion Lands Act*'s homestead provisions were similarly inapplicable, because the land was already occupied by the Métis in 1870, not land made available for homesteading by newcomers.

The government's handling of section 32 claims is yet another area of contention among historians. Some historians have argued that most section 32 (3) and (4) claims were disallowed in Winnipeg or Ottawa, and that when they were allowed the patents were for much smaller acreages than claimed. The principal cause of the denial of claims and the limitation of acreage was the same – lack of improvements such as fencing, home-building, and cultivation. These arguments are based on limited sample evidence and are contradicted by detailed empirical studies by others showing that some 95 *per cent* of 1870 occupants of river lots had their claims patented.[26] Although we think that the latter studies make the better case, we also find three criticisms of the government's handling of section 32 well founded. First, as with section 31, there were extensive delays in the implementation of section 32. Second, Mackenzie's Liberal government did strive to limit Métis entitlements by changing the law. Third, officials applied inappropriate legal doctrines in interpreting the meaning of possession. Correspondence between Ottawa and Dominion Lands officials in Winnipeg reveals much uncertainty among the local officials about what claims they should allow and the acreage that should be included when a claim was allowed. Correspondence between the Justice and Interior Ministries in Ottawa, a result of the many claims that were referred to Ottawa and not resolved in Winnipeg, shows that senior officials in both ministries insisted on an 'enhanced' view of what counted as possession, and on reduced acreages even when the claim was to be allowed.[27] An 1878 letter from Surveyor-General Dennis to Donald Codd, Dennis's right-hand man in Winnipeg, for example, stated that no claim under section 32 would be accepted unless there had been 'some really valuable improvements … made.' If not, the claim was 'not entitled to consideration.'[28]

That many section 32 claims were denied in the mid- to late 1870s was raised by one of the two Manitoba senators, Marc-Amable Girard, speaking in an 1878 debate on whether there should be an appeal from denial of a claim to the courts. Girard was a Québécois notary who had emigrated to Manitoba in 1870 and been a consistent supporter of Métis causes.* He was also a friend of Louis Riel and the first premier of the province under responsible government in 1874.[29] He complained that 'we hear of confiscation everywhere. The people are told they cannot remain any longer on the lands on which they have been settled for years.' He rhetorically asked 'why so many improvements are requisite when the law merely requires peaceable possession at the time of the transfer. Peaceable possession does not involve the cultivation of the land or any portion of it.… Everyone understands what the term "peaceable possession" means. It does not mean actual occupancy but ownership.' The government's response to such questions was that it was required to follow the law and that the minister of justice had given an opinion that 'the word "occupancy" means real possession.' Girard's view was supported by a number of senators, including former Minister of the Interior Campbell, who argued that it was important to be 'fair and reasonable.' Fair and reasonable meant that the government should accept customary rights as established by Métis practice. It was wrong to deny an application because Métis 'usages and customs are different from ours,' even if it seemed to the European mind that possession was 'very slight.' To base a decision on that European perspective 'would be inflicting an injustice upon those people [the Métis].'[30] This was an unusual example of the validation of customary law at a time when it was being widely delegitimated, especially in the Indigenous context. But the now Conservative government was unmoved, Macdonald confirming in 1879 that his administration would recognize only staked claims that 'have been followed by possession and improvement.'[31]

Despite the apparent finality of Macdonald's statement, claims continued to be processed, and disputes between Ottawa and the franco-Manitoban supporters of Métis land rights over the meaning of 'occupancy' and 'possession' continued through the 1880s. Joseph Royal, another Quebecker who heeded a call to go west in 1870 to support Riel and francophone Catholic rights and founded the first French-language newspaper, *Le Métis*, complained vigorously to Macdonald, who responded by summarily dismissing Codd but not by changing policy.[32] In 1880 a

---

* Girard was also the first person called to the Manitoba bar and is the only person mentioned in this book related to one of its authors. He is buried next to Louis Riel in Saint-Boniface.

limit of two more years for claims to be preferred was legislated and later extended. In 1883 the Dominion Lands Board classified outstanding claims in three categories and ordered that many of the outstanding claimants should receive either a grant of 160 acres or a homestead right of the same acreage. Four years later the same board could declare that section 32 claims 'have been nearly all finally closed' and that 'practically this branch of the business of the Department is closed.' It was not entirely closed, but rather than extend the application period further Ottawa announced that it would deal with any outstanding claims 'as a matter of grace.'[33] The Manitoba Métis population declined over the rest of the century because of migration to Saskatchewan, an issue discussed in chapter 10. They became very much a minority in Manitoba because of extensive white settlement, but some of those who stayed prospered and became a Métis middle class, engaged in a variety of occupations and able to leave significant assets to the next generation.[34]

Homestead Settlement: The Canada Land Survey, the *Dominion Lands Act*, and Provincial Homestead Laws

Attracting white settlers to the Prairie west was a key pillar of John A. Macdonald's National Policy, necessary to solidify Canadian control of the region, to enable the east-west exchange of grain and livestock for manufactured goods, to make the Pacific railway economically viable, and to put to rest any possibility of American annexation of the region. The law was a crucial component of white settlement, because it was the law that effected the transition from common to individual property, a transition famously dubbed 'The Great Transformation.'[35] As seen in the previous section, it was the federal government, not provincial or territorial administrations, that determined public land law and policy in the region because, as Macdonald put it, 'it would be injudicious to have a large province which would have control over lands and might interfere with the general policy of the Government in opening up communications to the Pacific.' In addition, locally enacted land regulations 'might be obstructive to immigration,' and thus 'all that vast territory should be for purposes of settlement under one control, and that the Dominion legislature.'[36] Federal jurisdiction over public lands in the prairie region was always controversial and became a party political issue at times but was confirmed when Alberta and Saskatchewan became provinces in 1905. Despite provincial protests it endured until 1930, when the Prairie provinces were given control of lands and natural resources by a constitutional amendment.[37]

Between the early 1870s and the First World War the prairie region was transformed by a tide of white settlers. From only the Red River colony in 1870, its white population rose to about 1,650,000 in 1916. A majority of the population of each Prairie province in 1911 was rural – 57 per cent in Manitoba, 63 per cent in Alberta, and 73 per cent in Saskatchewan, and 64 per cent in all three provinces combined. We have already seen that law, in the form of the numbered treaties, was the instrument by which Indigenous title to much of the West was extinguished. Here we examine how the state filled the space left by that extinguishment with white settlers.

A central aspect of the advance of private property across the prairies was the Canada Land Survey.[38] Starting in 1871, as Treaty 1 was being negotiated, teams of surveyors worked from east to west dividing the land into townships of six miles square, which took no account of any natural features. Nothing could better illustrate the contrast with Indigenous concepts of property: for Europeans, property in land was an abstraction that could be imposed anywhere on the earth's surface. Each township was further surveyed into 36 sections, a section being a square mile, or 640 acres, and each section was numbered, from one to 36, beginning at the southeastern corner. The Manitoba survey, which did not include the existing parishes and river lot system adjoining the Red and Assiniboine Rivers, was completed by the mid-1870s, and by 1881 over 1,200 townships in that province and the Territories, covering 27 million acres, had been completely surveyed, with more than as many again surveyed in outline. By the mid-1880s the task was essentially completed. The survey was, said Herbert Beresford, twice president of the Association of Provincial Land Surveyors, 'the greatest single factor in the development of Western Canada.'[39] Figure 19 shows how the townships were surveyed into sections and how the sections were numbered.

As the surveyors wielded their instruments on the ground, officials in Ottawa developed regulations for how the land was to be granted. Early in 1871 the administration of dominion lands was vested in the Secretary of State, within which department a Dominion Lands Branch was established, and these arrangements were confirmed in the *Dominion Lands Act* of 1872.[40] The branch was shifted to the Ministry of the Interior shortly afterwards. How the land was to be allocated was articulated in the 1871 'Memorandum on the Subject of the Public Lands in Manitoba,' discussed in the previous section. The essence of that memorandum dealing with white settlers, though not the parts concerned with the Métis land grant, was legislated in the *Dominion Lands Act*.

Much of the Act dealt with surveyors and the survey, and other parts with timber licences, and grazing, coal, and other leases. The sections that concern us begin at section 17, under the general heading 'Disposal of the Dominion Lands.' These laid down how land was to be allocated – to whom, and under what conditions.

In every township most of the even-numbered sections were set aside for white settlers, either through sales of land at $1 an acre with amounts limited to one section (640 acres) per person, or as homestead land, free grants to settlers, the precise meaning of which will be explained shortly. The exceptions were numbers 8 and 26, which were given to the HBC to satisfy a promise of one-twentieth of the land in the fertile belt contained in article 5 of the 1869 transfer agreement by which Canada acquired the HBC lands. All the odd-numbered sections, apart from sections 11 and 29, were set aside for grants to railway companies. The railways that received such grants could then sell or lease the land to settlers to pay for the construction of the line and related infrastructure. Sections 11 and 29 were set aside as school lands, an educational endowment to support local communities' schools. Land was also reserved for granting as military bounties and for use as town plots, markets, jails, courthouses, schools, and 'other like public purposes.' Finally, in section 105 of the Act the governor general was given the power 'to withdraw from the operation of this Act' whatever land was necessary to satisfy the Métis grant and 'land to such extent as may be required for Railway purposes.' 'Railway purposes' did not mean the land grants of even-numbered sections; it meant 'land to the width of three full Townships on each side of the line finally sanctioned for the Inter-Oceanic Railway.'[41] This later became the reservation of a 40-mile belt, 20 miles on each side of the line, to accommodate the Pacific railway and to pay for its construction.

For our purposes the most significant part of the Act was section 33, 'Homestead Rights or Free Grant Lands.' In a marked departure from imperially mandated pre-Confederation land settlement schemes since the 1820s,[42] land was to be granted for free to settlers. Ottawa thereby largely replicated the system in place in the United States since the *Homestead Act* of 1862; it had no choice if western Canada was to compete with the United States in attracting white settlers. It was simply assumed that free land was needed for effective settlement; there was no opposition to that policy and very little debate in Parliament over it. The starting point to claim a land grant of a maximum of a quarter section, 160 acres, was the 'entry,' which meant taking up residence on the land and filing within 30 days in the local Dominion Lands Office a

N O R T H

31	32	33	34	35	36
30	29	28	27	26	25
19	20	21	22	23	24
18	17	16	15	14	13
7	8	9	10	11	12
6	5	4	3	2	1

W E S T (left side)   **E A S T** (right side)

S O U T H

The Canada Land Survey divided each township
on the prairies into 36 sections, a section being 640 acres.

Credit: *Dominion Lands Act*, SC 1872, c. 23, s. 3 (2). Drawn by Christopher Hoyt.

claim to the parcel and paying a $10 fee. Any head of a family, or a single person 21 or over, and a British subject by birth or naturalization, could 'be entered for' a quarter section or a lesser amount (80 or 40 acres) 'for the purpose of securing a homestead right.'[43]

The claimant also had to provide affidavits, one attesting to 'proof of settlement and improvement' if the land had been surveyed, corroborated by 'two credible witnesses,' and another swearing that the claim was being made 'for his exclusive use and benefit, and for the purpose of actual settlement.' If the settler had simply squatted on unsurveyed land, he or she had three months after the survey was completed to file the application, again swearing an affidavit attesting to 'actual settlement and cultivation.' After three years of 'residence and cultivation' after entry, the settler was entitled to a patent for a fee simple. Homesteaders could receive the patent after just one year of residence and improvement by paying 1 shilling an acre, the price charged to a non-homesteader, and 'making proof of actual settlement and cultivation' by the same affidavit and supporting witness process laid out above. Homestead rights acquired within the three-year period were inheritable by the widow or, if there was no widow, the children.[44] The overriding theme in section 33 was that the government wanted land to be broadly owned by 'yeoman' farmers who would actually work the land, not taken up by speculators. Thus assignments and transfers of homestead rights prior to the patent issuing were null and void, a restraint on alienation. This was in contrast to allocations of land under the Métis grant, which could be alienated before a patent was issued and, as we saw in the previous section, often were. To further protect the homestead right and to prevent speculation, the land was exempt from being taken in execution during the three-year probationary period. If a settler did not fulfil the settlement conditions, the land could be given to another without encumbrances.[45]

Four significant amendments were made to the *Dominion Lands Act* within a few years. In 1874 the qualifying age for homesteading was lowered from 21 to 18. In 1876 single women were effectively excluded from becoming homesteaders, the qualifying criteria changing from 'any person' to 'any person, male or female, who is the sole head of a family, or any male who has attained the age of eighteen years.' Henceforth the vast majority of single women were disqualified because they would not have been heads of families; only widows with children were eligible. The requirement of being the 'sole' head of a family also eliminated from eligibility married women even if the husband had deserted the family or was incapable. These changes had been recommended by surveyor general Dennis, who did not believe that women had the physical strength to be productive homesteaders and that Canada would be better served by preserving the traditional family unit. This change has been aptly described as a conscious attempt to make the West a 'manly space,' built around the nuclear family unit and the authority of white males. Canadian officials often described American western settlement as chaotic, attributing it partially to polygamy and relaxed divorce laws and hoped to avoid these issues on their own frontier.[46]

Also in 1876, the minister was given the authority to waive the requirements of residence and cultivation 'in the case of settlements being formed of immigrants in communities (such as those of Mennonites or Icelanders).' This 'block system' had begun to be used in 1874 when tracts were set aside for settlements of francophones from Quebec and Massachusetts, and one was also allocated for Mennonites on Rat River. A second Mennonite settlement followed soon after, along with one for Icelanders at Gimli. Block settlement provisions were a feature of western settlement for decades and attracted a wide variety of ethnic and religious groups including, to the chagrin of Ottawa and local politicians, the fiercely independent Doukhobors and a group of Black Americans escaping Oklahoma's Jim Crow laws; the latter is discussed in more detail in chapter 16. Jewish immigrants were welcomed, but blocks were not set aside for them and they were required to integrate with other settlers. However, many acquired land near each other, thereby constituting their own de facto blocks.

Most importantly, in 1874 it became possible for settlers to acquire more than a quarter section by combining the homestead provisions with pre-emption rights. Although the term 'pre-emption' is sometimes used as a synonym for homestead, pre-emption in the *Dominion Lands Act* meant the first right to buy land, usually at a fixed price. Henceforth a settler who had obtained an entry for one piece of land could also receive an 'interim entry' for an unclaimed adjoining quarter section. When the settler had satisfied the requirements for a fee simple patent for the initial homestead entry, he or she could buy the adjoining quarter section for $1 an acre. This made it easier to leave some land fallow in some years, a technique in common use, and allowed settlers to expand production and/or to provide land for their children. It proved very popular, as more than half of homesteaders also pre-empted other land. It somewhat cut against the general principle of limiting what one individual could acquire, however, and was controversial with officials, some of whom argued that 160 acres was quite sufficient for one family. Others were concerned that settlers would over-reach their resources; having obtained a fee simple for the homestead land they would mortgage it to complete the purchase of the additional lot.[47]

The history of the homestead system is complex and interlinked to other aspects of the region's immigration and settlement history.

In the period of largely Conservative administrations down to 1896 about half of the white settlers were not homesteaders but people who settled in urban centres or, in rural and urban regions, bought land from the HBC, or, to a very large extent, the CPR and other railways – branch lines running north to Hudson's Bay, south to the American border, and various other places. Dominion lands policy in the quarter century after the *Dominion Lands Act* has been called the 'railway land grant period.'[48] Other than around railway hubs and termini the CPR sold its land cheaply because it was more interested in generating revenue from the traffic in goods and people that settlement would bring than in the money from land sales. In addition, the numbers of people who homesteaded fluctuated and the areas they went to changed. In the 1870s there were over 11,000 entries taken out in Manitoba, the Territories not being opened for homesteading until after the signing of Treaty 6 in 1876. In the 1880s the number of homesteaders more than doubled, to about 25,000, most of them settling in Manitoba. The relative lack of enthusiasm for the Saskatchewan district led the federal government to contract with colonization companies to bring in homesteaders from the early 1880s, but the numbers were still disappointing; settlers, mostly from Ontario, were thinly spread out along the CPR main line from Winnipeg to Regina.[49]

The role of the homestead in the white settlement of the prairies became much more important after the mid-1890s, 'the staple of Dominion land policy' in this later period.[50] By then there was no more homestead land available in the United States, increasing the demand for Canadian land. Equally important, the coming to power of the Liberals in 1896 brought a westerner to the Interior Ministry. Clifford Sifton believed fervently in the adage that the prairies were 'the last, best West.' He imbued one of his five sons with enough nationalist spirit that he left his daughter a trust fund from which payments were to be made 'only so long as she shall continue to reside in Canada.'[51] Sifton devoted substantial resources to advertising campaigns in Canada, Britain, and eastern Europe to attract experienced farmers. Thousands of people poured into southern Saskatchewan, including a large number of Ukrainians, and the district's population reached about 258,000 by the time Saskatchewan became a province in 1905. By 1911 Saskatchewan was the country's third most populous province, at over 490,000, and in the five years from 1906 to 1911 60 per cent of homestead entries nationally were taken out in Saskatchewan. In its first decade as a province the acreage patented for homesteads rose eightfold, from 2.78 million to 21.5 million.

The population of the district/province of Alberta also increased from the 1890s, but by not nearly as much and not primarily driven by homesteading but by leasing federal land for ranching. Indeed in 1881 Ottawa barred homesteading in what is now southern Alberta and instead offered leases of up to 100,000 acres for 1 cent per acre per year for 21 years. The success of ranching led to an 1897 amendment to the *Dominion Lands Act* that altered the 'cultivation' requirement to include stock farming. Henceforth it could be met by the cultivation of just one acre of land in each of the three years in addition to a 'substantial' fence around that acre, the keeping of at least forty head of cattle, and 'stables and outhouses sufficient to winter' them.[52] Ranching attracted eastern Canadian and British capital in large amounts, and within a few years a handful of large companies held leases on two-thirds of the stocked land.

Despite the differences between Saskatchewan and Alberta, the spin-off benefits from homesteading for the federal government were very substantial. Sifton's successor as interior minister, the Albertan Frank Oliver, stated in 1905 that the dominion 'can make millions out of the lands of the North-West and never sell an acre.... The increase in our customs returns, the increase in our trade and commerce, the increase in our manufactures, is to a very large extent due to the increase in settlement on the free lands of the Northwest Territories.... It is worth the while of the Dominion to spend hundreds of thousands of dollars in promoting immigration ... in surveying and administering these lands, and then to give them away.'[53] Oliver seized the opportunity presented by a decline in the Alberta ranching industry caused by cattle disease to allow grazing leases to lapse and more land to thereby become available for homesteads. One marked difference between Oliver and Sifton was that the former was much less enthusiastic about eastern European immigrants. He wanted settlers in order to establish 'a higher and better civilization,' by which he meant a community of 'like-minded neighbours.' People of Slavic origin did not fit; they were a 'millstone around our necks, could never be citizens of this country as we would wish them to be.' Oliver's views led him to dramatically reduce the spending on advertising in Europe and to sponsor restrictive immigration legislation, but he was unable to halt homesteaders coming in from eastern and southern Europe, whose numbers increased under his tenure relative to British and American settlers.[54]

The *Dominion Lands Act* only partially achieved its original objective of making the region one dominated by the modestly sized but successful and stable family farm. Many homesteaders failed because of the climate and lack of understanding in government circles of the variable suitability for agriculture of different regions within the Northwest.[55] The legal regime also played a role in thwarting the original vision, in particular the availability of pre-emption. Pre-emption allowed some settlers to acquire more than a quarter section. Between 1874 and 1890 there were some 21,420 interim entries in Manitoba and the Territories, involving a total of about 3.4 million acres. In 1883 what an individual could obtain was doubled when a successful homesteader, one who had earned a patent, was allowed to make a second entry onto homestead land. It thereby became possible for one person to obtain a full section: two quarter sections by homestead entries and two further quarter sections by pre-emption. This undermined the original policy of filling the West with moderately sized farms operated by permanently settled families, but was considered necessary to stop people migrating to the United States as soon as they had received their patents and could sell their land. This second entry right was controversial, as was pre-emption; critics argued that both led to speculators acquiring land, because homesteaders mortgaged the homestead as soon as the patent was received to pre-empt another quarter section and were then unable to make the payments. John A. Macdonald opposed pre-emptions, not because he objected to larger farms as such but because he saw pre-emption as favouring speculators: 'You do not get the 320-acre farmer,' he told the Commons in 1883, 'but you get the 160-acre homesteader, who is utterly unable to do anything with the pre-emption right, whilst the speculator gets hold of it.'[56] The Conservatives went back and forward on pre-emption, abolishing the right in 1883 as of 1885, then twice extending the grace period, and not until 1890 was it no longer available.[57]

Pre-emption was by no means the only cause of the increase in farm size from the original quarter section. Settlers could simply buy more land from railway companies or, less frequently because less was available, from the HBC or from school endowment lands, to augment their holdings. The Laurier government did not oppose larger farms. In 1908 the settlement conditions in the *Dominion Lands Act* were simplified and substantial discretion was given to the Interior Ministry. A homesteader still had to use the land for three years and to be resident on it for at least six months in every year, but the physical requirements became the building of a 'habitable house' and the cultivation of 'such an area of land in each year … as is satisfactory to the Minister.' Pre-emption, after being barred for a few years, was revived in 1908 but effectively limited to Alberta and Saskatchewan.[58]

Homestead policies under the *Dominion Lands Act*, applicable to the Prairie provinces, were by far the most important such laws in this period, but other provinces employed similar schemes to attract white settlers to their then outlying regions. Immediately after Confederation Ontario passed the *Free Grants and Homestead Act*, applicable to the Muskoka–Parry Sound region between the upper Ottawa River and Georgian Bay. Under it applicants could apply for a maximum lot of 100 acres, changed to 200 in 1869, provided they intended personally to use it for 'actual settlement and cultivation.' Successful applicants had five years to fulfil settlement conditions of cultivation and house building before receiving a fee simple patent, and in the interim the lot was not alienable, could not be mortgaged, and could not be taken in execution, except for non-payment of taxes. On meeting the settlement conditions a settler could acquire a second lot for 50 cents an acre. To ensure that land acquired under homestead laws was used for settlement, not simply exploited for its timber resources, homesteaders were prohibited from using pine forests other than for their own buildings. Further legislation later in the century extended homesteading to the Rainy River district and made it possible for those who had acquired a fee simple of their original homestead of less than 200 acres to take up a second, adjoining homestead to increase their holding to 200 acres, and, in 1908, reduced the probationary period from five years to three. For all the legislation and government pecuniary assistance these colonization schemes had a limited lasting effect. Most settlers in the north worked in lumbering and mining, and while 3 million acres was taken up by some 25,000 people in this period, the thin soil and lack of a market for agricultural produce meant that many of those acres ended up as abandoned farms within two generations.[59]

Free grant legislation was not limited to Ontario. New Brunswick, Quebec, and Nova Scotia all enacted similar schemes.[60] The most unusual provincial free grant statute of the period was a Quebec act of 1892, authorizing grants of 100 acres to married couples 'having twelve children living, born in lawful wedlock.' This was not a colonization provision as such, but more of a welfare measure, for the land was to come from any available Crown land where the parents were living or, if none was available, then from the nearest place.[61] The New Brunswick legislation dated from 1872 and designated land in certain areas as free grant land. Location tickets for 100 acres were issued to single men and for 200 acres to families. Applicants had to provide assurances that they personally wanted the land 'for the purpose of actual settlement and cultivation,' and settlement conditions included house building and cultivation of certain acreages for three years before a fee simple grant would be issued. Restrictions on alienation and mortgaging within the probationary period applied. Subsequent amendments allowed groups of 10 to apply to settle together in the same location. Homestead laws operated alongside other legislative initiatives to attract white settlers into the province, to persuade residents to move from one area to another within the province, and to cajole owners of 'unproductive' land to invest money in improvements.[62]

Title Registration: The Torrens System

In 1867 the confederating colonies all had long-established land registration regimes, which we will refer to as registry systems and were effectively mandatory because they made registered interests in land prevail over unregistered ones. Registry had been controversial only in Quebec, because it pitted middle-class commercial interests, anglophone and francophone, who wanted no incumbrances on freedom of property disposition, against traditional, principally francophone opinion that wanted to retain customary rights derived from French land law.[63] The new provinces added between 1870 and 1874, and the North-West Territories, also had land registries. Manitoba's first assembly in 1871 provided that each county registrar was required to record 'all Deeds, Mortgages, Certificates of Judgment, and other instruments affecting titles to Real Estate' presented to him, and to record all such instruments 'in the order in which they are deposited.' Federal legislation was passed to provide a similar system in the Territories.[64] Public registry offices were a substantial improvement on the traditional English conveyancing practice, which relied on deeds and other records kept by the vendor and was dominant until well into the twentieth century.

During the second half of the nineteenth century a new system of what we will call title registration was introduced and spread widely through the common law world, through parts of the empire that had mixed systems of law, and even to jurisdictions governed entirely by other legal systems. Known colloquially as the Torrens system, after its founder South Australian politician Robert Torrens, or the land titles system, after the fact that it guaranteed titles to land rather than simply provided a register of transactions, it was adopted in parts of Canada. By the end of the 1880s it was the sole system in operation in all western provinces with a limited exception in Manitoba, and co-existed in Ontario along with the registry system. Although there were some small differences in how title registration operated in different jurisdictions, they were all underpinned by three general principles, known as the 'mirror principle,' the 'curtain' principle,' and the 'insurance principle.' The first holds that a Torrens system should at all times be an accurate reflection of the legal status of the land. Claims on the land that threaten to contradict the official record in the land titles office may be ignored. The second ensures that buyers do not need to inquire about previous transfers of title or other interests in the property – a metaphorical curtain covers them, and the title is 'indefeasible.' The third refers to the fact that the state provides compensation in the event of an error.

The Torrens system was first introduced into British North America in the colony of Vancouver Island in 1861, an example of the international spread of ideas and institutions across the British Empire. Torrens convinced some influential officials in the Colonial Office of his system's merits, those officials asked Solicitor General Hugh Cairns to review the South Australian legislation, and one of Cairns's protégés, George Hunter Cary, was made attorney general of Vancouver Island shortly after it became a Crown colony. Cary put a bill through the island legislature that established the Torrens system on the island. It was different from the South Australian system in small ways, but it had the most important feature of a Torrens system – claims were investigated by a government official and, if satisfactory, the government guaranteed the title. It was successful because it provided for security of titles at a time when British policy was seeking to boost white settlement after a decade of HBC rule that had discouraged it. In the early 1860s over 2,000 people applied to have their titles confirmed and registered, and no dispute about titles occurred until 1870.

When mainland British Columbia was made a colony in 1858 it established a registry system, mainly because Governor Douglas thought that title registration would be too expensive in such a geographically large and thinly populated (by white settlers) colony. He saw it as requiring either many title registration offices in widely flung regions, or an expensive centralized system. When the colonies united in 1866 British Columbia therefore had two different systems in place. Nobody doubted that there should be only one, and against some opposition, mainly from mainland banks who held unregistered mortgages and from Douglas who feared that settlers with unregistered but valid interests would see them extinguished, Torrens won out.[65] The opposition carried the fight to London, but the Colonial Office refused to intervene. The problem of distance was solved by having local JPs serve as 'mailboxes' for applications for registration in a system in which investigations and the issuing of title certificates were carried out centrally. By 1880 almost all real estate transactions used the Torrens system.

Torrens spread beyond British Columbia in the 1880s, being implemented in Manitoba and the North-West Territories in 1885 and 1886.[66] The Canada Land Law Amendment Association (CLLAA), founded in 1883, was largely responsible for the spread of Torrens. It carried out an extensive campaign of lobbying and advocacy in person, in the press, and at public meetings, aimed at the federal and provincial governments, municipal leaders, and the general public. Its leading light was George Smith Holmested, whose wide interests in all areas of law were discussed in chapter 4, and its two other most prominent members were Beverley Jones, a real estate lawyer from Ontario, and John Herbert Mason, president of the Canada Permanent Building and Savings Company, who provided most of the funding.[67] All three believed that the Torrens system was cheaper and more efficient than a registry system. Politicians and lawyers in the West saw Torrens as offering greater security of title than a registry, and easier access to credit because lenders had more certain security. It was also seen as relatively easy to implement because chains of title were so much shorter than in central and eastern Canada.

In Manitoba also a combination of factors led to substantial dissatisfaction with registry in the 1870s. Despite the problems the agricultural community experienced in the 1870s, there was something of a land boom, which brought with it widespread speculation and subdivision, as well as confusion caused by dishonest or untrained conveyancers,[68] and when there was a land crash in 1882 many would-be buyers sought to cancel their contracts by claiming their titles were defective. The preferred solution was a Torrens system. Part of its attraction was the assumption that it would prevent Métis who, as we saw earlier, had often sold their future expectations, from ever reclaiming their land once the purchaser had registered. The CLLAA deluged the press and politicians in the press and public meetings. Premier John Norquay was quickly convinced in principle, but balked at the cost, and it took until 1885 to persuade him to replace the registry system.[69] When the Liberals came to power in 1888 they made the use of Torrens optional, but in 1889 further legislation had the effect of making it much preferred. Three new registration offices were established outside Winnipeg, fees for the assurance fund were reduced, and Torrens was made mandatory for newly patented land and for those close to a registration office. Within a decade most land in the province was registered with land titles.[70]

The Torrens system was adopted for the North-West Territories by federal politicians anxious to encourage immigration and settlement, with the strong support of Territorial officials. It was the sole and mandatory system of land registration. There was some resentment from the legislative assembly created in 1888 that it did not have the power to amend it, but Ottawa resisted and did not give up its jurisdiction until the formation of Alberta and Saskatchewan in 1905. The system worked well, except that there were many complaints about the inefficiency and fee-seeking of the first registrar, Thomas Alexander McLean, the son of Upper Canadian Queen's Bench Chief Justice Archibald McLean. An Ontario lawyer, McLean got the job because of his success at backroom organizing for the Conservatives and made the most of it. His remuneration was part salary and part fees, and he did everything he could to add to the latter. The subject of many complaints, McLean's political connections allowed him to keep his job until he died in 1896. The Territorial system remained in place after 1905, but most of the work and the assets in the assurance fund went to the new provinces of Alberta and Saskatchewan, which established their own land titles regimes.[71]

The CLLAA was also able to persuade the Ontario legislature to pass a *Land Titles Act* in 1885, which made Torrens optional and initially applied only to Toronto and York County. Its availability was widened in subsequent years, to northern Ontario in particular, but very few people in southern and central Ontario used it because the registry system had been in place a long time. Chains of title were consequently lengthy, meaning it was expensive to do the comprehensive title search required to switch from one system to the other. Torrens was cheaper in the long run, because once a property had been registered, only a quick title search was required thereafter, but any given purchaser had the choice of paying less in registry at the time of purchase or paying more to transfer, with the benefits going not to him or her but to all subsequent purchasers. In contrast, Torrens quickly became the preferred system in northern and western regions, where white settlement in substantial numbers occurred late in the century and chains of title were much shorter. It was supported officially because it was seen as a way to encourage white settlement.[72]

Resolving the Prince Edward Island Land Question

As discussed in *Volume 1*, Prince Edward Island's unique landholding structure, derived from the conveyance of the entire island to 67 landlords in 1769, was a constant source of economic friction and political protest throughout the second and third quarters of the nineteenth century. Confederation provided the means and the opportunity to finally resolve the problem by buying out the landlords through a mandatory purchase scheme.[73] The federal government put up the money, the opportunity came from the fact that with Confederation the remaining landlords could no longer exert sufficient influence in Britain to thwart local efforts at reform. Many had been bought out in the 1850s and 1860s in a voluntary scheme, and the land distributed to the occupiers. But in the early 1870s there were still about two dozen large landlords left, half of them resident in the United Kingdom, owning about 380,000 acres, some 16 per cent of the Island. Recalcitrant landowners were increasingly resented, and by the late 1860s there had emerged a powerful local lobby for mandatory purchase. The Colonial Office wanted the dispute ended, and although it would not agree to compulsion because it was an affront to the sanctity of private property, by the early 1870s it was prepared to wash its hands of the problem. If the Island joined Confederation it would be the federal government, not London, that would have to accept or disallow any local legislation. When Prince Edward Island did join Confederation in 1873 one of the terms was a federal loan of $800,000 for a buyout.[74]

In 1874 the provincial Conservative administration brought in the *Land Purchase Act*. Its preamble contained an unequivocal denunciation of the landlords, who as a class had failed to abide by the original settlement conditions, and of landlordism, which had 'proved seriously detrimental to the prosperity of this Province, and to the contentment and happiness of its people.'[75] The act provided for the mandatory government purchase of any estate of over 1,000 acres, or 500 acres if the owner did not personally occupy the estate. It affected two dozen or so remaining proprietors. Prices were to be determined by a three-man commission – one appointed by each landlord, one by the provincial government, and one by the other two. The commissioners were given criteria to use in fixing the price: what had been paid to those who had voluntarily surrendered their estates, the length and value of existing leases, the size of the estate and the acreage unleased, and any possible claims to title by adverse possession to any part of the estate. There was also a very strong privative clause preventing landlords from disputing the awards in court. The Liberals wanted the commissioners to be required also to take into account whether a particular landlord's original predecessor in title had fulfilled the 1769 settlement conditions, but the Conservatives, concerned about disallowance, did not wish to see the prices reduced so much.

The act was reserved by a cautious government, and the landlords organized campaigns directed at the imperial government and the governor general. They characterized the act as 'confiscation,' a 'violation of every principle of English law and common justice,' and 'tyranny that could emanate only from a Communistic and Socialist Assembly.' They argued that it would be used as precedent by agitators in Britain, particularly in Ireland, to demand land reform, and claimed that it would be found unconstitutional had the Island been an American state. Governor General Dufferin was convinced by these arguments, not surprisingly given that he was an absentee landlord of an estate in Ulster with over 7,000 tenants. He called the act 'unfair' and 'monstrous.' He believed that he could disallow the bill without the consent of the federal government but did not think the Colonial Office would support him in that. He therefore worked to amend it to get the landlords higher prices. The Island government compromised, passing another act in 1875 that omitted the pejorative language of the preamble and changed the 1874 scheme in two principal ways. First, the commissioners would be chosen by the lieutenant governor, the governor general, and the landlords. Dufferin chose his friend Hugh Culling Eardley Childers, an English politician who owned a railway in southwestern Ontario. The provincial appointee was Conservative MHA Dr. John Theophilus Jenkins, and the landlords appointed Robert Haliburton, who had been their legal counsel at the 1860 Land Commission, for which see *Volume 1*. Second, whether or not the original settlement conditions had been complied with was added to the valuation criteria as a factor to be investigated and if necessary taken into account. This was what the Liberal opposition had wanted in 1874.[76]

The commissioners toured the estates in the summer of 1875, then set up court in Charlottetown in August, where government and the landlords pleaded their cases. By September 1875 the five largest estates had been settled, at which point Childers resigned to attend to other business and was replaced by Lemuel Wilmot, lieutenant governor of New Brunswick. All estates but one were dealt with by the end of 1876, and the land was sold to tenants at a fixed price. That was not the end of the matter, for the compensation awards were challenged in the Island's Supreme Court, which ruled in the landlords' favour. The Supreme Court judges were hardly disinterested. Chief Justice Edward Palmer had been a major landlord until 1870 when he voluntarily sold to the government. Justice James Horsfield Peters had repeatedly opposed pro-tenant legislation in the legislative council and had worked as land agent on his father-in-law's estate, earning a reputation as ruthless. The court took the case despite the strong privative clause and found that because the commission had only provided the award amount, and not the formula by which they reached that amount, they had not acted within their statutory authority and the sales were void.[77] The provincial government took the case to the newly established SCC and won in the first reported case from that court.

The Island could not have had a more sympathetic bench in Ottawa[78] but neither did it need one. The court rejected arguments that it did not have jurisdiction because the appeal should have first gone to the defunct Island Court of Appeal, the governor in council, and ruled that the privative clause was abundantly clear, such that the Island Supreme Court had no jurisdiction to overturn the awards. The Prince Edward Island land question had always been a mixture of law and politics. Although neither Britain, nor its colonies, nor the Dominion of Canada, ever had a written constitutional protection of property rights, the political culture of all three showed great respect for property. The legal consequence was that while the state could take property or sanction its taking by others through expropriation, discussed in the next section, compensation for the taking was presumed as a matter of common law. While there had long been those on the Island who argued for an uncompensated taking, that was never achieved, the landlords having used their political clout in London and among local imperial officials to resist any taking, even with compensation. After the Island's entry into Confederation in 1873, the balance of power shifted so that it was now a national, rather than imperial, matter, and the landlords' power base had always been in London, not Ottawa. Land reform on

Prince Edward Island was a radical measure, taking land from one small elite and redistributing it to the people. Chief Justice Richards was well aware of the interests and issues at stake and made it clear that in appropriate circumstances private interest must yield to community good. The *Land Purchase Act* was not 'ordinary legislation.' It was 'the settling of an important question of great moment to the community … like the abolition of the Seigniorial tenure in Lower Canada, and the settling of the land question in Ireland.' In such cases 'private interests are made to yield to the public good.'[79]

Expropriation

Prior to Confederation all colonial governments and a wide variety of corporations, both business corporations and municipalities, had statutory powers to expropriate land on payment of compensation. Before and after 1867 a broad power of expropriation was seen as critical for the economic development of British North America, a necessary tool for activist administrations looking to help develop local industries and transportation networks. The right to expropriate for the public good was long recognized in UK law, as was the concomitant duty to pay compensation. In nineteenth-century Britain both parts of this equation were enacted in a series of *Land Clauses Acts*, which were imported into every legislative grant of expropriation power.[80] In Canada only British Columbia had similar legislation, originating in reception of the English statutes as of 1859, discussed in chapter 4. Even without received legislation the same quasi-constitutional principles applied in the new dominion, and among the first group of statutes passed by Parliament in 1867 was one that conferred expropriation power on the federal government. Like its colonial-era predecessors it was called the *Public Works Act*. It established a department by that name headed by a minister of public works, and section 24 gave that minister the power to 'acquire and take possession' of 'any land' that was 'necessary for the use, construction and maintenance of any Public Work or building.' The Act did not define 'public work,' but that deficiency was supplied by an 1872 statute that defined one very broadly as 'every canal, lock, dam, hydraulic work, harbour pier, public building or other work or property' of a similar nature 'that was acquired or constructed, or intended to be acquired or constructed,' or 'extended, enlarged, repaired or improved at the expense of' the federal government.' In subsequent years this list was expanded. The act contained no provision for challenging the taking, assumed a right to compensation and provided for arbitration by a government-appointed board of arbitration if the parties could not agree on the amount of compensation. The first federal statute actually termed an *Expropriation Act* was passed as part of the statutory revision of 1886 and essentially reproduced the expropriation sections of the earlier *Public Works Act*.[81] The *Expropriation Act* was amended a number of times in this period but its essential nature was not changed.

All provinces passed similar statutes, starting as *Public Works Acts* and being renamed *Expropriation Acts* at some point.[82] Expropriation powers were also included in other statutes, both federal and provincial. There were more of the latter for jurisdictional reasons – highway, municipal, mining, and railway acts. British Columbia's *Municipal Act*, for example, allowed for land to be taken 'by the [municipal] corporation in the exercise of any of its powers.'[83] Mining companies in Ontario were given the power to expropriate land for a road or tramway from their mines to 'the nearest navigable waters or railway or highway,' to a maximum of 20 miles. They could also do any work necessary to make navigable for their purposes any water course, provided they indemnified the riparian owners for any damage done.[84] With regard to other federal statutes conferring expropriation power, we saw in chapter 8 that the *Indian Act* sanctioned the taking of reserves in or near urban areas by the superintendent general of Indian affairs. The principal federal act conferring expropriation power was the *Railway Act*, which gave any railway incorporated by special act of Parliament the power to 'take of any corporation or person any land or other property necessary for the construction, maintenance and accommodation of the Railway.'[85] Only Crown land was exempt, although it could be taken with government permission. The Intercolonial Railway, a public work, was also granted power to 'take possession of any lands required for the purposes of the Railway,' and needed to pay compensation, the amount to be decided by agreement or arbitration.[86] Ontario's *Railway Act* was not just to the same effect, it was in many respects identically worded, as was Quebec's.[87] Canada's first provincial park to be created with the aid of expropriation, rather than by donations or the use of military lands, was Niagara Falls.[88]

The power to expropriate and the requirement to pay compensation was also given to many companies incorporated by federal and provincial special acts of incorporation. As we saw in chapter 11, there were a great many such special act corporations because some enterprises, especially railways, could not incorporate using general incorporation legislation and had to do so by private act. Many of the special acts conferred expropriation powers. The Canada and Detroit River Bridge Company, for example, was empowered by its 1873 federal incorporation statute to 'take … lands, waters, beaches, or other property necessary for constructing the Bridge,' and similarly to 'take, hold, use, and enjoy more land than is strictly necessary for stations, gravel pits, ballasting, or other purposes related to the Company's works if the greater amount of land is required to procure sufficient land for the same.' Compensation was to be paid according to the process laid out in the 1868 *Railway Act*. As it turned out the bridge was not built until 1929, so this power went unused. Similar powers were given to, inter alia, the Moncton Harbour Improvement Company in 1881, the Assiniboine Water Power Company in 1889, and the Shuswap and Thompson Rivers Boom Company in 1908.[89] Companies incorporated by provincial acts and given expropriation powers ranged from the South Shore Railway and Tunnel Company of Quebec, to the Winnipeg Water Power Company, to New Brunswick's Sackville Rural Cemetery Company, which could acquire private land if the cemetery needed to expand, and to the same province's Lepreau Mining Company, which was given the right to take 'so much of the land of private persons … as may be necessary' for the construction and operation of the trains that would transport the iron ore and other materials away from the mine.[90]

As we saw in the previous section on the Prince Edward Island question, courts did not question the substantive validity of expropriations, but they did ensure that corporations went no further than their constituting statutes allowed.[91] They also enunciated two principles familiar to the modern lawyer. First, that landowners were unable to claim compensation for loss of value of land that was not taken but was affected by the work for which other land was taken. In *Canada v Fowlds*, Falconbridge J, sitting as a judge of the Exchequer Court, rejected the damages claim of a mill owner based on a loss of water power because of the construction of the Trent Valley Canal. In doing so he relied on the leading US case and the major US text, *Lewis on Eminent Domain*. As noted in chapter 4, Canadian courts in this period relied mostly on English cases but used US ones in certain areas.[92] Second, that compensation should be based on the highest and best value of the land. In *Burton v The Queen*, for example, the plaintiffs challenged an arbitration award that was based on the value of the land for the agricultural purposes for which it had previously been used. Taschereau J held that the compensation should reflect the value of the land after it had been increased by the construction of the railway nearby. The amount awarded increased very substantially.[93] The level of compensation was also a matter of considerable contention following the expropriations to create the Queen Victoria Niagara Falls Park. Three landowners refused to accept the arbitrators' awards and took their cases to the Court of Appeal in 1885 and 1886, which upheld the arbitrators in each case.[94]

Before we leave this topic, it should be stressed that while Canadian governments were always required to pay compensation, in important respects their hands were freer than those of their US counterparts, where the relationships between the public interest and private rights in regard to property were defined in some measure by the Fifth and Fourteenth Amendments to the Constitution. In the United States there also emerged in the late nineteenth and early twentieth centuries a vigorous regulatory takings doctrine, which made some regulations in the public interest impermissible even if they did not take title to land. Canada developed a much weaker version of this doctrine, known as de facto expropriation, giving governments wider scope for action. When silver prospectors sued the Ontario government in the early twentieth century for compensation for their claims being located in an area that was then withdrawn from prospecting, they received a blunt denial from Justice Riddell of the King's Bench division. The legislature, he asserted, 'is restrained by no rule human or divine.' If the plaintiffs had acquired any rights, which he did not think they had, 'the Legislature had the power to take them away. The prohibition "Thou shalt not steal" has no legal force upon the sovereign body. And there would be no necessity for compensation to be given. We have no such restriction upon the power of the Legislature as is found in some States.' The Court of Appeal agreed.[95]

Land Use Regulation: Public and Private Law

The common law governing land use rested on the basic very general principle that landowners had the right to do whatever they wanted with the land, which stretched *cuius est solum, eius usque ad coelum ad est ad inferos.*[*] But as every property lawyer knew and knows, there have always been exceptions to this bedrock principle. These exceptions derived both from public law, largely in this period in the form of municipal by-laws, and private law, through restrictive covenants and nuisance law.

Limited land use regulations in the form of municipal by-laws predated Confederation and increased in volume and scope throughout

---

* Whosesoever is the soil, it is his up to the sky and down to the depths.

this period.[96] Such by-laws were either passed pursuant to a provincial authorizing statute, invariably called the *Municipal Act* and equally invariably constantly amended by the legislature, or were authorized by, and sometimes contained in, a city charter, such charters mostly originating in, and periodically renewed by, statutes passed by provincial assemblies.[97] Wherever their authority was derived from, urban by-laws in this period were ad hoc responses to what were seen as dangers to public health, or nuisances, or the felt need to improve building standards, or the danger posed by fire, or any one of a number of other concerns. The by-laws were not zoning regulations as we understand that term. Municipalities were not divided into districts that were residential or commercial/industrial, with the activities that could or could not be carried out within those districts specified. Rather activities, usually commercial activities, were either proscribed or limited by their proximity to other buildings. Similarly, the use of building materials, especially wood, was either prohibited entirely or limited, often depending on which area of a city the building was in. When enough of these kinds of regulations specific to certain parts of municipalities were in place it could be argued that ad hoc regulation had become de facto zoning. Informal zoning was also effected through the discretionary granting of licences. Officials often were persuaded to group certain businesses together in parts of the city away from wealthy residential neighbourhoods – neighbourhoods sometimes already partially protected by restrictive covenants, which are discussed immediately below. But it was not de jure zoning, the division of urban communities into residential, commercial, and industrial areas, with certain uses and activities permitted or prohibited in each. There is general agreement that this did not happen in the United States until 1916, and it has been argued that Canada's first true zoning regime was instituted in Kitchener, Ontario, in 1924.

There is no point in trying to decide how close the totality of urban land use regulations came to being a form of zoning in this period. What matters is that regulations became more numerous, affected an increasing number of activities and therefore people, and helped reinforce the class- and in some cases race-based residential segregation that was a feature of all towns and cities. Most urban by-laws did these things in two closely related ways. When they prescribed who could do what and where, they kept out what some saw as 'undesirable' trades and the undesirable people who worked in them, and made the neighbourhood consequently more salubrious for those from the 'better' social classes.

A Toronto by-law of 1866, number 431, for example, required the construction of slaughterhouses to be approved by the Board of Health and to be situated 'at least 100 feet from any public street and 300 feet from any residence or dwelling.' Thus residents did not have to spend their time in the immediate proximity of slaughterhouse workers, or the men who brought in the live animals and removed the carcasses. Nor did they have to endure the sounds and smells of the slaughtering process. Later by-laws dealt with the location, as well as the ventilation and cleanliness, of butchers' shops and the disposal of entrails. To similar effect, in 1881 BC's *Municipal Act* gave local councils the power to regulate slaughterhouses or bar them from particular locations, while in Newfoundland the slaughtering of animals required permission from a magistrate.[98]

Another example from the world of domesticated animals was stables. Toronto began regulating stables in the 1840s and a by-law of 1886, number 1702, made the construction of stables conditional on approval from the medical officer of health and the written consent of a majority of all the property owners within a 500-foot radius of the proposed site. Montreal in contrast had no regulations specific to stables under its general by-law on public health, number 105 of 1876, which required stables and other 'unwholesome or nauseous places' to be cleaned as often as ordered by the Board of Health. They were regularly inspected and occasionally shut down if they failed the inspection.[99] One effect of the widening web of regulation was that urban animal populations dropped precipitously in the late nineteenth century, in part because of increasingly strict by-laws passed to keep them out of downtown cores and in part as the result of other factors such as the fear of bovine disease and mechanization of transport, which made them redundant. In Montreal, for example, there were approximately six ungulates (horses, cows, pigs, and sheep) for every 100 humans in 1871, but less than one by 1911. By the early twentieth century free-roaming animals were entirely banned from all cities, and those that remained were heavily constrained by regulations in where they could be kept. Animal waste and carcasses were a major concern of public health and sanitation advocates. Winnipeg's by-law 12 of 1874, for example, outlawed the sale of water from sources commonly used to water animals and restricted the disposal of carcasses in public places and waterways.[100]

Other land use by-laws imposed what we would now term building codes. The earliest regulations were concerned principally with the constant danger of fire posed by the nineteenth-century wooden city. Halifax was perhaps the first to regulate in this area, following the New Year's Day fire of 1857. The council decreed that all new buildings higher than 26 feet had to be made of stone. In Toronto by-law 503 of 1869 was the first comprehensive response to this danger, requiring all buildings in the central core to be made of non-combustible materials. This kind of regulation, extended to other areas in the 1870s and 1880s, was also a form of segregation by class because the less wealthy could not afford to build with brick and stone. Winnipeg's 1902 charter gave the city council the power to prohibit the use of wooden fences and the construction of wooden buildings in specified parts of the city, and to require that buildings have main walls of brick, stone, or iron.[101] We have given just a few examples of land use by-laws in some cities here. A full study would include by-laws from all major urban centres dealing also with topics as varied as the storage of combustible material, the suppression of 'houses of ill-fame,' the width of streets, and the location of cemeteries.

As discussed above, this was not zoning, but a sign of things to come was that the phrase 'residential area' was appearing in by-laws by the late nineteenth century. An 1890 amendment to Ontario's *Municipal Act*, for example, gave municipalities the power to control where 'offensive and noxious trades' could be located, but limited that power by mandating that 'tanneries, slaughter houses, livery stables and laundries' were not to be located in 'residential areas.' The statute did not define residential area and the city did not designate which areas were residential, nor did the act or any by-law state which areas were not residential. In contrast Calgary did not designate residential areas but instead purchased land and made it available for industrial use, thus effectively zoning by incentives. This period therefore witnessed increasing land use differentiation in urban areas that was both de facto and de jure. In 1904 Ontario went one step further, at Toronto's request giving municipalities the power to control the location of 'laundries, butcher shops, stores and manufactories' without reference to residential areas.[102]

At the end of our period another, broader form of land use regulation was first legislated, what we now term land use planning. As its name implies, land use planning deals less with regulating existing uses and more with future development. It also generally kept the ultimate decision-making power at the provincial level, not the municipal, although municipalities were given the power to decide the details. The first such legislation was passed in both New Brunswick and Nova Scotia in 1912. The former permitted any town council to prepare 'a town planning scheme ... with respect to any land which is in the course of development.' The general object of any scheme, which required provincial approval, was to ensure that streets were laid out so that traffic was facilitated, sanitation could be provided, and future residents would enjoy 'amenity and convenience.' In 1912 Ontario passed legislation permitting the larger municipalities to regulate aspects of the subdivision of suburban land, and the following year Alberta passed a close copy of the New Brunswick Act.[103] Other provinces followed after 1914; we will have more to say about land use planning in *Volume 3*.

Moving from public to private law, the common law had two principal doctrines by which landowners could limit what other landowners could do with their land: nuisance and restrictive covenants. Nuisance law had been around for centuries, but restrictive covenants were an innovation by the English Court of Chancery in the mid-nineteenth century that was adopted by Canadian courts from the 1870s.[104] Restrictive covenants originate in an agreement between a vendor and purchaser of land by which the latter agrees not to do something with the land. The contract, always called a covenant because it is part of the conveyance, is enforceable between the contracting parties at common law, but not enforceable against a derivative owner of the affected land because he or she was not a party to the initial contract. In legal parlance there was no privity of contract. That changed with the 1848 case of *Tulk v Moxhay*, which concerned the toney London residential area Leicester Square.[105] The square was developed in the early nineteenth century by one Tulk, who owned several houses as well as vacant land in the middle of the square. In 1808 he sold the vacant land, the conveyance including a clause by which the purchaser agreed to 'keep and maintain the said piece of ground and square garden ... as square garden and pleasure ground, in an open state, uncovered with any buildings.' Title to the square passed through a number of hands before it was bought by someone who planned to develop it. The Court of Chancery held that despite the lack of privity it could be enforced if the purchaser had notice of the covenant. Chancery thereby created a new equitable interest in land, and over the rest of the nineteenth century other decisions elaborated on the requirements before a derivative owner could be sued: the covenant had to be negative in substance, to restrict the derivative owner in what he or she could do with the land; the covenantee had to own land to be benefitted by the covenant; and the covenant had to 'touch and concern' the land of the covenantee, to be about the use to which the land was put and not personal.

The first known restrictive covenant included in a Canadian land transaction actually predated *Tulk v Moxhay* by a decade and a half, an 1834 conveyance by William Forbes of New Glasgow, Nova Scotia, to one MacIntosh of the same town. Attached to the conveyance was an agreement that a defined part of the land 'should never be hereafter sold, but left to the common benefit of both parties and their successors.' Both lots went through various hands and in 1866 William MacLean placed a building on the burdened lot, and Alexander McKay sued to force its removal. The case was ruled on twice in Nova Scotia, by the Judge in Equity and the full court, and reached the JCPC in 1873. It is therefore the first reported restrictive covenant case emanating from Canada. The JCPC engaged in some disparaging remarks about 'popular language which unskilled men would employ,' noting that if the covenant was construed literally as one barring the sale of the land forever it would be invalid, presumably as a restraint on alienation. It ruled that the prohibition on sale could be severed from the rest of the clause, which made it a covenant not to develop the land falling within the *Tulk v Moxhay* doctrine.[106]

This was an unusual case, because the covenant preceded the English recognition of such interests and because it emanated from a small town in Nova Scotia and was not about protecting neighbourhoods in a major city. The first reported case that was similar to *Tulk* concerned a covenant made in 1860, discussed below in this paragraph. It was one of many responses to the growth of cities and the concomitant desire of the better-off to keep their parts of the city free from the effects of economic growth. These included the physical consequences of living near an abattoir or a noisy and odorous factory, and the social undesirability of living cheek-by-jowl with poorer people crammed into less salubrious housing. In the 1882 case of *Vankoughnet v Denison* a covenant had been attached in 1860 to Bellevue Square in Toronto, a green space bordered by four residential streets, which stated that the square was 'always to remain unbuilt on.' Chancellor Boyd issued an injunction against a development proposed by its derivative owner, Robert Brittain Denison, a landowner and developer whose Toronto landholdings were known as the Bellevue Estate.[107] The Court of Appeal upheld the trial decision, citing the leading English cases, and Bellevue Square remains an open space today.[108]

It is not possible to calculate how prevalent restrictive covenants were before the First World War. They remain 'hidden from view in countless documents of title locked away' in registry and land titles offices.[109] But we can say that they were used increasingly frequently in growing urban centres, assuming that an increase in the number of reported cases reflects a rise in their prevalence and resulting disputes over a small number of them. Restrictive covenant cases were decided by the Saskatchewan Supreme Court from 1909 on, just three years after the court first sat, and they were also used in Edmonton and Calgary.[110] In Ontario restrictive covenants were most commonly employed in Toronto, but they also appeared in other major urban centres such as Hamilton, London, and Windsor.[111] They typically prohibited trades and manufacturing in a given locale, limited the number of structures on any given lot, insisted on distances between lot lines and buildings, and laid down minimum costs for any structures, ensuring that cheap housing would not be built. Demonstrating that restrictive covenants and urban by-laws often overlapped, one covenant prohibiting non-residential uses was used against a derivative owner who in 1904 began to build a stable and carriage house on the land.[112] Covenants were used for parts of cities that had become, or wished to become, residential enclaves for the upper and upper-middle classes, such as Rosedale, Parkdale, and the Annex in Toronto. One quirky covenant, which would not be enforceable today precisely because it was so personal, prevented a person who bought part of leading Toronto lawyer Dalton McCarthy's land and thereby became his neighbour, not only from building on the lot but also doing, inter alia, 'anything which should annoy or tend to operate to the annoyance of McCarthy.'[113]

Pearson v Adams, a 1912 Ontario case that was taken to the SCC in 1914, aptly illustrates the use of restrictive covenants to effect residential segregation.[114] In 1888 one Maynard had sold off a number of lots on Maynard Avenue in Toronto, each sale with a covenant stipulating that the lot was 'to be used only as a site for a detached brick or stone dwelling house, to cost at least two thousand dollars, to be of fair architectural appearance and to be built at the same distance from the street line as the houses on the adjoining lots.' Obviously the purpose was to ensure that the area remained an aesthetically and socially homogenous upper-middle-class enclave, the 'minimum cost' provision preventing anybody who could not afford such a residence from moving in. Pearson bought a lot on the street and built 'a first-class private dwelling house.' Adams also bought a lot and proposed to construct a six-unit apartment building, which Pearson sought an injunction to prevent. The technical legal question before the court was whether the proposed apartment building was a 'dwelling house' within the meaning of the covenant, and a majority of the SCC said that it was not. This conclusion rested on the court's understanding of the context. Brodeur J stated that '[d]etached houses were necessarily more expensive than the others and were supposed to be used by a wealthier class of the community. There is no doubt that Mr. Maynard, when he opened the street in question and sold those lots, had in view the establishment of a nice residential quarter and those covenants were stipulated evidently for that purpose. He did not want to have any flats nor any tenements erected on those lots which would be occupied by two or three lessees.' Hence the term 'dwelling house' did not include apartment buildings – multi-occupant structures occupied by renters. Justice Brodeur was certainly correct in one of his observations. Apartment houses were opposed by middle-class urban reformers who believed they encouraged immorality, crowded living arrangements, and more ethnic diversity.[115]

Restrictive covenants segregated not only by class but also by ethnicity. In British Columbia the principal targets were people of Chinese or Japanese descent, an alignment of private law with the many discriminatory statutes of the period, discussed in chapter 16. In Ontario they were generally aimed at Jews, disfavoured southern and eastern Europeans, and, in the words of a covenant from just outside our period, in 1920, 'any person of a coloured race.' There was no judicial or legislative objection to such covenants in this period. That would come decades later, after the Second World War.[116] The one policy concern about restrictive covenants manifested in this period was their effect on the freedom of landowners to do what they wanted with the land – a key aspect of land ownership. In Ontario this concern was expressed in an 1887 amendment to the *Land Titles Act*, which gave a landowner the right to apply to court for a covenant to be 'modified or discharged,' the court needing to be satisfied that any change would be 'beneficial to the persons principally interested in the enforcement of the covenant.' Thus this was not a provision to serve the public interest or the private interest of those who owned burdened land, but only the private interests of those who owned land that at the time the covenant was created was thought to be benefitted by it.[117] It was also not a provision that applied to land in the registry system and thus had little effect in southern Ontario.[118] The courts' treatment of applications under this modification provision was true to the statutory language; they construed it narrowly and literally, refusing to interpret it as one allowing the public interest to prevail over the private. It was, as Middleton J said in 1911, an 'extraordinary' power and one to be 'exercised with the greatest caution.'[119]

Nuisance: The Shifting Boundary
between Public and Private Law

The law of nuisance exists to settle conflicts between neighbours where one engages in activities on one's land that diminish substantially the reasonable enjoyment of another's. These might involve discharges of various kinds into the air or water, or excessive noise or vibrations. Although also part of tort law, the common law of nuisance in effect regulated land use. By permitting some uses and prohibiting others in particular contexts, it defined the extent of property rights in land. In some cases damages were awarded but in others an injunction could issue, shutting down the offending activity permanently. The common law assumed that land was used primarily for agriculture and thus had a somewhat conservative bias. This was reflected in the traditional understanding that liability in nuisance was strict; the taking of reasonable care was not generally a defence, nor was the fact that the defendant had commenced activity first and the plaintiff 'came to the nuisance.' The Industrial Revolution and consequent urbanization led to environmental pollution on an unprecedented scale, presenting the courts with difficult choices to be made between the peaceable enjoyment of land by some individuals and the perceived benefits of large-scale economic development from lumbering, mining, manufacturing, and new energy facilities such as gasworks.

Scholars studying these conflicts in the more advanced industrial jurisdictions of Britain and the United States initially portrayed the courts as relaxing the common law of nuisance and related doctrines to permit industry to carry on more or less unimpeded, in the era before more assertive state regulation became the norm. The courts thus provided a subsidy to industry by allowing industries to externalize the costs of environmental degradation.[120] More recently this view has been challenged for the United Kingdom by an argument that 'nuisance law was consistently a robust constraint on polluting industrial enterprise.' Two related factors support this assertion. First, the effects of industrial and urban pollution were often experienced more in the countryside than in the city proper. Sewage outfalls were typically some distance outside towns, while higher smokestacks spread particulate matter outside city limits. Second, deep-pocketed plaintiffs lived in the countryside – large landowners who objected to the amenities of their estates being interfered with and were not reluctant to take legal action. These parties achieved some success through nuisance actions in forcing urban governments and industries to adopt new technologies that eliminated or largely abated their unpleasant and harmful effluents.[121]

Whatever the truth of these observations for Britain, they are not apposite for Canada, which lacked a wealthy land-owning class who might have been able to use nuisance law to push back against environmental degradation. Nonetheless, some scholars analysing the Canadian experience have argued that judges were motivated by a 'principled conservatism' that saw them protect traditional property rights against industrial polluters and fail to take up the flexibility offered by the newer English law, which was allegedly more favourable to industry. Others, analysing different sets of conflicts – those involving urban waste water rather than industrial pollutants – have found the record of Canadian courts more mixed on this score.[122] The Canadian example does not provide a 'pure' case study of the impact of industrialization on the common law of nuisance because the timing of its Industrial Revolution and large-scale water supply and sewerage works is considerably later than in comparator jurisdictions. By the time these conflicts arose in Canada in the late nineteenth century, legislatures were more active in trying to balance the perceived need for economic development with the rights of landowners to be free from undue environmental intrusions, reducing the pressure on the common law. If, in protecting traditional property rights, Canadian judges sometimes observed that it was up to the legislature to alter the common law if it was found insufficiently inhospitable to industry, such a stance was more justifiable when judges could see the legislature doing precisely that in conflicts of this kind.

This is not to say that 'balance' was always the order of the day when the legislature intervened. Take, for example, the conflict that opposed the interests of the lumber barons of the Ottawa Valley to those of downstream users who objected to the increasing flood of sawdust that impeded navigation, destroyed fisheries, rendered drinking water unsafe, and caused occasional explosions resulting from methane released by rotting wood debris. At Confederation about one million logs were cut annually at the Chaudière mills on the Ottawa River, which was apparently capable of handling the refuse produced with tolerable impacts on other uses. By 1884, however, that quantity had increased nearly fourfold. Antoine Ratté had bought property along the river and started a boating business in 1866, when the river was still relatively pristine. He alleged he had been making $2,000 per year at the time, which was reduced by half by the early 1870s and to $500 by the early 1880s as the growing tide of sawdust made recreational boating nearly impossible. Ratté went public with his complaints before suing the responsible mill owners in 1886, publishing an eight-page pamphlet detailing the degradation of the river and its impact on his business, and lamenting the aesthetic loss to the landscape. He offered to sell his property for $74,000 and retire from the boating business.[123]

Probably aware that some legal action was likely, the Ontario legislature had passed an act in 1885 effectively insulating the lumber operations on the Ottawa River from injunctions in nuisance actions. The act did not expressly forbid the granting of injunctions, but in directing the judge to 'take into consideration the importance of the lumber trade to the locality wherein such injury ... takes place, and the benefit and advantage, direct and consequential, which such trade confers on the locality and [its] inhabitants, ... and [to] weigh the same against the private injury ... complained of,' the legislature was sending a strong hint about the expected outcome. The act preserved a right to damages, which Ratté sought in his action against three mill owners.[124]

It was a David and Goliath struggle, contrary to the English cases described above. Ratté was not exactly poor, but one of the defendants, John Rudolph Booth, ran what in the 1890s would become the largest lumber operation in the world. He owned timber rights in some 640,000 acres in Ontario and Quebec, and his mills produced more than all the coastal mills of British Columbia combined. Ratté lost at trial on a technical issue related to the nature of the title to his property but succeeded at the Divisional Court, the Court of Appeal, and the JCPC. The matter then went to a master of the Ontario Supreme Court to determine damages. He ordered each defendant to pay $1,000 to Ratté, which Booth objected to as manifestly too high and appealed through several levels of court to the SCC, all of which dismissed the appeals. Ratté sued Booth again a decade later, and this time Booth settled for some $2,000. However, he apparently did not adopt the technology that would have considerably abated the sawdust problem until some time later, when his mill burned down and he was obliged to rebuild.[125] The relatively small damages awards were more of a licence fee to pollute than an incentive to invest in new technology.

In other cases where the courts were not statutorily prevented from granting injunctions they would often grant a stay before an injunction could be enforced to allow defendants time to adopt measures that would assist in abating the nuisance caused by their activities. This occurred in *Francklyn v Peoples Heat and Light Company*, where the defendant company had built a gasworks in 1897 on the site of an abandoned penitentiary adjoining Emscote, a stately Victorian home on Halifax's Northwest Arm. Emscote was owned by Gilbert Francklyn, who lived there with his mother, Sarah Jane Francklyn, a daughter of Sir Samuel Cunard. It was not disputed that the Francklyns were obliged to leave their home as result of the noxious vapours emanating from the company's operations, and they sought an injunction based on the alleged nuisance. An interim injunction was granted in January and confirmed on appeal on 1 March 1899, but the court suspended it for two weeks to allow the company to explore abatement; it also indicated that it would be receptive to further extensions. On 14 March a bill amending the company's act of incorporation was introduced in the assembly, insulating it from any suit for an injunction if it carried on business 'according to methods usually employed.' Moreover, it allowed only one suit for all damages, past, present, and future to be brought by any adjoining landowner. The bill was withdrawn when the company agreed to buy the Francklyn estate for what was rumoured to be $10,000 above the market price. A second bill was then brought forward that would have insulated manufacturers generally from nuisance suits; it passed the assembly but was rejected by the legislative council. The result was likely less than satisfactory for the Francklyns, whose home was essentially expropriated in spite of their success in court.[126]

It is not always possible to follow these injunction proceedings to their conclusion, but the liberal granting of extensions and the relatively low amounts of damages ordered point to attempts to balance the rights of landowners and economic development at the remedial stage, even if courts often pronounced themselves strongly in favour of property rights at the liability stage. Indeed, one might say that the courts employed a strict liability standard for liability but held defendants to a much less stringent standard when granting the remedy. And while public agencies began to be created with a mandate of balancing the interests of polluters and landowners, they found themselves facing dilemmas similar to those vexing the courts. Ontario's Public Health Board (PHB), for example, was established in 1882 to resolve conflicts created by the adoption of water closets and the new sewerage technology. These systems collected massive amounts of human waste and deposited it, often untreated, at outfalls in the countryside, out of sight of urbanites but not out of sight or other senses of the rural residents living nearby. In cases involving the board, the defendants were not private parties but municipalities or public institutions, which could pose problems for plaintiffs in nuisance litigation. In an 1875 suit, a farmer complained that the London Lunatic Asylum dumped all its sewage into a channel that ended in a stream that ran through his farm. The trial judge granted an injunction but the Court of Appeal disagreed, stating that it had no authority to order the statutorily created institution to spend the $30,000 allegedly required to transport its sewage directly to the Thames River, where in any case it would constitute a public nuisance rather than a private one. The asylum, no doubt fearing future litigation where it might not be so successful, proceeded to implement solutions to the sewage problem that effectively abated the nuisance.[127]

One of the board's tools was the power to sue municipalities for public nuisances such as fouling rivers, but this proved to be far from a panacea. The City of London was prosecuted in 1885 and ordered to take action, but did nothing for a decade, then took another six years to construct a new treatment facility, which opened in 1901 but proved unsatisfactory. In 1913, nearly 20 years after the initial PHB suit, the pipe dedicated to London's sewage could carry away only 30 per cent of the city's waste, the rest being discharged within city limits. Not until 1916 would the building of a second treatment plant and a separate storm sewer system bring some resolution to this long-standing problem.[128]

A final observation on the shifting role of private and public law in nuisance actions may be made on the zoning powers of cities, discussed in a previous section. Disputes such as that pitting the gas plant in Halifax against the owner of a neighbouring residence would not happen later because zoning by-laws would not have permitted the gas plant to build in such a place. During this period zoning by-laws were in their infancy, and their absence was a factor in a notorious 1896 Quebec case, *Drysdale v Dugas*.[129] Nuisance-type conflicts in Quebec law were dealt with under the rubric of neighbourhood obligations (obligations de voisinage) but the law was quite unsettled. In particular, it was not clear whether a fault standard or a strict liability standard should be employed. Drysdale had built a commercial stable in a residential area, employing the most recent techniques for ventilation and waste disposal. Nonetheless, his neighbour, Mr. Dugas, was vexed by the odours and sued for alleged loss of enjoyment of his property and diminution of its value.* He succeeded at all three court levels, including the SCC. While an injunction was not granted because its availability in Quebec was limited by statute to very specific situations prior to the enactment of a revised *Code of Civil Procedure* in 1897, the prospect of continuing actions for damages by Dugas or other neighbours persuaded Drysdale

---

* Dugas, a judge in Montreal, was encountered in chapter 3 in his later incarnation as a judge of the Territorial Court of the Yukon.

to discontinue using the property as a stable and he converted it to other purposes. The SCC did not clear up which standard was applicable, seeming to rely on the general fault provision of article 1053 but not allowing Drysdale the defence that he had acted with reasonable care by constructing the stable on the most up-to-date plan available.[130] The Quebec courts seem to have been motivated to provide a robust protection for property rights by the reference to the 'absolute' nature of such rights in article 406 of the *Civil Code*.[131]

It was the brief dissent by Justice Gwynne at the SCC that pointed out the conundrum resulting from the decision: if a stable according to the most approved plan could not be built without generating liability, then none could be built in Montreal, at least none in residential areas where they were needed in the pre-automobile era. In 1901 the city revised its by-laws to institute some control over the building of stables, prohibiting them altogether in some areas and subjecting others to strict standards of construction and periodic inspection. Conflicts over the location of such businesses would increasingly migrate to public law and away from private litigation as cities employed more sophisticated techniques of regulation.

Common law judges may have rhetorically embraced the protection of property rights over economic development in the later nineteenth century, but the remedies they afforded suggest that they were trying to avoid shutting down industries or urban water and sewage works if they could possibly avoid it. Legislatures did intervene at times to protect health as opposed to mitigating environmental harms more generally, but they too were wary of shutting down enterprises on which many depended for employment. Although captains of industry were well represented in Parliament and provincial legislatures, their views were not substantially different from those of the public at large. The idea that Canada's natural resources were inexhaustible and that streams, rivers, and air currents would naturally disperse pollutants and debris died hard, while public support for environmental protection was anaemic where it existed at all.

Succession Law

The law of succession does not move quickly, and reforms typically point to significant changes in societal views of which members of the family should be favoured, or in the nature of the assets typically held on death, or both. One major change in those views of family had already occurred by the time of Confederation. All common law provinces had moved away from primogeniture as the determinant of intestate succession to land, in favour of partible inheritance (equal division among an intestate's children), British Columbia being the last to do so just a year after it joined Confederation. Land was singled out for special treatment by the common law in another way. It did not go to the personal representative (the executor named in a will, or the administrator of an intestate's estate), but vested directly in the 'heir,' normally the eldest son of the deceased, subject to the dower interest of the widow. Seen as desirable in English society where large landholdings were the key to family honour, primogeniture was not suitable in North America, where land was much more widely held, personal labour was not stigmatized, and 'family capitalism' was the main form of economic organization. All children, it was thought, should be given a chance to make their way in life with a share of the family patrimony.[132]

Personal property (money, livestock, personal possessions) went to the personal representative of the deceased who shared it between the widow and children according to the *Statutes of Distributions 1670 & 1685*, which had been received in all the common law provinces. Hence the rules for intestate succession to real property and personal property were converging by the time of Confederation: equal division among the children of the deceased, subject to any claim by the widow or widower. Manitoba seems to have been the first province to treat all property of a deceased as a single fund, subject to the same rules, which it did almost immediately after provincehood in 1871. Ontario did so more elaborately in its *Devolution of Estates Act, 1886*, which declared that all property of a deceased person, in whatever form, was to devolve upon his or her personal representative for the payment of the debts of the deceased and distribution of the residue according to the will, if any, or the rules of intestate succession.[133] The heir, as a term of art in the common law, disappeared. Anyone who took by testate or intestate succession was now an heir.

After Confederation change in the law of succession was driven mainly by improvements in the legal status of married women, which are discussed in detail in the following chapter – reforms that not only authorized them to leave property by will as they saw fit but also elevated their position in the scheme of intestate succession relative to the children of the marriage. In addition, patterns of testation in the later nineteenth century, in Ontario at least, also reflected more generosity and less conditionality regarding gifts by will from husbands to their widows. We will consider first changes in the law of dower and intestate succession, then move on to broader changes in the law of testamentary succession, in particular those dealing with conditions attached to property in wills.

The common law treated widows as dependent pensioners who had to be supported for the remainder of their lives, while any productive assets in the husband's name were left to the children either by will or pursuant to the rules of intestate succession. In a largely agrarian society, if the assets left on death were not substantial, this difficult choice made sense. The children, typically young adults at the father's death, needed capital to assist in raising their own families, while the widow would have to make do with an income interest. The common law's mode of supporting widows was dower, a one-third interest for life in the real property her husband had left at death. Dower also provided an important right for women during marriage: they had to 'bar their dower' in any conveyance by the husband of land in his name, providing a veto on sale or mortgage of the family home, for example. All other interests in realty went to the children or the husband's blood relatives if no issue of the marriage survived. In England, dower was anathematized as interfering with conveyancing and virtually abolished in 1833, but it went in an entirely different direction in British North America, where it was strengthened and expanded to include equitable interests in land, including interests in mortgaged land. Even so, it applied only to realty and provided no sustenance for the widows of the landless – hence the importance of reforms to the law of intestate succession. Once again Manitoba led the way, its 1871 statute directing that a widow should receive an ownership interest (not just a life estate) in one-third of all her deceased husband's estate, the rest going to his children. The act said nothing new about the estates of married women themselves, the province having not yet reformed married women's property law. Ontario's *Devolution of Estates Act* of 1886 took the latter reforms into account. It made almost uniform the law of intestate succession for men and women by declaring that all assets would be distributed as if they were personal property. The surviving spouse would receive one-third of the estate of the deceased spouse, the rest going to the child or children; or one-half if there were no issue of the marriage, the other half going to the closest blood relatives of the deceased. And whereas at common law the personal property of married women would vest immediately in their husbands, leaving none to pass on their death, after the adoption of separate property by reforms to married women's property law it remained in their names and would pass on death according to the above scheme along with any realty they might have.[134]

A further improvement in the position of some Ontario widows was made in 1895. Copying an English act of 1890, Ontario enacted that where a husband died leaving a widow and no children, the widow would take the first $1,000 of his estate and the surplus would be distributed among his closest blood relatives. This was motivated as much by considerations of 'poor relief' as generosity to widows, but it nonetheless reflected a sentiment that the widow had a legitimate first claim on the estate of her husband ahead of his blood relatives, one that in time would put her 'preferential share' ahead of the children as well. Once again Manitoba had led the way, declaring in its 1871 act that a childless widow would receive all her husband's estate, regardless of its size, and the North-West Territories adopted this provision in 1901.[135]

Once a married woman was given the power to make a will pursuant to married women's property reforms of the 1880s and 1890s, she, like her husband, benefitted from freedom of testation. There were some minimal restraints on this freedom, which differed according to gender. If a husband dying with some real property purported to disinherit his wife entirely or leave her less than dower would have, she could nonetheless claim dower and reject the benefits under the will. If a wife died and likewise left little or nothing to her husband, he could claim an estate by the curtesy in her real property as well as his distributive share in her personal property 'as if this Act had not been passed,' according to Ontario's 1886 act. Curtesy was a life estate in all real property left by a wife at death, not just one-third, provided issue had been born alive of the marriage. Once reforms to intestate succession raised the share of the widow to at least a one-third ownership interest in both the real and personal property of the deceased, dower was rendered less relevant in that context, with one important exception: the claim to dower ranked ahead of creditors of the deceased. If a husband died insolvent, the widow could still claim her dower interest in any real property held by him. Otherwise, dower was relevant mainly as a 'safety net' where a husband died testate but left his widow little or nothing. It nonetheless remained an object of constant legislative solicitude in eastern Canada, as noted above, to the dismay of some. Treatise writer Malcolm Cameron observed in 1882 that 'the right of Dower in this Province [Ontario] has … been greatly extended, so that it may, with a great deal of force, be said that modern legislation is approaching the extreme.'[136]

Where the eastern provinces maintained and expanded dower, in Manitoba and the Territories it became entangled with the movement to adopt Torrens title, treated in an earlier section of this chapter. West of Ontario, common law dower did not exist, only the much-reduced version in the English Act of 1833 that was in force through the doctrine of reception. Even so, advocates of Torrens title were adamant that dower of any kind was inconsistent with the new system as an 'invisible' charge on title. It was abolished in Manitoba in 1885 and in the North-West Territories by federal statute in 1886.[137] British Columbia did not abolish it but re-enacted the English *Dower Act* of 1833 in its 1897 revised statutes to confirm that only this version of dower existed in the province. It also enacted a weak form of 'homestead law' in 1867, which provided that a homestead to the value of $2,500 was exempt from sale or seizure for the husband's debts, that a wife had to agree to its alienation, and that where a husband was survived by a widow and minor children, the widow was to manage the property until the youngest had reached the age of majority. At that point the children could deal with it as they wished, as the widow was not given a full life estate in the property.[138]

In all four western provinces, a movement by women activists to restore dower in the form of homestead rights (sometimes called homestead dower) began in the early twentieth century. In British Columbia the campaign sought to improve the minimal rights secured to widows under the existing dower and homestead laws. Their goal at first was to provide married women with a share of all property acquired during marriage, but this proposal ran into political headwinds. A much weaker form of protection was adopted in Alberta in 1910 and copied the next year in Saskatchewan. It allowed a widow to apply to court for a discretionary share of her husband's estate if he had left her by will less than the one-third she was entitled to pursuant to intestate succession. Eventually a more restricted form of homestead dower was adopted, mandating the consent of both spouses to the sale or mortgage of the family home, regardless of who held title, and providing succession rights in it (but not in any other property holdings of the husband) for the widow and children. These reforms occurred during or after the First World War and will be treated in *Volume 3*.[139]

Succession law traditionally aimed to uphold the sanctity of marriage by excluding from intestate succession illegitimate children and any intimate partner of the deceased to whom he or she was not married. Freedom of testation allowed testators to benefit such persons by will, however, if they so chose. Such gifts were not seen as contrary to public policy because they served two goals: preventing these beneficiaries from becoming public charges, and upholding male privilege by permitting a man to bestow his largesse on whomever he saw fit, even those with whom he had 'irregular' relationships. Allowing such gifts to illegitimate children also created a form of testamentary adoption at a time when formal adoption was not legally recognized.

Some modest relief was afforded to illegitimates in a few jurisdictions before the end of our period. Not surprisingly, these measures were adopted in western Canada, where children of Indigenous couples or mixed-race couples were more numerous and were often considered illegitimate if the parents were not formally married, although marriages according to accepted Indigenous customs could result in legitimate children. In 1901 the North-West Territories legislature provided that an illegitimate child was to be regarded as the legitimate child of its mother for the purposes of succession to personal, but not real, property, allowing each to inherit from the other on intestacy. British Columbia had passed bills aimed at alleviating the disadvantages of illegitimacy in the 1870s, but both were reserved by the lieutenant governor for the pleasure of the governor general and lapsed. Then it hit upon a solution that was not challenged. The *Destitute Orphans Act* of 1877 was an early form of dependents' relief statute. Where the 'concubine' and illegitimate children under the age of 16 of an intestate man had been supported by him prior to his death, they could apply to court for a share of his estate, to a maximum of $500 for the woman and the same amount for each child, or 10 per cent of the net estate, whichever was larger. Any award was at the discretion of the court, and virtually no guidance was provided to the judge. Somewhat surprisingly, the existence of a widow and/or legitimate children did not disentitle the 'concubine' or illegitimate children from applying. The only requirement was that the legitimate family had to be notified of any such application and be provided 'an opportunity of being heard thereon.' The act's lengthy preamble lamented that the country wives (unmarried partners) and illegitimate children of deceased men were 'thrown on the charity of their neighbours for support, … and the children are exposed to physical and moral deterioration.'[140] While attitudes towards illegitimacy were slowly softening, nowhere else in Canada was even this very modest form of recognition provided to female intimate partners in the context of succession. Again, however, the motivation for the reform grew out of concerns related to poor relief and public order rather than any validation of the status of such women.

The improved position of married women in the line of intestate succession found an echo in the practice of testate succession as well, at least in Ontario from which we have some evidence. Property law allowed wealth-holders to impose conditions on the largesse they dispensed by gift or will. In mid-nineteenth-century Ontario it was common for male testators to leave their widows a life interest in all or part of their property, on condition that it would be forfeited on remarriage. A study based on evidence from Guelph and the surrounding area revealed that some 90 per cent of widows took property under their husbands' wills subject to some condition at mid-century. The testator's assumption was that as the second husband had a legal obligation to support his wife, she no longer 'needed' the income from her first husband's estate, and the assets could pass to the children or other heirs. Moreover, prior to married women's property reform, he may have feared the second husband's mismanagement of her property. By the end of the nineteenth century only half the widows in the sample had conditions attached to property inherited from their husbands – a major shift over two generations.

The married women's property acts also seem to have inspired other changes in testamentary practice. By the end of the century, where a life estate was used, the trend was to bestow a life interest in all the husband's property upon the wife, rather than just a portion of it. Moreover, in significantly more cases than in earlier decades, the widow was granted a full fee simple interest rather than a life interest, demonstrating more confidence in a widow's ability to manage property. The adoption of separate property also meant that the spectre of the second husband was not as threatening: he now had no claim over his wife's property and could not dissipate it. This also applied to present or future sons-in-law, and many more male testators favoured daughters over sons in their wills after the married women's property acts than before.[141]

The law of conditions itself underwent significant change by the early twentieth century, in the direction of restricting the ability of testators to interfere with the key attribute of property so prized in a liberal society: freedom of alienation.[142] English law had long contained an inherent contradiction in this respect, as expressed by Robert Gordon: 'The power to alienate, as it expresses autonomy, becomes the instrument for the subversion of autonomy.'[143] The classic example in the English cases is the decision of the owner of a fee simple absolute to will it to his son, 'provided he never sells it out of the family.' While in

England such conditions often arose from dynastic concerns, in Canada they had a more prosaic purpose: maintaining economic security for future generations. Those who had worked hard to acquire a small patrimony wished to prevent their heirs from frittering it away. This could involve imposing direct restraints, as in an 1889 Ontario case where the court upheld a clause prohibiting the testator's sons from selling or mortgaging the devised properties during their lifetimes. Or it could involve behavioural prohibitions with the same goal, as in the will of Ann Fox. Should her son James not remain sober within five years of her death, her executors were to sell the land devised to him and donate the proceeds to charity. Another devisee was required by his father to 'be known as an industrious man 10 years after the death of his mother' or face forfeiting the property to other family members. Such clauses were regularly held not to be void for uncertainty, as judges understood and shared the motivations of the parental generation.[144]

These well-established lines of authority were overturned by the SCC in 1903 in *Blackburn and Cox v McCallum*. A father had left a farm to each of his sons with the stipulation that the land was not to be sold or mortgaged by them before 25 years after his death. One son had mortgaged the property and lost it to foreclosure (the father's fears apparently had some validity), but doubts arose about whether the property could be validly sold, given the clause in the will. The SCC set its face against such onerous restrictions. The son had made his bed and he must lie in it. In deciding that the clauses were invalid as excessive restraints on alienation, the court chose to follow one line of English authority in contrast to another that would have held them valid, the English law being in a state of flux at this point. Lower courts reluctantly fell into line with the results of this 'liberalization' of property law. Clauses that aimed to govern behaviour without directly restraining alienation, such as those limiting the choice of a spouse or of one's religion in order to inherit, continued to be held valid, however.

Succession to property for Indigenous individuals was subject to a distinct regime, one governed by the *Indian Act*. Where settler society highly valued freedom of testation, the DIA saw the disposition of reserve property by will as yet another area that it needed to control. Some provisions regarding wills were found in the 1857 *Gradual Civilization Act* and the 1869 *Enfranchisement Act*, but these applied mainly to enfranchised individuals, who were rare. The ability to dispose of property by will was eventually recognized in unenfranchised individuals and was a matter of frequent discussion between the Grand

General Indian Council of Ontario and the DIA. In 1884 it accepted the council's demands that 'Indians' be allowed to make a will, albeit subject to band council and DIA approval, and the *Indian Act* was amended accordingly. The provision allowed property to be devised to only a restricted circle of relatives, a limitation that was removed after lobbying by the council in 1894. The new section stated that property could be devised to anyone 'as long as the devisee of any property was allowed to reside on the reserve.'[145]

These successes also had caveats. The 1884 amendment specified that widows had to be of 'good moral character' in order to qualify for inheritance rights, subjecting them to increased surveillance by the local Indian agent. The 1894 amendment removed the requirement for band council approval, centralizing control in the superintendent general. Even after 1894, however, some bands at least continued to have a say in the approval of wills and inheritance matters in general, as noted for the Six Nations in chapter 10. Band council decisions were sometimes overruled by the DIA, but they remained engaged in this important aspect of community life. Disagreements often centred on a band's preference to uphold moral claims over claims of blood, following tenets of Indigenous law that emphasized responsibilities as much as rights. In 1882 the Oneida of the Thames dealt with a case where a childless woman on her deathbed verbally gave land she had inherited to her niece and two nephews, in preference to her husband. The council upheld her wishes, observing that the husband 'was never kind to her in health or sickness.' In this case the SG was willing to defer to the council because the *Indian Act* was silent on the claims of widowers. Increasingly, however, the DIA through local Indian agents sought to exercise the ultimate authority over Indigenous wills afforded them by the *Indian Act*.[146]

PART FOUR

Less Favoured by Law:
Women and Minorities

15

Women, the Family, and the Law

The underlying ideology governing the position of women in society during this period was the notion of separate spheres, the idea that the natural inclinations and abilities of women fitted them for a submissive role within the private world of the household, while men took on public duties in politics, economics, and society generally. The reality of women's economic lives was often very different, especially for rural women who toiled as much in fields as they did in farmhouses, and who, after bringing produce to maturity, often brought it to market as well. Urban working-class women similarly laboured in factories, while lower-middle- and middle-class women took part in public economic activity as boarding-house keepers, schoolteachers, shopkeepers, and the like. Women were also active in politics, even if they could not vote or be voted for. They were at the forefront of temperance and other social reform campaigns. Separate spheres nonetheless remained 'a powerful prescriptive ideology, elevated to the level of common sense' in this period and for much of the twentieth century.[1] Parallel to this belief in the separate roles and worlds of women was an equally potent ideology that elevated the family to the bedrock institution of society, provided it was the right kind of Judaeo-Christian family, the formal marriage of a man and a woman.

The ideologies of the family and of separate spheres underpinned much of the law in common law provinces, both common law and statute, which determined women's lives. Women's status in the civil law has been examined in chapter 5. Law was not, however, merely derivative of this social and ideological structure, it also reinforced it, exerting its own power and prescriptive force. The common law doctrine of coverture, the idea that husband and wife were one person in law, was never abolished in this period. An unmarried woman, or feme sole, had the same civil legal status as a man to own property, make contracts, sue and be sued, etc. But when a woman married she became a feme covert and all her legal rights and obligations were subsumed in her husband. Thus a married woman's rights to hold property, to make legally binding contracts, and to sue or be sued in court for torts committed by or against her were greatly reduced or negated. Law also limited women's (and men's) ability to escape by divorce from marriages that had not worked out, while coverture similarly constrained women's access to custody of the children resulting from such marriages if they were able to free themselves.

Many of the matters discussed in this chapter were relevant only to settler women, whether Black or white. The legal rights and responsibilities of Indigenous women in family and community were largely dealt with under the laws of their own people, discussed in chapter 10. While Indigenous societies had their own version of separate spheres, with distinct gender roles assigned to men and women, in some respects women's role was not as limited as that assigned to women in settler society. This was especially so with respect to participation in community leadership, while marriage, at least among non-Christian Indigenous peoples, was not as legally confining as in settler society, given the easier availability of divorce. Changes in married women's property law may have affected some Indigenous women who lived off-reserve and participated in the settler economy but were unlikely to have offered much to women living on reserve or on the land in traditional ways. The main law affecting Indigenous women was the *Indian Act*, which aimed to govern their lives in increasingly intrusive ways and, as we saw in chapter 8, expelled them and their children from membership in their own communities if they married non-Indigenous men, while bestowing membership on non-Indigenous women who married Indigenous men. Another area where the law took notice of Indigenous women was with regard to sex work, a topic discussed later in this chapter.

This chapter will not directly cover the suffrage movement, because it did not lead to votes for women at either the provincial or the federal level before the First World War. However, suffrage will be referred to when we examine the background to married women's property and custody legislation – the first 'women's movement' in Canadian history, which included, but was by no means limited to, a demand for the vote. Another topic not covered here is dower, which was examined in chapter 14.

Married Women's Property in Common Law Provinces

At Confederation the legal position of married women in relation to property in common law provinces was a hybrid of the common law of coverture and recent statutory change. The common law doctrine of marital unity held that a married woman did not own any personal property. It belonged to her husband, with some minor exceptions, whether she had entered the marriage with it or acquired it thereafter. A wife's real property, whether owned before marriage or acquired thereafter, did not become her husband's, and when she died it passed to her heirs. But during her lifetime her husband had the right to manage it and keep any income it generated, without accounting to her. If a husband predeceased his wife, her land reverted to being hers fully. Married women also did not have the capacity to make contracts, other than via the 'agency of necessity' by which they were permitted to pledge their husbands' credit for necessaries. Nor could they sue or be sued in tort.

In *Volume 1* we discussed two ways in which this common law regime was modified. One was via doctrines constructed by courts of equity, giving married women a trust interest in their property – property often settled on them by fathers or future husbands in the form of a transfer to trustees to a wife's 'separate use.' Such property was then referred to as her 'separate property' or 'separate estate.' Property so placed in trust could not be used by the husband, because rights to it were not common law rights but equitable ones. This relief through equity was largely of benefit to the better off, because to settle some substantial amount of property on trust, a person needed to own much of it in the first place. Equity therefore ameliorated the rigours of the common law for only a small minority of women.[2]

The other modification to the common law before Confederation came in the form of statutes passed by the Maritime colonies, Newfoundland, Upper Canada, and Vancouver Island, which limited the rigours of the common law.[3] We will not review that legislation again here but we will refer to it when necessary in dealing with post-Confederation statutes, in order to make clear the extent of developments in our period. For now suffice it to say that the common theme in the pre-Confederation statutory reforms was that a statutory separate estate for married women was created for some of their property. Which property became part of this separate estate and when varied. In some cases the separate estate applied only to women deserted by their husbands, and in yet other cases married women enjoyed some property as a separate estate and other property as her own on desertion or failure by the husband to provide for her or for some other reason. This colonial legislation was not intended to be a first step towards equal rights for married women. It was enacted to protect women and children from crises precipitated by husbands' failure to carry out their social and legal duty to provide shelter and support for them. As one study aptly puts it, it employed 'the language of morality and family responsibility, not the language of independent and equal spouses pursuing their individual goals.' Nonetheless, 'the idea that the state had a right to and a duty to intervene and protect the economic interests of the weaker party within the family sphere represented a significant break with traditional notions of male authority.' For the first time colonial states' roles were redefined from 'passive conservator of marital right' to 'active intervener in the spousal relationship.'[4]

In the first decade or so after Confederation, British Columbia, Manitoba, New Brunswick, and Ontario all enacted further legislation dealing with married women's property, and the federal government did likewise for the North-West Territories.[5] The legislation applicable to British Columbia, the Territories, and Ontario was identical, the former two copying the Ontario statute passed in 1872, and we will therefore begin with and focus on the Ontario act. Ontario's law in 1867 dated from 1859 and provided that a woman who married after the passage of the act would hold all her real and personal property 'free from the debts and obligations of her husband and from his control or disposition without her consent.' Women who were already married when the act passed held their real and personal property that had not already been taken possession of by the husband similarly 'free from his debts and obligations contracted after the passing of this Act, and from his control or disposition without her consent.' Thus all property a married woman already had in 1859, or that she acquired thereafter, could not be used to pay her husband's debts or be sold by him without her consent. It was, in the words of section 3 of the statute, her 'separate property.' But the act also provided that she was not entitled to her earnings or those of her minor children unless she obtained a protection order from a court. A protection order was available in a wide variety of circumstances, including desertion by her husband, which resulted in her husband neglecting or refusing 'to provide for her support and that of his family.' The statute therefore contained a contradiction: a married woman's personal property was her separate property and could not be used to pay her husband's debts, but her 'earnings,' which were personal property, could be used to pay her husband's debts if she did not have a protection order.[6] This contradiction caused confusion in the courts, discussed below.

The principal effect of Ontario's 1872 reform was to do away with the need for a protection order for a married woman to be entitled to all her 'wages and personal earnings … from any occupation or trade which she carries on separately from her husband.' She was also entitled to property she acquired with the money she had earned 'as fully as if she were a feme sole.' Again there was a lack of complete clarity, which led to conflicting judgments in the courts. The statute did not overturn the common law rule entirely, because it applied only to 'earnings,' not all personal property, and it applied only to earnings from employment or enterprises 'which she carries on separately from her husband.' The statute also left unclear one issue relating to her real property. Any real estate she owned, whether acquired before or after marriage, was to be held by her 'for her separate use, free from any … claim of her husband.' Married women were henceforth the owners of separate estates in their property, similar to women who held property as an equitable interest under a trust but without the requirement of a trustee. However, although a married woman was also made liable on any contract made regarding her real estate, the act did not state that she could alienate it without her husband's consent. That issue was settled the following year, a clarificatory statute stating that she could not do so unless 'the husband is a party to and executed the deed' of sale.[7]

The 1872 act allowed a married woman to insure her own life and that of her husband, hold stock in any company, maintain a bank account, and take a legal action in her own name to recover any wages or other property 'declared to be her separate property.' She could be sued separately from her husband over her ante-nuptial debts, with her separate property being liable for those debts, and her husband would not be liable for her debts incurred through any employment or business she undertook or on any contracts she made. She could be sued personally for any of her 'separate debts, engagements, contracts or torts as if she were unmarried.'

Some contemporary male critics deprecated the 1872 act, which was based on a UK statute of 1870,[8] as 'extraordinary' and 'extreme,' granting women 'equal rights' including 'the right to thrash their husbands' and leading to female suffrage. This fevered editorialist in the Hamilton *Spectator* even threw in 'free love' as an inevitable product of the act.[9] But the act was much less radical than he claimed. Christopher Patterson of the Court of Appeal stated for a unanimous bench in *Lawson v Laidlaw* that '[o]ur statutes have done for married women what was previously effected by the doctrines of equity and by the machinery of settlements and trusts, by creating or recognising the capacity to hold and enjoy property for their separate use.'[10] That the act's purpose was to protect the family unit rather than to advance married women's independence was emphasized in the assembly by Attorney General Adam Crooks and Premier Edward Blake. The latter, in responding to an assertion that the bill was about 'women's rights' and thus one that challenged the social order, pithily replied that his critic 'does not see the difference between women's rights and women's wrongs.' The act passed without difficulty because most assemblymen and the liberal press viewed it as protective of a woman's ability to take care of the family. Even the conservative Toronto *Daily Mail* approved its principal provisions, but not the granting of rights to hold bank accounts and company stock. Those provisions were 'reckless,' the 'first principles of revolution.'[11]

As noted above, the British Columbia statute of 1873 and the federal statute of 1875 for the North-West Territories were identical to the Ontario act of 1872.[12] The British Columbia act did away with the need for a protection order and, since it was identical to the Ontario legislation, contained the same uncertainties, as did the federal act. Before we discuss how those uncertainties played out in the courts, we will review the law at Confederation in the remaining provinces. Nova Scotia had the same regime as British Columbia had had, dating from 1866. A wife deserted by her husband could get a protection order from the Supreme Court for 'money or property she may have acquired, or may acquire, by her own lawful industry,' which shielded it from her husband and his creditors. This did not change until 1884. Prince Edward Island's legislation dated from 1860 and did not change until 1880. It provided that if a woman was deserted by her husband, or for some other reason had to support herself, any property she acquired 'shall vest in her, and be at her disposal, and not subject to the debts, interference or control of her husband,' without the need for a protection order.[13] New Brunswick had been the first colony to enact married women's property legislation, in 1851, and legislated further in 1869 and 1874, but the law as it stood at the first post-Confederation statutory consolidation in 1877 was effectively the same as it had been in 1851. All a married woman's real and personal property, whether acquired before or after marriage, with the exception of property she had been given by her husband during marriage, was her 'separate property' and 'exempt ... in any way for the debts and liabilities of her husband.' Nor could it be alienated without her consent. As with other protective legislation of the 1860s and 1870s the common law was modified but the fundamental reliance on coverture was not displaced, because non-alienation without her consent meant that her husband had the power to alienate with her consent. She did not have the same rights as a feme sole.

The other province that legislated in the 1870s, obviously for the first time, was Manitoba, and it did not adopt the provisions of the Ontario act of 1872, preferring to reproduce the earlier 1859 Upper Canada statute with its requirement for a protection order. This regime stayed in place until 1881, when a married woman was given the right to hold her wages or other earnings independently of her husband, 'as if she were a *feme sole*.' The same statute also made a married woman liable on any contract made by her 'respecting her real estate as if she were a *feme sole*.' In all other respects the law remained the same until 1900.[14] The Manitoba act obviously contained the same contradiction/uncertainty as the Upper Canada act, dealing inconsistently with earnings and 'all personal property.'

We turn to consider how these various statutes, especially the 1872 Ontario act, fared in the courts. Two general themes emerged. First, there was confusion in the courts, and among the legal profession and the public, about precisely what the law was. Second, the legislation had consequences that went beyond affording married women a greater degree of control over property and a greater ability to participate in the commercial world by involvement in business. Some married couples were able to exploit the uncertainties in the legislation to deprive creditors of the usual remedies against their debtors. Married women thereby demonstrated that they were indeed 'equal' to men in their capacity to engage in sharp practice. Indeed, very few of the reported cases involved disputes between husbands and wives. Most involved either or both of the husband and wife as one party, and creditors as the other.

Writing in 1883 George Smith Holmested, as we saw in chapter 4 one of the leading authorities on many aspects of Ontario law, asserted that '[t]here are few branches of law which are involved in more doubt than that embraced in the modern statute law related to married women.'[15] Holmested laid the blame for this partly on the legislature, which he thought had shown 'timidity' in drafting or a lack of understanding of what a statute needed to say to displace common law rules. Equally to blame were judges, Holmested rather inconsistently continued, who had 'misconstrued' the act by employing the rule of statutory interpretation that statutes were not to be read as altering the common law to a greater extent than was necessary to give effect to their provisions. Holmested cited a number of examples of confusion, and for current purposes we will use just two of them. First, could a married woman dispose of her personal property other than her earnings without her husband's consent? Section 2 of the 1872 act was abundantly clear that she could dispose of her earnings and any property acquired with those earnings without consent. But what about personal property other than earnings? That was not explicitly covered in the legislation. Holmested cited six cases in which the Ontario courts had held that the husband's consent was needed, and three in which they had held the opposite.

The second issue that caused confusion was a married woman's liability in debt or contract. Holmested discussed at some length whether, when a married woman was sued for a breach of contract involving her separate property, the successful plaintiff could enforce an execution to satisfy his claim. Two problems arose in the cases. One was whether any such judgment was in personam, against the woman herself, or in rem, against her separate property. The courts consistently held that it was the latter, because the doctrine of coverture still worked to block personal liability.[16] Holmested disagreed, insisting that holding a married woman personally liable was 'consonant with common sense and the fitness of things,' but his view counted for little when weighed against opinions from the bench. The second problem was whether, if it was in rem, the judgment could be enforced against any item of separate property, or had to be enforced against separate property the married woman had had at the time the contract was made and still had when sued. In *Lawson v Laidlaw* the Court of Appeal unanimously came down for the latter proposition.[17] Holmested disagreed with this, arguing that such decisions enabled married women to commit frauds 'with impunity, provided they can get anyone foolish enough to deal with them.' Opponents of both the 1859 and 1872 acts had argued that they would be used to evade debt obligations. A husband sued for money owing could render himself judgment proof by claiming that his apparent assets were his wife's separate property. The 1872 act contained an awkwardly worded provision apparently designed to deal with the problem, providing that if a husband put money into an account in his wife's name in order to shield it from his creditors that money did not become her separate property, but could be used to pay the husband's debts.[18] But this covered only transactions actually 'made in fraud of … creditors,' and this raised the always difficult issue of intent. If it could not be proved, creditors were unable effectively to sue the husband because, in the words of Justice John Douglas Armour of the Court of Queen's Bench, dissenting, 'the husband has contrived that the wife shall own everything, [and] his creditors are set at defiance.' More pertinently to the current discussion, in other cases the opposite problem was manifested. A wife had made a contract, the other party believing that she had separate property, which could be attached in the event of unpaid liabilities, but then her creditor was similarly 'set at defiance' because she had later alienated the property.[19]

The result, in the perhaps exaggerated language of Justice Armour, was that the legislation had been 'disastrous' to creditors, who in 'hundreds, I might say thousands, of cases throughout Ontario' had been defrauded by married couples. Over time third parties became more reluctant to deal with married couples. One historian has perceptively noted the irony that judges, 'haunted by the possibility that an innocent wife might be defrauded by her husband,' did not see women as economic actors with their own agency – an agency that could encompass unscrupulous behaviour.[20] Justice Armour did see the problem caused by what he termed the 'intelligent married woman,'[21] but many of his brethren regarded the phrase as something of an oxymoron, at least in the public world of economic behaviour. There certainly were instances of financial abuse by husbands, especially with regard to a wife's real estate, which she was unable to sell without her husband's consent, but the evidence from the reported cases is that at least as many women used the acts to evade their creditors, often with their husbands' connivance.

The British Columbia act also caused interpretive problems for the province's Supreme Court judges. But perhaps because there were only three of them the BC judges were more *ad idem* than their Ontario counterparts, more inclined to construe the statute as one that effected greater change to the common law. As a result, creditors fared a little better than they did in the Ontario courts. The court's 'expansive' rulings meant that colluding married couples were unable to succeed in their claims that the person who had contracted the debt was not the person who had property that could be used to satisfy it.[22]

By the mid-1870s, therefore, the Canadian law on married women's property varied significantly from province to province. The Maritime provinces all operated with their pre-Confederation protective legislation, albeit amended in minor ways in some cases.[23] Manitoba, with a clean slate on which to inscribe its law, chose something similar. Newfoundland, not previously discussed here, copied in 1876 with minor adaptations the English act of 1870, and most of the English 1882 Act in 1883, completing the job in 1895. These reforms were likely adopted because of a felt need in the legal profession to stay current with English norms, as there seems to have been little domestic movement in Newfoundland to reform the law in this area.[24] Ontario, British Columbia, and the North-West Territories had gone furthest, creating the married woman's separate estate applicable to all spouses without the need for protection orders. Between the mid-1880s and the early twentieth century all provinces went further.

Ontario took the lead in 1884. In the early 1880s it was widely agreed that the 1872 act had proved very difficult to administer, had failed to protect some women against abusive and irresponsible husbands, and had been bad for creditors.[25] The remedy for all these problems was legislation giving married women the same property rights as unmarried women. The 1884 act, based on the major UK statute of 1882,[26] began with a short and unequivocal statement that henceforth '[a] married woman shall ... be capable of acquiring, holding and disposing by will or otherwise, of any real or personal property as her separate property, in the same manner as if she were a *feme sole*.'[27] Thus all personal property, not just earnings, was separate property. Section 22 abolished the requirement for a husband's consent to a conveyance of land under the 1873 Act.[28] The Act also allowed a married woman to contract 'to the extent of her separate property,' and on this point went further than the 1872 act by stating that any contract entered into by a married woman was deemed to be with reference to her separate property, not only the separate property she owned when the contract was made, but also any that she acquired in the future. In 1897 this provision was amended to deem her contracts to bind her separate property 'whether she is or is not in fact possessed of' any at the time the contract was made.[29] Along with these equal rights provisions, the 1884 Act retained the availability of protection orders that had been first introduced in 1859, although in a very limited way. Section 18 provided a long list of circumstances, similar to those in other protection order provisions already discussed, in which a married woman could apply to court for a protection order entitling her to the earnings of her minor children. This provision showed that the act was about property, not about equalizing the position of men and women generally within the family. The husband's authority over the children and their earnings remained, except in the circumstances listed. The act was followed four years later by the first legislation in the province establishing a statutory right for a woman deserted by her husband to take him before magistrates and get an order for maintenance. This rendered much more accessible the previous right to claim alimony, available only from the High Court through somewhat cumbersome and expensive proceedings.[30]

The 1884 act was not controversial, with most of the impetus for reform coming from the legal community. In addition to its own experience with the 1872 act the profession was dealing with the fusion of common law and equity, which threatened to undermine common law rules in favour of equitable principles. The example of England also carried weight among an increasingly Anglophilic profession; one of Premier Oliver Mowat's justifications for his legislation was that it largely replicated the English act. But the assembly was also responding to an increasingly powerful middle-class woman's movement, which lobbied for social reforms, such as temperance, women's prisons, and child welfare, and legal reforms, principally married women's property law and suffrage. As in the previous decade judges tended not to grant married women more rights than the statute clearly prescribed, and as a result frustrated some creditors, who were again one of the parties in a majority of cases decided under the act, but the clearer statutory language meant that creditors fared better than they had done before 1884.[31]

The Ontario statutory reforms of the 1870s and 1880s did result in sharp increases in the ownership and disposition of property by married women. Studies of Guelph demonstrate that the wills written by all women went from 10 per cent of all wills in the 1860s to 40 per cent by 1900, and a substantial part of that increase must have been the result of married women doing so, because they had much more property to leave than before the reforms. In addition, a much greater number of parents left property equally to sons and daughters, either because it was no longer feared that a daughter's property would become her husband's and/or because women were seen as more capable of managing property. Statutory reform thus not only materially affected women's economic status, it also sparked a broader improvement in the status of women generally.[32] At the same time the reforms had less effect on the participation of women in the commercial world. They found it difficult to obtain credit for their independent businesses, and court decisions on whether they were carrying on businesses separate from their husbands tended to assume that the kinds of businesses they ran, often home-based, were at best in partnership with their husbands, at worst done under the husband's direction.[33]

As it had in the 1870s, British Columbia followed Ontario's lead, enacting in 1887 what was, with a few unimportant exceptions, a replica of the 1884 Ontario act. Like the Ontario act it was amended in 1897 to expand a married women's liability under contracts. There is evidence that married women in the province had difficulty obtaining credit despite having ample separate property, but this may have been as much to do with lenders' paternalistic attitudes towards women as with the law.[34]

It took considerably longer for the law in the Maritime and Prairie provinces to match that of Ontario and British Columbia. We will discuss principally Nova Scotia, which in 1884 passed a statute with the same title as the Ontario act. It was 'a compromise between conservative and liberal conceptions of the family' and a reflection of 'confusion over the appropriate role of the state in intra-familial disputes.'[35] Section 3 dealt with women married when the act came into force. Henceforth such a woman would 'have, hold and enjoy all her real estate' and personal property that was not in the possession of her husband. It was irrelevant whether such property had belonged to a woman before marriage or been acquired by her thereafter from someone other than her husband. In either event it was separate property, 'free from his [the husband's] debts and obligations, ... and from his control or disposition without her consent.' Sections 4 and 5 dealt similarly with women who married after the act came into force. These would appear to be assertions of a married woman's largely independent status with regard to property, but in later sections they were substantially cut down. Section 22 gave a married woman the right to convey her real estate, but only with the consent of her husband. Protection for a married woman was included; a judge or JP had to be satisfied that her own deed of conveyance had been executed 'without compulsion by her husband.' In addition, women could apply for a court order, dispensing with the need for the husband's consent if the circumstances were similar to those that triggered a protection order: the husband was in prison, or had deserted her, or had left the province, or was insane. In addition, a clear distinction was drawn between a married woman's personal property and her earnings from running a business. Section 52, in a part entitled 'A Married Woman's Separate Business,' began with a long recitation about a woman's earnings from any business she conducted independently of her husband being free from her husband's debts or control and able to be disposed of by her without her husband's consent. But the act also stated that for all this to occur the husband's consent in writing was needed, and that consent had to be filed in the registry of deeds.

That this was included to protect potential creditors by making them fully aware that they were dealing with the wife and not the husband, and could look for recourse only to her, is clearly evinced by section 53. It required a married woman intending to set up her own business not only to register her husband's consent but also to deposit with the clerk of the municipality a certificate stating her husband's name, the 'nature of the business,' and 'the place where it is or is proposed to be carried on, giving if practicable the street and the number on the street.' Failure to do this would make the property used in the business liable for the husband's debts. This section, unique in the Canadian legislation, was comparable, although more stringent, to the investor protection provisions of some provincial incorporation acts, discussed in chapter 11. The husband's consent could be dispensed with only if the wife obtained a protection order based on the usual criteria for one. Overall the act bore a much closer resemblance to the pre-Confederation statutes than to the contemporaneous 1884 Ontario statute. Not until 1898 did Nova Scotia enact legislation comparable to the latter.[36] There is no evidence of pressure for the 1884 legislation from the women's movement, which has been attributed to an ambivalence about reform as potentially undermining the family unit and/or a desire to concentrate on suffrage, which women activists considered more important. Nonetheless there was consensus among male legislators in favour. Their position was consistent with their opposition to female suffrage. If women were to be denied a place in the public sphere because their proper place was in the private world, they should have more equality within the home and in the family economy.

The 1884 act was a difficult statute for the judiciary to interpret, but the thrust of court decisions favoured husbands over wives and creditors over families. The SCC hewed to the same line in its one major decision on the act, *Crowe v Adams*, decided in 1892. A husband's judgment creditor had property seized by the sheriff, which the wife claimed was her separate property. She sued, and the case turned on who had the onus of proving that it was separate property. The SCC held that she did: 'Prima facie goods in the actual possession of the wife of an execution-debtor are the goods of the latter,' and 'it lies on the wife to show if she can that they are her separate property.'[37]

Elsewhere in the Maritimes, equivalent legislation was passed in New Brunswick in 1895 and Prince Edward Island in 1903, and between these two dates, in 1900, Manitoba also passed a similar act.[38] The evolution of North-West Territories law was more complex. The 1875 federal legislation regarding personal property stayed in place until 1890, but the provisions on real estate were replaced in 1886 by a federal statute similar to the 1884 Ontario act.[39] In 1890 the territorial assembly, which had the power to legislate in respect of property and civil rights, passed an ordinance declaring that 'in respect of personal property' a married woman was 'under no disabilities whatsoever … by reason of her coverture' but had 'all the rights and [was] subject to all the liabilities of a *feme sole*.'[40] This was very likely a response to *Brittlebank v Gray-Jones*, an 1888 case in which the Manitoba Court of Queen's Bench, which was the appeal court for the Territorial Supreme Court, held that 'separate property' in the 1875 act only included earnings derived from, and used for, running a business separate from her husband, and not all of a married woman's personal property.[41] Yet in a subsequent case a majority of the Territorial court found that the ordinance had not displaced the common law rule that a woman's personal property in general became her husband's on marriage. It relied on the principle that any statute changing the common law was to be construed strictly. Justice Thomas Wetmore's dissent was a subtle insult to his colleagues. In giving what he believed to be the correct interpretation of the ordinance he simply repeated the words used, in effect saying that the words were so plain that there was no doubt of their meaning. A year later the SCC agreed with Wetmore, and thereafter the Territorial court interpreted the ordinance more literally, and therefore liberally, in other areas involving husbands and wives and property.[42]

The Territorial legislation stayed in force in Alberta through the rest of this period, but Saskatchewan enacted its own provincial legislation in 1907.[43] It provided that 'all property standing in the sole name of any married woman shall be deemed unless and until the contrary is shown to be the property of such married woman.' Other sections defined real and personal property very broadly. One suspects that Chief Justice Wetmore drafted the act with an eye to any argument that could be made that some aspect of the common law regime was not covered. The act also gave married women full civil status in their own right in the courts and included a provision entitling a wife to a protection order by which she could claim the earnings of her infant children when the husband deserted her, went to prison, etc. Alberta's first Supreme Court bench did not have a Wetmore and interpreted the legislation conservatively in 1907 in *Fraser v Kirkpatrick*. The issue was whether a woman's earnings from running a business – a hotel – with her husband constituted 'separate property.'[44] Mr. Kirkpatrick had become insolvent in 1901, and to support the family his wife worked as a housekeeper and subsequently leased the hotel. She ran the business, her husband helped out, it worked out well, and Mrs. Kirkpatrick made some good investments with the profits. Under a pre-1901 execution creditors of her husband then stepped in and demanded those profits. In finding for the creditors Justice Horace Harvey, a lawyer of some eminence who had been deputy attorney general of the Territories, held that because Mrs. Kirkpatrick's husband had assisted with the business it was not separate property, it was her husband's and subject to being taken in execution. This was a somewhat eccentric result to say the least, because in *Conger v Kennedy*, the case mentioned above in which the SCC overturned the territorial Supreme Court, Chief Justice Strong had clearly said that the ordinance 'must be interpreted as having reference to all the personal property belonging to a married woman.' It seems likely that Harvey's attitude to women in business shaped his ruling. He expressed incredulity at the idea that the wife was running the business and the husband merely helping out. It was 'absurd' to think that he was 'doing nothing but loafing around there and living simply as a parasite on his wife.' Rather he was 'managing' the business and 'looking after the finances.' In fact, Mrs. Kirkpatrick had not suggested that her husband was a parasite, but that he was a subordinate. The only absurdity would have been having him, a failure in business still being pursued by his creditors, 'looking after the finances.' As elsewhere, statutory interpretation was influenced by judicial insistence on separate spheres and assumptions about the husband's role as head of the family.

Finally, it should be noted that in recognizing that married women could hold property in their own names and deal with it independently, the married women's property acts opened up a potential source of credit for their husbands. For men fortunate enough to marry women with inherited wealth, there was now nothing to prevent them from asking their wives to guarantee bank loans in support of their business ventures. This led in turn to a host of new questions about the nature of the husband–wife relationship. What circumstances might give rise to a presumption of undue influence? Was there a fiduciary duty between husband and wife in such transactions, such that they could be validated only if she had independent legal advice? Equity had traditionally been a protector of married women but had never gone so far as to say that the husband–wife relationship was a fiduciary one. Since the reform legislation redefined married women as independent legal subjects and economic actors, there was some ground for saying the wife was entitled to no more protection than any other third party would be when asked to serve as a guarantor. Indeed, after the statutory reforms, husband and wife were often described as 'strangers as to property.' But the ideology of separate spheres ran deep, and courts assumed, probably correctly, that most wives in the professional and business classes had little familiarity with commercial matters, giving rise to some unease about equating wives and third parties.

These conflicting views came to a head in a 1909 SCC case, *Stuart v Bank of Montreal*, in which the Court decided that a fiduciary relationship existed between husband and wife. John Stuart, who was president of the Bank of Hamilton and had many other business interests, was doing very well prior to 1896. In that year he needed money to support a pulp and paper mill he controlled in New Brunswick and persuaded his wife, Jane, to guarantee a very large loan from the bank. She had inherited some $250,000 from her father in 1886 and trusted her husband to manage it. The company became insolvent in 1901 and within a few years the bank had taken over all Jane's assets pursuant to the guarantee. There was found to be no deception involved in the guarantee, and Jane's counsel did not allege any. The SCC found that there was a fiduciary duty between husband and wife, one requiring that Jane Stuart have independent advice. Given its absence, she was entitled to set aside the conveyances to the bank and have her properties restored. The bank appealed to the JCPC, which upheld the decision but on entirely different grounds. They declined to label the relationship as fiduciary but found the actions of the husband and the bank's solicitor, Mr. Bruce, to be highly improper. Bruce was also Mr. Stuart's solicitor, and a director of and shareholder in the ill-fated pulp and paper mill. When more security was demanded by the bank, Bruce and the other shareholders declined to provide it once Stuart had 'offered up' his wife to do so. While it was not uncommon for a solicitor to act for both sides in such a transaction at the time, the fact that Bruce had a clear interest in finding others to help rescue his imperilled investment meant he could not act fairly to all parties and especially to Jane Stuart. The JCPC relied on previous jurisprudence stating that in transactions involving the interests of husband and wife, a wife was entitled to look to her husband's solicitor 'for advice and assistance until that solicitor repudiates the obligation to give such advice, and requires her to consult another gentleman.' Here, Bruce was in a clear conflict of interest owing to his own pecuniary interest in the company and should have recommended independent advice for Jane Stuart. They disagreed bluntly with the Supreme Court regarding the necessity of independent advice in all transactions between husband and wife. There simply was no such duty, the relief provided here arising from Bruce's improper actions.[45] The SCC's attempt at chivalry was no longer appropriate in a changed legal environment where married women were to be treated as independent actors with all the responsibilities as well as the liberties entailed in this new status. They deserved neither more nor less protection than non-spouses who might be imposed upon in commercial transactions.

Marriage

Residents of the new dominion were united in regarding marriage as the most fundamental institution of civil society. Protestants and Catholics alike did not hesitate to call it 'sacred,' and this label had some truth in it, given that virtually all marriages of non-Indigenous persons in Canada were solemnized by ministers of religion. 'Solemnization of Marriage' was given to the provinces in section 92 (12) of the *BNA Act*, while rules relating to the substantive validity of marriage fell under the federal power over 'Marriage and Divorce' in section 91 (26). Provincial acts typically authorized only members of the clergy to solemnize marriages. Nova Scotia, for example, authorized only Christian clergy to perform marriages, while Ontario's *Marriage Act* referred to clergy 'of every church and religious denomination,' which may have extended this authority to non-Christian clergy such as rabbis. Ontario also validated marriages of Quakers and 'Disciples of Christ,' neither of whom had clergy, if performed according to their own rites. While marriage was also in some respects a civil contract, its sacramental character for Roman Catholics raised particular issues in Quebec, discussed in chapter 5 and below, this chapter.[46]

Provincial rules relating to the substantive validity of marriage remained in place pursuant to section 129 of the *BNA Act* until the federal government chose to legislate. It entered this field only once during our period, on the much-debated issue of marriage with a deceased wife's sister. In the United Kingdom this prohibition, originating in Anglican canon law, was also the law of the land, and any alteration raised large issues of church-state relations. Bills on the topic were introduced annually for decades, only to be vetoed by the House of Lords until the law was finally changed in 1907. While the topic aroused passions in Canada as well, they were less vehemently expressed. Désiré Girouard, a Conservative, introduced a private member's bill on the topic in 1880 that would have legalized marriage with a deceased wife's sister and a deceased husband's brother. Outrage from church authorities led him to withdraw the latter part of the bill, after which it passed easily in 1882.[47]

Marriages according to Indigenous custom, whether both parties were Indigenous or only one of them, raised other issues. Here, the case of *Connolly v Woolrich*, discussed in *Volume 1*, although decided a few weeks after Confederation, long remained influential. In it the Superior Court and the Quebec Court of Queen's Bench upheld the validity of the 1803 marriage of a settler man with a Cree woman according to Cree custom in 'Indian territory.' Many years and several children later the couple moved to Montreal, where Connolly purported to divorce his wife via custom and married another woman. The 'divorce' was held invalid and hence so was the second marriage. The issue arose again in the 1880s in the Territories, regarding a marriage between two Indigenous persons according to their custom after the reception date of English law (15 July 1870). The North-West Territories Supreme Court noted that English laws were received only 'insofar as the same are applicable' and doubted that such laws were applicable '*quoad* the Indians' in any respect. The case was thus considerably stronger than *Connolly v Woolrich*, where there was no question of English law being applicable in the territory at the time.[48]

The issue of the (in)validity of such marriages was important for many reasons, not the least of which was the definition of status under the *Indian Act*, which defined 'Indian' as including any woman 'lawfully married' to a 'male person of Indian blood reputed to belong to a particular band.' The act also allowed a band to exclude 'illegitimate' children from membership with the approval of the SG. Thus, the DIA had to take a position on whether persons married according to Indigenous custom could be said to be 'lawfully married.' As of 1887, the department decided that such marriages would be recognized, on the basis of *Connolly v Woolrich*, though divorce according to Indigenous custom would not. Even after the UK High Court decided the next year that a customary marriage between an Englishman and a member of the Barolong people in South Africa was invalid under English law, the DIA stuck to its position until the 1951 *Indian Act* required a formal marriage for the transmission of status. The Canadian position was also distinct from that of the United States, which treated such questions as based completely on sovereignty. A marriage between two Indigenous persons on a reserve according to their customs, even if polygamous, was valid as an exercise of Native sovereignty. Any other marriage involving Indigenous persons could be valid only if it followed the relevant US law. On this particular issue, then, an older type of legal pluralism prevailed, whereby marriages according to Indigenous customs could be recognized by the settler state without being seen as a threat to its sovereignty.[49]

Marriages between Indigenous and non-Indigenous persons had a long history going back to the earliest days of contact and had given rise to a new people in the Canadian west, the Métis. Such marriages were tolerated if not exactly welcomed. This was not the case with other interracial marriages, such as those between Black and white or Asian and white persons. These marriages, especially the first, encountered strong social disapproval in white society. Efforts to outlaw them never gained traction in Canada, however, in contrast to the United States, where many types of interracial marriage were forbidden in a majority of states. In the US Black-white marriages could not be tolerated because they upset the racial hierarchy ingrained in so many areas of law and life, even though they also represented a constraint on the ability of white males to freely choose their spouses. In Canada the very small Black population was not considered a threat, but more generally, the failure to proscribe interracial marriages effectively maintained male privilege, especially white male privilege, in the choice of marriage partners.[50]

Divorce Law, Divorce Courts, and the Sanctity of Marriage

At Confederation judicial divorce was available in all three Maritime colonies by virtue of two eighteenth-century statutes and one passed in the early nineteenth century.[51] It was similarly available in British Columbia, the 1867 reception ordinance of the united colony declaring the colony's law to be the law of England as of 1858, thus including the *Divorce and Matrimonial Causes Act* of 1857, which instituted judicial divorce in the United Kingdom.[52] As we saw in chapter 4, whether English statutes were 'suitable' and therefore had been received was sometimes a contested and uncertain issue, and this was likely true for the 1857 act until 1877, when the BC Supreme Court held that it was received and granted its first divorce.[53] There was some judicial disagreement on this point thereafter, but the matter was finally settled in favour of the act's availability by the JCPC in 1908.[54] It contained a double standard: men could obtain a divorce on the ground of adultery alone, while women needed to show adultery in addition to some other fault, usually cruelty.[55]

Judicial divorce was simply not available anywhere else in the country in this period, nor in the one remaining British colony in northern North America, Newfoundland. Quebec's marriage law has been examined in chapter 5, and for current purposes what matters is that divorce was not available other than by an act of the federal Parliament. Ontario law was the English common law, and the reception date of 1792 meant that there was also no judicial divorce in that province, and resort had to be made to Parliament. Judicial divorces were also not available in this period in the region that became part of Canada in 1870. The 1857 UK act was believed not to have been received in Manitoba and the Territories, although the JCPC thought otherwise after the end of our period.[56] We discuss parliamentary divorce in the next section.

No provincial or territorial legislature could have instituted judicial divorce after Confederation because divorce was a matter of federal jurisdiction, but those provinces that had judicial divorce in 1866 retained it because the federal Parliament did not pass a *Divorce Act* for the whole country until 1968.[57] The Nova Scotia divorce court had operated since the 1750s, and as of 1866 divorce petitions were heard by the Court for Divorce and Matrimonial Causes, consisting of a Supreme Court judge sitting in his capacity as the 'Judge Ordinary' of the divorce court. The grounds for divorce were impotence, adultery, cruelty, and too close a degree of consanguinity,* and divorce was equally available to men and women on the same grounds. The English 'double standard' did not apply.[58] Procedures differed from those normally employed in the Supreme Court. The examination of witnesses was ordinarily to be done in writing by an examiner appointed by the court, but the court could take viva voce evidence from witnesses if the judge deemed it appropriate and necessary. Cases would generally be heard

---

* Degree of consanguinity means closeness of familial relationship by blood, as distinct from degree of affinity, which means a similar closeness by marriage. The first degree of consanguinity is the parent–child relationship, the second is siblings, the third uncle/aunt and niece/nephew, and the fourth first cousins. Marriage between those up to and including the third degree of consanguinity was prohibited.

in chambers, that is, not in open court, if the judge thought that 'expedient.' The court could order the payment of alimony and deal with all matters relating to the custody and maintenance of any children. There were no substantive changes to this regime before 1914.[59]

While a divorce could be obtained reasonably quickly in Nova Scotia, there were significant social and financial barriers to doing so.[60] Fear of societal disapproval deterred many from even trying to get one. Financial obstacles, though not excessive, meant that the majority of those who did petition were, if not wealthy, distinctly middle and upper middle class. Women petitioned slightly more often than men, and most petitions were successful. There was a marked gender difference in the grounds on which a divorce was sought. Between 1868 and 1888 all 23 male petitioners alleged adultery, while 19 of the 27 female petitioners did so as well. In addition, one woman gave impotence as the ground and, more significantly, 11 alleged cruelty, either by itself (seven) or in combination with adultery (four). When women did bring forward cruelty, they found a court that construed the word very strictly, requiring an 'extreme degree of physical violence.' Judges frequently responded to evidence of threats, beatings, kicking, and punching with questions about why the petitioner had put up with it for so long if it was that bad, and/or admonitions of wifely submission and obedience. There was some change in such judicial attitudes in the very late nineteenth century. The single most significant factor in determining the results in women's petitions was children. Women without them were much more likely to succeed because judges 'felt strongly that families should be kept intact, even with an abusive father.'

New Brunswick's divorce court was also an eighteenth-century creation and had, from 1860, the same name as its Nova Scotia counterpart and was also presided over by a Supreme Court judge. It had the power to subpoena witnesses and documents, and all witnesses were examined orally unless they were unable to attend, in which case a sworn deposition could be taken. There was an appeal to the full Supreme Court. The one material change to this regime after Confederation was that from 1902 issues of fact could be decided by a jury if the judge deemed it proper to do so. The grounds on which a divorce could be obtained were 'frigidity or impotence, adultery and consanguinity within the degrees prohibited.' As in Nova Scotia, there was no double standard.[61] Unlike Nova Scotia, no comprehensive study of the operation of the court has been done. We know of one divorce granted in 1883 to one Alberta Abell against a repeatedly violent husband, a husband who had also raped and/or seduced female residents of the boarding school for deaf children which he ran. Alfred Abell was himself deaf, but Alberta was not, and the presiding judge not only found her a highly credible witness but was also disgustedly disdainful of Alfred's disability. One cannot deduce much from one case, especially one larded with judicial prejudice, but judges were generally not sympathetic to allegations of cruelty, Justice Harrison McKeown opining in one case that 'the plaintiff must prove either actual bodily hurt or injury to health.'[62]

Prince Edward Island had a divorce court before Confederation but effectively not after. It had established one in 1835 consisting of the governor and council and listing the same grounds for divorce as New Brunswick. The court did grant one divorce in the early 1840s and another in 1864 but none thereafter. It was effectively moribund by the time that Elizabeth Rayner of Alma, Prince Edward Island, decided in about 1912 that she finally wanted to be rid of her husband, Benjamin, who had been living with Sarah Wells of Alberton, six kilometres from Alma, since 1892. She secured a parliamentary divorce. The Island government revived the court after the Second World War, using the 1835 Act.[63]

The lack of divorce courts did not go unnoticed and undebated after Confederation, and when the matter was raised in Parliament most MPs were very hostile to any suggestion that judicial divorce should be made more widely available. In 1870 John A. Macdonald introduced a bill to provide for an alternative judge to preside in the New Brunswick court if the Supreme Court judge commissioned to do so could not sit for some reason. This apparently minor housekeeping measure, made necessary by a potential conflict of interest involving Judge Charles Fisher, produced a heated debate, with opponents arguing that it was a first step to the establishment of a national divorce court, which the federal Parliament had the power to do under section 101 of the *BNA Act*. Indeed, an amendment was proposed not only not to pass the bill but to abolish the court altogether, and Macdonald withdrew his bill.[64] The issue came up again in 1875 when Amor De Cosmos, MP for Victoria and sometime premier of British Columbia, proposed that a divorce court should be established in each province. He knew that his own province had a divorce law but did not know that any court had jurisdiction to apply it. The immediate response he received, from François Béchard, a Liberal Quebec member, was a proposed 'amendment' that all existing divorce courts be abolished. He received a more measured response from Macdonald, to the effect that while he would not abolish existing courts, he did not wish to 'encourage' the obtaining of more divorces, despite the fact that some people endured 'domestic misery and unhappiness.' De Cosmos's motion was defeated 134 to 5. When in

1888 two Maritime MPs argued that the power to grant divorces should be given to one court, on the ground, among others, that publishing the evidence produced in parliamentary debates was putting out obscene material, MacDonald was again opposed. The experience in the United Kingdom since 1857, he said, had shown that the existence of a court increased the divorce rate, and a system that threw obstacles in the way of divorce was to be preferred.[65]

Whenever the issue of more divorce courts was raised, it was not infrequently pointed out that requiring a parliamentary procedure made divorce unavailable to the less well off.[66] Opponents really had no answer deeper than Macdonald's: divorce courts would mean more divorces, and that was a greater evil. In 1903 MP and moral crusader John Charlton argued that parliamentary divorces were 'unduly expensive, and often capricious and unreliable.' Prime Minister Laurier agreed that many countries had divorce courts, but it was not 'a blot upon the fair name of Canada' that it did not. On the contrary, 'it is to the credit of Canada that there are so few demands for divorce.' One of the few MPs who disagreed with this view was William Ross, MP for Boularderie, Nova Scotia, who praised his own province for having easier access to divorce and also expressed some admiration for the way Indigenous people handled relationship breakdowns. 'They confine their divorces to the same cause as our Savour did,' meaning presumably mostly adultery, and, 'particularly if the squaw is unfaithful, the Indian takes her to the camp where her people reside, and there the divorce is completed.' There is, Ross asserted, 'some decency in that, compared with the way in which we deal with the matter.'[67] In fact at least one case dealt with by the Nova Scotia Court for Divorce and Matrimonial Causes involved a Mi'kmaw couple.[68]

Discussions about divorce courts clearly demonstrate that divorce was widely and deeply unpopular in this period, not just among Quebec Catholics but across the country. It was not seen as a reasonable and broadly acceptable way for people to get out of marriages they no longer wanted, but as an existential threat to the social fabric. It was about fault, not unfortunate failure. When Macdonald opposed the establishment of a national divorce court, he did not then ask whether that was a good idea, a way of enabling escape from intolerable marriages. He was only concerned to limit its availability. For the vast majority of Canadians the family was the bedrock of society, assigning distinct social, economic, and political roles to men and women, and providing the ideal forum for the raising and education of children. The stability of families was intimately related to, and stood at the centre of, the stability of society. At a time when urbanization, industrialization, and rural depopulation were overturning the old world order, 'marriage breakdown operated as a ... negative symbol' of the greater undermining of the social order. Marriage 'represented a code of moral and sexual behaviour which was felt to have long ordered society; marriage breakdown, on the other hand, symbolized a wide variety of conduct that was considered immoral, anti-social, and unacceptable.'[69] To many, therefore, Catholics and Protestants alike, divorce undermined both women's roles as the nurturing care-givers of the next generation, and men's roles as responsible for the financial security of the family. Former Crown prosecutor and Nova Scotia senator Henry Kaulbach, who sat on many of the Senate's divorce committees, put it in 1889 that 'severing the sacred tie of Mat-rimony' was a matter of 'the gravest importance ... affecting not only the parties themselves but society at large.'[70]

The more prominent the parties involved, the greater the stigma and the perceived need for public shaming that went with divorce. In 1874 when John Sangster, the well-respected former principal of the Ontario Normal School for training teachers, was nominated for a seat on the Provincial Council of Public Instruction, it came out that he had divorced his wife in the United States and then married one of his students. The press attacked him relentlessly, the *Globe* running the headline 'For Sangster and Immorality' above a list of names of teachers supporting his candidacy, and a Kingston news-paper accused his supporters of debasing marriage 'from an honour-able state into casual cohabitation.'[71] Adeline Foster, second president of the Women's Christian Temperance Union and one of the leading female social reformers of her day, was another target. Deserted by her first husband, she fell in love with Conservative MP George Fos-ter and moved to Chicago to establish residence and obtain a divorce. Both she and Foster wishing to avoid the publicity of a parliamentary divorce. When he became minister of finance they were shunned by much of Ottawa society, including Governor General Lord Stanley, but later rehabilitated thanks to Prime Minister Sir John Thompson and Stanley's successor, Lord Aberdeen.[72]

Many marriages were far from idyllic, with wives invariably the ones who suffered in dysfunctional and abusive relationships, as demonstrated by studies of family violence and of alimony cases. Alimony could be obtained by wives whose husbands had deserted them, but when wives left because of the intolerable, often abusive, conduct of their husbands, many judges refused to order its payment

Table 15.1. Judicial divorces, 1867–1914

Province	1867–90	1891–1900	1901–14	Total
Nova Scotia	59	33	103	195
New Brunswick	52	22	56	130
British Columbia	21	27	168	216
Total	132	82	327	541

Source: *Canada Year Book 1921* (Ottawa: Dominion Bureau of Statistics, 1922), 825.

and instead blamed wives for provoking the conduct, or urged submission, forbearance, and wifely duty, or referred to a combination of these things.[73] In the late nineteenth century legislation was passed in most provinces providing a statutory right to maintenance for wives deserted by their husbands, a tacit admission that marriage practice did not match the ideal.[74] But none of this changed the attitude towards formal legal divorce. People confined to unacceptable marriages did have an option – what is often referred to as informal divorce, or sometimes self-divorce. The 'true' rate of 'divorce' was much higher than the statistics on formal divorces reveal, for many people simply left their spouses and lived elsewhere. Starting a new life in a new community was facilitated by the proximity of the United States, which not only provided a refuge from social disapproval, but much easier access to a divorce court.[75]

The statistics on judicial divorce in table 15.1 show how rare it was. Before about 1900 rather more divorces were granted in the Maritimes than British Columbia, but thereafter the figures were reversed. BC's higher absolute numbers also represent a much higher per capita divorce rate, likely attributable to the large number of new arrivals and transients. While many of the men who came were single, a significant number were husbands who came without their spouses and, whether or not they initially intended that their spouse would join them, found that that did not happen. Table 15.1 also shows that the number of judicial divorces grew, an increase roughly consonant with population growth down to about 1900 but considerably eclipsing it thereafter. These inter-provincial differences are less important than the fact that the Canadian divorce rate was very low compared to that of the United States, and equally low relative to later periods. The numbers rose steadily after the First World War, but that is a story for another volume.[76]

Parliamentary Divorce

The Canadian Parliament's jurisdiction over divorce was potentially unfettered, but it limited itself to granting full divorces, known as divorce *a vinculo matrimonii* (divorce from the bonds of marriage), only on the ground of adultery, the same basis as the House of Lords. It also gave the relief that the English ecclesiastical courts had given in the form of annulments for non-consummation, fraud, and lack of consent from a minor, but it called these divorces. The vast majority of the 262 divorce Acts passed by Parliament between Confederation and 1914 (table 15.2) were divorces *a vinculo matrimonii*, but one was for a divorce *a mensa et thoro* (separation from bed and board), and a small number were strictly speaking annulments. Among petitioners the male-female ratio was 142 to 120, or 54 to 46 per cent. In only six instances was there an overlap between cases. In 1906, for example, William Holmes of St. Francis, Quebec, a professor of music, divorced his wife, Alice, because of her desertion of him and her adultery with Dr. John Tompkins. Three years later Tompkins's wife, Hannah, divorced him, her own act citing the Holmes divorce.[77] The success rate for people who went as far as to have a bill introduced was very high, at 88 per cent, only 20 bills being voted down in either the Commons or the Senate and a further 15 being withdrawn by the petitioners.[78]

Some 60 per cent of the divorces were granted to residents of Ontario, the only province from which there were more female than male petitioners. Ontario residents obtained divorces at a much higher per capita rate than the next most populous province of Quebec, likely the result of Catholic aversion to divorce and the availability of judicial separation in the province, discussed in chapter 5. Although the acts do not give religious affiliation, it is reasonable to think that most applicants from Quebec were Protestant or Jewish. We deduce this from the names of the petitioners, the large number of applicants listed as being from Montreal or the Eastern Townships, and the fact that in some cases the venue of the marriage, always a Protestant church, was mentioned.[79]

Comparing table 15.2 with table 15.1 it is obvious that the number of divorces per capita for provinces where petitioners had to go to Parliament was much lower than in the provinces that had judicial divorce. The principal cause of this difference was simply that parliamentary divorces were much more difficult, especially financially difficult, to obtain. There was a filing fee, the cost of printing enough copies of the bill so that every parliamentarian could have one, the need to retain

ANNO TRICESIMO-PRIMO

VICTORIÆ REGINÆ.

CAP. XCV.

An Act for the relief of Joseph Frederick Whiteaves.

[Reserved for the signification of Her Majesty's pleasure thereon on the 22nd May, 1868; Royal assent given by Her Matesty in Council on the 7th July, 1868; Proclamation thereof made by His Excellency the Governor General on the 26th September, 1868.]

WHEREAS, Joseph Frederick Whiteaves, of the City of Montreal, Esquire, Curator of the Museum of the Natural History Society of Montreal, hath, by his petition humbly set forth, that on the eighteenth day of June, one thousand eight hundred and sixty-three, he was married to Julia Wolff; that they lived and cohabited together as husband and wife up to about the seventh day of March, one thousand eight hundred and sixty-six, when he discovered that she had been leading an irregular life, and had been committing adultery with a certain person named in the evidence within a year next preceding that date; that thereupon the said Julia Wolff left the house of the said Joseph Frederick Whiteaves and has ever since continued to live apart from him; that the said Julia Wolff had by her conduct dissolved the Bond of Matrimony on her part; that the said Joseph Frederick Whiteaves had taken measures to establish judicially the adulterous correspondence of the said Julia Wolff, and was ready to prove the allegations of his said petition; wherefore he humbly prayed that the said marriage might be dissolved so as to enable him to marry again, and that such further relief might be afforded him as might be deemed fit; And whereas the said Joseph Frederick Whiteaves hath since procured a judgment against the said Julia Wolff establishing the adultery above mentioned, and it is expedient that the prayer of the said petition should be granted: Therefore, Her Majesty, by and with the advice and consent of the Senate and House of Commons of Canada, enacts as follows :—

Preamble.

Case recited.

1.

Act for the Relief of Joseph Frederick Whiteaves, SC, 1869, c 95, the first divorce granted by the Parliament of Canada. Whiteaves was the curator of the Museum of the Natural History Society of Montreal and divorced his wife, Julia, because of her adultery.

Table 15.2. Parliamentary divorces, 1867–1914[80]

Province	Male petitioners	Female petitioners	Total
Ontario	79	83	162
Quebec	31	18	49
Manitoba (from 1892)	15	7	22
Alberta (Alberta District of NWT from 1892) and Province from 1906	10	8	18
Saskatchewan (Assiniboia District of NWT from 1903 and Province from 1906	6	2	8
Other	2	2	4
Total	143	120	263

Source: Annual volumes of the Statutes of Canada.

counsel, and the expenses associated with travel to Ottawa by petitioners and witnesses. Contemporary estimates of the total cost varied between $800 and $1,500.[81] As with judicial divorce, however, the
per capita rate increased after about 1900, as shown by table 15.3 on
the following page. Only 68 divorces were granted up to 1900, and 195
between then and 1914. Obviously, the country's population increased
also during the same period, but not threefold.

A parliamentary divorce was both a political and a legal process.[82] A
bill needed to be introduced by a member of Parliament – in this case
always a senator because all bills of divorce started in the Senate – and
had to go through all the standard procedures for any act of Parliament.
In the first decade after Confederation the governor general reserved
royal assent for London's approval under section 56 of the *BNA Act,*
which took three to six months. He did so pursuant to annual instructions from London not to assent to any divorce bill, which were a hang-
over from the pre-Confederation period. Minister of Justice Edward
Blake persuaded Westminster to change this practice, and no divorce
act was referred to London after 1877.[83] The process was also a legal
one, because when the bill went to a divorce committee the lawyer for
the petitioner had to present evidence to persuade the parliamentarians
that the facts which could justify a divorce were present.

Every act was largely identical in form. Each was either one or two
pages long, depending on the length of the preamble. The preamble
identified the parties, stated when and where they had been married,
and then recounted the fact of adultery, the sole ground for granting a
divorce. After detailing the accusation the preamble 'prayed that the

Table 15.3. Parliamentary divorces, 1867–1914

Period	Male petitioners	Female petitioners	Total
1867–90	18	14	32
1891–1900	22	14	36
1901–14	103	92	195
Total	143	120	263

said marriage may be dissolved and declared henceforth null and void to all intents and purposes whatsoever, so as to enable her [or him] to marry again.' The recounting of the reasons for seeking a divorce meant that the acts bore a resemblance to ordinary civil pleadings. The last sentence of the preamble was the verdict, stating that the petitioner 'has proved the allegations in her [or his] petition.' The acts then contained two substantive sections, one declaring the marriage dissolved and the other stating that the petitioner could marry again. Some acts also had a third clause, dealing with the legitimacy of living or future children of the husband or wife.

As in any civil legal proceeding, the first stage was the giving of notice. An advertisement had to be placed in two newspapers in the area in which the applicant usually resided, and in the *Canada Gazette*. This gave six months' notice of the applicant's intention to have a bill introduced, a long period but one designed to provide an opportunity for reconciliation. There were many more such notices posted than there were acts passed, and thus we know that a good number of separated people did not make it all the way through the process. We surmise that the reasons varied: some couples reconciled, while some applicants did not follow through for lack of funds or some other reason.

Once the notice requirements were met, the applicant petitioned the Senate, the petition was examined by the Senate divorce committee, and, if it met the formal requirements, it was submitted by the committee to the Senate as a whole. Once the Senate had adopted the committee's report, a bill was drawn up and immediately read for the first time. The investigation of the facts, the calling of witnesses, and the like then occurred on second reading in the Senate. Before standard rules were adopted in 1888, the committee was an ad hoc one; the sponsor of the bill would move for a committee and name the members he wanted.[84] After 1888 a standing committee of the Senate was established at the beginning of every session, the Select Committee on Divorce. The committee received the evidence, written and viva voce, and heard counsel on fact and law. The evidence was taken down in shorthand and later published, but only enough copies were made for distribution to all senators and MPs, given the private nature of the matter.

Details of the evidence were not routinely included in the *Journals* of either house, although there were exceptions. In the most unusual case of this period, one that began as a bill divorcing Whitby merchant Robert Campbell from his wife Elizabeth but ended four years later as an act granting Elizabeth a divorce *a mensa et thoro* from Robert, the evidence presented in over two weeks of committee hearings in 1876 was published in a 250-page appendix to the Senate *Journals*.[85] Even if the *Journals* were usually merely minutes of proceedings, the *Debates* of both houses often involved members referring to the evidence. Newspaper reporters were allowed into the committee room until 1885, but not thereafter.[86] There was, not surprisingly, tension between the principle of an open legislature and the attitude to divorce discussed above, for there were occasions when MPs and senators worried about the effect of open debates on public morality. In the 1888 case of Mary Matilda White there was a long discussion about whether the evidence in a case involving impotency should be published. White claimed that she had not had intercourse with her husband since their marriage in 1872, 'owing to his alleged malformation or incapacity to consummate the marriage.' Her husband denied this, and the committee ordered both to undergo a medical examination. The doctors gave evidence that 'there was no apparent malformation' in the husband and that 'the physical condition of the [wife] … was such as to contradict her statement that the marriage had not been consummated.' Her bill was rejected. Violet Dakin was more successful in arguing that her marriage to William Dakin had not been consummated. In a homophobic age her success had likely much less to do with any medical evidence than with the fact that a few months after the nuptials Dakin was convicted of 'attempting to commit unnameable offences with boys' and sentenced to six years in the Edmonton penitentiary.[87]

Mary White's failure was not unique. Between Confederation and 1888 34 bills were introduced, all from petitioners in Ontario and Quebec, resulting in 25 divorce acts. John Robert Martin, a barrister from Cayuga, Ontario, had two bills fail in 1871 and 1872, one because the preamble was 'not proved,' before getting his divorce in 1873. Three other petitioners failed to produce sufficient evidence to 'prove the preamble,' one man was shown to have colluded with his wife to get a divorce, an issue to which we will return, and two cases were postponed to the next session. As noted above, the vast majority of bills did become acts, even if they did not do so in the same session in which the bill was introduced. At least three of the male petitioners who were successful in the 1870s had sued the wife's lover for criminal conversation and won. Others likely did the same in later decades, but the acts did not say so.[88]

The easiest way to prove adultery was a conviction for bigamy. Five petitioners, four women and one man, were able to present evidence to this effect, which presumably included inmate records from Kingston penitentiary, where three of the men served two years. The only woman convicted of bigamy was Mary Stock, who after 18 years of marriage to David Stock and nine children, left him and married, also in Toronto, one William Jones. She was convicted by police magistrate George Denison and sentenced to just 60 days in jail. Once she had served her sentence she went back to living with Jones. It took David Stock another five years to divorce her, likely because he was a machinist and needed time to save up the money. At least four other people could have been prosecuted for bigamy. They had married someone else in Canada and still lived in the country. Ten had remarried elsewhere – in California, Chicago, New York, Seattle, North and South Dakota, Vermont, and, more romantically, Paris. There were also people who married outside Canada without getting a divorce but returned to live in the country. Abraham Aronsberg, an optician from Liverpool, England, had emigrated to Canada with his new wife Lottie and practised in Toronto. They separated a dozen years later when 'unhappy differences' arose between them, and only thereafter did he discover that she was having an affair with John Dunning, a commercial traveller. Aronsberg went to live in Montreal, she went to South Dakota and married Dunning, and then returned to Toronto, where she and Dunning were 'notoriously known' for their dubious living arrangement.[89] Lottie and John were unusual. It was much more common for respondents to have gone to the United States and remain there, often with their adulterous partner. Some got an American divorce and remarried. Others remarried in the United States, with no information given in the act about whether they had first divorced. Yet others were simply said to be living in the United States. Altogether some 50 respondents, about 20 per cent of the acts, were resident in the republic.

Although respondents were able to contest divorce bills, very few did. Lack of objection could be an issue – one also often to the fore in English parliamentary divorces before 1857 and in the divorce court thereafter. A bill would fail if there was connivance, condonation, or collusion.

Divorces were granted on the ground of adultery, and the adultery had to be real and an affront to the other spouse and the marriage bond. Connivance involved no such affront, because it meant encouraging or advising the adultery. Collusion was also an agreement between the spouses, but without the adultery. Evidence would be manufactured – renting a hotel room and spending the night there with someone of the opposite sex, perhaps for a fee, is the classic case. Both connivance and collusion were effectively ways to allow spouses to divorce just because they no longer wished to be husband and wife, and the law could not tolerate that. Condonation was harder to conceal, for it was effectively forgiveness of the fault with full knowledge of what the fault had been and an implied promise that it would not be repeated. In England the Queen's proctor was charged with investigating whether any of these things had happened or whether the petitioner's own conduct should debar him or her from a divorce. In Canada there was no similar official to oversee the parties. Parliamentary debates contain many comments on collusion as a problem, though rarely was the accusation levelled at particular individuals, and we know of just one bill being voted down on this basis, although there may well have been more.[90] Before the late 1880s clauses in bills denying connivance and/or collusion were rare – only two cases, both from Quebec, in 1878 and 1885. But when the rules were consolidated in 1888 Rule G required that the applicant's petition had to 'negative condonation, collusion and connivance.' Hence the 1890 divorce act for Christiana Filman Glover of Burlington alleged both that her grandiosely named contractor husband Christopher Columbus Glover had deserted her and their son and gone to live with another woman, and insisted that 'she has not in any way condoned the adultery ..., and that no collusion nor connivance exists between her and him to obtain a dissolution' of the marriage.'[91] Thereafter most, but not all, acts contained this clause.

Parliamentary divorce proceedings were relatively ill-attended. Many MPs and senators resented the time they took up or did not want to hear sordid details of marital breakdown. When members spoke it was not really to discuss the merits of individual cases but to use the occasion to ride a hobby horse – the class-biased nature of the procedure, the danger to the family and society that divorce posed, the iniquity of allowing the divorced guilty party the right to remarry, and the like. Finance Minister William Stevens Fielding understated in masterly fashion in 1903 that '[t]here is no great zeal on the part of members generally to deal with this question.'[92]

Not surprisingly, given what we have said about the difficulties of obtaining a parliamentary divorce, applicants came generally from among the better off. In the United Kingdom before 1857 about two-thirds of parliamentary divorces were granted to the upper classes,[93] and although Canada did not have the same class structure it too had significant social and economic stratification. Using occupational descriptions, which were included in most of the acts, both those of male petitioners and those of the husbands of female petitioners, we can say that some over 40 per cent of the petitioners came from the professional classes and from entrepreneurial and business backgrounds or were designated as 'gentlemen.' The above-mentioned cases of John Tomlins and Charles Holmes, the doctor and the professor, are examples. Such people made up a substantial part of the database, but slightly fewer than half of the total, and a range of occupations that can be termed small business and clerical and that included clerks, real estate agents, farmers, and many similar avocations, made up more than a third of the petitioners. Only 10 per cent consisted of people in artisanal and skilled trades and retailers – the above-mentioned machinist David Stock, a cabinet maker, a butcher, a locomotive engineer, a telegraph operator. It must be stressed that we have no information about personal wealth, and occupations are only a rough proxy to measure socio-economic status. A cabinet maker, for example, might have worked in a factory or had his own thriving business. Similarly, a farmer could work 200 acres or 2,000. But a clerk was a lower-middle-class clerical position, a mason was surely a tradesman, not a builder. Canadian parliamentary divorces were not solely 'law for the aristocracy,' as one English historian has termed it, but they were for the middle and upper middle classes. There were very few people who could be called working class – only five: four labourers and a bartender.

Getting a fuller and more nuanced picture of petitioners would require much more extensive research into a wide range of sources. Here we must content ourselves with the figures given above and some individual examples to make the point that those who obtained parliamentary divorces were far from representative of the population as a whole. They included leading Winnipeg lawyers James Manning Aikins and Isaac Pitblado, the former the founder of one of Winnipeg's major law firms, Aikins, MacAulay and Thorvaldson (now MLT Aikins), who is mentioned in chapter 6 as a leader of the bar. He was deserted by his wife in 1890. Ontario applicants included Albert Nordheimer, a prominent musician and music publisher whose wife, Edith May Vankoughnet, a niece of Ontario Chancellor Philip Vankoughnet, deserted him in 1893. Gertrude Mary Grantham, the daughter of Sir William Mackenzie, one of the country's pre-eminent railway entrepreneurs, divorced her husband, Toronto contractor Arthur Myles Grantham, in 1911 as a result of his multiple adulteries. From Quebec there was Joseph Whiteaves, curator of the Montreal Museum of Natural History, and Fanny Riddell, whose husband, Montreal physician George Field Herchmer, a relative of NWMP Commissioner Lawrence Herchmer, left her after four years of marriage and moved to western Canada.[94]

Child Custody in Common Law Provinces

For most of this period, in most provinces, the common law determined custody of minor children when the parents were not living together. There was little statutory change until the end of the nineteenth century. The common law gave women no rights to the custody of children while the marriage subsisted or upon divorce.[95] The same doctrine of marital unity that severely circumscribed married women's right to property operated to similar effect. As the husband was head of the household his authority extended to the children and sharing it with his wife would produce marital discord. The law permitted a father to choose his child's religion and education, to determine every aspect of his or her daily life, to take a minor's earnings, even to deprive a child of his or her mother's presence if the husband believed he had good reason to do so. The absoluteness of a father's right is perhaps best exemplified by the fact that a number of the cases discussed below, in which a father went to court to regain custody, were habeas corpus applications. The same writ to free illegally held prisoners was used to 'free' the child from the mother.

In extreme cases the Court of Chancery could intervene and act in loco parentis, but in this the court acted to protect the child, not to assert a mother's right. Even protection of the child was narrowly defined, nothing like the modern 'best interests' standard. Here, as seen in chapter 5, the civil law of Quebec had adopted this standard much earlier. The authority of the father largely outweighed consideration of the mother's and the child's interests. The father's prerogatives survived the grave, for he could appoint a guardian in his will to whom the wife had to submit. Every province had statutory law on guardianship to augment, or largely confirm, the common law, but statutory provisions on custody were rare. Manitoba's *Infants and their Estates Act*, for example, determined how guardians were to be appointed for infants (those under the age of majority) 'not having a father living.'[96] The mother could be appointed but had to petition the court for the right. The only modification to the common law in England was via a statute of 1839, *Lord Talfourd's Act*, and the *Divorce and Matrimonial Causes Act* of 1857. The former gave mothers the right to apply to court for custody of children under seven, but it provided no criteria for doing so, only for not doing so: a woman who had committed adultery could not apply. The 1857 Act gave the court broad discretion to issue orders that it 'deem[ed] just and proper with respect to the custody, maintenance and education of the children of the marriage,' including placing the children under the protection of Chancery.[97]

At Confederation Nova Scotia and Ontario had statute law on custody. The former simply adopted the provisions of the 1857 English act. Ontario's legislation originated in a Province of Canada statute of 1855. It differed from *Lord Talfourd's Act* in applying to children 12 and younger and in permitting a mother to apply to any Superior Court, not just Chancery, for custody when the child was in the custody of its father or a guardian. A woman who had committed adultery could not apply. The act also allowed for the award of maintenance payments, to the extent that the judge thought 'just and reasonable.' But like its English model it did not specify criteria for when custody would go to the mother beyond the fact that a judge thought it was 'fit' that this should happen. Thus it did not modify the common law beyond making it possible for a mother to apply for custody. Ontario enacted one additional piece of legislation after Confederation, also very limited in scope. No other province passed even this kind of legislation until the late nineteenth century.[98]

Despite the lack of substantive statutory guidance, over time some Ontario judges effectively shifted the balance between a father's rights and the interests of the mother and/or the child. It is reasonable to think that they did so from a combination of a greater sensitivity to the rights of women and children, as exemplified in things like protective workplace and anti-cruelty legislation, the 'child-saving' movement, the rise of maternal feminism, and an awareness that not all fathers lived up to their responsibilities to provide for and protect all 'weaker' members of the family.[99] In this latter regard judicial reform of child custody law mirrored statutory reform of married women's property law; it was a way of strengthening the family unit. The Ontario courts evinced this new approach slowly and with circumspection. In the first decade or so after Confederation they took the view that the provincial legislation had made very little difference to the common law. With some few exceptions, they agreed with Justice Adam Wilson of Queen's Bench, who insisted in 1871 that 'the general policy of the law with reference to father and child was not altered' by the legislation, and that 'if a father's marital duty and the interest of the child can be secured consistently with his retaining the custody of his children, his common law rights will not be interfered with.'[100] The same approach was taken in Nova Scotia, although direct comparison is made difficult by the fact that the reported Ontario cases did not involve divorcing couples, for obvious reasons, while the cases studied for Nova Scotia all arose out of divorce petitions.[101]

By the early 1880s a different approach emerged, as illustrated by the 1882 decision of Justice Featherston Osler of the Ontario Court of Common Pleas in *Re Murdoch*.[102] Mrs. Murdoch had left her husband to live with her parents, taking her four-year old daughter with her, and Mr. Murdoch brought a habeas corpus application for his daughter's return. (None of the parties was named, they were just the father, the mother, the child). Osler's decision, which caused him 'much pain and anxiety,' was an exercise in indecision. On the one hand, if it was 'in the interest of a child to be with its mother, it is hard towards the child that the mother should not have her.' On the other hand, if the wife had left a faultless husband because of 'mere caprice and wilfulness,' the father's common law right should prevail. But the common law right had been 'considerably modified … by statute,' and he was 'satisfied' that it was in the child's interest to be with her mother rather than with a father who, 'however affectionate and kind,' had many business dealings and was frequently absent from the home, all of which 'render it impossible for him to afford the constant care and attention which a child of such tender years demands.' While the husband admitted to 'some degree of actual personal violence to the wife,' Osler did not make much of this. Rather, it was the husband's inability to provide a home for his family that was determinative. If he had been able to do so, even if not a very good home in material terms, 'the wife must still share his fortunes, or if she will not, must submit up her child to its father,' but he could not manage even this. The judgment thus derogated in only a small degree from the absoluteness of a man's common law right to custody, but it did derogate. Most importantly, it did so because Osler J, adverting to some English decisions on that statute, placed some emphasis on the child's best interests as a factor to be considered when assessing the strength of a father's claim.

Decisions from other provincial courts also showed some movement away from the paramountcy of the common law and a father's prerogative. In *Jamieson v Jamieson* George Jamieson twice failed to win custody, once in a habeas corpus action after Marion Jamieson had left and taken the children with her, and again when she later successfully sued for divorce. In both proceedings ample evidence was produced to show that he drank excessively on occasion, was violent towards his wife, and had impregnated the children's nurse. Judge Ordinary of the Nova Scotia divorce court Alexander James concluded that he was 'an unfit person to have the care and custody of his children.' Unfortunately divorce cases were not reported, so we do not know how James J dealt with the relationship between the common law and his statutory discretion. In the only other Nova Scotia divorce case from the 1880s where a custody decision was rendered the father won custody against an adulterous mother.[103]

We can deduce rather more about the New Brunswick judges' changing but still conflicted approach to custody from *In Re Coram*, an 1886 case that produced a relatively long and split decision.[104] Finding himself in 'poor circumstances,' Joseph Coram, a father of four, had agreed with the McAfees, his wife's sister and her husband, that his youngest, Eva, would live with her aunt and uncle, and he went to Quebec with the rest of his family in search of work. The McAfees had no children and were comfortably off. It was agreed that they would raise Eva as their own and see to her education. Joseph returned to Saint John from Quebec after four years, having secured a job in the customs service, but at no time did he provide any material support to the McAfees. Four years after returning he decided he wanted Eva, now 15, back. Eva did not wish to go and Joseph brought a habeas corpus application before Judge in Equity Acalus Lockwood Palmer, who we saw earlier in this book was later forced off the bench for financial improprieties. At the hearing Eva testified to her reluctance to leave what she considered her home, and Joseph acknowledged that his principal reason for wanting her was that his wife was in poor health and he needed her help with the housekeeping. Palmer suggested a compromise whereby Eva would still consider the McAfee house her home but 'go to her father's house and assist there' yet '[be] at liberty to return at will to her uncle and aunt.' But Joseph would have none of it; he wanted full custody. Palmer could not decide and asked for a ruling from the full Supreme Court bench, on which he sat for the case – a practice common at the time.

A majority of the court found for the father 4:2. Chief Justice John Campbell Allen, for his colleagues George Edward King and William Henry Tuck, found the law simple to state. As the province had no statute on custody, a court had to apply the common law. It had 'no discretionary power to control the father in the exercise of his rights, except in extreme cases.' 'Extreme' circumstances were limited to 'danger to the child ... where there was an apprehension of cruelty,' or 'contamination in consequence of his [the father's] immorality or gross profligacy.' Allen discussed the difference between Chancery exercising its child protection jurisdiction, and a common law court hearing an application for habeas corpus, but thought there was essentially no difference if the latter was dealing with a habeas corpus application based on custody law. He quoted with approval the English case of *Re Fynn*:

> A man may be in narrow circumstances; he may be negligent, injudicious and faulty as the father of minors; he may be a person from whom the discreet, the intelligent, and the well disposed, exercising a private judgment would wish his children to be, for their sakes... removed; he may be all this without rendering himself liable to judicial interference.... Before this jurisdiction can be called into action between them it must be satisfied ... that the father has so conducted himself, ... or is placed in such a position as to render it not merely better for the children, but essential to their safety or to their welfare in some very serious and important respect.

Joseph Coram simply did not fit these criteria, even if he had given up his daughter to a better home for eight years and only wanted her back to help his wife with the housekeeping. As for what might be in the best interests of the child, that 'was not enough to justify ... interference with a parent's rights.' Allen backed up this assertion by approvingly quoting a UK decision in which a father had been given custody of a nursing infant when the mother had left because of his violence. It was a case that had 'never been questioned.' Allen ended by dismissing an argument that Joseph Coram could be said to have abandoned Eva and his parental rights. The courts had never considered a 'mere arrangement or consent' to constitute abandonment. He agreed that his decision might seem 'harsh' but only mentioned the McAfees as the victims of any apparent harshness, not Eva.

Justice Andrew Rainsford Wetmore wrote a very short concurring judgment, the principal point of which was to castigate Eva for not willingly doing her duty to obey a parent. She preferred her aunt's 'luxurious surroundings' to her parents' 'humbler home' and should 'be taught a wholesome lesson of the duty of children to their parents, and to go to the assistance of her mother who is in ill health.' Palmer, John James Fraser concurring, took a very different tack. He had no doubt that it was in Eva's best interests to stay with the McAfees and that Coram had freed Eva from her duty to submit to his control, 'both by his consent, and also by his conduct in entirely neglecting to provide for her.' He had no problem with the general proposition that a father was the best person to have custody, but a father's rights were 'qualified,' 'only given to enable him to discharge correlative duties; and he will be secured in such rights as long and no longer than he discharges such duties.' Palmer ignored the fact that the father actually sought to resume his duties by providing a home for and supporting his child, even if he also wanted her labour. But his general approach, that 'the principal thing to be looked to is the welfare of the child,' was a clear departure from common law authority. Palmer was also persuaded by the fact that Eva was 15 and could exercise her choice when she turned 16. But for the time his use of the phrase 'best interests of the child' was near revolutionary.

Osler J's decision in *Murdoch* and Palmer's dissent in *Coram* reflected, perhaps reinforced, a broader shift in societal attitudes, which in Ontario resulted in 1887 legislation changing the law to some degree. The Ontario act came just a year after UK legislation to the same effect and was an amendment to the province's guardianship statute, not its custody act. It very largely mirrored the English act's provisions. Section 1 fleshed out the court's power to make an order that was 'fit' regarding custody by providing new criteria: 'the welfare of the infant, … the conduct of the parents, and … the wishes as well of the mother as of the father.' The act also confirmed the court's power to order maintenance to be paid by the father and provided additional guardianship rights to the mother but did not legalize provisions in separation agreements dealing with custody. Any such clauses, if agreed to, could thus not be enforced by either party. Given its importance the act generated very little debate, although the *Canada Law Journal* shortly noted that it 'very properly gives the mother a voice in the custody of her children,' suggesting a consensus on the matter.[105]

The most significant Ontario case of the 1880s did not involve the 1887 act, because it was not retroactive and *Smart v Smart* began before it was passed.[106] The case nonetheless reflected a judicial approach similar to that taken by the legislators. David Smart was a lawyer in Port Hope, and in 1883, after 13 years of marriage and three children, Emilie Smart left him because of his habitual drunkenness. She moved to Toronto with the children, all under 12 years old, where she was able to support the family because she was independently wealthy. The following year she and David made a written agreement that they would resume cohabitation in Toronto, he would stop drinking, and she would pay his debts of $8,000 and support the family from her own money. The agreement also specified that if he started drinking again Emilie would be free to live apart from him with custody of the children. In 1885 he took up the bottle again, and when she filed suit for custody they made another agreement, in which she also undertook to maintain and educate the children and allow David access. In 1886 David sued for custody on a writ of habeas corpus. He lost at trial and at the Court of Appeal. The case was procedurally complicated, but what matters for our purposes is that while all judges agreed that the agreement was unenforceable, Emilie had a right to custody. Remarkably Ferguson J of the High Court bolstered his finding with the *Murdoch* case and with the fact that he had conferred with Justice Osler, who then wrote the majority decision in the Court of Appeal. The case ultimately went to the JCPC, which not only affirmed the Ontario courts but more generally acknowledged the extent to which judicial as well as societal views had changed. 'For many years,' wrote Lord Hobhouse, 'the tendency of legislative action and of judicial decision, as well as of general opinion, has been to give to married women a higher status both as regards property and person, and in family questions, to bring the marital duty of the husband and the welfare of the children into greater prominence, in both respects diminishing the powers accorded to the husband and the father.'

In the 1890s two other provinces passed legislation removing the common law's presumption of a father's right to custody. The New Brunswick provisions were just two sections of a very long 1890 statute on the practice of the Supreme Court in equity. They gave a mother the right to apply for access and/or custody and specified that when anybody applied for either or both the court's duty was 'to take into consideration the interests' of the child when deciding between the parents. This was a legislative overturning of, or at least a significant amendment to, *In Re Coram*, and it did not contain the adultery limitation on the right to apply of other legislation. The 1893 Nova Scotia statute was similar in principle. It authorized courts to award custody to mothers and delineated the criteria as 'the welfare of the infants, the conduct *or circumstances* of the parents, and the wishes of the mother as well as the father.' The two italicized words do not appear in any other legislation, suggesting that the assembly had in mind economic considerations. The act also provided for maintenance and, unlike Ontario's legislation, made separation agreements that dealt with custody enforceable so long as they were beneficial to the child.[107]

Neither British Columbia nor Manitoba went beyond the received English law. The latter's 1878 custody provisions were essentially those of the common law as modified by the 1839 English act. They stated succinctly and bluntly, 'As a rule the father shall have the custody and control of his infant children.' It allowed the court to hear a petition for access from a mother who did not have custody, either because the father had it or a third-party guardian did. A mother could request custody of any minor child younger than 12, which would be granted in 'a proper case.' No mother could ask for custody or access if she had committed adultery.[108] British Columbia legislated on the issue for the first time in the 1897 *Revised Statutes*. As discussed in chapter 4, many of the statutes contained replications of older English Acts, including the guardianship provisions. The BC statute was principally about guardianship, not custody, and affirmed the father's absolute right to assign a guardian by deed or will. The principal custody provision was a replica of the 1878 Manitoba act. The only innovation was that a mother's right to request custody was placed on the same footing as the father's if the child was under 21 and had been convicted of an indictable offence. In those circumstances mother, father, or anybody else was treated the same. Anybody who was willing 'to take charge of such infant, and to provide for his or her maintenance and education' could apply for custody. This section was about what might be termed the 'best rehabilitative interests' of the minor, for in assessing the application the court was to take into account the 'circumstances, habits and character of the parents.'[109]

Judicial decisions in the 1890s and the early twentieth century not surprisingly reflected the varied provincial legislation, although it has also been argued that New Brunswick judges were prone to ignore the 'best interests of the child' provision in the 1893 Act.[110] But Wallace Graham, Nova Scotia's Judge Ordinary and future chief justice, did not. He awarded custody to the mother in 28 of the 36 divorce cases he heard between 1893 and 1910 in which the mother was the petitioner and custody was an issue. One would, of course, expect the 'innocent' party to prevail in a case involving divorce and custody, but given the traditional common law position this was a marked departure from past assumptions about a father's right. Moreover, male petitioners for divorce did slightly less well on custody than their ex-wives. Despite the unusual wording of the 1893 statute discussed above, economic circumstances played only a minor role.[111] In contrast Manitoba judges, who lacked the same statutory guidance, agreed with Queen's Bench Judge Thomas Wardlaw Taylor in *Re Foulds* that 'the Court is always unwilling to interfere with the common law rights of the father.'[112]

By the end of our period the legal landscape on custody had changed considerably, albeit inconsistently, across the country. While mothers saw their legal position improve somewhat, these changes were not aimed at achieving equality. Rather, they were motivated in part by an even deeper commitment to the ideology of separate spheres as motherhood (and childhood) was sentimentalized and romanticized, in a trend furthered by the emergence of maternal feminism. In addition, various measures such as compulsory schooling and child labour laws began to reduce the economic value of children, making paternal control over them less crucial.[113] These changes heralded a new era of state intervention in the lives of better-off families (it had always intervened in the lives of poor families). The state no longer simply backed up paternal power but positioned itself above both parents in the interest of social order and creating 'better' citizens. The next logical step, promoted by middle-class reformers, was to question whether either parent was fit to keep the children or whether the state itself should assert its own right to custody or vest it in a third party. Once the best interests standard had infiltrated the traditional approach to custody, there was no necessary reason to entrust a child to either parent where both were deemed irresponsible or inadequate. The Victorian idea of childhood as a time of innocence and the anti-cruelty movement of the late nineteenth century combined to produce substantial legislation protecting children from exploitation and abuse, and permitting the removal of children from their parents' care. What began as a private-public partnership between the state and philanthropic organizations such as the Society for the Prevention of Cruelty in Nova Scotia and the Children's Aid Societies of Ontario in the 1880s and 1890s became an increasingly important governmental function, one that will be explored more fully in the next volume.[114]

The Female Body and the Law

The law's interest in women's bodies came in many forms, but all involved the exercise of power over them in some way: over women's reproductive choices, their decisions regarding sexual relations and sex work, and their ability to resist physical and sexual abuse by their husbands or other men. The criminal law was supposed to protect women's physical and sexual integrity but, in an era of all-male judges, juries, and police, often failed in this capacity. Reformers pressed for, and achieved, some changes in the criminal law itself regarding offences against women, but so long as the administration of criminal justice itself remained unchanged little progress could be expected. Not until the very end of this period, with the establishment of the Women's Court in Toronto in 1913, was there some willingness to experiment with new forms of justice delivery more cognizant of women's experience. When women's courts were also created in Edmonton and Calgary in 1916, the next logical step was taken when Emily Murphy was appointed police magistrate in the Alberta capital, the first woman in the British Empire to hold such a post.[115]

In the field of civil law, no area saw more women involved in litigation, at least in Ontario, than the tort of seduction. This action grew out of the old action *per quod servitium amisit*,* which permitted a master to sue the person who had injured a servant or otherwise deprived him of the servant's labour. As we saw in *Volume 1*, in the nineteenth-century common law world it was used by fathers against men who had impregnated their unmarried daughters. The harm alleged by the father was that, through his daughter's pregnancy and lying in, he had lost her services to which he was entitled. Despite calls by medical and legal critics in the 1880s for the action to be recognized as belonging to the woman herself, rather than her father (the mother could take the action only if the father were dead), this change did not occur. Prince Edward Island had been the only pre-Confederation jurisdiction where the law was amended to vest the action in the woman, but a court decision soon effectively nullified it by stating she could take the action only if she could show that she had a parent, master, or guardian who would have been able to maintain it at common law. The action had a very high success rate before Ontario juries, plaintiffs winning 90 per cent of the time and receiving an average award of damages of $663, a not inconsiderable sum. While appellate judges were much less keen on the action and allowed appeals by defendants half the time, only one-third of the cases featured appeals, leading to an overall success rate of 77 per cent. Allowing the aggrieved father rather than the unchaste daughter to take the action undoubtedly contributed to its runaway success, but at the cost of perpetuating antiquated ideas regarding a father's property right in his daughter's sexuality.[116]

---

* Literally 'whereby he lost the services of' a servant.

Quebec law also allowed an action in seduction, but its requirements were more stringent and became even more so after the adoption of the *Civil Code of Lower Canada*. Unlike the common law, consent of the woman was a defence to the action in Quebec unless she had been seduced under promise of marriage. Towards the end of the nineteenth century, judges began to demand some written evidence of the promise of marriage. Evidence by the woman or the oral testimony of witnesses no longer sufficed. In an 1881 case, for example, where an employer admitted having had sexual relations with his domestic servant who later gave birth, the suit failed because the woman could not produce written evidence of his marital intentions. A new requirement in the *Civil Code* for written evidence also led to decreased recourse by unmarried mothers to paternity actions whereby they could be awarded an alimentary pension for the child fathered by the defendant. Oral proof and circumstantial evidence had been freely accepted under French customary law, but article 232 of the 1866 Code required proof in writing to establish paternity – evidence not easily available in most cases. This change, along with the opening of charitable institutions for foundlings in Quebec City and Montreal after 1852, had the effect of removing most responsibility from men for their illegitimate offspring and placing it all on the mother. Only lying-in expenses (frais de gésine) could be recovered by the mother against the father on a virtual strict liability basis and with reduced evidentiary requirements. These changes had much to do with the appeal of the French example, where the *Code Napoléon* had forbidden paternity actions on the basis of a fear of women blackmailing men with such suits.[117]

Many of the women involved in seduction actions lived in rural communities where their families would take them back in their hour of need. This did not always happen with the increasing numbers of young women migrating to the cities in search of work, pleasure, and relationships. Finding oneself pregnant, unmarried, and poor in the city left a woman with few options, all of them unpalatable: abortion, giving up the child to an orphanage, paying to board it, or infanticide. At common law, abortion had not been considered a crime if accomplished before 'quickening,' around two or three months, but by Confederation most provinces had enacted laws making abortion a crime at any stage of pregnancy. This stricter position was taken into the 1869 consolidation of criminal law, which defined the crime as a felony with a maximum penalty of life imprisonment. However, if the woman died as a result of the abortion, the charge would be upgraded to murder, as any death occurring in the course of a felony was considered murder. Such a situation arose in the notorious abortion trial of 'Dr.' and Mrs. Arthur Davies in Toronto in 1875, when 23-year-old Jeannie Gilmour died after Davies performed an abortion. Both spouses were convicted of murder and sentenced to hang, but their sentences were commuted to life imprisonment, of which Alice Davies served five years and her husband 16. The *Criminal Code* of 1892 maintained the penalty of life imprisonment while making the woman herself liable to seven years' imprisonment, though no woman is known to have been charged under this provision. Unsurprisingly, given the desire of all concerned for secrecy, there are few accounts of such prosecutions. Generally, one was conducted only when the woman died as a result of the abortion, as with Jeannie Gilmour, or survived with serious medical complications, and in such cases the courts were severe on the offender.[118]

The severity with which abortion was viewed contrasted with attitudes towards infanticide, where judges and juries both empathized with the plight of women who felt obliged to take this extreme step. Prior to Confederation the colonies had created a lesser offence of 'concealment of birth' with a maximum penalty of two years' imprisonment, largely because it was difficult to prove that a newborn had died through human agency rather than from natural causes. This offence was reproduced in the 1892 *Criminal Code* and another with a more serious penalty was added, reflecting the increasing control the medical profession was seeking to exert over childbirth. Section 239 now made 'failing to obtain reasonable assistance during childbirth' a crime with a possible life sentence, if it could be shown that the woman's intent in forgoing assistance was that the child should not live. If she intended only to conceal the birth, the maximum penalty was still a stiff seven years. Yet acquittal rates remained high for prosecutions of both kinds, and sentences were relatively light upon conviction. Where, for example, an autopsy showed that the child of Quebec resident Denise D. had died from strangulation and skull fractures in 1910, she was prosecuted only for concealment and received a six-month sentence.[119]

While there is evidence of couples using artificial means of birth control in the later nineteenth century, social disapproval remained high and was reflected in section 179 of the *Criminal Code*, which prohibited the sale or advertisement of 'any medicine, drug or article intended or represented as a means of preventing conception or causing abortion.' Even feminist organizations did not advocate for access to birth control, and some began to participate in the discourse around 'race suicide' that emerged in response to a declining birth rate among whites in the later nineteenth century. Feminists advocated for male restraint as a means for women to space out their pregnancies, but moral suasion was a weak tool in the hands of most women. This was especially so when the *Criminal Code* defined rape for the first time in section 266 as 'the act of a man having carnal knowledge of a women not his wife without her consent,' or with consent vitiated by a variety of factors. While sexual crimes were being taken more seriously in the later nineteenth century, the assumption that marriage entitled the husband to unlimited sexual access to his wife was a backward step that, along with prohibitions on abortion and sale of contraceptive devices, impeded married women's efforts to control their fertility. The marital exemption also suggested that the husband had something like a property right in his wife's sexuality, analogous to the father's interest in his daughter's sexuality protected by the seduction action.[120]

The 1880s saw a dramatic increase in public and legislative attention to sexual offences, spurred on largely by concerns about the 'white slave trade' in which many young girls were thought to be employed. Other factors, both intellectual and material, were also at play, such as the increasing medicalization of sexuality with the emergence of the field of sexology, a term coined in the United States in 1867, and the presence of more single young women in cities, where their interactions with males could not be easily controlled. The definition of rape itself, outside the marital context, moved away from a preoccupation with reproduction, requiring penetration and emission, to a paternalist protection of women's sexual integrity. The 1869 consolidation of criminal law had included a provision deeming the act of rape to be complete 'on proof of any degree of penetration only,' one carried into the *Criminal Code*. As seen in chapter 13, Canada retained the death penalty for rape, but no one convicted of the crime was hanged after Confederation. Conviction rates for rape and related offences such as assault with intent to rape remained low. A study of prosecutions in York County, Ontario, between 1890 and 1930 shows that conviction rates varied inversely with the number of prosecutions brought. The moral panic of the 1890s around the white slave trade caused large numbers of prosecutions to be brought in response to public pressure. For many of these the evidence was weak, resulting in a high rate of acquittal. In the next decade, when many fewer prosecutions were brought more selectively, the conviction rate for rape (as opposed to lesser related offences) tripled from 7 to 23 per cent, while that for rape and lesser related offences doubled from 15 to 34 per cent. Even this rate meant that two-thirds of rape charges resulted in acquittals.[121]

A variety of other sexual offences added to the statute book in the 1880s and 1890s sought to protect young women from sexual predation. In 1886 seduction was criminalized for any girl of previously chaste character above 12 and under 16, and for any such unmarried female under 18 if under promise of marriage (raised to 21 in 1887), provided the male defendant was over 21. New offences in 1890 resurrected much older corporal punishments, following a North American trend. The age of consent for statutory rape was raised to 14 from 12 in 1890, rendering consent irrelevant for girls under that age. Those convicted faced imprisonment for a term ranging from five years to life and were liable to be whipped. Whipping was also a possible punishment for attempting the offence, and for the new offences of gross indecency by a male with a male or a female. Indecent exposure was criminalized in the same year for the first time, as was incest and seduction of a female ward or employee. While the protective impulse behind these measures was laudable in some respects, it also entrenched ideas about the passionless nature of women. And if such charges got to court, the treatment of female complainants, as in rape trials, sometimes featured stereotypical accusations of lying and blackmail and detailed probing into past sexual history. Such treatment, as well as legal barriers relating to corroboration and other evidentiary issues, kept conviction rates low. Much of the debate over sexual offences in the 1880s and 1890s was more theatre than law reform.[122]

Along with these new sexual offences came a new approach to prostitution, as moral reformers sought to replace the previous relatively tolerant approach to the 'social evil' with an unrelenting campaign to stamp it out. While legislators were reluctant to criminalize the act itself, they introduced a host of new offences relating to procuring, encouraging the defilement of young women, enticing women into prostitution, and the like. Provincial legislators got into the act as well, with Ontario, Manitoba, and Nova Scotia all passing laws that enabled judges to commit girls under 14 to institutions for delinquent girls if they were found 'wandering' or 'without salutary control,' aiming to reform them before they could fall into a life of prostitution. The most striking aspect of these new laws was their racial and ethno-religious discrimination. Not only were women from disadvantaged groups disproportionately charged with prostitution offences (Irish Catholic women in Toronto, Blacks in Calgary and Halifax, Asians in Vancouver), but the laws themselves began to encode these distinctions. The *Indian Act* was amended in the 1880s to address prostitution-related offences in several respects. It made the 'keeper of *any* house, tent or wigwam,' not just a bawdy house, guilty of an offence for suffering an 'Indian woman' to engage in prostitution-related activities therein. And an 'Indian woman [who] prostitutes herself' thereby committed an indictable offence, whereas such activity was rendered criminal for non-Indigenous women only indirectly via nuisance provisions that created summary conviction offences. A further *Indian Act* amendment in 1887 permitted the SG to withhold annuity payments from Indigenous women who 'lived immorally.' This replaced a provision that had allowed the SG to withhold annuity payments from Indigenous *men* who deserted their families.[123]

Roman Catholic women also found themselves singled out. Women of that faith convicted of vagrancy (the usual charge for prostitutes) in Nova Scotia were obliged to spend from one to four years in an institution run by the Sisters of the Good Shepherd, when the normal penalty at this time was six months in prison. A similar law of 1871 applicable only to Quebec did not specify religious affiliation but given the large majority of French-speaking Roman Catholics in that province, mostly women of that faith would have been consigned to the female reformatory prisons there. The law was concerned to distinguish between different types of female bodies but remained relatively uninterested in the demand side of the prostitution equation. Despite the best efforts of the moral reformers, the numbers of men charged with being customers in bawdy houses remained very low.

If legislators were attentive to the demands of moral reformers to protect the bodies of women, especially young, previously chaste women, from unwanted sexual interference, they responded with less alacrity to a parallel campaign to reduce the physical abuse of women by their husbands and domestic partners. Entering the domestic sphere that the reformers themselves had done so much to sacralize and sentimentalize was a more daunting proposition than protecting young girls from lustful men assumed to be strangers. The Woman's Christian Temperance Union (WCTU), which counted 10,000 members nationwide by 1900, was the most active group on the issue, clearly linking alcohol abuse and wife abuse in its campaigns. It made some headway, albeit slowly, in highlighting wife abuse as a public crime rather than a private misery to be endured or a legitimate exercise of marital 'rights.' An 1883 bill to imprison wife-beaters and make them liable to whipping died in Parliament, while an amendment to the *Criminal Code* to make wife-beating a distinct crime did not pass until a quarter-century later, in 1909. The provision was, somewhat oddly, tacked on to the indecent assault provision in the Code, making those convicted liable to the same punishment, up to two years imprisonment and possible whipping. The section was not limited to wives but referred to any man who 'assaults and beats his wife or any other female and thereby occasions her actual bodily harm.' Whether this change led to more effective protection for battered wives may be doubted, but its impact lies beyond the scope of this volume.[124]

Many men, and probably some women too, believed that husbands possessed a right of 'moderate correction,' as Blackstone had termed it, over their wives. This was widely considered a correlative to the wife's duty to 'obey' as articulated in the marriage ceremony but, unlike the position in Quebec civil law discussed in chapter 5, nowhere enshrined in positive law. The existence and extent of this 'right' was debated in the later nineteenth century as ideas of companionate marriage circulated more widely. Reformers sought to have the word 'obey' removed from the marriage ceremony, while in the celebrated English case of *R v Jackson* (1891), the Court of Appeal decided that a husband had no right to confine his wife or to physically discipline her. Reaction to the decision in the *Canada Law Journal* was mixed, some lauding the decision, others lamenting the seeming loss of the right of 'moderate correction,' but it has not been possible to discern whether *Jackson* had any measurable impact on the law or its implementation in Canada. Unless a judge positively directed a jury that a husband under no circumstances possessed a right to physically discipline his wife, their ability to render a verdict consonant with folk wisdom on the topic was unimpaired.[125]

A popular remedy with abused wives in Ontario was the protection order under the 1859 statute discussed in the first section of this chapter. A cache of 105 such orders made in Hamilton between 1860 and 1895 provides insights into the use of this device. Although directed mainly at ensuring that wives with absent or irresponsible husbands could support themselves by keeping their own and their children's wages, in practice most wives seeking such an order were from working-class families and had already fled abusive husbands with their children. An order could be obtained from a magistrate for $1.40, sparing the need for a woman to testify in the rowdy police courts. In granting a wife economic autonomy and, in effect, custody of her children, the protection order functioned as a more accessible analogue to the judicial

separation in Quebec. It remains to be seen whether it functioned similarly in other provinces with protection order regimes. Wife abuse was
also recognized expressly in an 1897 amendment to the 1888 Ontario
act for the maintenance of deserted wives noted earlier. The 1897 act
added that a married woman was deemed to have been deserted by
her husband 'when she is living apart from her husband because of
repeated assaults or other acts of cruelty,' or when he failed to supply
the necessaries of life. Attention to the issue of wife assault has tended
to focus on the difficulties in invoking the criminal law when it appears
that civil remedies, though far from perfect, were more accessible and
of greater practical utility to abused wives.[126]

16

Minorities and Civil Rights

Before Confederation the principal legal controversies in the area of minority rights concerned Catholicism and French language rights, which often went hand in hand. By 1867 both groups had achieved formal equality, and that equality was both confirmed and extended by the *BNA Act*. The French language had equal status with English in all operations of the federal Parliament, and minority language/religious educational rights in Ontario and Quebec were guaranteed by section 93. But issues concerning Catholic schools arose in this period, in New Brunswick and, most importantly and controversially, in Manitoba. This chapter deals with that question in the final section. Most of the chapter is concerned with ethnic minorities and illustrates the truth of Wilfrid Laurier's assertion that 'the people of Canada want to have a white country.'[1] We begin with the Chinese and Japanese, and with the British Columbia and the federal governments. Chinese and Japanese immigrants were entirely unwelcome to some in British Columbia and Ottawa, while to others they were accepted as cheap labour for dangerous work, but not as permanent immigrants. Exclusionary legislation, both federal and provincial, sought to bar East Asian immigration directly or indirectly. Other provincial legislation was discriminatory, treating Chinese and Japanese who were resident in the province very differently from the white population. There was some overlap between the two, because discriminatory legislation that was sufficiently onerous acted as, indeed was intended to be, exclusionary, a deterrent to further immigration. The distinction is nonetheless useful, and we have organized the first two sections of this chapter around these two themes.

The story told in these initial sections has one consistent theme – anti-Asian prejudice – and a number of subsidiary ones – a federal-provincial dispute over jurisdiction and, for a few brief years in the late 1870s and 1880s, a rift between the provincial legislature and the provincial judiciary over the substantive validity of discriminatory legislation. The BC Supreme Court struck down some of what the assembly enacted, the first time in Canadian legal history that a court held that parliamentary supremacy did not carry all before it, and to this day one of very few occasions that this was done before the advent of the *Charter of Rights* in 1982. There follows an account of exclusionary legislation, which implicated the Japanese as well as the Chinese and was also marked by a federal-provincial dispute about jurisdiction. Once the Japanese came into the story, international relations and Canada's subordinate place in the empire also became important. We also examine anti-Asian laws in other parts of Canada, especially Saskatchewan. The fifth section shifts the focus to South Asians and is set entirely in the twentieth century. The sixth section examines the legal treatment of another, much less numerous minority – Black Canadians. While the controversies over fugitive slaves ended with the northern victory in the US Civil War, Blacks faced unremitting racist prejudice and hostility in the new dominion – prejudice only occasionally mandated by law but at the same time never combatted by it.

The Chinese and Japanese in British Columbia: Discriminatory Legislation, International Relations, and the Courts and the Rule of Law

The vast majority of Chinese people living in Canada in this period resided in British Columbia, having either migrated north from California or journeyed across the Pacific to Canada's gateway to Asia.[2] The Chinese came in response to two major economic developments – the 1859 gold rush and the construction of the CPR in the 1880s. Immigration trailed off substantially once the railway through the Rockies was completed in 1885, but picked up again in the economic boom of the late 1890s. In 1867 the Chinese population in mainland BC was only about 2,000, but that was 40 per cent of the non-Indigenous population. Some had stayed when the gold rush was over, while others had arrived in the 1860s through recruitment schemes that brought people from Hong

Kong to Victoria via San Francisco. They worked in semi-skilled occupations, mostly in the mines and salmon canneries but also in sawmills, laundries, domestic service, vegetable gardening, road construction, and the like. Most importantly of all to employers, and a crucial part of understanding the legal story that follows here, the Chinese put up with long hours, seasonal work, and wage rates between half and two-thirds of what was given to white workers. The construction of the CPR through the mountains precipitated a wave of further Chinese immigration, some 15,000 entering BC between 1881 and 1885.

The Chinese were never welcome, never respected, and never considered an acceptable or desirable addition to the province. In this respect BC's history mirrored that of California.[3] As early as 1859 a Victoria newspaper asserted that they were 'not desirable as permanent settlers in a country peopled by the Caucasian race and governed by civilized enactments.'[4] The 'British' in 'British Columbia' was taken seriously by the vast majority of white British Columbians. White settler attitudes were often expressed in statutory preambles. The 1884 *Chinese Regulation Act*, for example, stated that the Chinese 'are not disposed to be governed by our law; are dissimilar in habits and occupation from our people; ... are governed by pestilential habits; are useless in instances of emergency,' and generally 'inclined to habits subversive of the comfort and well-being of the community.'[5] But despite these racist attitudes, no legal measures were passed against the Chinese before Confederation, and the 'Chinese question' was never mentioned in the negotiations that preceded BC's entry into the Union.

The coming of responsible government to the province with Confederation changed all this. Through the 1870s and early 1880s the BC assembly legislated to deny Chinese people many aspects of equality under the law, starting with the franchise. A franchise act of 1871 gave the vote to males 21 years old who were British subjects, had been resident in BC for six months, and met a property qualification. The province's first post-Confederation election saw the participation of Chinese voters in some districts. Almost immediately the new assembly disenfranchised 'Chinese or Indians,' although the act was reserved by Lieutenant Governor Joseph Trutch because he thought it might trench on the federal power over 'Indians' in section 91 (24) of the *BNA Act*. Ottawa gave its assent on the ground that the *BNA Act* gave the provinces the power to determine qualifications for the franchise. In 1874 and 1875 the province made it an offence for the officials compiling voting lists to place the name of any 'Chinaman or Indian' on an electoral register. In 1876 a further statute disqualified the Chinese from voting in municipal elections. Disenfranchisement had discriminatory spin-off effects; entry into a variety of professions, including law, was only for those with the vote.[6]

In 1878 BC passed its first piece of discriminatory legislation that went beyond denial of the franchise: the *Chinese Tax Act*. In the same year the Workingman's Protective Association was founded, with one of its principal objects being 'the mutual protection of the working class of British Columbia against the great influx of Chinese.'[7] The legislation imposed a discriminatory tax regime on the Chinese. Instead of paying taxes applicable to all as laid down in the *Assessment Act* and the *School Tax Act*, those statutes were declared inapplicable to the Chinese, 'large numbers' of whom supposedly 'evade the payment of such taxes,' and a 'more simple method' was adopted for the Chinese. It certainly was simple. Henceforth every Chinese person over 12 was required to acquire a licence, costing $10, every three months. It was not a tax on real property based on its value, or income based on what a person earned, or even on consumption, a sales tax. It was a poll tax, or head tax, an impost simply on being a Chinese person resident in the province. The *Chinese Tax Act* was struck down by Justice Gray of the BC Supreme Court, introduced in chapter 3, in a case discussed later in this chapter.

The Act was disallowed by Ottawa, after petitions to do so were received from a group of Victoria-based Chinese merchants and seven white salmon cannery owners, who argued that it offended the British constitution to tax people because of their ethnicity. They also claimed that it would destroy their business because 'Chinese labour is ... the only labour available for the prosecution of this business.' Canning needed to be done during the short period when the salmon were running, and non-Chinese would not work the long hours. The cannery owners also pointed out that some 1,500 white and Indigenous fishers would lose their livelihood if the canneries could not operate. The merchants' petition exposed a class divide among the white settlers, which always played a role in legislative responses to the 'Chinese question.' Employers and their allies blamed the 'popular cry against Chinese' on 'a class who have nothing at stake in the country,' that is, the non-propertied working class. There were few voices expressing respect for the Chinese, but employers wanted cheap labour while workers' groups added economic self-interest to their racial animosity. Federal Deputy Minister of Justice Zebulon Lash recommended disallowance, on the ground that, as discussed below, the BC Supreme Court had declared the Act ultra vires. It was one of 41 BC statutes disallowed between 1867 and 1911, 18 of them anti-Asian legislation.[8]

In 1884 two other pieces of discriminatory legislation were passed – a statute banning Crown land sales to, and the pre-emption of crown land by, Chinese, and another tax act. Sale and pre-emption of Crown land were how whites settled in the province, and thus the message was clear – the Chinese were not wanted for permanent settlement. The tax act required every Chinese person 14 and over to pay $10 annually in return for which they would receive a licence to remain. The fine for non-compliance was $40. The act included other provisions specifically aimed at the Chinese. For example, Chinese wishing to obtain a free miner's certificate had to pay $15, not the standard $5. Ottawa did not intervene in either of these statutes; Minister of Justice Alexander Campbell thought that the province had the authority to pass the land act and that the fate of the tax act should be judicially resolved.[9]

Further provincial legislation in the later 1880s and 1890s ran the gamut of ways to deny the Chinese equal rights. An 1885 amendment to the *Municipal Act* changed the business licence regulations previously in force so that anybody who kept a 'public washhouse or laundry' (virtually all of which were run by Chinese) was required to pay up to $75 every six months. Laundry licences had not been included in the regulations prior to this time, and most businesses that did not sell liquor had to pay much smaller licence fees. An 1888 act remarkable for its brevity forbade municipalities issuing pawnbrokers' licences to Chinese. A similarly brief and pointed 1890 amendment to the *Coal Mines Regulation Act* turned a child labour clause that boys under the age of 14 should not be employed underground into a child labour and anti-Asian clause, so that henceforth no boys under 14 'and no Chinaman' could be so employed. An 1888 Act allowing foreign mining corporations to register to operate in the province stated that no 'foreign Chinese company or association' could be registered.[10]

In 1895 the Japanese made their first appearance on the statute book, when they were excluded from the provincial franchise. The following year Japanese were similarly denied the municipal franchise, and in 1900 Vancouver's *Incorporation Act* specified that no Chinese, Japanese, or 'Indian' could vote.[11] Japanese migrants had first arrived in British Columbia in the late 1870s, and by the early to mid-1890s they numbered around only 1,000, the vast majority of them young men working in the Fraser River salmon fishery.[12] Their numbers grew significantly in the next few years, to about 4,500 in 1901, and double that by about 1911, some fishing, others turning to fruit farming, and yet others finding unskilled work in lumbering and saw milling. White British Columbians viewed them in broadly the same way that they viewed the Chinese (if indeed they could tell them apart). They had strange customs, spoke an unrecognizable language, tended to live in enclaves, and were considered not assimilable. The negative stereotypes of the Japanese were reinforced by the fact that many started small businesses, acquired land, and emerged as serious competitors, not just to the white working class but to white farmers and fishers. White British Columbians' image of the Japanese was 'peaceful penetration,' the 'quiet, relentless and insidious infiltration of Japanese immigrants into west coast society.'

The major legal assault on the Japanese came in the late 1890s, via their inclusion in two major employment discrimination statutes dealing with coal mines and public works. In 1897 the *Alien Labour Act* prohibited companies constructing and/or operating public works – railways, canals, bridges, turnpike roads, and telegraph lines were just a few of a long list – from employing Chinese or Japanese labour. This act was reserved by Lieutenant Governor Edgar Dewdney, and Ottawa decided simply to do nothing, given a protest by the Japanese consul-general in Vancouver, which left the act inoperative (we discuss Ottawa's response in more detail below). The statute was re-enacted the following year (renamed the *Labour Regulation Act*) with the offending clause included. In the 1898 legislative session 19 private acts of incorporation had the same clause added to them. In 1899 the process was repeated when the above-mentioned *Coal Mines Regulation Act* was amended to exclude Japanese as well as Chinese workers from working underground. Again, the same clause was added to a number of private act incorporations, this time of coal companies.[13]

Ottawa's approach to these employment discrimination statutes was cautious, the result of two contradictory pressures.[14] On the one hand, the statutes were arguably within provincial jurisdiction, being about local works and undertakings and the incorporation of companies with provincial objects. On the other hand, they could be characterized as trenching on the federal power over aliens and naturalization. As importantly, targeting the Japanese raised serious international relations concerns. After 30 years of modernization and industrial development following the Meiji restoration of 1868 Japan had become a significant economic power and a player in the geopolitics of the period. It had joined the ranks of the world powers, defeated a European nation, Russia, in the 1904–5 Russo-Japanese war, and posed a potential long-term threat to Britain's Asian empire. Most significantly for our purposes, it had a treaty with Britain that allowed nationals of each country to enter and reside in the other's territories. The discriminatory legislation was met with vigorous protests from Japan. When Dewdney reserved the *Alien Labour Act* the Japanese consul in Vancouver told Governor General Aberdeen that it was 'the most unjust and unfriendly measure ever taken by any civilized Government against a friendly nation.' Japanese officials were ironically concerned not only about the fact that Japanese were being discriminated against but also that they were being lumped in with the Chinese, given that, in the consul's words, 'it is a well-known fact [that] the education and character, customs and manners, of Japanese are entirely different from those of [the] Chinese.' Minister of Justice Oliver Mowat temporized, keenly aware of the diplomatic repercussions. Moreover, as the former premier of Ontario and effective leader of the provincial rights movement it is reasonable to think that he wanted to avoid using disallowance. He therefore advised doing nothing beyond expressing displeasure to Victoria about legislation concerning aliens. The act had been reserved and could not become law without royal assent. Standing pat would therefore have the same effect as disallowance.[15]

When the *Alien Labour Act* was re-enacted the following year as the *Labour Regulation Act*, thereby eliminating the word 'alien' from the title, the federal government procrastinated again. The new minister of justice, David Mills, wanted guidance from London about diplomatic relations with Japan but received an equivocal answer. Colonial Secretary Joseph Chamberlain did not sanction anti-Japanese legislation but also 'fully' appreciated BC's concerns and recognized 'the importance of guarding against the possibility of white labour in the province being swamped by the wholesale immigration of persons of Asiatic origin.' Ottawa did its best to bring British Columbia around, but the province was obdurate and the *Labour Regulation Act* was disallowed in November 1898. A year later the *Coal Mines Regulation Act* was also disallowed. Both were unacceptable to Ottawa principally because they would damage Canadian-Japanese and Anglo-Japanese relations, but it was also relevant, although not determinative, that they trenched on the federal powers relating to immigration and aliens. With one exception the private act incorporations were left as they were, because of the commercial confusion that would otherwise result from delegitimizing extant companies.

In the early twentieth century BC adopted a language test as a means of exclusion. A 1900 amendment to the public works employment legislation prohibited the employment of 'any workman' who could not read 'a language of Europe.' In 1901 and 1903 amendments to the *Coal Mines Regulation Act* specified English language proficiency for miners. As before, Japanese diplomats protested, one pointing out in reference to the coal mines act that it had been 'openly declared' in the provincial legislature that 'there was no use disguising the fact that the Bill aimed at the exclusion of … Orientals.' All these statutes were disallowed, the federal government seeing them as thinly disguised attempts to legislate on aliens and naturalization. For two years BC re-enacted the statutes annually, knowing that they would again be disallowed. Ironically the province's coal mining safety regulations were more advanced than health and safety legislation elsewhere in the country. As noted in chapter 13, it was in relative terms a good place to be a worker – as long as you were a white one.[16]

In addition to the federal government consistently exercising its disallowance power, five provincial statutes aimed at the Chinese were struck down by the BC Supreme Court between 1878 and 1888. The first case concerned the 1878 *Chinese Tax Act*. Twelve Chinese employers whose property had been seized for non-payment of the annual $40 tax/licence fee took their cases to the BC Supreme Court, where in *Tai Sing v Maguire*[17] the statute was struck down as ultra vires the provincial legislature by Justice John Hamilton Gray. At this very early period of courts grappling with sections 91 and 92, Gray thought his task was simple. A statute was within either one or the other, and the subsections of section 91 should be broadly defined, as 'extending to all matters coming within' them. As we saw in chapter 2, in this period he and other provincial judges viewed the *BNA Act* as a centralizing document that gave the provinces only limited authority appropriate for local governments. All residuary legislative power rested with the federal Parliament by the express terms of the opening paragraph of section 91. Gray relied largely on an 1862 California case, *Lin Sing v Washburn*,[18] which had dealt with a very similar statute enacted to protect white labour against competition and to curtail Chinese immigration. The California Supreme Court ruled the statute ultra vires because it trenched on the federal commerce power. Gray held that the same was true in Canada. 'Commerce,' he said, 'cannot be carried on without the agency of persons,' and a tax that limited 'personal intercourse' was 'a tax on commerce.' Indeed, Gray thought this even more true for Canada than for

California because in the United States the federal government only had the powers specifically given to it by the constitution. In Canada, by contrast, the provinces had only the powers specifically given them by the *BNA Act*. Gray cited other Canadian provincial court decisions on trade and commerce to the same expansive effect. This is not, of course, the current law on the trade and commerce power, and nor was it the view later in our period. But Gray was not an outlier in 1878; if anything, his was the dominant view. Gray's judgment discussed other issues as well, including Britain's mid-nineteenth-century treaties with China, which, even though they were effectively imposed on China, nonetheless gave each country's nationals the right to trade with and reside in the other's territory, and section 132 of the *BNA Act* required Canada to live up to Britain's treaty obligations. Gray also expressed distaste at the sweeping nature and underlying purpose of the *Chinese Tax Act*. It was a draconian measure not designed to raise revenue but to 'drive the Chinese from the country.'

In four further cases between 1885 and 1888 the BC Supreme Court struck down other provincial anti-Asian legislation. Two were solo decisions of Chief Justice Matthew Baillie Begbie, one was a solo decision of Justice Henry Pering Pellew Crease, and one was a decision of the full court, the court's newest member, John Foster McCreight, writing the decision for himself and Begbie, Crease, and Gray. Two of these decisions were based in part on a division of powers analysis. In 1885 in *R v Wing Chong* Crease struck down section 3 of the 1884 *Chinese Regulation Act*, which required every Chinese person to pay a $10 tax every quarter, on the grounds that it trenched on the trade and commerce and aliens and naturalization federal powers, as well as impeding Canada's ability to abide by the terms of Britain's treaty with China.[19] Even though his judgment could have rested solely on the division of powers, Crease went further. Section 28 of the act was a reverse onus provision, stating that in any prosecution under the act 'the burden shall lie on the defendant of proving that he is exempt from the operation of any of its provisions.' This, said Crease, 'reverses all the old law of England and one of the most cherished and priceless safeguards of the freedom from oppression won for us by our forefathers – that no one shall be deemed guilty until he has been proved so.' Everybody – 'white or yellow' – was entitled to 'the common law rights of the citizen.' He also said that the act 'looks like a bill of indictment as against a race,' and in discussing whether it infringed on the aliens and naturalization power he again invoked the principle of equality under the law.

In taxing and regulating a legislature could draw distinctions 'between and among different persons and occupations,' whether those persons where whites or not, but these were 'the only discriminations which the law allows.' The province had legislated in a way inimical to the equal rights of all residents under law.

The following year in *R v Mee Wah* Begbie CJ struck down section 11 of the 1885 *Municipal Act*, which required persons running a laundry business to pay a business licence fee of $150 a year, with the same mix of division of powers and rule of law analysis. Licences for laundries were not within the licensing power in section 92 (9) of the *BNA Act*, which was limited to 'shop, saloon, tavern, auctioneer, and other licences in order to the raising of a revenue for provincial, local, or municipal purposes.'[20] He also held that the statute subjected 'Chinamen to exceptional disadvantages,' which made it 'clearly unconstitutional.' As support for this conclusion he cited *Tai Sing v Maguire* and *R v Wing Chong*, as well as 'numerous decisions and arguments of Judges in United States Courts.' The United States had a different constitution, but 'the Judges in those foreign courts have had a much longer and more varied experience on these topics than ourselves; their institutions are closely analogous in many respects … [and] their opinions and reasonings … [are] founded on international law, and … on natural equity and common sense,' and as a result 'are entitled to great weight beyond the limits of their own jurisdiction.' Although his decision rested on the object of the statute being 'restriction [of the Chinese] and not revenue,' and interference with the federal power over immigration, he also stressed equality under the law: 'Any clause in a provincial statute or municipal by-law, which, though general in its terms, operates, or is intended to operate only upon one sect, race or class, is liable to be declared unconstitutional and void.'

The other two decisions of the court did not rely on the division of powers. The judges effectively decreed that discrimination against the Chinese was ultra vires the legislature. Section 14 of the *Chinese Regulation Act* of 1884, which set a higher cost for a free miner's certificate for Chinese than for others, was struck down in *R v Gold Commissioner of Victoria District*. In *R v Corporation of Victoria*, the section of the *Municipal Act* that forbade municipalities to issue pawnbrokers' licences to the Chinese, suffered the same fate.[21] In *Gold Commissioner* McCreight J's judgment cited *Wing Chong* and *Tai Sing v Maguire* simply for the fact that they had declared legislation unconstitutional and noted that their reasoning had not been seriously questioned in the argument. Rather, the government had argued that a free miner's licence was 'a privilege for going on lands of the Crown, and not like a store-keeper's licence.' McCreight was not persuaded, noting that it was not possible to operate as a free miner or to set up any kind of business in the goldfield region without a licence. Licences cost Chinese people more than whites, and 'it will scarcely be contended that such discriminating taxes would be constitutional.' Begbie's judgment in *Corporation of Victoria* was very similar, although he did make a fleeting reference to the trade and commerce power. The city's argument that the province had 'the right to eliminate nationalities or individuals from the capacity to receive … trade licences' had been 'entirely denied' by Gray, Crease, and himself in previous cases. None of those decisions had been appealed, and he could not 'disregard' them. He asserted that 'every person living under the protection of British law has a right … to exercise his industry and ability in any trade or calling he may select.' He further insisted that it was 'unnecessary even to state' the 'undoubted right, which is the boast of English law, that every person living under it has a right to his industry.' The prior cases decided by his court were based on the fact that the statutes in question were 'infringements at once of personal liberty, and of the equality of all men before the law.'

These judgments were remarkable, given that neither English nor Canadian law had a written rights-protecting constitution against which judges could test the substantive validity of legislation. They represented a 'short-lived period of judicial creativity in dealing with discriminatory, racist legislation.'[22] This creativity came in large measure from the personalities and judicial ideologies of Crease and Begbie in particular – ideologies that combined a traditional English belief in the rule of law with an acceptance of American, specifically Californian, judicial activism and economic liberalism. As discussed in chapter 3, the early British Columbia judges, Begbie and Crease, were hold-overs from the pre-Confederation period in which BC, though in northern North America, had nothing whatsoever to do with the central and eastern provinces to which it was joined in 1871.[23] Before 1871 BC did not have responsible government, and power lay with the official class whose natural ties were with Britain, not North America. Begbie and Crease were part of that official class and saw themselves as members of a providentially chosen leadership elite. As such the judges believed they had the right and duty to temper democratic excess when it clashed with what they saw as 'transcendent and enduring values.' Those values were principally tory paternalism, economic liberalism, and the rule of law – their idea of the rule of law embodying 'a set of underlying assumptions about the values of justice, the nature of law as the embodiment of reason, and how justice should be equally administered.'[24] Hence they variously drew on, using words from the cases, 'the common law rights of the citizen' and 'natural equity.' The *BNA Act*, while on its face concerned only with the division of powers, also included the rule of law. The BC judges did not consider the Chinese to be the moral equals of nineteenth-century Englishmen, but they were juridical equals.

The period of judicial creativity did not last long; Gray died in 1889, Begbie in 1894, and Crease and McCreight retired in 1896 and 1897 respectively. The judges who replaced them, and George Walkem, appointed in 1882 after the complement had been increased to five, were from different backgrounds – the provincial bar and provincial politics. In 1899 another anti-Asian statute was ruled intra vires by a differently constituted court, although that decision was overturned by the JCPC on division of powers grounds.[25] Three years later the exclusion of Japanese from the franchise was upheld by the JCPC, which made it clear that absent a division of powers argument the substantive validity of discriminatory legislation could not be challenged in court.[26]

Provincial and Federal Asian Exclusion Acts

The presence of increasing numbers of Chinese immigrants in BC in the 1880s led to repeated calls by BC politicians in Victoria and Ottawa for the federal government to curtail Chinese immigration – calls consistently and strenuously resisted by Macdonald's government. The Pacific railway was a key aspect of the national policy and was completed as far as Calgary by August 1883. But the most difficult section by far was the last, built from both the west and the east, through the succession of mountain ranges between the BC border and the ocean. Andrew Onderdonk, the principal contractor on the line through BC, told Macdonald in 1882 that over 8,000 men were needed, a workforce that could not be mustered 'without the Chinese.' Not having Chinese workers would delay completion of the railway for 12 years. Macdonald was persuaded, telling the Commons in 1882 that he did not want 'a Mongolian or Chinese population in our country,' that the Chinse race were 'an alien race in every sense' that 'could not be expected to assimilate with our Aryan population.' But the choice was simple: 'either you must have this labour, or you cannot have the railway.' He repeated the idea a year later: 'It will be all very well to exclude Chinese labour when we can replace it with white labour, but until that is done, it is better to have Chinese labour than no labour at all.'[27]

By 1884 things were looking different. The line was nearing completion, people in BC were aware that the Chinese workers were not going to return to China but settle in the province, in part because moving to the United States had been rendered nearly impossible by the 1882 *Chinese Exclusion Act*, and Macdonald had less and less need to resist provincial demands for legislative action. The province acted before the always-willing-to-wait-until-tomorrow Macdonald, in February passing an *Act to Prevent the Immigration of Chinese*.[28] A few months later, in response to a motion that the federal Parliament legislate to at least severely curtail further Chinese immigration, Ottawa established a royal commission on the question. The motion came from one of BC's most virulently anti-Chinese MPs, Noah Shakespeare, member for Victoria, former head of the Workingman's Protective Association, and founder of the Anti-Chinese Association. He did not want people in his province 'with their cheap and dirty mode of living and their capacity for living in swarms, in wretched dens where a white man would drop if he did not suffocate.' They were 'the lowest type of humanity,' 'slaves and criminals,' 'heathens' whose 'immorality … renders [them] … the most undesirable class to have in the province.'[29] The commission had just two members, both Macdonald supporters: John Hamilton Gray and Joseph Adolphe Chapleau, former premier of Quebec and now federal secretary of state.[30] The commissioners were to consider 'all those moral considerations which it is alleged make Chinese immigration undesirable.'[31] The government was much less interested in whether Chinese immigration should be restricted than in how that should be done. Macdonald parroted what BC politicians had often said: 'They are not of our people, they are not of our race, they do not mix kindly with us, and they do not even become settlers.' But he wanted to know the international relations and trade consequences of immigration restrictions, how much Chinese labour would continue to be needed by the CPR, and how cognate jurisdictions – California and Australia – had handled the 'problem.'

While the commission gathered evidence and opinions, Ottawa had to deal with the BC legislation, an eight-section statute baldly stating that it was henceforth 'unlawful' for any Chinese person 'to come into the Province of British Columbia, or any part thereof.' Violators were to be fined $50 or, if in default, imprisoned with hard labour for up to six months. There were similar penalties for anybody assisting a Chinese person to enter. Two classes were exempted: Chinese employed on ships where the total number of Chinese employees in the crew did not exceed 20, and 'bona fide' Chinese residents of BC who wished to be 'absent … for a temporary purpose.' They could re-enter the province if before leaving they obtained a certificate of exemption. The act was disallowed by Ottawa, although not with any great confidence. As discussed in chapter 2, the *BNA Act* included three areas of concurrent jurisdiction, outside sections 91 and 92. One was education, dealt with later in this chapter. The other two were agriculture and immigration, in section 95; a province could legislate in regard to 'immigration into the province.' Section 95 also had a repugnancy clause; provincial immigration legislation was valid 'as long … as it is not repugnant to' any act of Parliament. The preamble to BC's 1884 Act reproduced section 95 and asserted that it was 'not repugnant to any Act of the Parliament of Canada.' Whether or not it was repugnant to the 1869 *Immigration Act*, Justice Minister Alexander Campbell thought that section 95 gave the provinces only the power to promote and regulate immigration, not to prohibit it. In addition, such a prohibition potentially engaged imperial interests. In these circumstances, and because he found personally distasteful a measure that 'clearly discriminates against the Chinese,' Campbell recommended disallowance. It turned out that London said that its relations with the Chinese government did not require it to object to the act. In fact, it had already approved Australian legislation to the same effect.[32] But by then the die of disallowance was cast.

The following year both jurisdictions passed Chinese immigration legislation. BC's was an act of defiance, being substantially identical to the act disallowed the previous year. That defiance was expressed in a letter from the BC assembly criticizing the disallowance of the previous year and asserting that the need to prohibit Chinese immigration had not diminished:

The Chinese are alien in settlement and habits.… They do not become settlers in any sense of that word.… The Chinese population chiefly consists of male adults, and thus without the responsibility of providing for a family, they come in unfair competition with white labour. They are the slaves or coolies of the Chinese race, accustomed to live on the poorest fare and in the meanest manner, and hence their presence tends to the degradation of the white labouring classes.… They have a system of secret societies, which encourages crime among themselves, and which prevents the administration of justice.

'We urgently request,' the assembly concluded, aware that the legislation would probably be disallowed again, 'that some restrictive legislation be passed, to prevent our province from being completely over-run by Chinese.'[33]

The federal government again disallowed the legislation. Its action was not formalized for almost a year, by which time Ottawa was in an even stronger legal position, for it legislated on the question in July 1885. The Royal Commission reported in February 1885 and recommended imposing a $10 poll tax on Chinese immigrants, rather than a prohibition, because the Chinese were still needed. 'There is not in the province of British Columbia the white labour to do the required work,' it insisted, yet 'the work must be done or the country must stand still.' The commissioners preferred therefore a 'moderate' policy of restriction. The government's response was the 1885 *Chinese Immigration Act*, now one of the best-known pieces of legislation in Canadian history. Its centrepiece was the 'head tax' imposed upon Chinese immigrants, set at $50, five times more than the commission had recommended. The head tax applied to 'every person of Chinese origin' seeking to enter Canada, with some class-based exemptions for diplomats, merchants, and students. It also limited the number of new immigrants arriving by boat to one for every 50 tons of the boat's size. Substantial fines and/ or imprisonment were to be paid by individual immigrants and ship's captains who evaded the regulations. The same $50 levy was to be paid by any Chinese arriving by land. The act did not apply to Chinese residing in Canada who wished to leave temporarily and then return. They had to acquire a certificate of residence.[34]

In the debate over the bill Chapleau took the lead for the government, arguing that barring Chinese immigration altogether would be poor policy. He resisted some members' stereotypes, insisting that the Chinese were honest, brave, industrious, and as 'civilised' as white people. Hence the government did not want to bar the Chinese, just to limit their numbers and ensure that Canada only received people who could afford to pay the tax. Shakespeare thought the bill was better than nothing and would have preferred a ban on immigration, and he was joined in condemnation by the other member for Victoria, Edgar Crow Baker, who accused Chapleau of the crime of being pro-Chinese, said that the Chinese had 'a low scale of morality,' and asked if any member

THE PROPOSED CHINESE WALL.

The "proposed Chinese Wall" was the head tax of $500 that all Chinese persons wishing to enter Canada were required to pay from 1905. The head tax was $50 when this cartoon was published, but some people were lobbying for it to be raised.

Credit: *Globe and Mail*, 19 September 1896.

would like to live in the same room as a 'Chinaman.' When another MP interjected with 'yes,' Baker replied, 'You would? Then there is no accounting for taste.'[35]

The head tax legislation achieved its purpose very effectively, being amended only to exempt Chinese wives of non-Chinese residents of Canada and people travelling through Canada to some other destination.[36] In 1900 the head tax was doubled, to $100, and the fines and other penalties for non-compliance were also increased. According to Prime Minister Laurier the head tax had discouraged Chinese immigration for some years, but the numbers were rising again with the economic boom that began in the late 1890s. In 1886 only 211 Chinese had paid the tax, in 1897 roughly 2,500 did so. BC had pressed for an increase to $100 regularly since 1885, and in the later 1890s upped that demand to $500. Laurier argued that it would provide 'substantive justice' to the people of British Columbia to increase the tax. At the same time he announced the establishment of another royal commission, to look into both Chinese and Japanese immigration and a further increase in the tax. Three years later, following the report of the commission, the tax was raised to $500. The head tax legislation remained in force until 1923.[37]

In 1900, not having legislated to exclude Asians since its 1884 and 1885 statutes had been disallowed, BC re-entered the field with an act that did not refer to any ethnic group in its title. As had been done 15 years earlier, the statute's preamble reproduced section 95 of the *BNA Act*. Section 3 sought to do through the backdoor what had been tried and failed by the front, stating that it was 'unlawful' for a person to enter BC if he or she could not 'write out and sign, in the characters of some language of Europe,' an application to do so. Heavy penalties – a maximum fine of $500 or imprisonment for up to a year – were prescribed for violators. In addition, anybody who did enter the province by evading the act was barred from obtaining a licence to carry on any trade or profession, from acquiring land, from voting, and from getting a free miner's certificate.[38] By using the European language requirement the province sought to curtail Japanese as well as Chinese immigration. The legislation was certain to be disallowed, and was, on two grounds – it was a transparently obvious device to legislate in an area that the federal government had occupied, and because it applied to, although it did not name, Japanese people. Like the discriminatory legislation of the 1890s the *Immigration Act* was met with vigorous protests from the Japanese government, which could not be ignored because Japan brought all the diplomatic pressure it could on both Canada and

Britain.[39] Minister of Justice David Mills thought the language test 'not perhaps a very severe one,' but as the federal Parliament had legislated it was not 'desirable that the uniformity of the immigration laws should be interfered with by special provincial legislation.' He recommended disallowance, adding that an additional reason for doing so was the representations of the Japanese government. There followed a play in six additional acts, of the theatrical genre known as farce. Every year between 1902 and 1908, with the exception of 1906, the province passed the act, and every time Ottawa disallowed it.[40]

Ultimately the 'Japanese problem' was resolved by an international agreement in 1907.[41] But this did not prevent a vicious outpouring of white anger against Asians in Vancouver the same year. A substantial number of Japanese contract workers arrived to work for corporations that had recruited them in Japan. This only intensified anti-Asian sentiment, and later that same year a rally organized by the Asiatic Exclusion League turned into a full-scale riot in which thousands of whites ran amok, terrorizing Chinese and Japanese residents and destroying large amounts of property. The federal government dispatched the deputy minister of labour, William Lyon Mackenzie King, to Vancouver to report. In the end it effectively gave up its tepid resistance to racism and negotiated an agreement with Japan to limit immigration.[42]

Anti-Chinese Legislation: White Women's Labour Laws

British Columbia was not the only part of northern North America to legislate in a discriminatory manner towards Asian people. Newfoundland was still a British colony in this period and thus free to enact its own Asian exclusion legislation. It did so in 1906, copying the federal head tax scheme to the tune of $300. The same kinds of people were exempted as under the federal legislation – diplomats, clergymen, scientists, and students. A British subject who brought a Chinese servant with him had to pay, but the tax would be refunded on evidence that the servant was living with the employer.[43]

Other Canadian provinces besides BC passed discriminatory laws against Asians at the end of our period. Saskatchewan was the first to do so, disenfranchising the Chinese in 1908 and legislating in 1912 to prevent any business run by 'any Japanese, Chinaman or other Oriental person' from employing 'any white woman or girl.' An immediate protest from the Japanese consul in Vancouver citing the 1907 Treaty, and consequent federal government pressure, persuaded the province to amend the act by striking out the words 'Japanese' and 'other oriental person,' leaving only 'Chinaman.' The act stayed on the books until 1919, applicable to the thousand or so Chinese residents of Canada's third most populous province.[44] It was the product of attitudes we are familiar with – the largely single white male Chinese community were seen as gamblers, drug takers, and clients of prostitutes, disregarding and disrespectful of Canadian laws and morals. What made this alien presence especially dangerous to the Saskatchewan legislators, and the proximate cause of the legislation, was the white slave trade, the mythical but pervasive belief that 'orientals' would inveigle away white women and turn them into prostitutes. Saskatchewan's lead was followed by Manitoba in 1913, with an act identical to the original Saskatchewan statute, and Ontario in 1914. Municipal by-laws were passed in all these provinces, and in Quebec, to the same effect and/or to limit the operation of Chinese laundries. British Columbia, perhaps surprisingly, did not join in in the 'protection' of white women until 1919.[45]

The Saskatchewan statute gave rise to a case before the SCC, *Quong Wing v The King*.[46] Quong Wing, a naturalized British subject, ran a restaurant in Moose Jaw at which he employed two white women as waitresses. He was convicted and fined $5 by a magistrate, and unsuccessfully appealed to the Saskatchewan Supreme Court, Haultain JA dissenting on division of powers grounds. With the support of the local Chinese community he took the case to the SCC, where he again lost, four to one, Justice John Idington dissenting. Fitzpatrick CJ could not discern any significant difference between the *Female Labour Act* and provincial health and safety legislation. The two other judges who wrote in the majority all stressed two points. First, that there was no division of powers problem because the statute made no distinction based on naturalization, but on ethnicity, or as the court termed it, race. Second, the fact that it drew this distinction provided no grounds for a court to intervene. Davies J, for example, stated that once he had found the act to be intra vires the provincial legislature 'I cannot inquire into its policy or justice or into the motives which prompted its passage.'

Idington's dissent, though narrow in scope, was clearly motivated by his distaste for discriminatory legislation. He did not find the statute ultra vires, he found that it did not apply to Quong Wing because he was naturalized. He conceded that the word 'Chinaman' in the statute could be interpreted to mean all Chinese people, naturalized or not, but it could equally well not mean that. Given that, as it was a penal statute it should be construed narrowly, even if that meant departing from the plain words approach to statutory interpretation. The important question, therefore, is how Idington J reached the conclusion that the statute was not intended to apply to naturalized Chinese. Section 12 of the *Naturalization Act,* discussed in chapter 2, provided that a naturalized person was 'entitled to all political and other rights, powers and privileges ... to which a natural-born British subject is entitled.' Provincial legislatures could vary most of the political rights, but 'the "other rights, powers or privileges" of natural-born British subjects ... shared by naturalized British subjects, do not so clearly fall within the powers of the legislatures to discriminate ... as between classes or sections of the community.' Idington did not say which rights and privileges could be impaired and which could not, but they might include 'the highly prized gifts of equal freedom and equal opportunity before the law.' Idington asked if a legislature could introduce slavery and make naturalized subjects slaves, and continued, without answering his rhetorical question, to note that the *Female Labour Act* was a 'product of the mode of thought that begot and maintained slavery.' The broader point was that the rights given to naturalized subjects by the *Naturalization Act* were a guarantee of 'equality of freedom and opportunity,' and the *Female Labour Act* was ultra vires as applied to naturalized persons. He thus combined an exercise in statutory interpretation with the kind of rhetorical appeal to equality before the law voiced by the BC Supreme Court judges over twenty years before. He also observed that 'in a piece of legislation alleged to have been promoted in the interests of morality, it would seem a strange thing to find it founded upon a breach of good faith which lies at the root of nearly all morality worth bothering one's head about.'

It is not clear why Idington took this position. He is remarkable for his rapid ascent to the SCC, having been appointed to the Ontario High Court in March 1904 and to the SCC only eleven months later, and for being forced to retire against his will at the age of 88 in 1927 when Parliament enacted the first mandatory retirement legislation for SCC judges. More importantly, he was also known as a frequent dissenter and contrarian, often in the pursuit of laissez-faire liberal principles. It is likely that he disliked racist legislation for the same reason that he objected to regulation of the economy. Both offended his sense of 'British justice' and the rule of law. In this respect he was unusual, for many economic liberals could be intensely socially conservative.[47]

South Asians: Indirect Exclusion

Chinese and Japanese were not the only Asian people who were unwanted in Canada in this period. A small number of South Asians, almost all young men, mostly from the Punjab province of British India and predominantly followers of the Sikh religion, came to British Columbia in the late nineteenth and early twentieth centuries, brought by shipping companies and labour contractors looking to recoup their losses when the head tax took away Chinese business.[48] They found work as labourers in sawmills, lumber camps, and on railway construction in the lower mainland, and remitted their savings home to enable their families to increase their agricultural holdings. Given the seasonal nature of the work, they experienced periodic unemployment. A familiar story unfolded. Employers appreciated their work ethic and willingness to work for less than whites, organized labour saw them as a threat, and they were disenfranchised.[49] Racist and cultural prejudice resulted in vigorous campaigns in Victoria and Ottawa to at the very least severely restrict their numbers, especially after nearly 5,000 arrived in 1906–7. Even though they tended to move to the United States quite quickly, their expanded presence was one of the reasons that the latent simmering racial hostility towards Asians had exploded in 1907 in the Vancouver riots. In 1908 King, who had investigated those riots, recommended restrictions on Japanese immigration and on immigrants from India.[50]

By this time the federal government was perfectly willing to respond to anti-Asian pressure from BC and early in 1908 passed an Order in Council under the *Immigration Act* giving the minister of the interior the right to make regulations to prevent immigrants from landing in Canada 'unless they come from the country of their birth, or citizenship, by a continuous journey and on through tickets purchased before leaving the country of their birth, or citizenship.'[51] This created a problem for both Japanese and South Asians. The majority of Japanese came to Canada via Hawaii. For South Asians the problem was more than the cutting off of the preferred and established route. Few ships could make such a 'continuous journey' for that distance, invariably stopping at Japan or Hawaii. The regulation also required that immigrants bring with them a minimum of $25. The Order in Council did not long survive, challenged by a shipping company and being struck down two months later by Justice William Henry Pope Clement of the BC Supreme Court because section 30 of the *Immigration Act* gave the power to make the regulations to the governor general, not to the minister of the interior.[52]

The government responded in two ways. In April 1908 the *Immigration Act* was amended to authorize the governor general, 'whenever he considers it necessary and expedient,' to, inter alia, prohibit the landing in Canada of 'immigrants who have come to Canada otherwise than by continuous journey from the country of which they are natives or citizens and upon through tickets purchased in that country.'[53] Specific mention was made of 'Hindus' in the House of Commons, and Frank Oliver, MP for Edmonton, minister of the interior, and a keen supporter of large-scale immigration so long as it was white, emphasized that the amendment would allow the government to more easily deport 'undesirable' immigrants. The only way to turn back undesirables was to make them return on the ship that had brought them, but if that ship had not come from the immigrant's home country the undesirable could not be 'returned' that way.[54] This was a transparent subterfuge, because the issue was not deportation but preventing immigrants arriving in the first place. The government then repassed the January 1908 Order in Council without a reference to the minister of the interior, and upped the $25 requirement to $200 for all 'Asiatic immigrants.'[55] The government also pressed steamship companies not to provide a direct service from India to Canada or to sell through tickets in India. The rationale for the policy was that Canada was looking for 'immigrants of an agricultural class to occupy vacant lands,' and 'immigrants from Asia' were generally from 'labouring classes' and their 'language and mode of life' made them 'unsuitable for settlement,' especially because there were 'no colonies of their own people to ensure their maintenance in case of their inability to secure employment.' The unsuitability of migrants from hot countries to northern North America was a common trope among those who advocated immigration restrictions.

Both the continuous journey and the $200 requirements were stopgap responses to what was emerging as a serious problem for Ottawa. Canada could not simply ban immigration from the 'jewel in the crown' of the empire. There had already been vigorous protests from New Delhi when the Dominion of Australia, the colony of New Zealand, and some of the South African colonies enacted substantial restrictions on non-European immigration in the late nineteenth and early twentieth centuries. New Delhi's concern was not altruistic, as the Indian nationalist movement was gathering strength and would inevitably exploit any indication that Indians were discriminated against elsewhere in the empire. A Colonial Office minute of 1907 neatly summed up the 'problem' of South Asian immigration, to Canada and other parts of the empire: 'The whole subject is perhaps the most difficult we have to deal with. The colonies wish to exclude the Indians from spreading themselves all over the empire. If we agree, we are liable to forfeit the loyalty of the Indians. If we do not agree we forfeit the loyalty of the Colonists.'[56] King, who was seen as an expert on 'oriental' questions, having written the report on the 1907 Vancouver riots, became the government's point man as a flurry of consultations with London took place in 1908.[57] Laurier looked for a way both to live up to Canada's obligations as a member of the empire – a matter of the 'highest importance' – and to stop the flow of South Asian immigrants. He also claimed that migration to Canada was not good for South Asians, people 'wholly unsuited to this country' because they were 'accustomed to … a tropical climate.' South Asian immigration would cause 'much suffering and privation' to the migrants at the same time as it would 'result in a serious disturbance to industrial and economic conditions of the Dominion, … especially in … British Columbia.' Laurier's views about the economic conditions of South Asian migrants were shaped by King's report, which had said that many were unemployed and impoverished.

The $200 and continuous journey regulations were effective – between 1910 and 1920 only just over 100 South Asian immigrants arrived in Canada. The regulations were re-enacted in 1910 when the *Immigration Act* was consolidated, the continuous journey regulation known as PC 920 and the $200 requirement as PC 926.[58] Punjabi politicians and organizations did not quietly accept the situation but lobbied persistently in Ottawa, London, and New Delhi, and took cases to court. They had a breakthrough win in November 1913 when Chief Justice Gordon Hunter of the BC Supreme Court overturned an Immigration Department order for the deportation of 38 Sikhs.[59] They had come to Canada via Japan on a regularly scheduled Japanese liner, the *Panama Maru*, and been ordered deported because of the continuous journey rule and because they were not carrying $200. Hunter's decision was not based on any concern about the substance of the regulation. In response to an argument that Parliament knew that making a continuous journey was impossible, and that therefore the regulation was 'a subterfuge to place a ban on Hindus as a race,' Hunter said that courts were not concerned with 'questions of expediency and good faith,' but only with the 'validity and interpretation' of the regulation as a valid exercise in delegated legislation. Turning to that question, he found that PC 926 was invalid for two reasons, one of which was wrong and neither of which concern us here. He similarly found a problem with PC 920 – it did not use the word 'naturalized' before 'citizens,' which the Act did.

Faced with a deluge of white nativist protest, the federal government, now headed by Conservative Robert Borden, responded by quickly rewriting the regulations to meet the court's objections, and early in 1914 the continuous journey and $200 requirements were back in force. But before and after these events in Canada, a wealthy Sikh, Gurdit Singh Sirhali, had organized and financed an immigrant voyage of Sikhs to go to Canada from Hong Kong.[60] Their ship, the *Komagata Maru*, sailed from Hong Kong in April 1914 with 150 passengers. Others joined at ports in the Philippines, China, and Japan, and when it left Japan for the long trans-Pacific leg there were 376 passengers on board. The passengers had certain common characteristics that shaped events when the ship reached Vancouver. They were all Punjabis, the vast majority Sikhs, and all but six were young men. Almost all of them were from middle-class merchant backgrounds, and they did not bring their families because they were intent on exploiting the economic opportunities in British Columbia and remitting their money to extended families in the Punjab. They were also a politicized group, resentful of British rule over India, and these sentiments only grew stronger during the long weeks at sea through lectures and meetings organized by Sirhali. A number of their fellow Punjabis already in British Columbia also held strong anti-imperial feelings and were outspoken proponents of Indian nationalism. Although it was known that the exclusionary immigration regulations were back in force, Sirhali and other principals believed they could mount another successful court challenge. Alternatively, they relied on public opinion among Sikhs in India putting enough pressure on New Delhi, and then on London and Ottawa, to rescind the restrictions. Key to this political calculation was the fact that the massive British Indian army had long comprised a substantially disproportionate number of Sikhs, and it was hoped that dissatisfaction among those troops would persuade imperial authorities that there was some risk to the security of the empire.

The *Komagata Maru* dropped anchor in Vancouver harbour in late May 1914, and the passengers were met with a local population apoplectic at the prospect of the floodgates opening to immigrants from India and a Canadian government completely unwilling to compromise. Only 25 or so people were allowed ashore, mostly returning residents. The vast majority were confined to the ship throughout their two months in harbour. The government tried to force the ship to leave – limiting

Passengers on the *Komagata Maru*.

Credit: Vancouver Public Library.

communications with the outside world, refusing to supply food and water until things became desperate, and, on one occasion, trying to seize control of the ship with a boarding party of the local police force. But the passengers were not entirely alone. South Asians, mostly Punjabis, in Vancouver persuaded officials to allow a case to go to the courts to test the legality of the detention. The chambers judge refused the application for a writ of habeas corpus, and the recently created British Columbia Court of Appeal upheld that decision.[61] The applicants made arguments based on parsing the statutory language. They contended that the *Immigration Act* permitted regulations prohibiting the landing 'of immigrants of any specified class, occupation or character,' pursuant to which the government had enacted a regulation banning artisans and labourers, but the principal applicant, Munshi Singh, was a farmer. The Court of Appeal deferred to the finding of the Immigration Department that Singh came under the regulation. It could also have said, but did not, that the continuous journey regulation was sufficient to exclude in any event.

The court proceedings took place against a background of virulent local protest. If 300 could not be kept out, how could 300 million, the *Vancouver News Advertiser* expostulated, because they would all be able to make the same claim? A local Methodist magazine stressed profound and irredeemable differences between peoples. The 'social and moral aspects' made 'Asiatics ... so different that the two races are really incompatible.' Any attempt to 'fuse them as a common people is useless and would inevitably result in a lowered standard of civilization.'[62] The *Komagata Maru* left in late July with 355 passengers on board, under the watchful eye of Canadian naval vessel HMS *Rainbow*. By the time it reached the Indian port of Budge Budge near Kolkata on 29 September the First World War had begun. The continuous journey regulation stayed in force until 1947.

Black Canadians

In many respects the story of Black Canadians' legal experience during this period is one of stasis. Blacks remained a very small part of the Canadian mosaic, their numbers not augmented by an influx such as had occurred before 1860 with escaped slaves moving north or much earlier with the arrival of slaves and former slaves given their freedom in return for fighting with British forces. Indeed Canada's Black population decreased in this period, as many Blacks in Ontario returned to the northern states once the Civil War was over and as an equally significant proportion of the population joined the general exodus from the Maritimes in the late nineteenth century.[63] There was a brief upsurge in Black immigration in the first decade of the twentieth century, discussed later in this section, but the federal government acted decisively to curtail a further influx. Canada's Blacks were concentrated in the historical Black townships in rural Nova Scotia, 'Black districts' of Halifax, Montreal, and Toronto, and urban centres and rural townships in southwestern Ontario. The title we employed for one of the chapter sections in *Volume 1*, 'Not Slaves, but Not Equal,' remained apposite. The half-century after Confederation was the nadir of the Black experience in Canada; with the drama and turmoil of the Civil War over, Blacks in Canada were 'virtually forgotten, and they would not be a noticeable part of Canada to the non-Black population until the 1950s.[64]

Canada did not have Jim Crow laws – state-mandated residential segregation in housing, public services, and the like – except, as discussed in *Volume 1* and below, for segregated schools. At the same time two related themes dominated the lives of Black Canadians. First, they were a group of people living on the margins of society, disrespected, often despised, deprived of opportunity in every facet of social and economic life. Examples of racist social attitudes to Blacks abound. None is better known than the reason John A. Macdonald gave for retaining the death penalty for rape, noted in chapter 13. Macdonald epitomized racist attitudes in the new dominion: Blacks were almost sub-human, unable to control an animal instinct to rape. Such ideas were reinforced by emerging notions of 'race science,' which placed Black people on the lowest rung of the evolutionary scale.

While Blacks were not governed like their counterparts in the Jim Crow post-bellum southern United States, the law did nothing to assist them, to prevent private action against them. That private action ranged from threats of physical violence and actual violence to deter civic participation and generally cow this unwelcome minority, to being refused service in a host of establishments. Formal legal equality did not mean freedom from race-based restrictions. Canadian cities with Black populations had a distinct district where Blacks lived.[65] The proprietors of restaurants, bars, and other places of entertainment, landlords, homeowners, real estate agents, and transport operators, those who ran hospitals, orphanages, and cemeteries, simply refused to serve, rent to, sell to, employ, admit, or even bury Blacks, and the law permitted this, on the grounds that freedom of property and contract could not be interfered with. Employment opportunities were limited, with one of the few jobs available to the Black community being sleeping car porters on the railways.[66]

Very rarely did such discriminatory practices reach the courts. An exception was the suit brought in 1898 by Frederick Johnson, a black bellhop at Montreal's Queen's Hotel, who was able to buy two tickets in the orchestra section for a concert at the Academy of Music the following evening. When he and a lady friend turned up the usher refused to seat them, because house policy restricted Blacks to the dress circle. Johnson refused to comply and the couple were forcibly ejected. Johnson sued in Superior Court for $50 damages and won. Justice John Sprott Archibald, who had been a leading counsel and professor of constitutional law at McGill, denounced such 'invidious regulations' as 'a survival of prejudices created by ... negro slavery.' In language reminiscent of the early British Columbia judges, he insisted that 'our constitution ... does not admit of distinctions of races or classes. All men are equal before the law and each has equal rights as a member of the community.' Justice

Archibald also found a breach of contract, via an analogy with the civil law rule that a hotel was obliged to receive every traveller who arrived needing accommodation. Although the damage award was upheld by Queen's Bench, only the breach of contract holding was sustained. The court called the discrimination argument irrelevant.[67] In the few other similar cases judges found liability for breach of contract if a ticket had been bought, but no duty to sell the ticket in the first place. Indeed, in one Ontario case the damages were 25 cents, the cost of the ticket. The reliance on freedom of contract and a refusal to entertain broader considerations of anti-discrimination amounted to de facto if not de jure Jim Crow. The racism of the southern United States was 'a creation of social customs and legal support,' with the latter to the fore. In Canada 'the balance tipped towards Jim Crow as a function of social custom, while the law passively supported it.'[68]

What follows in this section is an account of Blacks and the law, not focused on the racism of the vast majority of the white population but necessarily written with an appreciation of it to the fore. In many ways it is an account of the law's silence, and silence always poses challenges for the historian. We deal here with the few areas where the law did, one might say, break that silence and speak. In turn we will look at segregated schools, the criminal justice system, and immigration policy. Segregated schools were endemic in the provinces with the largest Black populations: Ontario and Nova Scotia. Nova Scotia law had permitted the establishment of separate schools and the exclusion of Blacks from other schools by communities since 1836, but in the 1880s this regime was modified following protests to one in which segregated facilities could continue but Blacks could not be excluded from public schools in the district in which they lived. This had the not insignificant effect of making high school education available to Blacks. Nova Scotia Blacks invariably framed their claims to equality with reference to their British citizenship and the equal rights under the law that that entailed.[69]

In Ontario the *Common Schools Act* of 1850, which required any local government to establish a separate school for Protestants, Catholics, or 'coloured people' if 12 or more families resident in the area asked for one, stayed in force throughout this period. It was amended in 1869 only to limit the distance that any Black child had to go to school to three miles.[70] As noted in *Volume 1*, there were many separate schools established for Black children at the request of Black residents, not because they wanted separate schools as such, but because they wanted schools to which their children were guaranteed entry and in which they would not face daily disparagement and attempts to drive them away by white teachers and pupils. Half a loaf was better than no loaf or a mouldy loaf.

This point is illustrated by an 1883 case from Windsor.[71] Jane Anne Dunn had attended a separate school that had been unilaterally established by the school trustees, in violation of the legislation. That fact was not mentioned by Justice Thomas Ferguson when he heard an application by Dunn's parents for a mandamus compelling James Duncan, headmaster of the Public Central School, to admit her. Duncan had refused on the ground that there was no room for Jane. Justice Thomas Ferguson of the Chancery Division dealt with the case as a simple one involving the transfer regulations. These required a child registered at one school to stay at that school unless the school inspector and the trustees approved a transfer request. No such request had been made, and the court found the no vacancy argument supported by the evidence, and for both reasons refused the application. Ferguson J referred briefly to Jane's father's contention that 'the real reason for not admitting his child ... was that she is a coloured child,' but he found no evidence of that. Thus once a Black child had gone to a separate school the act and its regulations governed transfers, even if the act did not permit the separate school to be established in the first place without the approval of the Black members of the community. The court ignored earlier cases, one of which is discussed immediately below, which had held that without a properly established separate school Blacks had equal rights to common schooling.[72]

The Dunn case demonstrates that some Blacks did not accept the legitimacy of segregation and were prepared to try to combat it in court. It also makes clear that many white residents simply did not want Black children in the common schools and established separate schools within or without the legislative provisions. The racist attitudes of most white residents of areas with a Black population are starkly revealed in an 1871 case, *Re Hutchison and St Catharines School Board*, which also demonstrates that the courts were at times compelled to follow the law in favour of Blacks.[73] The town had established a school for Black children in 1846, before the *Common Schools Act* was amended to permit separate schools. Hutchison, a St. Catharines resident since 1855 and presumably a refugee from the United States, took his son Richard to the common school for the district and tried to register him there. He was rejected, the teacher asserting that he would not have a Black child, and the school trustees were equally open about their objections. Hutchison took the trustees to Queen's Bench, where they argued that there was a separate school that had always been well patronized by the local Black population and that all the other schools in the district were overcrowded. If the separate school was closed, they would be even more so. They supported their case with an affidavit from a physician to the effect that sending all the Black children to common schools 'would be attended with evil consequences from a sanitary point of view.' The trustees' arguments boiled down to the need for Hutchison père (his name is never mentioned) to know his place. His community had been treated fairly by having a separate school voluntarily provided, and his attitude was disruptive and the logical extension of his argument – all Black children could attend the common schools if they wished – would cause nothing but trouble. Justice Joseph Morrison held that because the separate school had been established before the permissive legislation was passed Hutchison had the right to send Richard to any local school. His judgment was a statement that Blacks were formally equal under law. But it did nothing to detract from the fact that separate schools were the norm and that that was the way the overwhelming majority of whites wanted it.

The limited research that has been done on Blacks and the criminal justice system in this period has shown that it reflected broader social attitudes. For all crimes, from vagrancy to murder, Blacks were more likely than whites to be arrested and prosecuted, more likely to be convicted, and more likely to receive harsher sentences. The only area where there was equality was in commutation decisions, as shown in chapter 13.[74] The ideology of equality under the law meant that it was often said that the legal system did not treat Blacks differently from whites, but such statements have to be regarded with caution. They were often invoked in high-profile cases involving serious crimes like rape and murder, and such statements were used to highlight the superiority of British justice over the extra-legal terror tactics often deployed in the southern United States. In the south a Black accused of a serious crime was lynched, in the Queen's dominion he was tried and convicted before being imprisoned or hanged. As we saw in chapter 13, the criminal justice system operated through formal legal rules overlaying many discretionary decisions made at every stage of the legal process. Policing authorities, prosecutors, and trial juries all exercised discretion that was opaque and did not require to be justified or explained.

Finally in this section we examine immigration law and policy. Blacks were never welcome as immigrants in this period, as some who sought to homestead in Saskatchewan and Alberta in the late nineteenth and early twentieth centuries discovered.[75] They came mostly from Oklahoma, where they had moved after Reconstruction ended in the older southern states and white supremacy reasserted itself through segregation and extra-legal violence. They found the same racism when they homesteaded in the Oklahoma territory, where white antipathy would lead to the destruction of the entire Black quarter of Tulsa in 1921 with the loss of dozens of lives. Blacks were attracted to Canada by advertisements placed in American newspapers for homesteaders to move north to the prairies. Very quickly the Canadian government moved to discourage this particular aspect of the migration: 'It is not desired that any negro immigrants should arrive in Western Canada,' Ottawa bluntly told its Kansas City agent in 1899. Arrive they nonetheless did, a few settling in the major cities of the Territories but most taking up homestead land and forming communities in Maidstone, Saskatchewan, and Amber Valley, Wildwood, Lobstick Lake, and Breton, Alberta. The best-known was John Ware, who accompanied the herds of cattle that were brought to southern Alberta by the area's early ranchers and established his own ranch south of Calgary. It did not take long for the inevitable reaction to appear. Newspapers ran articles about the danger Blacks posed, arguing that they did not assimilate, were unsuitable for the climate, and discouraged white settlers by their very presence.

The federal government responded with administrative measures. It stopped advertising in Black communities and subjected Blacks to unusually stringent medical checks at the border.[76] In 1911, with many thousands of Blacks nonetheless having arrived, Ottawa also resorted to law. An Order in Council banned Black immigration for a year, on the familiar rationale that Blacks were 'unsuitable to the climate and requirements of Canada.' The order was rescinded just two months later because Blacks had in any event stopped arriving, deterred by other measures taken and the hostility they encountered, word of which reached Oklahoma carried by, among others, agents of the Canadian government.[77]

Rekindling an Old Fire: Religious and Linguistic Minorities

Conflicts between the two principal branches of the Christian faith ran deep and wide in nineteenth- and early twentieth-century Canada, frequently, although not invariably, linked to linguistic animosities. Much of the sectarian animosity that afflicted the Canadas in the Union period was solved by the creation of two provinces from one colony in 1867,

and the guarantee of minority religious rights to education in Ontario
and Quebec in section 93 of the *BNA Act*. A similar guarantee was provided in the *Manitoba Act*. Nonetheless, religious and linguistic disputes
still infused society, politics, and law. Denominational schooling was
first an issue in this period in New Brunswick. Before Confederation
the province had a system of publicly supported non-sectarian parish
schools for young children. Education for older children was run by
the churches, principally the Catholic and the Anglican Churches, with
the former also operating francophone schools catering to the Acadian
community. In 1871 the provincial government enacted a thoroughgo-
ing reform, setting up a province-wide system of non-sectarian public
schools funded principally by property taxes and administered by a
provincial Board of Education.[78] The churches, especially the Catholic
Church, fought the act, asking Ottawa to disallow it on the basis of section 93 (1) of the *BNA Act*, which, while making education a matter of
provincial jurisdiction, also protected from provincial legislation 'any
right or privilege with respect to denominational schools which any
class of persons have by law in the province at the union.' The federal government refused to intervene in a matter of provincial jurisdiction because it did not believe that any group in New Brunswick had a
pre-1867 right to denominational schools 'by law.' The Catholic lobby
received essentially the same answer from both the provincial Supreme
Court and the JCPC: the denominational school system in New Brunswick was not established by law. The only legally sanctioned and state-
supported schools were the parish schools.[79]

The New Brunswick case was important locally, but it never became
a national issue. A similar dispute involving religion and language in
Manitoba did. The Manitoba schools crisis was 'one of the most ... divi-
sive issues ever to challenge the Canadian nation.'[80] To appreciate the
legal issues we must begin with the *Manitoba Act*, discussed in chapters 7 and 14, and section 22 in particular, which began by giving the
province the power to 'exclusively make laws in relation to education,'
a replication of the language of section 93 of the *BNA Act*. Like section
93, section 22 also contained limits on what a future provincial legislature could do. Subsection 1 provided that no provincial law could
'prejudicially affect any right or privilege with respect to denominational schools which any class of persons have by law or practice in the
Province at the Union.'[81] This broadly mirrored section 93 (1) of the *BNA
Act* but with the very important difference, noted above, that section 93
(1) protected rights to denominational schools established 'by law in the

province at the union.' Unlike section 22 of the *Manitoba Act*, it did not protect rights enjoyed 'by law or practice' at the union. The additional words 'by practice' made the Manitoba dispute different from the New Brunswick one.

Subsections 2 and 3 of the *Manitoba Act* section 22 went on to prescribe remedies for breaches of section 22 (1). Section 22 (2) provided an appeal to the governor general 'from any act or decision of the legislature of the province ... affecting any right or privilege of the Protestant or Roman Catholic minority ... in relation to education.' This was very similar to section 93 (3) of the *BNA Act*, which provided for an appeal to Ottawa in nearly identical language. The principal difference between the two was that under section 93 (3) the appeal was predicated on 'a system of separate or dissentient schools' existing, whereas the *Manitoba Act* simply referred to 'any right or privilege ... in relation to education.' A second distinction was that section 93 (3) specified that for there to be an appeal a denominational school system had to 'exist by law at the Union' or be 'thereafter established by the legislature of the Province'; section 22 (2) said nothing along these lines. Section 22 (3) provided a further remedy in the event that an appeal to the governor general succeeded but the province failed to remedy the default. In that case Parliament could enact 'remedial laws' to enforce the governor general's decision – laws that went 'as far only as the circumstances of each case require.' Again, this had its counterpart in section 93 (4) of the *BNA Act*. Both provisions were highly unusual in that they permitted the federal government to legislate in an area clearly within provincial jurisdiction.

The *Manitoba Act* also protected language rights, in section 23. Both French and English were made official languages, so that everyone had the right to use either in debates in the provincial assembly and in the courts. The proceedings of the assembly also had to be recorded in both languages. As we saw in chapter 7, sections 22 and 23 were part of the broad compromise hashed out in 1870 to end the Riel resistance and bring Manitoba into Confederation. They also reflected the equal linguistic and religious representation in the nascent province. By 1890 that balance had shifted dramatically. Two decades of immigration had increased the population from about 25,000 to over 150,000. A large proportion of the immigrants were Protestants from Ontario, and at the same time, as we saw in chapter 14, significant numbers of the Métis moved west to what became Saskatchewan. A combination of these two factors meant that in 1890 only 13 per cent of non-Indigenous Manitobans were Catholics and only 7 per cent were francophones.

The Manitoba school system, first established in 1871, was run from 1875 by a 21-member Board of Education, comprising a Protestant board of 12 members and a Catholic board of nine.[82] The province was divided into school districts, with most of the districts either exclusively or very largely Catholic or Protestant. In only eight school districts was the population both mixed and with sufficient numbers of each denomination to make separate schools economically feasible. There were separate schools in an additional four thinly populated districts with a mixed population. Schools were funded solely by a provincial grant until 1881, part of which came from transfers from Ottawa. Thereafter they were funded partly by the grant and partly by school taxes, with adherents of each denomination required to support their denomination's schools and exempted from being taxed for the other system.[83] Increasingly in the 1880s Protestants criticized the system as unfair and wasteful, mostly because the provincial grant given to Catholic schools represented a higher per capita expenditure on the Catholic population than that given to Protestant schools. But the real thrust of the critique was the very existence of separate schools and the fact that they helped to keep intact a separate community of francophone Catholics in Manitoba, a province that the increasing numbers of Protestant anglophones saw as their preserve.

In 1890 this system was abolished by the Liberal government of Thomas Greenway and replaced by a non-denominational public school system. A Department of Education and a seven-person advisory board were established. Four of the members were to be appointed by the Education Department and two elected by teachers. The advisory board's regulatory powers covered all aspects of public schools, including 'the forms of religious exercises to be used in schools.' Another statute, the *Public Schools Act*, permitted 'religious exercises' but limited them to 'just before the closing hour in the afternoon.' Parents could have their children opt out of such exercises. The statute was unequivocal about not wanting education and religion combined: 'The Public Schools shall be entirely non-sectarian, and no religious exercises shall be allowed therein' except for those held just before school closing. All property owners had to pay a tax to support the public school system, whether a person had children or not and whether or not he or she chose to send children to a public school. The *Public Schools Act* was almost an exact replica of the Ontario schools legislation. The assembly passed another statute on the same day as the *Public Schools Act*, one making English the sole official language of the province.[84]

There is an extensive literature on the origins of the 1890 acts, from which two principal points can be made to contextualize the ensuing legal battles.[85] First, the Manitoba schools question was part of a broader series of events that involved Quebec's relations with the Dominion. They included the execution of Riel, the coming to power in Quebec in 1887 of the Parti national (effectively the Liberal Party) led by Honoré Mercier, which had a nationalist orientation, and the imbroglio over the *Jesuit Estates Act* passed by that province in 1888 to restore lands once held by the Jesuits to the order.[86] That '[t]he relations between French and English-speaking Canadians' has been 'the most permanent theme in Canadian history' is a statement both obvious and profound, and the decade between 1885 and the coming to power in Ottawa of Laurier's Liberals in 1896 saw a succession of crises around this 'permanent theme.'[87] Second, while the Manitoba schools issue was played out against this background, it was very much a home-grown affair. It was influenced by opinion in Ontario, but that influence was largely indirect, transmitted through the many thousands of Ontarians who had moved west since 1870.

Local resentment at the amount of money spent on Catholic schools simmered from the late 1870s onwards and in the 1880s gained impetus from Territorial ordinances enacted between 1884 and 1887, which entrenched a similar system in the Territories.[88] Increasingly a belief took hold that the future of the Prairie west lay in cementing its status as not just anglophone but also as a loyal region of a dominion within the empire. As the Rev. George Bryce stated in a sermon given at Knox Presbyterian Church in Winnipeg in 1889, Manitoba was destined to be a 'British province' in which the 'civil and religious liberties' contained in the 1689 Bill of Rights must be upheld. Education was central to this vision, a key to creating a homogenous people united under one flag. Manitoba Attorney General Joseph Martin argued in an assembly debate over the 1890 act that '[t]here is no subject of greater importance to the people than ... education.' A year earlier he had conflated education, language, and loyalty in expressing his view at a public meeting that French was 'a foreign language' and all Manitobans should speak 'the language of the country.' In addition, it was argued that Catholic schools were simply not good schools, this assertion being linked to the language of instruction and the denominational divide. James Smart, provincial minister of public works and later the deputy SG under Clifford Sifton, produced statistics in the assembly purporting to show that in countries where education was controlled by the Catholic Church the literacy rate was lower than where national, non-denominational schooling was provided. The government expected a court challenge to the *Public Schools Act*, for on the same day that it received royal assent another statute was passed permitting the lieutenant governor to refer any issue to the Court of Queen's Bench.[89]

The French Catholic community in Manitoba had three options for fighting the legislation.[90] It could petition the federal government to disallow it, and although considerable lobbying for disallowance was conducted by the archbishop of St. Boniface, Alexander Taché, whom we last encountered during the 1869–70 Riel resistance, and James Émile Pierre Prendergast, a one-time Laurier loyalist in Quebec who had emigrated to Manitoba in 1882, this was a long shot. Macdonald knew that disallowance would anger Protestant Ontario, not just for religious reasons but because Oliver Mowat's provincial government played the leading role in the provincial rights movement. He rejected all efforts to persuade him to intervene. For similar reasons Macdonald had no interest in a second option, an appeal to the federal cabinet under section 22 (2) of the *Manitoba Act*. In any event he thought that the *Public Schools Act* was unconstitutional and would be found so in court.

That left the Manitoba Catholics with the third option, the courts, to which they resorted in late 1890, with a case taken by John Kelly Barrett, a Catholic resident of Winnipeg who had been assessed on the value of his real estate to pay school taxes. The central legal issue was simple. The *Public Schools Act* obviously affected Catholics' claim to a separate school system, whether one characterized it as a 'right' or a 'privilege.' But did Catholics have either in 1870? They could not have had it 'by law' because there was no school system established by law in 1870. But it could be argued that they had it 'by practice,' because the Catholic Church had established schools for Catholic children before 1870, and Protestant denominations had done the same. Barrett's application to quash the Winnipeg taxing by-law was initially heard by Justice Arthur Clements Killam of Queen's Bench, who rejected it, and was then reheard by the full court, a panel of three judges.[91] Chief Justice Thomas Wardlaw Taylor and Justice John Farquhar Bain upheld Killam, but Justice Joseph Dubuc, the only francophone on the court, dissented. Dubuc, discussed in chapter 7, was one of the first Québécois to travel west to support the Métis after the 1869–70 resistance. With Joseph Royal, a Quebec lawyer and journalist who had also been recruited by

Taché, Dubuc founded a French language weekly, *Le Métis*, in St. Boniface, was a member of the first provincial assembly and later a federal MP, and encouraged Québécois to emigrate to Manitoba. He knew the history of schools in Manitoba intimately, having served as a Catholic member of the Board of Education. He was a political conservative and in the 1870s distanced himself from Riel before being appointed to the bench in 1879.[92]

In the principal judgment upholding the *Public Schools Act* Taylor CJ devoted many pages to a comparison of section 22 of the *Manitoba Act* and section 93 of the *BNA Act*, from which he concluded that in drafting the *Manitoba Act* Parliament had not intended to give Catholics the same rights that section 93 gave to Catholics and Protestants in Ontario and Quebec. Had it intended to, Parliament would have said so in the *Manitoba Act*. Moreover, the fact that it had not simply incorporated section 93 meant that Parliament intended that Manitobans should be left to settle the issue for themselves. While doing so Parliament had 'naturally' included a provision in the *Manitoba Act* to ensure that the existing rights would not be abrogated by future legislation. Having decided that section 22 had not simply incorporated section 93 into the *Manitoba Act*, the next question was, what did section 22 do? It protected existing 'rights or privileges,' but were there any, and what were they? To answer these questions Taylor CJ returned to section 93. Section 93 (1) of the *BNA Act* and section 22 (1) of the *Manitoba Act* both protected 'any right or privilege with respect to denominational schools which any class of persons' had 'at the time of union.' If they were worded almost the same, they meant the same thing. Neither section meant Catholics or Protestants, they both meant 'any class of persons.' This was the interpretation given to section 93 (1) by the New Brunswick courts and the JCPC in the early 1870s. Taylor CJ stressed that the judge who delivered the principal opinion for the New Brunswick Supreme Court had been William Johnstone Ritchie, now the chief justice of Canada, and Ritchie's opinion had been confirmed by the JCPC. The flaw in Taylor's reasoning, of course, was that the two sections were worded very similarly but were not exactly the same. Section 22 (1) had two additional words, 'or practice,' after 'law.' Taylor went on to find that no community in Manitoba had a 'right or privilege' with respect to denominational schools 'by law' at the time of the Union. But he did not discuss practice.

Dubuc J wrote a long dissent. 'The whole question,' he asserted, 'turns on the construction of the words "or practice"' in the *Manitoba*

Act. They meant 'that the denominational schools, existing as a matter of fact at the time of the Union, were given by these words a legal *status,* so that they could not be interfered with by the Provincial legislature.' He argued that because in 1870 there were no laws protecting denominational schools as there had been in Ontario and Quebec before 1867, 'the words "or practice" were inserted in the Manitoba Act for only one and very manifest purpose,' to protect denominational schools of any group 'who might in the future find themselves in the minority.' Dubuc J supported this conclusion by discussing what 'privilege' the Catholics could be said to have had in 1870 if he was wrong. It was the 'privilege' of paying taxes for schools from which they received no benefit and then paying more money to support the schools they wanted. This was 'a very strange privilege indeed,' and while the legislature did have the authority to pass any, even 'unjust or absurd enactments,' it was unreasonable to think that Parliament had done so in 1870, had 'disregard[ed] and set at naught the well-known principles of natural justice and equity.' Dubuc J's final argument in his well-reasoned and powerful dissent drew on subsections 22 (2) and (3) of the *Manitoba Act.* Why provide for an appeal in case of a denial of a right or privilege if nobody in the province had one?

Dubuc's dissent convinced Manitoba's Catholics that they would win on appeal, and they eagerly took their case to Ottawa. At about the same time the federal government put through Parliament an amendment to the *Supreme Court Act* allowing it to direct a reference regarding 'the appellate jurisdiction as to educational matters vested in the Governor-in-Council' by the *BNA Act* or any other Act.[93] Shortly afterwards the SCC overturned the Manitoba court unanimously, a 5:0 decision from two Quebec judges and three from English Canada of Anglican and Presbyterian backgrounds.[94] Although their reasons were different in various respects, all judges homed in on the words 'or practice' and insisted that the only way to make sense of their inclusion was to hold that the factual if not the legal existence of a denominational school system on the ground before 1870 gave rise to a right or privilege that could not be undermined thereafter.

The victory was short-lived. A year later the JCPC overturned the SCC, having heard the case along with an appeal of *Logan v City of Winnipeg,* a suit launched by an Anglican angry at the SCC's decision and who argued that adherents of the Church of England also had a right to separate schools. The Court of Queen's Bench agreed, holding that Episcopalians were a 'class of persons' whose rights to denominational education had been 'prejudicially affected.' The JCPC overturned that decision as well, holding that section 22 was not infringed because the *Public Schools Act* did not compel any child to attend and allowed any group to establish and fund its own denominational school system. In what by the 1890s had become a standard mantra of the JCPC, it acknowledged that the issue before it was 'of serious moment' to Manitoba, and 'a matter of deep interest throughout the Dominion.' But as a legal question it was a matter of 'very narrow compass.' All the court had to do was find the 'true construction' of the *Manitoba Act*. Lord MacNaghten's 'true construction' of 'or practice' in section 22 was in fact somewhat baffling. On the one hand, these words must have been inserted to respond to the fact that prior to 1870 Manitoba had no laws 'properly so called.' On the other hand, the words were 'evidently … not to be construed as equivalent to "custom having the force of law."' Why this was 'evident' MacNaghten did not say, a surprising omission given that he had just acknowledged that the words were there because there was no formal state law. Nonetheless, having so comprehensively rendered 'in practice' effectively meaningless, it was easy to say that Catholics had only the right, along with everybody else, to establish and maintain denominational schools at their own expense.[95]

The JCPC decision in *Barrett* has been much criticized for its failure to give any meaning to the words 'in practice' and for its general lack of knowledge about Canada.[96] But such criticism, even though it was voiced at the time, did nothing for Manitoba's Catholics. Their only recourse was a section 22 (2) appeal to the federal cabinet. Led by their counsel in all the cases, John Skirving Ewart, a legal scholar of considerable ability and repute whom we discussed in chapter 6, and Archbishop Taché, they sent numerous petitions to Ottawa asking to invoke that appeal. In 1892 a subcommittee of the cabinet heard Ewart's arguments for the Catholic side and early in 1893 recommended that Manitoba be invited to present the other side. Manitoba, insistent that *Barrett* had settled the question, refused to do so.[97]

By this time the country was under different political leadership. Macdonald won his last majority in the March 1891 general election, but then died in May. He was succeeded by a reluctant John Abbott, whose legal career was discussed in chapter 6. Previously minister without portfolio, his brief tenure ended when he resigned for health reasons in December 1892. His successor was John Sparrow David Thompson, born a Presbyterian but a convert to Catholicism soon after he broke with convention and married a Catholic – a nineteenth-century 'mixed' marriage.[98]

Thompson, who features in chapter 13 as the architect of the *Criminal Code*, was personally sympathetic to the Catholic position, but the politics of the dispute were delicate. He moved cautiously, directing a reference to the SCC pursuant to the 1891 amendment to the *Supreme Court Act*. Ewart was again lead counsel for the Catholic side, with Frederick Wade, an Ontarian who had moved to Winnipeg in 1883 and equally prominent as a lawyer and advocate for Greenway's Liberal government and for English language public school education, appearing as counsel for Manitoba. On the Manitoba government's instructions Wade declined to make any arguments. The court appointed Christopher Robinson, son of John Beverly Robinson, lead prosecutor of Louis Riel, and frequently counsel for the federal government in constitutional cases before the SCC and the JCPC, to argue Manitoba's case.[99]

Five of the court's six judges heard the case; the sixth, Robert Sedgwick, had been appointed in 1893 and prior to his appointment had worked on the case in his capacity as deputy minister of justice. Six questions were asked, which effectively boiled down to whether the Catholics had a valid appeal under section 22 (2) of the *Manitoba Act*, which in turn required the court to find that a 'right or privilege … in relation to education' had been affected by the *Public Schools Act*. By a narrow majority of 3:2 the Court found there was no appeal available. Télesphore Fournier from Quebec and Edward King from New Brunswick were the two who found for the Catholic position. Fournier was critical of the JCPC in *Barrett* but was able to find his answer without resting his decision on that. *Barrett* had decided that no right or privilege existed at the 'time of union,' the words used in section 22 (1). Section 22 (2) did not contain those words, and thus Fournier found that an appeal could concern any local statute that derogated from rights enjoyed since 1870. Fournier thought it 'evident' that between 1870 and 1890 Catholics 'enjoyed the immunity of being taxed for other schools than their own, the right of organization, the right of self-government in this school matter, the right of taxation for their own people, the right of sharing in Government grants for education.' All these rights were taken away by the 1890 legislation. Thus, there was not only a right of appeal but, he thought, the power to pass remedial legislation, which he considered should be exercised. Fournier's opinion was perhaps not surprising, given that he was a francophone, and it was also in line with his Canadian nationalist belief, discussed in chapter 2, that appeals to the JCPC should be abolished. King said essentially the same thing, emphasizing the rights given in an 1881 Manitoba statute that empowered the

Catholic board to tax Catholics to maintain their schools and gave them an exemption from taxation for Protestant schools.

Henri-Elzéar Taschereau from Quebec and John Wellington Gwynne from Ontario came to the opposite conclusion, on the ground that they were bound by *Barrett*. That case had decided that Manitoba Catholics had no rights under section 22 (1), and section 22 (2) was an appeal from a denial of section 22 (1) rights. *Barrett* therefore precluded any appeal. Taschereau was not persuaded that section 22 (2) applied to post-1870 'rights' as enacted by local legislation. The *BNA Act* gave the provinces jurisdiction over education, and jurisdiction meant the power to legislate and to repeal legislation: 'It cannot be said that by adopting a system of separate schools, though not obliged to do so, they, forever, bound the future generations of the province to that policy.' It is tolerably clear that Taschereau, although not Gwynne, disagreed with the JCPC in *Barrett*, but he clearly also believed in *stare decisis*. Also arriving at a conclusion adverse to the Catholic position was Chief Justice Strong, whose reasoning was similar to Taschereau's.[100]

The SCC decision was appealed to the JCPC, which heard the case, named *Brophy*, late in 1894 and gave judgment early in 1895.[101] The Catholic position was again argued by Ewart, assisted by another leading light of the Canadian appellate bar, former minister of justice Edward Blake. Somewhat surprisingly, the JCPC found that a right of appeal did exist under section 22. In a single decision written by Lord Chancellor Herschell, the court cast some doubt on its own decision in *Barrett*, noting that it had 'narrowly restricted the protection afforded' by section 93 (1) of the *BNA Act*. That *Barrett* had 'narrowly restricted' rights was 'the inevitable result of the application of sound rules of construction.' On the question before it, the JCPC also employed what it thought were 'sound rules of construction,' homing in on the differences in wording between subsections 1 and 2 of section 93. The former referred to the right of 'any class of persons' to 'denominational schools' in 1867. The latter referred to 'the Protestant or Roman Catholic minority' and to a right or privilege 'in relation to education,' and specified no point in time. It would, the court concluded, 'do violence to sound canons of construction if the same meaning were to be attributed to the very different language employed in the two sub-sections.' Thus section 22 (2) was a 'substantive enactment,' not just a way to enforce section 22 (1) rights.

The *Brophy* decision, rendered almost five years after the *Public Schools Act* had been passed, thrust the Manitoba schools question firmly back into the political sphere. The prime minister was now Mackenzie Bowell, Thompson having died of a heart attack in December 1894 at Windsor Castle just after being knighted by the Queen, and a few weeks before the JCPC handed down its decision. Bowell was the country's third Conservative prime minister after Macdonald, an election was pending in 1896, and Bowell was in no position to introduce remedial legislation under section 22 (3) with the issue still controversial and the subject of heated emotions. He opted for another round of hearings before a cabinet committee held in late February and early March 1895. Dalton McCarthy and John Ewart made the arguments for each side. The cabinet found for the Catholic side: Roman Catholics in Manitoba had been deprived of their rights by the *Public Schools Act*, and the governor general should ask Manitoba to enact remedial legislation. On 21 March 1895 the remedial Order in Council was issued, asserting that the Catholics should have the right to 'build, maintain, equip, manage, conduct and support Roman Catholic schools, in the manner provided for by the said statutes which were repealed by the two Acts of 1890.' Premier Greenway was unmoved, however, and at the end of June Manitoba's official reply was received – the remedial order was ultra vires.[102] By then Charles Tupper had replaced Bowell as prime minister after a cabinet revolt.

If Manitoba would not act, then section 22 (3) allowed the federal Parliament to do so, and in February 1896 a remedial bill was introduced. It was modelled on the *Public Schools Act* but provided for the appointment of a separate Catholic school board. Catholics who wished to support separate schools were allowed to tax themselves for that purpose and were exempted from taxes for the public schools. Filibusters by an alliance of Liberal MPs and radical Protestants led by D'Alton McCarthy prevented its passage, and the government asked for a dissolution. The resulting June 1896 election was won by Laurier with a substantial majority. There were a number of factors responsible for the Conservative defeat, but a split in the Conservative Party over the Manitoba schools question was very significant. Everywhere their new leader Charles Tupper spoke he was heckled and interrupted by those strongly opposed to French Catholic rights. Laurier quickly negotiated a compromise with fellow liberal Greenway, the provincial government making three large concessions. First, that the teaching of religion was to be carried on between 3:30 and 4 p.m. each day, by any Christian clergyman when authorized to do so by a resolution of the local board of trustees or requested by the parents of 10 children in a rural or twenty-five in an urban school. Second, at least one Catholic teacher was to be employed in each urban school. Third, when 10 of the students in any school spoke French as their native language, the teaching of such students should be conducted in French and English. This settlement met with wide approval, and the dispute that had disturbed Canadian politics for more than half a decade was, at least temporarily, put to rest.

When Alberta and Saskatchewan became provinces in 1905, the acts creating them contained clauses similar to section 93 of the *BNA Act* and did not include the additional phrase 'or practice' that had become so controversial in Manitoba. These acts further clarified that the separate school rights to be protected were those – and only those – found in chapters 29 and 30 of the 1901 *Ordinances of the Northwest Territories*. The relevant sections set out a simple process whereby any three residents of a district (implicitly, those belonging to the minority religion in that district) could petition for a separate school. A vote would then be held in which only those of that religion would be able to vote. The 1905 Acts stated expressly that in the distribution of school monies by the province, 'there shall be no discrimination against schools of any class described in the said chapter 29' (that is, separate schools). These provisions seem to have worked well. When controversy next arose in Canada over schooling, the issue was language, not religion. In response to a rising tide of pro-British and anti-French sentiment, stimulated partly by the movement of large numbers of francophones into eastern and northern Ontario, the provincial government reacted with Regulation 17. Its restrictions on the use of the French language in schools galvanized the franco-Ontarian community. They challenged the law through litigation, but the JCPC ruled ultimately that only religion, not language, was protected by section 93 of the *BNA Act*. As this battle took place largely after our period, it will be taken up in *Volume 3*.[103]

Religion and education intersected in a unique way in Quebec, leading to much controversy during and after our period. Section 93, in making public education denominational in Quebec, left no place for non-Christian groups. This left the growing Jewish community of Montreal in a constitutional limbo, with no right to public education. While both Protestant and Catholic school boards accepted Jewish students out of 'Christian charity,' there were ongoing battles over the allocation of school taxes paid by Jewish property owners as between the two boards. The situation was exacerbated by the fact that many Jewish households were poor, rented rather than owned property, and hence did not pay school taxes. In the 1890s the Protestant board was educating most of the Jewish students but the Catholic board received most of the taxes paid by Jewish families, a matter that came to a head in the *Pinsler* case in 1903. At this time few Jewish students had access to education beyond the elementary level because of the fees levied on high school students. The Protestant school board did, however, offer scholarships in an annual competition. Jacob Pinsler, a Canadian-born Jewish boy, won one in 1901, but the board then refused to honour it because his parents did not pay taxes to them. When Jacob's father challenged the decision, the Superior Court held that the board had acted within its rights. Only Protestants and Catholics had constitutional rights to education in Quebec and the school boards had an unfettered right to deal with members of other religions as they chose. The case led immediately to an amendment to the *Education Act* requiring Jewish property owners to pay school taxes only to the Protestant board and providing Jewish children with 'the same right to be educated in the public schools of the province as Protestant children.' They were to be 'treated in the same manner as Protestants for all school purposes,' saving that they could not be compelled to participate in any religious exercises to which their parents objected. Jews now had a statutory right to have their children educated in Protestant schools as 'honorary Protestants' whether they paid taxes or not. This chapter in the saga of Jewish education in Quebec was now closed, but it only opened the door to further disputes in later years. Should there be Hebrew language instruction in Protestant schools with large Jewish populations? Should there be Jewish teachers? Should the Jewish holidays be observed? Some of these controversies will be explored in the next volume, as will the struggles of Mennonites and Doukhobors over educational issues.[104]

Postscript: Law and Legal Institutions on the Eve of the Great War

The roots of contemporary Canadian law were planted in the half century after 1867. Today we take for granted the dominant role played in our national life by the Supreme Court of Canada. We likewise accept without question that the civil law and common law are both fundamental parts of our system of law. We are not often concerned about whether a federal or provincial act falls within sections 91 or 92 of the *British North America Act*, the basic principles of the division of powers having been established by 1914, for better or worse. We have a well-established national *Criminal Code*, the laws that govern the economy, principally corporate law, are clear in their general outlines, and all those who own land rest easy that their titles are secure. The lawyers who operate our legal system have a clear trajectory towards professional qualification and advancement, featuring a university education and entry into a well-established and prestigious profession. When those lawyers represent their clients in court they encounter generally well-qualified and conscientious judges, on all rungs of provincial judicial hierarchies. Some, but by no means all, of these things were features of colonial legal systems before 1867, but all either came into being or were solidified in the half-century thereafter, as Canada emerged from a disparate collection of colonies into a nation of nine provinces and two territories encompassing almost all of northern North America. They did so contemporaneously with large changes in other areas of social and economic life, notably the industrialization of the economy and a transportation revolution, the centrepiece of which was the transcontinental railroad.

The period covered in this book, however, was more notable for building legal institutions – laying down the legal order, to advert to one dominating theme in *Volume 1* of this history – than it was for ensuring equal access for all to the benefits of that order. Liberty, another fundamental theme of *Volume 1*, that was sought to be balanced with order, was very unevenly distributed. By 1914 the status of women in common law provinces had been transformed by changes to married women's property laws and to the common law rules that defined their ability to launch actions in court. But despite some improvements in the law they did not have an equal right to the custody of their children. Protective labour and criminal laws had been enacted to their benefit. But only at the end of our period were they able to practise law, except for Quebec women, who would not be able to do so until 1941, and despite the efforts of some campaigners they were nowhere able to vote. They had more or less equal access to divorce with men, but that was relatively unimportant, given that divorce was beyond the reach of the vast majority of Canadians. The legal position of married women in Quebec had, for the most part, fallen behind that of their sisters in the other provinces. Across Canada the legal status and opportunities of all women were constrained by social, economic, and cultural norms, which would not change until well into the twentieth century. Women, especially single women, entered the paid labour force in large numbers in this period, but for many of these women and for male politicians and social critics new opportunities also brought new problems.

To similar effect, working-class Canadians were better off legally than they had been in 1867. They could strike for better wages and working conditions and rarely faced imprisonment for breaching their employment contracts. But the balance of power between labour and capital was tilted heavily towards the latter, and the law did not alter that balance. Indeed, in myriad ways it threw its weight behind the employer. Matters would continue that way after 1914; indeed in some respects they would worsen until changes introduced in the 1940s and 1950s.

Looking beyond gender and class to the social, economic, and legal status of ethnic and religious minorities in the white and mainly Protestant (outside of Quebec) dominion we have recounted here the many ways in which the Canada that took shape in the half-century after Confederation restricted the liberties of minorities. The very small Black population, although not generally subject to formal legal disadvantages, endured separate schools. In a host of other areas social discrimination was allowed to flourish behind a formal legal wall of freedom of contract and property. Nor did Canadians wish to see the numbers of Blacks increase, with restrictive immigration and land-granting policies keeping them out of the country and denying them as much as possible the right to acquire land in the Prairie west. It would be another half-century before positive state law would begin to intervene to protect some equality rights. Francophone and Catholic minorities had some protections enshrined in the *BNA Act*, but they did not extend to Manitoba in particular. Finally, Canada's newest communities, the Chinese, Japanese, and South Asians who entered Canada, principally British Columbia, in this period were subject to a host of discriminatory legal measures, enacted by provincial and federal governments, designed to persuade them to leave or to prevent more arriving. This too would change little until the 1960s.

The Canadian inhabitants whose lives were most affected by this half-century of building a new nation were the Indigenous people. Those living west of Ontario were added to the Canadian state in 1870 and 1871, in a process that saw them lose most of their land base to white settlers. On the prairies this was achieved in Canadian law by treaties embodying land surrenders, while in British Columbia there was no such veneer of legality. But the result was the same in both cases: the original inhabitants of the land were confined to reserves and substantial rights in land recognized by Canadian law were being vested in white settlers. In both regions the land reserved for Indigenous people was further reduced over time, and the same happened in central and eastern Canada. The Métis suffered much the same fate, in different ways and for different reasons.

Along with this great transformation affecting Indigenous peoples went another – the ever decreasing respect for Indigenous law. In *Volume 1* we highlighted the theme of legal pluralism before 1867. In this period the legal pluralism represented by two European-derived legal systems was confirmed, constitutionally protected, and even strengthened. But the tripartite legal pluralism of the seventeenth to nineteenth centuries was much reduced, even if it never disappeared. It was diminished by the simple fact that so many Indigenous people lived for the first time within the sovereignty of the Canadian state. It was even more reduced by the Canadian state's embrace and ardent pursuit of assimilation, its whole-hearted effort to eliminate Indigenous culture, language, beliefs, and the laws that were derived from and a crucial part of that culture. This 'civilization' policy had its roots in the mid-nineteenth century, and in this period it grew into the full-fledged 'Indian Act' system that is only now in the early stages of being dismantled. In *Volume 3* we will chart not just the continuation and hardening of these policies, but also their initial and tentative undermining, with two landmarks being the 1973 Supreme Court decision in the *Calder* case and the 1982 patriation of a constitution, which included aboriginal rights in section 35.

At various points in this book we have commented on the pre-1914 beginnings of a set of large changes that would profoundly reorient the liberal, white, male dominance of Canadian law. *Volume 3* will build on these beginnings and show how, at different moments in the twentieth century, Canadian law assumed a different shape. The loss of faith in the primacy of a liberal economic order, brought about by the Depression and two world wars, was the first of these large changes, bringing with it a welfare state and an economy regulated in the public interest in ways it never before had been. The second was the social, economic, and political revolution of the 1960s and 1970s. That revolution brought a profound loss of faith in the liberal idea of law as neutral and value-free, as women and ethnic and sexual minorities demanded positive support and substantive equality, not 'neutrality,' from judges and legislators. More recently, and with profound effects that are still incomplete, Canadian law has been reimagined and is being reimagined to be inclusive of Indigenous culture and values, reflected in law as well as many other aspects of our history. In this regard the current volume may be seen by future historians as being about an aberrant age, a period of discontinuity between eras marked by pluralism.

Abbreviations

Law Reports

AC	Appeal Cases (UK)
BCJ	British Columbia Judgments
BCR	British Columbia Reports
BR	Banc de la reine (Reports)
CNLC	Canadian Native Law Cases
CS	Cours supérieure (Quebec Superior Court Reports)
Ct Rev	Court of Revision
ER	English Reports
Grants	Grant's Chancery Reports (Ontario)
LCJ	Lower Canada Jurist
Man. LR	Manitoba Law Reports
MLR	Montreal Law Reports
NBR	New Brunswick Reports
NSR	Nova Scotia Reports
OAR	Ontario Appeal Reports
PEIR	Prince Edward Island Reports
OJ	Ontario Judgments
OR	Ontario Reports

QAC	Quebec Appeal Cases
QLR	Quebec Law Reports
RL and RL (n.s.)	Revue légale and Revue légale (new series).
SCJ	Supreme Court Judgments
SCR	Supreme Court Reports
Terr LR	Territories Law Reports
UCCP	Upper Canada Common Pleas Reports
UCQB	Upper Canada Queen's Bench Reports
UCR	Upper Canada Reports
UKPC	United Kingdom Privy Council Reports
WLR	Western Law Reports

Statutes

CCLC	Civil Code of Lower Canada
CSC	Consolidated Statutes of Canada [Province of Canada]
CSLC	Consolidated Statutes of Lower Canada [Province of Canada]
CSM	Consolidated Statutes of Manitoba
CSN	Consolidated Statutes of Newfoundland
CSNB	Consolidated Statutes of New Brunswick
CSUC	Consolidated Statutes of Upper Canada [Province of Canada]
ONWT	Ordinances of the Northwest Territories
RSBC	Revised Statutes of British Columbia
RSC	Revised Statutes of Canada
RONWT	Revised Ordinances of the Northwest Territories
RSM	Revised Statutes of Manitoba
RSNB	Revised Statutes of New Brunswick
RSNS	Revised Statutes of Nova Scotia
RSO	Revised Statutes of Ontario
SA	Statutes of Alberta
SBC	Statutes of British Columbia
SC	Statutes of Canada
SM	Statutes of Manitoba
SN	Statutes of Newfoundland

SNB   Statutes of New Brunswick
SNWT   Statutes of the Northwest Territories
SNS   Statutes of Nova Scotia
SO   Statutes of Ontario
SPC   Statutes of the Province of Canada
SPEI   Statutes of Prince Edward Island
SQ   Statutes of Quebec
SS   Statutes of Saskatchewan

Courts

CA   Court of Appeal
Ch   Chancery or Chancery Division
CP   Common Pleas
CS   Cour supérieure
Exch   Exchequer Court
JCPC   Judicial Committee of the Privy Council
MBQB   Manitoba Court of Queen's Bench
NBSC   New Brunswick Supreme Court
NSSC   Nova Scotia Supreme Court
NWTSC   Northwest Territories Supreme Court
PEISC   Prince Edward Island Supreme Court
QB   Queen's Bench
SC   Superior Court (Quebec)
SCC   Supreme Court of Canada

Journals

CBR   *Canadian Bar Review*
CHR   *Canadian Historical Review*
CJLS   *Canadian Journal of Law and Society*
CLJ   *Canada Law Journal*
CLR   *Canadian Law Review*
CLT   *Canadian Law Times*
Historical Papers *Canadian Historical Association, Historical Papers*
JCHA   *Journal of the Canadian Historical Association*

LHR   *Law and History Review*
OHLJ   *Osgoode Hall Law Journal*
RHAF   *Revue d'histoire de l'Amérique française*
UTLJ   University of Toronto Law Journal

Essays in the History of Canadian Law. 11 Volumes, All Published by the Osgoode Society for Canadian Legal History and the University of Toronto Press

EHCL I   David Flaherty, ed., *Essays in the History of Canadian Law: Volume I* (1981)

EHCL II   David Flaherty, ed., *Essays in the History of Canadian Law: Volume II* (1983)

EHCL III   Philip Girard and Jim Phillips, eds., *Essays in the History of Canadian Law Volume III – Nova Scotia* (1990)

EHCL IV   Carol Wilton, ed., *Essays in the History of Canadian Law Volume IV: Beyond the Law – Lawyers and Business in Canada, 1830–1930* (1990)

EHCL V   Jim Phillips, Tina Loo, and Susan Lewthwaite, eds., *Essays in the History of Canadian Law Volume V – Crime and Criminal Justice* (1994)

EHCL VI   Hamar Foster and John McLaren, eds., *Essays in the History of Canadian Law Volume VI – British Columbia and the Yukon* (1995)

EHCL VII   Carol Wilton, ed., *Essays in the History of Canadian Law Volume VII: Inside the Law – Canadian Law Firms in Historical Perspective* (1996)

EHCL VIII   G. Blaine Baker and Jim Phillips, eds., *Essays in the History of Canadian Law: Volume VIII – In Honour of R.C.B. Risk* (1998)

EHCL IX   Christopher English, ed., *Essays in the History of Canadian Law: Volume IX – Two Islands, Newfoundland and Prince Edward Island* (2005)

EHCL X   Jim Phillips, R. Roy McMurtry, and John T. Saywell, eds., *Essays in the History of Canadian Law: Volume X – A Tribute to Peter Oliver* (2008)

EHCL XI   G. Blaine Baker and Donald Fyson, eds., *Essays in the History of Canadian Law: Volume XI – Quebec and the Canadas* (2013)

Other

Annual Report	Annual Report of the Indian Affairs Branch of the Secretary of State (1868–1869), the Secretary of State for the Provinces (1869–1873), and the Ministry of the Interior (1873–1880). From 1880 Annual Report of the Department of Indian Affairs.
Census	Censuses of Canada, LAC
CN	Code Napoléon
Correspondence, Reports I	W.E. Hodgins, comp., *Correspondence, Reports of the Minister of Justice, and Orders in Council upon the Subject of Dominion and Provincial Legislation, 1867–1895* (Ottawa: Government Printer, 1896)
Correspondence, Reports II	Francis H. Gisborne and Arthur A. Fraser, comps., *Correspondence, Reports of the Minister of Justice, and Orders in Council upon the Subject of Provincial Legislation, 1896–1920* (Ottawa: Government Printer, 1922).
DIA	Department of Indian Affairs
HBC	Hudson's Bay Company
LAC	Library and Archives Canada
SG	Superintendent General of Indian Affairs
Terms of Union	Terms of Union for British Columbia's Entry into Confederation, UK Order in Council, 16 May 1871
Volume 1	Philip Girard, Jim Phillips, and Blake Brown, *A History of Law in Canada, Volume 1: Beginnings to 1866* (Toronto: Osgoode Society for Canadian Legal History and University of Toronto Press, 2018)

Notes

1. Introduction

1 The census of 1871 counted 23,000 Indigenous people living in the original four confederating provinces, although it is generally agreed that this is a substantial undercount. Here and throughout this book we use the term 'Indigenous' rather than 'aboriginal.' Neither term was employed in this period, when 'Indian' and 'half-breed' were used. Today Canadian law defines the Aboriginal peoples of Canada as Indians, Métis, and Inuit, so to avoid the confusion that 'aboriginal' might engender we use the terms we do, although we occasionally when appropriate refer to 'First Nations' rather than Indigenous people.

2 In the chapters that follow we draw extensively on many historians, of Canadian law as well as all other aspects of Canadian history. But of necessity only the most important of our sources appear in the notes to the various chapters.

3 On these themes generally in Canadian history, see Philip Girard, 'Liberty, Order, and Pluralism: The Canadian Experience,' in *Exclusionary Empire: English Liberty Overseas, 1600–1900*, ed. Jack P. Greene (New York: Cambridge University Press, 2010).

4 H.P. Glenn, 'Persuasive Authority,' *McGill Law Journal* 32 (1987): 261; Mark Walters, *A.V. Dicey and the Common Law Constitutional Tradition* (New York: Cambridge University Press, 2021); Philip Girard, 'The Contrasting Fates of French-Canadian and Indigenous Constitutionalism:

British North America, 1760–1867,' *Law & History* 7 (2020): 1. Dicey's liberal imperialism led him into certain contradictions where the rule of law was concerned. He espoused formal equality for all peoples regardless of race and was a member of the Jamaica Committee, which sought to prosecute the island's governor, Edward Eyre, for authorizing the execution of hundreds of rebels under the purported cover of military law. Yet he was obliged to concede that the strict principle of legality that governed the English polity could not always be observed in imperial possessions; see Dylan Lino, 'The Rule of Law and the Rule of Empire: A.V. Dicey in Imperial Context,' *Modern Law Review* 81 (2018): 739. We thank Bruce Ryder for drawing this reference to our attention.

5 Although England was only one region of the United Kingdom, contemporaries always referred to English law, and we have therefore mostly done the same.

6 Glenn, 'Persuasive Authority.'

7 SC 1920, c 46.

2. The Constitution: Confederation, The *British North America Act*, and Post-1867 Developments

1 See Peter Russell, *Canada's Odyssey: A Country Based on Incomplete Conquests* (Toronto: University of Toronto Press, 2017). The full title of the chapter is 'English Canada Gets a Dominion, French Canada Gets a Province, and Aboriginal Canada Gets Left Out.'

2 What follows in this section about the making of the Confederation pact is drawn from a limited selection of the very extensive literature on the subject, primarily works produced in the last two decades rather than earlier accounts. We have found very useful two volumes by Christopher Moore: *1867: How the Fathers Made a Deal* (Toronto: McClelland & Stewart, 1997), and *Three Weeks in Quebec City: The Meeting That Made Canada* (Toronto: Allen Lane, 2015). The leading study by a Quebec historian is Eugénie Brouillet, *La Négation de la Nation: L'identité culturelle québécoise et le fédéralisme canadien* (Sillery, QC: Sepentrion, 2005). Three excellent short accounts are chapter 27 of Russell, *Canada's Odyssey*; chapter 1 of John Saywell, *The Lawmakers: Judicial Power and the Shaping of Canadian Federalism* (Toronto: University of Toronto Press and Osgoode Society for Canadian Legal History, 2002); and chapter 1 of Robert Vipond, *Liberty and Community: Canadian Federalism and the Failure of the Constitution* (Albany: State University of New York Press, 1991). Also useful in presenting the Lower Canadian side of events, albeit at the expense of

other voices, *The Quebec Conference of 1864: Understanding the Emergence of the Canadian Federation*, ed. Eugénie Brouillet, Alain-G. Gagnon, and Guy Laforest (Montreal and Kingston: McGill-Queen's University Press, 2018). The book's main title is a misnomer; it is about much more than the Quebec conference.

3 Paul Romney, *Getting It Wrong: How Canadians Forgot Their Past and Imperilled Confederation* (Toronto: University of Toronto Press, 1999), 88. On the federal government succeeding to Britain's role, see below, this chapter.

4 As in *Volume 1* we refer to the constituent parts of the Province of Canada as Upper and Lower Canada rather than Canada West and East. In the early 1860s Upper Canada's approximately 1.5 million people outstripped Lower Canada's population by more than 400,000.

5 Quotations from Russell, *Canada's Odyssey*, 128 and 129–30.

6 Cited in J.M.S. Careless, *Brown of the Globe: Statesman of Confederation, 1860–1880*, 2 vols. (Toronto: Dundurn, 1959 and 1963), 2:156. Canada sent eight delegates to Charlottetown, including MacDonald, Brown, and Cartier. New Brunswick, Nova Scotia, and Prince Edward Island all sent five, led by their respective premiers Leonard Tilley, Charles Tupper, and John Hamilton Gray. For details, see Moore, *1867*, 44–8.

7 See especially Brouillet, *La Négation de la Nation*, 137 and 139; and John Dickinson and Brian Young, *A Short History of Quebec*, 4th ed. (Montreal and Kingston: McGill-Queen's University Press, 2008), 190.

8 Cited in Moore, *1867*, 50. For British attitudes and policies, see generally Ged Martin, *Britain and the Origins of Canadian Confederation, 1837–1867* (Vancouver: UBC Press, 1995); and for British business interests see Andrew Smith, *British Businessmen and Canadian Confederation* (Montreal and Kingston: McGill-Queen's University Press, 2008).

9 Moore, *1867*, 105.

10 This and the following sections are based on the general histories of Confederation, above note 2. They also make use of the primary sources available, which are far from comprehensive. Official minutes were taken at the Charlottetown conference by Charles Tupper and at Quebec by Hewitt Bernard, Macdonald's civil service secretary, but they are sparse and record what subjects were discussed on what day, but not what was said. Journalists were denied permission to attend. Two of the participants published memoirs and collections of documents in later years. One was John Hamilton Gray, *Confederation, or, the Political and Parliamentary History of Canada: From the Conference at Quebec in October, 1864, to the Admission of British Columbia, in July, 1871* (Toronto: Copp,

Clark, 1872). Gray was a New Brunswick conservative politician and pro-confederate who was a delegate to the Charlottetown and Quebec conferences. After 1867 he served a few years as a Conservative MP in the Commons and in 1872 was appointed a judge of the British Columbia Supreme Court: see C.M. Wallace, 'John Hamilton Gray,' *DCB* online. He should not be confused with his namesake, Colonel John Hamilton Gray, who was premier of Prince Edward Island in 1864 and thus the official host and chairman of the Charlottetown conference. Another collection of documents published by a contemporary is Edward Whelan, *The Union of the British Provinces* (Charlottetown: Haszard, 1865). See also Joseph Pope, ed., *Confederation: Being a Series of Hitherto Unpublished Documents Bearing on the British North America* Act (Toronto: Carswell, 1895). This has been recently republished as G.P. Browne and Janet Ajzenstat, eds., *Documents on the Confederation of British North America: A Compilation Based on Sir Joseph Pope's Confederation Documents Supplemented by Other Official Material* (Montreal and Kingston: McGill-Queen's University Press, 2009). Also useful are G.P. Browne, ed., *Documents on the Confederation of British North America* (Montreal and Kingston: McGill-Queen's University Press 2009); and Peter B. Waite, *The Life and Times of Confederation* (Toronto: University of Toronto Press, 1962). The debates in the Province of Canada assembly are collected in *Parliamentary Debates on the Subject of the Confederation of the British North American Provinces* (Quebec: Hunter, Rose, 1865).

11 Ineligibility Act, SO 1871–72, c 4; Ineligibility Act, SC 1873, c 2.

12 See *Volume 1*, 530–1, for elective legislative councils.

13 There was a difference between the two prospective provinces. Newfoundland's four senators would be in addition to those provided in sections 21–2, whereas Prince Edward Island's would be part of the 24 allocated to the Maritime provinces, reducing the Nova Scotia and New Brunswick allocations to 10 each.

14 Moore, *1867*, 104. What follows is largely based on this source and on Russell, *Canada's Odyssey*.

15 Indeed when Island delegates intimated that if they could not get provincial equality they might prefer to stay out of Confederation, the central Canadian delegates made it a 'take it or leave it' issue, and the Islanders were the only dissenters from the final resolution on the Senate: Moore, *1867*, 106.

16 See *Volume 1*, 529–31.

17 Cited in Moore, *1867*, 111.

18 Cited in ibid., 112–13.

19 Alternative views are discussed below, this chapter.

20 Cited in Browne, *Documents*, 202.

21 Pope, *Confederation*, 53.

22 Debate at the Quebec conference, 21 Oct. 1864, cited in Browne and Ajzenstat, *Documents*, 119. See also Moore, *Three Weeks*, 142.

23 Gray, *Confederation*, 63.

24 A point made in Robert Vipond, '1787 and 1867: The Federal Principle and Canadian Confederation Reconsidered,' *Canadian Journal of Political Science* 22 (1989): 3 .

25 Education was listed among other provincial powers in the Quebec resolutions, with no suggestion that it would not be part of the eventual section 92 with all the others. As late as December 1866 it was still listed under section 92. The reason for its removal to its own section may have been that it became more complicated and verbose over time as the delegates grappled with separate schools.

26 Brouillet, *La Négation de la Nation*.

27 For an extended version of this argument, see Jim Phillips and Tom Collins, 'The Colonial Origins of the Division of Powers,' in *Law, Life and the Teaching of Legal History: Essays in Honour of G. Blaine Baker*, ed. Ian Pilarcyk, Angela Fernandez, and Brian Young (Montreal and Kingston: McGill-Queen's University Press, 2022).

28 Legislative Assembly Debate, 6 Feb. 1865, in *Parliamentary Debates*, 30.

29 Legislative Assembly Debate, 22 Feb. 1865, cited in Gray, *Confederation*, 265.

30 Legislative Assembly Debate, 16 Feb. 1865, in *Parliamentary Debates*, 263–4.

31 Whelan, *Union of the British Provinces*, 197.

32 For the Ontario court structure before 1867, see *Volume 1*, chap. 22, which also explains the distinction between county and district courts.

33 *Volume 1*, 401.

34 For the limited very early efforts to do something with section 94, see Saywell, *Lawmakers*, 14–15.

35 Gray, *Confederation*, 63. There is considerable irony, therefore, in the fact that Gray himself, a New Brunswicker who had never set foot in British Columbia, was Ottawa's first appointment to that province's Supreme Court, in 1872.

36 Hector Langevin argued that federal appointment was preferable because local governments wishing to rid themselves of a troubling opponent, or indeed a supporter, would appoint that person to the bench: see *Parliamentary Debates*, 387. See also Browne, *Documents*, 47. See generally

E. Robert Edwards, 'Section 96: The Historical Rationale,' *Advocate* 42 (1984): 541.

37 See *Volume 1*, 525.

38 Peter Russell, *Canada's Trial Courts: One Tier or Two?* (Toronto: University of Toronto Press, 2007), 7. For the rest of this paragraph, see Moore, *Three Weeks*, 172; and William H. Angus, 'Judicial Selection in Canada: The Historical Perspective,' *Canadian Legal Studies* 1 (1967): 221–2. For patronage and judicial appointments, see chapter 3.

39 *Parliamentary Debates*, 388.

40 This section on disallowance is largely based on Robert Vipond, 'Alternative Pasts: Legal Liberalism and the Demise of the Disallowance Power,' *University of New Brunswick Law Journal* 39 (1990): 126. See also Russell, *Canada's Odyssey*, 141–2 and 153; Moore, *1867*, 125; and Vipond, *Liberty and Community*, 75–6. For tables of all disallowed statutes, see *Correspondence, Reports I* and *II*.

41 This paragraph is from Pope, *Confederation Documents*, 31; and *Parliamentary Debates*, 108, 123, 361, 364, 407, 433, and 876.

42 Circular by Macdonald, 8 June 1868, in Canada, *Sessional Papers*, 1869, no. 18.

43 The figures given here and elsewhere in this section are from *Correspondence, Reports I*, Table of Disallowed Acts by province, 1327–35.

44 *Common Schools Act*, SNB 1871, c 21; *Correspondence, Reports I*, 662–702. This latter source contains extensive correspondence on many other Acts not disallowed.

45 *Commons Debates*, 29 Apr. 1872, 75.

46 Report of the minister of justice, 28 Sept. 1870, in *Correspondence, Reports I*, 475.

47 *Parliamentary Debates*, 34.

48 See entries for Princess Louise and Prince Arthur in the *Oxford Dictionary of National Biography Online*.

49 David E. Smith, 'The Crown and the Constitution: Sustaining Democracy?,' in *The Evolving Canadian Crown*, ed. Jennifer Smith and D. Michael Jackson (Montreal and Kingston: McGill-Queen's University Press, 2012), 60.

50 David E. Smith, *The Invisible Crown: The First Principle of Canadian Government* (Toronto: University of Toronto Press, 1995), 32 and 34.

51 Barbara Jane Messamore, 'The Line over Which He Must Not Pass: Defining the Office of Governor General, 1878,' *CHR* 86 (2005): 453. Note

also that London exercised the prerogative of pardon in Canada once after 1867, in the case of Ambroise Lépine, discussed in chapter 7.

52 J.T. Saywell, 'The Crown and the Politicians: The Canadian Succession Question, 1891–1896,' *CHR* 37 (1956): 309. The taming of the lieutenant governors was a rather more fraught experience. Lieutenant Governor Thomas McInnes of British Columbia dismissed two premiers before being himself dismissed by the government of Sir Wilfrid Laurier in 1900. The last dismissal of a provincial premier by vice-regal decision occurred in 1903, by McInnes's successor, Sir Henri-Gustave Joly de Lotbinière: see Marcel Hamelin, 'Henri-Gustave Joly de Lotbinière' and Réal Bélanger, 'Sir Wilfrid Laurier,' both in *DCB* online. The right to do so under exigent circumstances is one of the few reserve powers of the Crown's representative that can be exercised without advice.

53 J.R. Mallory, 'The Appointment of the Governor General: Responsible Government, Autonomy, and the Royal Prerogative,' *Canadian Journal of Economics and Political Science* 26 (1960): 96, quotation from Macdonald at 96; A. Berriedale Keith, *The Dominions as Sovereign States: Their Constitutions and Governments* (London: Macmillan, 1938), 207.

54 [1892] AC 437 at 443.

55 *North-West Territories Act, 1875*, SC 1875, c 49, s 2; *Yukon Territory Act*, SC 1898, c 6, s 4.

56 *R v Taylor* (1875) 36 UCQB 183; Bradley Miller, 'Political Imagination, in Its Most Fervid and Patriotic Flights: Copyright and Constitutional Theory in Post-Confederation Canada,' *JCHA* 20 (2009): 85; Peter C. Oliver, *The Constitution of Independence: The Development of Constitutional Theory in Australia, Canada, and New Zealand* (Oxford: Oxford University Press, 2005), 190–208. And see generally Andrew Heard, *Canadian Constitutional Conventions: The Marriage of Law and Politics* (Toronto: Oxford University Press, 1991).

57 Hugh Keenleyside and Gerald Brown, *Canada and the United States: Some Aspects of Their Historical Relations* (New York: Knopf, 1952), 178–89.

58 See Peter Neary, 'Sir George Gibbons,' *DCB* online; and Alan O. Gibbons, 'Sir George Gibbons and the Boundary Waters Treaty of 1909,' *CHR* 34 (1953): 124. Gibbons was knighted by King George V for his work on the treaty, which was implemented by SC 1911, c 21.

59 Philip Girard, 'If Two Ride a Horse, One Must Ride in Front: Married Women's Nationality and the Law in Canada 1880–1950,' *CHR* 94 (2013): 28, esp. 35–7; *Naturalization Act*, SC 1881, c 13, and 1914, c 44.

60 This account of British Columbia's accession to Confederation is based
principally on Jean Barman, *The West beyond the West: A History of British
Columbia*, 3rd ed. (Toronto: University of Toronto Press, 2007); Margaret
Ormsby, *British Columbia: A History* (Toronto: Macmillan, 1958); Patricia
Roy and John Herd Thompson, *British Columbia: Land of Promises*
(Toronto: Oxford University Press, 2005). See also Patricia Roy, 'John
Robson,' and Robert Macdonald and Keith Ralston, 'Amor De Cosmos,'
both in *DCB* online.

61 Responsible government was implicit in the Terms of Union, clause 10,
which stated that the *BNA Act* would apply to British Columbia 'in the
same way and to the like extent' as it applied to the other provinces, 'as if
the Colony of British Columbia had been one of the Provinces originally
united by the said Act.'

62 For Prince Edward Island's accession, see Francis W.P. Bolger, *Prince
Edward Island and Confederation, 1863–1873* (Charlottetown: St. Dunstan's
University Press, 1964); Frank MacKinnon, *The Government of Prince
Edward Island* (Toronto: University of Toronto Press, 1951); Ian Robertson,
'James Colledge Pope,' and Andrew Robb, 'Robert Haythorne,' both in
DCB online.

63 For the Prince Edward Island land question, see *Volume 1*, 596–600, and
this volume, chapter 14.

64 *Prince Edward Island Act*, SC 1873, c 40.

65 For this paragraph and the next see, inter alia, Bill Waiser, *Saskatchewan:
A New History* (Calgary: Fifth House, 2005), chap. 1; Howard Palmer with
Tamara Palmer, *Alberta: A New History* (Edmonton: Hurtig, 1990), esp.
chap. 6; Lewis Herbert Thomas, *The Struggle for Responsible Government
in the North-West Territories, 1870–1897*, 2nd ed. (Toronto: University of
Toronto Press, 1978); *North-West Territories Act*, SC 1875, c 49; *North-West
Territories Act*, SC 1880, c 25, ss 15–22; *North-West Territories Representation
Act*, SC 1886, c 24.

66 See *Alberta Act*, SC 1905, c 3; and *Saskatchewan Act*, SC 1905, c 42. For the
details of the various proposals, see Waiser, *Saskatchewan*, 5–10.

67 Gordon W. Smith, 'The Transfer of Arctic Territories from Great Britain
to Canada in 1880, and Some Related Matters, as Seen in Official
Correspondence,' *Arctic* 14, no. 1 (1961): 53; quotation at 69 from H.R.
Holmden, 'Memo re the Arctic Islands.' The 1880 Order in Council is
reproduced in the *Canada Gazette* 14, no. 15 (9 Oct. 1880).

68 General information from Kenneth Coates and William Morrison, *Land of
the Midnight Sun: A History of the Yukon* (Montreal and Kingston: McGill-
Queen's University Press, 2005), quotation at 77. On miners' meetings, see

Thomas Stone, 'The Mounties as Vigilantes: Perceptions of Community and the Transformation of Law in the Yukon, 1885–1897,' *Law and Society Review* 14 (1979): 83; *Yukon Act*, SC 1898, c 6.

69 Michael Gordon, 'The Andrew G. Blair Administration and the Abolition of the Legislative Council of New Brunswick, 1882–1892' (master's thesis, University of New Brunswick 1964); SNB 1891, c 6; SPEI 1893, c 1; Frank Mackinnon, *The Government of Prince Edward Island* (Toronto: University of Toronto Press, 1951), 210–17.

70 *The Queen v Chandler* (1869) 12 NBR 556 at 560, cited in R.C.B. Risk, 'Canadian Courts under the Influence,' *UTLJ* 40 (1990): 687.

71 The legal literature is extensively reviewed in R.C.B. Risk, 'Constitutional Thought in the Late Nineteenth Century: Making Federalism Work,' *UTLJ* 46 (1996): 427.

72 On the provincial rights movement and constitutional litigation, see Vipond, *Liberty and Community,* and below, this chapter.

73 Cited in Moore, *1867,* 126.

74 Risk, 'Canadian Courts,' 689, calculates that about a quarter of the cases on the division of powers decided before 1900 were liquor-related. For temperance after Confederation, see principally Dan Malleck, *Liquor and the Liberal State: Drink and Order before Prohibition* (Vancouver: UBC Press, 2022); Malcolm Decarie, 'Something Old, Something New: Aspects of Prohibitionism in Ontario in the 1890s,' in *Oliver Mowat's Ontario,* ed. Donald Swainson (Toronto: University of Toronto Press, 1972); and Saywell, *Lawmakers.*

75 This chronology, and this section, is based principally on the work of two authors: Saywell, *Lawmakers,* a detailed study that uses not just the cases but a wide range of sources, including facta and oral arguments; and articles by Richard Risk, especially 'Canadian Courts.'

76 *Hodge v The Queen,* (1883) 9 AC 117 (PC).

77 *AG Ontario v AG Canada,* [1896] AC 348 (PC).

78 See in particular two essays by William Lahey: 'Confederation, Adjudicative Culture, and the Law of the Constitution: The Late Nineteenth-Century Persistence of Local Autonomy in the Nova Scotia Supreme Court,' in *The Supreme Court of Nova Scotia 1754–2004: From Imperial Bastion to Provincial Oracle,* ed. Philip Girard, Jim Phillips, and J. Barry Cahill (Toronto: Osgoode Society for Canadian Legal History and University of Toronto Press, 2004); and 'Constitutional Adjudication, Provincial Rights, and the Structure of Legal Thought in Late Nineteenth-Century New Brunswick,' *University of New Brunswick Law Journal* 39 (1990): 185. An example is Charles Fisher, a former New Brunswick premier and a delegate to the

Quebec and London conferences elevated to the Bench in 1868, who stated in one case, 'As I was party to the various discussions relating to the Union, and know the object of placing the fisheries under the control of the Dominion, I may have allowed myself to be influenced by that consideration': *Robertson v Steadman* (1876) 16 NBR 621 at 635 (SC).

79 Thomas Jean Jacques Loranger, *Letters upon the Interpretation of the Federal Constitution* (Quebec: Morning Chronicle, 1883). For more on Loranger and his arguments, see Risk, 'Constitutional Thought.'

80 This brief section on the compact theory is based on Paul Romney, *Getting It Wrong*; Romney, 'Provincial Equality, Special Status and the Compact Theory of Canadian Confederation,' *Canadian Journal of Political Science* 32 (1999): 21; and Romney, 'Why Lord Watson Was Right,' in *Canadian Constitutionalism, 1791–1991*, ed. Janet Ajzenstat (Ottawa: Canadian Study of Parliament Group, 1992).

81 Among the critics of the compact theory is one who calls it 'ideologically inclined to provincial rights': Bradley Miller, 'Confederation in Court: The BNA Act as Legal History,' *CHR* 98 (2017): 712. Risk succinctly states that the compact theory is 'vulnerable to the simple claim that it was fundamentally inaccurate': R.C.B. Risk, 'The Late Nineteenth Century: Canadian Courts under the Influence,' in *Canadian Constitutional Law*, ed. Patrick Macklem et al., 5th ed. (Toronto: Emond Montgomery, 2017), 110. Jean-François Caron has labelled the compact theory an ahistorical fiction: 'Le Québec et la Confédération: le fédéralisme et la théorie du pacte,' in *Le Canada français et la Confédération: Fondements et bilan critique*, ed. Caron and Marcel Martel (Quebec: Presses de l'Université Laval, 2016).

82 For this paragraph, in addition to the cases cited below, see Saywell, *Lawmakers*, 17–25.

83 The cases cited in this paragraph are *L'Union St-Jacques v Belisle*, (1874) 29 LCJ 29 at 38; *Ex Parte Dansereau* (1875) 19 LCJ 210 at 224 (Dorion CJ); *Re Goodhue* (1872) 19 Grants 366 at 418; *Ryan v Devlin* (1875) 30 LCJ 77 at 83; *Leprohon v Corporation of the City of Ottawa* (1877) 40 UCQB 478 at 488.

84 *Keefe v McLennan* (1876) 11 NSR 5 (SC); *Re Slavin and Orillia* (1875) 36 UCQB 159.

85 *R v Justices of the Peace for the County of Kings* (1875) 15 NBR 535 (SC); *Hart v Missisquoi* (1876) 3 QLR 170; *Cooey v Broome* (1877) 21 LCJ 182. There is some confusion over the Quebec position, because *Cooey* was appealed and overturned on a different ground. At the same time the Court of Queen's Bench judges apparently discussed the constitutional question and disagreed with it. But the appeal decision was not reported and presumably remained largely unknown until it appeared in an 1892

case, *Lepine v Laurent*, Legal News 14 (1892) 369. For all this, see Risk, 'Canadian Courts,' 692. The trade and commerce power was also invoked by the Quebec Superior Court to invalidate a provincial tax on federally or British-incorporated insurance companies: *Angers v The Queen Insurance Company* (1877) 22 LCJ 307.

86 (1875) 36 UCQB 183 (CA); quotation below at 199–200.

87 *Smith v The Merchants Bank* (1881) 28 Grants 629 at 638.

88 (1878) 2 SCR 70; quotations below in this and the next paragraph at 92 and 95.

89 Quotation from Risk, 'Canadian Courts,' 695, summarizing Mowat's argument. For an analysis of Mowat's argument, see also Saywell, *Lawmakers*, 37–40.

90 (1879) 3 SCR 1, quotation at 2.

91 *R v Fredericton* (1879) 19 NBR 139 (SC); (1880) 3 SCR 505; quotation by Gwynne below in this paragraph at 561. The legislation was *Traffic in Intoxicating Liquors Act*, SC 1878, c 16. For a comprehensive account of the New Brunswick Supreme Court decision, see Lahey, 'Constitutional Adjudication.'

92 (1879) 3 SCR 575; quotation below at 610.

93 Saywell, *Lawmakers*, 50. Another case decided around the same time, *Mercer v AG Ontario* (1881), 5 SCR 538, also found that provincial lieutenant governors did not exercise the prerogative, in this instance in the context of escheats.

94 (1881) 4 SCR 215; quotation below at 295; (1881), 7 AC 96 (PC). For the history of insurance regulation behind *Parsons*, see Saywell, *Lawmakers*, 46.

95 Saywell, *Lawmakers*, 49; and Risk, 'Canadian Courts,' 704.

96 Saywell, *Lawmakers*, 82.

97 For these subjects see ibid., chap. 4.

98 Ibid., 76–7.

99 (1881) 7 AC 96 (PC); quotations below at 107–9 and 111–13. There is much information on the case in Ontario, *Sessional Papers*, 1882, no. 31, Report of the Attorney-General with respect to certain proceedings before the Privy Council.

100 Saywell, *Lawmakers*, 85. Another author has similarly but more colourfully described this part of Smith's judgment as 'a rambling and unnecessary disquisition': Miller, 'Confederation in Court,' 715.

101 (1882) 7 AC 829 (PC); quotations below at 839–40 and 842.

102 Risk, 'Canadian Courts,' 709.

103 Quoted in Saywell, *Lawmakers*, 92. Macdonald seemed to believe that *Russell* had not only upheld the *Canada Temperance Act* but also invalidated Ontario's *Crooks Act*, discussed immediately below.

104 SO 1876, c 26.

105 (1882) 7 OAR 246 (CA); (1883) 9 AC 117 (PC).

106 *Hodge* (CA), at 278. Risk, 'Canadian Courts,' 710, is the author of the 'effective sovereignty' point.

107 The JCPC's *Russell* decision was handed down on 23 June 1882, and the Ontario Court of Appeal gave its judgment in *Hodge* on 30 June: Risk, 'Canadian Courts,' 711. For the arguments in *Hodge*, see Canada, *Sessional Papers*, 1884, no. 30E, Judgments of the Supreme Court and the JCPC in *Hodge v The Queen*, and related papers.

108 *Hodge* (PC) at 131.

109 *The Liquidators of the Maritime Bank v The Receiver-General of Canada*, [1892] AC 437 at 441–2 (PC). This case is fully discussed in Saywell, *Lawmakers*, 125–8.

110 Since neither court gave reasons in reference cases, there are no judgments. This account is based on the oral arguments detailed in Saywell, *Lawmakers*, 100–7. The arguments at the Supreme Court are reproduced in Canada, *Sessional Papers*, 1885, no. 85A, Copies of factums and other papers presented to the Supreme Court in argument over the *McCarthy Act* reference.

111 *Liquor Licence Act*, SC 1883, c 30.

112 Both quotations from Risk, 'Canadian Courts,' 716 and 719.

113 Risk, 'Canadian Courts,' 719. Risk discusses the cases at 722–9, quotation below at 729.

114 (1895) 24 SCR 145.

115 Saywell, *Lawmakers*, 111. For the Act and the court decisions, see *Direct Taxes on Certain Commercial Corporations Act*, SQ 1882, c 22; *North British & Mercantile Fire & Life Insurance Co v Lambe*, (1884) 1 MLR (QB) 122; *Bank of Toronto v Lambe* (1887) 12 AC 575 at 587 (PC).

116 Saywell, *Lawmakers*, 114, quotation below at 118.

117 [1892] AC 437 (PC).

118 *Liquidators*, 441–2.

119 *AG Ontario v AG Canada* [1894] AC 189 (PC); quotation below at 200–1.

120 *AG Ontario v AG Canada* (1895) 24 SCR 170. The legislation was the *Liquor Licence Laws Act*, SO 1890, c 56.

121 (1895), 24 SCR 145. For an explanation, see Risk, 'Canadian Courts,' 727.

122 *AG Ontario v AG Canada* [1896] AC 348 (PC), quotations below at 360–1 and 362–3.

123 Saywell, *Lawmakers*, 136.

124 Risk, 'Canadian Courts,' 735.

125 See Romney, 'Why Lord Watson Was Right'; F. Murray Greenwood, 'Lord Watson, Institutional Self-Interest, and the Decentralisation of Canadian Federalism in the 1890s,' *UBC Law Review* 9 (1974): 244.

126 What follows is a necessarily much truncated description of the
relationship between division of powers cases and legal thought. It
is drawn from Risk, 'Canadian Courts'; Saywell, *Lawmakers*; Vipond,
'Alternative Pasts,' 139; R.C.B. Risk, 'Blake and Liberty,' in Ajzenstat,
Canadian Constitutionalism; R.C.B. Risk and Robert Vipond, 'Rights Talk
in Canada in the Late Nineteenth Century: "The Good Sense and Right
Feeling of the People,"' *LHR* 14 (1996): 1.

127 A.H.F. Lefroy, *The Law of Legislative Power in Canada* (Toronto: Toronto
Law Book and Publishing, 1897–8). For Lefroy, and an extended treatment
of his thought and its relation to the developments described here, see
R.C.B. Risk, 'A.H.F. Lefroy: Common Law Thought in Late Nineteenth-
Century Canada – On Burying One's Grandfather,' *UTLJ* 41 (1991): 307.

128 This argument is most strongly made by David Schneiderman, who provides
a very good analysis of the rise of legal liberalism. See his 'Constitutional
Interpretation in an Age of Anxiety: A Re-consideration of the Local
Prohibition Case,' *McGill Law Journal* 41 (1996): 411; and 'A.V. Dicey, Lord
Watson, and the Law of the Canadian Constitution,' *LHR* 16 (1998): 495.

129 For the rivers and streams dispute, see Vipond, 'Alternative Pasts'; and
Jamie Benidickson, 'Private Rights and Public Purposes in the Lakes,
Rivers and Streams of Ontario, 1870–1930,' in *EHCL II*. The legislation
at issue was the *Rivers, Streams and Creeks Act*, SO 1881, c 11; 1882, c 4;
and 1882–3, c 10. Many of the documents in the case are reproduced in
Correspondence, Reports I, 177–93.

130 *Commons Debates*, 14 Apr. 1882, 924.

3. Creating the Dominion Court System

1 *Manitoba Act*, SC 1870, c 3. The following discussion of the Manitoba
courts is based principally on Dale Brawn, *The Court of Queen's Bench of
Manitoba: A Biographical History* (Toronto: Osgoode Society for Canadian
Legal History and University of Toronto Press, 2004); and Dale and
Lee Gibson, *Substantial Justice: Law and Lawyers in Manitoba, 1670–1870*
(Winnipeg: Manitoba Legal Research Institute, 1972), chaps. 2 and 3.
Judicial appointments to the Manitoba courts, and to all other Canadian
superior, district, and county courts in this period, can be located in
Narcisse O. Cote, *Political Appointments, Parliaments and the Judicial Bench
in the Dominion of Canada*, vol. 1, *1867–1895* (Ottawa: Thoburn, 1896)
(hereafter *Political Appointments* I); and Gibson and Gibson, *Political
Appointments, Parliaments and the Judicial Bench in the Dominion of Canada,
1896–1917* (Ottawa: Thoburn, 1918) (hereafter *Political Appointments* II).

2 *Supreme Court Act*, SM 1871, c 2, and 1872, c 3.

3 For the court system of the North-West Territories, see Shelley Gavigan, *Hunger, Horses and Government Men: Criminal Law on the Aboriginal Plains, 1870–1905* (Vancouver: Osgoode Society for Canadian Legal History and UBC Press, 2012), chap. 1.

4 SC 1875, c 49, ss 64–73; *North-West Territories Act*, SC 1885, c 51. In this period the Territories were called the North-West Territories, and we have retained that form when we refer to statutes or other contemporary institutions, such as the North-West Territories Supreme Court. When we refer generically to the region we use 'the Territories.'

5 *North-West Territories Act*, RSC 1886, c 50.

6 *Yukon Act*, SC 1898, c 6. The first judge of the court was Thomas Maguire, from the NWTSC, but the next two were Calixte Aimé Dugas, a Montreal police magistrate, and James Craig, an Ontario lawyer.

7 See *North-West Territories Act*, SC 1905, c 27; *Alberta Act*, SC 1905, c 3, s 16(2); *Saskatchewan Act*, SC 1905, c 42, s 16(2); *Supreme Court Act*, SS 1907, c 8; *District Courts Act*, SS 1907, c 9; *Supreme Court Act*, SA 1907, c 3; *District Courts Act*, SA 1907, c 4. The Supreme Court of Saskatchewan's name was changed to King's Bench in 1915: *King's Bench Act*, SS 1915, c 10; and *Court of Appeal Act*, SS 1915, c 9. No new Supreme Court was created for the area still called the North-West Territories. Instead Parliament re-established a system of stipendiary magistrates: *North-West Territories Act*, SC 1905, c 27, s 8. For the early history of the Alberta and Saskatchewan courts, see also *The Alberta Supreme Court at 100: History and Authority*, ed. Jonathan Swainger (Edmonton: Osgoode Society for Canadian Legal History and University of Alberta Press, 2007); and David Mittelstadt, *The Court of Appeal for Saskatchewan: The First Hundred Years* (Regina: University of Regina Press, 2018).

8 For the British Columbia Supreme Court's early years as part of Canada, see Hamar Foster, 'The Struggle for the Supreme Court: Law and Politics in British Columbia, 1871–1885,' in *Law and Justice in a New Land: Essays in Western Canadian Legal History*, ed. Louis A. Knafla (Toronto: Carswell, 1986).

9 See *Civil Service Act*, SC 1872, c 20, s 5. Begbie's salary was $5,820, with no other chief justice being paid more than $5,000; Crease received $4,850, more than any other puisne judge. Both salaries were to last 'so long as the present incumbents remain in office.' Begbie received a personal assurance from Macdonald that he would retain his salary so long as he was the incumbent: David R. Verchere, *A Progression of Judges: A History of the Supreme Court of British Columbia* (Vancouver: UBC Press, 1988), 49.

10 C.M. Wallace, 'John Hamilton Gray,' *DCB* online; *Puisne Judge Act*, SBC 1872, c 24.

11 Crease to Edward Blake, 10 July 1877, cited in Foster, 'Struggle for the Supreme Court,' 180.

12 *Better Administration of Justice Act*, SBC 1878, c 20.

13 Quotations from Crease to Zebulon Lash, 9 Sept. 1878, and 18 Jan. 1879, both cited in Foster, 'Struggle for the Supreme Court,' 183.

14 SBC 1879, c 13. The three residence locations designated were New Westminster, Clinton, and Barkerville. To the Supreme Court judges, the last two 'might as well have been in Siberia': Foster, 'Struggle for the Supreme Court,' 190.

15 *Sewell v BC Towing Co* (1883) 1 BCR Part 1 153 (BCSC and SCC). The SCC's decision was not published in the *Supreme Court Reports* but was included in the report of the BCSC's decision in the BC Reports. The SCC decision is approximately 1 page long and follows the 215-page judgment of the BCSC: Foster, 'Struggle for the Supreme Court,' 209.

16 Foster, 'Struggle for the Supreme Court,' 211.

17 This section on the Supreme Court is based principally on James Snell and Frederick Vaughan, *The Supreme Court of Canada: History of the Institution* (Toronto: Osgoode Society and University of Toronto Press, 1985), chaps. 1–4, quotations below in this paragraph and the next at 5 and 7.

18 Sir John Young to Colonial Secretary Granville, 11 Mar. 1869, in Canada, *Sessional Papers*, 1870, no. 35, Correspondence Touching Provincial Legislation.

19 *Commons Debates*, 4 Feb. 1875, cited in John T. Saywell, *The Lawmakers: Judicial Power and the Shaping of Canadian Federalism* (Toronto: Osgoode Society for Canadian Legal History and University of Toronto Press, 2005), 32.

20 *Supreme and Exchequer Courts Act*, SC 1875, c 11. The Exchequer Court was created to deal with revenue claims against the federal Crown. Until 1886 its judges were the Supreme Court judges. In 1887 a separate judge, George Wheelock Burbidge, was appointed to hear trials in the court: *Supreme and Exchequer Courts Act*, SC 1887, c 16. Burbidge, a leading New Brunswick lawyer until appointed deputy minister of justice in 1882, served until his death in 1908. He was succeeded by Sir Walter Cassels, and in 1912 an assistant judge to Cassels was added, Louis Arthur Audette. For the Exchequer Court, see Ian Bushnell, *The Federal Court of Canada: A History, 1875–1922* (Toronto: Osgoode Society for Canadian Legal History and University of Toronto Press, 1997), parts 1–3; and Desmond Brown, 'George Wheelock Burbidge,' *DCB* online.

21 *Supreme and Exchequer Court Act*, SC 1879, c 39, s 5.

22 See, for example, *References to the Supreme Court of Canada Act*, SO 1877, c 5; *Supreme Court of Canada Act*, SNS 1879, c 2; *Supreme Court of Canada Act*, SNB 1888, c 9.

23 *Commons Debates*, 29 Apr. 1890, 4089–90; *Supreme and Exchequer Courts Act*, SC 1891, c 25, s 4; *In Re References by the Governor-General in Council*, (1910) 43 SCR 536; [1912] AC 571 (PC). The section was slightly but not materially amended in *Supreme and Exchequer Courts Act*, SC 1906, c 50, s 2. For the history of the reference power, see Carissima Mathen, *Courts without Cases: The Law and Politics of Advisory Opinions* (New York: Hart, 2019), 45–57 and 63–4.

24 For proposed amendments generally, see the table in Snell and Vaughan, *Supreme Court*, 11; and for the civil law, see Yves Hébert, 'Henri-Thomas Taschereau'; and Sylvio Normand, 'Michel Mathieu,' both in *DCB* online.

25 The direct appeal is known as a *per saltum* appeal, literally 'hopping.'

26 For patronage and judicial appointments, see the section below, this chapter. For these men, see Michèle Brassard and Jean Hamelin, 'Télesphore Fournier'; Ian MacPherson, 'Sir William Buell Richards'; Jamie Benidickson, 'Sir Samuel Henry Strong'; Christine Veilleux, 'Jean-Thomas Taschereau'; Phyllis Blakeley, 'William Alexander Henry'; Gordon Bale and E. Bruce Mellett, 'Sir William Johnstone Ritchie'; all in *DCB* online.

27 Snell and Vaughan, *Supreme Court*, 12–15.

28 Blakeley, 'William Alexander Henry.'

29 (1879) 3 SCR 1 at 10–11.

30 Fournier retired in 1895 after 20 years on the Court. Gwynne died in 1902 at the age of 88. Strong resigned in 1902 at the age of 77, not that old but a man of 'violent and bullying temperament': Benidickson, 'Sir Samuel Henry Strong.'

31 For the individuals mentioned in this paragraph, see Philip Girard, 'Robert Sedgwick'; T.W. Acheson, 'George Edward King'; David Howes, 'Sir Henri-Elzéar Taschereau'; and Michael Smith, 'Désiré Girouard,' all in *DCB* online. For Patterson, see Robert Sharpe, *The Lazier Murder: Prince Edward County 1884* (Toronto: Osgoode Society for Canadian Legal History and University of Toronto Press, 2011), 56–9 and 128–9.

32 See Snell and Vaughan's chapter title for the 1902–18 period, 'The Court in Decline.'

33 Snell and Vaughan, *Supreme Court*, discuss Laurier's appointments at 82–93. For patronage and judicial appointments under Laurier and other prime ministers, see the section below on judicial appointments. For the

individuals mentioned in this paragraph, see J.M. Bumsted, 'Sir Louis Henry Davies'; Robert Vipond, 'David Mills'; and C. Ian Kyer, 'Wallace Nesbitt,' all in *DCB* online, and for Fitzpatrick the website of the Supreme Court of Canada.

34 Snell and Vaughan, *Supreme Court*, 94.

35 This section on courts of appeal does not deal with the appeals available lower down provincial court systems, from justices of the peace and stipendiary magistrates to county courts, and from county courts to superior courts.

36 For the Ontario Court of Appeal, see Christopher Moore, *The Court of Appeal for Ontario: Defining the Right of Appeal, 1792–2013* (Toronto: Osgoode Society for Canadian Legal History and University of Toronto Press, 2014), chap. 2. For the legislation discussed here, see *Court of Error and Appeal Act*, SO 1868–1869, c 24; *Administration of Justice Act*, SO 1874, c 7; *Court of Appeal Act*, SO 1897, c 13.

37 The newly organized court was initially still named Error and Appeal, but the name was changed to Court of Appeal in 1876: *Statute Law Reform Act*, SO 1875–1876, c 7, s 22.

38 *Judicature Act*, SO 1881, c 5.

39 *Court of Appeal Act*, SO 1897, c 13; *Judicature Act*, SO 1904, c 11. In addition, the *Law Reform Act*, SO 1909, c 28, not in force until 1913, formalized the 1881 arrangements whereby a separate appeal court of elected trial judges could also hear appeals; it was formally named the Second Appellate Division.

40 *Political Appointments* I, 338–9.

41 Philip Girard, 'The Supreme Court of Nova Scotia: Confederation to the Twenty-First Century,' in *The Supreme Court of Nova Scotia, 1754–2004: From Imperial Bastion to Provincial Oracle*, ed. Philip Girard, Jim Phillips, and J. Barry Cahill (Toronto: Osgoode Society for Canadian Legal History and University of Toronto Press, 2004), 159–61, 179–80, and 192; *Judicature Act*, SNB 1909, c 23, not proclaimed in force until 1913.

42 Saskatchewan (1918) and Alberta (1921) established separate appeal courts outside the period covered by this volume.

43 *Supreme Court Act*, SM 1872, c 3, s 2; *Court of Appeal Act*, SM 1906, c 18; Brawn, *Court of Queen's Bench*, 18–20.

44 What follows is drawn principally from Christopher Moore, *The British Columbia Court of Appeal: The First Hundred Years* (Vancouver: Osgoode Society for Canadian Legal History and UBC Press, 2010); quotation below at 11. See also *Court of Appeal Act*, SBC 1907, c 10, in force 1909.

45 Hunter to Laurier, 15 Sept. 1909, cited in Moore, *British Columbia Court of Appeal*, 12.

46 For these men, see Christopher Moore, 'Archer Evans Stringer Martin'; and Louis A. Knafla, 'James Alexander Macdonald,' both in *DCB* online; Moore, *British Columbia Court of Appeal*, 21–46; *Court of Appeal Act*, SBC 1913, c 13.

47 The best overviews of Canadian developments in this area are Philip Girard, 'At the Crossroads of Fusion: British North America/Canada, 1750–1900,' in *Equity and Law: Fusion and Fission*, ed. John Goldberg, Henry Smith, and Peter Turner (Cambridge: Cambridge University Press, 2019); and Girard, 'History and Development of Equity,' in *The Law of Trusts: A Contextual Approach*, ed. Mark Gillen and Faye Woodman, 4th ed. (Toronto: Emond, 2021).

48 UK Statutes, 1809, c 27; and 1824, c 67.

49 This section on fusion in Ontario is principally from Elizabeth Brown, 'Equitable Jurisdiction and the Court of Chancery in Upper Canada,' *OHLJ* 21 (1983): 275.

50 These figures are from Ontario, *Sessional Papers*, 1877, no. 14.

51 'Chancery Reforms,' *CLJ* 6 (1870): 29; Michael Lobban, 'Preparing for Fusion: Reforming the Nineteenth-Century Court of Chancery, Part 1,' *LHR* 22 (2004): 389; and Lobban, 'Preparing for Fusion: Reforming the Nineteenth-Century Court of Chancery, Part II,' *LHR* 22 (2004): 565. For Buell, who was associated with the rebels of 1837 and arrested but never tried for treason, see Leo Johnson, 'Andrew Norton Buell,' *DCB* online.

52 See *Volume 1*, 409–10.

53 'Equity in Common Law Courts,' *CLJ* 8 (1872): 130.

54 SO 1873, c 8; quotation below from section 1. The Mowat quotation is from Brown, 'Equitable Jurisdiction,' 305.

55 *Administration of Justice Act*, SO 1874, c 7, s 23.

56 *Kennedy v Bown* (1874), 21 Grants 95 at 96; *Bank of Hamilton v Western Assurance Company* (1876) 38 UCQB 609 at 616.

57 UK Statutes, 1873, c 24; Lobban, 'Preparing for Fusion Part II.'

58 'Legislation of Last Session,' *CLJ*, 15 Apr. 1881, 164; untitled, *CLJ*, 1 Sept. 1881, 312. The general thrust of commentary comes from a survey of the *Canada Law Journal*, Feb. 1880 to Aug. 1882.

59 *Judicature Act*, SO 1881, c 5.

60 As one editorial stated in 1881, 'Our act has been mainly based on the English Judicature Act, and we much doubt the wisdom of departing from it in this matter': *CLJ*, 1 Oct. 1881, 358.

61 For Nova Scotia and New Brunswick, see *Equity Judge Act*, SNS 1864, c 10; *Supreme Court Act*, SNB 1879, c 7; and SNB 1894, c 7; *Political Appointments*

I, 360 and 367; and II, 268; *Judicature Act*, SNS 1884, c 25, esp. s 14(9);
Judicature Act, SNB 1909, c 5, esp. s 19(11).

62 For Prince Edward Island and Newfoundland, see *Chancery Act*, SPEI
1884, c 3; *Vice Chancellor Act*, SPEI 1869, c 4; *Chancery Jurisdiction Transfer
Act*, SPEI 1974, c 65; *Judicature Act*, SN 1889, c 29.

63 For Chancery in Manitoba, see Brawn, *Court of Queen's Bench*, 16–18. For
the statutes in some provinces, see *Court of Queen's Bench Act*, SM 1886,
c 14 and SM 1895, c 6, esp. s 39(15); *Supreme Court Act*, SBC 1879, c 12, s
3(11); *Judicature Ordinance*, SNWT 1886, No 2.

64 For British Columbia, see below this chapter. For Newfoundland, see
Central District Court Act and *Harbour Grace District Court Act*, CSN 1874, c
15 and 16.

65 See Canada, *Sessional Papers*, 1868, no. 29, Return to an Address of the
House of Commons, … for Information Respecting County Courts in
Ontario. For the earlier history see *Volume 1*, 400–2. For the number of
judges in 1914, see *Political Appointments* II.

66 *County Courts Act*, SNB 1867, c 10. For Ontario County and District courts
and judges, see *Political Appointments* I, 315–36; and II, 223–44.

67 The statutes discussed here are *Judicial Organization Act*, SQ 1893, c 24;
and *Court of Review Act*, SPC 1864, c 39.

68 *County Court Ordinance*, BC Ordinances, 1867, no. 95. This section on
the remarkably convoluted early history of the British Columbia county
courts is based principally on Foster, 'Struggle for the Supreme Court,'
171. For the quotation below, see *County Courts Act*, SBC 1877, c 22, s 27.
For Ottawa's role, see *Report of Minister of Justice*, 16 Mar. 1875; and Order
in Council, 16 Mar. 1875, in *Correspondence, Reports I*, 1030–5, 1037–9, and
1054–8.

69 *Volume 1*, 398–404.

70 For the Manitoba County Courts, see generally Brawn, *Court of King's
Bench*, 15–16; *Supreme Court Act*, SM 1872, c 3; *Judicial Districts Act*, SM
1881, c 28; *Political Appointments* I, 286–7; and II, 281–7.

71 For the Prince Edward Island County Courts, see Ian Robertson,
'Edward Palmer,' *DCB* online; *County Courts Act*, SPEI 1873, c 3; *Political
Appointments* I, 279–80.

72 For what follows on Nova Scotia county courts, see Girard, 'Supreme
Court of Nova Scotia,' 148–51; G. Patterson, 'The Establishment of the
County Court in Nova Scotia,' *CBR* 21 (1943): 405–6; *County Courts Act*,
SNS 1874, c 18, quotation below from section 32; *Political Appointments* I,
363–6.

73 Girard, 'Supreme Court of Nova Scotia,' 149 and 150.

74 *Provincial Courts Judges Act*, SC 1882, c 12, s 2. For the colonial and
provincial provisions, see *Upper Canada County Courts Act*, SPC 1857, c 58,
ss 10–12; *County Courts Act*, SNB 1867, c 10, s 2; *County Courts Act*, SPEI
1873, c 3, s 9; *County Courts Act*, SNS 1874, c 18, s 3. The Manitoba county
court judges were the Queen's Bench judges until 1881 and therefore had
good behaviour tenure.

75 Report of the Deputy Minister of Justice, 28 Feb. 1878, in *Correspondence,
Reports I*, 1055.

76 Campbell to Sir John A. Macdonald, 11 July 1885, cited in Gibson and Gibson,
Substantial Justice, 149; Philip Girard, 'Politics, Promotion and Professionalism:
Sir Wilfrid Laurier's Judicial Appointments,' in *EHCL X*, 175.

77 For the statutes discussed here, see *County Courts Act*, SPEI 1873, c 3, ss
8 and 53; *County Courts Act*, SNS 1874, c 18, s 55; *Parish Courts Act*, SNB
1876, c 5; *Towns Incorporation Act*, SNS 1895, c 4, s 197; *Civil Jurisdiction of
Magistrates Act*, SBC 1895, c 13; *Small Debts Recovery Act*, SS 1913, c 31.

78 *Colonial Courts of Admiralty Act*, UK Statutes 1890, c 27, s 17; *Admiralty
Act*, SC 1891, c 29, ss 3 and 20; *Maritime Jurisdiction Act*, SC 1877, c 21;
Cote, *Political Appointments*, I, 302–5, 314, and 359; R. Gregory Cox, 'The
Maritime Court of Ontario,' *CLT* 8 (1888): 1.

79 *Volume 1*, 397–8. Here we use the same definition of 'Superior Court'
that we employed in *Volume 1*: the highest courts in each province
and territory and the two federal courts, but not county and district
courts.

80 The figures here are compiled from *Political Appointments* I and II.

81 This section on judicial salaries is based on *Civil List Act*, SC 1868, c 33;
Official Salaries Act, SC 1873, c 31; *Civil List Act*, SC 1872, c 20; *Prince
Edward Island Salaries Act*, SC 1874, c 4; *Supreme and Exchequer Court Act*,
SC 1875, c 11; *BC Judges Salaries Act*, SC 1880, c 4; *Prince Edward Island
Judges Salaries Act*, SC 1881, c 6; *Judges Salaries Act*, SC 1882, c 11; *Provincial
Court Judges Act*, RSC 1886, c 138; *North-West Territories Act*, SC 1886, c
25, s 10; *Supreme and Exchequer Court Act*, SC 1887, c 16, s 5; *Provincial
Court Judges Act*, SC 1898, c 52; *Judges Act*, SC 1905, c 31; *Manitoba Court
of Appeal Act*, SC 1906, c 4; *Alberta and Saskatchewan Statute Amendments
Act*, SC 1907, c 45; *Provincial Court Judges Act*, SC 1898, c 52. Various
individuals received additional small sums, not included here, for serving
as admiralty judges or judges of courts of marriage and divorce in the
provinces that had them.

82 Snell and Vaughan, *Supreme Court*, 45.

83 Canada, *Sessional Papers*, 1874, no. 45, Correspondence between the
Government of Canada and the Judges of the Superior Courts of Nova

Scotia, New Brunswick, and British Columbia, Touching the Inequality of the Salaries of the Judges … in the Different Provinces.

84 *Judges Salaries Act*, SC 1869, c 8, s 5. For figures compiled for the federal government in 1868 of payments from the fee fund, see Canada, *Sessional Papers*, 1868, no. 29, Return to an Address of the House of Commons, … for Information respecting County Courts in Ontario, and Fee Fund, since 1868. For the other information here on county court judges salaries, see *Civil List Act*, SC 1872, c 20; *Official Salaries Act*, SC 1873, c 31; *Judges Salaries Act*, SC 1874, c 4; *Nova Scotia County Court Salaries Act*, SC 1876, c 29; *PEI County Court Salaries Act*, SC 1879, c 4; *Judges Salaries Act*, SC 1882, c 11; *Judges Salaries Act*, SC 1883, c 9; *Manitoba County Court Judges Act*, SC 1885, c 55; *Provincial Court Judges Salaries Act*, SC 1895, c 38; *Provincial Court Judges Act*, SC 1898, c 52.

85 See *Volume 1*, 389; and Canada, *Sessional Paper*, 1881, no. 55, Statement of the Number of Judgeships in Each Province … Entitled … to Retiring Allowances. Similar information is contained in the pensions section of Canada, *Sessional Papers*, 1868, no. 80, Statement of the Total Expenses of the Judiciary.

86 *Civil List Act*, SC 1868, c 33, s 3. The judges of the Ontario Court of Error and Appeal were omitted from the 1868 Act, an omission remedied by *Ontario Judges Pension Act*, SC 1876, c 28.

87 *Judges Pension Act*, SC 1903, c 29, s 1. A judge could retire on full salary who was 75 and had been on the bench for 20 years, or was 70 and had been on the bench for 25 years, or had been on the bench for 30 years. See also for this paragraph Snell and Vaughan, *Supreme Court*, 55–6; and Gordon Bale, 'John Idington,' *DCB* online.

88 For this paragraph, see *Official Salaries Act*, SC 1873, c 31, s 12; *Judges Salaries Act*, SC 1874, c 4, s 8; *Judges Salaries Act*, SC 1877, c 23, s 1; *Judges Salaries Act*, SC 1913, c 28, s 25.

89 Macdonald to Timothy Anglin, 10 Jan. 1871, quoted in Jonathan Swainger, 'Judicial Scandal and the Culture of Patronage in Early Confederation,' in *EHCL X*, 222. The other quotations above are from *EHCL X*, 222 and 225.

90 Macdonald to J. Robson, 30 May 1888, cited in David Bell, 'Judicial Crisis in Post-Confederation New Brunswick,' *Manitoba Law Journal* 20 (1991): 184.

91 Goldwin Smith, *Reminiscences* (New York: Macmillan, 1910), 428–9.

92 For studies of patronage and appointments to administrative posts generally and the awarding of government contracts, not just judicial appointments, see especially Gordon T. Stewart, 'Political Patronage under Macdonald and Laurier, 1878–1911,' *American Review of Canadian*

Studies 10 (1980): 3–26, esp. 8–9. See also Stewart, 'John A. Macdonald's Greatest Triumph,' *CHR* 62 (1982): 3; and Stewart, *The Origins of Canadian Politics: A Comparative Approach* (Vancouver: UBC Press, 1986). General political histories invariably make the same point. Peter Waite, *Canada 1874–1896: Arduous Destiny* (Toronto: McClelland and Stewart, 1971), 96, argues that throughout Macdonald's years as prime minister from 1878 to 1891 his 'principal preoccupation was patronage.'

93 Swainger, 'Judicial Scandal,' 225; and Swainger, *The Canadian Department of Justice and the Completion of Confederation, 1867–1878* (Vancouver: UBC Press, 2000).

94 Girard, 'Politics, Promotion,' 170; Moore, *BC Court of Appeal*, 47.

95 Swainger, 'Judicial Scandal,' 226–9.

96 Peter B. Waite, *Macdonald: His Life and World* (Toronto: McGraw-Hill Ryerson, 1975), 188–9.

97 Quoted in Swainger, 'Judicial Scandal,' 238.

98 For numerous examples of individual patronage appointments, see the entries in *DCB* online. For a case study in addition to those already cited, see James G. Snell, 'Frank Anglin Joins the Bench: A Study of Judicial Patronage, 1897–1904,' *OHLJ* 18 (1980): 664. For a review of all New Brunswick Supreme Court appointments, see Bell, 'Judicial Crisis.' For a general statistical study, see William J. Klein, 'Judicial Recruitment in Manitoba, Ontario, & Quebec, 1905–1970' (PhD diss., University of Toronto, 1975), chap. 5.

99 Appointments to, and promotions within, all superior courts are listed in *Political Appointments* I and II.

100 Indeed much of the literature on patronage involves county court appointments. 'County judgeships,' states one account, 'were sought-after plums in the legal profession' and 'were given by the party in power primarily on the basis of the candidate's service to the party': Stewart, 'Political Patronage,' 8.

101 The designations of judicial appointments as one of the three categories discussed immediately below is based on a wide variety of sources too numerous to detail here. The principal sources used are the *DCB* online, the histories of courts already cited in this chapter, and other court histories not cited. Also extensively employed are judicial and general biographical dictionaries, and other disparate sources too numerous to list.

102 An example is Alexander Casimir Galt, appointed to the Manitoba Court of Queen's Bench in 1912 by Borden. He took no interest in politics, but the Conservative minister of the interior, Robert Rogers, convinced

Borden to appoint Galt. Rogers was probably acting at the behest of James Stewart Tupper (the son of Rogers's political associate, Charles Tupper), who had recently hired Galt at Tupper, Tupper, Minty & McTavish and was deeply regretting the decision. Galt's intransigence alienated clients, increased costs, and impeded the collection of fees. See Brawn, *Court of King's Bench*, 246–59.

103 See Tina Loo, 'John Foster McCreight,' *DCB* online. For British Columbia politics in the first thirty years after Confederation, see, inter alia, John Belshaw, 'Provincial Politics, 1871–1916,' in *Pacific Province: A History of British Columbia*, ed. Hugh M. Johnston (Vancouver: Douglas & McIntyre, 1996); David Ricardo Williams, 'Theodore Davie,' *DCB* online; Foster, 'Struggle for the Supreme Court.'

104 There are some differences between the figures given here for appointments made by Laurier and those given in Girard, 'Politics, Promotion,' but they are not important and turn on different definitions of 'vacancies.'

105 This argument draws on Stewart's analysis of Macdonald's party-building efforts in the 1870s: see Stewart, *Origins of Canadian Politics*, 64–7.

106 For the term 'parachuting' and the figures given here, see Girard, 'Politics, Promotion,' 178.

107 Girard, 'Politics, Promotion,' 173; and Philip Girard, 'Sir Charles Townshend,' *DCB* online.

108 Girard, 'Politics, Promotion,' 178.

109 Snell and Vaughan, *Supreme Court*, 91.

110 One of his non-partisan appointments stemmed from the 1913 establishment of an appeal division in New Brunswick. Borden promoted Albert Scott White to it, who had been a provincial liberal assemblyman for fourteen years before being appointed by Laurier in 1908. On the other hand, a year later, when Frederick Barker retired from his post as chief justice of the appeal division, he was replaced by Ezekiel McLeod, until then a Conservative MP.

111 This paragraph is largely based on Girard, 'Politics, Promotion'; quotations below at 171, 172, and 189. Also very useful on Macdonald and Mackenzie in the 1870s is Swainger, *Canadian Department of Justice*, and the many studies of individual judges in *DCB* online.

112 See, for example, the 'Atlantic seat' on the SCC, discussed in Philip Girard, 'The "Atlantic Seat" on the Supreme Court of Canada: An Endangered Species,' in *In Furtherance of Justice: The Judicial Life of Thomas A. Cromwell*, ed. Stephen Aylward and Pam Hrick (Toronto: Lexis-Nexis, 2017).

113 The examples in this paragraph are taken from Girard, 'Politics, Patronage,' 174 and 182.

114 Swainger, 'Judicial Scandal,' 223; quotation below at 229. What follows is
    based on this source unless other references are given.
115 Jonathan Swainger, 'A Bench in Disarray: The Quebec Judiciary and the
    Federal Department of Justice, 1867–1878,' *Les Cahiers de Droit* 34 (1993):
    59, quotations below at 83.
116 For the Mondelet affair, see also Elizabeth Nish, 'Charles Elzear
    Mondelet,' *DCB* online.
117 SC 1875, c 16; and SC 1874, c 9.
118 Bell, 'Judicial Crisis,' 186 and 190–1; Jennifer Allaby, 'John Valentine
    Ellis,' *DCB* online; David Bell, *Legal Education in New Brunswick: A History*
    (Fredericton: University of New Brunswick, 1992), 53–4 and 80.
119 For Martin, see Christopher Moore, 'Archer Evans Stringer Martin,' *DCB*
    online; and David Ricardo Williams, 'Judges at War: Mr Justice Martin and
    Chief Justice Hunter,' *Law Society of Upper Canada Gazette* 16 (1982): 292.
120 'Shall We Stop Appealing to the Privy Council,' *CLT* 32 (1912): 804.

4. Sources of Law: Statutes, Codes, and Case Law

1 English Law Ordinance, 1867, in *The Laws of British Columbia* (Victoria:
  Queen's Printer, 1871), no. 70; Hamar Foster, 'British Columbia: Legal
  Institutions in the Far West, from Contact to 1871,' in *Canada's Legal
  Inheritances*, ed. W. Wesley Pue and DeLloyd J. Guth (Winnipeg:
  University of Manitoba, 2001), 309 and 311.
2 *Temporary Government of Rupert's Land and North-Western Territory Act*, SC
  1869, c 3, s 5; *North-West Territories Act*, SC 1871, c 16, s 4.
3 *Supreme Court Act*, SM 1871, c 2, s 1; *North-West Territories Act*, SC 1886,
  c 25, s 3; *Application of Laws to Manitoba Act*, SC 1888, c 33, s 1; *Sinclair v
  Mulligan*, (1886) 3 Man LR 481 and (1888) 5 Man LR 17; *Consolidation of the
  Statutes Act*, SM 1878, c 3, s 3; *Consolidated Statutes of Manitoba* (Winnipeg:
  Government Printer, 1880).
4 On this and the next paragraph, see Louis Massicotte, 'Le Parlement du
  Québec en transition,' *Canadian Public Administration* 28 (1985): 550; Pierre
  Issalys, 'La rédaction législative et la réception de la technique française,'
  in *Droit québécois et droit français. Communauté, autonomie, concordance*, ed. H.
  Patrick Glenn (Cowansville, QC: Éditions Yvon Blais, 1993), at 147–57. The
  Manitoba private acts are SM 2020, c 29 and c 30. At the federal level much
  more control was exerted. Fewer than 10 per cent of federal bills in the first
  20 years after Confederation were initiated by individual members.

5 See, for example, *Consolidation of the Statute Laws Act*, SBC 1886, c 19, s 1; *Revised Statutes of Canada Act*, SC 1886, c 4, preamble. See, for a contemporary affirmation, W. Martin Griffin, 'The Course of Statute Revision in Canada,' *CLJ* 32 (1896): 383; and generally Norman Larson, 'Statute Revision and Consolidation: History, Process and Problems,' *Ottawa Law Review* 19 (1977): 321.

6 See *Volume 1*, 439–46.

7 *Revision and Consolidation of the Statutes Act*, SNB 1900, c 9.

8 *An Act to Amend and Consolidate the Laws respecting Indians*, SC 1876, c 18; *An Act to Amend and Consolidate the Laws respecting Indians*, SC 1880, c 28.

9 *Revised Statutes of Canada Act*, SC 1903, c 61, s 3; *Consolidation of Public Statutes Act*, SNB 1877, c 13, s 3.

10 'The Independence of the Judiciary,' *CLJ* 39 (1903): 539.

11 For the information in this paragraph, see the various consolidations, which often named the commissioners and/or included statutes authorizing the consolidation that did so: *CLR* 2 (1903): 172; Second Report of the Commissioners, in Ontario, *Sessional Papers*, 1875–6, no. 37; Report of the Commissioners, in Ontario, Sessional Papers, 1888, no. 46.

12 Quotation from Second Report of the Commissioners, Ontario, *Sessional Papers*, 1875–6, no. 37. For the 1859 and 1860 consolidations, see Jim Phillips and Tom Collins, 'The Colonial Origins of the Division of Powers,' in *Law, Life and the Teaching of Legal History: Essays in Honour of G. Blaine Baker*, ed. Ian Pilarczyk, Angela Fernandez, and Brian Young (Montreal and Kingston: McGill-Queen's University Press, 2022).

13 *Statute Consolidation Acts*, SQ 1876, c 8, and SQ 1880, c 2; *Revised Statutes Act*, RSQ 1887, c 5.

14 These examples are from the annual volumes of the *Statutes of Canada*, 1867–9.

15 For a discussion of one example, see Paul Craven, '"The modern spirit of the law": Blake, Mowat, and the Breaches of Contract Act, 1877,' in *EHCL VIII*, 145–8.

16 Second Report of the Commissioners, Ontario, *Sessional Papers*, 1875–6, no. 37.

17 Third Report, *Sessional Papers*, 1877, no. 20; RSO 1877, appendixes B and C; RSNS 1873, appendix B; CSNB 1877, appendix; Stepan Wood, 'Premier Davie, Meet King Rex: Reconsidering Reception in Light of British Columbia's Forgotten 1897 Consolidation of English Statute Law' (unpublished, 2022, on file with the authors).

18 The reception rules are discussed in *Volume 1*, 338–41. See also
J.E. Côté, 'The Reception of English Law,' *Alberta Law Review* 15
(1997): 29.

19 *Revised Statutes Act*, SBC 1895, c 50, s 2. What follows on RSBC 1897
is from Wood, 'British Columbia's Forgotten 1897 Consolidation.' We
are grateful to Professor Wood for permission to cite this paper, and all
quotations from primary sources that follow in this section are from it.
See also David Ricardo Williams, 'Theodore Davie,' *DCB* online; and *The
Revised Statutes of British Columbia 1897 Being a Consolidation and Revision
of the Statutes Applicable to British Columbia, and within the Power of the
Legislature to Enact*, 2 vols. (Victoria: Queen's Printer, 1897).

20 For the debate over Begbie's legacy, see Hamar Foster, 'Sharp as a
Knife: Judge Begbie and Reconciliation,' in *Voicing Identity: Cultural
Appropriation and Indigenous Issues*, ed. Kent McNeil and John Borrows
(Toronto: University of Toronto Press, 2022).

21 *Revised Statutes Act*, SBC 1897, c 41.

22 *Consolidation of the Statutes of Ontario Act*, SO 1897, c 3; Order in Council,
17 Dec. 1902, in Ontario, *Sessional Papers*, 1902, no. 49; *The Revised Statutes
of Ontario, 1897, Volume III, Being a Consolidation and Revision of Certain
Imperial Statutes Relating to Property and Civil Rights Incorporated into the
Law of Ontario by Virtue of Provincial Legislation up to the End of the year
1897, with an Appendix Containing (1) Imperial Constitutional Statutes, (2)
Imperial Statutes of General Practical Utility in Force in Ontario ex proprio
vigore, (3) The Habeas Corpus Act, and (4) a Table of Imperial Statutes in Force
in Canada at the End of the Year 1901, ex proprio vigore* (Toronto: Queen's
Printer, 1902).

23 For the *BNA Act 1871*, see chapter 14. The other four were the *Petition of
Right* (1628), the *Bill of Rights* (1688), the *Act of Settlement* (1701), and the
Colonial Laws Validity Act (1865).

24 'Revised Statutes of Ontario, Vol III,' *CLJ* 38 (1902): 65 at 65–6.

25 For all the statutes referred to here, see chapter 15.

26 For all the statutes referred to here, see chapter 11.

27 Some of these moves are discussed elsewhere in this volume, such as the
successful attempt to create a uniform law governing the British subject
status of persons naturalized in the dominions, in chapter 2. On attempts
to impose on Canadian courts the duty to follow English precedent, see
later in this chapter. Patterns of mimesis in legal culture are explored
in Philip Girard, 'The Supreme Court of Nova Scotia, Responsible
Government, and the Quest for Legitimacy, 1850–1920,' *Dalhousie Law
Journal* 17 (1994): 429.

28 These factors and others are noted by Bernard J. Hibbitts, 'Her Majesty's Yankees: American Authority in the Supreme Court of Victorian Nova Scotia, 1837–1901,' in *The Supreme Court of Nova Scotia, 1754–2004: From Imperial Bastion to Provincial Oracle*, ed. Philip Girard, Jim Phillips, and Barry Cahill (Toronto: University of Toronto Press for the Osgoode Society for Canadian Legal History, 2004) .

29 Young CJ, in *Fraser v Salter* (1869) 7 NSR 424 at 441; second quotation at 423, per Wilkins J; see Hibbitts, 'Her Majesty's Yankees,' 330–1.

30 *Re Missouri Steamship Co* (1889) 42 Ch D 321 at 330.

31 J.M. McIntyre, 'The Use of American Cases in Canadian Courts,' *UBC Law Review* 2 (1964–6): 478; S.I. Bushnell, 'The Use of American Cases,' *University of New Brunswick Law Journal* 35 (1986): 157.

32 *Pledge v Carr* [1895] 1 Ch 51.

33 *London Street Tramways v London County Council* [1898] AC 375 at 381.

34 *Judicature Act*, SO 1895, c 12, s 79; P.B. Mignault, 'The Authority of Decided Cases,' *CBR* 3 (1925): 1.

35 (1909) 41 SCR 516, quotations at 549 and 550. The bank appealed to the JCPC, which disagreed with the law as stated by the SCC but upheld the result on other grounds and did not advert to the stare decisis issue: [1911] AC 120. The substantive point at issue in *Stuart* is addressed in chapter 15.

36 *Ross v The Queen* (1896) 25 SCR 564, 566–7; *Salvas v Vassal* (1897) 27 SCR 68; Michel Morin, 'Des juristes sédentaires? L'influence du droit anglais et du droit français sur l'interprétation du *Code civil du Bas Canada*,' *Revue du barreau* 60 (2000): 247 at 318, 336.

37 *Stuart v Bank of Montreal*, at 549.

38 Frank Hodgins, 'The Authority of English Decisions,' *CBR* 1 (1923): 470 at 484.

39 Bora Laskin, *The British Tradition in Canadian Law* (London: Stevens & Sons, 1969), 60.

40 G. Blaine Baker, 'The Reconstitution of Upper Canadian Legal Thought in the Late-Victorian Empire, *LHR* 3 (1985): 219. Baker based his conclusions almost entirely on legal texts (where they are arguably apposite), not on case law, and others have tended to generalize the Ontario case posited by him to Canada at large.

41 Hibbitts, 'Her Majesty's Yankees,' 342.

42 Richard A. Danner, 'Law Libraries and Laboratories: The Legacies of Langdell and His Metaphor,' *Law Library Journal* 107 (2015): 7.

43 Edmond Lareau, *Histoire du droit canadien: depuis les origines de la colonie jusqu'à nos jours*, 2 vols. (Montreal: A. Périard, 1889), 2:298 (authors' translation). Especially useful for what follows are Morin, 'Des juristes

sédentaires'; Sylvio Normand, 'Le Code civil et l'identité,' in *Du Code civil du Québec: contribution à l'histoire immédiate d'une codification réussie*, ed. Serge Lortie, Nicholas Kasirer, and Jean-Guy Belley (Montreal: Thémis, 2005); Sylvio Normand, 'La codification de 1866: contexte et impact,' in *Droit québécois et droit français*; Sylvio Normand, 'Une culture en redéfinition: La culture juridique québécoise durant la seconde moitié du XIXe siècle,' in *Transformation de la culture juridique québécoise*, ed. Bjarn Melkevik (Quebec: Presses de l'Université Laval, 1998) ; Brian Young, 'Overlapping Identities: The Quebec Civil Code of 1866, Its Reception and Interpretation,' in *Le Code Napoléon, un ancêtre vénéré? Mélanges offerts à Jacques Vanderlinden*, ed. R. Beauthier and I. Rorive (Brussels: Bruylant, 2004); *Quebec Civil Law: An Introduction to Quebec Private Law*, ed. J.E.C. Brierley and R.A. Macdonald (Toronto: Emond Montgomery, 1993), 24–45.

44 M. Bibaud, *Exégèse de jurisprudence* (privately published, n.d.), cited in Normand, 'La codification de 1866,' 58; E. Bellefeuille, *Le Code civil annoté ...* (Montreal: Beauchemin & Valois, 1879), vii (authors' translation); J-J Beauchamp, 'De l'étude et de la pratique du droit: Théorie,' *Revue légale*, n.s., 1 (1895): 8 at 9; R. McGibbon, *The Revision of the Civil Code of the Province of Quebec: An Address Delivered before the Junior Bar Association of Montreal, December 4th, 1905* (Montreal, 1906), 8, all cited in Normand, 'Le Code civil et l'identité,' 621–3. On Beauchamp, see Sylvio Normand, 'Jean-Joseph Beauchamp,' *DCB* online.

45 Thomas Jean-Jacques Loranger, *Commentaire sur le Code civil du Bas-Canada*, 2 vols. (Montreal: Des Presses à Vapeur de la Minerve, 1873–79), both quotations at 1:22.

46 Jetté's work was not published until 1922–37 in the *Revue du droit*. On Mignault's work, see Sylvio Normand, '*Le droit civil canadien de Pierre-Basile Mignault* ou la confection d'un palimpseste,' in *Le faux en droit privé*, ed. Nicholas Kasirer (Montreal: Les Éditions Thémis, 2000). On Jetté, see Sylvio Normand, 'Sir Louis-Amable Jetté,' *DCB* online.

47 François Langelier, *Cours de droit civil* (Montreal: Wilson & Lafleur, 1905), 1:xii. For an example of Langelier's bold ideas, see Eric Reiter, *Wounded Feelings: Litigating Emotions in Quebec, 1870–1950* (Toronto: University of Toronto Press and Osgoode Society for Canadian Legal History, 2019), 37–40. See also Jocelyn Saint-Pierre, 'Sir François Langelier,' *DCB* online.

48 Vilbon took part only in the first three volumes, hence subsequent references are to de Lorimier only.

49 De Lorimier and Vilbon, *La bibliothèque du Code civil de la province de Québec* (Montreal: La Minerve, 1871–90), 21 vols., 1:5. De Lorimier's uncle was a notary prominent in the rebellions of 1837–8 who was convicted of treason and executed in 1839. His father was also active in the rebellion but managed to escape to Iowa, where de Lorimier was born, before the family returned to Montreal in 1842: Brian Young, 'Charles-Chamilly de Lorimier,' *DCB* online.

50 Jean-Joseph Beauchamp, *Répertoire général de jurisprudence canadienne*, 4 vols. (Montreal: Wilson & Lafleur, 1914–15). On Mathieu, see Sylvio Normand, 'Michel Mathieu,' *DCB* online.

51 On Girouard's bill, see Normand, 'Le Code civil et l'identité'; Pierre-Basile Mignault, 'Le Code civil au Canada,' in *Société d'études législatives, Le Code civil 1804–1904, Livre du centenaire* (Paris: Librairie Edouard Duchemin, 1904), 731.

52 Pierre-Gabriel Jobin, 'L'influence de la doctrine française sur le droit civil québécois: le rapprochement et l'éloignement de deux continents,' *Revue internationale de droit comparé* 44 (1992): 381, reports that during the 1900–39 period, 42 per cent of judgments (in selected areas of law) contain reference to French authors, but only 31 per cent to doctrinal works. On reference to modern French authors, see Morin, 'Des juristes sédentaires,' 373–6.

53 F.P. Walton, *The Scope and Interpretation of the Civil Code of Lower Canada* (Montreal: Wilson & Lafleur, 1907). On Walton, see the entry by H.G. Hanbury, rev. Eric Metcalfe, in *Oxford Dictionary of National Biography Online*.

54 Jobin, 'L'influence de la doctrine française.'

55 David Howes's seminal article on this topic, 'From Polyjurality to Monojurality: The Transformation of Quebec Law, 1875–1929,' *McGill Law Journal* 32 (1987): 523, has been effectively critiqued by H. Patrick Glenn, 'Le droit comparé et l'interprétation du Code civil du Québec,' in *Le nouveau Code civil*, and especially by Morin, 'Des juristes sédentaires.'

56 Beauchamp, *Repertoire général*, 1:xi (authors' translation).

57 The French Revolution had abolished all intermediary entities between the individual and the state, such as corporations, which thus did not appear in the 1804 Code but were authorized by special legislation later in the century.

58 For an empirical study of the implementation of these articles, see Thierry Nootens, *Fous, prodigues et ivrognes: Familles et déviance à Montréal au XIXe siècle* (Montreal and Kingston: McGill-Queen's University Press, 2007).

59 SC 1882, c 42, recognized in an amendment to article 125 of the *Code* via RSQ 1888, art 6230; in 1890, marriage with the daughter of a deceased wife's sister was also authorized: SC 1890, c 36. Marriage with a deceased husband's brother would have to wait until 1923: SC 1923, c 19. For more on this issue, see chapter 15.

60 The trust: SQ 1879, c 29, added to the Code in the statutory revision of 1888. In France, married women were given control over their own salaries in 1907; Quebec would wait until 1931 (to be treated in Volume 3 of this work). The 1868 Act is SC 1868, c 7, discussed in Brierley and Macdonald, *Quebec Civil Law*, at 30.

61 SQ 1906, c 38. Such forfeiture had been eliminated in two stages by federal legislation, partly by SC 1869, c 29, and completely in the *Criminal Code* of 1892, but in *Dumphy v Kehoe* (1891) 21 *Revue légale* 119 the Quebec Superior Court found the 1869 provision unconstitutional as relating to property and civil rights in the province. Hence, forfeiture to the provincial Crown still applied, but unlike English law, subject to the payment of debts of the convict or executed person. The 1906 Act rendered provincial and federal law on this topic uniform.

62 SQ 1893–4, c 46, completed by SQ 1916, c 52; such privileges are analogous to mechanics' liens in the common law; see Thierry Nootens, 'Droit civil, condition ouvrière et transition au capitalisme industriel au Québec,' *CJLS* 31 (2016): 47.

63 Articles 1569a–e, added by SQ 1910, c 39; further amendments were made to these articles by SQ 1913–14, c 63.

64 Antonio Perrault, *Traité de droit commercial*, 3 vols. (Montreal: A. Lévesque, 1936–9).

65 Nicholas Kasirer, 'Si La Joconde est au Louvre, où trouve-t-on le Code civil du Bas-Canada?,' *Cahiers de droit* 46 (2005): 481. The most thorough edition of the *Civil Code* showing 'point in time' versions of all articles is Paul Crépeau and John E.C. Brierley, eds., *Code Civil – Civil Code 1866– 1980* (Montreal: Chambre des Notaires du Quebec and SOQUIJ, 1981).

5. Quebec Civil Law: A Mixed Legal System in Confederation

1 Jack Jedwab, 'Sir Rodolphe Forget,' *DCB* online. Forget's daughter Thérèse Casgrain would become an indefatigable champion of women's and workers' rights from the 1920s until her death in 1981.

2 On Kahnawà:ke, see chapter 10. For the Hurons, see John Dickinson and Brian Young, *A Short History of Quebec* (Montreal and Kingston: McGill-Queen's University Press, 2003), 207–8.

3 In the most prominent of these, *Brassard et al v Langevin* (1877) 1 SCR 145, the trial judge, the ultramontane Adolphe-Basile Routhier, had found the actions of the clergy unobjectionable, but the SCC found them to be a violation of the *Dominion Elections Act* of 1874.

4 Dickinson and Young, *Short History*, 174.

5 On Easter duty, René Hardy, *Contrôle social et mutation de la culture religieuse au Québec 1830–1930* (Montreal: Boréal, 1999), 142; on ensuring order, based on extensive correspondence between Catholic clergy and the clerk of the peace for the district of Mauricie, 171–86.

6 Rainer Knopff, 'Quebec's "Holy War" as "Regime" Politics: Reflections on the Guibord Case,' *Canadian Journal of Political Science* 12 (1979): 315; Lovell Clarke, *The Guibord Affair* (Toronto: Holt, Rinehart & Wilson, 1971). The JCPC decision is reported at 1874 UKPC 70.

7 A number of the issues to be discussed in what follows are treated in Michel Morin, 'Des juristes sédentaires? L'influence du droit anglais et du droit français sur l'interprétation du Code civil du Bas Canada' *Revue du Barreau* 60 (2000): 247.

8 *Fisher v Webster* (1894) 6 CS 25; *Lafontaine v Poulin* (1912) 18 *Revue légale*, n.s., 378 (CS); re housing, *Janvey v Cree* (1895) 8 CS 19. In civil law, a married woman kept her maiden name for legal purposes but used her husband's surname socially. Thus, the plaintiff here would be identified as Dame Fisher in a lawsuit but Madame Webster socially.

9 W.A. Baker, 'Incapacité de la femme mariée: dissertation sur les articles 176 à 184 C.C.,' *RL* (*n.s.*), 1 (1895): 154 ('human dignity' requires that the person in charge of the household be the husband). For Louis Loranger, in his doctoral thesis *De l'incapacité légale de la femme mariée* (Montreal: Eusèbe Senécal & Cie, 1899), God had placed man in this position.

10 See *Volume 1*, 697; P.-B. Mignault, *Le droit civil canadien basé sur les 'Répétitions écrites sur le Code Civil' de Frédéric Mourlon, avec revue de la jurisprudence de nos tribunaux*, 9 vols. (Montreal: C. Théoret, 1895–1917), VI (1902), 405–65. Patterns of dower are explored in Bettina Bradbury, *Wife to Widow: Lives, Laws, and Politics in Nineteenth-Century Montreal* (Vancouver: UBC Press, 2011). On the comparison with common law Canada, see Thierry Nootens, *Genre, patrimoine et droit civil: Les femmes mariées de la bourgeoisie québécoise en procès, 1900–1930* (Montreal and Kingston: McGill-Queen's University Press, 2018), 19–21.

11 *McFarran v Montreal Park & Island Railway* (1900) 30 SCR 410. For an in-depth analysis of the choice of matrimonial regime made by spouses, its consequences, and variations in these trends over the course of the century, see Bradbury, *Wife to Widow*.

12 An important exception was the purchase of life insurance after marriage, provided for in the *Husbands and Parents Life Insurance Act*, SPC 1865, c 17, but never incorporated into the *Civil Code* itself.

13 Nootens, *Genre, patrimoine et droit civil*, chap. 2.

14 *Odell v Gregory* (1894) 5 CS 348.

15 *Proulx v Klineberg and Sheffer* (1906) 30 CS 1.

16 *Fox v Lamarche* (1907) 16 BR 83.

17 The cases in this and the next paragraph are discussed in Nootens, *Genre, patrimoine et droit civil*, chaps. 5 and 7.

18 *Courville v Paquette* (1916) 50 CS 94; see generally Thierry Nootens, 'L'abnégation comme fondement de l'ordre juridique et social: l'expérience des femmes mariées au Québec, 1866–1930,' in *L'abnégation en droit civil*, ed. Anne-Sophie Hulin and Robert Leckey (Montreal: Thomson Reuters, 2017).

19 This would finally be modified in 1915, to be dealt with in Volume 3. Relatives of the twelfth degree are those with whom one shares one set of great-great-great-great-grandparents. These provisions were written in gender-neutral fashion but in practice it was the widow rather than the widower who was likely to be affected by them.

20 For example, an Ontario act of 1895 entitled a childless widow to succeed to her late husband's entire estate where it was valued at $1,000 or less, or to take $1,000 'off the top' if it was worth more, the excess going to other relatives of the husband: *Intestates' Estates Act*, SO 1895, c 21.

21 See chapter 15.

22 *Delpit v Côté* (1901) 20 CS 338. The husband was the son of the famous French novelist Édouard Delpit and the private secretary to the lieutenant governor of Quebec. *In re Marriage Act* (1912) 46 SCR 132; *Despatie v Tremblay* [1921] 1 AC 702. See generally Michel Morin, 'De la reconnaissance officielle à la tolérance des religions: l'état civil et les empêchements de mariage de 1628 à nos jours,' in *Le droit, la religion et le 'raisonnable': Le fait religieux entre monisme étatique et pluralisme juridique*, ed. Jean-François Gaudreault-Desbiens (Montreal: Éditions Thémis, 2009).

23 *Gladston v Slayton* (1913) 21 BR 440 at 443 (authors' translation). Where a husband left his wife, however, and she was seen as blameless, he could still be obliged to support her via an alimentary pension.

24 Marie-Aimée Cliche, 'Les Séparations de corps dans le district judiciaire de Montréal de 1900 à 1930,' *CJLS* 12 (1997): 71. For unknown reasons, it appears that the rate of petitioning for separation from bed and board was declining in Quebec City over the same period. On court fees, see *Des Troismaisons v Tellier* (1909) 35 CS 501.

25 Mignault, *Le droit civil canadien* (1896), 2:10. On moral judgments on wives' behaviour, see Nootens, *Genre, patrimoine et droit civil*, chap. 6.

26 *Bonneau c Circé* (1890) 19 RL 437 at 439 (QB) (authors' translation).

27 *Cote v Daudelin* (1904) 11 CS 519 (deprivation allowed); *Drolet v Lapierre* (1889) 16 BR 1 and *L'Heureux v Boivin* (1881) 7 CS 220 (deprivation not allowed: 'she cannot be allowed to starve' at 223).

28 In theory, and contrary to English law, either spouse could be compelled to pay an alimentary pension to the other, depending on their respective resources. On the common law regarding custody, see chapter 15.

29 *Lafleur v Gagnon* (1910) 16 *RL* (n.s.), 398. Such actions for 'freestanding' pensions had been allowed as early as 1878: *Lachapelle v Beaudoin* (1878) 1 *Legal Notes* 581 (SC).

30 *Fournier v Paradis* (1894) 6 CS 116 at 117; Nootens, *L'abnégation*, makes this point at 67.

31 *Wheeler v Smith* (1885) 19 *RL* (n.s.), 575 (SC). Formal amendment of article 188 to remove the double standard would have to wait until 1954. Where, however, the adultery took place discreetly in the home after the wife had left it, the court blamed her for her husband's 'faiblesses' and refused to grant a judicial separation: *Tudor v Hart* (1888) 4 MLR 348 (SC).

32 *Lebeau v Plouffe* (1894) 5 CS 59.

33 *Laperrière v Ribardy* (1874) 5 *RL* (n.s.) 742 at 743. Adrian Popovici, 'De l'aliénation d'affection: essai critique et comparative,' *CBR* 48 (1970): 236. The property argument was completely unnecessary, given that wives could also take such action; clearly, they had no property interest in their husbands. In *Gober v Agnew* (1907), the female plaintiff had married Augustus Agnew when he was underage and had not sought the consent of his parents. When his parents sought the annulment of the marriage, she sued them and his sister for alienation of her husband's affection: Eric Reiter, *Wounded Feelings: Litigating Emotions in Quebec, 1870–1950* (Toronto: University of Toronto Press for the Osgoode Society for Canadian Legal History, 2019), 138–40.

34 Mignault, *Le droit civil canadien* (1896), 2:141.

35 *Barlow v Kennedy* (1871) 17 LCJ 257 (QB).

36 Cynthia S. Fish, 'La puissance paternelle et les cas de garde d'enfant au Québec 1866–1928,' *RHAF* 57 (2004): 509.

37 (1900) 2 Rapports de pratique 539 (SC).

38 (1900) 2 Rapports de pratique 554.

39 *Mission de la Grande Ligne v Morissette* (1889) 33 LCJ 227 (SC). The Code provided in articles 314–22 for minors to be emancipated from paternal authority by a judge or prothonotary, but this process had not been invoked in this case.

40 CN, art 1134.

41 P.P.C. Haanappel, 'Contract Law Reform in Quebec,' *CBR* 60 (1982): 393; Brigitte Lefebvre, 'L'évolution de la justice contractuelle en droit québécois: une influence marquée du droit français quoique non exclusive,' in *L'acculturation en droit des affaires*, ed. Jean-Louis Navarro and Guy Lefebvre (Montreal: Éditions Thémis, 2007).

42 CN, art 1674; the other examples dealt with partition in the context of succession, where one or more heirs received less property than they should have.

43 *Bernard v JA Hurteau & Co* (1906) 30 CS 184.

44 *Grange v McLennan* (1883) 9 SCR 385; *Salvas v Vassal* (1897) 27 SCR 68. In *Grange*, for example, Justice Fournier wrote for the majority, while Justice Taschereau strongly dissented.

45 *Glengoil SS Co v Pilkington* (1897) 28 SCR 146. The Court found nonetheless against the shipper by interpreting the clause narrowly: the damage was due to negligent stowage, which, according to the Court, was not covered in the exculpatory clause.

46 SQ 1906, c 40, and see below. Armand Lavergne, *Trente ans de vie nationale* (Montreal: Éditions du Zodiaque, 1934), 121–31, 147–52; SQ 1910, c 40.

47 S.W. Jacobs, *The Railway Law of Canada* (Montreal: John Lovell & Son, 1909), 527–8.

48 Yves Roby, *The Franco-Americans of New England: Dreams and Realities* (Montreal: Septentrion, 2004), 1.

49 Statistics derived from Quebec, *Sessional Papers*, Inspection of Factories (1889–94); *Sessional Papers*, Inspection of Industrial Establishments and Public Buildings (1905–9).

50 Mignault, *Le droit civil canadien* (1901), 5:684.

51 SQ 1885, c 32. The long title of the act was *An Act to Protect the Life and Health of Persons Employed in Factories*. Various sections stated that where the precaution in question was not taken, the factory 'shall be deemed to be kept unlawfully … so that the health of any person employed therein is likely to be permanently injured' – arguably deeming the 'fault' required by article 1053 to exist.

52 A federal act of 1903 outlawed such clauses altogether in the railway industry: SC 1903, c 81.

53 *Shawinigan Carbide Co v Doucet* (1909) 42 SCR 281, 19 KB 271. On earlier Quebec case law adopting this approach, see David Howes, 'Faultless Reasoning: Reconstructing the Foundations of Civil Responsibility in Quebec since the Original Codification,' *Dalhousie Law Journal* 14 (1991): 90.

54 On these trends in the Quebec case law, see Katherine Lippel, *Le droit des accidentés du travail à une indemnité: analyse historique et critique* (Montreal: Éditions Thémis, 1986), 16–35; quotation from J. Cléophas Lamothe, *Responsabilité du Patron dans les Accidents du Travail* (Montreal: S. Carswell, 1905), 23 (authors' translation).

55 Frederick Parker Walton, *The Workmen's Compensation Act 1909 of the Province of Quebec* (Montreal: John Lovell & Son, 1910), 21–2.

56 Mignault, *Le droit civil canadien* (1901), 5:372–6.

57 (1898) 13 CS 471.

58 (1888) 22 SCR 721.

59 SPC 1847, c 6. The Canadian version broadened the class of persons who might bring the action.

60 *Ravary v Grand Trunk Railway* (1860) LCJ 49 (QB); this paragraph and the next rely on Reiter, *Wounded Feelings*, chap. 6.

61 *Couillard v Jeannotte* (1891) 3 BR 461 at 471–2 (SC).

62 (1894) 3 BR 496 at 498.

63 *Robinson v CPR* (1891) 19 SCR 292, [1892] AC 491. Re aid from the Conseil des métiers, see *La Presse*, 31 Oct. 1891, 8; 14 Nov. 1891, 4. We thank Eric Reiter for these references.

64 (1909) 42 SCR 205.

65 Not until after the adoption of the *Civil Code of Quebec* in 1991, which deleted the former article 1056, did the Quebec Court of Appeal affirm that moral damages, including those for grief, were fully recoverable; *Augustus v Gosset* (1995) 68 QAC 127, affd [1996] 3 SCR 268.

66 [1906] AC 187, reversing (1903) 34 SCR 45; *Reg v Grenier* (1899) 30 SCR 42.

67 *Asbestos and Asbestic Co v Durand* (1900) 30 SCR 285.

68 *McArthur v Dominion Cartridge Co* [1905] AC 72 at 77, reversing (1901) 31 SCR 392.

69 On the law prior to the enactment of the *Workmen's Compensation Act, 1909,* see Frederick Parker Walton, *The New Laws of Employers' Liability in England and France and Their Bearing on the Law of the Province of Quebec*

(Montreal: C. Théoret, 1900); Walton, *Workmen's Compensation Act 1909*; Lamothe, *Responsabilité du Patron*; Lippel, *Le droit des accidentés du travail*; Andrew Stritch, 'Power Resources, Institutions and Policy Learning: The Origins of Workers' Compensation in Quebec,' *Canadian Journal of Political Science* 38 (2005): 549. 'Workmen' included women workers.

70 Lippel, *Le droit des accidentés du travail*, 41. Mignault, *Droit civil canadien*, vol. 5 (1901) states that there were '800 or 900' such cases, but it is not clear whence he derives this figure. The rate of success in the Quebec courts was somewhat higher than that reported by R.C.B. Risk for Ontario in the same period: '"This Nuisance of Litigation": The Origins of Workers' Compensation in Ontario,' in *EHCL II*, 426–36.

71 Lamothe, *Responsabilité du Patron*, 117. 'The Supreme Court has become a nightmare for victims of workplace accidents.'

72 Walton, *New Laws*, 2.

73 *Montreal Rolling Mills v Corcoran* (1896) 26 SCR 595.

74 *Gauthier v Wertheim* (1905) CS 280 (Ct Rev), 283–5 (authors' translation).

75 Mignault, *Le droit civil canadien* (1901), 9:685–6.

76 See the summing up by Duff J in *Montreal Light, Heat and Power Co v Regan* (1908) 40 SCR 580.

77 Lippel, *Le droit des accidentés du travail*, 47, relying on Lamothe and the *Rapport de la Commission d'enquête sur les accidents du travail* (Quebec, 1908) (Globensky Commission), which led to the adoption of the *Workmen's Compensation Act* in 1909.

78 Walton, *New Laws*, 2; Lamothe, *Responsabilité du Patron*, 116. On the percentage of unionized workers see Stritch, 'Power Resources,' 559.

79 Terence Ison, *The Forensic Lottery: A Critique on Tort Liability as a System of Personal Injury Compensation* (London: Staples, 1968).

80 SQ 1909, c 66.

81 Walton, *Workmen's Compensation Act, 1909*, 22. For examples, see *Desrosiers v St-Lawrence Furniture Co* (1905) 27 CS 73; *Gauthier v Wertheim* (1905) 28 CS 280; *Shawinigan Carbide Co v Doucet* (1909) 35 CS 385 (reversed in the Court of Appeal but restored by the SCC (1910) 42 SCR 281).

82 The Canadian Manufacturers' Association reported that jury awards of $8,000 to $10,000 had been made against its members: Stritch, 'Power Resources,' at 559. However, only one reported case is known to have made an award as high as $10,000 in a wrongful death suit, being $6,000 to the widow and $1,000 each to the deceased's four minor children, while the maxima were more usually in the $4,000 to $5,000 range; *Miller v Grand Trunk Railway* [1906] AC 187 (PC), overturning dismissal by the SCC and restoring jury award.

83 How this operated in practice remains to be investigated.

84 Madeleine Cantin Cumyn, 'Le droit privé des biens: à l'enseigne de la continuité,' in *Droit québécois et droit français: communauté, autonomie, concordance*, ed. H. Patrick Glenn (Cowansville, QC: Yvon Blais, 1993) .

85 Thomas Jean-Jacques Loranger, *Commentaire sur le Code civil du Bas-Canada*, 2 vols. (Montreal: Presses à vapeur de la Minerve, 1873–79), 1:36 (authors' translation).

86 SPC 1858, c 85, applicable to both Upper and Lower Canada. Previous laws allowing incorporation had been limited to particular types of business, but the 1864 law covered a wide range of enterprises as well as certain non-profit activities such as mechanics' institutes, libraries, exhibition halls, and the like: SPC, c 23. See also *Volume 1*, 636–40.

87 *Money-Lenders Act, 1906*, SC 1906, c 32; *Dallaire v Jacques* [1953] CS 304 (on 12 per cent interest as usurious). See generally Mary Anne Waldron, 'A Brief History of Interest Caps in Consumer Lending: Have We Learned Enough from the Past?,' *Canadian Business Law Journal* 50 (2011): 300.

88 SQ 1914, c 51; Suzanne Le Bel, 'Les émissions d'obligations dans le droit de la province de Québec de 1890 à nos jours,' *Cahiers de droit* 21 (1980): 43. 'Obligations' are bonds.

89 SC 1890, c 31, ss 74–6.

90 Sylvio Normand and Alain Hudon, 'Confection du cadastre seigneurial et du cadastre graphique,' *Revue du notariat* 91 (1988–9): 184.

91 SQ 1854, c 3. This and the next paragraph rely on Benoît Grenier, '"Le dernier endroit dans l'univers": À propos de l'extinction des rentes seigneuriales au Québec, 1854–1974,' *RHAF* 64 (2010): 75–98. On commutation in Montreal, see Robert Sweeny, 'Paysans et propriété: Les commutations montréalaises, 1840–1859,' in *Famille et marché XVIe–XXe siècles*, ed. Christian Dessureault et al. (Sillery, QC: Septentrion, 2003). For the effect of commutation at Kahnawà:ke, see chapter 10.

92 Luc Lépine, *Répertoire Numérique du Fonds des seigneuries de la région de Montréal* (Montreal: Ministère des Affaires culturelles, Archives nationales du Québec à Montréal, 1984).

93 On these provisions and the origins of the 1879 trust, see Marcel Faribault, *Traité théorique et pratique de la fiducie ou trust du droit civil dans la province de Québec* (Montreal: Wilson & Lafleur, 1936), 21–50; Madeleine Cantin Cumyn, 'L'origine de la fiducie québécoise,' in *Mélanges Paul-André Crépeau* (Cowansville, QC: Yvon Blais, 1997).

94 *Abbott v Fraser* (1874) 20 LCJ 197. The library was the first free public library in Montreal, maintained purely through the funds from Fraser's estate and other private donations until 2003.

95 SQ 1879, c 29.
96 On Langstaff, see Ian C. Pilarczyk, *'A Noble Roster': One Hundred and Fifty Years of Law at McGill* (Montreal: McGill University Faculty of Law, 1999), 58–68; Mary Jane Mossman, *The First Women Lawyers: A Comparative Study of Gender, Law, and the Legal Professions* (Portland, OR: Hart, 2006).

6. The Legal Professions, Legal Education, and Legal Literature

1 Philip Girard, 'Benjamin Russell,' *DCB* online.
2 Elizabeth Bloomfield, 'Lawyers as Members of Urban Business Élites in Southern Ontario, 1860 to 1920,' in *EHCL IV*, 113.
3 Curtis Cole, 'A Developmental Market: Growth Rates, Competition and Professional Standards in the Ontario Legal Profession, 1881–1936,' *Canada-US Law Journal* 7 (1984): 231; Philip Girard and Jeffrey Haylock, 'Stratification, Economic Adversity, and Diversity in an Urban Bar: Halifax, Nova Scotia, 1900–1950,' in *The Promise and Perils of Law: Lawyers in Canadian History*, ed. Constance Backhouse and W. Wesley Pue (Toronto: Irwin Law, 2009), 80; André Vachon, *Histoire du notariat canadien 1621–1960* (Quebec: Presses de l'Université Laval, 1962), 172; H.J. Morgan, ed., *The Canadian Legal Directory: Guide to the Bench and Bar of the Dominion of Canada* (Toronto: Carswell, 1878).
4 Bennett to Shannon Bowlby, 5 Apr. 1903, cited in Louis Knafla, 'Richard "Bonfire" Bennett: The Legal Practice of a Prairie Corporate Lawyer, 1898–1913,' in *EHCL IV*, 353. On 'systemic stabilization' and lawyerly migration, see Girard and Haylock, 'Stratification,' 79.
5 Quotations from Christopher Moore, *The Law Society of Upper Canada and Ontario's Lawyers 1797–1997* (Toronto: University of Toronto Press, 1997), 147; W. Wesley Pue, *Lawyers' Empire: Legal Professions and Cultural Authority, 1780–1950* (Vancouver: UBC Press, 2016), 80; and Vachon, *Histoire du notariat canadien*, 135–55.
6 Christopher Moore, 'Megafirm: A Chronology for the Large Law Firm in Canada,' in Backhouse and Pue, *Promise and Perils of Law*, 105–7; Dale Brawn, 'Dominant Professionals: The Role of Large-Firm Lawyers in Manitoba,' in *EHCL VII*; Girard and Haylock, 'Stratification.'
7 Wayne Hobson, 'Symbol of the New Profession: The Emergence of the Large Law Firm, 1870–1915,' in *The New High Priests: Lawyers in Post–Civil War America*, ed. Gerard W. Gawalt (Westport, CT: Greenwood, 1984) . Figures derived from Curtis Cole, *Osler, Hoskin & Harcourt: Portrait of a Partnership* (Toronto: McGraw-Hill Ryerson, 1995), appendix II. On the DBS cutoff, see Moore, 'Megafirm,' 110.

8 Moore, 'Megafirm,' 106.

9 C. Ian Kyer, *Lawyers, Families, and Businesses: The Shaping of a Bay Street Law Firm, Faskens 1863–1963* (Toronto: Osgoode Society for Canadian Legal History and Irwin Law, 2013), 51; Philip Girard, 'William Bruce Almon Ritchie,' *DCB* online; Cole, *Osler, Hoskin & Harcourt*; Christopher Moore, *McCarthy Tétrault: Building Canada's Premier Law Firm 1855–2005* (Vancouver: Douglas & McIntyre, 2005); and Jeffrey Haylock, 'Cravath by the Sea: Recruitment in the Large Halifax Law Firm, 1900–1955,' *Dalhousie Law Journal* 31 (2008): 401.

10 Cole, *Osler, Hoskin & Harcourt*, 48; Kyer, *Faskens*, 92.

11 D'Alton Lally McCarthy fonds, Law Society of Ontario Archives, draft memoir (n.p., n.d.), file 994-1-002. We thank Christopher Moore for this reference. McCarthy appeared in JCPC appeals from 1900 until the 1940s.

12 Carman Miller, 'Sir John Joseph Caldwell Abbott,' *DCB* online; Brawn, 'Dominant Professionals,' 405–6.

13 *Toronto Daily Star*, 6 Feb. 1901. On Osler's role in the prosecution of Louis Riel, see chapter 7; Patrick Brode, 'Britton Bath Osler,' *DCB* online.

14 W.R. Riddell, 'The Lawyer: An Address to the Ontario Bar Association,' *CLT* 27 (1907): 785 at 788.

15 *CLJ* 33 (1897): 307; Philip Girard, 'The Making of the Canadian Legal Profession: A Hybrid Heritage,' *International Journal of the Legal Profession* 21 (2014): 145 at 155–8.

16 Ibid., 160–3.

17 Ibid., 145; Michael Burrage, *Revolution and the Making of the Contemporary Legal Profession: England, France and the United States* (Oxford: Oxford University Press, 2006). On the clerkship proposal, see Robert Stevens, *Law School: Legal Education in America from the 1850s to the 1980s* (Chapel Hill: University of North Carolina Press, 1983), 120.

18 *Acte concernant le barreau de la province de Québec*, SQ 1886, c 14, art 49. Sylvio Normand, 'La transformation de la profession d'avocat au Québec, 1840–1900,' in *Entre justice et justiciables: les auxiliaires de la justice du Moyen Âge au XXe siècle*, ed. Claire Dolan (Quebec: Presses de l'Université Laval, 2005), 428–30. On the 1890 law, see Sylvio Normand, *Le droit comme discipline universitaire: Une Histoire de la Faculté de droit de l'Université Laval* (Quebec: Presses de l'Université Laval, 2005), 80.

19 Normand, *Le droit comme discipline universitaire*, 74; Vachon, *Histoire du notariat canadien*, 142–4.

20 D.G. Bell, *Legal Education in New Brunswick: A History* (Fredericton: University of New Brunswick, 1992), 70.

21 John Willis, *A History of Dalhousie Law School* (Toronto: University of Toronto Press, 1979). On the degree privilege, see Barry Cahill, *Professional Autonomy and the Public Interest: The Barristers' Society and Nova Scotia's Lawyers, 1825–2005* (Montreal and Kingston: McGill-Queen's University Press, 2019), 169–74; and Philip Girard, 'Richard Chapman Weldon' and 'Benjamin Russell,' both *DCB* online.

22 See the treatment of these scandals in chapter 3.

23 Bell, *Legal Education in New Brunswick*, 90; D.G. Bell, 'Slamming the Door on Brains: Two Early Twentieth-Century Law Schools and the Narrowing of Educational Opportunity,' in Backhouse and Pue, *Promise and Perils of Law*.

24 W. Wesley Pue, '"The Disquisitions of Learned Judges": Making Manitoba Lawyers, 1885–1931,' in *EHCL VIII*, 517.

25 W. Wesley Pue, *Law School: The Story of Legal Education in British Columbia* (Vancouver: UBC Faculty of Law, 1995); John P.S. McLaren, 'The History of Legal Education in Common Law Canada,' in *Legal Education in Canada*, ed. Roy J. Matas and Deborah McCawley (Montreal: Federation of Law Societies of Canada, 1987).

26 Walton (1858–1948), a member of the Scottish bar and former lecturer in Roman law at Glasgow, resigned the deanship in 1915 to become director of the Khedival School of Law in Cairo; see the entry by H.G. Hanbury in the *Oxford Dictionary of National Biography Online*. His treatise on the *Civil Code* was republished by Butterworths with an introduction by Professor Maurice Tancelin in 1980.

27 Ivan Wotherspoon, *A Manual of the Practice and Procedure in the Several Courts Having Civil Jurisdiction in the Province of Quebec* (Montreal: Dawson, 1870).

28 Cornelius Masten, *Canadian Company Law: A Treatise of the Law of Joint Stock Companies in Canada* (Toronto: Canada Law Book, 1901); Masten, *The Canadian Law of Partnership* (Montreal: Snow Law Publishing, 1900).

29 These figures are derived by counting the titles in *A Legal Bibliography of the British Commonwealth of Nations*, vol. 3, *Canadian and British-American Colonial Law from Earliest Times to December 1956*, 2nd ed. (London: Sweet and Maxwell, 1964).

30 Joseph Boivin, *Loi corporative des compagnies à fonds social, Québec avec les formules en usage* (Quebec: Jos. E. Vincent, 1901).

31 Examples of many such books include R.E. Kingsford, *Collection of Such of the Revised Statutes of Ontario and of the Acts of the Legislature ... Passed in ... 1878, as Relate to Municipal Matters* (Toronto: Hunter Rose, 1878); and J.J. Kehoe, *The Municipal and Assessment Guide* (Toronto: Hunter Rose, 1900).

32 S.R. Clarke, *A Treatise on Criminal Law* (Toronto: Carswell, 1872); Henri-Elzéar Taschereau, *The Criminal Law Consolidation and Amendment Acts of 1869, … for the Dominion of Canada, as Amended and in Force on the 1st day of November 1874*, 2 vols. (Montreal: Lovell, 1875), iii; George Wheelock Burbidge, *A Digest of the Criminal Law of Canada (Crimes and Punishments): Founded by Permission on Sir James Fitzjames Stephen's Digest of the Criminal Law* (Toronto: 1890); Henri-Elzéar Taschereau, *The Criminal Code of Canada as Amended in 1893, with Commentaries, Annotations, Precedents of Indictments, Etc.* (Toronto: Carswell, 1893); James Crankshaw, *Criminal Code of Canada and the Canada Evidence Act* (Montreal: Théoret, 1894).

33 Loranger's book was published in Quebec City, and Travis's by Sun Publishing, Saint John. The other three were published in Toronto by J.C. Stuart, Carswell, and Canada Law Book. For these authors, see R.C.B. Risk, 'Constitutional Thought in the Late Nineteenth Century: Making Federalism Work,' *UTLJ* 46 (1996): 427.

34 Sir Edward Fry, *A Treatise on the Specific Performance of Contracts … Including Notes on the Canadian Law by Hon. Mr Justice Russell of the Supreme Court of Nova Scotia* (London: Stevens and Sons and Canada Law Book, 1911); W.B. Odgers, *Principles and Practice of the Law of Evidence … with Canadian Notes by Hon. Mr Justice Russell* (London: Butterworths, 1911).

35 W. Wyatt-Paine, *A Commentary on the Canadian Law of Simple Contracts* (Toronto: Carswell; and London: Sweet and Maxwell, 1914).

36 Joseph MacDougall, *Law Lectures on the Subject of Torts and Negligence* (Toronto: Rowsell and Hutchison, 1882). Quotation from Introduction, n.p.; J.F. Clerk and W.H.B. Lindsell, *A Canadian Edition of the Law of Torts; Being the Latest English Edition as Revised by Wyatt Paine; With Canadian Notes on the Decisions and Statutes of the English-Speaking Provinces of the Dominion by A.T. Hunter* (London: Sweet and Maxwell and Carswell, 1908).

37 Joshua Williams, *Principles of the Law of Real Property Intended as a First Book for the Use of Students in Conveyancing, Adapted to the Laws in Force in the Province of Ontario by Alexander Leith* (Toronto: Rowsell & Hutchison, 1882); Edward Armour, *A Treatise on the Law of Real Property Founded on Leith and Smith's Edition of Blackstone's Commentaries on the Rights of Things* (Toronto: Canada Law Book, 1916).

38 Herbert C. Jones, *The Torrens System of Transfer of Land: A Practical Treatise of the Land Titles Act of 1885, Ontario, and the Real Property Act of 1885, Manitoba* (Toronto: Carswell, 1886); Douglas Thom, *The Canadian Torrens System, with Special Reference to the Statutes of Manitoba, Saskatchewan, and*

Alberta (Calgary: Burroughs, 1912); Lewis William Coutlee, *A Manual on the Law of Registration of Titles to Real Estate in Manitoba and the North-West Territories* (Toronto: Carswell, 1890).

39 For Winnipeg and Victoria, see two very different books by Archer Martin, who is discussed in chapter 3: *The Hudson's Bay Company's Land Tenures and the Occupation of Assiniboia by Lord Selkirk's Settlers* (London: W. Clowes, 1898); and *Reports of Mining Cases Decided by the Courts of British Columbia … with an Appendix of Mining Statutes* (Toronto: Carswell, 1903). For the Saint John Law School, see the discussion below of Bell, *Legal Education in New Brunswick*, chap. 3. For a Halifax example, see the career of Benjamin Russell, whose principal scholarly contribution was *A Commentary on the Bills of Exchange Act … with References to English, Canadian and American Cases, and the Opinions of Eminent Jurists* (Halifax: McAlpine Publishing, 1909); he also wrote Canadian footnotes for other leading English texts, mentioned in note 33 above.

40 This account of Armour is principally from Christopher Moore, 'Edward Douglas Armour,' *DCB* online; and editions of the *Canadian Law Times*. See also Anon, 'The Late Mr Justice Armour,' *CLR* 2 (1903): 593. *Armour on Titles* was published by Canada Law Book. His other books include an edition of *Leith and Smith's Adaptation of Part of Blackstone's Commentaries*, noted above; *Essays on the Devolution of Land upon the Personal Representative and Statutory Powers Relating Thereto: With an Appendix of Statutes* (Toronto: Canada Law Book, 1903).

41 The familial relationship among these men can be traced through Judson Purdy, 'John George Hodgins'; and Kerry Badgley, 'William Egerton Hodgins,' both *DCB* online; and Henry J. Morgan, *Canadian Men and Women of the Time: A Handbook of Canadian Biography*, 2nd ed. (Toronto: W. Briggs, 1912), 538. For the titles mentioned here, see *Correspondence, Reports I*; Thomas Hodgins, *Guide to Counting Marked Ballots at Elections for the House of Commons* (Toronto: Rowsell and Hutchison, 1878); Hodgins, *Handybook on the Dominion and Ontario Franchises* (Toronto: Carswell, 1889); and Hodgins, *The Bills of Exchange Act, 1890* (Toronto: Carswell, 1890); Frank E. Hodgins and W. Ewing, *The Life Insurance Contract in Canada: A Treatise on the Scope, Making, Character and Effect of the Contract for the Insurance of Life in Canada* (Toronto: Canada Law Book, 1902). William Hodgins's book on corporations was published in Toronto in 1888 by Carswell.

42 R.C.B. Risk, 'John Skirving Ewart: The Legal Thought,' *UTLJ* 37 (1987): 335 at 335. Much of what follows is drawn from this article, quotations below at 337 and 338.

43 For these examples, see *CLT* (1881): 71; and 14 (1894): 177.

44 John Skirving Ewart, *An Exposition of the Principles of Estoppel by Misrepresentation* (Toronto: Carswell, 1900). His articles were published in *CLT* 16 (1896): 205, 229, 260, and 283; 17 (1897) 229 and 282; and in the English *Law Quarterly Review* 15 (1889): 383; and 16 (1900) 135.

45 For this 'scientific' movement, see David Sugarman, 'Legal Theory, the Common Law Mind, and the Making of the Textbook Tradition,' in *Legal Theory and Common Law*, ed. William Twining (Oxford: Basil Blackwell, 1986).

46 See 'George Smith Holmested: An Appreciation,' *CBR* 6 (1928): 451.

47 Charles Morse, *Apices Juris and Other Legal Essays in Prose and Verse,* (Toronto: Canada Law Book, 1906).

48 Margaret Center Klinglesmith, 'The Continuity of Case Law,' originally published in the *University of Pennsylvania Law Review*; and Klinglesmith, 'Stonore Said,' a wide-ranging historical piece, in *CLT* 30 (1910): 605; and 33 (1913): 600. Klinglesmith was likely a law librarian at the University of Pennsylvania.

49 His early career is summarized in George MacLean Rose, ed., *A Cyclopedia of Canadian Biography* (Toronto: Rose Publishing, 1888), 101–2. See generally Bell, *Legal Education in New Brunswick*, 76.

50 Alfred Henry Marsh, *History of the Court of Chancery and of the Rise and Development of the Doctrines of Equity* (Toronto: Carswell, 1890).

51 Admissions by private act peaked in Ontario in the 1870s and 1880s and declined thereafter but did not cease until 1939: Curtis Cole, '"A Learned and Honorable Body": The Professionalization of the Ontario Bar, 1867–1929' (PhD diss., University of Western Ontario, 1987), 87–109.

52 Cameron Harvey, ed., *The Law Society of Manitoba, 1877–1977* (Winnipeg: Peguis, 1977); A.J. Watts, *History of the Law Society of British Columbia 1869–1973* (Vancouver: A.J. Watts, 1973).

53 Iain Mentiplay, *A Century of Integrity: The Law Society of Saskatchewan 1907 to 2007* (Regina: Law Society of Saskatchewan, 2007), 18–21; Peter Sibenik, 'The Doorkeepers: The Governance of Territorial and Alberta Lawyers, 1885–1928' (LLM thesis, University of Calgary, 1984).

54 Cited in Moore, *Law Society*, 136.

55 Cahill, *Professional Autonomy*, 44–6; D.G. Bell, *The Law Society of New Brunswick: An Historical Sketch* (Fredericton: Law Society of New Brunswick, 1999), 13–14; SN 1889, c 22.

56 Moore, *Law Society*, 149–51; SBC 1874, c 18, s 10; SN 1889, c 22.

57 Moore, *Law Society*, 131–3; Girard and Haylock, 'Stratification,' 85–6; Brawn, 'Dominant Professionals,' 415–17.

58 RSQ 1888, title X, c 1; RSQ 1909, title X, c 2.
59 Watts, *History of the Law Society of BC*, 106.
60 John D. Honsberger, *The County of York Law Association: A History of the First Hundred Years, 1885–1985* (Toronto: County of York Law Association, 1989).
61 Vachon, *Notariat canadien*, 139–54, 179.
62 J. Barry Cahill, 'Abraham Beverley Walker'; and Judith Fingard, 'James Robinson Johnston,' both *DCB* online; see also Barry Cahill, 'The Colored Barrister: The Short Life and Tragic Death of James Robinson Johnston, 1876–1916,' *Dalhousie Law Journal* 15 (1992): 336; Justin Johnston, *James Robinson Johnston: The Life, Death and Legacy of Nova Scotia's First Black Lawyer* (Halifax: Nimbus, 2005); Deidré Rowe Brown, 'Robert Sutherland: Celebrating the Legacy,' *Queen's Law Journal* 35 (2010): 401.
63 On early Jewish lawyers in Ontario, see Moore, *Law Society of Upper Canada*, 179–80; Sylvio Normand, 'Samuel William Jacobs,' *DCB* online; on Davis, Kyer, *Faskens*, 115, 139, 148, and 175; on Green, obituary in *Winnipeg Free Press*, 16 Apr. 1969; Phyllis Senese, 'Samuel Davies Schultz,' *DCB* online. Schultz died prematurely in 1917 and hence little is known about him.
64 Della M. Stanley, *Au service de deux peoples: Pierre-Amand Landry* (Fredericton: Barreau du Nouveau-Brunswick, 1987); Jacques Paul Couturier, 'Perception et pratique de la justice dans la société acadienne, 1870–1900,' in *Économie et société en Acadie 1850–1950*, ed. Jacques Paul Couturier and Phyllis E. Leblanc (Moncton, NB: Éditions d'Acadie, 1996), 47–48; F.-X. Ribordy, *Les avocats de Sudbury, 1891–1981* (Sudbury, ON: Université Laurentienne, 1982); G.O. Rothney, 'Marc-Amable Girard,' *DCB* online; Dale Brawn, *The Court of Queen's Bench of Manitoba: A Biographical History* (Toronto: Osgoode Society for Canadian Legal History and University of Toronto Press, 2006).
65 Constance Backhouse, '"To Open the Way for Others of My Sex": Clara Brett Martin's Career as Canada's First Woman Lawyer,' *Canadian Journal of Women and the Law* 1 (1985–86): 1; Lois Yorke, 'Mabel Penery French (1881–1955): A Life Re-created,' *University of New Brunswick Law Journal* 42 (1993): 3; Mary Jane Mossman, *The First Women Lawyers: A Comparative Study of Gender, Law, and the Legal Professions* (Portland, OR: Hart, 2006).
66 French's paper, presented at the 1909 International Congress of Women in Toronto, was published in its proceedings and is reproduced in the *University of New Brunswick Law Journal* 42 (1993): 49. Martin's paper was published in National Council of Women, *Women of Canada: Their Life and Work* (n.p., 1900; reprint Ottawa: National Council of Women of

Canada, 1975). On Gérin-Lajoie, author of *Traité de droit usuel* (1902) and
its English version *Treatise on Everyday Law*, published the same year,
see generally Nicholas Kasirer, 'Apostolat Juridique: Teaching Everyday
Law in the Life of Marie Lacoste Gérin-Lajoie (1867–1945),' *OHLJ* 30
(1992): 427.

67 Canada, with a unitary court system, has no distinct federal bar. A lawyer
belonging to any provincial or territorial law society is entitled to practise
before any federally created court or tribunal.

68 Girard, 'Hybrid Heritage,' 151–2.

7. Canadian Law and Indigenous Peoples I: The Métis, the Numbered Treaties, British Columbia, and the Rebellion

1 J.R. Miller, *Skyscrapers Hide the Heavens: A History of Indian-White Relations
in Canada* (Toronto: University of Toronto Press, 1989), ix.

2 In addition to the specific sources cited below, this account of the events
surrounding the origins of Manitoba as a province is based on Gerhard
J. Ens and Joe Sawchuk, *From New Peoples to New Nations: Aspects of Metis
History and Identity from the Eighteenth to the Twenty-First Centuries* (Toronto:
University of Toronto Press, 2016), esp. chaps. 4 and 6; J.M. Bumsted, *Trials
and Tribulations: The Red River Settlement and the Emergence of Manitoba*
(Winnipeg: Great Plains Publications, 2003); George Stanley, *The Birth
of Western Canada: A History of the Riel Rebellions* (Toronto: University of
Toronto Press, 1960); and W.L. Morton, ed., *Manitoba: The Birth of a Province*
(Winnipeg: Manitoba Record Society, 1984). The *DCB* online entries for
leading participants John Bruce, Simon Dawson, Jean-Baptiste Lepine,
William MacDougall, Louis Riel, Noel-Joseph Ritchtôt, John Christian
Schultz, Thomas Scott, and Garnet Wolseley have also been used, as have
the many contemporary documents reproduced by MacInnes J in the trial
judgment in *Manitoba Métis Federation v Canada*, [2007] MBQB 293.

3 *Commons Journals*, 6, 9, 12, 16, and 18 Dec. 1867, 53–4, 59, 65–8, 98, 108.

4 *Government of Rupert's Land and the North-Western Territory Act*, SC 1869, c 3.

5 Macdonald to Cartier, 27 Nov. 1869, cited in Donald Creighton, *John A.
Macdonald: The Old Chieftain*, repr. ed. (Toronto: University of Toronto
Press, 1998), 46–7.

6 Some people contend that Métis should have a more restricted meaning,
but in this book we use the word to describe all people of mixed ethnicity,
anglophone and francophone, living in what is now western Canada,
before and after 1870.

7 *Volume 1*, 537–8.

8 *Correspondence and Papers Connected with the Recent Occurrences in the North-West Territories*, in Canada, *Sessional Papers*, 1870, no. 12 (hereafter *Correspondence and Papers*), 79. The four Lists of Rights, compiled by Lawrence Barkwell, can be accessed at www.metismuseum.ca.

9 The Declaration is reproduced in a number of sources. See *The Red River Journal of Alexander Begg and Other Papers Relative to the Red River Resistance of 1869–1870* (Toronto: Champlain Society, 1956 reprint), 218–20.

10 Cited in Colin Read, 'John Stoughton Dennis,' *DCB* online.

11 Proclamation of Young, 6 Dec. 1869, in *Correspondence and Papers*, 44.

12 Cited in Bumsted, *Trials and Tribulations*, 208.

13 *Manitoba Act*, SC 1870, c 3.

14 *Commons Journals*, 4, 7, 9, and 10 May 1870, 289–91, 316–41; *Commons Debates*, 9 May 1870, 446–7.

15 *Commons Debates*, 12 May 1870, 1174.

16 Cited in N.E. Allen Ronaghan, 'John Bruce,' *DCB* online.

17 K.G. Pryke 'Sir Adams George Archibald,' *DCB* online.

18 The pressure from Quebec included a Commons motion in April 1873 for production of all communications between the government and Riel or any other person about an amnesty for people involved in the death of Scott. Secretary of State for the Provinces J.C. Aikins responded that there was no such correspondence in either his department or the Department of Justice: see 'Return to an Address,' 6 May 1873, in Canada, *Sessional Papers*, 1873, no. 64.

19 See Louis Knafla, 'Treasonous Murder: The Trial of Ambroise Lépine, 1874,' in *Canadian State Trials*, vol. 3, *Political Trials and Security Measures, 1840–1914*, ed. J. Barry Wright and Susan Binnie (Toronto: Osgoode Society for Canadian Legal History and University of Toronto Press, 2009). For Wood and his political and financial connections, see J. Daniel Livermore, 'Edmund Burke Wood,' *DCB* online.

20 These were the *Canada Jurisdiction Acts* of 1803 and 1826.

21 *Commons Journals*, 11 and 12 Feb. 1875, 68–9 and 74–81. The amnesty and banishment included Lépine, but he refused it and served out his sentence.

22 *North-West Territories Act*, SC 1871 c 16; SC 1873, c 5.

23 For these pre-Confederation treaties, and for the different policies pursued in the other central and eastern colonies, see *Volume 1*, 245–8 and 488–95. The transfer terms are contained in UK Order in Council, 23 June 1870.

24 *Report of the Minister of Justice*, 19 Jan. 1875, in *Correspondence, Reports I*, 1026–7; quotations below from the same source at 1028. For Bernard, see P.B. Waite, 'Hewitt Bernard,' *DCB* online.

25 For the *St. Catherine's Milling* case, the definitive work is Kent McNeil, *Flawed Precedent: The St Catherine's Case and Aboriginal Title* (Vancouver: UBC Press, 2019). For Calder, see [1973] SCR 313.

26 There is a very large literature on the context in which the numbered treaties were signed. See, inter alia, J.R. Miller, *Compact, Contract, Covenant: Aboriginal Treaty-Making in Canada* (Toronto: University of Toronto Press, 2009), chaps. 6 and 7; and Miller, *Skyscrapers Hide the Heavens*, chap. 9; David J. Hall, *From Treaties to Reserves: The Federal Government and Native Peoples in Territorial Alberta* (Montreal and Kingston: McGill-Queen's University Press, 2015), chap. 1; Maureen K. Lux, *Medicine That Walks: Disease, Medicine and Canadian Plains Native People, 1880–1940* (Toronto: University of Toronto Press, 2001), 20–32.

27 Report of Deputy SG Spragge, 18 Mar. 1874, in *Annual Report, 1873*.

28 Alexander Morris, *The Treaties of Canada with the Indians of Manitoba and the North-West Territories, Including the Negotiations on Which They Were Based, and Other Information Related Thereto* (Toronto: Belfords Clarke, 1880), 144.

29 For the decline in the buffalo population, in addition to the general sources already cited, see, inter alia, Bill Waiser, *A World We Have Lost: Saskatchewan before 1905* (Markham, ON: Fifth House Limited, 2016).

30 Hall, *From Treaties to Reserves*, 26–7.

31 SC 1875, c 49.

32 Morris, *Treaties of Canada*, contains the text of all treaties. The treaties are also accessible on the government of Canada website and the numerous websites devoted to each treaty.

33 See *Volume 1*, 246–7.

34 Morris, *Treaties of Canada*, 92 and 183–5.

35 Ibid., 262.

36 What follows on the negotiations is based on a variety of sources, including those listed above in note 26. The fullest source written from a Canadian participant is Morris, *Treaties of Canada*, which contains reports on the negotiations and correspondence with Ottawa, all of which are also reproduced in the *Annual Reports* and in the sessional papers of the federal Parliament. We have also drawn on Robert J. Talbot, *Negotiating the Numbered Treaties: An Intellectual and Political*

Biography of Alexander Morris (Saskatoon: Purich, 2009), on the series of *Treaty Research Reports* published by the federal government, and on the *DCB* online entries for many of the participants, including Adams Archibald, Peter Erasmus, David Laird, James McKay, Alexander Morris, Isapo-muxik (Crowfoot), Kamīyistowesit (Beardy), Kāpeyakwāskonam (One Arrow), Paskwāw (The Plain), Pītikwahanapiwīyin (Poundmaker), Mistahimaskwa (Big Bear), and Minahikosis (Little Pine).

37 Jean Friesen, 'Alexander Morris,' *DCB* online.

38 John Taylor, 'Two Views on the Meaning of Treaties Six and Seven,' in *The Spirit of the Alberta Indian Treaties*, ed. Richard Price (Edmonton: Pica Pica, 1987), 6 and 13.

39 Morris, *Treaties of Canada*, 33. Other quotations in this paragraph are from the same source, at 34 and 71.

40 Quotations from ibid., 83, 101, and 133.

41 See Derek Whitehouse Strong, 'Everything Promised Had Been Included in the Writing: Indian Reserve Farming and the Spirit and Intent of Treaty Six Reconsidered,' *Great Plains Quarterly* 27 (2007): 25.

42 Michael Payne, 'Peter Erasmus,' *DCB* online.

43 The scholarship includes Peter Allan Barkwell, 'The Medicine Chest Clause in Treaty No. 6,' *Canadian Native Law Reports* 4 (1981): 1; Bob Beal, 'An Indian Chief, an English Tourist, a Doctor, a Reverend, and a Member of Parliament: The Journeys of Pasqua's Pictographs and the Meaning of Treaty Four,' *Canadian Journal of Native Studies* 27 (2007): 109; Aimée Craft, 'Living Treaties, Breathing Research,' *Canadian Journal of Women and the Law* 26 (2014): 5; and Craft, *Breathing Life into the Stone Fort Treaty: An Anishinaabe Understanding of Treaty One* (Saskatoon: Purich, 2013); Walter Hildebrandt, Sarah Carter, and Dorothy First Rider, *The True Spirit and Original Intent of Treaty 7* (Montreal and Kingston: McGill-Queen's University Press, 1996); Brittany Luby, '"The Department Is Going Back on Its Promises": An Examination of Anishinabee and Crown Understandings of Treaty,' *Canadian Journal of Native Studies* 30 (2010): 203; Lux, *Medicine That Walks*, 20–32; Delia Opekokew, *The First Nations: Indian Government and the Canadian Confederation* (Saskatoon: Federation of Saskatchewan Indians, 1979); Taylor, 'Two Views'; Kate Gunn, 'Agreeing to Share: Treaty 3, History and the Courts,' *UBC Law Review* 51 (2018): 75; Sharon Venne, 'Understanding Treaty Six: An Indigenous Perspective,' in *Aboriginal and Treaty Rights in Canada: Essays on Law, Equality and Respect for Difference*, ed. Michael Asch (Vancouver: UBC Press, 1977);

Whitehouse-Strong, 'Everything Promised'; Miriam Wing, 'Divisions in Treaty 6 Perspectives: The Dilemma of Written Text and Oral Tradition,' *Muse* 3 (2016): 200; 'Interviews with Elders,' in *Spirit of the Alberta Treaties*, ed. Price.

44 Molyneux St John to William Spragge, 24 Feb. 1873, cited in Craft, 'Living Treaties,' 6.

45 *Report of a Committee of the Privy Council*, 30 Apr. 1875, in Morris, *Treaties of Canada*, 338–9, and accompanying agreements, 339–42.

46 Morris made this promise when asked about land for the 'rising generation': *Manitoban*, 12 Aug. 1871. We thank Roger Townshend for this reference.

47 Wayne E. Daugherty, *Treaty Research Report: Treaty Three (1873)* (Ottawa: DIAND, 1986), 25–7.

48 Opekokew, *First Nations*, 11.

49 Whitehouse Strong, 'Everything Promised,' 25 and 31.

50 See especially Sarah Carter, *Lost Harvests: Prairie Indian Reserve Farmers and Government Policy* (Montreal and Kingston: McGill-Queen's University Press, 1990).

51 See in particular on food shortages and health, Lux, *Medicine That Walks*; Hugh Shewell, *Enough to Keep Them Alive: Indian Welfare in Canada, 1873–1965* (Toronto: University of Toronto Press, 2004); and James Daschuk, *Clearing the Plains: Disease, Politics of Starvation, and the Loss of Aboriginal Life* (Regina: University of Regina Press, 2012).

52 Kenneth S. Coates and William R. Morrison, *Treaty Research Report: Treaty Five (1875)* (Ottawa: DIAND, 1985), 10.

53 Luby, '"Department Is Going Back"' 207–8; Craft, 'Living Treaties,' 11; Gunn, 'Agreeing to Share,' 80 (emphasis in original).

54 This brief account of Treaties 8–10 is based on the relevant *Treaty Research Reports*, on Arthur J. Ray, 'Treaty 8: A British Columbian Anomaly,' *BC Studies* 122 (1999): 5; and John Long, *Treaty No. 9: Making the Agreement to Share the Land in Far Northern Ontario in 1905* (Montreal and Kingston: McGill-Queen's University Press, 2010).

55 For the treaties of the early 1850s, see *Volume 1*, 538–42. For the rest of this paragraph, see Hamar Foster, 'Letting Go the Bone: The Idea of Indian Title in British Columbia,' in *EHCL VI*; Sarah Pike, 'The Colony of British Columbia's Unsurveyed Land System,' in *To Share Not Surrender: Indigenous and Settler Visions of Treaty-Making in the Colonies of Vancouver Island and British Columbia*, ed. Peter Cook et al. (Vancouver: UBC Press, 2022); Robin Fisher, 'Joseph Trutch and

Indian Land Policy,' *BC Studies* 12 (1971–2): 3; and Fisher, 'Sir Joseph William Trutch,' *DCB* online. Pre-emption was the right to purchase public land when it was put on the market. By the terms of the 1860 *Land Ordinance* anybody could pre-empt 160 acres on the coast or 320 acres in the interior. But after 1864 Indigenous people could do so only with permission of the executive, which was given in a very few cases before 1871, and not thereafter.

56 Memorandum of David Laird, 4 Nov. 1874, in *Annual Report,* 1875.

57 What follows on British Columbia's policy regarding Indigenous land rights draws heavily on two principal sources: Cole Harris, *Making Native Space: Colonialism, Resistance and Reserves in British Columbia* (Vancouver: UBC Press, 2002), chaps. 4–7; and Foster, 'Letting Go the Bone.' Other sources are cited where appropriate.

58 For Powell, see John Lutz, 'Israel Wood Powell,' *DCB* online. For his reports to Ottawa in the early to mid-1870s, from which the quotations below are taken, see Abstract of the Report of J.W. Powell, 11 Jan. 1873; and Powell to Minister of Interior, 4 Feb. 1875, in *Annual Reports,* 1874 and 1875.

59 Walkem's memorandum, 18 Aug. 1875, in *Annual Report,* 1875.

60 SBC 1873–4, c 2.

61 Quotations from Report of the Minister of Justice, 19 Jan. 1875, in *Correspondence, Reports I,* 1024–8; *Annual Report,* 1874 and 1875; Harris, *Making Native Space,* 122.

62 Mills's report, 15 Jan. 1877, in *Annual Report,* 1876.

63 For Anderson, see W. Kaye Lamb, 'Caulfield Anderson,' *DCB* online. For extended discussions of Sproat's views and his career, see Foster, 'Letting Go the Bone,' 32–3 and 61–5; Foster, 'Gilbert Malcolm Sproat,' *DCB* online; and Sarah Pike, 'Gilbert Malcolm Sproat, British Columbia Indian Reserve Commissioner (1876–1880), and the "Humanitarian Civilizing" of Indigenous Peoples' (LLM diss., University of British Columbia, 2018).

64 SC 1877, Orders in Council, cxxvii. The surrender requirement is discussed more fully in chapter 8.

65 Harris, *Making Native Space,* 104.

66 Douglas C. Harris, *Landing Native Fisheries: Indian Reserves and Fishing Rights in British Columbia, 1849–1925* (Vancouver: UBC Press, 2008).

67 Harris, *Making Native Space,* 107. The accounts of the first and second circuits are from 104–33.

68 Foster, 'Gilbert Sproat.'

69 Douglas Harris, 'The Nlha7lapmx Meeting at Lytton, 1879, and the Rule of Law,' *BC Studies* 108 (1995–6): 5.

70 Robin Fisher, 'An Exercise in Futility: The Joint Commission on Indian Land in British Columbia, 1875–1880,' *Historical Papers* (1975): 79.

71 For O'Reilly, see David Ricardo Williams, 'Peter O'Reilly,' *DCB* online.

72 Cited in Foster, 'Letting Go the Bone,' 47.

73 *Commons Debates*, 11 Mar. 1881, 1348.

74 *A.G. and I.B. Nash v John Tait (4 Metlakatla Indians)*, unreported but preserved in the Begbie Benchbooks and cited in Foster, 'Letting Go the Bone,' 66.

75 For O'Meara and Clark, and the complexities of the legal procedure, see Hamar Foster, 'We Are Not O'Meara's Children: Law, Lawyers and the First Campaign for Aboriginal Title in British Columbia, 1908–1928,' in *Let Right Be Done: Aboriginal Title, the Calder Case, and the Future of Indigenous Rights*, ed. Foster, Heather Raven, and Jeremy Webber (Vancouver: UBC Press, 2007); and Foster, 'If Your Life Is a Leaf: Arthur Eugene O'Meara's Campaign for Aboriginal Justice,' in *The Promise and Perils of Law: Lawyers in Canadian History*, ed. Constance Backhouse and W. Wesley Pue (Toronto: Irwin Law, 2009).

76 [1973] SCR 313. See Hamar Foster, 'A Romance of the Lost: The Role of Tom MacInnes in the History of the British Columbia Indian Land Question,' in *EHCL VIII*.

77 For these men, see E. Brian Titley, 'James Andrew Joseph McKenna'; and Patricia Roy, 'Richard McBride,' both in *DCB* online. McBride took very little part in the commission's work and resigned before it was concluded.

78 See Lux, *Medicine That Walks*, which includes tables detailing population decline on reserves. On food insecurity generally in this and later periods, see Daschuk, *Clearing the Plains*.

79 The following brief account of the legal proceedings against persons other than Louis Riel is largely based on Bob Beal and Barry Wright, 'Summary and Incompetent Justice: Legal Responses to the 1885 Crisis'; and Bill Waiser, 'The White Man Governs: The 1885 Indian Trials,' both in Wright and Binnie, *Canadian State Trials Volume* 3. Other sources are cited below where appropriate. For those convicted, see Beal and Wright, 'Summary and Incompetent Justice,' 615–17.

80 Campbell to prosecutors, 20 June 1885, in Canada, *Sessional Papers*, 1886, no. 43B, 12.

81 For these proceedings, see Sandra Estlin Bingaman, 'The Trials of the "White Rebels,"' *Saskatchewan History* 25 (1972): 41.

82 *Better Security of the Crown and Government Act*, SC 1868, c 69. For the history of the treason-felony statutes, see Beal and Wright, 'Summary and Incompetent Justice,' 357–8.
83 Waiser, 'White Man Governs,' 474; other quotations below in this paragraph at 451 and 458.
84 As noted above, the literature on the Riel trial is very substantial. The account offered here relies principally on J.M. Bumsted, 'Another Look at the Riel Trial,' in Wright and Binnie, *Canadian State Trials*, 3.
85 See Desmond Brown, 'George Wheelock Burbidge'; Patrick Brode, 'Britton Bath Osler'; Brode, 'Christopher Robinson'; Louis Knafla, 'David Lynch Scott'; and René Castonguay, 'Thomas Chase Casgrain,' all in *DCB* online.
86 See Andrée Désilets, 'Sir Françoise-Xavier Lemieux,' *DCB* online; Sir Charles Fitzpatrick, Supreme Court of Canada website.
87 Canada, *Sessional Papers* 1886, no. 43C. The indictment, pleading, jury selection, and preliminary arguments are at 1–47. The prosecution evidence is at 48–143, and the defence case at 143–76, quotations used below at 144–5. The remainder of the trial, including closing arguments and Riel's speech to sentence, is at 177 to the end.
88 (1843) 8 ER 718 (HL).
89 Thomas Flanagan and Neil Watson, 'The Riel Trial Revisited: Criminal Procedure and the Law in 1885,' *Saskatchewan History* 34 (1981): 57. Flanagan is the principal defender of the government's conduct of the trial. See also his *Riel and the Rebellion: 1885 Reconsidered* (Saskatoon: Western Producer Prairie Books, 1985).
90 Bumsted, 'Another Look,' 421.
91 *North-West Territories Act*, SC 1886, c 25.
92 *Commons Debates*, 11 May 1886, 1203.
93 For this paragraph, see Thomas Flanagan, 'Hugh Richardson,' *DCB* online; Shelley Gavigan, *Hunger, Horses and Government Men: Criminal Law on the Aboriginal Plains, 1870–1905* (Vancouver: Osgoode Society for Canadian Legal History and UBC Press, 2012); Beal and Wright, 'Summary and Incompetent Justice,' 360–5; Bumsted, 'Another Look,' 426.
94 *North-West Territories Act*, SC 1875, c 49, s 94.
95 Beal and Wright, 'Summary and Incompetent Justice,' 364.
96 Connor was tried in 1885 for the murder of one Henry Mulaski at Moose Jaw. For the appeal based on the jurisdictional question, see Man. LR 2 (1885) 235.

97 The Crown repeated this argument before the JCPC: Beal and Wright,
'Summary and Incompetent Justice,' 359.

98 Initial confusion over what criminal law was in force west of Ontario in
1870 had been resolved in 1873 by a federal statute, which stated that
some 20 federal statutes passed in 1868 and 1869 unifying substantive
criminal law and procedure were in force in the Territories: *North-West
Territories Act*, SC 1873, c 34, and chapter 13. One of those statutes dealt
with treason, and in addition to providing a list of which acts were
treasonous it also specifically stated that the 1352 statute was in force in
Canada: *Security of the Crown and Government Act*, SC 1868, c 69, s 1. See
generally Desmond Brown, 'Unpredictable and Uncertain: Criminal Law
in the Canadian North West before 1886,' *Alberta Law Review* 18 (1979):
497; and Brown, 'The Meaning of Treason in 1885,' *Saskatchewan History*
28 (1975): 65.

99 *LawlessAggressions Act*, SC 1867, c 14.

100 For this argument,see Beal and Wright, 'Summary and Incompetent
Justice,' 357.

101 Cited in Bumsted, 'Another Look,' 428. For the subject and allegiance
questions, see Jeremy Ravi Mumford, 'Why Was Louis Riel, a United
States Citizen, Hanged as a Canadian Traitor in 1885,' *CHR* 88
(2007): 237.

102 See Bumsted, 'Another Look,' 425–6; and Lewis Thomas, 'A Judicial
Murder: The Trial of Louis Riel,' in *The Settlement of the West*, ed. Howard
Palmer (Calgary: University of Calgary Press, 1977).

103 As noted above, on 21 July, the second day of the trial, the defence
requested an adjournment to find witnesses who would come, most of
whom had fled to Montana, and also asked for money to bring witnesses
to Regina. The affidavit supporting the request stated that the evidence
was required to 'prove that the agitation in the North-West Territories
was constitutional and for the rights of the people of the said North-
West': Bumsted, 'Another Look,' 429.

104 Riel's spiritual beliefs are briefly examined in Bumsted, 'Another Look,'
435–7. For a review of the debate, see Gregory Betts, 'Non Compos
Mentis: A Meta-Historical Survey of the Historiographic Narratives
of Louis Riel's "Insanity,"' *International Journal of Canadian Studies* 38
(2008): 15. For the insanity defence, see Simon Verdun-Jones, 'Not Guilty
by Reason of Insanity: The Historical Roots of the Canadian Insanity
Defence, 1843–1920,' in *Crime and Criminal Justice in Europe and Canada*,
ed. Louis A. Knafla (Waterloo, ON: Wilfrid Laurier University Press,

1981); and Alison Kirk-Montgomery, 'Courting Madness: Insanity and Testimony in the Criminal Justice System of Victorian Ontario' (PhD diss., University of Toronto, 2001).

105 Flanagan, *Riel and the Rebellion*, 136; Bumsted, 'Another Look,' 431–2.

106 See Ronald Olesky, 'Louis Riel and the Crown Letters,' *Canadian Lawyer*, Feb. 1998. For Wallbridge, see Bruce Hodgins, 'Lewis Wallbridge,' *DCB* online.

107 Diane Payment, 'Sir Joseph Dubuc,' *DCB* online.

108 The Manitoba Queen's Bench decision is *The Queen v Louis Riel*, (1885) 2 Man. LR 321, and the JCPC decision is at *Riel v The Queen* [1885] AC 675 (PC).

109 Canada, *Sessional Papers* 1886, nos. 43E and 43F; Castonguay, 'Thomas Casgrain.'

110 What follows is from Canada, *Sessional Papers* 1886, no. 43A, Report of the Medical Men Appointed by the Government to Enquire into the Mental Condition of Louis Riel; Peter Oliver, 'Michael Lavell,' *DCB* online; Bumsted, 'Another Look,' 443; Flanagan, 'Riel and the Rebellion,' 135–45. Flanagan is critical of the government's actions in this instance.

111 Carolyn Strange, 'The Lottery of Death: Capital Punishment 1867–1986,' *Manitoba Law Journal* 23 (1995): 603. See also Cyril Greenland, 'The Last Public Execution in Canada: Eight Skeletons in the Closet of the Canadian Justice System,' *Criminal Law Quarterly* 29 (1987): 415.

8. Canadian Law and Indigenous Peoples II: The *Indian Act*, the Reserve System, and Assimilation

1 *Volume 1, 608–14.*

2 *Department of the Secretary of State Act, SC 1868, c 42, ss 1, 5–8, 15, and 31–3; Department of the Interior Act, SC 1873, c 4, ss 1 and 3; Indian Act, SC 1880, c 28, s 4.*

3 For these people, see Douglas Leighton, 'A Victorian Civil Servant at Work: Lawrence Vankoughnet and the Canadian Indian Department, 1874–1893,' in *As Long as the Sun Shines and the Water Flows: A Reader in Canadian Native Studies*, ed. Ian Getty and Antoine Lussier (Vancouver: UBC Press, 1983); E. Brian Titley, *Duncan Campbell Scott and the Administration of Indian Affairs in Canada* (Vancouver: UBC Press, 1986); Titley, 'Hayter Reed,' *DCB* online; John Leslie and Ron Maguire, eds., *Historical Development of the Indian Act* (Ottawa: DIAND, 1978).

4 *Extension of Laws Relating to Indians to Manitoba and British Columbia Act*, SC 1874, c 21; *Department of the Secretary of State Act*, s 15; *Gradual Enfranchisement Act*, SC 1869, c 6, s 6; *Commons Debates*, 27 Apr. 1869, 84.

5 *Indian Act*, SC 1876, c 18, ss 1, 3, and 97 [hereafter *Indian Act 1876*].

6 John Milloy, *A National Crime: The Canadian Government and the Residential School System, 1879–1986* (Winnipeg: University of Manitoba Press, 2017), 3; Return to an Order of the House of Commons, 2 May 1887, in Canada, *Sessional Papers*, 1887, no. 20B. Note that Macdonald distinguished Indigenous people from 'the inhabitants of the Dominion,' not from the 'other inhabitants of the Dominion.' Indigenous people were not considered true 'inhabitants' of the new country until they had been assimilated.

7 For the pass system, see F. Laurie Barron, 'The Indian Pass System in the Canadian West, 1882–1935,' *Prairie Forum* 13 (1988): 25; John Jennings, 'The North West Mounted Police and Indian Policy after the 1885 Rebellion,' in *1885 and After: Native Society in Transition*, ed. F. Laurie Barron and James B. Waldram (Regina: Canadian Plains Research Center, 1986).

8 *Royal Commission on Aboriginal Peoples*, vol. 1, *Looking Forward Looking Back* (Ottawa: Government of Canada, 1997), 325 and 350. The Royal Commission report provides a good general summary of the issues discussed in this chapter. See also John Leslie and Ron Maguire, *The Historical Development of the Indian Act*, 2nd ed. (Ottawa: DIAND, 1978); John S. Milloy, 'The Early Indian Acts: Developmental Strategy and Constitutional Change,' in Getty and Lussier, *As Long as the Sun Shines*; and John L. Tobias, 'Protection, Civilization, Assimilation: An Outline History of Canada's Indian Policy,' in *Sweet Promises: A Reader on Indian-White Relations in Canada*, ed. J.R. Miller (Toronto: University of Toronto Press, 1991).

9 SPC 1857, c 26; *Volume 1*, 531–7; *Gradual Enfranchisement Act*, SC 1869, c 6. For enfranchisement, see Coel Kirkby, 'Reconstituting Canada: The Enfranchisement and Disenfranchisement of "Indians," c 1837–1900,' *UTLJ* 69 (2019): 497; and Kirkby, 'Paradises Lost: The Constitutional Politics of "Indian" Enfranchisement in Canada,' 1857–1900,' *OHLJ* 56 (2020): 606.

10 Tobias, 'Protection, Civilization, Assimilation,' 132.

11 *Commons Debates*, 27 Apr. 1869, 83–4; *Extension of Laws relating to Indians to Manitoba and British Columbia*, SC 1874, c 21, ss 10 and 12.

12 'Return to an Address of the House of Commons,… for a Return Showing
the Number of Indians in the Different Counties of the Dominion to
Whom Letters Patent Have Been Issued Granting a Life Estate in Lands
Allotted Them,' in Canada, *Sessional Papers*, 1873, no. 23.

13 This section on Indigenous responses to enfranchisement is based on
Kirkby, 'Reconstituting Canada'; Susan Hill, *The Clay We Are Made Of:
Haudenosaunee Land Tenure of the Grand River* (Winnipeg: University of
Manitoba Press, 2017), 39–43; and *The General Council of the Six Nations and
Delegates from Different Bands in Western and Eastern Canada, June 10 1870*
(Hamilton, 1870).

14 *Indian Act 1876*, s 3(3) and 86–93; *Commons Debates*, 2 Mar. 1876, 342–3.

15 Laird's Report, 31 Jan. 1876, in *Annual Report*, 1875; Order in Council,
20 May 1886. For further extensions in the 1890s, see Kirkby, 'Paradises
Lost,' 7.

16 *Commons Debates*, 2 and 21 Mar. 1876, 342–3 and 749–53.

17 Report of David Mills, 15 Jan. 1877, in *Annual Report*, 1876; John Jacobs to
Laird, 12 July 1876, cited in Kirkby, 'Reconstituting Canada,' 511.

18 *Commons Debates*, 31 Mar. 1879, 844.

19 Report of Ebenezer Watson, superintendent, Western Superintendency,
Sarnia, 12 Dec. 1878; Reports of SG Macdonald, 31 Dec. 1882 and 1 Jan.
1884, in *Annual Reports* 1878, 1882, and 1884; Peter Dembski, 'Solomon
White,' *DCB* online; Kirkby, 'Paradises Lost,' 9–10.

20 *Indian Act*, SC 1884, c 27, ss 19 and 20; Reports of SG Macdonald, 31 Dec.
1881 and 31 Dec. 1882, in *Annual Reports*, 1881 and 1882.

21 Kirkby, 'Reconstituting Canada,' 513; and Kirkby, 'Paradises Lost'; Hill,
The Clay We Are Made Of, 203; *Enfranchisement of Jamieson Webster Lewis
Act*, SC 1906, c 25.

22 Calculations by scholars and our own reading of the *Annual Reports* come
up with slightly different totals, but all show a small number: see Kirkby,
'Paradises Lost,' 7; *Annual Reports*; Tobias, 'Protection, Civilization,
Assimilation,' 137; Hill, *The Clay We Are Made Of*, 203.

23 The issue of the provincial franchises and Indigenous men in this period
is summarized in Kirkby, 'Reconstituting Canada,' 535–7. See also chapter
16, on the British Columbia franchise.

24 SC 1885, c 40. This account of the Act is from Gordon T. Stewart, 'John A.
Macdonald's Greatest Triumph,' *CHR* 63 (1982): 3; and Richard Bartlett,
'Citizens Minus: Indians and the Right to Vote,' *Saskatchewan Law Review*
44 (1980): 163.

25 *Commons Debates*, 1 May 1885, 1575.

26 *Electoral Franchise Act*, SC 1898, c 14. For analyses of Indigenous peoples'
exercise of the franchise, see Kirkby, 'Reconstituting Canada,' 519–38;
and Malcolm Montgomery, 'The Six Nations Indians and the Macdonald
Franchise,' *Ontario History* 57 (1965): 13.

27 SC 1868, c 42, ss 6, 8, and 10; *Indian Act 1876*, ss 4, 25, and 26; *Commons
Debates*, 24 Mar. 1868, 395 (Langevin) and 12 June 1872, 1223.

28 See, inter alia, Address to the Commons on the Subject of the Tobique
Reserve in New Brunswick, upon Which White Settlers Are Residing, in
Canada, *Sessional Papers* 1873, no. 23. Squatting continued to plague the
Whycogomah reserve on Cape Breton, discussed in *Volume 1*, where 'the
most stringent legal measures' had to be taken: Vankoughnet's Report, 28
Jan. 1875, in *Annual Report, 1874*.

29 *Black v Kennedy*, in *Reports of Cases Argued and Determined in the Court of
Queen's Bench in Manitoba*, ed. E. Douglas Armour (Toronto: Carswell,
1884), 144–9.

30 SC 1868, c 42, ss 17, 22, and 25; *Indian Act 1876*, ss 6, 8, 11, 16, 26, 31–4, and
42; *Railway Act*, SC 1868, c 68, s 9.

31 Douglas C. Harris, 'Property and Sovereignty: An Indian Reserve and a
Canadian City,' *UBC Law Review* 50 (2017): 321.

32 Reports of Spragge, 14 Mar. 1873 and 18 Mar. 1874; Reports of
Vankoughnet, 31 Dec. 1875 and 31 Dec. 1876, in *Annual Reports, 1872,
1873, 1875, and 1876*.

33 D.J. Hall, 'Clifton Sifton and Canadian Indian Administration, 1896–1905,'
in Getty and Lussier, *As Long as the Sun Shines*, 136; Vic Satzewich and
Linda Mahood, 'Indian Affairs and Band Governance: Deposing Indian
Chiefs in Western Canada, 1896–1911,' *Canadian Ethnic Studies* 26 (1994):
45 at 57; *Commons Debates*, 18 July 1904, 6952; *Royal Commission*, 358; and
R.C. Daniel, *A History of Native Claims Processes in Canada, 1867–1979*
(Ottawa: DIAND, 1980), 113. Another example of pressure for a surrender
can be found in Robert Irwin, 'No Means No: Ermineskin's Resistance to
Land Surrender, 1902–1921,' *Canadian Journal of Native Studies* 22 (2003):
165.

34 *Indian Act*, SC 1894, c 32, s 3; and SC 1895, c 35, s 1. The 1894 amendment
also gave the SG the power to lease the land of infants, widows, the aged,
or the infirm; the purpose was to reduce welfare costs.

35 *Indian Act*, SC 1898, c 34, s 6; and SC 1906, c 20, s 1; David Hall, 'Frank
Oliver,' *DCB* online; *Commons Debates*, 30 Mar. 1906, 950.

36 *Indian Act*, SC 1911, c 14; *Commons Debates*, 26 Apr. 1911, 7827. For
expropriation, see chapter 14.

37 *Songheees Indian Reserve Act*, SC 1911, c 24. The next occasion it was used, after Victoria, was for Sydney, NS, in 1915. The judge who granted the application held that it was in the public interest because 'removal would make the property in that neighbourhood more valuable,' given the 'racial inequalities of the Indians': *Re Indian Reserve, City of Sydney, NS* (1918) 42 DLR 314 at 316 (Exch, Audette J).

38 W. Daugherty and D. Madill, *Indian Government under Indian Act Legislation* (Ottawa: DIAND, 1980), 41. We cannot provide more than this short summary of traditional Indigenous leadership structures: see, inter alia, Heidi Bohaker, *Doodem and Council Fire: Anishinaabe Governance through Alliance* (Toronto: Osgoode Society for Canadian Legal History and University of Toronto Press, 2020); *Volume 1*, chaps. 2 and 7; Satzewich and Mahood, 'Band Governance,' 46–7; Terry Lyn Poucette, 'Spinning Wheels: Surmounting the Indian Act's Impact on Traditional Indigenous Governance,' *Canadian Public Administration* 61 (2018): 501–2. See also chapter 10, below.

39 Cited in Daugherty and Madill, *Indian Government*, 10.

40 Quotations from Report of William Spragge, 2 Feb. 1871, in *Annual Report*, 1870. See also *Extension of Laws re Indians to Manitoba and British Columbia Act*, SC 1874, c 21, s 10; Kathleen Jamieson, *Indian Women and the Law: Citizens Minus* (Ottawa: Minister of Supply and Services, 1971).

41 Quotations from Report of William Spragge, 2 Feb. 1871, in *Annual Report*, 1870. On the low take-up rate, see Tobias, 'Protection, Civilization, Assimilation,' 133–4. For the Six Nations, see Hill, *Clay We Are Made Of*, esp. at 28 and 191–2; and, for the internal split over elections, Sally Weaver, 'The Grand River Reserve in the Late Nineteenth and Early Twentieth Centuries, 1875–1945,' in *Aboriginal Ontario: A History of the First Nations*, ed. Edward S. Rogers and Donald B. Smith (Toronto: Dundurn, 1994). The lobby advocating elections was the 'Dehorner' group, a collection of non-chiefly men educated at the Mohawk Institute, an industrial school (discussed in the next chapter) who worked as tradesmen, shopkeepers, and the like off-reserve. The DIA did not impose elections until 1924.

42 Order in Council, 7 Apr. 1877; James Phipps, visiting superintendent, Manitowaning, to SG, 14 Oct. 1878, in *Annual Report*, 1878; Tobias, 'Protection, Civilization, Assimilation,' 133.

43 SC 1880, c 28, s 72; Report of SG Macdonald, in *Annual Report*, 1880; Reports of Francis Ogletree, Indian agent, Portage La Prairie Agency, 30 Aug. 1884, and of H. Martineau, Indian agent, Manitoba House Agency,

30 Aug. 1884, both in *Annual Report*, 1884; Daugherty and Madill, *Indian Government*, 10–11; *Commons Debates*, 26 Feb. 1884, 539.

44 *Indian Act*, RSC 1886, c 43, s 76.

45 Report of SG Macdonald, 1 Jan. 1886, in *Annual Report*, 1885; Matthew Marchello, 'Band Governance under the Indian Acts, 1869–1930' (unpublished, 2019, on file with the authors).

46 SC 1884, c 28. The particular sections discussed here are 5–10. There were some consultations with Indigenous leaders: see Daugherty and Madill, *Indian Government*, 14–15.

47 *Commons Debates*, 29 Jan. 1884, 67.

48 *Commons Debates*, 31 Mar. 1890, 2725 and 2729.

49 *Commons Debates*, 28 Feb. 1884, 542.

50 Daniel Rûck, *The Laws and the Land: The Settler Colonial Invasion of Kahnawa:ke in Nineteenth-Century Canada* (Vancouver: UBC Press and Osgoode Society for Canadian Legal History, 2021), 206–11. See generally, for the low take-up rate, Daugherty and Madill, *Indian Government*, 17; and Weaver, 'Grand River Reserve,' 243–5.

51 Orders in Council, 15 June 1895 and 6 May 1899; Daugherty and Madill, *Indian Government*, 6.

52 Both quotations cited in Satzewich and Mahood, 'Band Governance,' 5.

53 Reed to SG Dewdney, 5 Mar. 1891, cited in Daugherty and Madill, *Indian Government*, 29. For the rest of this paragraph and the next, see 17–19, 29–35, and 57; and Satzewich and Mahood, 'Band Governance.'

54 For this incident, see Daugherty and Madill, *Indian Government*, 39–45.

55 Sifton to governor-general, 11 Sept. 1897, cited in Hall, 'Clifford Sifton,' 130; Satzewich and Mahood, 'Band Governance,' 6–7, 8, and 19–20; Daugherty and Madill, *Indian Government*, 57; John Tobias, 'Star Blanket,' *DCB* online.

56 Acting Deputy SG Mclean to Indian agent, 30 Oct. 1912, cited in Satzewich and Mahood, 'Band Governance,' 7. See generally for this paragraph, Daugherty and Madill, *Indian Government*, 58–9.

57 Order in Council, 17 July 1883; *Indian Act*, SC 1884, c 27, s 3.

58 There is a large body of literature, anthropological and historical, on the potlatch, which we do not comprehensively review here because our purpose is to examine the reactions of white settlers to Indigenous culture. For what follows, see Douglas Cole and Ira Chaikin, *An Iron Hand upon the People: The Law against the Potlatch on the Northwest Coast* (Vancouver: UBC Press, 1990); and Cole and Chaikin, 'A Worse Than Useless Custom: The Potlatch Law and Indian Resistance,' *Western Legal History* 5 (1992): 187; Tina Loo, 'Dan Cranmer's Potlatch: Law as

Coercion, Symbol and Rhetoric in British Columbia, 1884–1951,' *CHR* 73 (1992): 125; Peggy Brock, 'Moveable Feasts: Chronicles of Potlatching among the Tsimhain, 1860s–1900s,' *Ethnohistory* 59 (2012): 390. Examples below from Brock, 'Moveable Feasts,' 393; and Powell's report, 1 Sept. 1876, in *Annual Report*, 1876.

59 There is much less written about the Tamanawas than about the potlatch, and its exact nature remains obscure. The description here is taken from Christopher Bracken, *The Potlatch Papers: A Colonial Case History* (Chicago: University of Chicago Press, 1997), 167. See also Cole and Chaikin, 'Worse Than Useless Custom,' 188: it was 'the winter secret-society ceremony typified by the Kwakiutl *hamatsa*, or cannibal ritual.'

60 Brock, 'Moveable Feasts,' 394; Powell's report, 1 Oct. 1875, in *Annual Report*, 1875.

61 Quotations from Loo, 'Dan Cranmer's Potlatch,' 140 and 143; and Sproat to Macdonald, 17 Oct. 1879, cited in Cole and Chaikin, 'Worse Than Useless Custom,' 188.

62 SG Macdonald's Report, 1 Jan. 1884, in *Annual Report*, 1884.

63 Donckele to William Lomas, 2 Feb. 1884, cited in Loo, 'Dan Cranmer's Potlatch,' 139.

64 *Commons Debates*, 24 Mar. and 7 Apr. 1884, 1063 and 1399.

65 All of the quotations in this paragraph are from Indigenous letters and petitions cited in Cole and Chaikin, 'Worse Than Useless Custom,' 189. There are many similar quotations in the same source, and others to the same effect in Loo, 'Dan Cranmer's Potlatch.'

66 Cited in Loo, 'Dan Cranmer's Potlatch,' 141. We thank Hamar Foster for insight into this case.

67 *Indian Act*, SC 1895, c 35, s 6.

68 Sapir to Scott, 11 Feb. 1915, cited in Loo, 'Dan Cranmer's Potlatch,' 160.

69 What follows is from Katherine Pettipas, *Severing the Ties That Bind: Government Repression of Indigenous Religious Ceremonies on the Prairies* (Winnipeg: University of Manitoba Press, 1994); and Constance Backhouse, 'Bedecked in Gaudy Feathers: The Legal Prohibition of Aboriginal Dance, Wanduta's Trial, Manitoba, 1903,' in Backhouse, *Colour-Coded: A Legal History of Racism in Canada, 1900–1950* (Toronto: Osgoode Society for Canadian Legal History and University of Toronto Press, 1999).

70 Quotations from Backhouse, 'Bedecked,' 67.

71 One source claims 50 arrests and 20 convictions between 1900 and 1904, another seven and four between 1895 and 1897: Pettipas, *Severing the Ties*, 122; and Backhouse, 'Bedecked,' 68–9.

72 Backhouse, 'Bedecked,' 70.
73 *Indian Act*, SC 1914, c 35.

9. Canadian Law and Indigenous Peoples III: Education and Assimilation: The Origins and Expansion of Residential Schools

1 See *Volume 1*, 531–7; and J.R. Miller, *Shingwauk's Vision: A History of Native Residential Schools* (Toronto: University of Toronto Press, 1996), chap. 3.
2 SG Dewdney's Report, 13 Jan. 1891, in *Annual Report, 1890*.
3 The figures given in this chapter for the number of schools for Indigenous children are from two principal sources, the *Annual Reports* and *Final Report of the Truth and Reconciliation Commission of Canada*, vol. 1, *The History, Part 1, Origins to 1939* (Montreal and Kingston: McGill-Queen's University Press, 2012). For general accounts of Indigenous education policy and residential schools, see Miller, *Shingwauk's Vision*; John Milloy, *Suffer the Little Children: The Aboriginal Residential School System, 1830–1992* (Ottawa: Royal Commission on Aboriginal Peoples, 1996); and Milloy, *A National Crime: The Canadian Government and the Residential School System, 1879–1986*, 2nd ed. (Winnipeg: University of Manitoba Press, 2017). Other secondary sources are cited when appropriate.
4 For this paragraph, see Report of Deputy SG Spragge, 10 Apr. 1869, in *Annual Report, 1868*; and Report of SG Joseph Howe, n.d., in *Annual Report, 1870*; Elizabeth Graham, *The Mush Hole: Life at Two Indian Residential Schools* (Waterloo, ON: Heffle Publishing, 1997). The New England Company was a non-denominational Protestant missionary organization, which had moved its operations north after the American Revolution. It is described in Miller, *Shingwauk's Vision*, 64–6; and in Neil Hitchin, *'Come Over and Help Us': The New England Company and Its Mission, 1649–2001* (Ely, UK: St. Pancras Books, 2002). We do not have a precise figure for schools in the HBC territories, but missionary societies ran most of them, including two residential schools: Miller, *Shingwauk's Vision*, 95–6.
5 Report of SG Langevin, 10 Apr. 1869; Report of Deputy SG Spragge, 14 Mar. 1873; Report of Deputy SG Vankoughnet, 31 December 1876; Report of David Mills, 15 Jan. 1877, in *Annual Reports, 1868, 1872, 1873,* and *1876*; Vankoughnet to Macdonald, 26 Aug. 1877, cited in Milloy, *National Crime*, 7. For the grant figures, see Peter Bryce, *Report on the Indian Schools of Manitoba and the North-West Territories* (Ottawa: Government Printer, 1907), 8.
6 The Wikwemikong Industrial School was first listed as such in *Annual Report, 1879*. For the establishment of Shingwauk Home and Wawanosh

House, see Miller, *Shingwauk's Vision*, 3–7; and Janet Chute, 'George Shingwauk,' *DCB* online. Shingwauk was opened in 1873, burned down six days later, and was relocated closer to Sault Ste. Marie and reopened in 1875. Wawanosh House opened in 1879 a few miles away but was later relocated to the same site as Shingwauk.

7 For the grants system, see Orders in Council, 23 Oct. 1873, 1 Apr. 1874 (Manitoba and the Territories), and 7 Apr. 1874 (British Columbia). Schools in Manitoba and the Territories had to have an attendance of 25, those in British Columbia 30. In 1876 six schools in British Columbia were closed, 'owing to the inability of those charged with their management to maintain the required average': Report of Deputy SG Vankoughnet, 31 Dec. 1877, in *Annual Report, 1877*.

8 Quotations from J.R. Miller, 'Troubled Legacy: A History of Native Residential Schools,' *Saskatchewan Law Review* 66 (2003) 357 at 361; and Milloy, *National Crime*, 26. See generally Miller, *Shingwauk's Vision*, 97–100.

9 The first mention we have found of 'residential schools' in the *Annual Reports* appears in 1907 and then not in the main report, by Deputy SG Frank Pedley, but in one of the additional documents printed, the report of the Indian agent for the Hobbema agency in Alberta, James Gibbons. Gibbons used the word three times, the only uses of the word in the entire report, and he also referred to boarding and industrial schools. In general up until the First World War it remained uncommon for officials to refer to residential schools, and instead to use the names of, and to distinguish between, boarding and industrial schools. Only from 1923 did the DIA use the term 'residential schools' for all such institutions.

10 For industrial schools, see Charlotte Neff, 'The Ontario Industrial Schools Act of 1874,' *Canadian Journal of Family Law* 12 (1994): 142; Paul Bennett, 'Turning Bad Boys into Good Citizens: The Reforming Impulse of Toronto's Industrial Schools Movement, 1883 to the 1920s,' *Ontario History* 78 (1986): 205; *Industrial Schools Act*, SQ 1869, c 17; *Halifax Industrial School Act*, SC 1870, c 32. See also Milloy, *National Crime*, 13–14.

11 Statement of Boarding Schools in the Dominion, in *Annual Report*, 1910.

12 Laird to Minister of Interior, 17 Apr. 1878, cited in Miller, *Shingwauk's Vision*, 100.

13 Report of SG Edgar Dewdney, 27 Jan. 1892, in *Annual Report*; letter from SG Frank Oliver, 21 Mar. 1908, cited in Milloy, *National Crime*, 25.

14 Reports of Deputy SG Vankoughnet, 31 Dec. 1876 and 31 Dec. 1877; Report of BC Superintendent Powell, 31 Oct. 1877; Report of SG Edgar Dewdney, 1 Jan. 1890, in *Annual Reports*, 1876, 1877, and 1890.

15 Anonymous letter from a Duck Lake resident, possibly Fourmond, to SG
Hayter Reed, 18 Jan. 1893, cited in Trevor John Williams, 'Compulsive
Measures: Resisting Residential Schools at One Arrow Reserve, 1889–1896,'
Canadian Journal of Native Studies, 34 (2014): 200.

16 Macaulay's Minute on Indian Education, 1835, in H. Sharp, ed., *Selections
from Educational Records, Part 1, 1781–1839* (Calcutta: Government Printer,
1920), 117.

17 Quotations from Report of Deputy SG Spragge, 14 Mar. 1873; Report of
Israel Powell, 1 Sept. 1876; Report of SG Macdonald, n.d. 1880: *Annual
Reports*, 1872, 1876, and 1880.

18 *Report to the Minister of the Interior on Industrial Schools for Indians and Half-
Breeds, 14 March 1879* (Winnipeg, 1879); John Herd Thompson, 'Nicholas
Flood Davin,' *DCB* online.

19 Order in Council, 19 July 1883, Industrial Schools for Indians, Northwest
Territories; Reports of SG Macdonald, 1 Jan. 1883 and 1 Jan. 1884, in
Annual Reports, 1883 and 1884.

20 Douglas Leighton, 'A Victorian Civil Servant at Work: Lawrence
Vankoughnet and the Canadian Indian Department, 1874–1893,' in Getty
and Lussier, *As Long as the Sun Shines*, 108. The figures are from Bryce,
Report on the Indian Schools, 9. During Clifford Sifton's tenure as SG from
1895 to 1905 the national budget nearly doubled, the Interior Department
budget quadrupled, but the DIA budget went up by less than 30 per cent.
For these figures, see David Hall, 'Clifton Sifton and Canadian Indian
Administration, 1896–1905,' in Getty and Lussier, *As Long as the Sun
Shines*, 121.

21 Information and quotation from Order in Council, 22 Oct. 1892, Industrial
Schools in Manitoba and the North-West Territories.

22 *Annual Report*, 1896. The Moore pictures were reused on more than one
occasion. Milloy, *National Crime*, has them at 4–5, referenced to the 1904
Annual Report.

23 The commission was established in 2008 and completed its work in 2015.
Its final *Report* consists of six volumes, the first of which outlines the
history of residential schooling.

24 The major studies of residential schools noted above, including the *TRC
Report*, are replete with examples of what is described here. We have
also relied on the detailed examination of the conditions at Qu'Appelle
Industrial School in Jacqueline Gresko, 'White "Rites" and Indian "Rites":
Indian Education and Native Responses in the West, 1870–1910,' in
Western Canada Past and Present, ed. A.W. Rasporich (Calgary: McClelland
and Stewart, 1975); and Maureen Lux, *Medicine That Walks: Disease,*

Medicine and Canadian Plains Native People, 1880–1940 (Toronto: University of Toronto Press, 2001), chap. 3.

25 Report of Deputy SG Reed, 2 Dec. 1896, in *Annual Report*, 1896.

26 See, for example, *Registration of Births, Deaths and Marriages Act*, SBC 1872, c 13, s 8; *Registration of Births, Marriages and Deaths Ordinance*, SNWT 1888, No 6, s 7.

27 Report of Deputy SG Vankoughnet, 11 Jan. 1893, in *Annual Report*, 1892. Hall, 'Clifford Sifton,' calculated that the $300 a year paid in residential schools was half of what could be earned in urban schools for teaching white children.

28 Cited in *TRC Report*, 521–2.

29 Diana Castillo, '*Miller v Ashton*: A Story of Resistance' (unpublished, 2020, on file with the authors).

30 The *TRC Report's* chapter 22, 'Covering Up Sexual Abuse, 1867–1939,' is the shortest in its detailed history of residential schools, just 12 pages, of which only four concern the period prior to the 1920s.

31 For these incidents, see *TRC Report*, 560–2.

32 Miller, *Shingwauk's Vision*, 118–19. The contract included clauses that 'while children are young and at school they shall not be baptized without the consent of their parents,' and that 'little children (under 8 years) shall not be given heavy work.'

33 Report of SG Dewdney, 1 Jan. 1890, in *Annual Report,* 1889; Report of Deputy SG Vankoughnet, 31 Dec. 1892, in *Annual Report*, 1892.

34 *Indian Act*, SC 1890, c 29, s 10.

35 Report of SG Dewdney, 13 Jan. 1891, in *Annual Report*, 1890; Reed to Wright, 31 Jan. 1891, cited in Miller, *Shingwauk's Vision*, 129, 128; Jonathan Wright, acting Indian agent, file Hills, to SG, 4 Aug. 1891, in *Annual Report*, 1891.

36 *Indian Act*, SC 1894, c 32, s 11.

37 *Commons Debates*, 9 July 1894, 5552.

38 Order in Council, 10 Nov. 1894.

39 Miller, *Shingwauk's Vision*, 129–30.

40 Report of Deputy SG Smart, 31 Dec. 1898, in *Annual Report*, 1898; Williams, 'Compulsive Measures,' 197–8 and 201.

41 *Manitoba Free Press*, 29 Dec. 1896, cited in Hall, 'Clifford Sifton,' 125; *Commons Debates*, 18 July 1904, 6948.

42 Report of Duncan C. Scott, superintendent of Indian education, 1910, in *Annual Report*, 1910.

43 *Indian Act*, SC 1914, c 35, s 1; *Commons Debates*, 18 July 1904, 6946–8. The figures given here and in the next paragraph are from the *Annual Reports* for 1895, 1900, 1908, and 1914.

44 For Bryce, see Maureen K. Lux, 'Peter Henderson Bryce,' *DCB* online; and Lux, *Medicine That Walks*, 122–35; Megan Sproule-Jones, 'Crusading for the Forgotten: Dr. Peter Bryce, Public Health, and Prairie Native Residential Schools,' *Canadian Bulletin of Medical History* 13 (1996): 199. Quotations below in this paragraph from Bryce's *Report on the Indian Schools*, 7.

45 See generally Bryce, *Report on the Indian Schools*, 17; quotations from 17–19.

46 *Evening Citizen*, 15 Nov. 1907, cited in Travis Hay, Cindy Blackstock, and Michael Kirlew, 'Dr. Peter Bryce (1853–1932): Whistleblower on Residential Schools,' *Canadian Medical Association Journal* 192 (2020): E224. The remainder of this paragraph draws principally on Miller, *Shingwauk's Vision*, 140–1; and Lux, 'Peter Henderson Bryce.'

47 Peter Bryce, *The Story of a National Crime; Being a Record of the Health Conditions of the Indians of Canada from 1904 to 1921* (Ottawa: James Hope and Sons, 1922), 4, 5, and 14. Historian John Milloy used the main title for his book on residential schools, cited above. For a similarly negative assessment of Scott, see E. Brian Titley, *Duncan Campbell Scott and the Administration of Indian Affairs in Canada* (Vancouver: UBC Press, 1986).

10. Indigenous Law and European Law: Adaptation, Resistance, Avoidance

1 Jones, *History of the Ojebway Indians, with Especial Reference to Their Conversion to Christianity* (London: A.W. Bennett, 1861); Copway, *The Traditional History and Characteristic Sketches of the Ojibway Nation* (London: Charles Gilpin, 1850; Boston: Benjamin Mussey, 1851).

2 Philip Girard, 'The Contrasting Fates of French-Canadian and Indigenous Constitutionalism: British North America, 1760–1867,' *Law & History* 7 (2020): 1. On cultural defences, see chapter 13; on family law, chapter 15.

3 Irene Spry, 'The Great Transformation: The Disappearance of the Commons in Western Canada,' in *Man and Nature on the Prairies*, ed. Richard Allen (Regina: Canadian Plains Research Center, University of Regina, 1976) ; John Lutz, *Makúk: A New History of Aboriginal-White Relations* (Vancouver: UBC Press, 2008), 279.

4 Daniel Rück, '"Où tout le monde est propriétaire et où personne ne l'est": droits d'usage et gestion foncière à Kahnawake, 1815–1880,' *RHAF* 70 (2016): 31 at 51 (authors' translation).

5 The fullest account of these interactions in this period is found in Jeremy Williams, 'A History of Gitxsan Relations with Colonial and Canadian Law, 1858–1909' (master's thesis, University of Victoria, 2000). See also Robert Galois, 'The History of the Upper Skeena Region, 1850–1927,' *Native Studies Review* 9 (1993–4): 113. On Gitxsan law generally, see Valerie Napoleon, 'Ayook: Gitksan Legal Order, Law, and Legal Theory' (PhD diss., University of Victoria, 2009), where examples of Gitxsan law in action at a later period are given.

6 On drowning death, see Williams, 'History of Gitxsan Relations,' 33–4; Robert Galois, 'The Burning of Kitsegukla, 1872,' *BC Studies* 94 (1992): 39.

7 Williams, 'History of Gitxsan Relations,' 40.

8 Ibid. See also Hamar Foster, '"The Queen's Law Is Better Than Yours": International Homicide in Early British Columbia,' in *EHCL V*.

9 Quotation from Williams, 'History of Gitxsan Relations,' 40.

10 Ibid., 60–1.

11 Douglas C. Harris, *Landing Native Fisheries: Indian Reserves & Fishing Rights in British Columbia, 1849–1925* (Vancouver: UBC Press, 2008), 7.

12 Cited in Douglas C. Harris, *Fish, Law & Colonialism: The Legal Capture of Salmon in British Columbia* (Toronto: University of Toronto Press, 2001), 46.

13 Ibid., 62.

14 Ibid., 66–71.

15 See the table constructed by Douglas C. Harris, 'Indian Reserves Allotted for Fishing Purposes in British Columbia, 1849–1925,' https://www .ubcpress.ca/asset/13402/1/9780774814195_HarrisD_IndianReservesBC_ WebTable.pdf.

16 *British Columbia Fisheries Act*, SBC 1901, c 25. See generally Harris, *Landing Native Fisheries*, 130–1, quotation at 142, who confirms that canneries were heavily reliant on Indigenous labour, especially that of women. The court cases culminated in *AG BC v AG Canada* [1914] AC 153.

17 Lutz, *Makúk*, 281.

18 Galois, 'History of the Upper Skeena Region,' 118–28, quotations at 125 and 133.

19 David Ricardo Williams, *Simon Peter Gunanoot, Trapline Outlaw* (Victoria, BC: Sono Nis, 1982), 80–1.

20 On the post-1900 situation, see Neil Sterritt, *Mapping My Way Home: A Gitxsan History* (Smithers, BC: Creekstone, 2016), 175–81; Galois, 'History of the Upper Skeena,' 140; Williams, *Simon Peter Gunanoot*, 82, quotation from *Omineca Miner*, 11 Jan. 1913 at 81.

21 Daniel Rück, *The Laws and the Land: The Settler Colonial Invasion of Kahnawà:ke in Nineteenth-Century Canada* (Vancouver: Osgoode Society for Canadian Legal History and UBC Press, 2021), 48–50.

22 Ibid., 118–20. There was at least one benefit from the building of the CPR Bridge on the reserve in 1886: men from Kahnawà:ke became interested in high steel and riveting work. They displayed such aptitude for it that the railway trained a dozen of them, who trained others, beginning a tradition of work in this industry that endures today. See 'The Mohawks Who Built Manhattan,' ASWA, https://www.aswa.ca/mohawks-who-built-manhatten [*sic*].

23 Daniel Rueck, 'Commons, Enclosure, and Resistance in Kahnawà:ke Mohawk Territory, 1850–1900,' *CHR* 95 (2014): 352.

24 Gerald F. Reid, *Kahnawà:ke: Factionalism, Traditionalism, and Nationalism in a Mohawk Community* (Lincoln: University of Nebraska Press, 2004), 24, 30–6. See also Matthieu Sossoyan, 'Les Indiens, les Mohawks et les Blancs: Mise en contexte historique et sociale de la question des Blancs à Kahnawake,' *Recherches amérindiennes au Québec* 39 (2009): 158.

25 Rück, *Laws and the Land*, chap. 5.

26 Rück, *Laws and the Land*, chaps. 6, 7. Reid, *Kahnawà:ke*, 38–49, has a detailed analysis of the tribunal's decisions.

27 Ibid., 231–2.

28 Ibid., 201–11; Reid, *Kahnawà:ke*, chap. 3.

29 Reid, *Kahnawà:ke*, 91, quotation at 103–4.

30 Ibid., 230 (quotation), 201–11.

31 Susan Hill, *The Clay We Are Made Of: Haudenosaunee Land Tenure on the Grand River* (Winnipeg: University of Manitoba Press, 2017), 190.

32 Keith Jamieson, *History of Six Nations Education* (Brantford, ON: Woodland Indian Cultural Education Centre, 1987); Alison Norman, '"True to My Own Noble Race": Six Nations Women Teachers at Grand River in the Early Twentieth Century,' *Ontario History* 107 (2015): 5; and Norman, 'Race, Gender and Colonialism: Public Life among the Six Nations of the Grand River, 1899–1939' (PhD diss., Ontario Institute for Studies in Education, 2010).

33 The Six Nations Council employed a secretary from the 1870s to record minutes of their meetings. Meetings were held in the Haudenosaunee languages, but the minutes were written in English and are held by the Woodland Cultural Centre on the Six Nations reserve. Copies were sent to the DIA and are held by Library and Archives Canada, though some sections were intentionally left out of the copies supplied to Ottawa: Hill, *Clay We Are Made Of*, 10–11.

34 Ibid., 193–6. On the New England Company, see F. Hitchin, *Come Over and Help Us: The New England Company and its Mission, 1649–2001* (Ely, UK: St Pancras Books, 2002).

35 Hill, *Clay We Are Made Of*, 196–7.

36 Ibid., 199.

37 Mike Brogden, 'Rise and Fall of the Western Métis in the Criminal Justice Process,' in *The Struggle for Recognition: Canadian Justice and the Métis Nation*, ed. S. Corrigan and L. Barkwell (Winnipeg: Pemmican Publications, 1991), 44; quotation from Lawrence Barkwell, 'Early Law and Social Control among the Métis,' in the same volume, 21.

38 Code and Resolutions in this and the next paragraph are reproduced in Barkwell, 'Early Law and Social Control,' 23–8. The formation of a 'people's' government to remedy a legal vacuum has much in common with a similar attempt in St. John's, NL, in 1723: see *Volume 1, 257*.

39 George Woodcock, *Gabriel Dumont: The Métis Chief and His Lost World* (Edmonton: Hurtig Publishers, 1975), quotation at 110.

40 Lynne Champagne, 'Pascal Bréland,' *DCB* online.

41 Woodcock, *Gabriel Dumont*, 126–8; Gerhard Ens and Joe Sawchuk, *From New Peoples to New Nations: Aspects of Métis History and Identity from the Eighteenth to Twenty-First Centuries* (Toronto: University of Toronto Press, 2016), 243–55. The saga of land for the Manitoba Métis is dealt with in chapters 7 and 14.

42 Janique Dubois and Kelly Saunders, 'Unfinished Business: Bringing the Métis into Confederation,' in *Surviving Canada: Indigenous Peoples Celebrate 150 Years of Betrayal*, ed. Kiera L. Ladner and Myra J. Tait (Winnipeg: ARP Books, 2017).

11. Law and Economy: Corporate and Commercial Law and Regulation

1 What follows in this introduction is drawn principally from the leading text, Ken Norrie, Douglas Owram, and J.C. Herb Emery, *A History of the Canadian Economy*, 4th ed. (Toronto: Thomson-Nelson, 2008). Other sources are cited when appropriate.

2 Marvin McInnis, 'Canadian Economic Development in the Wheat Boom Era: A Reassessment' (unpublished, 2020), 1, http://qed.econ.queensu .ca/faculty/mcinnis/Cdadevelopment1.pdf. See also, to similar effect, McInnis, 'The Economy of Canada in the Nineteenth Century,' in *The Cambridge Economic History of the United States*, vol. 2, *The Long Nineteenth*

Century, ed. Stanley Engerman and Robert E. Gallman (Cambridge: Cambridge University Press, 2000).

3 Railway statistics are from Canada, *Sessional Papers*, 1915, no. 20b, Railway Statistics of the Dominion of Canada.

4 M.C. Urquhart, *Gross National Product, Canada, 1870–1926: The Derivation of the Estimates* (Montreal and Kingston: McGill-Queen's University Press, 1993), 11–14.

5 Jamie Benidickson, 'John Rudolphus Booth,' *DCB* online. For a major enterprise that for many years preferred partnership to incorporation because it maintained family control over the partners' affairs, see C. Ian Kyer, 'Gooderham and Worts: A Case Study in Business Organization in Nineteenth-Century Ontario,' in *EHCL VIII*. No Canadian treatise on partnerships appeared before 1900: R.B. Henderson and Peers Davidson, *The Canadian Law of Partnership* (Montreal: Snow Law Publishing, 1900).

6 This chapter is only about what we term 'business organizations,' not all corporations. A host of religious, educational, municipal, and other non-profit corporations formed for a wide variety of purposes were created before and after Confederation, but we will not further discuss them here. The historical literature on incorporation in Canada is very limited, except for Nova Scotia: see Barbara Patton, 'From State Action to Private Profit: The Emergence of the Business Corporation in Nova Scotia, 1796–1833'; and Jonathan Davidson, 'Industry and the Development of Company Law in Nineteenth-Century Nova Scotia,' *Nova Scotia Historical Review* 15 (1995) 86, and 16 (1996) 21. In addition to these we have relied on Fenner L. Stewart, 'A History of Canadian Corporate Law: A Divergent Path from the American Model,' in *Research Handbook on the History of Corporate and Company Law*, ed. Harwell Wells (London: Edward Elgar, 2018), and Thomas Mulvey, 'Some Phases of Canadian Company Law,' *CLT* 20 (1920): 832.

7 Charles Henry Stephens, *The Law and Practice of Joint Stock Companies* (Toronto: Carswells, 1881), viii; C.A. Fleming, *The Laws of Business with Forms of Common Business and Legal Documents* (Toronto: n.p., 1897), 178.

8 For pre-Confederation business incorporation, see *Volume 1*, 628–45. For federalism and incorporation, see John T. Saywell, *The Lawmakers: Judicial Power and the Shaping of Canadian Federalism* (Toronto: Osgoode Society for Canadian Legal History and University of Toronto Press, 2002), 169–70.

9 *Citizens Insurance Company v Parsons* [1881–1882] 7 AC 96; *Joint Stock Companies Act*, SO 1874, c 35, s 3. See Mulvey, 'Some Phases of Canadian Company Law'; John D. Spence, 'The Status of Provincial Corporations'; and R.A. Reid, 'Company Incorporation Jurisdiction in

Canada under the British North America Act,' in *CLT* 28 (1908) 239 and 32 (1912) 749 and 944.

10 Section 91(15), banking, incorporation of banks, and the issue of paper money, and 91(16) savings banks. Section 92(11) gave the provinces jurisdiction over 'local works and undertakings' except for 'lines of steam or other ships, railways, canals, telegraphs, and other works and undertakings connecting [a] … Province with any other or others of the Provinces, or extending beyond the limits of [a] … Province.'

11 RSO 1877, Title 11, Companies and Corporations, c 151–5, 157–8, and 164. These statutes were still in force in 1897: see RSO, 1897, Title 13, Companies and Corporations, c 192–6 and 199–202; SO 1879, c 24.

12 *Corporations Act*, SNB 1862, c 28, s 1; *Joint Stock Companies Act*, RSNS 1873, c 54, s 1; Davidson, 'Company Law in Nova Scotia,' 101; *Re Nash Brick and Pottery Manufacturing Company*, (1873) 9 NSR. 254.

13 *Joint Stock Companies Patent Act*, SC 1869, c 13. The role of the different departments is summarized in Charles Holt, 'The Canada Companies Act,' *CLT* 2 (1902): 71.

14 *Joint Stock Companies Act*, SC 1877, c 43, s 78.

15 *Companies Act*, SO 1874, c 35; SM 1875, c 28; SNB 1875, c 30; SQ 1881, c 11; SNS 1883, c 24; SPEI 1888, c 14; *Companies Ordinance*, ONWT 1886, No 3. All of these statutes were later amended in various ways, but only significant amendments are discussed in this chapter. In the 1906 *Revised Statutes of Canada* the *Companies Act* and the *Companies Clauses Act*, discussed below, were merged: RSC 1906, c 79.

16 *Incorporation of Joint Stock Companies Act*, SQ 1868, c 25. Twelve sectors were listed, with two more added in 1875: SQ 1875, c 39.

17 *Senate Debates*, 8 Apr. 1902, 171. The federal legislation discussed by Scott was *Companies Act*, SC 1902, c 15, s 13. For provincial legislation, see *Registration of Foreign Companies Act*, SBC 1872, c 36; *Out of Province Corporations Act*, SO 1876, c 27; *Companies Incorporated under Imperial Statutes Act*, SO 1880, c 19; *Corporations Incorporated outside the North-West Territories Ordinance*, ONWT 1884, No 22; *Companies Act*, RSQ 1888, vol 2, c 3, art 4764; *Companies Act*, SNS 1898, c 57; *Extra Provincial Corporations Act*, SNB 1903, c 25; *Extra-Provincial Companies Act*, SPEI 1913, c 22.

18 The exception was New Brunswick before 1885, where the provincial secretary granted a certificate of incorporation. This was changed to the letters patent system in 1885: *Corporations Act*, SNB 1862, c 28 and 1865, c 30; *Joint Stock Companies Act*, SNB 1885, c 9.

19 For the meaning of letters patent, and the British and American approaches, see A.W. Currie, 'The First Dominion Companies Act,'

Canadian Journal of Economics and Political Science 28 (1962): 387 at 400–5;
John D. Turner, 'The Development of English Company Law before
1900,' in Wells, *Research Handbook*; Ron Harris, *Industrializing English
Law: Entrepreneurship and Business Organization* (Cambridge: Cambridge
University Press, 2000).

20 *Companies Act*, SN 1899, c 10; 1856, c 18; *Alberta Act*, SC 1905, c 3, s 16(4);
Saskatchewan Act, SC 1905, c 42, s 20.

21 *Joint Stock Companies Ordinance*, BC Ordinances 1866, No 5; *Companies
Ordinance 1866*, BC Ordinances 1869, No 129; *Companies Act*, UK Statutes
1844, c 110, and 1862, c 89; *Corporations Act*, SBC 1878, c 5; *Companies Act*,
CSBC 1888, c 21, s 2; *Corporations Act*, RSBC 1897, c 44, quotations from
preamble and sections 4 and 9.

22 Unless otherwise referenced, the exclusions were all contained in the
general incorporation statues cited above, note 15.

23 *Joint Stock Companies Act*, RSNS 1900, c 128, s 6; *Joint Stock Companies Act*,
SO 1912, c 31, s 3; Fleming, *Laws of Business*, 177.

24 *Companies Act*, RSNS 1900, c 128, s 6; *Companies Act*, RSO 1887, c 157, s 4;
SO 1887, c 26, s 4; RSO 1897, c 191, s 9; and SO 1908, c 43, s 1; *Mutual Fire
Insurance Companies Act*, RSO 1877, c 161; *Mutual Insurance Companies Act*,
SQ 1884, c 74.

25 *Companies Act*, SC 1902, c 15, s 5; *Companies Act*, SO 1897, c 28, s 8;
Companies Act, RSNS 1900, c 128, s 6; *Statute Law Amendment Act*, SNS
1913, c 28, s 16; SS 1906, c 31; *Companies Act*, RSM 1902, c 25, s 4; and RSM
1913, c 35, s 4; *Companies Act*, SBC 1895, c 55; *Statute Law Amendment Act*,
SA 1907, c 5, s 13.

26 *Companies Act*, SC 1869, c 13, s 48; and SC 1877, c 43, s 78; *Limited Liability
Act*, SO 1889, c 26.

27 In addition to the Hansard for the Senate and the Commons, this
statement is also based on a reading of the *Canada Law Journal* and the
Canadian Law Times.

28 *Corporations General Provisions Act*, RSNS 1864, c 87, s 13; also in RSNS
1873, c 53, s 13; RSNS 1884, c 78, s 13; and RSNS 1900, c 127. The 1900
Revised Statutes thus contradicted the general incorporation statute passed
in 1883 and re-enacted in RSNS 1884, c 79; and RSNS 1900, c 128.

29 What follows is from *Senate Debates*, 4 May 1869, 84–6.

30 *Corporations Act*, SNB 1862, c 28, s 10.

31 *Declarations by Incorporated Companies Act*, SQ 1876, c 15.

32 *Protection of Investors in Companies Act*, SQ 1884, c 73, quotations from ss
3 and 7; SPEI 1888, c 14, s 69. 'Watering' stock was, and is, the practice
of defrauding investors by offering shares at a higher value than they

are worth by overstating the company's book value. Those who bought watered stock generally found that the market quickly realized that it was overvalued, and investors could not sell it other than at a greatly reduced price. They also became personally liable for the corporation's debts if they had not paid in full for their stock and a creditor or creditors pushed the company into insolvency. A capital surplus is the amount raised on an initial share offering that exceeds the par or face value of a share. It could create the same problem as watered stock – an inflated share price, which the market then discounts, with the investor ending up the loser.

33 *Companies Act*, SC 1902, c 15, ss 10 and 18; Report of the Secretary of State for 1903, in Canada, *Sessional Papers*, 1904, no. 29; *Senate Debates*, 22 Apr. 1902, 270. For a brief description and approval of the 1902 legislation, see Holt, 'Canada Companies Act.'

34 Stephens, *Joint Stock Companies*, viii.

35 Report of the Secretary of State for 1902, in Canada, *Sessional Papers*, 1903, no. 29.

36 Report of the Secretary of State for 1880, in Canada, *Sessional Papers*, 1881, no. 10.

37 Report of the Secretary of State for 1902, in Canada, *Sessional Papers*, 1903, no. 29.

38 Not all locations are known. All details in this paragraph are from Report of the Secretary and Registrar of Ontario for 1895, in Ontario, *Sessional Papers*, 1896, appendix 3.

39 *Metropolitan Bank Act*, SC 1871, c 39; *Fredericton and St Mary's Railway Bridge Company Act*, SC 1871, c 51; *St Clair and Lake Erie Navigation Company Act*, SC 1880, c 63; *Lake Superior Mineral Railway Company Act*, SC 1886, c 81; *Calgary Street Railway Company Act*, SC 1893, c 40; *St LawrencePower Company Act*, SC 1901, c 111; *Arnprior and Pontiac Railway Company Act*, SC 1909, c 44.

40 *Companies General Clauses Act*, SQ 1868, c 24; *Companies Clauses Act*, SC 1869, c 12; *Companies Incorporated by Special Act General Provisions Act*, RSO 1877, c 149; *General Provisions Respecting Domestic and Foreign Companies Act*, RSNS 1900, c 127; *Corporate Bodies Act*, SPEI 1852, c 4; *Companies Clauses Act*, SPC 1861, c 18; *General Provisions Respecting Corporations Act*, RSNS 1864, c 87.

41 *Railway Act*, SC 1868, c 68, s 18.

42 William E. Hodgins, *Synopsis of the Provisions of the Companies Act relating to the Incorporation of Joint Stock Companies* (Toronto: Carswell, 1883), v.

43 For this paragraph, see Davidson, 'Development of Company Law.'

44 *Volume 1*, 647–52.

45 See Thomas G.W. Telfer, *Ruin and Redemption: The Struggle for a Canadian Bankruptcy Law, 1867–1919* (Toronto: Osgoode Society for Canadian Legal History and University of Toronto Press, 2014), 6–7; and the first federal bankruptcy statute, *Insolvency Act*, SC 1869, c 16.

46 See, for example, *Suits against Absent or Absconding Debtors Act*, RSNS 1864, c 141.

47 *Insolvent Debtors Relief Act*, RSNS 1864, c 137, s 3; *Insolvent Debtors Relief Act*, SNS 1878, c 8; *Insolvent Debtors Relief Act*, SNS 1884, c 19; *Imprisonment for Debt Act*, SNS 1890, c17, ss 1 and 3; *Collection Act*, SNS 1894, c 4; *Collection Act*, RSNS 1914, c 182.

48 *Fraser v Kirkpatrick*, (1907) 5 WLR 287 (NWTSC); *Imperial Debtors Act*, SA 1908, c 6; *Statute Law Amendment Act*, SA 1909, c 4, s 20. Saskatchewan passed similar legislation, but not until a decade later: *Imperial Debtors Act*, SS 1918–1919, c 83.

49 The remainder of this section, on bankruptcy, relies principally on Telfer, *Ruin and Redemption*. Other sources are cited when appropriate. Telfer's work deals with the federal legislation, with debates over bankruptcy, and with the operation of the law in Ontario. He does not discuss the other provinces.

50 *Insolvent Act*, SC 1869, c 16, 1873, c 2, 1874, c 46, and 1875, c 16; *Insolvent Act Repeal Act*, SC 1880, c 1; *Bankruptcy Act*, SC 1919, c 36.

51 *Insolvent Act*, SC 1877, c 41.

52 *Commons Debates*, 11 May 1869, 253; *Senate Debates*, 18 June 1869, 359–60.

53 See Michael Bliss, *A Living Profit: A Study in the Social History of Canadian Business, 1883–1911* (Toronto: McClelland and Stewart, 1974).

54 The figures are from Telfer, *Ruin and Redemption*, 29, based on Ontario county court records.

55 Cited in ibid., 39.

56 Ibid., 85.

57 Ibid., 44–5. The cases mentioned in the following paragraph are from the same source, at 46 and 50–1.

58 Ibid., 84.

59 *Execution Creditors Act*, SO 1880, c 10; *Assignments for the Benefit of Creditors Act*, SO 1885, c 26; *Assignments for the Benefit of Creditors Act*, SM 1886, c 45; *Assignments and Preferences Act*, SNB 1895, c 6; *Assignments and Preferences Act*, SNS 1898, c 11. Quebec had pro rata distribution as part of the Civil Code: Telfer, *Ruin and Redemption*, 104. For federalism and insolvency see Thomas Telfer and Virginia Torrie, *Debt and Federalism: Landmark Cases in Canadian Bankruptcy and Insolvency Law, 1894–1937* (Vancouver: UBC Press, 2022), introduction and chap. 1.

60 Margot Priest, W.T. Stanbury, and Fred Thompson, 'On the Definition of Economic Regulation,' in *Government Regulation: Scope, Growth, Process,* ed. W.T. Stanbury (Montreal: Institute for Research on Public Policy, 1980), 5. For governments and the economy before 1867, see *Volume 1,* 626–8.

61 H.V. Nelles and Christopher Armstrong, *Monopoly's Moment: The Organisation and Regulation of Canadian Utilities, 1830–1930* (Toronto: University of Toronto Press, 1938); and H.V. Nelles, *The Politics of Development: Forests, Mines and Hydro-Electric Power in Ontario, 1849–1891* (Montreal and Kingston: McGill-Queen's University Press, 1974). See generally Alex Corry, *The Growth of Government Activities since Confederation* (Ottawa: Royal Commission on Dominion-Provincial Relations, 1939); and Carman D. Baggaley, *The Emergence of the Regulatory State in Canada, 1867–1939* (Ottawa: Economic Council of Canada, 1981).

62 *Combines Act,* SC 1889, c 4. For this legislation, and common law restraint of trade doctrines, see, inter alia, Charles P. Hoffman, 'A Reappraisal of the Canadian Anti-Combines Act of 1889,' *Queen's Law Journal* 39 (2013): 127; and Brian Cheffins, 'The Development of Competition Policy, 1890–1940: A Re-evaluation of a Canadian and American Tradition,' *OHLJ* 27 (1989): 449.

63 For the origins of this phrase in Canadian legal historiography, see R.C.B. Risk, 'Lawyers, Courts and the Rise of the Regulatory State,' *Dalhousie Law Journal,* 9 (1984): 31.

64 Respectively public debt and property, the borrowing of money on the public credit, currency and coinage, savings banks, bills of exchange and promissory notes, interest, and legal tender.

65 Christopher Kobrak and Joe Martin, *From Wall Street to Bay Street: The Origins and Evolution of American and Canadian Finance* (Toronto: University of Toronto Press, 2018). In addition to the sources cited below, we have relied for this section on Edward Peter Neufeld, *The Financial System of Canada: Its Growth and Development* (Toronto: Macmillan, 1972); Ronald Rudin, *Banking en français: The French Banks of Quebec, 1835–1925* (Toronto: University of Toronto Press, 1985); and A.J. Glazenbrook, 'Finance and Banking: Economic Development of Canada, 1867–1921,' in *Cambridge History of the British Empire,* ed. J. Holland Rose (Cambridge: Cambridge University Press, 1930), 6:625–41.

66 *Bank Act,* SC 1867, c 11; *Bank of Upper Canada Act,* SC 1867, c 17; *Bank Amalgamation Act,* SC 1867, c 18; *Amalgamation of Banks Act,* SC 1868, c 84.

67 *Bank Act,* SC 1870, c 11, and 1871, c 5. See generally Robert M. MacIntosh, 'Origins of Financial Stability in Canada: The Bank Act of 1871,' in

Relentless Change: A Case Book for the Study of Canadian Business History, ed. Joe Martin (Toronto: University of Toronto Press, 2010).

68 *Farmers Bank Incorporation Act*, SC 1904, c 77.

69 James D. Frost, 'The "Nationalization" of the Bank of Nova Scotia, 1880–1910,' *Acadiensis* 12 (1982): 3.

70 *Bank Act*, SC 1900, c 25, ss 33–9.

71 Laurence B. Mussio, *A Vision Greater Than Themselves: The Making of the Bank of Montreal, 1817–2017* (Montreal and Kingston: McGill-Queen's University Press, 2016), 45–8. For another merger/acquisition, James D. Frost, 'From the Merchants' Bank of Halifax to the Royal Bank of Canada: 1864–1908,' *Journal of the Royal Nova Scotia Historical Society* 21 (2018): 48.

72 *Bank Act*, SC 1880, c 22; *Bank Act*, SC 1890, c 31; *CBA Incorporation Act*, SC 1900, c 93; John Anthony Turley-Ewart, 'Gentlemen Bankers, Politicians and Bureaucrats: The History of the Canadian Bankers Association, 1891–1924' (PhD diss., University of Toronto, 2000).

73 For this paragraph, see *Currency Act*, SC 1910, c 14; *Dominion Notes Act*, SC 1870, c 10, and 1914, c 4; *Bank Act*, SC 1870, c 11; George Rich, 'The Gold-Reserve Requirement under the Dominion Notes Act of 1870: How to Deceive Parliament,' *Canadian Journal of Economics* 10 (1977): 447.

74 Andrew Smith, 'Continental Divide: The Canadian Banking and Currency Laws of 1871 in the Mirror of the United States,' *Enterprise & Society* 13 (2012): 491; *Quebec Syndicates Act*, SQ 1906, c 33, quotation at s 5. See generally Ronald Rudin, *In Whose Interest? Quebec's Caisses populaires, 1900–1945* (Montreal and Kingston: McGill-Queen's University Press, 1990).

75 *Union Bank Notes Act*, SN 1895, c 1; *Commercial Bank Notes Act*, SN 1895, c 2.

76 Smith, 'Continental Divide,' 458.

77 Urquhart, *Gross National Product*, 11–14.

78 There is a substantial literature on mining in Canada, most of it devoted to particular provinces/regions and/or to what was mined. For general overviews, see Jeremy Mouat, *Metal Mining in Canada, 1840–1950* (Ottawa: National Museum of Science and Technology, 2000); Bernard L. McEvoy, *Canada's Buried Treasures: The Story of Minerals and Their Discovery* (Toronto: McClelland and Stewart, 1968); Del Muise and Robert G. McIntosh, *Coal Mining in Canada: A Historical and Comparative Overview* (Ottawa: National Museum of Science and Technology, 1996).

79 RSNS 1864, c 25.

80 For these points, and for much of what follows, see Donald McLeod, 'Colliers, Colliery Safety and Workplace Control: The Nova Scotia Experience, 1873–1910,' *Historical Papers* 18 (1981): 226.

81 RSNS 1873, c 9 and 10.

82 SNS 1881, c 5; 1884, c 21; 1885, c 6; 1890, c 19; 1891, c 9.

83 The principal source for what follows is Nelles, *Politics of Development*.

84 *Mines and Minerals Act*, SPC 1864, c 25; *Gold and Silver Mining Act*, SO 1868, c 19, ss 25 (grant of minerals with patents) and 27 (royalties); *Gold and Silver Mining Act*, SO 1869, c 34, s 3.

85 *General Mining Act*, SO 1891, c 8, quotations from ss 3 and 9.

86 *Mining Regulations Act*, SO 1890, c 10, quotation from s 23; SO 1892, c 9.

87 *Mines Act*, SO 1900, c 13, ss 2 and 3; David G. Burley, 'Sir George William Ross,' *DCB* online.

88 SC 1868, c 68; *Railway Act*, CSC 1859, c 66. Ontario did not pass its own *Railway Act* until its statutes were first consolidated in 1877: *Railway Act*, RSO 1877, c 165.

89 SC 1868, c 68, s 23; *Railway Act*, SC 1888, c 29. Per section 8 of the latter, the railway committee consisted of the minister of railways and canals, the minister of justice, and any two other members of Cabinet.

90 The following account of the development and operation of federal railway legislation is from Ken Cruikshank, *Close Ties: Railways, Government and the Board of Railway Commissioners, 1851–1933* (Montreal and Kingston: McGill-Queen's University Press, 1991); and Jamie Benidickson, 'The Canadian Board of Railway Commissioners: Regulation, Policy and Legal Process at the Turn of the Century,' *McGill Law Journal* 36 (1990–1): 1222.

91 For these disputes, which there is not space to detail here, see, inter alia, Ken Cruikshank, 'The Transportation Revolution and Its Consequences: The Railway Freight Rate Controversy of the Late Nineteenth Century,' *Historical Papers* (1987): 12; and H. Darling, *The Politics of Freight Rates: The Railway Freight Rate Issue in Canada* (Toronto: McClelland and Stewart, 1980).

92 John S. Willison, *The Railway Question in Canada, with an Examination of the Law in Iowa* (Toronto: Warwick Brothers, 1897), 6–7. For Willison, see Richard Clippingdale, 'Sir John Stephen Willison,' *DCB* online.

93 See, inter alia, Herbert Hovenkamp, 'Regulatory Conflict in the Gilded Age: Federalism and the Railroad Problem,' *Yale Law Journal* 97 (1988): 1017.

94 Canada, *Sessional Papers*, 1902, No 20A, Reports upon Railway Commissions, Railway Rate Grievances, and Regulative Legislation; Benidickson, 'Canadian Board,' 1230–3; *Railway Act* 1903, s 8.

95 Risk, 'Rise of the Regulatory State,' 35; *Railway and Municipal Board Act*, SO 1906, c 31.

96 *CLJ* 40 (1904): 449–50, cited in Benidickson, 'Canadian Board,' 1234–5.
97 Benidickson, 'Canadian Board,' 1251–5. For the statutory provisions, see *Railway Act*, SC 1905, c 35. For the individuals named here, see D.M. Young, 'Andrew George Blair'; Margaret Derry, 'James Mills'; and Lee Gibson, 'Albert Clements Killam,' all in *DCB* online.
98 (1916) 53 SCR 583 at 599.
99 Risk, 'Rise of the Regulatory State,' 37–9.

12. Labour and Employment Law

1 British Columbia legislation limited underground work in mines to eight hours in every 24: *Inspection of Metalliferous Mines Act*, SBC 1899, c 49, s 4. See also *Labour Regulation Act*, SBC 1907, c 23.
2 This paragraph summarizes *Volume 1*, 677–81. What follows on master and servant law after Confederation is based principally on Paul Craven, 'Canada, 1670–1935: Symbolic and Instrumental Enforcement in Loyalist North America,' in *Masters, Servants and Magistrates in Britain and the Empire, 1562–1955*, ed. Craven and Douglas Hay (Chapel Hill: University of North Carolina Press, 2004); and on Craven, 'The Law of Master and Servant in Mid-Nineteenth-Century Ontario,' in *EHCL I*, and 'The Modern Spirit of the Law: Reconsidering the Breaches of Contract Act, 1877,' in *EHCL VIII*. For all aspects of labour law in Ontario, including master and servant, see Jeremy Webber, 'Labour and the Law,' in *Labouring Lives: Work and Workers in Nineteenth-Century Ontario*, ed. Paul Craven (Toronto: University of Toronto Press, 1995).
3 See *Masters, Apprentices and Servants Act*, RSNS 1873, c 88; RSNS 1883, c 98; and *Apprentices Act*, RSNS 1900, c 117. For New Brunswick, see *Minors and Apprentices Act*, CSNB 1877, c 70.
4 The Quebec law was complex, involving by-laws made by JPs in Montreal and a Lower Canada statute applicable to rural areas that prescribed fines and imprisonment on workers who breached contracts: *Masters and Servants in Country Parts Act*, CSLC 1860, c 27, and SPC 1866, c 34; Craven, 'Canada, 1670–1935,' 189–90. For the other provinces, see *Servants Act*, SPEI 1833, c 26, s 3; *Masters and Servants Act*, SM 1871, c 14; *Masters and Servants Ordinance, 1877*, ONWT 1879, No 5, RONWT 1886, c 36, and SNWT 1904, c 3. For British Columbia, see *Master and Servant Act*, SBC 1897, c 26.
5 SC 1877, c 35. The other legislation discussed in this paragraph was *Punishment of Officers and Servants of Railway Companies Act*, SPC 1856, c 136; and *Master and Servant Act*, RSO 1914, c 144.

6 See Craven, 'Modern Spirit of the Law'; and, for the political activities of labour groups and for trade unionism in this period, Gregory Kealey, *Toronto Workers Respond to Industrial Capitalism, 1867–1892* (Toronto: University of Toronto Press, 1980), 148–53.

7 See Craven, 'Canada, 1670–1935,' 206; *Master and Servant Act*, SM 1883, c 33, RSM 1891, c 96. Imprisonment was also a sanction available for use against apprentices and those to whom they were apprenticed: *Apprentices and Minors Act*, SM 1877, c 26.

8 See generally Craven, 'Canada, 1670–1935,' esp. at 190 and 193. The legislation was *Master and Servant Act*, SQ 1881, c 15; and SQ 1894, c 40; quotations from s 1 in each case. See also *Montreal City Charter*, SQ 1899, c 58, s 300(105), which stated that among the city council's voluminous powers was the authority '[t]o regulate the respective duties of masters, apprentices, servants, domestics, journeymen and labourers.' See also *Montreal City Charter Act*, SQ 1912, c 56, s 23.

9 This and the following paragraph on enforcement patterns are based on Craven, 'Canada, 1670–1935'; quotations and figures below at 194, 199, 207, and 215; Craven, 'Law of Master and Servant,' 200–4; and Harris, *Fish, Law and Colonialism*, 49–55.

10 The extensive literature on pre- and immediately post-Confederation labour conflicts is comprehensively summarized in Bryan D. Palmer, 'Labour Protest and Organization in Nineteenth-Century Canada, 1820–1890,' *Labour/Le Travail* 20 (1987): 61. That literature is about more than unions; as Palmer notes at 62, '[b]efore there were unions, there were strikes.'

11 An excellent survey of this debate can be found in Eric Tucker, 'That Indefinite Area of Toleration: Criminal Conspiracy and Trade Unions in Ontario, 1837–1877,' *Labour/Le Travail* 27 (1991): 15.

12 For this use of master and servant law, see especially Craven, 'Canada, 1670–1935,' 201 and 207–8; and Tucker, 'Indefinite Area of Toleration,' 33–4.

13 *Upper Canada Law Journal* 3 (1867): 57, cited in Tucker, 'Indefinite Area of Toleration,' 37.

14 For the printers strike and the legislation, see SC 1872, c 30 and 31, and 1876, c 37, and the following secondary sources: Michael Chartrand, 'The First Canadian Trade Union Legislation: An Historical Perspective,' *Ottawa Law Review* 16 (1984): 267; Bernard Ostry, 'Conservatives, Liberals and Labour in the 1870s,' *CHR* 41 (1960): 93; Donald Creighton, 'George Brown, Sir John Macdonald, and the "Workingman,"' *CHR* 24 (1943): 362; and Tucker, 'Indefinite Area of Toleration,' quotation at 42.

15 Cited in Tucker, 'Indefinite Area of Toleration,' 49.
16 The phrase is from Judy Fudge and Eric Tucker, *Labour before the Law: The Regulation of Workers' Collective Action in Canada, 1900–1948* (Toronto: Osgoode Society for Canadian Legal History and Oxford University Press, 2001), 2. Much of what follows is based on chapters 2 and 3 of this book.
17 *Union Colliery v John Bryden*, [1899] AC 580; Clarence Karr, 'James Dunsmuir,' *DCB* online; Rod Mickleburgh, *On the Line: A History of the British Columbia Labour Movement* (Madeira Park, BC: Harbour Publishing, 2018), 38–9.
18 Douglas Cruikshank and Gregory S. Kealey, 'Strikes in Canada, 1891–1950,' *Labour/Le Travail* 20 (1987): 85; table at 86.
19 Rande Kostal, 'Conservative Insurrection: Great Strikes and Deep Law in Cleveland, Ohio, and London, Ontario, 1898–1899,' in *EHCL VIII*, quotation at 309.
20 *Criminal Code*, SC 1892, c 29, s 523(f).
21 *Vulcan Ironworks Company v Ironmoulders Union* (1909) 10 WLR 421, cited in Fudge and Tucker, *Labour before the Law*, 25. For Mathers, see Dale Brawn, *The Court of Queen's Bench of Manitoba, 1870–1950: A Biographical History* (Toronto: Osgoode Society for Canadian Legal History and University of Toronto Press, 2006), 185–99.
22 *Criminal Code Amendment Act*, SC 1905, c 9, s 3.
23 For the origins of these torts, see, inter alia, A.W.J. Thompson, 'The Injunction in Trade Disputes in Britain before 1910,' *Industrial and Labour Relations Review* 19 (1965–6): 21; Michael J. Klarman, 'The Judges versus the Unions: The Development of British Labour Law, 1867–1913,' *Virginia Law Review* 75 (1989): 1487.
24 See the table in Fudge and Tucker, *Labour before the Law*, 20. See also generally Judy Fudge and Eric Tucker, 'Forging Responsible Unions: Metal Workers and the Rise of the Labour Injunction in Canada,' *Labour/Le Travail* 37 (1996): 96.
25 *Trade Unions Amendment Act*, SBC 1902, c 66, s 1.
26 *Trade Unions Act*, SBC 1902, c 66; Judy Fudge and Eric Tucker, '"Everybody Knows What a Picket Line Means": Picketing before the British Columbia Court of Appeal,' *BC Studies* 162 (2009): 53.
27 The litigation stemming from this strike resulted in at least five reported cases: [1903] OJ No 92; [1905] OJ No. 110 (CA), quotations in this paragraph at paras. 6, 25, and 31; [1906] OJ No 43 (Div Ct); [1907] OJ No 122; and [1908] AC 514 (JCPC). The case is discussed in Fudge and Tucker, *Labour before the Law*, 29–30.

28 *Trades Arbitration Act*, SO 1873, c 26; Margaret McCallum, 'Labour and Arbitration in the Mowat Era,' *CJLS* 6 (1991): 65, quotation at 83.

29 *Trades Arbitration Amendment Act*, SO 1890, c 40; *Trade Disputes Act*, SO 1894, c 42; *Trade Disputes Act*, SQ 1901, c 31; *Industrial Disputes Conciliation and Arbitration Act*, SBC 1893, c 21. A further 1897 amendment to the Ontario legislation sought to have arbitration used more frequently by imposing a duty on the arbitration councils to intervene in disputes, but this proved equally ineffective: *Trade Disputes Amendment Act*, SO 1897, c 25.

30 *Railway and Municipal Board Act*, SO 1906, c 31, ss 58–9.

31 We cannot discuss here in any detail the politics of workers' movements in this period. Suffice it to say that most unions were trade-based and thus the CLU and its successor, the Canadian Labour Congress (CLC), largely comprised craft unions. The principal rival organization was the Knights of Labour, a branch of an American union oriented to socialism, which sought to draw its membership from both skilled and unskilled workers. Ontario was at the centre of Canadian trade unionism from the 1870s until the 1890s. See, inter alia, Gregory S. Kealey and Bryan Palmer, *Dreaming of What Might Be: The Knights of Labour in Ontario, 1880–1900* (Cambridge: Cambridge University Press, 1982).

32 SNS 1888, c 3. For this discussion of the *Act*, see Margaret McCallum, 'The Mines Arbitration Act 1888: Compulsory Arbitration in Context,' in *EHCL III*.

33 For the PWA, see K. Abbott, 'The Coal Miners and the Law in Nova Scotia: From the 1864 Combination of Workmen Act to the 1947 Trade Union Act,' in *Workers and the State in Twentieth-Century Nova Scotia*, ed. Michael Earle (Fredericton: Acadiensis, 1989).

34 What follows on the federal government's labour policies and legislation in this period is based principally on Paul Craven, *'An Impartial Umpire': Industrial Relations and the Canadian State, 1900–1911* (Toronto: University of Toronto Press, 1980). Federal policy is also discussed in Fudge and Tucker, *Labour before the Law*, 34–50; Jeremy Webber, 'Compelling Compromise: Canada Chooses Conciliation over Arbitration, 1900–1907,' *Labour/Le Travail* 28 (1991): 15; and Margaret McCallum, 'Labour and the Liberal State: Regulating the Employment Relationship, 1867–1920,' in *Canada's Legal Inheritances*, ed. Wesley Pue and D. Guth (Winnipeg: University of Manitoba, 2001), 586–9.

35 *Conciliation Act*, SC 1900, c 24, quotations from ss 3 and 4. As pointed out in Craven, *Impartial Umpire*, 147–50, people at this time used 'conciliation' to mean both third-party assistance and third-party intervention at the bargaining table, the latter now called mediation.

36 *Railway Labour Dispute Act*, SC 1903, c 55. This and the *Conciliation Act* were consolidated in the *Conciliation and Labour Act*, RSC 1906, c 96.

37 SC 1907, c 20; William Baker, 'The Miners and the Mediator: The 1906 Lethbridge Strike and Mackenzie King,' *Labour/Le Travail* 11 (1983): 89.

38 McCallum, 'Labour and the Liberal State,' 588; *Toronto Electric Commissioners v Snider* [1925] AC 396 (PC).

39 SBC 1877, c 15.

40 *Threshing and Other Machines Safety Act*, SM 1877, c 37. There is not space here to provide a full listing of such legislation, but examples include the *Railway Accidents Act*, SO 1881, c 22.

41 *Factories Act*, SO 1884, c 39, quotations below from sections 2, 5, and 14. This section on the origins of the 1884 Act relies principally on Eric Tucker, *Administering Danger in the Workplace: The Law and Politics of Occupational Health and Safety Regulations in Ontario, 1850–1914* (Toronto: University of Toronto Press, 1990); and Lorna F. Hurl, 'Restricting Child Factory Labour in Late Nineteenth-Century Ontario,' *Labour/Le Travail* 21 (1988): 87.

42 Royal Commission on Mills and Factories, Canada, *Sessional Papers*, 1882, no. 42.

43 *Factories Act*, SO 1889, c 43.

44 *Compulsory School Attendance Act*, SO 1891, c 50, s 5; *Factories Act*, SO 1895, c 50, s 2.

45 *Shops Regulation Act*, SO 1888, c 33; *Protection of Persons Employed in Places of Business Act*, SO 1892, c 54.

46 *Factories Act*, SQ 1885, c 32; SM 1900, c 13; SNS 1901, c 1; SNB 1905, c 7; SBC 1908, c 15; SS 1909, c 10.

47 See, for example, *Shops Regulation Act*, SM 1888, c 32.

48 *Mining Operations* Act, SO 1890, c 10.

49 *Prevention of Accidents by Fire Act*, SO 1888, c 34.

50 Cited in Tucker, *Administering Danger*, 138. What follows on enforcement is based on this source, chap. 6, quotation below at 152, on Tucker, 'Making the Workplace Safe in Capitalism: The Enforcement of Factory Legislation in Nineteenth-Century Ontario,' *Labour/Le Travail* 21 (1988): 45; and on Hurl, 'Restricting Child Factory Labour.'

51 For employers' liability for workplace injuries, see R.C.B. Risk, 'This Nuisance of Litigation: The Origins of Workers' Compensation in Ontario,' in *EHCL II*.

52 150 ER 1030 (Exch, 1837); (1842) 4 Mass (4 Met) 49.

53 For this argument, see Lawrence Friedman and Jack Ladinsky, 'Social Change and the Law of Industrial Accidents,' *Columbia Law Review* 67

(1967): 50; and Michael Lobban, 'Torts,' in *The Oxford History of the Laws of England*, vol. 12, *1820–1914: Private Law*, ed. Lobban et al. (Oxford: Oxford University Press, 2010).

54 Figures from Risk, 'This Nuisance of Litigation,' 422.

55 *Deverill, Administratrix of Deverill v Grand Trunk Railway* (1866), 25 UCQB 517 at 525.

56 For this case, see Rande Kostal, 'Legal Justice, Social Justice: An Excursion into the Social History of Work-Related Accident Law in Ontario, 1880–1886,' *LHR* 6 (1988): 1. The Court of Appeal decision is (1887) 14 OAR 261.

57 SO 1886, c 28, s 3. This and later amendments were consolidated in 1892: *Compensation to Workmen Act*, SO 1892, c 30.

58 *Workmen's Compensation for Injuries Act*, SO 1889, c 23, s 7; *Employers Liability Act*, SBC 1891, c 10; *Workmen's Compensation for Injuries Act*, SM 1893, c 39; *Employers Liability for Injuries Act*, SNS 1900, c 1; *Workmen's Compensation for Injuries Act*, SNB 1903, c 11. Saskatchewan did likewise later, in 1911: *Workmen's Compensation Act*, SS 1910–1911, c 9.

59 Quotations from Risk, 'This Nuisance of Litigation,' 434, and conclusions at 462–4.

60 For these international developments, see ibid., 452–3, and the sources cited in note 53 above.

61 *Workmen's Compensation Act*, UK Statutes 1897, c 37; David G. Hanes, *The First British Workmen's Compensation Act of 1897* (New Haven, CT: Yale University Press, 1968). Newfoundland also introduced the 'English model' in 1908: *Workmen's Compensation for Injuries Act*, SN 1908, c 5.

62 *Workmen's Compensation Act*, SBC 1902, c 74, quotations below from s 2; *Workmen's Compensation Act*, SA 1908, c 12; *Workmen's Compensation for Injuries Act*, SN 1908, c 5; *Workmen's Compensation Act*, SM 1910, c 81; *Workmen's Compensation Act*, SS 1910–1911, c 9; *Workmen's Compensation Act*, SNS 1910, c 3; *Responsibility for Accidents Suffered by Workmen Act*, SQ 1909, c 66. The Quebec legislation followed an inquiry into the issue, established by *Commission of Inquiry into Labour Accidents Act*, SQ 1907, c 5. For the debates in Quebec, see J. Terry Copp, *The Anatomy of Poverty: The Condition of the Working Class in Montreal, 1897–1929* (Toronto: McClelland and Stewart, 1974), 123–6; and for more on the Quebec legislation and its relationship to the Civil Code, see chapter 5.

63 *Workmen's Compensation Act*, SO 1914, c 25. The following account of the act is based on Risk, 'This Nuisance of Litigation.' See also Michael Piva, 'The Workmen's Compensation Movement in Ontario,' *Ontario History* 68 (1975): 39; and Dennis Guest, *The Emergence of Social Security in Canada* (Vancouver: UBC Press, 1980), chap. 4.

64 See Charles Humphries, 'Sir James Pliny Whitney,' *DCB* online.
65 Cited in Risk, 'This Nuisance of Litigation,' 456. For Meredith, see R.C.B. Risk, 'Sir William R. Meredith, CJO: The Search for Authority,' *Dalhousie Law Journal* 7 (1983) 713; Peter Dembski, 'Sir William Ralph Meredith,' *DCB* online.
66 Risk, 'This Nuisance of Litigation,' 458.
67 Guest, *Emergence of Social Security*, 39; Risk, 'This Nuisance of Legislation,' 418.
68 *Workmen's Compensation Act*, SNS 1915, c 1; SM 1916, c 25; SNB 1918, c 37.

13. Criminal Justice: Criminal Law, Criminal Procedure, and Punishment

1 Compare Donald Fyson, *Magistrates, Police and People* (Toronto: Osgoode Society for Canadian Legal History and University of Toronto Press, 2006); and John M. Beattie, *Crime and the Courts in England, 1660–1800* (Princeton, NJ: Princeton University Press, 1986).
2 See, inter alia, *Parliamentary Debates on the Subject of the Confederation of the British North American Provinces* (Quebec: Hunter Rose, 1865), 41.
3 We will not give the titles of all of these statutes. They are SC 1867, c 14; 1868, c 68, 70 and 72; 1869, c 18–28. The following discussion of this legislation relies on Desmond Brown, *The Genesis of the Canadian Criminal Code of 1892* (Toronto: Osgoode Society for Canadian Legal History and University of Toronto Press, 1989), 67–9 and chap. 5. See also, for useful details from the parliamentary debates, Anthony Wan, 'A Century of Pain and Violence: Judicial Corporal Punishment in Canada, 1867–1972' (unpublished, 2018, on file with the authors), 8–16.
4 For Gowan, see Desmond Brown, 'James Robert Gowan,' *DCB* online. Wicksteed had held the same position for the Province of Canada assembly before Confederation.
5 Brown, *Criminal Code*, 67 and 93, citing the examples of killing pigeons and stealing from oyster beds. See also *Senate Debates*, 15 May 1868, 320–1.
6 For a full listing, see *Criminal Laws Repeal Act*, SC 1869, c 36, Schedule B.
7 Piracy was also a capital offence under an imperial statute, prosecutable in Canadian Admiralty courts, which sat under the authority of the same statute: Brown, *Criminal Code*, 213, n185. Four men were convicted of piracy in Victoria in 1872, but not executed: Carolyn Strange, 'The Lottery of Death: Capital Punishment, 1876–1976,' *Manitoba Law Journal*, 23 (1995): 601n20. Piracy was made a capital offence under Canadian law with its inclusion in the *Criminal Code* of 1892 (SC 1892, c 29, s 127), although death was not mandatory.

8 Macdonald to Ritchie, 8 June 1868, cited in Constance Backhouse, *Petticoats and Prejudice: Women and Law in Nineteenth-Century Canada* (Toronto: Osgoode Society for Canadian Legal History and Women's Press, 1991), 98.

9 *Offences against the Person Act*, SC 1873, c 50, s 1; and 1877, c 28, ss 1 and 2; Carolyn Strange, *The Death Penalty and Sex Murder in Canadian History* (Toronto: Osgoode Society for Canadian Legal History and University of Toronto Press, 2020), 17.

10 'Race, Rape, and the Death Penalty,' Death Penalty Information Center, https://deathpenaltyinfo.org/policy-issues/race/race-rape-and-the -death-penalty.

11 See Samuel R. Clarke, *A Treatise on the Criminal Law as Applicable to the Dominion of Canada* (Toronto: Carswell, 1872), with a further edition in 1882, with H.P. Sheppard; and Henri-Élzear Taschereau, *The Criminal Law Consolidation and Amendment Acts* (Montreal: Lovell Printing, 1874), with a further edition in 1888.

12 For a brief but useful summary of Bentham and later criminal law codifications, see J. Barry Wright, 'Renovate or Rebuild? Treatises, Digests and Criminal Law Codification,' in *Law Books in Action: Essays on the Anglo-American Legal Treatise*, ed. Angela Fernandez and Markus Dubber (Oxford: Hart Publishing, 2012).

13 *A Digest of the Criminal Law (Crimes and Punishments)* (London: Macmillan, 1877). For Stephen, see K.J.M. Smith, *James Fitzjames Stephen: Portrait of a Victorian Rationalist* (Cambridge: Cambridge University Press, 1988). For a useful brief summary of the criminal law codification movement in Britain, see William Cornish et al., *Law and Society in England, 1750–1950*, 2nd ed. (London: Hart, 2019), 579–87.

14 What follows on the origins and enactment of the criminal code is taken from Brown, *Criminal Code*, chap. 6; Brown, 'George Wheelock Burbidge,' *DCB* online; and Brown, 'Parliamentary Magic: Sir John Thompson and the Enactment of the Criminal Code,' *Journal of Canadian Studies* 27 (1992): 26; Graham Parker, 'The Origins of the Canadian Criminal Code,' in *EHCL I*, quotation in this paragraph at 259; Peter B. Waite, 'Sir John Sparrow David Thompson,' *DCB* online; Philip Girard, 'Robert Sedgwick,' *DCB* online.

15 George Burbidge, *A Digest of the Criminal Law of Canada (Crimes and Punishments)* (Toronto: Carswell, 1890).

16 See his article in *Legal News* 16 (1893): 36. It has been argued, probably correctly, that Taschereau's critiques were motivated at least partly by the fact that the changes made by the Code made the 1888 revised edition

of his book on the criminal law obsolete: R.C. McLeod, 'The Shaping of
Canadian Criminal Law, 1892–1902,' *Historical Papers* (1978): 64 at 67.

17 *The Criminal Code*, 1892, SC 1892, c 29.

18 See Martin L. Friedland, 'R.S. Wright's Model Criminal Code: A Forgotten
Chapter in the History of the Criminal Law,' *Oxford Journal of Legal Studies*
1 (1981): 307.

19 Norman W. Hoyles, 'The Criminal Law of Canada,' *CLJ* 38 (1902): 225.

20 Girard, 'Robert Sedgwick.'

21 *Criminal Code Act*, SC 1900, c 29; 1909, c 9. See generally McLeod, 'Shaping
of Canadian Criminal Law,' 70.

22 There is no history of criminal procedure in this period, although aspects
of it have been studied, and there are many studies of particular cases, too
numerous to cite here. That work is cited below where appropriate. This
introduction is a distillation of those studies, on what we said in *Volume
1*, chap. 29, and on the best study of the post-Confederation period of
one jurisdiction – Hamilton, Ontario: John Weaver, *Crime, Constables and
Courts: Order and Transgression in a Canadian City, 1816–1970* (Montreal
and Kingston: McGill-Queen's University Press, 1995).

23 *Crown Attorneys Act*, SM 1875, c 13.

24 The United Kingdom's director of public prosecutions was not
established until 1879 and was a small department for dealing only with
serious and difficult cases: Cornish et al., *Law and Society in England*, 588.

25 *Manitoba and British Columbia Laws Act*, SC 1871, c 13; *Manitoba Criminal
Law Act*, SC 1871, c 14.

26 See *Magistrates Act*, SM 1871, c 9; *Supreme Court Act*, SM 1871, c 2; *Queen's
Bench Act*, SM 1872, c 3; *County Court Act*, SM 1873, c 6.

27 *North-West Territories Act*, SC 1873, c 35.

28 Shelley Gavigan, *Hunger, Horses and Government Men: Criminal Law on the
Aboriginal Plains, 1870–1905* (Vancouver: Osgoode Society for Canadian
Legal History and UBC Press, 2012), quotation at 35. There is a vast
literature on the NWMP and the controversies over its role in the white
settlement of the prairies. This account relies on Gavigan's summary
in chap. 1. For the similarities between the NWMP and the Royal Irish
Constabulary, see Greg Marquis, 'Policing Two Imperial Frontiers: The
Royal Irish Constabulary and the North-West Mounted Police,' in *The
Mounted Police and Prairie Society, 1873–1919*, ed. Louis A. Knafla and
Jonathan Swainger (Vancouver: UBC Press, 2005).

29 *North-West Territories Act*, SC 1875, c 49.

30 *North-West Territories Acts*, SC 1877, c 7; 1880, c 25; 1885, c 51; 1886, c 25;
Juries Ordinance, ONWT 1886, No 4, and RONWT 1888, c 62.

31 *North-West Territories Act*, SC 1905, c 27, s 8.

32 R. Blake Brown, *A Trying Question: The Jury in Nineteenth-Century Canada* (Toronto: Osgoode Society for Canadian Legal History, 2009), v. The following account of juries relies principally on this work, chapters 7 and 8; and Brown, *Criminal Code*, 61–5.

33 *County Incorporation Act*, SNS 1879, c 1.

34 *Senate Debates*, 25 Feb. 1889. Gowan's principal speech is at 52–64, and the rest of the debate at 64–9; quotations below at 53, 55, 65, and 69.

35 Canada, *Sessional Papers*, 1891, No 66, Correspondence between the Department of Justice and the Judges and Attorneys-General respecting the Grand Jury.

36 *Commons Debates*, 12 Apr. 1892, 1314–15. For this interpretation, see McLeod, 'Shaping of the Criminal Law,' 66.

37 In addition to the statutes cited below, this account of the speedy trials legislation and its operation is based on Nancy Parker, 'Reaching a Verdict: The Changing Structure of Decision-Making in the Canadian Criminal Courts, 1867–1905' (PhD diss., York University, 1999); and Parker, 'Swift Justice and the Decline of the Criminal Trial Jury: The Dynamics of Law and Authority in Victoria, BC, 1858–1905,' in *EHCL VI*.

38 SC 1869, c 32.

39 *Speedy Trials in Ontario and Quebec Act*, SC 1869, c 35.

40 A word is in order here about junior and deputy judges of the Ontario county courts. When the districts of Ontario were abolished in 1849 and the administrative subdivisions became counties, the district courts were renamed county courts. But some counties comprised more than one district, with the result that they had two county court judges. In 1852 legislation was passed providing that in such circumstances the judge first appointed should be known as the county court judge, the other the junior county court judge. There was little difference between them. When the *Speedy Trials Act* was passed, conferring criminal jurisdiction on county courts, nothing was said about them being a new kind of criminal court, but they quickly became known as county judges criminal courts, a name they were actually given in the *Administration of Justice Act*, SO 1873, c 8. See chapter 3 and, for a great deal more detail, Margaret Banks, 'The Evolution of the Ontario Courts, 1788–1981,' in *EHCL II*, 513–23.

41 *Criminal Procedure Act*, SC 1869, c 29, s 12; *Offences against the Person Act*, SC 1869, c 20, s 48; *Larceny Act*, SC 1869, c 21, ss 76–92.

42 *Senate Debates*, 25 Feb. 1889, 56.

43 *Speedy Trial before Police and Stipendiary Magistrates in Ontario Act*, SC 1875, c 47; *Extension of Speedy Trials to Manitoba Act*, SC 1875, c 54; *Extension of*

Speedy Trials to British Columbia Act, SC 1884, c 42; *Speedy Trials Act*, SC 1889, c 47.

44 *Commons Debates*, 21 May 1869, 419, and 28 June 1892, 4348.

45 Brown, *Trying Question*, 196.

46 SC 1876, c 13. The statistics collected were published annually in the federal *Sessional Papers*.

47 These figures are from Parker, 'Swift Justice,' 196n10. See also Parker, 'Reaching a Verdict,' for very detailed analyses of the figures for Halifax, London, and Victoria.

48 Philip Girard, Jim Phillips, and J. Barry Cahill, eds., *The Supreme Court of Nova Scotia, 1754–2005: From Imperial Baston to Provincial Oracle* (Toronto: Osgoode Society for Canadian Legal History and University of Toronto Press, 2004), 156.

49 SC 1869, c 29; *Witnesses in Criminal Trials Act*, SC 1876, c 36.

50 This paragraph is based principally on Ronald D. Noble, 'The Struggle to Make the Accused Competent in England and Canada,' *Osgoode Hall Law Journal* 8 (1970): 249.

51 *Witnesses Act*, SC 1878, c 18; *Criminal Evidence Act*, UK Statutes 1898, c 36.

52 *Commons Debates*, 27 July 1891, 2956.

53 For the debate on second reading in which these issues were extensively aired, see *Commons Debates*, 3 Mar. 1893, 1674–1701.

54 In addition to the sources cited below, this account of criminal appeals is from Vincent M. Del Buono, 'The Right to Appeal in Indictable Cases: A Legislative History,' *Alberta Law Review* 16 (1978): 446; Benjamin Berger, 'Criminal Appeals as Jury Control: An Anglo-Canadian Historical Perspective on the Rise of Criminal Appeals,' *Canadian Criminal Law Review* 10 (2005): 1; Paul Romney, *Mr Attorney: The Attorney-General for Ontario in Court, Cabinet and Legislature, 1791–1899* (Toronto: Osgoode Society for Canadian Legal History and University of Toronto Press, 1986); and Brown, *Criminal Code*, 68–9.

55 James Fitzjames Stephen, *A History of the Criminal Law of England*, cited in Berger, 'Criminal Appeals,' 6.

56 UK Statutes, 1848, c 78; *Administration of Criminal Law Act*, SPC 1851, c 13; *Of Trial*, RSNB 1854, c 159, ss 22–4; *Administration of Criminal Law Act*, SNS 1862, c 6; *Court of Queen's Bench Act*, CSLC 1861, c 77, ss 56–62. A somewhat broader right of appeal had been available in Upper Canada from 1857, but this was repealed by the 1869 *Criminal Procedure Act*: *Appeal in Criminal Cases Act*, SPC 1857, c 61, s 1; SC 1869, c 29, s 80.

57 *Supreme and Exchequer Court Act*, SC 1875, c 11, s 49.

58 SC 1889, c 41, s 5.

59 *Commons Debates*, 27 June 1892, 4268–71.

60 *Offences against the Person Act*, SC 1869, c 20, ss 20–1 and 53. Whipping was prescribed for additional offences on the same basis in the Criminal Code: see Wan, 'Century of Pain and Violence,' 23–7.

61 See *Criminal Procedure Act*, SC 1869, c 29, ss 93 and 96.

62 H.G. Needham, 'Historical Perspectives on the Federal-Provincial Split in Jurisdiction in Corrections,' *Canadian Journal of Criminology* 22 (1980): 298 at 299.

63 SC 1868, c 75, quotations from ss 3, 7, 31, 32, and 62. For the pre-Confederation history, see *Volume 1*, 554–60. Penitentiary sentences were also required to include hard labour by the terms of the *Criminal Procedure Act*, SC 1869, c 29, s 97. In addition to the statutes and other sources cited, what follows on prison regimes is based principally on Peter Oliver, *Terror to Evil-Doers: Prisons and Punishments in Nineteenth-Century Ontario* (Toronto: Osgoode Society for Canadian Legal History and University of Toronto Press, 1998), chap. 8; quotations below at 281, 311, and 314.

64 *Penitentiary Act*, SC 1875, c 44; 1876, c 24.

65 Report of the Inspector of Penitentiaries for 1877, in Canada, *Sessional Papers*, 1878, No 12, 7.

66 *Penitentiary Act*, SC 1883, c 37; 1906, c 38.

67 This paragraph and the next are also based on, inter alia, W.A. Calder, 'Convict Life in Canadian Federal Penitentiaries, 1867–1900,' in *Crime and Criminal Justice in Europe and Canada*, ed. L.A. Knafla (Waterloo, ON: Wilfrid Laurier University Press, 1985); Ted McCoy, *Hard Time: Reforming the Penitentiary in Nineteenth-Century Canada* (Edmonton: Athabasca University Press, 2012); *Report of the Royal Commission on Penitentiaries* (Ottawa: King's Printer, 1914); R. Neufeld, 'Cabals, Quarrels, Strikes and Impudence: Kingston Penitentiary, 1890–1914,' *Histoire sociale* 31 (1998): 95; Lee Gibson, 'Samuel Lawrence Bedson'; H. Pearson Gundy, 'John Creighton'; and Peter Oliver, 'James George Moylan,' all in *DCB* online.

68 Macdonald to John Creighton, warden of Kingston, 31 Oct. 1871, cited in Oliver, *Terror to Evil-Doers*, 310.

69 Tyler Wentzell, 'Prison Disturbances and Canada's Militia' (unpublished, 2021, on file with the authors).

70 SC 1899, c 49.

71 *Who's Who in Canada* (Toronto: International, 1914), 926; Queen's University Encyclopedia, online; Wikipedia entry for Downey.

72 Peter Oliver, 'John Langmuir,' *DCB* online. Langmuir's post was created by the *Inspection of Prisons Act*, SO 1868, c 21.

73 For the central prison, see Joseph Berkovits, 'Prisoners for Profit: Convict Labour in the Ontario Central Prison,' in *EHCL V*, quotation below at 478;

Oliver, *Terror to Evil-Doers*, 399–424; and Oliver, 'A Terror to Evil Doers: The Central Prison and the Criminal Class in Late Nineteenth-Century Ontario,' in *Patterns of the Past: Interpreting Ontario's History*, ed. Roger Hall, Laurel Sefton MacDowell, and William Westfall (Toronto: Dundurn, 1988).

74 For the Mercer, see Peter Oliver, 'To Govern by Kindness: The First Two Decades of the Mercer Reformatory for Women,' in *EHCL V*; and Carolyn Strange, 'The Criminal and Fallen of Their Sex: The Establishment of Canada's First Women's Prison, 1872–1901,' *Canadian Journal of Women and the Law* 1 (1985): 79.

75 See Frederick Armstrong, 'Andrew Mercer,' *DCB* online.

76 This figure, and all of the statistics used in this section and the next, are from Lorraine Gadoury and Antonio Lechasseur, *Persons Sentenced to Death in Canada, 1867–1976* (Ottawa: National Archives, 1994). They differ from those used by other scholars because they do not include death sentences for offences other than murder, all of which were commuted, and because they are limited to the 1867–1914 period. A summary table of death sentences and executions/commutations is in Guy Favreau, *Capital Punishment: Material Relating to Its Purpose and Value* (Ottawa: Information Canada, 1965), appendix D, but it gives no details of the individuals other than their gender.

77 Carolyn Strange, 'Comment: Capital Case Procedure Manual,' *Criminal Law Quarterly* 41 (1998): 184 at 188; Jack Jedwab, 'Robert Bickerdike,' *DCB* online.

78 See John T. Saywell, *The Lawmakers: Judicial Power and the Shaping of Canadian Federalism* (Toronto: Osgoode Society for Canadian Legal History and University of Toronto Press, 2002), 51 and 121–7.

79 Jonathan Swainger, 'A Distant Edge of Authority: Capital Punishment and the Prerogative of Mercy in British Columbia, 1872–1880,' in *EHCL VI*, 205.

80 See Cyril Greenland, 'The Last Public Execution in Canada: Eight Skeletons in the Closet of the Canadian Justice System,' *Criminal Law Quarterly* 29 (1987): 415; Strange, 'Lottery of Death,' 603n24; Gadoury and Lechasseur, *Persons Sentenced to Death*, 65; Girard et al., *Supreme Court of Nova Scotia*, 153. For other examples, see Ken Leyton-Brown, *The Practice of Execution in Canada* (Vancouver: UBC Press, 2010).

81 For what follows, see especially Strange, 'Lottery of Death'; Strange, *Death Penalty and Sex Murder*, chap. 1; Strange, 'Comment: Capital Case Procedure Manual'; and Strange, 'Stories of Their Lives: The Historian and the Capital Case File,' in *On the Case: Explorations in Social History*, ed. Franca Iacovetta and Wendy Mitchinson (Toronto: University of Toronto Press, 1998).

82 See Martin Friedland, *The Case of Valentine Shortis: A True Story of Crime and Politics in Canada* (Toronto: Osgoode Society for Canadian Legal History and University of Toronto Press, 1985).

83 There were 27 death sentences for rape after Confederation, the last in 1877, so judges obviously stopped giving that sentence although they could have done so. Four Indigenous people were convicted of piracy in Victoria in the early 1870s for acts committed in 1862, and sentenced to death, but those sentences were all commuted to five years' 'surveillance.'

84 Karen Dubinsky and Franca Iacovetta, 'Murder, Womanly Virtue and Motherhood: The Case of Angelina Napolitano, 1911–1922,' *CHR* 72 (1989): 505.

85 For Riel, see chapter 7. For Workman, see Scott Gaffield, 'Justice Not Done: The Hanging of Elizabeth Workman,' *CJLS* 20 (2005): 171; and F. Murray Greenwood and Beverly Boissery, *Uncertain Justice: Canadian Women and Capital Punishment, 1754–1953* (Toronto: Osgoode Society for Canadian Legal History and Dundurn Press), chap. 7.

86 Strange, *Death Penalty and Sex Murder.*

87 Robert J. Sharpe, *The Lazier Murder: Prince Edward County, 1884* (Toronto: Osgoode Society for Canadian Legal History and University of Toronto Press, 2011), 120.

88 Kenneth Avio, 'The Quality of Mercy: Exercise of the Royal Prerogative in Canada,' *Canadian Public Policy* 13 (1987): 366; and Avio, 'Capital Punishment in Canada: Statistical Evidence and Constitutional Issues,' *Canadian Journal of Criminology* 30 (1998): 331.

89 We say 'probably' here because we are relying on the identification of convicted persons as Black given in Gadoury and Lechasseur, *Persons Sentenced to Death.* Their identification numbers are not always reliable. They identify six people sentenced to death in Ontario in this period as Black, while Barrington Walker, *Race on Trial: Black Defendants in Ontario's Criminal Courts, 1858–1958* (Toronto: Osgoode Society for Canadian Legal History and University of Toronto Press, 2010), chap. 2, found eight cases, including two people in Gadoury and Lechasseur not identified as Black. We have added those two to get to the number of 19 used here, but it seems likely that individuals from other provinces were also not labelled as Black when they were, and thus that the number for the whole dominion was slightly higher. Perhaps more importantly, of the two additional cases discussed in *Race on Trial*, one person was hanged and one had his sentence commuted, meaning that finding more cases would not necessarily mean finding a different pattern of commutation based on race.

90 Strange, 'Lottery of Death,' 608. The low rate of execution of women held true in the long run. Only 12 of the 57 women condemned to death between 1867 and 1962 were hanged: 607.

91 See Constance Backhouse, 'Desperate Women and Compassionate Courts: Infanticide in Nineteenth-Century Canada,' *UTLJ* 34 (1984): 447; and Marie-Aimée Cliche, 'L'infanticide dans la région de Québec 1660–1969,' *RHAF* 44 (1990): 31.

92 See Ian Radforth, *Jeannie's Demise: Abortion on Trial in Victorian Ontario* (Toronto: Between the Lines, 2020).

93 For the Viau and Blake cases, see Clément Fortin, *L'affaire Cordélia Viau, la vraie histoire* (Montreal: Wilson & Lafleur, 2013); Reinhold Kramer and Tom Mitchell, *Walk towards the Gallows: The Tragedy of Hilda Blake, Hanged 1899* (Toronto: University of Toronto Press, 2016); and Tom Mitchell, 'Blood with the Taint of Cain: Immigrant Labouring Children, Manitoba Politics, and the Execution of Emily Hilda Blake,' *Journal of Canadian Studies* 28 (1994): 39.

94 For this case, see Hamar Foster, 'The Queen's Law Is Better Than Yours: International Homicide in Early British Columbia,' in *EHCL V*, 41–5; and Tina Loo, 'Savage Mercy: Native Culture and the Modification of Capital Punishment in Nineteenth-Century British Columbia,' in *Qualities of Mercy: Justice, Punishment and Discretion*, ed. Carolyn Strange (Vancouver: UBC Press, 1996), quotation at 112.

95 For these cases, see Sidney Harring, *White Man's Law: Native People in Nineteenth-Century Canadian Jurisprudence* (Toronto: Osgoode Society for Canadian Legal History and University of Toronto Press, 1998), 221–36; and Harring, 'The Windigo Killings: The Legal Penetration of Canadian Law into the Spirit World of the Ojibwa and Cree Indians,' in *Violent Crime in North America*, ed. Louis A. Knafla (Westport, CT: Praeger, 2003). For windigos. see Shawn Smallman, *Dangerous Spirits: The Windigo in Myth and History* (Ottawa; Heritage House Publishing, 2014); and Hadley Friedland, *The Wetiko (Windigo) Legal Principles: Cree and Anishinabek Responses to Violence and Victimization* (Toronto: University of Toronto Press, 2018).

96 This account is from Catherine Evans, 'Heart of Ice: Indigenous Defendants and Colonial Law in the Canadian North-West,' *LHR* 36 (2018): 199; quotations below at 223 and 226.

97 Cornelia Schuh, 'Justice on the Northern Frontier: Early Murder Trials of Native Accused,' *Criminal Law Quarterly* 22 (1973): 74.

14. Property Law

1 *Commons Debates*, 2 May 1870, 1302, and 6 July 1885, 3113–14.

2 The following account of the administration of the land grant is based on a large and contentious historiography, so that it is difficult to produce a succinct account. We have drawn what follows from authors critical of the federal government and those who take a different

view. D.N. Sprague is the principal critic of the federal government: see principally 'The Manitoba Land Question, 1870–1882,' *Journal of Canadian Studies* 15 (1980): 74; Sprague, 'Government Lawlessness in the Administration of Manitoba Land Claims, 1870–1877,' *Manitoba Law Journal* 10 (1980): 415; and Sprague, *Canada and the Métis, 1869–1885* (Waterloo, ON: Wilfrid Laurier University Press, 1988). Thomas Flanagan has provided an opposing view: see principally *Metis Lands in Manitoba* (Calgary: University of Calgary Press, 1991); Flanagan, 'The Market for Métis Lands in Manitoba: An Exploratory Study,' *Prairie Forum* 16 (1991): 1; and Flanagan, 'Métis Land Grants in Manitoba: A Statistical Study,' *Social History / Histoire sociale,* 27 (1994): 65 (with Gerhard Ens). For the most recent account, see Gerhard Ens and Joe Sawchuk, *From New Peoples to New Nations: Aspects of Métis History and Identity from the Eighteenth to the Twenty-First Centuries* (Toronto: University of Toronto Press, 2016). The historiographical controversies are well reviewed in Brad Milne, 'The Historiography of Métis Land Dispersal, 1870–1890,' *Manitoba History* 30 (1995): 31. The government's handling of the Métis grant has also been recently litigated to the SCC: *Manitoba Métis Federation Inc v Canada (Attorney-General),* [2013] 1 SCR 623. The trial judgment of the Manitoba Court of Queen's Bench in that case is a very useful source of voluminous primary documents: *Manitoba Metis Federation Inc v Canada (Attorney General),* [2007] MJ No 448 [hereafter *MMF-QB*].

3 Howe to Archibald, [Apr.] 1871, cited in Sprague, 'Government Lawlessness,' 418; Order in Council, 7 Mar. 1871.

4 Order in Council, 1 Mar. 1871.

5 For the census, see Canada, *Sessional Papers,* 1871, No 20.

6 See generally Ens and Sawchuk, *From New Peoples,* 138, and map showing the areas reserved the Métis land grant, at 144.

7 See esp. *Commons Debates,* 5 and 10 May 1870, 1387 and 1501; 6 and 13 Apr. 1871, 343 and 398.

8 Order in Council, 3 Apr. 1873; SC 1873, c 38.

9 Ens and Sawchuk, *From New Peoples,* 136–7, 142–3, and 145–7; Orders in Council, 6 Sept. 1873, 26 Apr., and 5 May 1875; Report of the Secretary of State of 1873, in Canada, *Sessional Papers,* 1874, No 8; Report of the Surveyor-General for 1874, in Canada, *Sessional Papers,* 1875, No 8; *MMF-QB,* paras 221–4 and 227.

10 Wood to Alexander Mackenzie, 3 July 1874 and 25 May 1875, cited in Sprague, *Canada and the Métis,* 112.

11 SC 1874, c 20. To be consistent with section 30 of the *Manitoba Act*, the preamble of the *Appropriation Act* stated that it was passed to extinguish 'the Indian title' of 'half-breed heads of families' resident in the province in 1870. If section 30 now applied only to the children, heads of families had not had their title extinguished.

12 Order in Council, 7 Sept. 1876; Ens and Sawchuk, *From New Peoples*, 143–8; Reports of the Surveyor-General of Canada, in Canada, *Sessional Papers*, 1876–80.

13 *Commons Debates*, 6 July 1885, 3113. There is not space here to detail the evidence of these transactions. In addition to many of the secondary works cited above, it includes, but it is by no means limited to, the legislation passed by the Manitoba assembly in 1873, discussed below, and the evidence collected by an 1881 Commission to Investigate the Administration of Justice in the Province of Manitoba relating to Half-Breed Lands, in Canada, *Sessional Papers*, 1882, No 124.

14 SM 1873, c 44.

15 Early Manitoba had an assembly of 12 members from the anglophone ridings/parishes and 12 from francophone ones, with the lieutenant governor the head of the executive and commanding a majority of moderates from both linguistic groups in the assembly. Moderates wished to see Riel's influence among the francophones reduced and that of John Christian Schultz, the leader of the 'Canada Firsters,' similarly kept to a minimum among the anglophone members. See Gerald Friesen, 'Homeland to Hinterland: Political Transition in Manitoba, 1870–1879,' *Historical Papers* 14 (1979): 33. On disallowance, see *Correspondence, Reports I*, 776–8.

16 See Order in Council, 23 Mar. 1876.

17 SM 1885, c 30, s 1. For the other legislation referred to here, see *Half-Breed Land Protection Act*, SM 1875, c 37; and 1877, c 5; *Children of Half-Breed Heads of Families Conveyancing Act*, SM 1878, c 20; *Infants and Their Estates Act*, SM 1878, c 7; *Children of Half-Breed Heads of Families Conveyancing Act*, SM 1879, c 11; *Half-Breed Lands Act*, CSM 1880, c 42, 1881, c 19, and 1883, c 29. For the discussions of disallowance, see reports of Dorion, Edward Blake, Rudolph LaFlamme, and Zebulon Lash, in *Correspondence, Reports I*, 779, 804–5, 816, and 821–2.

18 See principally, on one side, Sprague, 'The Manitoba Land Question'; Sprague, 'Government Lawlessness'; Sprague, 'Dispossession vs. Accommodation in Plaintiff vs. Defendant Accounts of Métis Dispersal from Manitoba, 1870–1881,' *Prairie Forum* 16 (1991): 137; and Sprague

and P.R. Mailhot, 'Persistent Settlers: The Dispersal and Resettlement of the Red River Métis, 1870–1885,' *Canadian Ethnic Studies* 17 (1985): 1. For the opposing view, see Flanagan, *Métis Lands in Manitoba*, who finds support from Ens and Sawchuk, *From New Peoples*, chap. 6; and from Gerhard Ens, *Homeland to Hinterland: The Changing Worlds of the Red River Métis in the Nineteenth Century* (Toronto: University of Toronto Press, 1996).

19 In addition to the primary sources cited below, this analysis of section 32 is based on *MMF-QB*, paras. 27–50 and 259–343; the work of Sprague, Flanagan, and Ens cited above; and that of Nicole St-Onge, 'The Dissolution of a Métis Community: Pointe à Grouette, 1860–1885,' *Studies in Political Economy* 18 (1983): 162.

20 A comprehensive list of these grants was published later by Archer Martin, the BC Supreme Court judge discussed in chapter 3, work begun during his brief sojourn practising law in Winnipeg: *The Hudson's Bay Company Land Tenures and the Occupation of Assiniboia by Lord Selkirk's Settlers, with a List of Grantees under the Earl and the Company* (London: William Clowes, 1898).

21 Quotations from Howe to Alexander McDougall, 7 Dec. 1869, Macdonald to Smith, 3 Jan. 1870, and Cartier to Ritchot and Scott, 23 May 1870, all cited in *MMF-QB*, paras. 263, 264, and 268.

22 Order in Council, 11 Nov. 1872.

23 This summary is based on the annual reports of the surveyor-general in the *Sessional Papers*. The provincial *Highways Act*, SM 1871, c 31, and 1872, c 12, designated the footpaths and cart trails that ran from farm to farm as public highways and required them to be 120 feet wide.

24 SC 1875, c 52.

25 *Commons Debates*, 24 Apr. 1874, 189, and 17 Feb. 1875, 196.

26 See the sources cited above in the discussion of section 31.

27 These statements summarize the extensive evidence reproduced in *MMF-QB*.

28 Dennis to Codd, 24 Oct. 1877, cited in *MMF-QB*, para. 311. See also the correspondence between the two men cited in D.N. Sprague, 'Donald Codd,' *DCB* online.

29 G.O. Rothney, 'Marc-Amable Girard,' *DCB* online.

30 The quotations in this paragraph are from *Senate Debates*, 8 Mar. 1878, 115–17, and 11 Apr. 1878, 559–63.

31 *Commons Debates*, 5 May 1879, 1755.

32 Sprague, 'Donald Codd'; A.I. Silver, 'Joseph Royal,' *DCB* online.

33 For this paragraph, see *MMF-QB*, paras. 315–33. For the legislation, see *Manitoba Land Claims Act*, SC 1880, c 7; 1884, c 26.

34 See Daniel Murchison, 'Alice Payette's Piano and Fur Coat: Views of Métis Life from the Manitoba Surrogate Court, 1870 to 1930' (unpublished, 2021, on file with the authors).

35 Irene Spry, 'The Great Transformation: The Disappearance of the Commons in Western Canada,' in *Man and Nature on the Prairies*, ed. Richard Allen (Regina: University of Regina Press, 1976).

36 *Commons Debates*, 2 May 1870, 1328.

37 *Alberta Act*, SC 1905, c 3, s 20; *Saskatchewan Act*, SC 1905, c 42, s 20; *Natural Resources Transfer Agreement Act*, UK Statutes, 1930, c 26.

38 For the survey, see James Grierson McGregor, *Vision of an Ordered Land: The Story of the Dominion Land Survey* (Saskatoon: Western Producer Prairie Books, 1981). See also Bill Waiser, *Saskatchewan: A New History* (Calgary: Fifth House Publications, 1905), 102–4, for a succinct account of the grid system employed. In addition to the specific sources cited in this section, the following discussion of land-granting law and policy is based on the *Dominion Lands Act* and two monographs: Kirk N. Lambrecht, *The Administration of Dominion Lands, 1870–1930* (Regina: Canadian Plains Research Center, 1991); and Chester Martin, *Dominion Lands Policy*, 2nd ed. (Toronto: University of Toronto Press, 1973).

39 Cited in John Friesen, 'Expansion of Settlement in Manitoba, 1870–1900,' in *Historical Essays on the Prairie Provinces*, ed. Donald Swainson (Ottawa: Macmillan, 1978), 122. For Beresford, see James D. Mochoruk, 'Herbert Grahame Beresford,' *DCB* online.

40 SC 1872, c 22.

41 The quotation is not from the *Dominion Lands Act*, which did not specifically mention the Pacific railway, but from the 1871 Order in Council, which was preserved in force by section 108 of the *Act*.

42 For pre-Confederation land settlement policies, see *Volume 1*, 601; and Hugh Morrison, 'The Background of the Free Homestead Law of 1872,' *Report of the Annual Meeting of the Canadian Historical Association* 14 (1935): 58.

43 *Dominion Lands Act*, SC 1874, c 19, s 2.

44 Section 33 dealt with a variety of other issues as well, which for reasons of space we do not discuss here.

45 For cases in which this provision was applied, from both Manitoba and the Territories, see Lambrecht, *Administration of Dominion Lands*, 23.

46 Sarah Carter, 'Daughters of British Blood or Hordes of Men of an Alien Race: The Homesteads for Women Campaign in Western Canada,' *Great*

Plains Quarterly 29 (2009): 267. For the legislation, see *Dominion Lands Acts*, SC 1874, c 19, s 8; and 1876, c 19, s 4.

47 *Dominion Lands Acts*, SC 1874, c 19, s 8; and 1876, c 19, s 9. For block settlements, see Ryan Eyford, *White Settler Reserve: New Iceland and the Colonization of the Canadian West* (Vancouver: UBC Press, 2016); and, for Black settlers, chapter 16. For summer fallowing, see Friesen, 'Settlement in Manitoba,' 124–5.

48 Martin, *Dominion Lands Policy*, 145. For the CPR and railway land grants, see 142–4. For homesteading compared to land purchases, see the 1902 statement by Clifford Sifton, minister of the interior, that half of the settlers in western Canada had taken up purchased land, not homesteads, cited in 172.

49 The figures for homestead entries given here and below are from Martin, *Dominion Lands Policy*, esp. table on 170. They are stated as approximations because the author presents them poorly and makes it difficult to distinguish between Manitoba and the Territories.

50 Martin, *Dominion Lands Policy*, 150.

51 *Sifton v Sifton*, [1938] 3 All ER 435 (PC).

52 *Dominion Lands Act*, SC 1897, c 29, s 4.

53 *Commons Debates*, 24 Mar. 1905, 3157–8.

54 Quotation and information from David Hall, 'Frank Oliver,' *DCB* online.

55 Briefly, for reasons too complicated to go into in any detail, both the government and the CPR were inadequately informed about the climate and topography of the Territories when the settlement frontier started to go beyond Manitoba in the later 1870s and 1880s. This lack of knowledge lay behind the CPR's decision to build the main line directly southwest from Winnipeg to Regina and Calgary rather than follow the more northerly route along the North Saskatchewan River to Edmonton, through the 'fertile belt' characterized by well-watered wooded prairie.

56 *Commons Debates*, 27 Apr. 1883, 863; *Dominion Lands Act*, SC 1883, c 17, s 37.

57 *Dominion Lands Acts*, SC 1883, c 17, s 39; 1884, c 25, s 4; 1886, c 27, s 10; 1887, c 54, ss 31(2), 32(3), and 38(5).

58 *Dominion Lands Act*, SC 1908, c 20, ss 16 and 24. The statute did not limit the application to the two provinces in terms, but designated tracts of land in which pre-emption applied, all of them in the two provinces.

59 Joseph Schull, *Ontario since 1867* (Toronto: McClelland and Stewart, 1978), 43–4 and 57; *Free Grants and Homestead Acts*, SO 1869, c 8; 1869, c 20; 1871, c 5; RSO 1877, c 24; SO 1886, c 7; 1884, c 7; 1890, c 6; 1908, c 17.

60 For reasons of space, only the New Brunswick legislation is discussed in any detail here. Quebec continued in force aspects of the pre-

Confederation *Public Lands Act*, SPC 1860, c 2, which also initially applied to Ontario: *Encouragement of Settlers Act*, SQ 1868, c 20.

61 *Free Grants to Parents of Twelve Children Act*, SQ 1892, c 19.

62 *Free Grants Act*, SNB 1872, c 17, 1873, c 20, and 1879, c 4; *Crown Lands Act*, SNB 1899, c. 6; *Wilderness Land Tax Act*, SNB 1872, 1881, c 23, and 1885, c 24; *ColonizationCompany of the Maritime Provinces Incorporation Act*, SNB 1890, c 72; *Settlement of Crown Lands Act*, SNB 1898, c 19; *Settlement of Farm Lands Act*, SNB 1912, c 28.

63 See *Volume 1*, 592–3.

64 *Registration of Deeds Act*, SM 1871, c 7; Greg Taylor, *The Law of the Land: The Advent of the Torrens System in Canada* (Toronto: Osgoode Society for Canadian Legal History and University of Toronto Press, 2008), 115–16. Much of what follows in this section is taken from this source.

65 *An Ordinance to Assimilate the Law relating to the Transfer of Real Estate, and to Provide for the Registration of Titles to Land, throughout the Colony of British Columbia*, BC Ordinance 1870, No 143.

66 *Real Property Act*, SM 1885, c 28; *Real Property in the Territories Act*, SC 1886, c 26.

67 See Holmested's contributions to *Canadian Law Times* on Torrens title, in 3 (1883) 536 and 581, 4 (1884) 20, and those of Jones, at 3 (1883) 475 and 29 (1909) 354, the last on the system in Ontario.

68 As in many provinces before and after Confederation, conveyancing was not the sole preserve of lawyers. The problems in Manitoba led to regulation of conveyancing in 1881, with only those who were legally trained or had passed an examination being allowed to do so for money: *Conveyancers Act*, SM 1881, c 25.

69 *Real Property Act*, SM 1885, c 28.

70 *Real Property Acts*, SM 1888, c 21 and 1889, c 16. By 1891 almost 8,000 lots were registered with the land titles offices. Land titles never entirely displaced the registry of deeds: Taylor, *Law of the Land*, 154.

71 *Real Property Act*, SA 1906, c 24; *Land Act*, SS 1906, c 24; *Assurance Fund Act*, SC 1908, c 42.

72 *Land Titles Act*, SO 1885, c 22; and 1887, c 15 and 16; Taylor, *Law of the Land*, 107–9.

73 *Volume 1*, 596–600. The principal source for this section is Rusty Bitterman and Margaret McCallum, 'Upholding the Land Legislation of a "Communistic and Socialist Assembly": The Benefits of Confederation for Prince Edward Island,' *CHR* 87 (2006): 1. See also Margaret McCallum, 'The Sacred Rights of Property: Title, Entitlement and the Land Question in Nineteenth-Century Prince Edward Island,' in *Essays Volume VIII*; and

Preetmohinder Aulakh, 'British Empire, Land Tenure and the Search for an Ideal Proprietor' (PhD diss., Osgoode Hall Law School, 2022), chap. 5.

74 *Prince Edward Island Act,* SC 1873, c 40.

75 SPEI 1874, c 3.

76 *Land Purchase Act,* SPEI 1875, c 32.

77 *Kelly v Sulivan, Stewart and Fane* (1876) 2 PEIR 3.

78 Chief Justice Richards had been a reformer in the United Canada Assembly, where he had argued for commutation of Quebec's seigneurial tenure to freehold tenure, referring to this as a precedent in his decision. Justice Ritchie was the only Maritimer and was sympathetic because he knew the history of leasehold property on the island. Justice Fournier had been a *rouge* politician who also opposed Quebec seigneuries, and a minister in Mackenzie's government that had recommended the approval of the 1875 *Land Purchase Act.*

79 *Kelly v Sulivan* (1877) 1 SCR 3; quotations at 34–5.

80 *Lands Clauses Consolidation Act,* UK Statutes, 1845, c 18.

81 *Public Works Act,* SC 1867, c 12; and 1874, c 24, s 1; *Expropriation Act,* RSC 1886, c 39.

82 We cannot list them all here. Ontario's various statutes authorizing expropriation are summarized in Tyler Wentzell, 'The Creation of the Queen Victoria Niagara Falls Park and the Ontario Court of Appeal,' *Ontario History* 106 (2014): 109–12. See also British Columbia's first *Public Works Act,* SBC 1872, c 28, which remained so named in the statutory consolidations of 1877 and 1888; *Board of Works Act,* CSNB 1877, c 20, and *Expropriation Act,* CSNB 1903, c 14; *Public Works and Agriculture Act,* SQ 1869, c 15; *Public Works and Labour Act,* RSQ 1888, Title 4, c 8, art 1776.

83 SBC 1881, c 16, s 105. See also *Municipal Act,* RSO 1877, c 174.

84 This statute was a pre-Confederation enactment, CSUC, c 64, and stayed in force thereafter – see *Mining Companies Act,* RSO 1877, c 156.

85 SC 1868, c 68, s 7.

86 *Intercolonial Railway Act,* SC 1867, c 13, ss 7, 13, and 14.

87 *Railway Act,* RSO 1877, c 165; *Railway Act,* SQ 1869, c 51.

88 *Niagara Falls Park Act,* SO 1885, c 21, ss 9–10. See generally Wentzell, 'Creation of the Queen Victoria Niagara Falls Park.'

89 SC 1873, c 90, ss 6 and 17; SC 1881, c 52, s 7; SC 1889, c 88, s 6 and 10; SC 1908, c 155, s 13.

90 *South Shore Railway and Tunnel Incorporation Act,* SQ 1880, c 47, s 22; *Winnipeg Water Power Company Incorporation Act,* SM 1883, c 84, s 3(d); *Sackville Rural Cemetery Company Expropriation Act,* SNB 1894, c 80; *Lepreau Mining Company Incorporation Act,* SNB 1895, c 73, s 8.

91 See Silas Alward, 'Expropriation of Property,' *CLT* 18 (1899): 233.

92 (1893) 4 Exch Court Reports 1. Falconbridge was chief justice of the Ontario Court of Queen's Bench.

93 (1883) 1 Exch Court Reports 87. As noted in chapter 3, in this period the Supreme Court judges sat singly as the Exchequer Court judges.

94 Wentzell, 'Creation of the Queen Victoria Niagara Falls Park.'

95 *Florence Mining Company v Cobalt Lake Mining* (1908) OLR 274 (CA) at 280.

96 The literature on land use controls in the nineteenth century is not large but we have found useful Raphael Fischler, 'Development Controls in Toronto in the Nineteenth Century,' *Urban History Review* 36, no. 1 (2007): 16; Sean Kheraj, 'Urban Environments and the Animal Nuisance: Domestic Livestock Regulation in Nineteenth-Century Canadian Cities,' *Urban History Review* 44 (2015): 37; David Hulchanski, *The Evolution of Ontario's Early Land Use Planning Regulations, 1900–1920* (Toronto: University of Toronto Centre for Urban and Community Studies, 1982).

97 The Toronto Charter originated in the city's incorporation in 1834: SUC 1834, c 22. Halifax's Charter was conferred in 1841: SNS 1841, c 55. Winnipeg was incorporated in 1873: SM 1874, c 7.

98 SBC 1881, c 16, s 45; *Of Nuisances and Municipal Regulations*, CSN 1896, c 36.

99 For the Toronto by-laws cited here and below, see Fischler, 'Development Controls.' For Montreal, see Eric Reiter, 'Nuisance and Neighbourhood in Late Nineteenth-Century Montreal,' in *Property on Trial: Canadian Cases in Context*, ed. Eric Tucker, James Muir, and Bruce Ziff (Toronto: Osgoode Society for Canadian Legal History and University of Toronto Press, 2011), 42.

100 Kheraj, 'Urban Environments,' 40 and 49.

101 Philip Girard, *Lawyers and Legal Culture in British North America: Beamish Murdoch of Halifax* (Toronto: Osgoode Society for Canadian Legal History and University of Toronto Press, 2011), 141; SM 1903, c 45, s 28.

102 *Municipal Amendment Act*, SO 1890, c 50, s 21; Max Foran, 'Land Development Patterns in Calgary, 1884–1985'; and Peter W. Moore, 'Zoning and Planning: The Toronto Experience, 1904–1970,' both in *The Usable Urban Past: Planning and Politics in the Modern Canadian City*, ed. A.F. Artibise and Gilbert A. Stelter (Toronto: Macmillan, 1979).

103 *Town Planning Act*, SNB 1912, c 19, s 1; *Town Planning Act*, SNS 1912, c 6; *Town Planning Act*, SA 1913, c 18; *City and Suburbs Plans Act*, SO 1912, c 43.

104 The development of restrictive covenant law in England and its reception in Ontario is laid out in Jim Phillips, 'Restrictive Covenants: The Law and Practice in Ontario, c. 1850–1930' (unpublished, 2016). See also Bruce

Ziff, 'Bumble Bees Cannot Fly, and Restrictive Covenants Cannot Run,' in *Public Interest, Private Property: Law and Planning Policy in Canada*, ed. Marcia Valente and Anneke Smit (Vancouver: UBC Press, 2016), 59–63.

105 (1848), 41 ER 1143 (Ch).

106 *McLean v McKay*, (1873) 40 NSR 111, 7 AC 1 (PC). The New Brunswick Supreme Court upheld a covenant in 1872, but it was a positive covenant and the case was decided before the need for a covenant to be negative was laid down by the English courts: *Ryan v Lockhart* (1872), 14 NBR 127.

107 See David Gagan, *The Denison Family of Toronto* (Toronto: University of Toronto Press, 1973).

108 (1882) 1 OR 349 (Ch); [1885] 11 OAR 699. Note, 'Vankoughnet v. Denison,' *CLT* 2 (1882): 307. See also R.S. Cassels, 'Restrictive Covenants: Purchasers' Right to Enforce Inter Se,' *CLT* 10 (1890): 1, citing numerous English cases; Note, 'Restrictive Covenants'; and Note, 'Restrictive Covenants Respecting Stables and Garages,' *CLT* 29 (1909): 1121; and 32 (1912): 523. Restrictive covenants are, however, not mentioned in the 1901 or 1916 editions of *Armour on Titles*, discussed in chapter 4. See also *Ross v Hunter*, 1882 SCJ No 6.

109 Ziff, 'Restrictive Covenants Cannot Run,' 62.

110 See in particular *Sawyer-Massey Co v Bennett*, (1909) 10 WLR 539, 12 WLR 249, (1910) 46 SCR 622, which was appealed to the full court and then to the SCC; Ziff, 'Restrictive Covenants Cannot Run,' 62 and 79.

111 This summarizes Phillips, 'Restrictive Covenants'; and Iain Wilson, 'Restrictive Covenants in Toronto' (unpublished, 2020, on file with the authors). For the development of Toronto's residential neighbourhoods, see Barbara Sanford, 'The Political Economy of Land Development in Nineteenth-Century Toronto,' *Urban History Review* 16 (1987): 17; and Isobel K. Ganton, 'Land Sub-Division in Toronto, 1851–1883,' in *Shaping the Urban Landscape: Aspects of the Canadian City Building Process*, ed. Gilbert Stelter and Alan Artibise (Ottawa: Carleton University Press, 1982).

112 *Hime v Lovegrove*, [1905] OJ No 34 (CA).

113 *Cosmopolitan Club v Lavine* (1909) OJ No 643 (HC).

114 (1914) 50 SCR 204.

115 Nicholas Lombardo, 'White Collar Workers and Neighbourhood Change: Jarvis Street in Toronto, 1880–1920,' *Urban History Review* 43 (2014): 16.

116 There is no study of such covenants in this period, but there were occasional references to them in reported cases and legal literature in this period and later: see H.S. Robinson, 'Limited Restraints on Alienation,' *Advocate* 8 (1950): 250; Ziff, 'Restrictive Covenants Cannot Run,' 69; and James W. St. G. Walker, 'Noble and Wolf v. Alley,' in Walker, '*Race*,'

Rights and the Law in the Supreme Court of Canada: Historical Case Studies (Waterloo, ON: Wilfrid Laurier University Press, 1997).

117 *Land Titles Act*, RSO 1887, c 116, s 86. A very similar provision was in the first *Land Titles Act*, s 86, discussed above in the section on land registration, but referred only to conditions. The omission from the 1885 *Act* of covenants presumably reflects their very recent acceptance by courts of the restrictive covenant as a new interest in land. It stayed in the Act thereafter: see *Land Titles Act*, RSO 1897, c 138, s 104(2); and RSO 1914, c 126, s 99(2).

118 A similar provision was introduced for land under the Registry system in 1922, by the *Conveyancing and Law of Property Act*, SO 1922, c 53, s 2.

119 *Re Baillie*, (1911) OJ No 816 (HC), quotation at para. 10.

120 For the United Kingdom, see Joel Brenner, 'Nuisance Law and the Industrial Revolution,' *Journal of Legal Studies* 3 (1974): 403; and John McLaren, 'Nuisance Law and the Industrial Revolution: Some Lessons from Social History,' *Oxford Journal of Legal Studies* 3 (1983): 155. For the United States, see Morton Horwitz, *The Transformation of American Law, 1780–1860* (Cambridge, MA: Harvard University Press, 1977).

121 Ben Pontin, 'Nuisance Law and the Industrial Revolution: A Reinterpretation of Doctrine and Institutional Competence,' *Modern Law Review* 75 (2012): 1010, quotation at 1010.

122 The former include Jennifer Nedelsky, 'Judicial Conservatism in an Age of Innovation: Comparative Perspectives on Canadian Nuisance Law 1880–1930,' in *EHCL II*. The latter include Jamie Benidickson, 'Ontario Water Quality, Public Health and the Law, 1880–1930,' in *EHCL VIII*.

123 *The Sawdust Nuisance in the River Ottawa* (Ottawa: Evening Journal, 1886); published in French as *Dommages causés par la sciure dans la rivière Ottawa*; John McLaren, 'The Tribulations of Antoine Ratté: A Case Study of the Environmental Regulation of the Lumbering Industry in the Nineteenth Century,' *UNB Law Journal* 33 (1984): 203. See also Jamie Benidickson, 'Private Rights and Public Purposes in the Lakes, Rivers, and Streams of Ontario,' in *EHCL II*, for a detailed discussion of legal conflicts involving the timber industry.

124 *Saw Millson the Ottawa River Act*, SO 1885, c 24.

125 Jamie Benidickson, 'John Rudolph Booth,' *DCB* online.

126 (1899) 32 NSR 44; Kyle Jolliffe, 'A Saga of Gilded Age entrepreneurship in Halifax: The People's Heat and Light Company Limited, 1893–1902,' *Nova Scotia Historical Review* 15 (1995): 10. The case is also discussed in Nedelsky, 'Judicial Conservatism.' It is not clear whether effective abatement was accomplished, but B.F. Pearson, the moving force behind

People's Heat and Light, soon moved into Emscote and died there in 1912: Gregory Marchildon, 'Benjamin Franklin Pearson,' *DCB* online.

127 *Hiscox v Lander* [1876] OJ No 216 (Ch).

128 Charlie Hatt, 'Nuisance in the Age of Progress: The Legal History of London, Ontario's Waterworks and Sewer System, 1870–1916' (unpublished, 2014, on file with the authors). On the PHB see Benidickson, 'Ontario Water Quality,' and more generally Benidickson, *The Culture of Flushing: A Social and Legal History of Sewage* (Vancouver: UBC Press, 2007).

129 (1896) 26 SCR 20. The treatment here relies on Reiter, 'Nuisance and Neighbourhood.'

130 This matter was not clarified by the SCC until the twenty-first century: *St Lawrence Cement v Barrette* [2008] 3 SCR 392.

131 This section does not discuss the issue of riparian rights in Quebec, which were relevant to the kinds of conflicts discussed here; for an overview, highlighting the complex interplay among Roman law, old French law, English law, and American law in the Quebec jurisprudence, giving rise to solutions that were adopted by the JCPC in Quebec cases and arguably re-exported to the empire, see David Schorr, 'Riparian Rights in Lower Canada and Canada East: Inter-imperial Legal Influences,' in *Imperial Co-operation and Transfer, 1870–1930: Empires and Encounters*, ed. Roland Cvetskovski and Volker Barth (London: Bloomsbury, 2015).

132 Amor De Cosmos had tried to get bills passed to this effect while a member of the Legislative Assembly of Vancouver Island in the mid-1860s, only to see them vetoed by the legislative council. The united colony of British Columbia had no upper house when it entered Confederation, and the bill passed easily: SBC 1872, c 29. See *Volume 1*, 615–16, for similar action in other provinces.

133 SO 1886, c 22; SM 1871, c 6.

134 On the expansion of dower in eastern Canada, see Philip Girard, 'Land Law, Liberalism, and the Agrarian Ideal: British North America, 1750–1920,' in *Despotic Dominion: Property Rights in British Settler Societies*, ed. John McLaren, A.R. Buck, and Nancy E. Wright (Vancouver: UBC Press, 2005), 122–7.

135 SM 1871, c 6; ONWT 1901, c 13; the latter provision carried over into Alberta and Saskatchewan after they achieved provincehood. See Louise Mimnagh, 'A History of Preferential Share in Ontario: Intestacy Legislation and Conceptions of the Deserving and Undeserving Widow,' *Dalhousie Journal of Legal Studies* 23 (2014): 1.

136 Malcolm Graeme Cameron, *A Treatise on the Law of Dower* (Toronto: Carswell, 1882), 3.

137 The claim of incompatibility was false. Ontario specifically preserved dower and curtesy when it adopted the Torrens system for northern Ontario in 1885: *Land Titles Act*, SO 1885, c 21, s 22.

138 The 1867 ordinance is reproduced in CSBC 1877, c 84. Newfoundland also adopted a homestead law in the 1880s. It applied only to those who occupied 'wilderness land' up to twenty acres and erected a dwelling house thereon, exempting such land from sale or seizure by creditors. On the husband's death it would be held for the benefit of the widow and minor children, 'if some one of them occupies the premises' until the youngest was twenty-one and 'until the marriage or death of the widow': CSN 1896, c 78.

139 SC 1886, c 26; SM 1885, c 28; SA 1910, c 18; SS 1911, c 13; Catherine Cavanaugh, 'The Limitations of the Pioneering Partnership: The Alberta Campaign for Homestead Dower, 1909–1925,' *CHR* 74 (1993): 198; Margaret E. McCallum, 'Prairie Women and the Struggle for a Dower Law, 1905–1920,' *Prairie Forum* 18 (1993): 19; Chris Clarkson, *Domestic Reforms: Political Visions and Family Regulation in British Columbia, 1862–1940* (Vancouver: UBC Press, 2007), 97.

140 SBC 1877, c 28; Clarkson, *Domestic Reforms*, 55–61. The 'concubines' referred to in the Act were often, though not invariably, Indigenous women, and in common parlance were referred to as 'country wives.'

141 On this and the previous paragraph, see Kris Inwood and Sarah van Sligtenhorst, 'The Social Consequences of Legal Reform: Women and Property in a Canadian Community,' *Continuity and Change* 19 (2004): 165.

142 Conditions could also be attached to *inter vivos* transfers and to leases, but the issue of their validity came up most often in testamentary contexts.

143 Robert Gordon, 'Paradoxical Property,' in *Early Modern Conceptions of Property*, ed. John Brewer and Susan Staves (London: Routledge, 1995), 103.

144 On this and the next paragraph, see Girard, 'Land Law, Liberalism'; *Re Northcote* (1889) 18 OR 107 (Ch); *Re Fox Estate* (1885) 8 OR 489 (Ch); *Dunn Estate v Dunn* (1887) 13 OR 267 (QB).

145 SC 1884, c 27; SC 1894, c 32. On this paragraph and the following, see Chandra Murdoch, 'Inheritance and the *Indian Act*: Political Action and Women's Property on Southern Ontario Indian Reserves, 1857–1900' (unpublished, 2021, on file with the authors).

146 Murdoch, 'Inheritance,' 12.

15. Women, the Family, and the Law

1 Janet Guildford and Suzanne Morton, 'Introduction,' in *Separate Spheres: Women's Worlds in the 19th-Century Maritimes*, ed. Guildford and Morton (Fredericton: Acadiensis, 1994), 10. The literature on women's history in this period is now very substantial and sophisticated, too substantial to cite extensively here.

2 We know little about the use of marriage settlements in nineteenth-century Canada, but they were employed: see *Volume 1*, 684–5; Philip Girard and Rebecca Veinott, 'Married Women's Property Law in Nova Scotia, 1850–1910,' in Guildford and Morton, *Separate Spheres*, 72–3; Lori Chambers, *Married Women and Property Law in Victorian Ontario* (Toronto: Osgoode Society for Canadian Legal History and University of Toronto Press, 1997), chap. 3.

3 For this and the following paragraph, see *Volume 1*, 686–91. See also a protective statute not discussed in *Volume 1*, *Of the Protection of Married Women*, CSN 1864, c 107.

4 Girard and Veinott, 'Married Women's Property Law,' 74 and 77. For other studies of the pre-Confederation legislation making the same argument, see Constance Backhouse, 'Married Women's Property Law in Nineteenth-Century Canada,' *LHR* 6 (1988): 217–19 and 221–2; Chambers, *Married Women*, chap. 4; Chris Clarkson, *Domestic Reforms: Political Visions and Family Regulation in British Columbia, 1862–1940* (Vancouver: UBC Press, 2007), chaps. 1 and 2.

5 *Rights of Property of Married Women Act*, SBC 1873, c 29; *Separate Rights of Property of Married Women Act*, SM 1875, c 25; *Real and Personal Property of Married Women Act*, SNB 1869, c 33, and *Property of Married Women Act*, CSNB 1877, c 72; *Rights of Property of Married Women Act*, SO 1872, c 16; *North-West Territories Act*, SC 1875, c 49, ss 48–53.

6 *Married Women Separate Rights of Property Act*, SPC 1859, c 34, ss 1–3, 5, and 6.

7 *Conveyance of Real Estate by Married Women Act*, SO 1873, c 18, s 3.

8 *Married Women's Property Act*, UK Statutes, 1870, c 93.

9 *Spectator* (Hamilton), 2 Apr. 1872, cited in Chambers, *Married Women*, 92.

10 (1878) OAR 77 at 87.

11 Cited in Chambers, *Married Women*, 100–2.

12 *Property of a Wife Deserted by Her Husband Act*, CSBC 1871, c 116, s 1. This was originally passed by the Vancouver Island legislature in 1862 and was later extended to apply to the United Colony of British Columbia.

13 *Protection of Married Women Act*, SNS 1866, c 33, s 1; *Rights of Married Women Act*, SPEI 1860, c 35, s 2.

14 See *Married Women's Act*, CSM 1880, c 65; and RSM 1891, c 95.

15 George Holmested, 'Married Women's Rights of Property,' *CLT* 3 (1883): 63; quotations in this and the next paragraph at 64, 66, 75, and 76.

16 See *Consolidated Bank v Henderson*, (1879) 29 UCCP 549; *Kerr v Stripp*, (1876) 40 UCR 125 (QB).

17 (1878) 3 OAR 77 (CA).

18 Section 7 stated, 'Nothing hereinbefore contained in reference to moneys deposited, or investments made by any married woman shall, as against creditors of the husband, give validity to any deposit or investment of moneys of the husband made in fraud of such creditors, and any moneys so deposited or invested may be followed as if this Act had not passed.'

19 *Griffin v Patterson and Wife* (1881) 45 UCQB 536 at 555.

20 Chambers, *Married Women*, 107.

21 He used the phrase in *Clarke v Creighton* (1881) 45 UCQB 514 at 526.

22 See Clarkson, *Domestic Reforms*, chap. 3; and Sheri Allen, 'One Hundred Years of Solicitude: Judicial Resistance to Reform of Married Women's Property Law in the West,' *Dalhousie Journal of Legal Studies* 4 (1995): 175. This very brief summary greatly simplifies the arguments made by Clarkson, as the result of space constraints.

23 For New Brunswick, see *Married Women's Property Act*, RSNB 1864, c 114; CSNB 1877, c 72. The Acts were differently worded and organized from the Act of 1851, but their substance was essentially the same. No more significant reform was enacted until 1895, discussed below. The only changes between 1860 and 1903 to the PEI legislation were an 1880 Act allowing a married women to convey her real estate with her husband's concurrence, and an 1881 statute making a married woman with separate property (which was only one who had been deserted or abandoned) liable to be sued in respect of it: *Conveyance of Real Estate by Married Women Act*, SPEI 1880, c 6; *Rights of Married Women Act*, SPEI 1881, c 12. No amendments were made to the Nova Scotia legislation until 1884, discussed below.

24 For Newfoundland, see *Married Women's Property Law Act*, SN 1876, c 11; 1883, c 11; 1895, c 17; and Trudi Johnson, 'Matrimonial Property Law in Newfoundland to the End of the Nineteenth Century' (PhD diss., Memorial University of Newfoundland, 1998).

25 In addition to the specific references below, this section on the 1884 Ontario *Act* relies on Chambers, *Married Women*, chaps. 8 and 9; Backhouse, 'Married Women's Property Law.'

26 *Married Women's Property Act,* UK Statutes, 1882, c 75.

27 *Married Women's Property Act,* SO 1884, c 19, s 2.

28 See also the amended version of the 1873 act in *Married Women's Real Estate Act,* RSO 1887, c 134. The SCC recognized the importance of this change in *Moore v Jackson* (1892) 22 SCR 210.

29 *Married Women's Property Act,* SO 1897, c 22, s 1. This was based on a UK statute of 1893: *Married Women's Property Act,* UK Statutes 1893, c 63.

30 *The Married Women (Maintenance in Case of Desertion) Act,* SO 1888, c 23. On the earlier law, see *Volume 1,* 685–6.

31 For examples see Backhouse, 'Married Women's Property Law,' 233; and Chambers, *Married Women,* chap. 9.

32 Susan Ingram and Kris Inwood, 'Property Ownership by Married Women in Victorian Ontario,' *Dalhousie Law Journal* 23 (2000): 405; Kris Inwood and Sarah Van Sligtenhorst, 'The Social Consequences of Legal Reform: Women and Property in a Canadian Community,' *Continuity & Change* 19 (2004): 165.

33 Lori Chambers, 'Married Women and Businesses,' *Ontario History* 104 (2012): 45.

34 *Married Women's Property Act,* SBC 1887, c 20. Allen, 'One Hundred Years of Solicitude,' 187, cites the case of Margarette Boechofsky who, despite owning property appraised at three times the value of what she was seeking, was refused a loan because her husband had a bad credit rating.

35 Girard and Veinott, 'Married Women's Property Law,' 79; SNS 1884, c 12, RSNS 1884, c 94.

36 *Married Women's Property Act,* SNS 1898, c 22. For the background to this Act, see Girard and Veinott, 'Married Women's Property Law,' 85.

37 (1892) 21 SCR 342, quotation below at 344–5, cited in Girard and Veinott, 'Married Women's Property Law,' 79.

38 See *Married Women's Property Act,* SNB 1895, c 24; *Married Women's Property Act,* SPEI 1903, c 9; *Married Women's Property Act,* SM 1900, c 27.

39 *Territories Real Property Act,* SC 1886, c 26. Section 13 stated, 'A married woman shall, in respect of land acquired by her after the coming into force of this Act, have all the rights and be subject to all the liabilities of a feme sole, and may alienate and, by will or otherwise, deal with land as if she were unmarried.' For the retention of the personal property legislation of 1875, see the *North-West Territories Act,* SC 1886, c 50, ss 36–40.

40 SNWT 1890, Ordinance 20.

41 (1888) 5 Man LR 33 (QB).

42 *Conger v Kennedy,* (1895) 2 Terr LR 186; (1896) 26 SCR 397. The case is well treated in Allen, 'One Hundred Years of Solicitude,' 200–2, and later she also discusses subsequent cases.

43 *Married Women's Property Act*, SS 1907, c 18. Alberta legislated in 1922: *Married Women's Property Act*, SA 1922, c 10.

44 (1907) 5 WLR 581 (Alta SC)

45 (1909) 41 SCR 516; [1911] AC 120, quotation at 138.

46 *Of the Solemnization of Marriage*, RSNS 1884, c 93; *Solemnization of Marriages Act*, RSO 1887, c 131.

47 *Marriage Act*, SC 1882, c 42. In 1890 the Act was amended to also allow marriages between a man and the daughter of his deceased wife's sister: SC 1890, c 36. Marriage with a deceased husband's brother (or such brother's son) was not permitted until 1923: SC 1923, c 19.

48 On *Connolly*, see *Volume 1*, 437–9. The court decided that once the couple moved to Montreal, any divorce would be governed by the *lex loci*, Quebec civil law, rather than Cree law: *R v Nan-e-quis-e-ka* (1889) 2 CNLC 368. Another way of analysing such marriages was to regard them as valid consensual marriages under English common law, or to rely on the presumption of validity of marriage arising from long cohabitation: *Robb v Robb* (1891) 20 OR 591 (HC); and see Brad Morse, 'Inuit and Indian Family Law and the Canadian Legal System,' *American Indian Law Review* 8 (1980): 199–258.

49 *Indian Act, 1876*, SC 1876, c 18, s 3; *Bethel v Hildyard* (1888) 13 Ch D 220; Philip Girard with Jim Phillips, 'Rethinking "the Nation" in National Legal History: A Canadian Perspective,' *LHR* 29 (2011): 607, 611–13; Sarah Carter, *The Importance of Being Monogamous: Marriage and Nation Building in Western Canada to 1915* (Edmonton: University of Alberta Press, 2008).

50 Girard and Phillips, 'Rethinking "the Nation."'

51 This summary of divorce law in 1867 is based on *Volume 1*, 352–3 and 694–5; James Snell, *In the Shadow of the Law: Divorce in Canada, 1900–1939* (Toronto: University of Toronto Press, 1991), chap. 3; John Alexander Gemmill, *The Practice of the Parliament of Canada upon Bills of Divorce* (Toronto: Carswell, 1888), chap. 4; and Gemmill, 'Parliamentary Divorce in Canada,' *CLT* 8 (1888): 52; and Kimberley Smith Maynard, 'Divorce in Nova Scotia, 1750–1890,' in *EHCL III*.

52 UK Statutes 1857, c 85.

53 *M, falsely called S v S* (1877) 1 BCR 25. See the discussion below of the lack of knowledge of former British Columbia premier Amor De Cosmos in 1875 about his own Supreme Court's jurisdiction in this area.

54 *Watts v Watts* [1908] AC 573 (PC). The judicial history was reviewed by Justice Archer Martin in *Sheppard v Sheppard* (1908) 13 BCR 486.

55 The double standard was not abolished until 1925: *Marriage and Divorce Act*, SC 1925, c 41.

56 In 1919 the JCPC held that whatever may have been the status of English law in Manitoba in 1870, a federal statute of 1888 (*Manitoba Reception Act*, SC 1888, c 33), had set the date for the reception of English statutes in Manitoba in areas that were within federal jurisdiction as 15 July 1870: *Walker v Walker* [1919] AC 947 (PC). In a decision released the same day the court held the same in relation to Alberta, by virtue of the *North-West Territories Law Amendment Act*, SC 1886, c 25. The Alberta decision clearly implicated Saskatchewan law as well: *Board v Board* [1919] AC 956 (PC). As in British Columbia, this meant that the double standard applied until 1925.

57 See section 91(26) of the *BNA Act*. As noted above, Parliament did legislate pursuant to this head of power in 1925 to eliminate the double standard in BC, and it also legislated in 1930 to give the Supreme Court of Ontario jurisdiction over divorce, obviating the need for Ontario residents to seek a parliamentary divorce: *Divorce Act (Ontario)*, SC 1930, c 14.

58 *Court of Marriage and Divorce Act*, RSNS 1864, c 126, s 4; *Divorce and Matrimonial Causes Act*, SNS 1866, c 13, s 8.

59 In 1886 the appeal was made one to the NSSC *en banc*: *Divorce Court Act*, SNS 1886, c 49.

60 What follows in this paragraph is from Maynard, 'Divorce in Nova Scotia'; quotations below at 250 and 254; see also Rebecca Veinott, 'Child Custody and Divorce: A Nova Scotia Study,' in *EHCL III*.

61 *Divorce and Matrimonial Causes Court Act*, CSNB 1877, c 50, s 19; SNB 1902, c 19, s 5.

62 Constance Backhouse, *Petticoats and Prejudice: Women and Law in Nineteenth-Century Canada* (Toronto: Osgoode Society for Canadian Legal History and Women's Press, 1991), 181–99; (1910) 40 NBR 196.

63 *Court of Divorce Act*, SPEI 1835, c 10; *An Act for the Relief of Elizabeth Adelaide Rayner*, SC 1913, c 183; Wendy Owen and J.M. Bumsted, 'Divorce in a Small Province: A History of Divorce on Prince Edward Island from 1833,' *Acadiensis* 20 (1991): 86. All parliamentary divorce Acts were named 'An Act for the Relief of …; henceforth we omit this phrase and just provide the name and statute citation.

64 Prior to his appointment Fisher was involved in a case that was headed for the Divorce Court, and he could see that he would have to recuse himself: *Commons Debates*, 23 Mar. 1870, 672–81; C.M. Wallace, 'Charles Fisher,' *DCB* online.

65 *Commons Debates*, 22 Mar. 1875, 858–61; 14 May 1888, 1414–15.

66 See, for example, *Commons Debates*, 13 Mar. 1901, 1412–14.

67 *Commons Debates*, 26 Mar. 1903, 576–8.

68 *Halifax Daily Echo*, 22 July 1908.

69 James G. Snell, '"The White Life for Two": The Defence of Marriage and Sexual Morality in Canada, 1890–1914,' *Histoire sociale/Social History* 16 (1983): 112. See similarly and for what follows in the next few pages, Constance Backhouse, 'Pure Patriarchy: Nineteenth-Century Canadian Marriage,' *McGill Law Journal* 31 (1986): 264.

70 *Senate Debates*, 21 Feb. 1889, 41.

71 For this anecdote see Robert Pike, 'Legal Access and the Incidence of Divorce in Canada: A Socio-Historical Analysis,' *Canadian Review of Sociology and Anthropology* 12 (1975), 115–16, citing *Globe*, 22 July and 3 Aug. 1874.

72 Sharon Cook, 'Adeline Davis,' *DCB* online; Peter B. Waite, *The Man from Halifax: Sir John Thompson Prime Minister* (Toronto: University of Toronto Press, 1985), 391.

73 Chambers, *Married Women*, chap. 2.

74 See, for example, *Maintenance of Deserted Wives Act*, SO 1888, c 23.

75 See James G. Snell, 'The International Border as a Factor in Marital Behaviour: A Historical Case Study,' *Ontario History* 81 (1989): 289.

76 See the table in Snell, *In the Shadow of the Law*, 10–11. There is not space here to discuss US divorce rates in any detail, but the historical literature and contemporary commentary demonstrate much higher rates than Canada.

77 *Charles William Holmes*, SC 1906, c 108; *Hannah Ella Tomkins*, SC 1909, c 142. See also the divorce granted to Isabelle Brewster of Calgary in 1913 because her husband, William, had deserted her for and committed adultery with Sylvia Alberta Froste, and the divorce granted to William Froste of the same city on the ground of Sylvia's adultery: *Isabelle Lee Brewster*, SC 1913, c 73, and *William Froste*, SC 1913, c 115. See similarly the divorce granted to Mary Young of Calgary because her husband John had run off to Spokane with Isabel Crooks, and the cognate case of George Crooks, whose divorce Act did not mention Isabelle's paramour: *Mary Arabella Young*, SC 1913, c 209, and *George Andrew Crooks*, SC 1913, c 162.

78 This figure is from Leah Kelly, 'Parliamentary Divorce, 1892–1919' (unpublished, 2021, on file with the authors). Despite its title, this paper includes summary statistics from 1867 on.

79 In Nova Scotia also the 'overwhelming majority' of divorce litigants in court were Protestant: Maynard, 'Divorce in Nova Scotia,' 246.

80 Almost all the petitioners were from provinces without judicial divorce, but two were from British Columbia (*Hugh Forbes Keefer*, SC 1890, c 108; *James Wright*, SC 1892, c 82) during a period of judicial uncertainty about whether judicial divorce was available. One was from Prince Edward Island (*Elizabeth Adelaide Rayner*, SC 1913, c 183), and one was from a woman resident in the United Kingdom who had returned there after a short period living with her husband in Edmonton, where he still resided (*Ella Rose Morris*, SC 1914, c 177).

81 Snell, *In the Shadow of the Law*, 51.

82 The following account of parliamentary divorce procedure is derived from Gemmill, *Practice of the Parliament of Canada*; Snell, *In the Shadow of the Law*, 50–1; a reading of the divorce Acts; and from a far from comprehensive perusal of the Senate *Debates*.

83 J.G. Bourinot, 'Prefatory Note,' in Gemmill, *Practice of the Parliament of Canada*, xi–xii. For s 56, see chapter 2, above.

84 Gemmill, *Practice of the Parliament of Canada*, 26 and 77. The rules are reproduced in Gemmill.

85 See Jim Phillips, 'The Trials and Travails of Elizabeth Campbell' (forthcoming in *Essays in the History of Canadian Law Volume XII: Women and the Law*, eds. Lori Chambers and Joan Sangster, 2023).

86 *Senate Journals*, 16 Mar. 1885, 323.

87 Gemmill, *Practice of the Parliament of Canada*, 191; *Violet Jane Dakin*, SC 1911, c 71.

88 The information on failed bills in this paragraph is from Gemmill, *Practice of the Parliament of Canada*, table on 150–1. See also *John Robert Martin*, SC 1873, c 126; *Elisa Maria Campbell*, SC 1879, c 79; *Henry Peterson*, SC 1875, c 98; *Walter Scott*, SC 1878, c 188.

89 *David Stock*, SC 1899, c 134; *Suzan Ash*, SC 1887, c 127; *Thomas Bristow*, SC 1891, c 132; *James Pryor*, SC 1905, c 150; *Frank Parsons*, SC 1909, c 119; *Abraham Aronsberg*, SC 1899, c 132.

90 Gemmill, *Practice of the Parliament of Canada*, 113–17; Gemmill instances only one case between 1868 and 1888 where the Senate rejected a bill because of collusion. For these issues in England, see Sybil Wolfram, 'Divorce in England, 1700–1857,' *Oxford Journal of Legal Studies* 5 (1985) 155; and Gail Savage, 'The Divorce Court and the Queens/Kings Proctor: Legal Patriarchy and the Sanctity of Marriage in England, 1861–1937,' *Historical Papers* (1989): 210.

91 *Christiana Filman Glover*, SC 1890, c 109.

92 *Commons Debates*, 26 Mar. 1903, 578.

93 Wolfram, 'Divorce in England.' See also to similar effect Gail Savage, 'The Operation of the 1857 Divorce Act, 1860–1910: A Research Note,' *Journal of Social History* 16 (1983): 103.

94 *James Albert Manning Aikins*, SC 1892, c 78; *Albert Nordheimer*, SC 1896, c 16; W.L. Morton, 'Philip Vankoughnet,' *DCB* online; *Joseph Frederick Whiteaves*, SC 1868, c 95; *Gertrude Mary Grantham*, SC 1911, c 85; T.D. Regehr, 'Sir William Mackenzie,' *DCB* online; *Fanny Margaret Riddell*, SC 1887, c 31.

95 This section is based on Constance Backhouse, 'Shifting Patterns in Nineteenth-Century Canadian Custody Awards,' in *EHCL II*; and Backhouse, *Petticoats and Prejudice*, chap. 7; Susan Boyd, *Child Custody, Law and Women's Work* (Don Mills, ON: Oxford University Press, 2003); Veinott, 'Child Custody and Divorce.'

96 SM 1878, c 7, s 1.

97 UK Statutes 1839, c 54; 1857, c 85, s 35.

98 *Divorce and Matrimonial Causes Act*, SNS 1866, c 13, s 10; *Custody of Infants Act*, SPC 1855, c 126. With minor unimportant variations, this became the *Appointment of Guardians and Custody of Infants Act*, CSUC, c 74; and, after Confederation, the *Custody of Infants Act*, RSO 1877, c 130; *Law Amendments Act*, SO 1877, c 8, s 31.

99 There is a large literature on child-related social reform movements in this period. See especially Neil Sutherland, *Children in English Canadian Society: Framing the Twentieth-Century Consensus* (Toronto: University of Toronto Press, 1976); Joy Parr, *Childhood and Family in Canadian History* (Toronto: McClelland and Stewart, 1982); Nancy Janovicek and Joy Parr, eds., *Histories of Canadian Children and Youth* (Don Mills, ON: Oxford University Press, 2003). Most provinces passed child protection Acts in the late nineteenth and early twentieth centuries: see, for Ontario and Nova Scotia, *Prevention of Cruelty Act*, SO 1893, c 45; *Child Protection Act*, SNS 1882, c 18; and 1884, c 95.

100 *In Re Allen* (1871) 31 UCQB 458 at 499–500. For similar decisions, see Backhouse, 'Shifting Patterns,' 224–6.

101 Sometimes the two routes to custody claims were conflated. In the 1873 case of *Desbrisay v Desbrisay*, unreported, Anne Desbrisay sued for divorce on the ground of cruelty, and despite strong evidence thereof her husband denied many of the allegations and the court concluded that it could not grant the divorce. There was therefore no custody issue to decide consequent on divorce, and the father won custody on a writ of

habeas corpus, also an unreported decision. See Veinott, 'Child Custody,' 278–9.

102 [1881] OJ No 327 (CP); quotations at paras 5, 7, 13, and 23.

103 See Veinott, 'Child Custody,' 280–2.

104 (1886) 25 NBR 404 (Supreme Court *en banc*); quotations below at 404, 405, 407, 408, 410, 411, 414–17, 419, 421, 423.

105 Cited in Backhouse, 'Shifting Patterns,' 233. For the legislation discussed here, see *Guardianship of Infants Act,* SO 1887, c 21, based on *Guardianship of Infants Act,* UK Statutes 1886, c 27. The prior Ontario legislation was *Appointment of Guardians and the Custody of Infants Act,* CSUC, c 74; and *Guardians of Infants Act,* RSO 1877, c 132.

106 For what follows, see *Re Smart Infants* (1886) OJ No. 348 (HC); (1887) OJ No 367 (HC); (1888) OJ No 354 (CA); [1892] AC 425, quotation below at 432.

107 *Supreme Court in Equity Act,* SNB 1890, c 4, s 183; *Custody of Infants Act,* SNS 1893, c 11, s 2.

108 *Infants and Their Estates Act,* SM 1878, c 7, s 11.

109 *Guardians Appointment Act,* RSBC 1897, c 96.

110 For a brief review of cases from Manitoba, Ontario, and New Brunswick, see Backhouse, 'Shifting Patterns,' 239. For a good example of a New Brunswick case, see Backhouse, *Petticoats and Prejudice,* 200–17.

111 For this account of Nova Scotia, see Veinott, 'Child Custody.'

112 (1893) 6 Man LR 23 at 28, cited in Backhouse, *Petticoats and Prejudice,* 201.

113 Boyd, *Child Custody,* 30–4.

114 There is a large literature on this shift. See, inter alia, Andrew Jones and Leonard Rutman, *In the Children's Aid: J.J. Kelso and Child Welfare in Ontario* (Toronto: University of Toronto Press, 1980); Judith Fingard, *The Dark Side of Life in Victorian Halifax* (Porters Lake, NS: Pottersfield, 1989).

115 Amanda Glasbeek, *Feminized Justice: The Toronto Women's Court, 1913–34* (Vancouver: UBC Press, 2009).

116 *Volume 1,* 691–3; Constance Backhouse, 'The Tort of Seduction: Fathers and Daughters in Nineteenth-Century Canada,' *Dalhousie Law Journal* 10 (1986): 45; *McInnis v McCallum* (1854) Peter's PEI Reports 72 (SC). The North-West Territories also gave the woman the right to take the action: ONWT 1903, c 8.

117 Marie-Aimée Cliche, 'Les filles-mères devant les tribunaux du Québec, 1850–1969,' *Recherches sociographiques* 32 (1991): 9.

118 See, generally, Constance Backhouse, 'Involuntary Motherhood: Abortion, Birth Control and the Law in Nineteenth-Century Canada,' *Windsor*

Yearbook of Access to Justice 3 (1983): 61. On the Davies case, see Ian Radforth, *Jeannie's Demise: Abortion on Trial in Victorian Toronto* (Toronto: Between the Lines, 2020). In spite of the risk, Mr. and Mrs. Davies seem to have operated their business more or less openly. On another notorious trial, that of Robert Notman, brother of the famous photographer William Notman, for procuring his paramour's abortion, see Elaine Kalman Naves, *The Portrait of a Scandal: The Abortion Trial of Robert Notman* (Montreal: Véhicule, 2013).

119 For more detail, see Constance Backhouse, 'Desperate Women and Compassionate Courts: Infanticide in Nineteenth-Century Canada,' *UTLJ* 34 (1984): 447; Marie-Aimée Cliche, 'L'infanticide dans la région de Québec 1660–1969,' *RHAF* 44 (1990): 31, example of Denise D. at 52.

120 Constance Backhouse, 'Nineteenth-Century Canadian Rape Law 1800–1892,' in *EHCL II*; whether a marital exemption existed at common law was not clear. On 'race suicide,' Mariana Valverde, '"When the Mother of the Race Is Free": Race, Reproduction, and Sexuality in First-Wave Feminism,' in *Gender Conflicts: New Essays in Women's History*, ed. Mariana Valverde and Franca Iacovetta (Toronto: University of Toronto Press, 1992).

121 Backhouse, 'Canadian Rape Law'; Carolyn Strange, 'Patriarchy Modified: The Criminal Prosecution of Rape in York County, Ontario, 1880–1930,' in *EHCL V*.

122 Backhouse, 'Canadian Rape Law.' The statutes were SC 1886, c 52; 1887, c 48; 1890, c 37.

123 For this and the next paragraph, see Constance Backhouse, 'Nineteenth-Century Canadian Prostitution Law: Reflections of a Discriminatory Society,' *Histoire sociale/Social History* 18 (1985): 387; SC 1884, c 27; RSC 1886, c 43; SC 1887, c 33. The prostitution sections of the *Indian Act* were brought into the *Criminal Code 1892*, s 190. The Quebec Act was SC 1871, c 30, the Nova Scotia Acts SC 1891, c 55 and SC 1895, c 43. In 1893 Children's Aid Societies in Ontario were allowed to take charge of delinquent or unsupervised girls and commit them to foster care instead of industrial refuges, unless they were 'unfit' for life in private homes: SO 1893, c 45.

124 Lorna McLean, '"Deserving" Wives and "Drunken" Husbands: Wife Beating, Marital Conduct, and the Law in Ontario, 1850–1910,' *Histoire sociale/Social History* 35 (2002): 50; SC 1909, c 9.

125 [1891] 1 QB 671; *CLJ* 27 (1891): 356; C 11 (1891): 134.

126 McLean, '"Deserving" Wives,' at 77–80; SO 1897, c 14. The 1872 Act that abolished the need for married women to seek protection orders for their own earnings did not repeal the 1859 Act that allowed them to be sought

for children's earnings, and protection orders for children's earnings were maintained in the 1884 Ontario Act, as noted above.

16. Minorities and Civil Rights

1 *Commons Debates*, 1 June 1914, 4562.
2 In addition to specific sources discussed below, this brief survey of the history of the Chinese in British Columbia is drawn from Kay Anderson, *Vancouver's Chinatown: Racial Discourse in Canada, 1875–1980* (Montreal and Kingston: McGill-Queen's University Press, 1991); Patricia E. Roy, *A White Man's Province: British Columbia Politicians and Chinese and Japanese Immigrants, 1858–1914* (Vancouver: UBC Press, 1989); W. Peter Ward, *White Canada Forever: Popular Attitudes and Public Policy towards Orientals in British Columbia*, 2nd ed. (Montreal and Kingston: McGill-Queen's University Press, 1990); James W. St. G. Walker, *'Race,' Rights and the Law in the Supreme Court of Canada: Historical Case Studies* (Waterloo: Wilfrid Laurier University Press and Osgoode Society of Canadian Legal History, 1997), chap. 2; and John A. Munro, 'British Columbia and the "Chinese Evil": Canada's First Anti-Asiatic Immigration Law,' *Journal of Canadian Studies* 6 (1971) 42.
3 See Jay M. Perry, '"The Present of California May Prove the Future of British Columbia": Local, State and Provincial Immigration Policies Prior to the American Chinese Exclusion Act and Canadian Chinese Immigration Act,' *BC Studies* 201 (2019): 13.
4 Cited in Anderson, *Vancouver's Chinatown*, 37.
5 SBC 1884, c 4, preamble.
6 *Voters Act*, SBC 1871, no. 156, s 3; 1872, c 39, s 13; 1874, c 12, s 3; 1875, c 2; and 1876, c 1, s 9; Walker, *'Race,' Rights and the Law*, 70. For Ottawa's approval, see *Correspondence, Reports I*, 1011–12.
7 SBC 1878, c 35; Munro, 'British Columbia and the "Asiatic Evil,"' 42.
8 Report of Minister of Justice John A. Macdonald, 15 Aug. 1879, in *Correspondence, Reports I*, 1065–8. For the other documents mentioned here, see the same source, 1061–5. For the figures on disallowance, see Bruce Ryder, 'Racism and the Constitution: The Constitutional Fate of British Columbia Anti-Asian Immigration Legislation, 1884–1909,' *OHLJ* 29 (1991): 619 at 629.
9 *Crown Lands Act*, SBC 1884, c 2; *Chinese Regulation Act*, SBC 1884, c 4; Report of Alexander Campbell, minister of justice, 29 Mar. 1885, and accompanying documents, in *Correspondence, Reports I*, 1093–5.

10 *Municipal Amendment Act*, SBC 1885, c 21, s 10; *Municipality Act*, SBC 1881, s 110; *Pawnbrokers Act*, SBC 1888, c 25; *Coal Mines Regulation Act*, SBC 1877, c 15, s 4; *Coal Mines Regulation Amendment Act*, SBC 1890, c 33, s 1; *Foreign Mining Companies Act*, SBC 1888, c 12.

11 *Provincial Voters Act*, SBC 1895, c 20, s 2; *Municipal Elections Act*, SBC 1896, c 38, s 7; *Vancouver Incorporation Act*, SBC 1900, c 54, s 7.

12 This brief summary of the Japanese experience in British Columbia is from Ward, *White Canada Forever*, chap. 6, quotation below at 107; Roy, *White Man's Province*; and Roy, 'The Oriental "Menace" in British Columbia,' in *Studies in Canadian Social History*, ed. Michiel Horn and Ronald Saborin (Toronto: McClelland and Stewart, 1974).

13 SBC 1897, c 1; and SBC 1898, c 28. For the coal mines Act, see *Coal Mines Regulation Act*, SBC 1899, c 46. The private Acts of incorporation referred to here are SBC 1898, c 30, 44, 46–8, 50, and 52–64; and 1899, c 4–5, 7–9, 12–17, 19–21, 26, 28, 37, 39, and 41. Typical was *An Act to Incorporate the Vancouver Northern and Yukon Railway Company*, SBC 1899, c 89, s 37, of which stated that 'No Chinese or Japanese persons shall be employed in the construction of the undertaking or the working of the railway.'

14 What follows in this and the next paragraph is drawn largely from *Correspondence, Reports II*, 529–57 and 848; quotations below in this paragraph and the next at 529, 541, and 555.

15 See chapter 2 for the provincial rights movement and for the reservation/disallowance process.

16 *Employment on Private Act Works Act*, SBC 1900, c 14, s 4; *Coal Mines Regulation Act*, SBC 1901, c 36, s 2; 1902, c 48, s 2; and 1903, c 47, s 2; *Employment on Private Act Works Act*, SBC 1902, c 38, s 4; 1903, c 14, s 4; *Correspondence, Reports II*, 586 and 848.

17 (1878) 1 BCR (part 1) 101.

18 (1862) 20 Cal 534 (Sup Ct).

19 *R v Wing Chong* [1885] BCJ No 1; quotations below at paras 25, 36, and 42. The cases are discussed in John McLaren: 'The Early British Columbia Supreme Court and the "Chinese Question": Echoes of the Rule of Law,' *Manitoba Law Journal* 20 (1991) 109; McLaren, 'The Early British Columbia Judges, the Rule of Law and the "Chinese Question": The California and Oregon Connection,' in *Law for the Elephant, Law for the Beaver: Essays in the Legal History of the North American West*, ed. Hamar Foster and John McLaren (Regina: Canadian Plains Research Center, 1992); and McLaren, 'The Head Tax Case and the Rule of Law,' in *Calling Power to Account: Law, Reparations and the Chinese Canadian Head Tax Case*, ed. David Dyzenhaus and Mayo Moran (Toronto: University of Toronto Press, 2005).

20 *R v Mee Wah* (1886) 3 BCR 403; quotations below at para 16.

21 [1886] BCJ No 4, quotations at paras 5 and 13; [1888] BCJ No 3, quotations at paras 1–3 and 5.

22 McLaren, 'Early British Columbia Supreme Court,' 144; quotation below from 131. This explanation of the judicial interventions in these cases relies on this and the other articles by MacLaren cited above.

23 For Begbie, see chapter 3. For Crease, see Tina Loo, 'Sir Henry Pering Pellew Crease,' *DCB* online.

24 McLaren, 'Head Tax Case and the Rule of Law,' 93.

25 This was *Union Colliery Company v Bryden* [1899] AC 580 (PC), which concerned the 1890 *Coal Mines Regulation Act*, which banned the employment of Chinese underground. It was a suit launched by John Bryden, a shareholder in Union Colliery, for a declaration that the company had no right under the law to employ Chinese workers, as it had done, and an injunction restraining it from continuing to do so. It was a collusive action, giving the company the opportunity to argue that the law was ultra vires. The BC Supreme Court held the legislation intra vires, but the JCPC held that the reference to the Chinese included aliens not yet naturalized and came under the federal power in section 91(25).

26 *Cunningham v Homma*, [1903] AC 151 at 156.

27 Onderdonk to Macdonald, 14 June 1882, cited in Munro, 'British Columbia and the "Asiatic Evil,"' 43; *Commons Debates*, 12 May 1882, 1477; 30 Apr. 1883, 905. See generally Patricia Roy, 'A Choice between Evils: The Chinese and the Construction of the Canadian Pacific Railway in British Columbia,' in *The CPR West: The Iron Road and the Making of a Nation*, ed. Hugh A. Dempsey (Vancouver: Douglas and McIntyre, 1984).

28 SBC 1884, c 3.

29 *Commons Debates*, 19 Mar. 1884, 974, quotations below from 975 and 976, and 2 Apr. 1884, 1284. For Shakespeare, see Jamie Morton, 'Noah Shakespeare,' *DCB* online.

30 For Chapleau, see Andrée Désilets, 'Joseph Adolphe Chapleau,' in *DCB* online. What follows in this paragraph is from *Commons Debates*, 2 Apr. 1884, 1282–9, quotation at 1287.

31 *Report of the Royal Commission on Chinese Immigration: Report and Evidence* (Ottawa, 1885), in Canada, *Sessional Papers*, 1885, No 54A, vi.

32 Report of the Minister of Justice, 8 Apr. 1884, in *Correspondence, Reports I*, 1092–3, quotation at 1093. For the other documents mentioned here see the same source.

33 John Andrew Mara, Speaker of the Legislative Assembly, to Governor
   General Lansdowne, 3 Mar. 1885, in *Correspondence, Reports I*,1098–1099.
   The Act was *Chinese Immigration Act*, SBC 1885, c.13.
34 SC 1885, c. 71; *Royal Commission Report 1885*, lxxxvi.
35 *Commons Debates*, 2 July 1885, 3002–22; quotations below at 3006–7 and
   3016–17.
36 *Chinese Immigration Act*, SC 1887, c. 35; SC 1892, c. 25.
37 *Chinese Immigration Act*, SC 1900, c. 32, and *Commons Debates*, 14 June
   1900, 7406–8; *Chinese Immigration Act*, SC 1903, c. 8; Report of the Royal
   Commission on Chinese and Japanese Immigration 1902, in Canada,
   Sessional Papers, 1903, no. 54; *Chinese Immigration Act*, SC 1923, c 38.
38 *Immigration Act*, SBC 1900, c 11.
39 For the disallowance campaign, see *Correspondence, Reports II*, 586–604;
   quotations below in this paragraph at 595.
40 *Immigration Act*, SBC 1902, c 34; 1903, c 12; 1904, c 26; 1905, c 28; 1907, c
   21A; 1908, c 23.
41 Parliament enacted the *Japanese Treaty Act*, SC 1907, c 50, which applied
   to Canada the provisions of the 1894 Treaty of Commerce and Navigation
   between Britain and Japan. Article 1 of the treaty guaranteed British and
   Japanese subjects 'full liberty to enter, travel or reside in any part of the
   dominions and possession of the other.'
42 Roy, *White Man's Province*; H.H. Sugimoto, 'The Vancouver Riots of 1907:
   A Canadian Episode,' in *East across the Pacific: Historical and Sociological
   Studies of Japanese Immigration and Assimilation*, ed. H. Convoy (Santa
   Barbara, CA: American Bibliographical Centre–Clio, 1972); Report
   by W.L. Mackenzie King, Deputy Minister of Labour, Commissioner
   Appointed to Investigate into the Losses Sustained by the Chinese
   Population of Vancouver, B.C., on the Occasion of the Riots in That City
   in September 1907, in Canada, *Sessional Papers*, 1907, No 74F.
43 *Chinese Immigration Act*, SN 1906, c 2, s 1.
44 *Election Act*, SS 1908, c 2, s 11; *Female Labour Act*, SS 1912, c 17; 1912–13, c
   18. See generally, for what follows, Walker, *'Race,' Rights and the Law*, chap.
   2; and Constance Backhouse, 'The White Women's Labour Laws: Anti-
   Chinese Racism in Early Twentieth-Century Canada,' *LHR* 14 (1996): 315.
45 *Female Labour Act*, SM 1913, c 19; *Factory, Shop and Office Building Act*, SO
   1914, c 40, s 2 (1); Walker, *'Race,' Rights and the Law*, 55 and 70.
46 (1914) 49 SCR 440.
47 See generally, Gordon Bale, 'John Idington,' *DCB* online.
48 What follows in this section is based on Ward, *White Canada Forever*, chap.
   5; Narindar Singh, *Canadian Sikhs: History, Religion and Culture of Sikhs in*

North America (Ottawa: Canadian Sikhs Studies Institute, 1994), chaps. 2 and 3; and Hugh Johnston, *The East Indians in Canada* (Ottawa: Canadian Historical Association Booklet, 1984). Most writing on South Asians focuses on the *Komagata Maru* affair, discussed below.

49 *Provincial Elections Act*, SBC 1907, c 16, s 3, excluding 'Hindus' from voting; *Municipal Elections Act*, SBC 1908, c 14, s 13(1), excluding 'Chinese, Japanese, Other Asiatics and Indians.' Sikhs were commonly referred to as Hindus, occasionally as East Indians to distinguish them from Indigenous people.

50 Report by W.L. Mackenzie King on Mission to England to Confer with the British Authorities on the Subject of Immigration to Canada from the Orient and Immigration from India in Particular, in Canada, *Sessional Papers*, 1908, No 36A [hereafter *Mackenzie King Report*].

51 Order in Council, 8 Jan. 1908. The regulation was purported to be made as a supplement to sections 26–30 of the *Immigration Act*, the first four sections being bans on the immigration of the insane, the disabled, the diseased, the destitute, prostitutes, and their pimps. Section 30 was a much more general provision, allowing the governor-general, if he considered it 'necessary or expedient,' to 'prohibit the landing in Canada of any specified class of immigrants.'

52 *Canada v Behari Lal*, [1908] BCJ No 23.

53 *Immigration Act*, SC 1908, c 33, s 1.

54 *Commons Debates*, 8 Apr. 1908, 6429.

55 Orders in Council, 27 Mar. and 3 June 1908. It is not clear why the government re-passed a regulation that mirrored a provision that was now contained in the statute itself, especially since Oliver said that the government wanted it to be in the statute rather than in a regulation: *Commons Debates*, 8 Apr. 1908, 6430.

56 Cited in Walker, *'Race,' Rights and the Law*, 253.

57 This account of the federal government's deliberations and actions is from the Orders in Council of 2 Mar., 5 May, 13 June, and 13 July 1908, and attached reports. Quotations below in this paragraph are from the 2 Mar. order. See also *Mackenzie-King Report*.

58 Order in Council, 9 May 1910; *Immigration Act*, SC 1910, c 27, s 82.

59 *Re the Hindus and Immigration Act* (1913), 15 DLR 189 (BCSC). In a case two years earlier, *Canada v Rahim (No 2)*, [1911] BCJ No 74, Morrison J of the BC Supreme Court granted a writ of habeas corpus to free Hussain Rahim, a radical Indian politician who had lived in Honolulu and come to Canada before the passage of the 1910 *Immigration Act* and the 1910 re-enactment of the continuous journey Order in

Council. He did so on the basis that the 1910 *Immigration Act* was not retroactive.

60 The following account of the *Komagata Maru* affair relies principally on Hugh Johnston, *The Voyage of the* Komagata Maru*: The Sikh Challenge to Canada's Colour Bar* (Vancouver: UBC Press, 2014). See also Renissa Mawani, *Across Oceans of Law: The* Komagatu Maru *and Jurisdiction in Time of Empire* (Vancouver: UBC Press, 2018).

61 *In Re the Immigration Act and Munshi Singh*, (1914) 20 BCR 243 (CA).

62 *Vancouver News-Advertizer*, 2 June 1914; and *Western Methodist Recorder*, July 1914, both cited in Ward, *White Canada Forever*, 90.

63 Robin Winks, *The Blacks in Canada: A History*, 2nd ed. (Montreal and Kingston: McGill-Queen's University Press, 1997), 289. For Black history in Canada in this period, see also Walker, *'Race', Rights and the Law*, 124–43; population figure at 125; and Walker, *A History of Blacks in Canada: A Study Guide for Teachers and Students* (Ottawa: Minister of State for Multiculturalism, 1981); Dorothy W. Williams, *Blacks in Montreal, 1628–1986: An Urban Geography* (Montreal: Éditions Yvon Blais, 1989); Ida Greaves, *The Negro in Canada* (Orillia, ON: Packet-Times, 1930). The census of 1871 gave the number of Blacks in Canada as 21,500, and that of 1911 showed a decrease to 16,900. These figures must be taken with considerable scepticism, however, because of undercounting. But even allowing for this, Blacks were a very small part of the national population, which increased from 3.69 million in 1871 to 7.2 million in 1911.

64 Winks, *Blacks in Canada*, 288.

65 For the best-known example – Halifax – see Donald H. Clairmont and Dennis William Magill, *Africville: The Life and Death of a Canadian Black Community*, 3rd ed. (Toronto: Canadian Scholars, 1999).

66 See Cecil Foster, *They Called Me George: The Untold Story of Black Train Porters and the Birth of Modern Canada* (Windsor: Biblioasis, 2019); and Agnes Calliste, 'Sleeping Car Porters in Canada: An Ethnically Submerged Split Labour Market,' *Canadian Ethnic Studies* 19 (1987): 1. Examples of the many kinds of 'social discrimination' abound in the literature and are usefully summarized in Walker, *'Race,' Rights and the Law*, 131–7 and 140–6.

67 (1899) 15 CS 104 and 8 QKB 379. This account, and the discussion of the two cases in the following paragraph, are taken from Walker, *'Race,' Rights and the Law*, 144–7. For Archibald, see, inter alia, Pierre-George Roy, *Les Juges de la province de Quebec* (Quebec: Redempti Paradis, 1933), 21.

68 Barrington Walker, 'Introduction: From a Property Right to Citizenship Rights – The African Canadian Legal Odyssey,' in *The African Canadian Legal Odyssey: Historical Essays*, ed. Walker (Toronto: Osgoode Society for Canadian Legal History and University of Toronto Press, 2012), 28. See also Walker, 'Finding Jim Crow in Canada,' in *A History of Human Rights in Canada: Essential Issues*, ed. Janet Miron (Toronto: Canadian Scholars Press, 2009).

69 *Schools Act*, SNS 1836, c 92, s 5; *Of Public Instruction*, RSNS 1884, c 29, s 3(10). See also Robin Winks, 'Negro School Segregation in Ontario and Nova Scotia,' *CHR* 50 (1969): 164; and Judith Fingard, 'Race and Respectability in Victorian Halifax,' *Journal of Imperial and Commonwealth History* 20 (1992): 169.

70 *Separate Schools Act*, RSO 1877, c 206, s 2; *Common Schools Act*, SO 1869, c 44, s 9. See also Harry Arthurs, 'Civil Liberties – Public Schools – Segregation of Negro Students,' *CBR* 41 (1963): 453.

71 *Dunn v Windsor Board of Education* [1883] OJ No 221 (Ch).

72 *In re George Stewart and the Trustees of School Section No. 8 of the Township of Sandwich East*, [1864] OJ No 125 (QB).

73 [1871] OJ No 55 (QB).

74 This briefly summarizes a large literature, the most notable of which is Barrington Walker, *Race on Trial: Black Defendants in Ontario's Criminal Courts, 1858–1958* (Toronto: Osgoode Society for Canadian Legal History and University of Toronto Press, 2010).

75 For what follows, see principally R. Bruce Shepard, *Deemed Unsuitable: Blacks from Oklahoma Move to the Canadian Prairies in Search of Equality in the Early 20th Century Only to Find Racism in Their New Home* (Toronto: Umbrella, 1996), chaps. 5 and 6; quotation below at 69. See also Winks, *Blacks in Canada*, 300–12; Harold Troper, 'The Creek Negroes of Oklahoma and Canadian Immigration,' *CHR* 53 (1972): 272; Stewart Grow, 'The Blacks of Amber Valley: Negro Pioneering in Northern Alberta,' *Canadian Ethnic Studies* 6 (1974): 17.

76 The *Immigration Act*, SC 1906, c 19, listed a wide set of 'immigrants prohibited,' including those with mental and physical disabilities, paupers, prostitutes, and those carrying contagious diseases. Although these sections referred to people travelling to Canada by sea, other sections of the Act effectively incorporated these criteria into the screening of those who arrived by land.

77 Orders in Council, 12 Aug. and 5 Oct. 1911.

78 *Common Schools Act*, SNB 1871, c 21.

79 *Correspondence, Reports I*, 661–702. For the litigation, see *Ex parte Renaud*, (1873) 1 NBR 273 (SC); *Maher v Town Council of Portland* [1874] UKPC 83.

80 Gordon Bale, 'Law, Politics and the Manitoba Schools Question: Supreme Court and Privy Council,' *CBR* 63 (1985): 462.

81 Although schools west of Manitoba never became embroiled in controversy, religious minorities in the North-West Territories were also granted separate denominational schools in 1875: *North-West Territories Act*, SC 1875, c 49, s 11.

82 Initially the board had fewer members and half Protestants and half Catholics. The change to 12 and nine was made in 1875: see *Education Acts*, SM 1871, c 12; and SM 1875, c 27, s 1.

83 *Public Schools Act*, SM 1881, c 4; *Aid to Manitoba Schools Act*, SC 1878, c 13.

84 *Department of Education Act*, SM 1890, c 37, esp. ss 5–7 and 14; *Public Schools Act*, SM 1890, c 38, ss 6 and 8; *Official Language Act*, SM 1890, c 14.

85 See, inter alia, Lovell Clark, *The Manitoba Schools Question: Majority Rule or Minority Rights* (Toronto: Copp Clark Publishing, 1968); J.R. Miller, 'D'Alton McCarthy, Equal Rights, and the Origins of the Manitoba Schools Question,' *CHR* 54 (1973): 369.

86 *Jesuit Estates Act*, SQ 1888, c 13; J.R. Miller, *Equal Rights: The Jesuit Estates Act Controversy* (Montreal and Kingston: McGill-Queen's University Press, 1979).

87 Ramsay Cook, *Watching Quebec: Selected Essays* (Montreal and Kingston: McGill-Queen's University Press, 2005), 157. For a more extended treatment of this idea, see Cook's *Canada and the French-Canadian Question* (Toronto: Macmillan, 1966).

88 The *North-West Territories Act*, SC 1875, c 49, s 11, permitted the religious minority in any district to establish a separate school, tax themselves for its support, and make regulations for its curriculum. In 1884 the system was made more formal, a Territorial Board of Education established with Catholic and Protestant sections responsible for their own schools: *School Ordinances*, SNWT 1884, No 5, and SNWT 1887, No. 2. But this system came under frequent attack and was abolished in 1892 and replaced with a government-run Council of Public Instruction: *School Ordinance*, SNWT 1892, c 22. Section 4 permitted only the establishment of certain 'classes of schools,' two of which were 'public schools' and 'separate schools.' In both there was to be 'instruction … in the elements of English and commercial education.'

89 *Constitutional and Other Provincial Questions Act*, SM 1890, c 16. For the quotations in this paragraph, see *Manitoba Free Press*, 7 and 12 Aug. 1889, 5 and 6 Mar. 1890, all in Clark, *Manitoba School Question*, 37, 39, 54, and 58.

90 In addition to the sources already cited, this account draws on Paul Crunican, *Priests and Politicians: Manitoba Schools and the Election of 1896* (Toronto: University of Toronto Press, 1974).

91 There is only one case report for the two Manitoba decisions, which
   includes the reasons of Killam J and of his three colleagues: *Barrett v City
   of Winnipeg* (1891) 7 Man LR 273. Killam J's reasons are at 282–304; Taylor
   CJ's at 308–30; Dubuc J's at 330–64; and Bain J's at 364–80. Quotations
   in the following paragraphs are at 317, 318, 321, 338–9, 345, and 349. All
   cases reviewed in what follows are discussed in Bale, 'Manitoba Schools
   Crisis,' an excellent account of what was said in the cases but one marred
   by an editorial re-litigation of them.
92 For Dubuc and Royal, see Diane Paulette Payment, 'Sir Joseph Dubuc,'
   and A.I. Silver, 'Joseph Royal,' both in *DCB* online.
93 *Supreme and Exchequer Courts Act*, SC 1891, c 25.
94 *Barrett v Winnipeg (City of)*, (1891), 19 SCR 374.
95 *Winnipeg (City) v Barrett*, [1892] AC 445; *Logan v City of Winnipeg* (1891) 8
   Man LR 3 (QB); quotations from the JCPC decision are at paras 2 and 7.
96 See Clark, *Manitoba School Question*; Crunican, *Priests and Politicians*, 17.
97 Many of the petitions, and the Cabinet documents discussing them, are
   reproduced in the judgment of the SCC in the reference case, discussed
   immediately below.
98 For Thompson see Peter B. Waite, *The Man from Halifax: Sir John Thompson,
   Prime Minister* (Toronto: University of Toronto Press, 1985); and Waite, 'Sir
   John Sparrow David Thompson,' *DCB* online.
99 For Wade, see Brad R. Morrison and Christopher J.P. Hanna, 'Frederick
   Choate Wade,' and for Robinson see Patrick Brode, 'Christopher
   Robinson,' both *DCB* online. In *Barrett*, Manitoba's counsel had been
   Attorney-General Joseph Martin. Wade later published two pamphlets
   supporting the *Public Schools Act: National Schools for Manitoba* (Winnipeg,
   1892), and *The Manitoba School Question* (Winnipeg, 1895).
100 *Re Certain Statutes of the Province of Manitoba relating to Education*, (1894) 22
   SCR 577; quotations below at 661, 672–3, and 686.
101 *Brophy and Others v Attorney-General of Manitoba*, [1895] AC 202 (PC);
   quotations below at paras 12, 15, and 17.
102 For all of this, see Crunican, *Priests and Politicians*; Clark, *Manitoba School
   Question*, 139–70; 'Extracts from the Arguments of John S. Ewart and
   Dalton McCarthy before the Federal Cabinet, Feb. 26 and Mar. 5, 6, and
   7, 1895'; Report of Minister of Justice Sir Charles Tupper, 19 Mar. 1895;
   'Remedial Order-in-Council, 21 Mar. 1895; and Reply of the Government
   and Legislature of Manitoba, 25 June 1895, all in Canada, *Sessional Papers*,
   1895, Nos 20 and 20C.
103 *Alberta Act*, SC 1905, c 3; *Saskatchewan Act*, SC 1905, c 42. On Regulation
   17, see Marcel Martel and Martin Pâquet, *Speaking Up: A History of*

Language and Politics in Canada and Quebec, trans. Patricia Dumas (Toronto: Between the Lines, 2012); *Mackell v Ottawa (Roman Catholic Separate School Board)* [1917] AC 62.

104 David Fraser, *'Honorary Protestants': The Jewish School Question in Montreal, 1867–1997* (Toronto: Osgoode Society for Canadian Legal History and University of Toronto Press, 2015); *Education Act*, SQ 1903, c 16; *Pinsler v The Protestant Board of School Commissioners*, (1903) 23 CS 365.

Statute and Proclamation Index

Federal Statutes

Act for the Relief of Joseph Whiteaves
  (1869), 545
Alberta Act (1905), 611
Appropriation Act (1874), 467, 472;
  (1875), 472

Bank Act (1870), 381; (1880), 382;
  (1890), 179; (1900), 382
Bankruptcy Act (1869), 15; (1919), 373
*Better Security of the Crown and
  Government Act* (1868), 256
Bills of Exchange Act (1890), 6, 136, 148
Breaches of Contract Act (1877),
  396–7, 400

*Canada and Detroit River Bridge Company
  Incorporation Act* (1873), 494
Canada Temperance (Scott) Act (1878),
  61, 64, 69
Chinese Immigration Act (1885), 583
Combines Act (1889), 380, 443
Companies Act (1869), 360–1; (1877), 360

Conciliation Act (1900), 410
Construction Act (1873), 466
Criminal Code (1892), 8, 122, 192, 198,
  265, 402–4, 425–8, 436, 438, 441–4,
  451, 563–4, 567, 608, 613
Criminal Law Amendment Act (1876),
  399–400, 403
Criminal Procedure Act (1869), 433,
  440, 444, 451
Criminal Statistics Act (1876), 439

Dominion Election Act (1874), 113;
  (1920), 9
Dominion Lands Act (1872), 7, 319,
  346, 462, 467, 472–3, 476–9, 481,
  483–4; (1874), 479–80; (1876),
  479–80; (1897), 482; (1908), 483

Enfranchisement Act (1869), 13, 273–8,
  290, 293, 515
Expropriation Act (1886), 493

Federal Franchise Act (1885), 282–3
Fisheries Act (1877), 332

Immigration Act (1869), 582, 589;
(1908), 590; (1910), 591, 593
Indian Act (1876), 5, 13, 14, 120, 250,
271–2, 277–80, 291–2, 328, 339–40,
342–3, 347, 516, 536
Indian Act Amending Acts (1884), 281,
298, 300, 516; (1886), 293; (1894),
286, 319; (1895), 286, 301–2; (1898),
286; (1906), 207; (1911), 287–9;
(1914) 323; (1920), 321
Indian Act Consolidation (1880), 120,
270, 292
Indian Advancement Act (1884), 293, 340
Industrial Disputes Investigation Act
(1907), 411
Insolvent Act (1869), 373–4, (1873),
373; (1874), 373–4; (1875), 113, 374,
376, 378; (1877), 374
Insolvent Act Repeal Act (1880), 371

Lawless Aggressions Act (1867), 263–4

Manitoba Act (1870), 12, 19, 76, 188,
225–6, 228–9, 255, 462–3, 467,
469–72, 600–1, 605–7
Marriage Act (1912), 159
Money-Lenders Act (1906), 178

Naturalization Act (1881), 46, 588;
(1914), 46
North-West Territories Act (1870), 231;
(1875), 76, 524; (1877), 459;
(1901), 511

Penitentiary Act (1868), 445
Public Works Act (1867), 492–3

Railway Act (1868), 284, 366, 389, 493;
(1903), 391
Revised Statutes of Canada (1886), 122;
(1906), 124

*Speedy Trials in Ontario and Quebec
Act* (1869), 8, 437–9
Summary Proceedings Act (1869), 437
Supreme and Exchequer Courts Act
(1875), 80
Supreme Court Act (1879), 80; (1891),
81, 606

Ticket of Leave Act (1899), 448
Trades Union Act (1872), 399–400

Yukon Act (1898), 53

Provincial and Other Statutes – UK, Colonial, US – and Proclamations

Act Concerning Uses (ON 1897), 129,
131–2. See also *Statute of Uses*
*Act for the abolition of feudal rights and
duties in Lower Canada* (PC 1854), 179
*Act for the Prevention of Frauds and
Perjuries* (ON 1897), 132. See also
Statute of Frauds
Act of Union (UK 1840), 25–6
Act Respecting Real Property
(ON 1897), 132
Alien Labour Act (BC 1897), 574–5
Assessment Act (BC 1878), 572
Attorneys' and Solicitors' Act
(UK 1870), 192

Better Administration of Justice Act
(ON 1873), 91
Better Administration of Justice Act
(BC 1878), 79
British Columbia Fisheries Act
(BC 1901), 333
British North America Act (1867), 9–10, 18,
126, 147, 333, 354, 371, 380, 392, 410,
421, 444, 463, 535, 540, 546, 569, 571,
576, 580, 582, 600–1, 606, 609, 613, 615

Chinese Exclusion Act (USA 1882), 581
Chinese Regulation Act (BC 1884), 571,
    577–8
Chinese Tax Act (BC 1878), 572, 576
Civil Code of Lower Canada (PC 1866),
    5, 11, 117, 146–50, 154–6, 159,
    165–8, 177–83, 562
Coal Mines Regulation Act (BC 1877),
    412; (BC 1899), 574–5; (BC 1901), 576
Code Napoléon (FRA 1804), 149, 163,
    165–6, 177
Code of Civil Procedure (QUE 1866),
    148, 182; (QUE 1897), 149
Common Law Procedure Act (PC 1856), 91
Common Schools Act (NB 1871), 39
Companies Act (UK 1844), 358;
    (UK 1862), 358
Compensation to Workmen Act
    (ON 1892), 704n57
Consolidated Statutes (PC 1859), 439
Consolidated Statutes (NB 1877), 125
Consolidated Statutes (MB 1880), 119
Consolidated Statutes (BC 1888), 127
Constitutional Act (UK 1791), 56, 132
Corporations Act (BC 1878), 358
Councils of Conciliation Act (UK
    1867), 407–8
County Court Act (BC 1883), 96
Criminal Law Consolidation Acts
    (Greaves' Acts) (UK 1861), 424–5
Crown Lands Act (BC 1874), 230, 249

De Donis Conditionalibus
    (UK 1285), 132
Destitute Orphans Act
    (BC 1877), 513
Devolution of Estates Act (ON 1886),
    509, 510
Divorce and Matrimonial Causes Act
    (UK 1857), 18, 537, 553
Dower Act (UK 1833), 512

Education Act (QUE 1903), 612
Employers' Liability Act (UK 1880), 174

Factories Act (ON 1895), 413
Female Labour Act (SK 1912), 587
Free Grants and Homestead Acts
    (ON 1869), 484

Gaming Act (UK 1845), 139
General Mining Act (ON 1891), 389
Gold and Silver Mining Act
    (ON 1868), 387
Gradual Civilization Act (PC 1857),
    274–6, 515
Grantees of Reversions Act
    (UK 1540), 129

Habeas Corpus Act (UK 1679), 129
Half-Breed Land Grant Protection Act
    (MB 1873), 468–9
Highways Act (MB 1871, 1872), 716n23
Homestead Act (USA 1862), 477

Interpretation Act (QUE 1868), 148

Jesuit Estates Act (QUE 1888), 603
Judicature Act (UK 1873), 92–3
Judicature Act (BC 1879), 94
Judicature Act (ON 1881), 92–3;
    (ON 1895), 138
Judicature Act (NS 1884), 93
Judicature Act (MB 1895), 94
Judicature Act (NFLD 1899), 93
Judicature Act (NB 1909), 93
Judicial Districts Act (BC 1879), 79

Land Clauses Consolidation Act
    (UK 1845), 492
Land Purchase Act (PEI 1874), 489;
    (PEI 1875), 492
Larceny Act (UK 1861), 424

Law Society Act (MB 1877), 205
Legal Profession Act (AB 1907), 206
Legal Profession Act (SK 1907), 206
Liquor License (Crooks) Act
  (ON 1876), 65–6
Lord Campbell's Act (UK 1846), 170
Lord Talfourd's Act (UK 1839), 553

Magna Carta (ENG 1245), 129
Master and Servant Act (ON 1914), 396
Mines Act (ON 1902), 389
Mines and Minerals Act (NS 1864),
  385–6
Mines Arbitration Act (NS 1888), 409
Mines Regulation Act (NS 1873),
  386, 389
Mining Regulations Act (ON 1890),
  386, 389
Municipal Act (BC 1881), 493, 547;
  (BC 1885), 573
Municipal Amendment Act
  (ON 1890), 498

Ordinance Respecting the Legal
  Profession (NWT 1885), 225

Public Works Act (BC 1872), 543

Quebec Act (UK 1774), 132
Quia Emptores (UK 1290), 129, 132

Railway Act (ON 1877), 493
Real Property Act (UK 1845), 129

Revised Statutes Act (BC 1895), 129
Revised Statutes of Manitoba 1913, 123
Revised Statutes of New Brunswick
  1903, 120
Revised Statutes of Nova Scotia
  1873, 125
Revised Statutes of Nova Scotia 1900, 123
Revised Statutes of Ontario 1897, 129, 132
Rivers and Streams Act (ON 1884), 71
Royal Proclamation (UK 1763), 230, 341

Sale of Goods Act (UK 1893), 136
School Tax Act (BC 1878), 572
Sex Disqualification (Removal) Act
  (UK 1919), 212
Sheriffs Act (BC 1897), 128
Special Corporate Powers Act
  (QUE 1914), 179
Statute of Frauds (UK 1677), 132
Statute of Uses (UK 1535), 132
Statutes of Distributions (UK 1670),
  509; (UK 1685), 509

Titles of Half-Breed Lands Act (MB
  1885), 469

Vancouver Incorporation Act
  (BC 1900), 641

Workmen's Compensation Act
  (UK 1897), 418
Workmen's Compensation Act
  (QUE 1909), 175

Case Index

Abbott v Fraser (1874), 659n94
*Angers v The Queen Insurance
    Company* (1877), 59, 633n85
Asbestos and Asbestic Co v Durand
    (1900), 173, 201n67

Barrett v City of Winnipeg (1891),
    604–9
Black v Kennedy (1876), 284
Blackburn and Cox v McCallum
    (1903), 515
Board v Board (1919), 730n56
Brassard et al v Langevin (1877), 653n3
Brittlebank v Gray-Jones (1888), 532
*Brophy and Others v Attorney-General
    of Manitoba* (1895), 609–10
Burton v The Queen (1883), 494–5

*Calder v Attorney-General of British
    Columbia* (1973), 218, 231, 254,
    255, 616
Canada v Fowlds, (1893), 494–5
Canada v Rahim (No 2) (1911), 740n59

*Canadian Pacific Railway Co v
    Chalifoux* (1888), 170
*Certain Statutes of the Province of
    Manitoba relating to Education,
    Re* (1894), 608–9
Citizens Insurance Company v Parsons
    (1881–2), 62, 63, 64–5, 68
Conger v Kennedy (1895), 533
Connolly v Woolrich (1867), 536–7
Cooey v Broome (1877), 632n85
Coram, In Re (1886), 555–9
Couillard v Jeannotte (1891), 171
Courville v Paquette (1916), 157
Cox v Adams (1904), 138–9
CPR v Chalifoux, 170
CPR v Lachane, 185
Crowe v Adams (1892), 531–2
Cushing v Dupuy (1880), 378

Daoust v Schiller (1900), 163–4
Davidson v Ross (1876), 377–8
Delpit v Côté (1901), 654n22
Desbrisay v Desbrisay (1873), 733n101

Despatie v Tremblay (1921), 159
Drysdale v Dugas (1896), 507–8
Dumphy v Kehoe (1891), 652n61
Dunn v Windsor Board of Education
    (1883), 597, 742n71

Farwell v Boston and Worcester
    Railroad Corporation (1842), 415–16
Fisher v Webster (1894), 154, 653n8
Foulds, Re (1892), 560
Francklyn v Peoples Heat and Light
    Company (1899), 505–6, 723n126
Fraser v Kirkpatrick, (1907), 533
Fynn, Re (1848), 556

Glengoil SS Co v Pilkington (1897),
    656n45
Gober v Agnew (1907), 655n33

Hindus and Immigration Act, Re, The
    (1913), 591, 740n59
Hiscox v Lander (1876), 506–7
Hodge v The Queen (1883), 55, 65–7,
    634n107
Huson v South Norwich (1895), 67, 69
Hutchison and St Catharines School
    Board, Re (1871), 597–8

Immigration Act and Munshi Singh,
    Re, The (1914), 592–3
Indian Reserve, City of Sydney, NS, Re
    (1918), 680n37
Ingersoll Telephone Company v Bell
    Telephone Company (1916), 392

Jamieson v Jamieson (1921), 555
Janvey v Cree (1895), 653n8
Johnson v Sparrow (1899), 595–6
Jones, Re (1868), 376

Lachapelle v Beaudoin (1878), 655n29
Lafleur v Gagnon (1910), 161, 199n29
Lafontaine v Poulin (1912), 154, 653n8
Lawson v Laidlaw (1878), 524, 526–7
Lenoir v Ritchie (1879), 61–2, 68
Lepine v Laurent (1891), 632n85
Liquidators of the Maritime Bank of
    Canada v Receiver-General of New
    Brunswick (1892), 43
Liquidators of the Maritime Bank of
    Canada v The Receiver-General of
    Canada (1892), The, 68
Local Prohibition Reference, 55, 69,
    70–1
Logan v City of Winnipeg (1891),
    606–7, 744n95

Manitoba Métis Federation Inc v
    Canada (Attorney-General)
    (2013), 713n2
McCrae v White (1893), 377–8
McFarran v Montreal Park & Island
    Railway (1900), 156
McLean v McKay, 500, 722n106
Mercer v A.G. Ontario (1881),
    62, 633n93
Metallic Roofing Company v
    Amalgamated Sheet Metal Workers
    International, Local Union No. 30
    (1903), 405–6, 701n27
Miller v Ashton, 316–17, 686n29
Miller v Grand Trunk Railway (1906),
    172–3, 174, 658n82
Mission de la Grande Ligne v
    Morissette (1889), 164
Murdoch, Re (1881), 554, 557, 558

North British & Mercantile Fire & Life
    Insurance Co. v Lambe (1884), 67–8

Pearson v Adams (1912), 501–2
Pineo v Gavazza (1885), 377
Priestley v Fowler (1837), 415–16

Queen v Louis Riel, The (1885), 257–69, 676n108
Quong Wing v The King (1914), 587–8

R v Corporation of Victoria (1888), 578–9
R v Fredericton (1879), 61–2, 64, 66
R v Gold Commissioner of Victoria District (1886), 578–9
R v Grenier (1899), 172
R v Jackson (1891), 567
R v Mee Wah (1886), 578
R v Nan-e-quis-e-ka (1889), 729n48
R v Taylor (1875), 59
R v Wing Chong (1885), 577–8, 737n19
Ranger c. Cie du Grand Tronc, 170
Riel v The Queen (1885), 267, 676n108
Robb v Robb (1891), 538, 729n48
Robinson v CPR (1891), 171–2
Russell v The Queen (1882), 64–7, 69, 633n103, 634n107

Ryan v Lockhart (1972), 722n106
Rylands v Fletcher (1868), 203

Severn v The Queen (1878), 59–61, 66
Smart Infants, Re (1886), 557–8
Smart v Smart (1883), 557–8
St Catherines Milling and Lumber Company v The Queen, (1888), 230–1
St Lawrence Cement v Barrette (2008), 724n130
Stuart v Bank of Montreal (1909), 138–9, 534–5, 649n35

Tai Sing v Maguire (1878), 576–7, 578–9
Trimble v Hill (1879), 6–7, 139
Tudor v Hart (1888), 199n31
Tulk v Moxhay (1848), 499–500

Union Colliery Company v Bryden (1899), 738N25

Valin v Langlois (1879), 60–1, 85
Vankoughnet v Denison (1882), 500

Walker v Walker (1919), 730n56

Name Index

Abbot, John, 107, 109, 189–90, 373, 607
Abell, Alberta, 539–40
Abell, Alfred, 539–40
Achuchwahauhhatohapit (Star
    Blanket), 297
Agnew, Augustus, 655n33
Ahtahkakoop (Star Blanket), 240–1, 319
Aikins, James Cox, 464, 668n18
Aikins, James Manning, 190, 551
Albert, Prince Arthur William
    Patrick (Duke of Connaught and
    Strathearn), 41
Allan, Hugh, 189
Allen, John Campbell, 556
Alverstone, Baron, Richard Webster 45
Alward, Silas, 203
Anderson, Alexander Caufield, 250, 332
Anglin, Francis Alexander, 138–9
Anglin, Timothy, 39, 104
Archambeault, Horace, 111
Archibald, Adams George, 76, 226–7,
    233, 239, 241, 464, 466
Archibald, John Sprott, 595–6

Armour, Archibald, 200
Armour, Edward Douglas, 200,
    202, 204
Armour, John Douglas, 200, 527
Aronsberg, Abraham, 549
Aronsberg, Lottie, 549
Ashton, Nelles, 317
Austin, John, 5

Baker, Edgar Crow, 583
Ballendine, Peter, 345
Barber, Robert, 414
Beauchamp, Jean-Joseph, 141, 144,
    146, 202
Béchard, François, 540
Bedson, Samuel, 447
Begbie, Matthew Baillie, 78, 79, 94,
    101, 127, 253, 301, 577, 578–80,
    636n9
Bennett, Richard Bedford, 186
Bentham, Jeremy, 5, 425, 428
Benwell, Frederick, 452
Beresford, Herbert, 476

Bergin, Darby, 412
Bernard, Hewitt, 230–1, 249, 424, 625n10
Bibaud, Maximilien, 141
Bickerdike, Robert, 450
Big Bear, 241, 256, 261
Birchall, Reginald, 452
Black, John, 223
Blair, Andrew, 392
Blake, Edward, 42, 81, 82, 83, 104, 105, 112, 114, 223, 261, 294, 300, 345, 378, 400, 426, 524, 546, 609
Blake, Hilda, 454, 456
Blake, Samuel Hume, 105
Blake, William Hume, 91
Blanchard, Richard, 118
Booth, John Rudolph, 353, 505
Borden, Robert, 51, 89, 107, 108, 109, 110, 208, 592, 644n102
Bourassa, Henri, 111
Bowell, Mackenzie, 105, 107, 109, 229, 610
Boyd, John Alexander, 407, 500
Bradford, Samuel, 204
Bréland, Pascal, 346
Brodeur, Louis-Philippe, 502
Brown, George, 25, 26, 29, 30, 34, 38, 108, 399, 400, 625n6
Brown, James, 414
Bryant, Cornelius, 300
Bryce, Peter Henderson, 321, 323–7, 329–33
Buell, Andrew Norton, 90
Burbidge, George Wheelock, 198, 258, 426–8, 637n20
Burdett, Samuel, 300

Cairns, Hugh, 486
Cameron, E.R., 124
Cameron, Malcolm, 440, 551

Campbell, Alexander, 99, 256, 361, 474, 573, 582
Campbell, John (Marquess of Lorne), 41, 42
Campbell, Phoebe, 457
Campbell, Robert, 548
Carmack, George Washington, 52
Cartier, George-Étienne, 25, 188, 219, 225, 378, 471, 625n6
Cary, George Hunter, 486
Casgrain, Thérèse, 652n1
Casgrain, Thomas Chase, 193, 258, 268
Cassels, Walter, 637n20
Chamberlain, Joseph, 575
Chandler, Edward Barron, 36
Chapleau, Joseph Adolphe, 581, 583
Charlton, John, 320, 541
Childers, Hugh Culling Eardley, 490
Clah, Arthur Wellington, 299
Clark, Daniel, 259
Clark, John Murray, 253–4
Clarke, Lawrence, 345
Clarke, Samuel Robinson, 198
Clement, William Henry Pope, 99, 198, 589
Codd, Donald, 473, 474
Connolly, Suzanna, 536
Connolly, William, 536
Connor, James, 263, 674n96
Cook, Jane, 300
Copway, George (Kahgegagahbouwh), 329
Coram, Eva, 555–7
Coram, Joseph, 555–7
Courville, Godfrey, 157
Courville, Marie Anne, 157
Craig, James, 636n6
Crease, Henry Pellew, 78–9, 94, 458, 577, 579, 580, 638n9
Creighton, John, 447

Crofton, Walter, 445
Crooks, Adam, 523
Crop-Eared Wolf, 285
Crozier, Leif, 345
Cunard, Samuel, 506

D., Denise, 563
Dakin, Violet, 554
Daly, T. Mayne, 320
Davidson, Peers, 197
Davie, Theodore, 120, 126–9, 132, 436
Davies, Alice, 563
Davies, Arthur, 563
Davies, Louis Henry, 85
Davin, Nicholas Flood, 311–12
Davis, Amanda Esther, 158
Davis, Delos Rogest, 210
Davis, Frederick, 210
Davis, Lionel, 212
Davis, Samuel, 158
Dawson, Simon, 280
De Cosmos, Amor, 47, 540, 724n132
de Lorimier, Charles-Chamilly, 143,
    651n49
De Sola, Joseph, 158
Dease, William, 220
Denison, George, 403, 549
Denison, Robert Brittain, 500
Denison, Shirley, 204
Dennis, John, 220, 222
Dennis, John Stoughton, 473, 479
Dewdney, Edgar, 257, 296, 304, 310,
    318, 319, 574, 575
Dicey, A.V., 5
Ditchburn, William, 302
Dorion, Antoine Aimé, 34, 38, 83,
    113, 188, 276, 469
Douglas, James, 47, 247, 486–7
Douglas, Thomas (5th Earl of Selkirk),
    464, 470

Downey, Joseph, 448
Drake, Montague Tyrwhitt, 128,
    457–8
Draper, William Henry, 44
Drummond, Lewis Thomas, 113
Drysdale, Arthur, 110
Dubuc, Joseph, 267, 604–5
Ducharme, Charles, 459
Dufferin, Lord, 228, 250, 490
Dugas, Calixte Aimé, 507, 636n6
Dumont, Gabriel, 344–6
Duncan, James, 597
Dunn, Jane Ann, 597
Dunning, John, 549
Duval, Jean-François, 57

Ellis, John, 114
Erasmus, Peter, 240
Etherington, Frederick, 448
Ewart, John Skirving, 201, 203, 204,
    267, 607–8, 609, 610

Falconbridge, John Delatre, 204, 494
Fasken, David, 188
Ferguson, Thomas, 558, 597
Fielding, William Stevens, 110, 550
Fisher, Charles, 540, 631n78
Fitzpatrick, Charles, 86, 258–9, 260,
    266, 587
Forbes, William, 500
Forget, Amédée, 206, 321
Forget, Rodolphe, 151
Foster, Adeline, 542
Foster, George, 542
Fourmond, Vital, 310
Fournier, Télesphore, 80, 83, 85, 103,
    249, 608, 638n30, 656n44
Fox, Ann, 515
Fox, James, 515
Fox, Sarah, 157

Francklyn, Gilbert, 506
Francklyn, Sarah Jane, 506
Fraser, Hugh, 181
Fraser, John James, 557
French, Mabel Penery, 211, 213
Fry, Edward, 137

Gage, Thomas, 336
Galliher, William Alfred, 89
Galt, Alexander Casimir, 644n102
Geddum-Cal-Doe, 331
Gérin-Lajoie, Marie Lacoste, 213
Gibbons, George, 45, 629n58
Gibbons, James, 684n9
Giffard, Hardinge (1st Earl of
    Halsbury), 137
Gilmour, Jeannie, 563
Gilpin, Edward, 387
Girard, Marc-Amable, 212, 473–4
Girouard, Désiré, 85, 144, 148, 167,
    174, 536
Globensky, Arthur, 176
Glover, Christiana Filman, 550
Glover, Christopher Columbus, 550
Gordon, John Hamilton (Lord
    Aberdeen), 42, 542, 575
Gordon, Robert, 514
Gouin, Lomer, 149
Gowan, James Robert, 424, 426,
    434–6, 438–9, 440
Graham, Wallace, 194, 559
Grantham, Arthur Myles, 552
Grantham, Gertrude Mary, 552
Gray, John Hamilton, 32, 35–6,
    78, 79, 572, 576–7, 579, 580, 581,
    625n10, 627n35
Greaves, Charles, 424
Green, Solomon Hart, 212
Greenshields, James, 259, 263
Greenway, Thomas, 602, 608, 610

Guibord, Joseph, 113, 153
Gwynne, John Wellington, 61, 62, 67,
    85, 103, 508, 609, 638n30

Haatq, 331, 457–8
Hagarty, John, 416
Hale, Matthew, 264
Haliburton, Robert, 490
Hallam, George, 325
Halliday, William, 302
Hamasack, 301
Harley, Herbert, 214
Harrison, Eli, 96
Harrison, Robert, 57, 91, 108, 399, 400
Harvey, Horace, 533
Haultain, Frederick, 50–1, 587
Haviland, Thomas Heath, 31
Haythorne, Robert, 49, 50
Helmcken, John Sebastian, 128
Henderson, Robert B., 197
Henry, William Alexander, 62, 83, 112
Herbert, Henry (Lord Carnarvon), 345
Herchmer, George Field, 552
Herchmer, Lawrence, 552
Herschell, Farrer (1st Baron
    Herschell), 138, 609
Hobhouse, Arthur, 558
Hodgins, Eleanor, 200
Hodgins, Frank, 139, 203
Hodgins, Frank Egerton, 201
Hodgins, John George, 200
Hodgins, Thomas, 200
Hodgins, William Egerton, 200, 368
Holker, John, 62
Holmes, Alice, 544
Holmes, Charles, 544, 551
Holmes, Simon Hugh, 110
Holmested, George Smith, 132, 203,
    487, 525–6
Holton, Luther, 276

Howe, Joseph, 220, 270, 304, 464, 471
Howell, Hector, 286
Hoyles, Hugh, 192
Hoyles, Newman Wright, 192, 204, 428
Hunter, Gordon, 89, 114–15, 591
Hutchison, Richard, 597–8

Idington, John, 587–8
Irving, Paulus Aemilius, 81–2, 89

Jacobs, Samuel, 211
James, Alexander, 555
Jamieson, Marion, 555
Jenkins, John Theophilus, 490
Jetté, Louis-Amable, 142, 149, 171
Johnson, Festus, 342
Johnson, Francis Godschall, 57, 76
Johnson, Frederick, 595
Johnston, James Robinson, 210–11
Johnston, James William, 93
Johnstone, Thomas Cooke, 258, 264
Joly de Lotbinière, Henri-Gustave,
    38, 629n52
Jones, Beverly, 487
Jones, Peter (Kahkewaquonaby), 329
Jones, William, 549
Jukes, Augustus, 259, 268

Kaa Gox (Dawson Charlie), 52
Kaulbach, Henry, 436, 542
Keish (Skookum Jim), 52
Kelly, Peter, 300
Killam, Albert Clements, 392, 604
King, Edward, 608
King, George Edward, 85, 556
King, John, 192
King, William Lyon Mackenzie,
    410–11, 586, 589, 591
Klinglesmith, Margaret Center, 203,
    665n48

L'Heureux, Jean, 317
Laflamme, Rodolphe, 220, 469
Lafleur, Anastasie, 161
Lafleur, Eugène, 188
Lafontaine, Aimé, 113
Laird, David, 234, 238, 247, 270, 277,
    278, 279, 280, 303, 316, 472
Lamothe, J.C., 169–70, 174, 175
Landry, Pierre-Amand, 111, 212
Lane, Mary, 456–7
Lane, Robert, 457
Langdell, Christopher Columbus, 140
Langelier, François, 143, 149
Langevin, Hector Louis, 36, 270, 274,
    276, 279, 306, 627n36
Langmuir, John, 449, 710n72
Langstaff, Annie Macdonald, 183, 212
Lareau, Edmond, 140–1
Lash, Zebulon, 99, 572–3
Laskin, Bora, 139
Laurier, Wilfrid, 19, 42, 51, 52, 70,
    71, 72, 85–6, 89, 99, 103, 107, 108,
    109–11, 153, 254, 258, 294, 322, 336,
    390, 392, 410, 411, 457, 483, 541, 569,
    585, 591, 603, 610, 629n52, 645n110
Lavell, Michael, 268
Lavergne, Armand, 111, 167
Lavergne, Joseph, 111
Le Jeune, Henry, 262
Lefebvre de Bellefeuille, Édouard, 141
Lefroy, Augustus Henry, 71, 203, 204
Leggo, William, 197
Leith, Alexander, 200
Lemieux, François-Xavier, 258, 265, 267
Leo XIII, 152
Lépine, Ambroise, 220, 223, 227–8
Lewis, Jamieson, 282
Longley, James Wilberforce, 206, 436
Loranger, Thomas Jean-Jacques, 56,
    141, 142, 143, 177, 198

Lougheed, James, 186
Louis, Chief Petit, 251
Louise Caroline Alberta, Princess, 41
Lynch, David Scott, 258

Macaulay, Thomas Babington, 311
Macdonald, James Alexander, 89
Macdonald, John A., 25, 29, 30, 31,
    32, 33–4, 36, 38–9, 40, 42, 50, 65, 66,
    71, 72, 80–1, 83, 84, 89, 104, 105,
    106, 107, 108, 109, 110, 113, 219,
    222, 223, 225, 227, 230, 253, 257,
    266, 268, 269, 270, 272, 279. 281,
    282, 283, 290, 292, 293, 294, 300,
    307, 311, 312, 373, 390, 400, 412,
    424, 425, 426, 434, 438, 447–8, 452,
    463, 466, 468, 471, 474, 475, 483,
    540–1, 580–1, 595, 604, 607, 610,
    625n6, 636n103, 636n9, 677n6
Macdonald, John Sandfield, 438
MacDonald, William, 196
Macdonnell, George Milnes, 448
MacDougall, Joseph, 199
MacInnes, T.R.E. (Tom), 254
MacKay, Ira, 196
Mackenzie, Alexander, 80, 82, 105,
    107, 109, 230, 374, 396
Mackenzie, Robert, 310, 321
Mackenzie, William, 552
MacLean, Simon J., 390–1
MacLean, William, 500
MacLeod, James, 432
MacNaughten, Lord Edward, 173, 613
Mactavish, William, 221
Maguire, Thomas, 77, 636n6
Mansfield, Arabella, 212
Marsh, Alfred Henry, 204
Martin, Archer, 89, 114
Martin, Clara Brett, 213
Martin, John Robert, 548

Mason, John Herbert, 487
Massie, James, 449
Masson, Luc-Hyacinthe, 113
Masten, Cornelius, 197
Masters, C.H., 426
Mathers, Thomas, 403
Mathieu, Michel, 144, 163, 164, 202
McAfees, 555–6
McArthur, Archibald, 173
McCarthy, D'Alton, 501, 610
McColl, Ewan, 295
McCreight, John Foster, 106, 577,
    578, 579, 580
McCully, Jonathan, 29, 361
McDougall, Joseph, 100
McDougall, William, 219, 220, 221
McFarran, Sarah, 156
McGee, D'Arcy, 31
McGibbon, Robert Davidson, 141, 145
McInnes, Thomas, 629n52
McKay, Alexander, 500
McKenna, James, 254
McKeown, Harrison, 540
McKinlay, Archibald, 250
McLean, Archibald, 488
McLean, Thomas Alexander, 488
McLeod, James, 76
McMahon, Hugh, 406
McMartin, Daniel, 246
McMullen, James, 362
McPhillips, Albert Edward, 89
Meloche, Osias, 338
Mercer, Andrew, 449
Meredith, William Ralph, 419
Mignault Pierre-Basille, 142, 143,
    144, 149, 160, 163, 169, 170, 174,
    181, 182
Miller, Hazel, 316
Miller, Mary, 172
Miller, Ruth, 316

Mills, David, 70, 85, 249, 307, 438,
    575, 586
Mills, James, 392
Mistahimawaska, 458
Mistawsis (Big Child), 240
Mitchell, Peter, 375
Molson, John Thomas, 189
Monck, Charles Stanley (4th Viscount
    Monck), 25
Mondelet, Charles, 113–14
Monk, Samuel Cornwallis, 163
Moore, Thomas, 313–14
Morris, Alexander, 123, 231, 233,
    237–41, 253, 466, 467, 468
Morris, Christine, 239
Morse, Charles, 203
Mourlon, Frédéric, 142
Mowat, Oliver, 29, 37, 55, 62, 69,
    80, 87, 91, 105, 123, 201, 213,
    388, 389, 407–8, 419, 434, 436,
    529, 575, 604
Moxon, Arthur, 196
Moylan, James Gorge, 447
Munro, George, 194
Musgrave, Anthony, 48

Napolitano, Angelina, 454, 456
Nault, André, 227
Nesbitt, Wallace, 86
Newcombe, E.L., 124
Nolin, Joseph, 242
Nordheimer, Albert, 551–2
Norton, John, 281, 282

O'Meara, Arthur, 254
O'Reilly, Peter, 252
O'Sullivan, Dennis, 198
Oliver, Frank, 111, 286, 287, 482, 590
Onderdonk, Andrew, 580
One Arrow, 261

Osler, Britton Bath, 190, 258, 259,
    263, 265
Osler, Featherston, 406, 554, 557, 558

Pagnuelo, Siméon, 154
Palmer, Acalus Lockwood, 93, 114,
    555, 557
Palmer, Edward, 97, 491
Pambrun, Pierre Chrysologue, 459
Papineau, Louis Joseph, 26
Paquette, Clara, 157
Parslow, Samuel, 456
Pasqua, Chief Joseph, 242
Paterson, William, 279
Patterson, Christopher, 85, 524
Pedley, Frank, 271, 684n9
Peguis, Chief, 470
Peters, James Horsfield, 491
Pidcock, Reginald, 301
Pinsler, Jacob, 612
Pitblado, Issac, 551
Poole, Henry, 386
Pope, James, 49
Poulin, Dame, 154
Poundmaker, 241, 255, 256, 261
Powassin, Chief, 242
Powell, Israel Wood, 248–9, 292,
    299, 311
Power, Augustus, 124, 452
Prendergast, James Emile Pierre, 99, 604
Prince, William Stratton, 449
Prud'homme, Louis Arthur, 99
Pyke, Loran, 290

Ramsden, Richard, 172
Ratté, Antoine, 504–5
Rayner, Benjamin, 540
Rayner, Elizabeth, 540
Reed, Hayter, 271, 290, 295, 315,
    317, 319

Reeve, William Albert, 192, 202, 204
Richards, William Buell, 59, 60, 83, 84, 85, 492, 720n78
Richardson, Hugh, 77, 257–64, 266, 268
Richtôt, Noël-Joseph, 225
Riddell, Fanny, 552
Riddell, William Renwick, 191, 495
Riel, Jean-Louis, 220
Riel, Louis, 7, 12, 17, 19, 77, 153, 190, 218, 220–1, 222–3, 225, 227, 228, 229, 255–6, 257–69, 344, 346, 422, 426, 427, 450, 451, 453, 454, 474, 601, 603, 605, 608, 668n18
Riskeyak (She Wins), 458
Ritchie, William Bruce Almon, 186
Ritchie, William Johnstone, 54, 62, 82, 83, 84, 85, 188, 200, 425, 605
Robinson, Agnes, 171
Robinson, Christopher, 204, 258, 608
Robinson, John Beverly, 258, 608
Roblin, Rodmond, 51
Robson, John, 47, 458
Roque, O.A., 414
Rose, John, 34, 38
Ross, George William, 389
Ross, William, 541
Rouleau, Charles Borromée, 257, 459
Routhier, Adolphe-Basile, 162, 174, 653n3
Roy, Francois, 259
Royal, Joseph, 474, 604
Russell, Benjamin, 184, 195
Ryan, Matthew, 77
Ryerson, Egerton, 200

Sangster, John, 542
Sapir, Edward, 302
Schiller, Victoria, 163
Schultz, John Christian, 220, 222, 227, 229, 715n15

Schultz, Samuel Davies, 212, 666n63
Scott, Alfred, 223
Scott, Duncan Campbell, 271, 302, 316, 322, 325
Scott, Richard, 357, 436
Scott, Thomas, 7, 222–3, 256
Sedgwick, Robert, 85, 194, 426, 608
Seymour, Frederick, 47
Shakespeare, Noah, 581, 583
Sharpe, W. Prescott, 459
Shingwauk, Chief, 281
Shortis, Valentine, 452
Sifton, Arthur, 111
Sifton, Clifford, 286, 322, 323, 340, 457, 481, 482, 604
Simmons, William, 111
Simpson, Wemyss, 239
Singh, Munshi, 593
Sirhali, Gurdit Singh, 592
Smart, David, 557–8
Smart, Emilie, 558
Smart, James, 271, 321, 603
Smith, Donald, 223
Smith, Goldwin, 105
Smith, Montagu, 64
Smith, William (Amor De Cosmos), 47
Smith, William, 98
Smithe, William, 253
Spragge, John, 59
Spragge, William, 270, 285, 291, 306, 307, 311
Sproat, Gilbert, 250, 251, 252, 300
St-Laurent, Louis, 182
Stanley, Lord Frederick Arthur, 542
Steele, Sam, 53
Stephen, James, 8, 426, 442
Stephens, Charles, 353
Stock, David, 549, 551
Stock, Mary, 549

Strong, Samuel Henry, 66–7, 83, 84,
  85, 103, 124, 533, 609, 638n30
Stuart, Jane, 534
Stuart, John, 534
Sutherland, Robert, 210

Taché, Alexander, 604, 605, 607
Talbot, Peter, 111
Taschereau, Henri-Elzéar, 62, 85, 86,
  167, 198, 426, 494, 609
Taschereau, Jean-Thomas, 83, 84
Thévenot d'Essaule de
  Savigny, Claude-François, 144
Thibault, Joseph, 452
Thompson, John Sparrow David, 107,
  109, 114, 194, 261, 426, 428, 436,
  441, 443, 459, 494, 542, 607–8, 610
Thomson, Daniel, 188
Tilley, Leonard, 26, 30, 36, 83, 625n6
Tobias, George, 282
'Tom,' Chief, 297
Tomlins, John, 551
Tompkins, Hannah, 544
Tompkins, John, 544
Torrens, Robert, 486
Townshend, Charles, 110
Travis, Jerimiah, 198
Trudel, François-Xavier, 436
Trutch, Joseph, 247, 249, 252, 253,
  331, 571
Tuck, William Henry, 556
Tupper, Charles, 26, 30, 42, 103, 105,
  107, 109, 610, 616, 625n6, 625n10,
  644–5n102
Tyrwhitt-Drake, Montague, 128

Valade, François-Xavier, 268
Vankoughnet, Edith May, 551
Vankoughnet, Lawrence, 270–1, 280,
  285, 307, 310, 313, 316, 317, 318

Vankoughnet, Philip, 552
Vanwart, James A., 114
Viau, Cordelia, 456
Vilbon, Charles-Albert, 142, 651n48
von Savigny, Freidrich, 141
Vowell, Arthur, 302

Wade, Frederick, 608
Wahsahgamass, 459, 460
Walbank, William McLea, 338–9
Walkem, George, 78, 128, 249, 580
Walker, Abraham, 210
Wallace, James, 259
Wallbridge, Lewis, 105, 266
Walton, Frederick Parker, 141, 145,
  170, 182, 196
Wananosh, William, 280
Wandering Spirit, 255
Wanduta, 303
Watson, Lord William, 68, 69, 70, 71
Wawasehowein, 459, 460
Webster, Dame, 154
Weldon, Richard Chapman, 195, 196
Wells, Sarah, 540
Wetmore, Andrew Rainsford, 556
Wetmore, Edward Ludlow, 77
Wetmore, Thomas, 531–2
White Pup, 317
White, Albert Scott, 645n110
White, John, 283
White, Mary Matilda, 548
White, Solomon, 280
White, Thomas, 290
Whiteaves, Joseph, 545, 552
Whitney, Henry Melville, 385
Whitney, James P., 418
Wicksteed, Gustavus, 424, 705n4
Willison, John Stephen, 390
Wilmot, Lemuel, 361, 375, 491
Wilson, Adam, 59, 554

Wilson, R.N., 285–6
Wolseley, Garnet, 226–7, 667n2
Wood, Edmund Burke, 227, 228,
     284, 467
Workman, Elizabeth, 454
Wotherspoon, Ivan, 197

Wright, Robert, 428
Wurtele, Jonathan, 181

Youmans, Amos, 331, 457–8
Young, John (1st Baron Lisgar), 44, 222
Young, William, 36, 136–7, 356

Topical Index

agriculture, 4, 31, 151, 168, 176, 232, 237–8, 352, 376, 394, 412, 419, 482–4, 494–5, 503, 574, 590; and Indigenous peoples, 232, 236–8, 241, 243, 245, 252, 255, 297, 302–3, 304, 306, 309–10, 311–12, 319, 334, 338, 344, 347, 464

allegiance, 46, 221, 264–5

Arctic Islands, 51–2

banking, 15, 64, 67–8, 125, 138, 155, 179, 198, 354, 359, 378, 523, 524, 533–4; federal regulation of, 380–4, 412–16; Newfoundland bank crisis, 383–4

bilingualism, 83–4, 150, 182–3, 221, 223, 569

Black Canadians: and criminal justice, 19, 455, 598–9; discrimination in court, 425, 595–6, 660–1; segregated schools, 596–8, 614–15; settlement, 594. *See also* immigration; lawyers

boundaries: Alaska, 45, 47; provincial changes, 50–3; Yukon, 52–3

British Columbia: anti-Asian discrimination, 12, 19, 209, 569–70, 576–8, 589; Chinese, 137, 570–3, 576–86; Indigenous policy, 247–55; Japanese, 72, 573–5, 585–6; South Asians, 589–94

Canada Land Law Amendment Association, 487–9

Canada Land Survey, 243, 475–9

Canadian Bar Association, 12, 186–7, 190; and national legal culture, 213–14

Canadian Pacific Railway, 151, 170–2, 189, 252, 284, 285, 380, 381–2, 388, 390, 416, 481, 570–1, 580–1, 689n22, 718n55

Canadian Party (Manitoba), 219, 220, 222, 223, 226, 227

capital punishment: Indigenous peoples, 450–1, 453, 457–60;

capital punishment (*cont.*)
pardon process, 450–4; pardon statistics, 452–4, 456; public hanging, 451–2; women, 454, 456–7
case law: case reports, 135, 137, 202; courts of coordinate rank and stare decisis, 137–9, 608; English Court of Appeal decisions and stare decisis in Canadian courts, 139–40; influence of British and American cases, 135–8, 145–7
Catholic church, 25, 346, 535, 599–600, 603–4; influence in Quebec, 113–14, 152–4. *See also* residential schools
Charlottetown Conference, 25–6, 27, 49, 625n6
children. See *Civil Code of Lower Canada*; enfranchisement; marriage
citizenship. *See* nationality
Civil Code of Lower Canada, 5–6, 11, 117–18, 121–2, 140–2, 146–7, 151, 562; amendments, 149; corporations, 651n57; and English law, 145–6; family law, 154–64; and French-Canadian identity, 144–5; legal literature, 11, 141–5; obligations, 165–77; property, 177–82, 508
common law: in imperial context, 6; and relationship to the economy, 379–80
Confederation: accession of British Columbia, 41–4, 46–9; accession of Manitoba, 12, 225–6; accession of Prince Edward Island, 49–50; creation of Alberta and Saskatchewan, 50–1; creation of Northwest Territories, 43–4, 50–1; creation of Yukon Territory, 52–3; economic and demographic changes, 3, 351–2, 370; historical background, 24–7; Lower Canada, 25–6, 33–4. *See also* federalism
corporate law
—general incorporation: defined, 134–5; exclusions, 359; federal and provincial jurisdiction, 353–6, 360–2; incorporation process and regulations, 356–8, 362; number of incorporations, 363–5
—limited liability, 134, 352, 356–7, 360–1, 366–7, 370
—special act incorporations: defined, 365–6; in the Maritimes, 370–1; number of special act incorporations, 367–70
Council of Assiniboia, 220, 228, 470–1
courts, Chancery: in BC and Manitoba, 93–4; fusion of equity and common law courts in Ontario, 90–2, 92–5; in the Maritimes and Newfoundland, 93
courts, county and district, 34–5, 37, 75, 78–9, 429, 430, 708n4; absence in Quebec, 95; appointments and reputation of judges, 35, 99, 102–4, 212; and the *BNA Act*, 34–5; Manitoba, PEI, and NS, 96–8; Ontario, 92–3, 94–5, 97; small claims courts, 100–1
courts, Judicial Committee of the Privy Council, 6–7, 10, 11, 19, 43, 55, 57, 62–71, 81–2, 115, 135–6, 139–40, 189, 228–9, 230–1, 378–9, 500, 534–5, 538, 558, 580, 600, 605, 606–9, 611; and Indigenous land rights, 230–1, 246; and industrial liability in Quebec, 171–3, 174, 416; and property in Quebec, 181; and Quebec, general, 145–6, 153, 182; and the Riel trial, 267–8

courts, specialized: divorce courts,
537–41; women's court
(Ontario), 561
courts, Superior Courts General,
34, 429–30; Court of Queen's
Bench (Manitoba), 76, 263,
266, 431–2, 532, 606–7; Court
of Queen's Bench (New
Brunswick), 54; Court of Queen's
Bench (Ontario), 597–8; Court
of Queen's Bench (Quebec), 11,
67, 88, 171, 173–4, 536; Superior
Court of Quebec, 159, 162,
173–4; Supreme Court of British
Columbia and discriminatory
legislation, 577–80; Supreme
Court of PEI, 491; Supreme
Court of the North-West
Territories, 77–8
courts, Supreme Court of Canada,
6, 10, 11, 19, 254–5, 377–8,
391–3, 443, 501–2, 507–8, 515,
531–2, 587, 607–9, 613, 653n3;
and courts of coordinate rank,
139; and the division of powers,
59–65, 68–9; early judges,
82–3, 85; early reputation, 81–2,
84–7; founding, 75, 79–80; and
Indigenous land rights, 231,
254–5; liability and Quebec
civil law, 170–4; and married
women's property, 138, 532–5;
reference power, 81; and the
Supreme Court of BC, 78–9; and
US cases, 137. See also judges
Cree, 232, 233–4, 239, 240–1, 245, 255,
310, 319, 344, 457, 458–9, 536
criminal law: capital offences, 16–17,
424–5; codification movement, 425;
development of the Criminal Code,
426–8; establishment of criminal

justice systems in Manitoba and BC,
431; establishment of the criminal
justice system in the Northwest
Territories, 431–3; federalism, 421;
and 'liberty,' 8–9, 16–17; post-
Confederation legislation, 423–6,
469–71; prosecution, 429–31; types
of offences, 423. See also Criminal
Code of Canada
criminal trial: accused's rights,
439–41, 484–6; appeal, 441–4. See
also capital punishment; juries
Crown: federalizing of, 35–9, 40–4;
relation to Indigenous peoples,
5, 40; royal prerogative, 41–3,
52, 61–2, 68, 82, 229, 260, 421,
450–1. See also governors general;
lieutenant governors
currency, 32, 382–3, 384

debt, 48, 50, 97, 100, 167, 178, 185–6,
384, 526–7
debtor creditor law: bankruptcy and
insolvency distinguished, 371–2,
373–8; and commercial morality,
374–6; federal and provincial
jurisdiction, 371–2, 378–9, 403,
409–10; imprisonment for debt,
149, 371–3; usury laws, 383
Department of Indian Affairs, 270–1,
273, 286–7, 292, 295–6, 302, 311,
312–13, 317, 318–19, 321, 323–6,
338, 339–41, 342–3, 347, 515–16,
536–7; policies in Western Canada,
296–8, 320. See also Indigenous
peoples and Canadian law
disallowance, 27–8, 31, 37–9, 53,
71–3, 96, 99, 575, 576, 582, 604.
See also federalism; lieutenant
governors
division of powers. See federalism

divorce: judicial divorce, 537–43;
public opinion of, 18, 541–2, 601–2;
in Quebec, 158–60
—parliamentary divorce, 544–52;
adultery, 548–50; demographics,
551–2; figures, 544–7, 548–9;
process, 546–8; public opinion of,
18, 541–2, 601–2

economy: banks and credit unions,
151–2, 155, 178–9; economic
development, 26–7, 49–50, 492,
503, 504, 506; Montreal Stock
Exchange, 151–2. *See also* banking
employment law: *Breaches of
Contract Act*, 396–7; common law
of employment, 395–6; master
and servant law, 395–8. *See also*
labour law
enfranchisement (Indigenous
persons), 273–83; and children,
276–7; Indigenous reception of,
276–7, 280–2; life estates, 274–6,
342; process, 277–80, 281; property
and land rights, 273–4, 277–8,
279–80; and women, 276–7

farming. *See* agriculture
federalism: compact theory and,
55–7, 632n81; criminal law power,
64–5; division of powers, 18–19,
25–30, 30–6, 61–2, 64; legislative
power, 28, 54, 576; licensing
power, 59–60, 65–7; peace, order,
and good government power,
30–1, 57, 69–70; police power,
59; property and civil rights,
33–4, 35, 57–9, 62, 63–4; provincial
rights movement, 37, 55, 62, 70,
71–3; regulation, 379–80, 392–3;

residuary power, 30–1; royal
prerogative, 41, 61–2; taxation,
67–8; trade and commerce power,
32, 54–6, 59–61, 62, 64–5, 68,
577, 632n85. *See also* banking;
disallowance; labour laws;
mining; railways
Fenians, 27, 227, 264

Gitxsan: and criminal law, 331–2;
European encroachment and
settler disputes, 330–2, 334–6. *See
also* Indigenous law
governors general, 28, 34, 37, 40–1,
42–3, 44–5, 81, 97, 99, 228–9, 357–8,
421, 451, 477, 490, 546, 590, 601

homestead settlement: beyond the
prairies, 484–5; block settlement,
480; criteria, 479–80; Dominion
Land Survey, 466, 476–8;
objectives and goals, 479–80,
483; pre-emption, 480, 483–4;
ranching, 482
Hudson's Bay Company, 218–22,
232, 240, 470
Huron-Wendat: Wyandot of
Anderdon, 280

immigration: Blacks, 598–9; Chinese
in BC, 570–1, 580–1; federal
policies, 590–2; Sikhs in BC, 589,
590–3
imprisonment: establishment of
federal penitentiaries, 446; Kingston
Penitentiary, 445–6, 447–8; Mercer
Reformatory for Women, 448–50;
Ontario Central Prison, 448–9;
parole, 448; prison reform, 447–8;
purpose, 16–17, 446–7; reform

advocates, 447; Royal Commission
on Penitentiaries, 448–9
Indian agents, 13, 76, 285–6, 294,
297–8, 299–302, 312, 320, 336, 516
Indian reserves, 235–6, 247–8,
249–54, 255, 274, 293–4, 309,
615; railways, roads, and public
works, 284, 287; relocation, 287–9;
surrender of reserve lands, 285–6;
surrender requirement, 283–4,
286–7; Walbank Survey, 336–41;
white squatters, 270, 284, 679n28
Indigenous law, 14, 328–50; chiefs
and matriarchs, 339–40; dispute
resolution, 330–1, 342–5; and
European settlement, 329; fishing
in BC, 332–3; impact of legal
positivism, 329; and the *Indian
Act*, 341–3, 347; and land rights,
334–6, 338–9, 346; land tenure and
timber laws, 338–9; leadership and
governance structures, 289–90;
succession laws, 339, 342
Indigenous peoples and Canadian
law, 689; assimilationist policies,
general, 5, 13–14, 273–4, 304,
306, 317–18; 'civilization' and
progress, 152, 219, 223, 227, 247,
251, 272, 278, 291–2, 297–9, 307–9,
313–14, 321–3; criminalization of
prairie dances, 302–3; deposition
of chiefs, 296–8; franchise, 282–3;
governance structures, 289–92,
292–4, 340–1; hunting and fishing
rights, 236, 243, 246, 250–1;
Indigenous land title at common
law, 229–30, 233, 244, 247–9, 253–5,
461; legal definition of 'Indian,'
271; pre-Confederation legislation,
270. *See also* capital punishment;

enfranchisement; Indian reserves;
Métis; numbered treaties; potlatch;
Tamanawas dance
industrialization, 16, 402, 503; and
the family, 413–14, 449; in Quebec,
151. *See also* labour laws
insurance, 172, 175, 176, 259, 419–20;
regulation of, 62

judges: appointment power, 36;
criminal procedure, 437–8;
judiciary provisions of the
BNA Act, 34–6; patronage and
appointments, 10, 87–9, 104–11,
112; reputation of the judiciary
and scandals, 112–16; salaries,
101–4, 105–6; tenure, 35, 75, 98–9.
See also Name Index
juries, 98, 147, 171–2, 430–1; grand
juries, decline and abolition
movement, 434–6; in the Northwest
Territories, 431–2; trial juries,
decline in significance, 6, 437–9.
See also trial of Louis Riel

Kahnawà:ke, 152, 295, 330, 336–41,
347, 689n22. *See also* seigneuralism
Komagata Maru, 592–4

labour laws: arbitration and
conciliation, 408–11; child labour,
386, 388–9, 412–15, 560, 573;
employers' liability, 415–18; health
and safety, 16, 401, 411–13, 414,
576, 587; industrial employers
and liability, 169–75; liability law
reforms (Quebec), 175–7; strikes
and workplace disputes, 15–16,
396, 401–7. *See also* trade unions;
workers' compensation

land law: expropriation, 237,
287, 389, 492–5; land and
improvement, 472–4, 478–9;
owner-occupier model, 461–2;
registration, 462, 485–6; Torrens
system, 7–8, 199, 208, 485–9.
See also land use regulation;
Métis; Prince Edward Island;
succession law

land use regulation: building codes,
497–8; nuisance, 499, 503–7;
planning, 498–9, 548–9; restrictive
covenants, 499–502; zoning
bylaws, 496–7, 507–8

large law firms: emergence of, 11–12,
187–8; partnerships and salaries,
188; work and clients, 188–90

law journals: *Canadian Bar Review*,
201–2; *Canadian Law Times*, 201,
202–3, 204–5; *La Revue Légale*, 202;
short lived journals, 202; target
audience, 197–8

lawyer-scholars, emergence of,
199–200; influence of French law
in Quebec, 142–3, 144–5; local law,
198; use of English and American
texts, 199

lawyers: Black, 210–11; county
attorneys, 430; demographics, 209,
213; family, 190–1; Francophone,
182–3, 212; Jewish, 211–12;
number of and demographics,
184–7, 205–7; as political
representatives, 185–6; voluntary
associations, 186–7, 190; women
lawyers, 211, 212–13. *See also*
provincial law societies

legal education: authority of law
societies over, 192, 193, 194–6; in
common law Canada, 192, 194–7;

notaries, 194, 209; professoriate,
192, 194–5, 199–200, 204; in
Quebec, 141, 193–4; US influence,
192–3, 194, 195, 197. *See also*
university legal education

legal literature: case law
compilations in Quebec, 144;
commentaries on Civil Code,
141–3; growth in output, 197–8

liberalism, 588, 616; economic,
140, 165, 178, 579; laissez
faire, 415; legal, 70–1; liberal
individualism, 57, 401, 407; in
Quebec, 140, 151–2, 153–4. *See
also* trade unions

liberty and the law, 5, 8–9, 16–17

lieutenant governors, 76, 97, 218–20,
229–30, 233–4, 247, 331, 357–8,
450–1; powers of, 37, 38–9, 40,
43–4, 50, 629n52; and royal
prerogative, 41–2, 61–2, 68, 450–1,
633n93

linguistic minorities, 599–600, 603,
610–11, 614–15. *See also* Manitoba
schools crisis

Manitoba schools crisis, 19–20, 201,
246, 600–11

marriage: between Indigenous and
non-Indigenous persons, 271, 343,
536–7; child custody, presumption
of father's right, 552–60; child
custody, Quebec, 162–4; child
support, Quebec, 156–7; federal/
provincial jurisdiction, 535–6;
husband's duties in Quebec,
154–5; Indigenous custom, 513,
536–7, 541; judicial separation,
Quebec, 160–2, 164; and
property in Quebec, 155–7;

solemnization, 535–6; spousal abuse, 566–8. *See also* Civil Code; divorce; married women's property; succession law

married women's property: debt, 526–7; interprovincial statutory borrowing, 133–4; judicial interpretation (problems), 526–8, 532–3; post-confederation statutory reforms, 9, 17–18, 522–5, 528–33; pre-confederation, 522. *See also* succession law

Métis: Buffalo hunt, legal framework, 343–4; and Confederation, 9, 219; Declaration of the People of Rupert's Land and the North West, 221–3; definition, 667n6; and Indigenous title, 17, 462–3; land grant in Manitoba Act, 462, 467–9, 477; land grants based on customary law, 470–5; land surveys and allotments, 346–7; laws of St Laurent, 344–6; List of Rights, 221, 225; Métis National Committee, 220; Rebellion of 1885, 8, 12, 227–9, 255–7; Red River Resistance, 218–27; Scrip, 467; trial of Ambroise Lépine (1874), 227–8; trials after 1885 rebellion, 256–7. *See also* trial of Louis Riel

mining, 246, 335, 370, 384–5, 503; expropriation, 493; provincial Workmen's Association, 387; public-private revenue (Ontario), 387–8; safety, 385–7, 388–9, 412; strikes and workplace conflict, 405, 409–11. *See also* trade unions

Mohawk Institute, 306, 309, 312, 316, 341–2

Mohawks, 290, 297, 336, 339–40. *See also* Kahnawà:ke

national policy, 187, 351, 370, 390, 426, 475, 580

nationality, 45–6

naturalization, 32, 45–6, 71, 264–5, 577

Northwest Mounted Police, 8, 52–3, 76, 239, 321, 345–6; establishment, 431–2; role in criminal justice system, 432–3

Northwest Territories, 16, 43–4, 50, 53, 74, 76–7, 118, 205–6, 218–19, 226, 229–31, 260–1, 346, 357, 433

Orange Order, 219, 223, 226–7, 267

police magistrates, 429, 561

potlatch: Christian converts, 300; description of, 298–9; European reception and criminalization of, 299–302, 303, 329, 334

Prince Edward Island: landholding system, 489; landlord buyouts, 489–92

Prohibition, 57–60, 64, 65–7, 69

prostitution, 450, 565–6

Protestantism, 25, 164, 213, 219, 220, 300

provincial law societies: county and local law associations, 208–9; establishment of, 205–6; governing bodies, 207–8; influence in the United States, 214; in the North-West Territories, 2–5, 6; in Quebec, 208; resistance in Nova Scotia and Ontario, 2–7, 8, 206–7; statutory powers, 205, 207

provincial rights movement, 37, 55, 62, 70, 71–3, 575, 604

Quebec: francophone nationalism, 153–4, 603; mixed legal tradition, 5–6, 181–2. *See also* liberalism
Quebec civil code. See *Civil Code of Lower Canada*
Quebec conference, 26, 28, 30–1, 49

racial discrimination: anti-Black discrimination, 594–9; Asiatic Exclusion League, 586; discriminatory statutes in BC, 18–19, 572–4, 581–3, 650–1; discriminatory statutes in Newfoundland and Saskatchewan, 586–7; federal response to discriminatory provincial statutes, 574–5, 581–2, 587–8; head tax, 572, 583–5, 586, 589; and language, 576, 585–6; white slave trade, 586–7. *See also* immigration
railways, 7, 168–9, 170, 171–2, 232, 284, 329, 334–6, 359, 367, 404–5, 574; Board of Railway Commissioners, 353, 380–1; expropriation, 493–4; federal regulation of, 389–92; and homesteaders, 477, 481; intercontinental, 26–7; PEI debt, 50; rates, 391; safety regulations, 414; transcontinental, 48–9. *See also* Canadian Pacific Railway
religious minorities: Jewish students in Quebec, 611–12. *See also* Manitoba schools crisis
residential schools, 13–14; attendance and resistance to sending children, 319–22; boarding and industrial schools, 308–9; Bryce's report, 323–6; conditions, 314–15; establishment of, 312; federal funding and cost, 312–13, 322–3, 327; gender roles, 309; Indigenous leadership, 307–8, 319; lack of regulation and oversight, 305, 312; missionary societies, 306, 310; numbers and locations, 304–6, 322; physical and sexual abuse, 316–17; psychological abuse, 317–18; quality of teachers, 315–16; role of churches, 311–12, 326–7; stated goals, 309–12
Rupert's Land, 51, 118, 218, 221, 227–8

seigneurialism, 178, 179–81, 720n78; Mohawks of Kahnawà:ke, 336
Senate: composition of, 27–30
Six Nations, 277, 290–1, 295; day schools, 341; governing autonomy, 343; Grand Council, 342–3; population growth, 372; The Great Law of Peace, 342–3. *See also* Indigenous law
sole proprietorships and partnerships, 353
statute law: copying of statutes between provinces, 133–5; legislative process, 119; number of statutes, post Confederation, 121–2; reception of, 118–19
statutory consolidations, post Confederation: in British Columbia, 126–31; commissioners of, 123–4; complications, 124–6; in Ontario, 132–3; organization and naming, 120–3; purpose, 120
succession law: campaign to restore homestead dower, 512; illegitimate

children, 513; Indigenous peoples,
515–16; land, 509; married women,
widows, and dower, 509–13; move
to partible inheritance, 508–9;
personal property, 509; testate
succession, 514–15
Superintendent-General of Indian
Affairs, 13, 238, 248, 270, 274, 278,
281, 282, 286–7, 291, 292, 294, 302,
303, 322, 340, 493, 516, 536, 566

Tamanawas dance, 298, 299, 300,
301, 682n59
temperance and social/moral reform
movements, 58, 64, 519, 529;
Women's Christian Temperance
Movement, 542, 566–7
trade unions: Canadian Labour
Union, 409, 702n31; *Criminal
Law Amendment Act*, 399, 400–1,
403; early history, 398; legality
of, 398–9; Provincial Workmen's
Association, 409–10; Trades and
Labor Congress of Canada, 177,
404, 409, 411, 414
treaties with Indigenous peoples,
5, 12, 32; Indigenous and
European understandings of
treaties, 233, 241–5; Indigenous
goals and motivations, 232, 246;
negotiations, 238–41; protocol,
239; settlement and resource
development, 231–2, 234–5, 265;
terms, 234–9, 255–9
treaties with other states: Canadian
power with respect to, 39–40,
44–5; international, 45

trial of Louis Riel, 12, 431; appeals,
266–7; evidence and witnesses,
259–60; execution, 268–9; fitness
and insanity, 265–6, 268; judge and
lawyers, 258–9, 261–2; jury, 262–3;
statute and charges, 263–5; venue,
260–1
trusts: and Indigenous peoples,
286–7, 342; in Quebec, 148, 180–1,
194–5; role in married women's
property, 521, 523, 524
Truth and Reconciliation
Commission, 314, 686n30,
865n24

university legal education: in Alberta,
Saskatchewan, and BC, 195–6;
in the Maritimes, 192–3, 194–5; in
Ontario and Quebec, 193–4, 196–7

Windigos, 458–9, 460
women: abortion, 456, 562–3,
564; feminism, 563–4; maternal
feminism, 163, 553, 560; National
Council of Women, 213; seduction,
561–3, 564–5; separate spheres,
519–20, 533–4, 560; sexual
offences, 565–6; suffrage, 520–1,
524, 529, 531, 591. See also *Civil
Code of Lower Canada*; divorce;
lawyers; marriage; married
women's property
workers' compensation, 393, 401,
418–20; in Quebec, 169, 170–1,
173–7
Workingman's Protective
Association, 572, 581

2022   Jim Phillips, Philip Girard, and R. Blake Brown, *A History of Law in Canada Volume Two: Law for the New Dominion, 1867–1914*
Barry Wright, Susan Binnie, and Eric Tucker eds., *Canadian State Trials Volume 5: World War, Cold War, and Challenges to Sovereignty, 1939–1990*
Constance Backhouse, *Reckoning with Racism: Police, Judges, and the RDS Case*

2021   Daniel Rück, *The Laws and the Land: The Settler Colonial Invasion of Kahnawà:ke in Nineteenth-Century Canada*
Martine Valois, Ian Greene, Craig Forcese, and Peter McCormick, eds., *The Federal Court of Appeal and the Federal Court: 50 Years of History*
Colin Campbell and Robert Raizenne, *A History of Canadian Income Tax Volume I: The Income War Tax Act 1917–1948*
Lyndsay Campbell, *Truth and Privilege: Libel Law in Massachusetts and Nova Scotia, 1820–1840*

2020   Heidi Bohaker, *Doodem and Council Fire: Anishinaabe Governance through Alliances*
Carolyn Strange, *The Death Penalty and Sex Murder in Canadian History*

2019   Harry W. Arthurs, *Connecting the Dots: The Life of an Academic Lawyer*
Eric H. Reiter, *Wounded Feelings: Litigating Emotions in Quebec, 1870–1950*

2018   Philip Girard, Jim Phillips, and R. Blake Brown, *A History of Law in Canada Volume One: Beginnings to 1866*
Suzanne Chiodo, *The Class Actions Controversy: The Origins and Development of the Ontario Class Proceedings Act*

2017   Constance Backhouse, *Claire L'Heureux-Dubé: A Life*
Dennis G. Molinaro, *An Exceptional Law: Section 98 and the Emergency State, 1919–1936*

2016   Lori Chambers, *A Legal History of Adoption in Ontario, 1921–2015*
Bradley Miller, *Borderline Crime: Fugitive Criminals and the Challenge of the Border, 1819–1914*
James Muir, *Law, Debt, and Merchant Power: The Civil Courts of Eighteenth-Century Halifax*

2015   Barry Wright, Eric Tucker and Susan Binnie eds., *Canadian State Trials Volume 4: War Measures and the Repression of Radicalism, 1914–39*
David Fraser, *Honorary Protestants: A Socio-Legal History of the Jewish School Question in Montreal*
C. Ian Kyer, *A Thirty Years War: The Failed Public/Private Partnership that Spurred the Creation of the Toronto Transit Commission, 1891–1921*
Dale Gibson, *Law, Life, and Government at Red River: Settlement and Governance, 1812–1872*

2014   Christopher Moore, *The Court of Appeal for Ontario 1792–2013*
Paul Craven, *Petty Justice: Low Law and the Sessions System in Charlotte County, New Brunswick, 1785–1867*
Thomas GW Telfer, *Ruin and Redemption: The Struggle for a Canadian Bankruptcy Law, 1867–1919*
Dominique Clément, *Equality Deferred: Sex Discrimination and British Columbia's Human Rights Code, 1953–1984*

2013   Roy McMurtry, *Memoirs and Reflections*
Charlotte Grey, *The Massey Murder: A Maid, Her Master, and the Trial that Shocked a Nation*
C. Ian Kyer, *Lawyers, Families, and Businesses: The Shaping of a Bay Street Law Firm, 1863–1963*
G. Blaine Baker and Donald Fyson, eds., *Essays in the History of Canadian Law Volume XI: Quebec and the Canadas*

2012   R. Blake Brown, *Arming and Disarming: A History of Gun Control in Canada*
Eric Tucker, James Muir, and Bruce Ziff, eds., *Property on Trial: Canadian Cases in Context*
Barrington Walker, ed., *The African Canadian Legal Odyssey: Historical Essays*
Shelley Gavigan, *Hunger, Horses, and Government Men: Criminal Law on the Aboriginal Plains, 1870–1905*

2011   Robert J. Sharpe, *The Lazier Murder: Prince Edward County, 1884*
Philip Girard, *Lawyers and Legal Culture in British North America: Beamish Murdoch of Halifax*
John McLaren, *Dewigged, Bothered, and Bewildered: British Colonial Judges on Trial 1800–1900*
Lesley Erickson, *Westward Bound: Sex, Violence, the Law, and the Making of a Settler Society*

2010   Judy Fudge and Eric Tucker, eds., *Work on Trial: Canadian Labour Law Struggles*
Christopher Moore, *The British Columbia Court of Appeal: The First Hundred Years*
Frederick Vaughan, *Viscount Haldane: `The Wicked Step-father of the Canadian Constitution'*
Barrington Walker, *Race on Trial: Black Defendants in Ontario's Criminal Courts, 1858–1958*

2009   William Kaplan, *Canadian Maverick: The Life and Times of Ivan C. Rand* R. Blake Brown, *A Trying Question: The Jury in Nineteenth-Century Canada*
Barry Wright and Susan Binnie, eds., *Canadian State Trials Volume 3: Political Trials and Security Measures 1840–1914*

Robert J. Sharpe, *The Last Day, the Last Hour: The Currie Libel Trial* (paperback edition with a new preface)

2008   Constance Backhouse, *Carnal Crimes: Sexual Assault Law in Canada, 1900–1975*
Jim Phillips, R. Roy McMurtry, and John T. Saywell, eds., *Essays in the History of Canadian Law Volume X: A Tribute to Peter N. Oliver*
Greg Taylor, *The Law of the Land: The Advent of the Torrens System in Canada*
Hamar Foster, Benjamin Berger, and A.R. Buck, eds., *The Grand Experiment: Law and Legal Culture in British Settler Societies*

2007   Robert Sharpe and Patricia McMahon, *The Persons Case: The Origins and Legacy of the Fight for Legal Personhood*
Lori Chambers, *Misconceptions: Unmarried Motherhood and the Ontario Children of Unmarried Parents Act, 1921–1969*
Jonathan Swainger, ed., *A History of the Supreme Court of Alberta*
Martin Friedland, *My Life in Crime and Other Academic Adventures*

2006   Donald Fyson, *Magistrates, Police, and People: Everyday Criminal Justice in Quebec and Lower Canada, 1764–1837*
Dale Brawn, *The Court of Queen's Bench of Manitoba, 1870–1950: A Biographical History*
R.C.B. Risk, *A History of Canadian Legal Thought: Collected Essays*, edited and introduced by G. Blaine Baker and Jim Phillips

2005   Philip Girard, *Bora Laskin: Bringing Law to Life*
Christopher English, ed., *Essays in the History of Canadian Law Volume IX – Two Islands: Newfoundland and Prince Edward Island*
Fred Kaufman, *Searching for Justice: An Autobiography*

2004   Philip Girard, Jim Phillips, and Barry Cahill, eds., *The Supreme Court of Nova Scotia, 1754–2004: From Imperial Bastion to Provincial Oracle*
Frederick Vaughan, *Aggressive in Pursuit: The Life of Justice Emmett Hall*
John D. Honsberger, *Osgoode Hall: An Illustrated History*
Constance Backhouse and Nancy Backhouse, *The Heiress versus the Establishment: Mrs Campbell's Campaign for Legal Justice*

2003   Robert Sharpe and Kent Roach, *Brian Dickson: A Judge's Journey*
Jerry Bannister, *The Rule of the Admirals: Law, Custom, and Naval Government in Newfoundland, 1699–1832*
George Finlayson, *John J. Robinette, Peerless Mentor: An Appreciation*
Peter Oliver, *The Conventional Man: The Diaries of Ontario Chief Justice Robert A. Harrison, 1856–1878*

2002   John T. Saywell, *The Lawmakers: Judicial Power and the Shaping of Canadian Federalism*
Patrick Brode, *Courted and Abandoned: Seduction in Canadian Law*

David Murray, *Colonial Justice: Justice, Morality, and Crime in the Niagara District, 1791–1849*

F. Murray Greenwood and Barry Wright, eds., *Canadian State Trials, Volume 2 Rebellion and Invasion in the Canadas, 1837–1839*

2001 Ellen Anderson, *Judging Bertha Wilson: Law as Large as Life*

Judy Fudge and Eric Tucker, *Labour before the Law: The Regulation of Workers' Collective Action in Canada, 1900–1948*

Laurel Sefton MacDowell, *Renegade Lawyer: The Life of J.L. Cohen*

2000 Barry Cahill, 'The Thousandth Man': A Biography of James McGregor Stewart

A.B. McKillop, *The Spinster and the Prophet: Florence Deeks, H.G. Wells, and the Mystery of the Purloined Past*

Beverley Boissery and F. Murray Greenwood, *Uncertain Justice: Canadian Women and Capital Punishment*

Bruce Ziff, *Unforeseen Legacies: Reuben Wells Leonard and the Leonard Foundation Trust*

1999 Constance Backhouse, *Colour-Coded: A Legal History of Racism in Canada, 1900–1950*

G. Blaine Baker and Jim Phillips, eds., *Essays in the History of Canadian Law Volume VIII: In Honour of R.C.B. Risk*

Richard W. Pound, *Chief Justice W.R. Jackett: By the Law of the Land*

David Vanek, *Fulfilment: Memoirs of a Criminal Court Judge*

1998 Sidney Harring, *White Man's Law: Native People in Nineteenth-Century Canadian Jurisprudence*

Peter Oliver, 'Terror to Evil-Doers': Prisons and Punishments in Nineteenth-Century Ontario

1997 James W. St.G. Walker, 'Race,' Rights and the Law in the Supreme Court of Canada: Historical Case Studies

Lori Chambers, *Married Women and Property Law in Victorian Ontario*

Patrick Brode, *Casual Slaughters and Accidental Judgments: Canadian War Crimes and Prosecutions, 1944–1948*

Ian Bushnell, *The Federal Court of Canada: A History, 1875–1992*

1996 Carol Wilton, ed., *Essays in the History of Canadian Law Volume VII: Inside the Law: Canadian Law Firms in Historical Perspective*

William Kaplan, *Bad Judgment: The Case of Mr Justice Leo A. Landreville*

Murray Greenwood and Barry Wright, eds., *Canadian State Trials: Volume 1 – Law, Politics, and Security Measures, 1608–1837*

1995 David Williams, *Just Lawyers: Seven Portraits*

Hamar Foster and John McLaren, eds., *Essays in the History of Canadian Law Volume VI: British Columbia and the Yukon*

W.H. Morrow, ed., *Northern Justice: The Memoirs of Mr Justice William G. Morrow*

Beverley Boissery, *A Deep Sense of Wrong: The Treason, Trials, and Transportation to New South Wales of Lower Canadian Rebels after the 1838 Rebellion*

1994 Patrick Boyer, *A Passion for Justice: The Legacy of James Chalmers McRuer*

Charles Pullen, *The Life and Times of Arthur Maloney: The Last of the Tribunes*

Jim Phillips, Tina Loo, and Susan Lewthwaite, eds., *Essays in the History of Canadian Law Volume V: Crime and Criminal Justice*

Brian Young, *The Politics of Codification: The Lower Canadian Civil Code of 1866*

1993 Greg Marquis, *Policing Canada's Century: A History of the Canadian Association of Chiefs of Police*

Murray Greenwood, *Legacies of Fear: Law and Politics in Quebec in the Era of the French Revolution*

1992 Brendan O'Brien, *Speedy Justice: The Tragic Last Voyage of His Majesty's Vessel Speedy*

Robert Fraser, ed., *Provincial Justice: Upper Canadian Legal Portraits from the Dictionary of Canadian Biography*

1991 Constance Backhouse, *Petticoats and Prejudice: Women and Law in Nineteenth-Century Canada*

1990 Philip Girard and Jim Phillips, eds., *Essays in the History of Canadian Law Volume III: Nova Scotia*

Carol Wilton, ed., *Essays in the History of Canadian Law Volume IV: Beyond the Law: Lawyers and Business in Canada, 1830–1930*

1989 Desmond Brown, *The Genesis of the Canadian Criminal Code of 1892*

Patrick Brode, *The Odyssey of John Anderson*

1988 Robert Sharpe, *The Last Day, the Last Hour: The Currie Libel Trial*

John D. Arnup, *Middleton: The Beloved Judge*

1987 C. Ian Kyer and Jerome Bickenbach, *The Fiercest Debate: Cecil A. Wright, the Benchers, and Legal Education in Ontario, 1923–1957*

1986 Paul Romney, *Mr Attorney: The Attorney General for Ontario in Court, Cabinet, and Legislature, 1791–1899*

Martin Friedland, *The Case of Valentine Shortis: A True Story of Crime and Politics in Canadaå*

1985 James Snell and Frederick Vaughan, *The Supreme Court of Canada: History of the Institution*

1984 Patrick Brode, *Sir John Beverley Robinson: Bone and Sinew of the Compact*

David Williams, *Duff: A Life in the Law*

1983   David H. Flaherty, ed., *Essays in the History of Canadian Law Volume II*
1982   Marion MacRae and Anthony Adamson, *Cornerstones of Order:*
        Courthouses and Town Halls of Ontario, 1784–1914
1981   David H. Flaherty, ed., *Essays in the History of Canadian Law Volume I*

Milton Keynes UK
Ingram Content Group UK Ltd.
UKHW021341030124
435409UK00017B/81/J